DATABASE SYSTEMS

CONCEPTS, MANAGEMENT, AND APPLICATIONS

ALDEN C. LORENTS
NORTHERN ARIZONA UNIVERSITY

JAMES N. MORGAN
NORTHERN ARIZONA UNIVERSITY

THE DRYDEN PRESS
HARCOURT BRACE COLLEGE PUBLISHERS

Fort Worth   Philadelphia   San Diego   New York   Orlando   Austin   San Antonio
Toronto   Montreal   London   Sydney   Tokyo

Publisher	George Provol
Executive Editor	Wesley Lawton
Product Manager	Federico Arrieta
Developmental Editor	Larry Crowder
Project Editor	Rebecca Dodson
Art Director	Jeanette Barber
Production Manager	Eddie Dawson
Electronic Publishing Coordinator	Lisa Rawlinson

ISBN: 0-15-500029-2
Library of Congress Catalog Card Number:97-065944

Address for Editorial Correspondence
Harcourt College Publishers, 301 Commerce Street, Suite 3700, Fort Worth, TX 76102

Address for Domestic Orders
Harcourt, Inc.,
6277 Sea Harbor Drive,
Orlando, FL 32887-6777
1-800-782-4479

Web Site Address
http://www.harcourtcollege.com

Printed in the United States of America

0 1 2 3 4 5 6 7 8 9   039   13 12 11 10 9 8 7 6 5 4

Harcourt College Publishers

To my wife, Olivia, for your love and support, and to our children, Heidi (Bill) and Troy (Renee), and our grandchildren, Darby, Abby, Olivia, Brianna, and Troy, Jr.—for all their everyday contributions and inspirations.

Alden

To my wife, Teresa, and our children, Angelee and Adam, for their love, support, and understanding, and to my parents, for the foundation they gave me and the love and support they continue to provide.

Jim

The Dryden Press Series in Information Systems

Fenrich
Practical Guidelines for Creating Instructional Multimedia Applications

Forcht
Management Information Systems: A Casebook

Gordon and Gordon
Information Systems: A Management Approach

Gray, King, McLean, and Watson
Management of Information Systems
Second Edition

Harrington
Database Management for Microcomputers: Design and Implementation
Second Edition

Harris
Systems Analysis and Design: A Project Approach
Second Edition

Head
An Introduction to Programming with QuickBASIC

Larsen
Using Microsoft Works 4.0 for Windows 95: An Introduction to Computing

Laudon and Laudon
Information Systems and the Internet: A Problem-Solving Approach
Fourth Edition

Laudon and Laudon
Information Systems: A Problem-Solving Approach
(A CD-ROM interactive version)

Lawlor
Computer Information Systems
Third Edition

Licker
Management Information Systems: A Strategic Leadership Approach

Martin
Discovering Microsoft Office 97

Martin/Parker
PC Concepts

Mason
Using Microsoft Access 97 in Business

Mason
Using Microsoft Excel 97 in Business

McKeown
Living with Computers
Fifth Edition

McKeown
Working with Computers
Second Edition

McKeown
Working with Computers with Software Tutorials
Second Edition

McLeod
Systems Analysis and Design: An Organizational Approach

Millspaugh
Business Programming in C for DOS-Based Systems

Morgan and Lorents
Database Systems: Concepts, Management, Applications

Morley
Getting Started with Computers

Parker
Understanding Computers: Today and Tomorrow
98 Edition

Parker
Understanding Networking and the Internet

Spear
Introduction to Computer Programming in Visual Basic 4.0

Spear
Visual Basic 3.0: A Brief Introduction
Visual Basic 4.0: A Brief Introduction

Sullivan
The New Computer User
Second Edition

Thommes and Carey
*Introduction to CASE Using Visible Analyst Workbench
v4.3 for DOS*
*CASE Tools: Using Visible Analyst Workbench for
Windows*

Martin and Parker
Mastering Today's Software Series

Texts available in any combination of the following:

Disk Operating System 5.0 (DOS 5.0)
Disk Operating System 6.0 (DOS 6.0)
Windows 3.1
Windows 95
Microsoft Office 97
Microsoft Office for Windows 95 Professional Edition
WordPerfect 5.1
WordPerfect 5.2 for Windows
WordPerfect 6.0 for DOS
WordPerfect 6.0 for Windows
WordPerfect 6.1 for Windows
Corel WordPerfect 7.0 for Windows 95
Word 6.0 for Windows
Word 7.0 for Windows 95
Word 97
Lotus 1-2-3 (2.2/2.3)
Lotus 1-2-3 (2.4)
Lotus 1-2-3 for Windows (4.01)
Lotus 1-2-3 for Windows (5.0)
Lotus 1-2-3 97
Excel 5.0 for Windows
Excel 7.0 for Windows 95
Excel 97
Quattro Pro 4.0
Quattro Pro 6.0 for Windows
dBASE III PLUS
dBASE IV (1.5/2.0)
dBASE 5 for Windows
Paradox 4.0
Paradox 5.0 for Windows
Access 2.0 for Windows
Access 7.0 for Windows 95
Access 97

PowerPoint 7.0 for Windows 95
PowerPoint 97
A Beginner's Guide to BASIC
A Beginner's Guide to QBASIC
Netscape Communicator

The Harcourt Brace College Outline Series

Kreitzberg
Introduction to BASIC

Kreitzberg
Introduction to Fortran

Pierson
Introduction to Business Information Systems

Veklerov and Pekelny
Computer Language C

ABOUT THE AUTHORS

Alden C. Lorents

Alden (Al) graduated with a bachelors degree from Concordia College (1960, Accounting), an MBA (1963, Accounting and Finance), and a PhD (1971, MIS and Accounting) from the University of Minnesota. He started his career in 1960 doing programming and systems work for Honeywell Aerospace in Minneapolis. He moved to Bemidji State University in 1966, as Director of the Computer Center and part-time instructor. Al left this position in 1969 to complete his PhD and accepted a teaching position in the College of Business (CIS/MIS) at NAU in 1971. During his tenure at NAU, he has been on various interim assignments that have included Sandia National Labs, Lawrence Livermore Labs, Kuwait University, Arizona Public Service (APS), Texas Instruments (TI), and Allied Signal. Projects at APS and TI included building client-server systems using the Composer (IEF) tools.

James N. Morgan

Jim graduated with a bachelors degree from Southwest Missouri State University (1970, Economics) and a PhD from the University of Missouri, Columbia (1978, Economics). He moved to NAU in 1977 to accept a teaching position in economics. He completed additional information systems study at both Arizona State University and the University of Arizona and has been teaching in the information systems field at NAU since 1984. Jim has completed research relating to distributed database systems, chargeback systems, and a variety of information systems teaching and curriculum issues. His research has appeared in a number of IS Journals, including *Information and Management* and the *Information Resources Management Journal*. His current research interests include Data Warehousing and Data Mining.

PREFACE

This database book has been written to serve the introductory database course in most CIS major programs, and to support any program where there is an emphasis on information systems design beyond the introductory course in CIS. Normally it is helpful for students to have a course in programming before taking a CIS major course in database systems. Students with some programming experience have more background in data structures such as bytes, data types, field names, records, and files. Programming also helps students understand host language constructs that are used in conjunction with IMS, IDMS, and embedded SQL. However, an introductory database course that concentrates primarily on relational implementations without host language implementations, can be successfully completed by students who have had a good introductory CIS course that include projects using a PC database such as Access or Paradox.

A major objective of this book is to get students involved in database activities early in the course. It is our belief that students learn more effectively when they are actively involved in learning activities that reinforce the theories that are being discussed in class. The primary emphasis of the book is on relational databases. Students can start working on selecting data from a database early in the course by starting on the airline case early, depending on the sequencing preferences of the instructor. Chapter 6 has an introductory section on SQL and an advanced section on SQL. The introductory section can be covered any time after covering Chapters 1 and 2.

Another objective of this book is to keep students involved in various applied activities that continue to reinforce the concepts covered in the conceptual chapters. The amount of applied activities somewhat depends on the software available to students and the design of the course. At a minimum students should have access to a good relational database. It is helpful if students have access to design software that supports the design of entity relationship (ER) diagrams. This book supports ANSI SQL and the specifics of using ACCESS, ORACLE, DB2, and XDB SQL. Other relational databases can easily be used by supplementing any SQL differences. XDB and DB2 have the same SQL since XDB is a DB2 clone that runs on the PC. XDB was originally developed as a database to support PC development of applications that run using DB2.

The other database systems covered in the text are IMS (Hierarchical Structure) and IDMS (Network Structure). These database systems are heavily embedded in legacy enterprise-wide systems in most larger organizations. Students can benefit from the discussions on hierarchical and network structures even if they are not able to get access to systems that support IMS and IDMS.

This book is structured to support the various design dimensions of database systems including normal forms, E-R diagramming, database planning, data and database administration. The design section centers around the use of entity relationship diagrams which are supported by a number of software tools today. In addition two chapters support the applied aspects of converting these designs into physical database systems. The one chapter covers the physical aspects of storage and access methods such as VSAM, linked list, various pointer structures, and different B-Trees. The other chapter covers the conversion of a database design to a relational database complete with indexes, referential integrity constraints, security, and space allocation.

One unique feature of this text is the coverage of application development that includes forms, windows, reports, and menus. Database systems today are supported by front end tools using Windows and the open database connectivity (ODBC) interfaces. Examples are shown using Access, XDB, and Oracle. Application development tools are a major part of prototyping and building client-server based systems.

Another important feature is the coverage of client-server, distributed, and object oriented database development. Most new systems developed today are designed in a client-server environment using database systems like DB/2, Oracle, and SYBASE. The text provides an extensive set of examples on client-server and distributed applications using Oracle with Access as a Client. Other client-server examples are illustrated using a windows based front end to a host language with embedded SQL to either DB2 or Oracle. Embedded SQL is a major part of database applications using tools such as C++, COBOL, and Case products like Composer.

CHAPTER ORGANIZATION

Chapter 1 introduces students to the basic concepts of data and information and how a database is used to support the information needs of an organization. The chapter covers the fundamental characteristics of databases, the different types of databases, and how databases are linked with various software tools to access the data.

Chapter 2 gives students a very detailed explanation of data, data modeling, and the characteristics of data. This chapter introduces the concepts of the relationship of data to entities, and how these entities can be related to each other in a one to many relationship. Entity relationship diagramming is used to provide a graphical way of modeling. The chapter introduces the initial concepts associated with the hierarchical, network, and the relational models.

Chapter 3 is an extension of some of the concepts in data modeling and database design that were introduced in Chapter 2. It covers the rules, benefits, drawbacks, and various examples of data normalization. Examples of the various normal forms are covered including Boyce-Codd and Domain/key.

Chapter 4 is a more conceptual chapter that covers data planning, the interaction of system development and database development, and some of the tools that can be used to enhance these activities. One of the CASE tools introduced in this chapter is Composer (IEF) from Texas Instruments. Composer is an integrated CASE tool that supports business system modeling, data modeling, systems design, and system construction.

Chapter 5 is a case oriented chapter that develops a database application for Air West Airlines. The airline database case is used here to get away from the traditional production, student, and hospital database examples that have been overused. Most students use airlines today as a mode of transportation so they are somewhat familiar with the business systems. Chapter 5 illustrates some of the business systems used in an airline setting, and provides the framework for all of the airline database illustrations used throughout the book.

Chapter 6 is an extensive chapter on using SQL to retrieve data from the airline database. The intent of the book is to get the student to interact with databases early in the course, and to use projects as a means to reinforce the concepts covered in class. The chapter is divided into two parts. The first part covers the easier parts of SQL that the student can pick up on quite rapidly. It can be used in the first few weeks of a course to get students started early on retrieving data from a relational database. The second part goes into the more advanced concepts of using SQL. Depending on how the course is structured, some instructors may want to delay portions of the second part until more concepts have been covered from other parts of the text.

Chapter 7 covers the concepts of building a relational database. The student is introduced to the SQL that builds the physical spaces, tables, indexes, and views associated with a relational database. It also covers the SQL used to add, delete, and update data in the tables. It gives the student an opportunity to map the design ideas presented in Chapters 2 through 5 into building an actual database.

Chapter 8 is an introduction to application development. It covers examples of setting up forms, windows, menus, and reports that interface the users and the database. Although this chapter is not directly related to database development, it is an important chapter, because these are the tools that allow students to design applications that interact with the database they design. The examples are windows-based using XDB, Oracle, and Access. Some of the Access examples illustrate the linking of Access to Oracle tables with open database connectivity (ODBC) drivers.

Chapter 9 covers the use of SQL in host language systems using COBOL. Students who are looking for positions in larger organizations will encounter systems that are developed around databases like DB2 and ORACLE using COBOL and C. There are many concepts related to using embedded SQL that are different from the SQL covered in Chapter 3 such as precompilers, declaring host variables, defining SQL cursors, and using dynamic SQL.

Chapter 10 covers the concepts of data and database administration giving the student some basics related to administrative functions of maintaining databases in an organization. It covers standards, database controls, data dictionary maintenance, data planning, database monitoring, loading and recovery, and the overall data responsibilities to the various departments within an organization. There are a number of issues that complicate the multi-user environment over a single user environment. Some of the issues covered include access control, concurrent updates of the same data or data areas, commits and rollbacks, database recovery, and various forms of locking.

Chapter 11 can be covered at anytime in the course depending on the content and organization set up by the instructor. Chapter 11 covers some of the fundamental concepts of data structures, data organization, physical storage devices, and a few layout strategies for storing data on disk. Basic structures of ISAM, VSAM, linked list, trees, rings, B-Trees, hashing, and indexing are a part of this chapter.

Chapter 12 covers concepts related to client-server systems and introduces the topic of distributed database systems. Topics covered include various ways of distributing a database, complexities in managing a distributed database, and some of the advantages and disadvantages of using distributed database systems. The primary orientation of this book is to learn how to develop database systems in various multi-user and client-server environments.

Chapter 13 is an introduction to object-oriented database management systems. The chapter is primarily a conceptual presentation with some examples. Some of the topics covered include the semantic object model, characteristics of objects, basic components of the object-oriented model, and some discussion of the current use of object-database systems.

Chapter 14 covers the Hierarchical model and IMS for those courses that want to include this orientation. The chapter can be used in part, just to get the concepts, or it can be used in total to set up a small database using IMS. The easiest way to do this is to install Micro Focus COBOL with the IMS option. The chapter presents examples of designing and setting up schemas to construct an IMS database, along with examples of maintaining data and accessing that data.

Chapter 15 covers the network model and IDMS. This chapter can also be used in part to cover the concepts, or in total to implement a small database using IDMS. This easiest way to gain access to IDMS is to implement the PC version of IDMS from Computer Associates along with Micro Focus COBOL. The chapter presents examples of designing and setting up schemas to construct an IDMS database, along with examples of maintaining data and accessing that data.

LEARNING AIDS AND SUPPLEMENTS

One of the unique features of the text is the use of the "Air West Airlines" case throughout most of the chapters in the text. The Air West case is described in detail in Chapter 5 and is used for most of the database examples and implementations. Additional case examples are used in various other illustrations to add variety and to provide a different basis for the illustration. Database files for the airline case are available on the Web at **www.dryden.com/infosys/lorents.** These files support Access, Oracle, and XDB/DB2 implementations. Each chapter has the following features to support the learning objectives.

Chapter Outline: A quick overview of the content of each chapter.

Learning Objectives: A summary of what the student should know or be able to do after reading each chapter.

Key Terms: Terms are highlighted throughout the chapter as they are used to make it easy to refer to them as the student is reading the chapter, or reviewing for exams.

Diagrams and Examples: Each chapter is illustrated with a large number of diagrams, examples, and short applications to make it easier for the student to view and comprehend what is being presented.

Chapter Summary: A short summary overview of the main points covered by each chapter.

Review Quiz: A matching review quiz is included at the end of each chapter to reinforce some of the terms and concepts that were a part of that chapter.

Review Questions and Exercises: Each chapter ends with a series of questions and exercises that can be used for discussion, homework, in-class exercises, and review. These exercises include Web-based activities to research and report on recent technologies in database and client-server computing.

The supplements include an instructor's manual, database support on diskette, and up-to-date Web support that students can access for readings and additional research related to each chapter. From our Web page (www.dryden.com/infosys/lorents), you can also download PowerPoint slides for each chapter that include chapter diagrams and teaching outlines. A separate case book will be available to supplement the course with additional case material that can be used as projects, as examples, and as support for questions covered on exams.

ACKNOWLEDGMENTS

A book of this type does not come together without the contributions of many individuals. Initial support for this project came from Richard Bonacci, former editor with Harcourt Brace. We respect his knowledge and still call on him from time to time for advice. We appreciate the leadership of Scott Timian, Vice President of Custom Publishing, and Wesley Lawton, Executive Editor at Dryden, in maintaining their commitment to the project.

We are grateful for the expert editorial and review work that was done by Joni Harlan of La Mesa, California and Rebecca L. Johnson of Bradford, Massachusetts. They did an excellent job of structuring the reviews, coordinating the review process, and summarizing the results of the reviews. We are also very indebted to all of the reviewers who gave us very detailed feedback on the chapters. The reviewers included:

Professor Kevin Gorman
University of North Carolina at Charlotte

Prof. Tom Farrell
Dakota State University

Professor Wullianallur R. Raghupathi
California State University, Chico

Professor Hilary L. Ives
DeVry Institute

Professor Kirk P. Arnett
Mississippi State University

Professor Alexis Koster
San Diego State University

Professor David Olsen
University of Akron

Professor William R. Cornette
Southwestern Missouri State University

Professor Bijan Mashaw
California State University, Hayward

Karen Watterson
Independent Consultant

Other reviewers who have contributed comments and improvements include CIS students at Dakota State University and Northern Arizona University. We thank them for their patience and willingness to work with manuscript copies.

The contributions by Troy Lorents and Mac Bosse at Northern Arizona University, and Norm Stevens of Boise, Idaho have been outstanding in helping us with the support materials. Norm built the test bank of questions for each chapter. Troy put together the end-of-chapter solutions, built most of the Oracle and Access support files, and put together the Powerpoint slides. Mac did a lot of the initial manuscript review and assisted with software testing.

We are especially grateful to the staff at Dryden Press for their diligence in dealing with all of the details of editing and converting rough manuscripts into final production layouts. Our thanks to Larry Crowder, Developmental Editor, and Rebecca Dodson, Senior Project Editor, for all of their work in editing the manuscripts and making sure that all of the pieces were in place. We also want to thank Jeanette Barber, Art Director, Lisa Rawlinson, Electronic Publishing Coordinator, and Eddie Dawson, Production Manager, for their contributions in the design, final layout, and production of the book.

Last and most important is our gratitude to our families for hanging in, caring, understanding, being patient, having confidence, and giving us support over an extended period of time.

Alden C. Lorents
James N. Morgan

BRIEF CONTENTS

CONTENTS

CHAPTER 3
TOOLS AND METHODS FOR CONCEPTUAL DESIGN   69

CHAPTER 4
THE PROCESS OF DATABASE PLANNING AND DEVELOPMENT   115

CHAPTER 5
THE AIRLINE DATABASE: A CONCEPTUAL DESIGN CASE   149

CHAPTER 6
INTRODUCTION TO RELATIONAL TABLES AND SQL RETRIEVAL   195

SECTION 1: RELATIONAL TABLES AND SQL   197

SECTION 2: ADVANCED APPLICATIONS USING SQL   233

CHAPTER 7
IMPLEMENTING A RELATIONAL DATABASE   261

CHAPTER 8
CLIENT-SERVER APPLICATION DEVELOPMENT   313

CHAPTER 9
EMBEDDED SQL PROGRAMMING FOR CLIENT-SERVER APPLICATIONS   355

CHAPTER 10
CONTROL AND ADMINISTRATION OF DATABASE SYSTEMS   389

CHAPTER 11
PHYSICAL DATA ORGANIZATION FOR DATABASE SYSTEMS   435

CHAPTER 12
DISTRIBUTED DATABASE SYSTEMS   475

CHAPTER 13
OBJECT-ORIENTED DATABASE SYSTEMS   515

CHAPTER 14
THE HIERARCHICAL MODEL—IMS   551

AN OVERVIEW OF DATABASE MANAGEMENT SYSTEMS

LEARNING OBJECTIVES

After completing this chapter, you should be able to

- Define the terms *database, database management system,* and *database system.*
- List the key advantages and limitations of database systems.
- Describe the following key features of database systems:
  - Data Dictionary
  - Query Language
  - Host Language Interface
  - Application Generator Software
- Briefly describe hierarchical, network, relational, and object-oriented databases and discuss where each might be used.
- Describe how alternative levels of centralization and decentralization can be supported by database systems.

DATABASES IN ACTION

A sales representative calls her headquarters and asks to have information about all customers in the area she will be visiting the next day downloaded to her portable PC. The information she receives can be used to plan her sales stops for the next day and includes details about sales to each customer over the past year. The sales rep is also able to transmit information about today's sales to her company's headquarters so that processing of the orders can begin immediately.

A department store chain uses information gathered when customers buy appliances to improve customer service and marketing. Free service calls for customers who have purchased a service agreement are scheduled by the store's service representatives one year after purchase of the appliance. The customer information gathered at the time of the sale is also used to create a list of customers for marketing mailings and phone calls, so that extensions to service agreements can be target marketed to those customers whose warranties are about to expire.

A credit card company is able to process millions of transactions a day. For each credit card purchase, the validity of the card is checked (Is the number valid? Has the expiration date passed? Has the customer's credit limit been exceeded?) and the amount of the purchase is added to the customer's balance. This processing is performed "on-line" and an approval of the purchase is transmitted usually within a few seconds.

A corporate executive is able to examine summary sales trends for his organization. He can examine trends by region and by product line. By clicking on the figures for an individual region or a specific product line, he can get a more detailed listing of trends in that element of the business.

All the information systems described above are commonly available today and all of them require well-organized database systems. The ever-expanding range of information needed to manage modern organizations can be provided effectively only if the organization has a well-organized and integrated set of databases.

INTRODUCTION

Database systems have become the primary mechanism used by most organizations to store and manage important organizational data. With the continuing expansion in the capabilities of PC-based computer systems, even small businesses are beginning to make extensive use of database systems.

Prior to the emergence of database systems, key organizational data were kept in numerous files, which had to be independently maintained and managed. When data stored in different files needed to be processed together, application programs were used to manage the interrelationships.

Database systems provide several important advantages. Well-designed database systems implemented using appropriate database management software can provide better control of sensitive data, broader access to organizational data, improved data accuracy, and improved productivity.

This chapter provides a brief overview of the key features of database systems. Vignettes describing typical business situations are presented. These vignettes identify key features of database systems and highlight the key advantages of database processing. Following the vignettes, key features of database systems and the environments they support are briefly described.

WHAT IS A DATABASE?

What is a database? What gives database-oriented processing so many apparent advantages over file-oriented systems? A **database** is an integrated collection of data. This collection of data describes sets of "things" that are interrelated and are of interest to the organization. The database also must describe how the "things" it contains are interrelated. For example, students and courses are "things" of interest to a university. A logical relationship exists between them because students enroll in particular courses. Thus, a database might contain data describing both students and courses along with information defining the enrollment relationship between students and courses. Such a database would also likely contain data about numerous other **entities,** such as professors, departments, and classrooms.

Database
A database is an integrated, self-describing collection of data about related sets of things and the relationships among them.

Entity
A person, place, thing, or event of importance to the organization. Anything that can be a noun can be an entity.

Database management system

The set of software used to develop, implement, manage, and maintain the data stored in a database.

Database system

A database system includes the data stored in the database, the DBMS used to develop it, and the applications developed to create and maintain the data of the database.

Databases are expected to be self-describing. That is, the statements that define what the database contains and how it is organized are a part of the database itself. This contrasts with file-oriented processing in which descriptions of the file structure are written in the applications programs that process the file (for example, the COBOL data division).

Databases are also expected to have additional features designed to *integrate the collection of data* that we call a database. These features are provided by a set of software called a **database management system,** or DBMS. DBMSs are software packages used to develop, implement, manage, and maintain databases. The DBMS software is distinct from the databases that are developed with it in the same way that a COBOL program is distinct from the COBOL compiler used to execute it.

The term **database system** is used to describe an information system that utilizes a database. A database system encompasses the database, the DBMS used to manage it, and all the applications needed to implement the system (the applications may be developed either using tools of the DBMS software package or using procedural languages, such as COBOL or C++).

To get a feel for these characteristics, let's take a look at a hypothetical company, Apex Products. We will present four vignettes describing how that company would respond to a variety of events requiring adjustments to its information systems. Two alternative responses will be presented for each event. The first response will assume that Apex uses database management systems. The second response will assume that Apex does not use database technology. This side-by-side comparison is designed to highlight some of the key capabilities of database management systems. It should be noted that these capabilities can be achieved only when database systems are designed and used very effectively.

■ VIGNETTE 1: **A Customer Moves to a New Address**

One of Apex's customers, Al's Auto Parts (Customer Number 1056), recently moved to a new address, 8922 S. Pine Street. Al's sent a letter to all its vendors indicating the new address and the effective date. The manager in Apex's Customer Services Department received this letter.

With Database Systems Figure 1.1 shows how this address change might be handled under a database system. The manager of the Customer Services Department is responsible for maintaining this data. When the address change is received, she makes the address change on the customer master table. This one customer master table is used to supply customer address data to all applications throughout the company that need this type of data. Thus, users in the Marketing, Shipping, and Accounts Receivable departments all access the same master table.

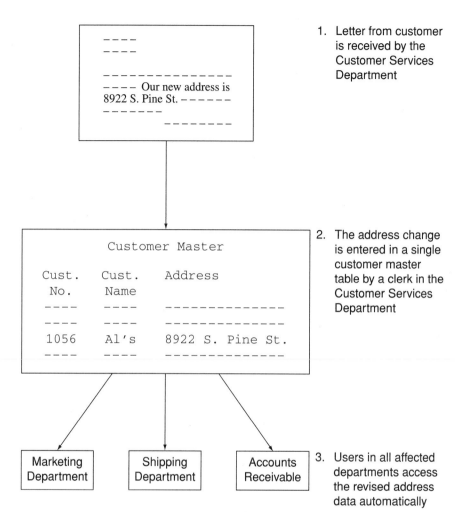

1. Letter from customer is received by the Customer Services Department

2. The address change is entered in a single customer master table by a clerk in the Customer Services Department

3. Users in all affected departments access the revised address data automatically

FIGURE 1.1

Processing a Customer Address Change Using Database Systems

Without Database Systems   Figure 1.2 shows how the same address change might be handled without the use of database systems. The manager of the Customer Services Department fills out a manual change of address form when the address change is received. This form has three carbon copies that are sent to the other departments that use customer address data: Marketing, Shipping, and Accounts Receivable. A clerk in each department enters the address change on that department's customer master file.

In this instance, the carbon copy sent to Accounts Receivable was very faint, and the clerk read the address as 3922 S. Vine Street. Al's Auto Parts became more than 60 days in arrears in its payments.When Mr.Brown, the manager of the Accounts Receivable Department, called the customer requesting immediate payment, he was very embarrassed

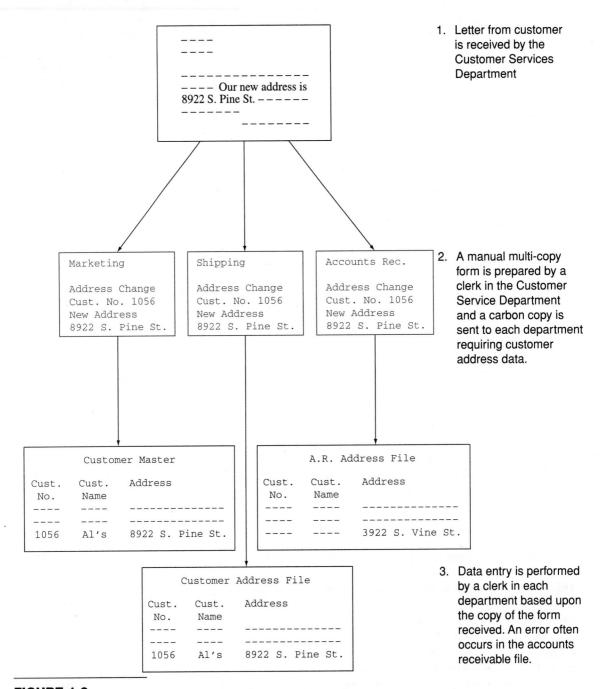

1. Letter from customer is received by the Customer Services Department

2. A manual multi-copy form is prepared by a clerk in the Customer Service Department and a carbon copy is sent to each department requiring customer address data.

3. Data entry is performed by a clerk in each department based upon the copy of the form received. An error often occurs in the accounts receivable file.

FIGURE 1.2
Processing a Customer Address Change without Database Systems

to learn that the billings had not been received because of the error in his department's data. Soon after this, Al's Auto Parts switched its account to another vendor.

■ VIGNETTE 2: **Retrieving a Selected List of Customer Addresses**

Alice Davis, an engineer working on modifications to one of Apex's products, a portable PC—Product Number AD12, wants to send a survey to all customers who have purchased that product in the past year. She is a fairly sophisticated computer user, but is not familiar with Apex's customer and order data.

With Database Systems As Figure 1.3 illustrates, Alice Davis was able to use the data dictionary features of the DBMS to retrieve descriptions of the tables she needed. Data dictionary information for the Customer table is shown in Figure 1.3, but similar information was available for all data that Alice was authorized to access. Using these descriptions, Alice was able to quickly retrieve the names and addresses of the customers who had purchased product AD12 in the preceding year. To do this she used a feature of the DBMS called a query language. Although Customer table data needed to be matched with products ordered in a different table, Alice was able to use a single query language statement to pick out the data she needed. Once she had retrieved the data she wanted, Alice used a report generator that was part of the database management software to print a set of address labels. The whole process required less than 45 minutes. Alice was able to access this data from another part of the company because it was not considered to be sensitive data. However, she would not have been allowed to make any changes to this data, nor to access more sensitive data from areas outside her primary responsibility.

Without Database Systems Alice Davis had no effective way of finding out for herself how or where the data she needed were stored. She requested assistance from Apex's information systems (IS) staff. They indicated that there were two ways to meet her request. The IS staff could write an applications program that would involve merging customer and order data files. Given the backlogs they faced, they could not promise to deliver in less than 6 weeks. Alternatively, someone could manually search through an existing printout maintained in the marketing department which listed annual sales of each product to each customer.

Because she needed the survey results as soon as possible, Alice chose the latter alternative. The steps she went through are

FIGURE 1.3
Identifying a Selected
Group of Customers
Using Database
Systems

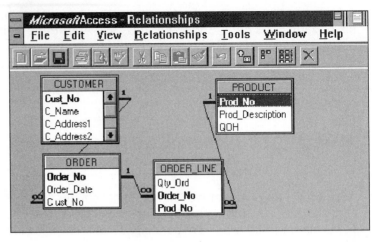

(a)

Alice Davis browses the
database's data dictionary
to find the data she needs
to see the set of tables
available to her (a), and to
get information about the
data fields in those tables (b).

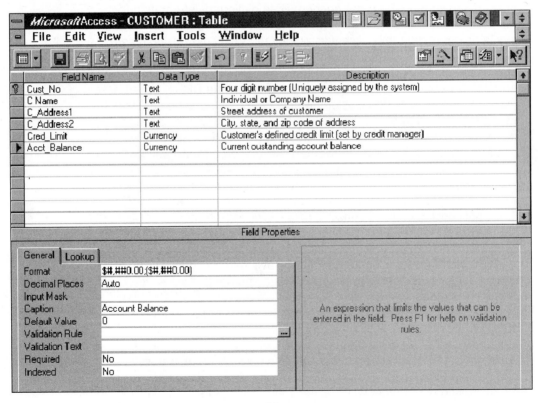

(b)

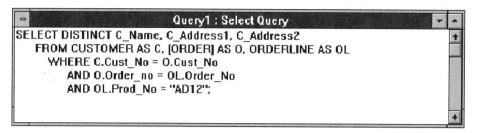

(c)

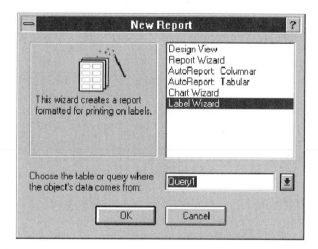

(d)

(c) Based on this information, Alice is able to write a single statement using the query language of the database to retrieve the list of names and addresses she needs.

(d) Alice uses a fourth generation language report generator that is a part of the database management software package to quickly format and print the needed labels.

| Chris Pike |
| 1427 N. Mockingbird |
| Flagstaff, AZ |
| 36002 |

| Rodney Taylor |
| 2655 Collinwood |
| Scottsdale, AZ |
| 83651 |

(e)

FIGURE 1.4
Identifying a Selected
Group of Customers
without Database
Systems

1. Consultation with the IS Department reveals they can't produce the information in less than six weeks. The alternative is to manually search a marketing department printout and record the names and addresses.

2. The marketing manager allows the printout to be used, but only by Alice and only in the office of the marketing manager.

3. Alice spends most of a working day searching the printout for customers who have purchased the product she is interested in. She writes their names and addresses in pencil on a notepad.

4. Alice's secretary types out a set of mailing labels from the pencil-and-paper list Alice gives her. Four addresses are recorded incorrectly on the typed labels.

summarized in Figure 1.4. When Mr. Barnes, the Marketing manager, was contacted, he was hesitant to allow anyone from another department to see this printout because it also contained information about customers that was considered private and sensitive. Mr. Barnes would agree to give access to the printout only if it remained in his office. Also, he insisted that only Alice and not her secretary could look at this listing.

Alice spent most of a working day identifying and transcribing the list of names and addresses. Her secretary then spent another four hours converting Alice's lists back into computerized form to produce the address labels for the survey. In the process, erroneous addresses were recorded for four of the customers.

■ VIGNETTE 3: **Revising Marketing Sales Reports**

The product mix of Apex's sales has changed sharply in recent years. Apex establishes quotas and provides bonuses to sales staff based on sales performance in each product line. Mr. Barnes, the Marketing manager at Apex, feels that the product lines need to be restructured to consolidate lines that now represent a small percentage of total sales, and to split expanding lines so that appropriate emphasis can be placed on the expanding portions of the business. In conjunction with these changes, he also wants revisions in the layout of several reports used by the sales staff.

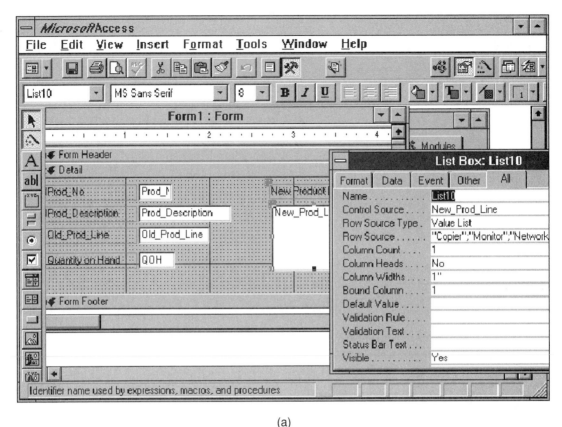

(a)

(a) IS staff add a new field to the Product table and use a 4GL package to create a data entry form for this field.

(b) A clerk enters the new product line data for each product. Existing sales reports continue to operate without revision.

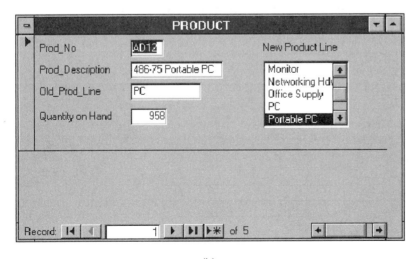

(b)

FIGURE 1.5
Revising Marketing
Sales Reports Using
Database Systems

FIGURE 1.5 (Cont.)
Revising Marketing
Sales Reports Using
Database Systems

(c)   The IS staff use
the DBMS's 4GL report
generator and a
prototyping approach
to generate most of
the needed new
reports (d).

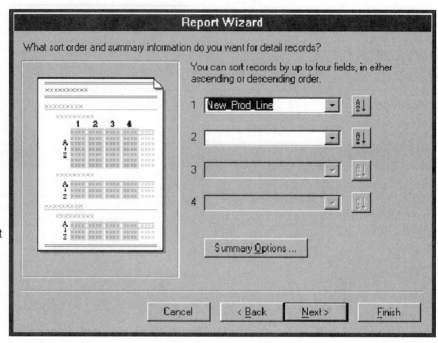

(c)

Sales Trends 1995-97

Year	New_Prod_Line	SumOfSales ($1,000)
1995	Monitor	2347
	Network Hdwr	1010
	PC	4074
	Portable PC	2402
	Printer	1430

Summary for 'Year' = 1995 (5 detail records)

Sum   *11263*

1996	Monitor	2482
	Network Hdwr	1380
	PC	4781
	Portable PC	3050
	Printer	1480

Summary for 'Year' = 1996 (5 detail records)

Sum   *13173*

(d)

(e) Two reports cannot be produced by the report generator. These are written in COBOL, but use data supplied by the DMBS's host language interface to simplify the required programing.

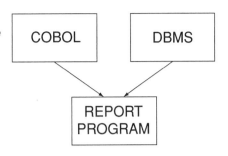

(f) The required set of reports is operational in 2 months.

FIGURE 1.5 (Cont.)
Revising Marketing
Sales Reports Using
Database Systems

During a transition period, sales will continue to be reported using the old product line classifications, but reports of sales using the new categories will also be produced to help establish quotas and to let sales staff see how the new system will affect them. During the transition, two sets of product line information will be recorded for each sale—the old and the new.

Apex's CEO feels that these changes are extremely crucial and has told the IS staff to give them top priority and begin implementation immediately.

With Database Systems   Figure 1.5 illustrates the steps needed to meet these requirements using database systems. Powerful tools using a Windows-like graphical interface and point-and-click methods are a part of most database management system (DBMS) software packages. These typically include at least a form generator and a report generator. These tools are used extensively in addressing the requirements of this Vignette.

A new field called NEW_PROD_LINE was added to the product table of the database. A form to add data for this field was quickly created using the form generator module of Apex's DBMS software. A clerk quickly entered the new product line for each product based on the Marketing manager's specifications. The existing sales reports were unaffected by this change and no modifications to them were required.

Apex's IS staff was able to produce most of the new reports using the report generator software of Apex's DBMS. The IS staff was able to use a prototyping approach to rapidly generate these reports with constant feedback from the users.

Two reports that could not be produced by the report generator software were developed by linking the database to COBOL. A software module of the DBMS called host language interface software supplied database data to COBOL programs that performed the processing needed to produce the report applications. Using this approach, the database software handles the data description and manipulation tasks

FIGURE 1.6
Revising Marketing
Sales Reports without
Database Systems

1. A clerk enters a set of transactions to create the new product code for each product.

2. A COBOL program is written to rewrite the product master file with the new field added.

3. The new field changes the structure of the new product master file. All sales reports programs using the product master file must be modified to reflect this change.

4. The IS staff writes COBOL programs to produce all the new reports. Programming complexities cause delays of many weeks between the initial specification of report requirements and production of sample results for most of the reports.

5. More than 6 months go by before the set of reports is operational.

for the COBOL program. This keeps data storage and manipulation functions independent of programs using the data.

Using this approach the programs were written rather quickly. The new system was completed within 2 months.

Without Database Systems   The steps involved in implementing the new approach in the absence of database systems are shown in Figure 1.6. A set of transactions establishing the NEW_PROD_CODE field for each product was created by a clerk based on the Marketing manager's specifications. A COBOL program was written to regenerate the product master file with the new field added. Because the addition of this field changed the length and structure of the product master file, the data definition sections of all the programs producing the sales reports currently used by Apex had to be modified to reflect the new file structure.

Apex's IS staff had to write COBOL programs to produce all the new reports. They worked as closely as possible with users. However, because of the complexity of the programming required, a delay of many weeks occurred between the initial specification of program require-ments and the production of results to which the users could respond. Many of the new reports required data from multiple files. Various com-binations of product, customer, salesperson, and order data had to be accessed. Each program using data from multiple files needed complex data handling operations to sort and merge the required data.

The IS staff found it difficult to maintain the users' interest and to remember all the nuances of the users' requests through this lengthy development period. Thus, in several cases, users did not feel that the new reports met their expectations. Some users requested major changes requiring more weeks of programming and the staff felt that some other users had simply turned off and would probably make little use of their reports. More than 6 months elapsed before the new system was operational, and there was a substantial amount of dissatisfaction with the results.

■ VIGNETTE 4: **Strategic Use of Sales Data**

Mr. Barnes recently attended a conference where the use of organizational data to strategically target marketing efforts was discussed. He would like to have access to summary information about each company's sales, credit, and maintenance/servicing history with Apex, as well as demographic information about the customer. This set of data would be used by computer literate market research staffers to generate lists of prospective customers for particular products and service agreements, to determine the levels of discounting to be offered to customers, and to allocate personal sales calls more effectively. He requests that the IS department create an application that will produce a summary file or database containing this set of information on a monthly basis.

   With Database Systems   Figure 1.7 illustrates the process used to develop this system. The first step for the IS staff assigned to this project was to use the data dictionary feature of the DBMS software to retrieve screen displays describing the nature and structure of the data

1. The development team searched the data dictionaries of several databases to find the requested data.
2. Sessions were held with interested parties to find ways to provide the marketing research staff with the needed data without disclosing sensitive data. An acceptable compromise was reached.
3. The development teams worked with the marketing research staff to design and implement the new database using a PC-based database package that could be operated primarily by the marketing research staff.
4. The IS staff wrote applications to extract the necessary summary data from various organizational databases and download it to the new strategic marketing database.
5. The strategic marketing database was turned over to the marketing research staff for their operation using 4GL reporting and query language capabilities of the DBMS.
6. The database was operational within 3 months.

FIGURE 1.7
Developing a Strategic Marketing Information System Using Database Systems

in the database. Using these displays, staff members were able to quickly identify where the requested data were stored. They found that data from several databases would be required. However, this did not pose a substantial problem, because common data standards had been established for all important organizational databases. These standards meant that it would be relatively easy to extract and pull together data from the various databases.

It was determined that the requested data was best handled by creating a new database to store just this strategic summary data. Several members of the market research staff were proficient in the use of personal computer-based relational database products. Some of the requested data was considered to be sensitive. Sessions were held between the marketing research staff, the individuals responsible for the administration of the databases involved, and personnel in the various departments responsible for the requested data to find ways to give the marketing research staff access to as much information as possible without compromising the security of sensitive data.

The IS staff then worked with the marketing research staff to develop the design for the new strategic marketing database. They implemented the database structure using a PC-based relational DBMS package, and created applications to extract the required data from its various sources, translate it into the required form, and download it to the PC to populate the new database. The database was then turned over to the marketing research staff who plan to use report generation and query language features of the DBMS to produce outputs as needed. The project was completed in about 3 months.

FIGURE 1.8
Developing a Strategic Marketing Information System without Database Systems

1. The development team began the process of assembling data by consulting the individuals responsible for managing key files located in several different departments.

2. In several instances, managers of key files were unwilling to grant access because they felt there was no way to protect the confidentiality of sensitive data.

3. Where access was permitted, the developmental team found that files were often poorly documented.

4. Some departments used different names for the same data. Also, inconsistent reporting periods and coding methods were found among departments using related data.

5. Because of these problems, the development team was not able to find an acceptable method for retrieving data.

6. After 9 months the project was abandoned.

Without Database Systems   Figure 1.8 illustrates the key steps involved in the attempt to develop this system without the presence of database systems. When this project was proposed to the IS staff, they indicated that pulling together the required data might take some time, but was certainly feasible. After getting the go-ahead to proceed, they began seeking out the required data. They went to the IS staff responsible for maintaining files likely to contain the needed data. Several obstacles were encountered. In some instances, access to information about the files was restricted and those responsible for it were reluctant to grant access to *their* files. In other instances, the contents of the files were not well documented.Staff members found that different departments often used different terms for the same data. They also found that reporting periods and identification codes used were not always identical across different departments using related data. After 9 months, no acceptable mechanism for retrieving the requested information had been established and the project was abandoned.

ADVANTAGES OF DATABASE PROCESSING

The vignettes presented highlight several advantages of database processing. A summary of these is presented in Figure 1.9. In our first vignette, unless a database system is used, four separate files need to be updated when address information changes. With these multiple copies, inconsistencies could occur in the address stored. Under database processing the new address is stored only once, thus eliminating data redundancy. Eliminating redundancy reduces data entry time and the amount of storage space required and, more important, guarantees that there can be no conflicting or inconsistent values for the customer's address. With just one address entry, it is easier to ensure that the address is correct.

The second Apex vignette illustrates that broader sharing of organizational data is promoted by the database approach. Under the database approach, the engineer has

1. Reduced data duplication and improved data consistency
2. Broader sharing of organizational data
3. Integrated systems for protecting the integrity and privacy of data
4. Improved programmer and end user productivity in developing and maintaining applications
5. Ability to use data as an organizational resource

FIGURE 1.9
Advantages of
Database Processing

FIGURE 1.10
Limitations of
Database Processing

1. Cost of software acquisition and user training
2. Higher cost of processing routine batches of transactions data
3. Increased magnitude of potential loss due to disaster
4. User resistance to loss of control of data

access to a data dictionary to help her find the required data from other parts of the organization and to a data query language that allows her to retrieve the data for herself.

The existence of integrated systems for the protection of the integrity and privacy of data under database processing is also very important in Vignette 2. Some of the customer data was of a sensitive nature and access to it needed to be restricted. The database system provided controls that allowed the engineer to see and retrieve all nonsensitive data while protecting the sensitive data from view.

Both the second and the third vignettes illustrate the fourth advantage of database processing listed in Figure 1.9. The query language available to the engineer improves her productivity in developing her list of customers. Several features of the database system help boost the productivity of the information systems staff in developing the revised marketing reports. First, the host language interface software allows the maintenance and retrieval of data required for an application to be independent of the program using the data. This program-data independence means that programs do not have to be rewritten each time there is a change in the structure of the data. This reduces maintenance requirements substantially. Beyond this, the availability of 4GL application generator software and the use of the data dictionary to quickly identify needed data also speeded development.

The fourth vignette illustrates the fact that database processing can help a company use its data as a corporate resource. Here, Apex Products wants to use data, originally gathered for other purposes, to support strategic marketing efforts. With well-developed database systems, it is possible to rapidly generate a new database to support this strategic thrust. Indeed, Apex's databases themselves can be thought of as a strategic resource ready to provide this type of support wherever it is needed within the organization.

LIMITATIONS OF DATABASE PROCESSING

We have seen that many strong advantages can be gained by the use of database systems. However, these advantages do come at a cost. Limitations of database processing are listed in Figure 1.10.

Database systems require sophisticated software. This software may be more expensive than that required for file-oriented processing, although this factor is becoming less important. In addition to the cost of the software, there may be substantial costs in training users to effectively utilize the DBMS package.

Use of database systems to process routine transactions is more costly, in terms of processing time, than processing those same transactions using sequential batch file processing. The rich storage structures that allow databases to support flexible access to their data add some overhead to routine sequential processing activities. Where the processing to be performed on a set of data is very routine and needs for ad-hoc access to it are minimal, the additional processing costs associated with database systems are not justified.

A third consideration is the fact that database processing exposes the organization to the risk of large-scale losses due to a disaster. Although DBMS packages are designed to counteract this risk with their recovery software, there is no doubt that the magnitude of possible loss due to a disaster is increased when large volumes of crucial organizational data are integrated into a single database. Expensive backup and recovery procedures are needed to counteract this risk.

Finally, there may be user resistance to the loss of control associated with database systems. Database processing requires centralized control of its data. Users who are responsible for a set of data and whose job performance depends upon its integrity are understandably reluctant to surrender control of that data. They must be convinced that the control features of the DBMS software will provide adequate protection for their data and will make their jobs easier.

These limitations are outweighed by the advantages of database processing in most cases. However, database storage is probably not appropriate for infrequently used sets of data, or for sets of data not requiring ad-hoc access. Also, the increased risk exposure cautions us to limit the scope of databases. At some point this increased risk, and the increased complexity, from adding more entities to a database outweighs the benefits from integrating the data. Thus, organizations create sets of subject area databases rather than one immense database containing all organizational data.

KEY FEATURES OF DATABASE SYSTEMS

Figure 1.11 describes some of the key features of modern DBMSs. Not all DBMSs used in organizations possess all these features. However, all the features described here are widely available in DBMS software. We will discuss each of these features in turn.

The first feature, a cross-entity linking mechanism, allows different related files or entities in a database to be linked together. The linkage of related data across entities or files is established either by pointers or by the repetition of unique identifying data.

Regardless of the method used, the DBMS establishes permanent linkages between related entities that can be used to efficiently retrieve sets of related data across these multiple entities. This capability has several implications. It means that we can treat the collection of data across these entities as an integrated whole. If a need arises to bring together related data from separate entities, we can quickly do so. Therefore, we do not need to keep multiple copies of the same data. As we saw in Vignette 1, instead of keeping a customer's address in four different files,

FIGURE 1.11
Key Features of
Database
Management Systems

1. A cross-entity linking mechanism
2. A data dictionary
3. A query language
4. Mechanisms for management of access to data
5. Host language interface software
6. A high-level data manipulation language
7. 4GL application development software
8. Disaster recovery and concurrency control capabilities

Data redundancy
Data redundancy occurs when more than one copy of the same item of information is stored and maintained by an organization. Data redundancy can lead to *data inconsistency* in which different copies show different values for the same item.

Data dictionary
Information describing the structure of a set of data that can be readily retrieved by users. A data dictionary is a common feature of DBMS software.

Query language
A user-friendly language designed to support retrieval of selected data from a database.

the address is recorded only once and the linkages between entities allow it to be retrieved for all needed uses. This reduces **data redundancy** and ensures data consistency.

The second feature is the data dictionary. The **data dictionary** allows users to readily access information about the structure of the data they are using. Definitions and descriptions of all data available to a user are provided by the data dictionary. Thus, a user can consult the data dictionary to familiarize himself or herself with previously unknown parts of the database. The data dictionary listings also provide descriptions of restrictions on the values of data items. For instance, a customer ID number may be required to be unique, or a quantity on hand may not be allowed to be negative. Many DBMSs feature *active* data dictionaries. This means that the rules and restrictions on data described in the data dictionary are automatically enforced by the DBMS. The data dictionary provides users with information only about the parts of the database they are authorized to use, thus preserving data integrity and privacy. An example of a data dictionary listing can be seen in Figure 1.3.

The **query language** is a feature most prominently associated with relational DBMSs, although some query language-like capabilities have been added to hierarchical and network database systems. The query language is simple enough to be used extensively by end-users. It focuses on providing the ability to retrieve selected data from the database needed to satisfy ad-hoc queries. An example of a query language statement designed to answer just such an ad-hoc question can be seen in Figure 1.3.

Because database systems broaden the access to data, they must provide strong measures to control that access so that the integrity and privacy of data are not compromised. Important components of the DBMS software are devoted to this task. Database systems typically are able to control access down to the field level—that is, a user can be allowed to see certain fields in a file but not others. The type of action that a user can perform on the data he or she accesses can also be controlled. For instance, some users can be allowed to read an item but not to make changes to it.

The **host language interface** allows the database to supply data to traditional high-level languages that can then be used to develop applications programs. As we have seen, this can simplify the programming required by allowing the database to handle the data-oriented portions of the application. A program is written that contains a combination of valid statements in the host language, COBOL for instance, and database commands recognized by the host language interface software. When the program is completed, it is first run through a precompiler that idenifies the database-oriented commands and converts them to a set of calls. These calls are valid statements in the host language and can be used to supply the needed data to the host language program in the desired form.The program is then compiled using the host language compiler and executed. Host language interface capabilities are not present on some PC-oriented relational DBMSs, but are available on almost all DBMSs designed for operation on minicomputers or mainframes.

Host language interface
A software component of the DBMS that allows commands to manipulate a database to be combined with standard programming language commands to create applications.

Many DBMSs also provide their own internal high-level language called a data manipulation language (DML). The DML can be used to develop applications entirely within the software of the DBMS.

Fourth-generation (4GL) application development software is also increasingly available in DBMSs. Form Generators and Report Generators are two of the most common types of 4GL software bundled in DBMSs. The use of this type of software for Report and Form Generation was briefly described in conjunction with Vignettes 2 and 3, and sample screens were shown in Figures 1.3 and 1.5. Fourth-generation language software generally provides a visual interface, and it eliminates the need to specify detailed, line-by-line instructions for the production of routine forms or reports. Instead, the user specifies the key parameters for application and the 4GL software handles the routine processing required to produce the needed result.

Procedures for disaster recovery and control of concurrent access are extremely important. Because database processing has encouraged us to treat large amounts of related organizational data as an integrated unit, it has also increased the magnitude of the potential loss if that set of data is damaged or destroyed. DBMSs must contain sophisticated software for disaster recovery. This includes maintenance of a transactions log that contains a listing of each transaction and its impact on the database. DBMS recovery software is designed to process the transactions log, in conjunction with a backup copy of the database if necessary, to recover a database to its position at the time the disaster occurred. Most DBMSs are designed to support simultaneous access by multiple users—concurrent access.The DBMS must have software to manage this type of use and to ensure that concurrent access to a data item by different users does not compromise the accuracy of the data.

It is important to note that the advantages of database processing can be achieved only if the databases that are used have been designed effectively. The features of database management software that were described earlier will not be able to provide efficient and effective processing of a poorly designed database. Good database design requires that the designers have a full understanding of the information needs of the prospective users of the database. Appropriate data structures to meet those needs are first designed at a conceptual level and then implemented using the database software tools described in the previous section.

FIGURE 1.12
Alternative Data
Models

Model	Description	Common Uses
Hierarchical	Uses pointer-based retrieval; allows only hierarchical data structures	High-volume legacy systems
Network	Uses pointer-based retrieval; allows network data structures	High-volume legacy systems
Relational	Links data by repetition of unique identifying data and features a user-friendly query language	Broad—from personal use to high-volume systems
Object-oriented	Combines data and methods (processes) used with the data into objects and features inheritance of properties from higher level objects	Emerging technology with limited current use in business systems

ALTERNATIVE TYPES OF DATABASES

A variety of DBMS software is available to assist the implementation of database systems. This software varies both in terms of the data model used to implement the database system and in the degree of decentralization of system resources that is supported.

DATA MODELS FOR IMPLEMENTING DATABASE SYSTEMS

Figure 1.12 lists the alternative data models that are available for the development of database systems. The first database systems were developed to support high-volume organizational transaction processing systems. These applications strained the capacities of the largest mainframe computers available at the time they were developed. These databases were developed using the hierarchical or **network data models,** which utilize highly efficient pointer-based retrieval methods. On the downside, **hierarchical** and network databases tend to be inflexible to changes in the structure of a database, and they do not provide a user-friendly mechanism to allow nontechnical users to access data.

The **relational database model** emerged in the 1970s and became prevalent during the 1980s. It uses the repetition of unique identifying information to link related data. This method is somewhat slower and less machine efficient than pointer-based retrieval. However, changes in the structure of a database can be accommodated relatively easily under the relational model. In addition, the relational model has a strong theoretical basis, rooted in a few relatively simple principles. A standard language called structured query language (SQL) has emerged for retrieval and processing of relational databases. SQL is a query language that makes it relatively easy for end-users to access a database and retrieve selected data to answer ad-hoc questions.

The relational model is by far the most prevalent model in use today. Due to continuing increases in the capacity and processing speed of computers, the slower data retrieval of the relational model is no longer a major disadvantage for most systems.

Network data model
A database model that uses pointer-based data retrieval and supports network data structures.

Hierarchical data model
A database model that uses pointer-based data retrieval and supports only hierarchical data structures.

Relational data model
A database model that uses the repetition of key identifying data to link related data and features a query language widely accessible to end-users.

At the same time, the flexibility and ease of use of the relational model become more and more important over time.

The relational model was initially used primarily for low- to medium-volume databases. It opened up the ability to apply database technology to support individuals and work groups. Relational database technology can now provide adequate processing power even for many high-volume databases. Hierarchical and network databases have been relegated largely to the role of **legacy systems**—technologies that are no longer viable for use in new systems, but are embedded in important ongoing systems that must be maintained. Given the scope of some of the systems developed under the hierarchical and network models, and the cost involved in replacing them, it is likely that databases based on the hierarchical and network models will continue to be used well into the next century (Burleson, 1995).

In recent years, the **object-oriented data model** has emerged. Object-oriented concepts were first incorporated in object-oriented programming languages. In object-oriented systems, methods or procedures that can be performed on data are stored, along with the data, in objects. Object-oriented systems also emphasize the idea that objects inherit characteristics from higher level classes of objects to which they belong. Incorporating these concepts into database systems adds to the power of the systems, but also adds to their complexity. Although databases incorporating the concepts of the object-oriented model are commercially available, thus far, object-oriented databases have been implemented primarily in engineering rather than business-oriented systems.

Because the relational model is most commonly used for business systems developed today, most of this textbook will focus on it. The hierarchical, network, and object-oriented models are covered in Chapters 13 through 15.

Legacy system
A system that uses older technology that is no longer used in systems currently under development.

Object-oriented data model
A database model based upon objects that combine methods (processes) to be applied to data with the data itself, and which includes the concept that objects can inherit the properties of other (higher level) objects.

Category	Description	Common Uses
Centralized	DBMSs designed to operate on a central mainframe or mini-computer with all related processing activities performed on that central processor	Widely used for most medium- to large-scale databases
Personal Use	DBMSs designed to reside on a microcomputer and to meet the needs of a single user	Widely used for personal applications and for small-business applications
Client-Server	DBMSs designed to support the sharing of processing activities between a server and a set of clients connected by the network	Increasingly used for small- to medium-scale databases supporting work groups and departments
Distributed	DBMSs that distribute data across multiple computers, but manage it as a single database	Limited current use due to complexity of processing

FIGURE 1.13
Distribution Alternates among Database Systems

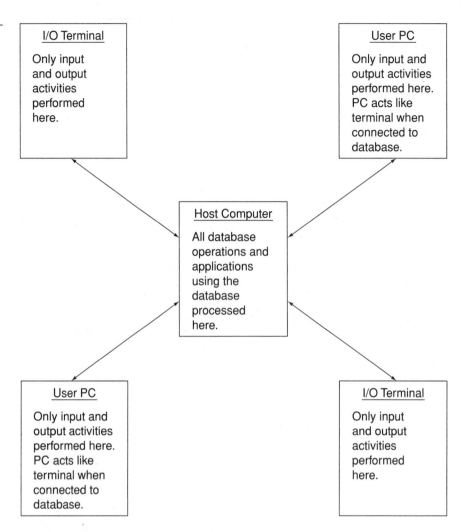

FIGURE 1.14
Resource Utilization in
a Centralized
Database System

DECENTRALIZATION IN DATABASE SYSTEMS

Databases can also be divided into categories based upon the degree of centralization or decentralization of processing that they support, as shown in Figure 1.13. The first databases were all designed to operate as centralized systems running on a mainframe computer. All processing activities, database access and retrieval, any required programming or manipulation of the data retrieved, and conversion of the results to the form required by the user were all to take place on the central computer. Computer terminals might be used to provide distributed access to the database, but all of its processing was performed at the central computer (see Figure 1.14). This type of database structure is still prevalent. The processing speed of mainframe computers remains necessary for high-volume, transactions-processing systems. Centralized mainframe-based databases also offer greater control than other systems over access to the database.

Personal use databases based on the relational data model began to appear a few years after development of the personal computer. In a sense these systems represent the opposite end of the spectrum from the centralized mainframe database. Any individual with a PC on his or her desk could develop and maintain his or her own databases. These databases were designed to be easy for nontechnical individuals to use. Many of the early products in this category had a rather limited set of database management features, which did not fully qualify them as relational DBMSs. Over time, the features of these systems have expanded and many of them have been adapted so that they can support multiple users on PC networks. In many small businesses this type of PC database may extend beyond personal use applications to manage crucial organizational data. Prominent examples of this type of database product include DBASE, RBASE, PARADOX, ACCESS, and Foxbase.

As the networking capabilities of computers have increased, a need has arisen for a type of database between the centralized mainframe system and the personal use system residing on a single PC. Systems are needed that can facilitate coordinated access to data by multiple users while still taking advantage of the distributed computing power of PCs and distributing some of the control over the system to individual users. Two new types of database are emerging to fill this need. They are client-server databases and distributed databases.

Client-server databases utilize the concept of cooperative processing. The database is still stored at one central location on a computer called the *server*. However, much of the processing of the database data (manipulating data that has been retrieved, summarizing it, and converting it to the desired form for presentation to the user) can be moved to client computers (see Figure 1.15). Each user with a PC connected to the network can be a client. Allowing applications to manipulate and present the data to be placed on client machines reduces the workload on the database server. This allows higher volumes of transactions to be handled with a given capacity of server. Spreading the processing load across the network provides greater flexibility to incrementally expand systems. It also gives individual users a greater sense of control over the system, since their applications are developed and run on their own computers (Friend,1994).

Use of client-server computing is expected to expand rapidly over the next few years, paralleling the expanding role of networked microcomputers. Oracle and Sybase are two prominent examples of DBMS products designed to support client-server operations.

Distributed database systems move a step beyond the client-server approach in that they actually distribute the data of the database across multiple computers. Data are distributed across various computers in a fashion designed to store each unit of data at the location where it is most frequently used (see Figure 1.16). By doing this, the load on the communications network is minimized and users have a sense of custody over the data they use most frequently. However, allowing distribution of the data in a database adds greatly to the complexity of database processing, because distributed databases must allow users to access all data in the database

Client-server database
A database designed to support cooperative processing. All direct database operations are handled by a server computer that stores the database data. Related processing to manipulate data and present it appropriately is performed on client computers.

Distributed database
A database configuration in which data are distributed across multiple computers but managed as a single database.

FIGURE 1.15
Distribution of
Activities in a Client-
Server Database
System

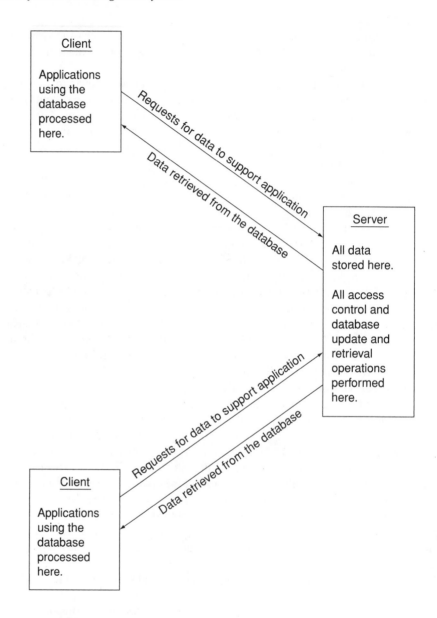

transparently (as if it were located at their local computer) while still maintaining adequate controls. For this reason, distributed database systems have seen only limited use thus far.

Because centralized and client/server databases are prevalent in business database systems developed today, we will discuss both types throughout the text. Distributed database concepts will be covered in Chapter 12.

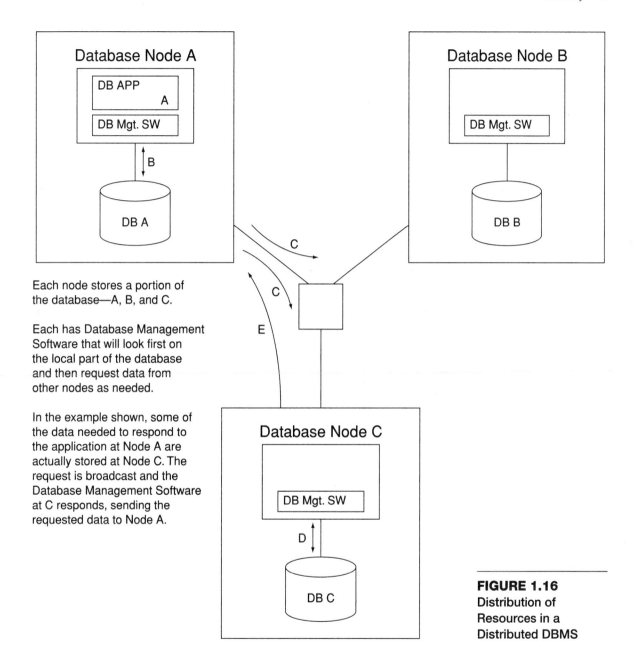

FIGURE 1.16
Distribution of
Resources in a
Distributed DBMS

SUMMARY

A database may be defined as an integrated, self-describing collection of data describing sets of related entities and the relationships that interconnect them. Database systems have several advantages, including: reduced data redundancy, broader sharing of organizational data, improved productivity in the development and maintenance of applications, and the ability to use data as an organizational resource. Limitations or disadvantages to database systems include: the cost of software acquisition and user training, increased cost of processing routine transactions data, increases in the magnitude of potential loss due to a disaster, and user resistance to the loss of control over data.

Modern database management systems (DBMSs) are expected to have a number of important features. A linking mechanism to bring together related data from different entities must be provided. Data dictionaries allow users to easily locate descriptive information about a database. Query languages allow users to retrieve tables of related data using a single command. Mechanisms to control access to the database must be provided. Most DBMSs provide a host language interface that allows the database to be used in conjunction with a standard programming language. Many DBMSs also provide high-level data manipulation languages and/or 4GL application development software to support the development of applications within the DBMS environment itself. Finally, DBMSs must provide disaster recovery and concurrent access control capabilities.

DBMSs may be categorized by the type of data model on which they are based. DBMSs have been developed based on the hierarchical, network, relational, and object-oriented models. The relational model is most widely used currently, while the potential of the relatively new object-oriented model has not yet been fully developed.

DBMSs can also be categorized by their degree of centralization or decentralization. Categories include centralized mainframe databases, personal use databases, client-server databases, and distributed databases. Client-server databases feature cooperative processing wherein the client and the server share the processing work of an application.

REVIEW QUIZ

_____ Systems using technology no longer used in currently developed systems.

_____ An integrated, self-describing collection of data about related entities.

_____ A listing describing the structure of a set of data.

_____ A user-friendly language supporting retrieval of selected data from a database.

_____ A set of software that supports the storage, maintenance, and operation of databases.

_____ Storage of more than one copy of the same data item.

_____ Type of database that supports cooperative processing.

_____ A person, place, thing, or event of importance to an organization.

_____ Allows database commands to be embedded in programs in an external language, e.g., COBOL.

_____ Places data on multiple computers but manages them as an integrated database.

_____ Two or more users accessing a database at the same time.

_____ Uses repetition of identifying data to link entities and features a query language.

1. Database
2. Database management system
3. Entity
4. Data dictionary
5. Query language
6. Host language interface
7. Data redundancy
8. Legacy systems
9. Client-server database
10. Distributed database
11. Relational database
12. Concurrent access

---

1. Describe and distinguish among the terms *database, database management system,* and *database system.*
2. What do we mean when we say that a database is self-describing?
3. What is data redundancy? What problems does data redundancy cause?
4. What do we mean by program-data independence? Why is this concept important?
5. How do database systems support the ability of organizations to treat data as an organizational resource?
6. What is the function of host language interface software?
7. What does a query language do?
8. What is the role of a data dictionary in a database system?
9. Briefly describe and distinguish among the hierarchical, network, relational, and object-oriented data models.
10. What are the principal advantages and disadvantages of the relational data model? Why has it become the most widely used data model?

REVIEW QUESTIONS AND EXERCISES

11. Briefly describe and distinguish among centralized, personal use, client-server, and distributed databases.

12. Client-server databases support cooperative processing. What do we mean by cooperative processing, and how does the client-server model support this type of processing?

13. Describe a situation in which a file-oriented system would be superior to a database system.

14. The D. E. Fitness Company currently uses a file-oriented system. They have a master customer file that contains the customer's name, account number, address, phone number, and account balance. Another file is used to maintain a list of customers who have signed up for each class. This file contains the class name, the time the class meets, and the customer's account number, name, and phone number.

    a. Describe the data redundancy involved in this system. Describe the problems this redundancy causes. How would a move to a database system eliminate these problems?

    b. Based on the preceding description, how would you describe information in this system in terms of its scope and type?

    c. Assuming D. E. Fitness were to develop a database system for this application, what type of database would you recommend? Why?

15. What questions would you ask if you were brought in as a consultant to help determine the type of DBMS to be used in an organization?

16. What measures would you use to overcome user resistance to the development of a new database system?

17. For each of the following situations, indicate the DBMS feature or features you would use to address the problem and describe why you think its (their) use is appropriate.

    a. You are asked to convert some reports to the new database environment. A set of COBOL programs to produce these reports based on the prior file-oriented system is available.

    b. You are asked to build some forms and menus to maintain a portion of a database that you have never used before.

    c. You have a database containing, among other things, project status information. Your boss asks you to bring summary information about the status of one of the projects to a meeting that will begin in 20 minutes.

18. Find an organization that maintains several databases and identify at least three.

    a. Describe the scope and type of information maintained by each database.

    b. Indicate the type of DBMS used for each database, and suggest alternative DBMS types that might be appropriate, if any.

    c. For at least one of the databases, indicate which staff perform each of the developer and user roles described in Figure 1.15.

DATA AND ITS REPRESENTATION IN DATABASE SYSTEMS

LEARNING OBJECTIVES

After completing this chapter, you should be able to

■ Identify the basic metadata units—attributes, entity occurrence, and entity class—and relate them appropriately to associated units in tables or files.

■ Describe the domain of an attribute.

■ Describe functional determination, indicate how functional determination relates to the primary key, and describe how it is used to link related data elements.

■ Examine sample data or reports and identify:
  ■ One to one, one to many, and many to many relationships between entities.
  ■ Fixed, mandatory, and optional relationships between entities.
  ■ Class, subclass, and intra-table relationships.

■ Draw an appropriate entity–relationship diagram for a small example database.

■ Create an appropriate set of table structure diagrams for a small example database.

Organizations must maintain data about a wide variety of persons, things, and activities of importance to them. As we noted in Chapter 1, the data collected and maintained by an organization should provide an effective model of the organization and its components, which can be used to monitor and control the organization's resources and operations. To use data effectively, appropriate methods must be in place for generation, storage, and retrieval. In addition, information must be organized in a manner that supports the ways in which the organization accesses and uses its data.

In designing databases we begin by examining the physical persons, things, and processes that are important to the organization, and then create a conceptual data model of those physical realities. This model is designed to capture the key characteristics of the entities we are representing and the relationships among them. It does not specify how the data will be physically stored or even the type of database model that will be used to implement the database. Once this conceptual data model is completed, it is converted to a database model with appropriate structures capable of implementing the database.

In this chapter, we first describe the fundamentals of how units of data are logically organized or structured. Next, we examine how those structures are represented in the most commonly used conceptual data model—the entity-relationship model. Finally, we provide a brief overview of how the conceptual data model is implemented under the relational database model.

METADATA—DATA ABOUT DATA

Before we can begin to build a data model of a system, we must understand the types of logical relationships or structures that can exist among physical elements and that must be represented in our data models. This type of information is commonly referred to as **metadata.** Metadata encompasses all information about the structure of data, and restrictions on the values and structures that data can have—it is "data about data." The data dictionary of a database can be thought of as containing metadata for that database.

Metadata
Information describing the nature and structure of an organization's data; data about data.

Although no universally accepted terminology exists to describe metadata structures, the most popular set of terms is used in the entity-relationship model. We will use that terminology to describe the components of metadata. Later in this chapter, we will formally discuss the entity-relationship model.

In building a data model a number of questions must be addressed. What **entities** (e.g., customers, employees, products) need to be described in the model? What characteristics or attributes of these things need to be recorded (e.g., the *names* of employees and the *unit price* of products)? Can an attribute or a set of attributes be identified that will serve as a primary key to uniquely identify one specific occurrence of an entity (e.g., there is only one product whose product number is L682C, and there cannot possibly be more than one employee with the social security number 396-28-1273). What associations or relationships exist between entities that should be recognized and incorporated in the database model in order to effectively process interrelated groups of data? Entities, attributes, primary key identifiers of entities, and relationships between entities are all important types of metadata and must be identified and described when modeling data to be stored in a database.

Entity
A person, place, thing, or event *of importance to the organization.* Anything that can be a noun can be an entity.

Metadata also provides information about limits on the values data should be allowed to take and about the allowable relationships between entities and attributes. The **domain** of an attribute defines the attribute's data type and its set of valid values (Flemming and Van Halle, 1990). For example, social security numbers must be nine numeric digits and grades issued by a university might be restricted to only the values A, B, C, D, F, and I. Beyond this, various additional restrictions may be needed to make the data model support and conform to business rules. A variety of rules may limit the valid values of an attribute based on the value of some other attribute or set of attributes. For example, suppose that *Product ID#* and *Product Class* are attributes of the product entity. The *Product ID#* whose *Product Class* is "Computers" may be required to have a C as its first digit, but a *Product ID#* beginning with P might be allowed in some other *Product Class* such as "Printers."

Domain
The domain of an attribute is the set of all data types and all possible values that an attribute can validly have.

The basic metadata building blocks of the structure of databases are discussed in more detail in the following sections. More complex examples of metadata structures and restrictions will be presented in subsequent chapters on logical and physical design.

THE ENTITY/ATTRIBUTE STRUCTURE

ENTITIES

Let's assume that the Apex Products Company, which we introduced in Chapter 1, takes orders through a traveling sales staff and ships the products it sells through the mail. Clearly, one important system for this firm will be order processing. *Customers* of Apex Products place orders for the *products* they want. The orders are placed with salespersons who are *employees* of Apex Products. These customers, products, and employees are all *entities* of importance to our firm. Any person, place, thing, or event that the organization keeps information about can be thought of as an entity. Basically, anything that can be a noun can be an entity.

The entities identified above represent physical persons or things; however, entities also can be intangible or conceptual objects. What about the process of *ordering* products? Is there an order entity? Is an order a thing? The word *order* can be used as either a verb or a noun. We can say "the customer *ordered* three boxes of computer paper" or "the customer *placed an order* for three boxes of computer paper." In the first instance the word *ordered* is a verb describing the action or process of a customer requesting something. In general, actions or processes cannot be represented as entities, but are instead represented as computer processes that change the status of the entities involved in those processes.

In the second example above, the word *order* is used as a noun. It stands for an event, which can be represented as an entity. The *order event* records the fact that, at a particular point in time, a customer requested some units of one or more products. This request triggers a set of processes that results in products being shipped to the customer and payment for them being received by the firm. Note that the order is not the customer who placed it or the product that was ordered. It is not a physical, tangible thing, but rather an intangible representation of an event.

There can also be intangible entities which are not events. Take, for instance, a *department.* What is a department? Is it the manager's office, the physical facilities that the workers use, the workers themselves, or the functions or activities that the workers perform? When we talk about a department, we might mean any of these things. The department is a conceptual unit rather than a specific physical object, and it can encompass all the components just described.

ATTRIBUTES

Attribute
An individual characteristic or property of an entity.

Each entity has a number of characteristics or properties called **attributes.** If entities are nouns, we can think of attributes as adjectives describing characteristics of entities. If our organization's customers are individuals, attributes of interest to our organization might include their names, social security numbers, addresses, and, if we extend credit to our customers, their account balances. Our data model should include all the attributes of the customer entity that are important to our organization. As physical beings, these customers have many additional attributes—hair color, eye color, age—which are not important to our organization. For some other organization, a firm selling cosmetics for instance, these attributes might be very important and should be included in that firm's data model of the customer entity.

ENTITY CLASS VERSUS ENTITY OCCURRENCE

We can talk about an individual *occurrence* of an entity, such as an individual customer or a particular product. Sets of these **entity occurrences** that have the same types of characteristics constitute **entity classes.** For example, we might refer to the set of all our customers as the customer entity class for our organization, and the set of all products we produce would represent the product entity class. When we refer to an attribute of an entity class, we mean the type of characteristic which that attribute represents and not its value. *Address* is an attribute of the Customer entity class, but "223 Main Street" is a *value* of the Address attribute for a particular Customer occurrence.

Entity occurrence
One individual instance of a type of entity—the set of data describing an instance of an entity.

Entity class
The set of all occurrences of a given type of entity.

ENTITIES AND ATTRIBUTES AS A FILE OR TABLE STRUCTURE

When we create the conceptual design for a database, we are creating a model of selected elements of these entities. Our model uses data to identify and describe physical or conceptual entities, and attributes of those entities, that are important to our organization. Like all models, the data model we create is not designed to be a complete representation of reality. If employees' cars are not needed to effectively model the functions of our organization, we do not include a car entity in our data model. Similarly, if we do not need to know the hair color of our customers to meet any current or potential organizational need, we will not include this attribute in our data model of the customer entity class.

The idea of building data models of entities and their attributes is not new or unique to database management systems. These data units underlie file-oriented processing and can be represented in standard tabular presentation of data as well. As Figure 2.1 indicates, the idea of an attribute corresponds to the unit of data that we called a field in file-oriented processing. An occurrence of an entity corresponds to a record in a file, and an entity class corresponds to an entire file in a file-oriented system.

Figure 2.1 also shows that an entity class and its attributes and occurrences can be represented as a table. In this tabular representation, the entire contents of the table represent the entity class, each column represents the set of values for a specific attribute of the entity, and each row represents the set of attribute values for a specific occurrence of the entity. Figure 2.2 presents a sample table for the Customer entity. Note that the metadata units (entity class, entity occurrence, and attribute) correspond

Entity-Relationship Model	File-Oriented Model	Tabular or Relational Model
Attribute	Field	Column
Entity occurrence	Record	Row
Entity class	File	Table

FIGURE 2.1
Representations of Data Units in Alternative Data Models

FIGURE 2.2
Sample Data Table for
Apex Products

C_Id#	C_Name	C_Address	Account_Balance
2475	Chris Moss	147 Dale Tr.	$752.34
6789	Bob Bates	382 Locust St.	$386.54
1905	Al Vest	1701 S. Market St.	$0.00
5182	Mike Adams	286 Front St.	$1,826.54

to features of the structure of the table rather than its contents. Tables contain the data itself, but their structure is a representation of metadata.

This tabular representation is a very user-friendly way to represent these data units. We are used to the idea that the data in a specific row or column of a table belong together, and that column headers describe the type of data stored in the remainder of the column. Thus, we read across a row of the Customer table to find all the information we have about a particular customer using the column headings to identify the attributes or characteristics recorded in each cell: The customer whose ID# is 6789 is named Bob Bates, lives at 382 Locust Street, and has an account balance of $386.54.

The relational database model utilizes a tabular structure. In fact, all data in relational databases must be stored in ways that can be represented as rectangular tables like those shown in Figure 2.2. Because this tabular representation is easy to understand and is the method of representation most commonly used for relational databases, we will use tables of this type throughout this textbook to present entity structures and samples of the data they might contain.

ENTITY CLASSES AND SUBCLASSES

The scope of an entity class depends on the context in which it is defined. If we deal with all our customers in essentially the same way, we will need information about the same characteristics (attributes) for each customer and will need to perform the same types of processes on the data for each customer. All our customers should be treated as members of a single customer entity.

Now suppose some of our customers are individuals and others are organizations. We may need to deal with these types of customers in very different ways. Perhaps we will use social security numbers to identify individual customers, but will assign our own customer number to organizational customers, or perhaps we will extend credit only to organizational customers.

If these two categories of customers interact with our organization in different ways that require us to store different types of information about them, we should treat them as separate entity classes. It is quite possible that some attributes will be common to both individual and organizational customers, whereas others will apply to only one category or the other. In this case, we might want to define a CUSTOMER entity class that encompasses all customers and contains only the attributes common to both classes of customers. Additionally, we would define subclasses of the CUSTOMER entity class to record attributes specific only to individual customers and attributes specific only to organizational customers.

ASSOCIATIONS

Associations exist between data items and between entity occurrences. Between any two items a pair of associations can exist: an association from the first to the second, and a reverse association from the second item back to the first. Some associations link to only one occurrence of the related item while others allow multiple associated occurrences. For example, a child can have no more than one biological mother, but as a student can have several teachers. If there can be no more than one occurrence of B for a given occurrence of A, we say that there is a *one association* from A to B. If there can be more than one occurrence of B for each occurrence of A, we say that there is a *many association* from A to B.

The maximum number of occurrences of B that can be associated with A is called the *cardinality* of the association from A to B. If a maximum of one B can be associated with a given occurrence of A, the association has a cardinality of one. If a maximum of two B occurrences can be tied to a single occurrence of A, the association has a cardinality of two, and so on. For most purposes, however, we need only distinguish between associations with a cardinality of one (one associations), and associations whose cardinality is anything greater than one (many associations).

Saying that there is a one association from X to Y is equivalent to saying that X functionally determines Y. In common notation, this is expressed as X→Y. Figure 2.3 presents a set of association diagrams. In part A of the figure, if I know that the value of A is 12, then I also know that the value of B is 18. Similarly, the *one association* between CHILD and BIOLOGICAL MOTHER shown in part B ensures that I can uniquely identify the BIOLOGICAL MOTHER associated with any known occurrence of CHILD. If the CHILD is Sue Smith, the BIOLOGICAL MOTHER must be Sally Smith: CHILD→BIOLOGICAL MOTHER.

Part C demonstrates that one item does *not* functionally determine another item when there is a many association from the first item to the second. Knowing the PROFESSION of the PERSON we are interested in does not allow us to uniquely identify that person because there is more than one person associated with a single value of profession. In our example, if PROFESSION is Lawyer, the PERSON could be Sue Smith or Ann Adams. Thus the value of X functionally determines the value of Y *if and only if* there is a one association from X to Y.

Notice also that the reverse associations in our example are not always one associations. The association from Y to X and the association from BIOLOGICAL MOTHER to CHILD are both a many association. Thus Y does not uniquely determine X; when Y is 16, X can be 3 or 5, and similarly the BIOLOGICAL MOTHER Sally Smith has more than one CHILD.

An important extension of **functional determinaton** is the fact that if A functionally determines B and B functionally determines C, then A functionally determines C. This logic can be extended through any number of intermediate associations (e.g.,

Associations
An association can exist from one set of objects to another. There is a one association from set A to set B if only one item in B may be associated with a given item in A. There is a many association from A to B if more than one item in B can be associated with a given item in A.

Functional determination
X functionally determines Y if there is only one possible value for Y associated with each value of X.

FIGURE 2.3
Three Types of
Associations

a. A One Association from Set A to Set B

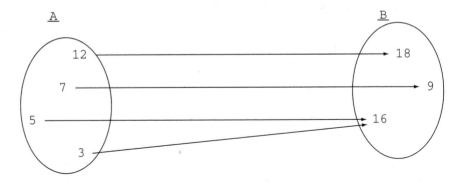

b. A One Association from Child to Biological Mother

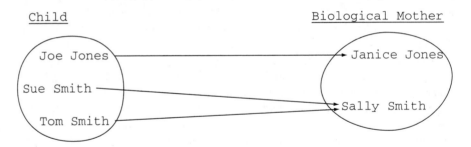

c. A Many Association from Occupation to Person

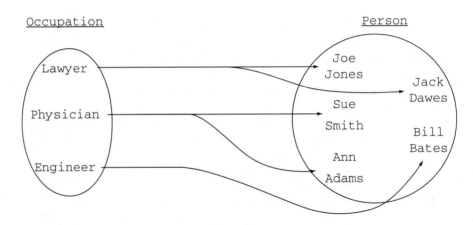

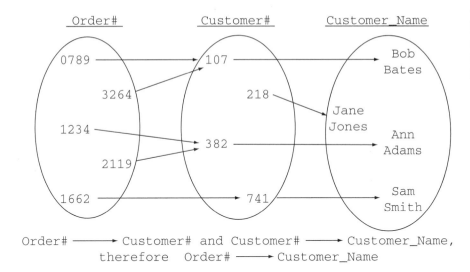

FIGURE 2.4
An Example of a
Chain of Functional
Determination

Order# ──────▶ Customer# and Customer# ──────▶ Customer_Name,
        therefore Order# ──────▶ Customer_Name

A→B, B→C, C→D, and D→E, implies A→E). In Figure 2.4, since each Order# is associated with only one Customer# and each Customer# is associated with only one Customer_Name, we can infer that knowing an Order# allows us to uniquely identify the name of the Customer who placed it; Order# 1662 was placed by Sam Smith.

ASSOCIATIONS AMONG ATTRIBUTES OF AN ENTITY

If an entity has been properly defined, all its attributes must be associated with one another. Figure 2.5 presents a table of sample data for the employee entity, with a set of association diagrams for a portion of the table. Because each row of that table gives the set of attribute values describing a particular employee, the attribute values in each row are obviously associated with one another. However, some attributes may have the same data values in multiple occurrences. For example, Pay_Class C occurs three times in the sample data. Thus, there is an association from the value C in Pay_Class to the values of the other attributes associated with all three of those occurrences. Pay_Class C is associated with three different values of E_ID# (2874, 4081, and 1870) and with two different Departments (Shipping and Assembly). In fact, the Pay_Class attribute has a many association with all the other attributes of the employee table. This means that knowing the value of Pay_Class does not allow us to determine the value of any other attribute. Similarly, the value Assembly occurs as the Department attribute on three different rows of the table, so it is associated with multiple occurrences of other attributes; knowing the value of Department does not allow us to infer the value of any other attribute.

In contrast to the Department and Pay_Class attributes, the employee ID number, E_ID#, has a unique value for each row of the employee table. Because there are never two entity occurrences with the same value for E_ID#, each E_ID# value must have a one association with all the other attributes of the employee table. The E_ID# attribute functionally determines the values of all other attributes in the table.

E_Id#	E_Name	Pay_Class	Department
2874	Bill Jones	C	Shipping
9138	Sue Tibbots	A	Assembly
4081	Tom Turner	C	Assembly
7238	Ann Davis	B	Order Entry
1870	Nat Evans	C	Assembly

FIGURE 2.5
Associations among
Attributes of Apex
Products Employees

Association Diagrams

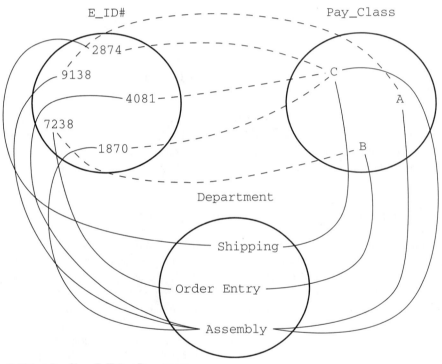

E_ID# → Pay Class, E_ID# → Department
Pay_Class ↛ E_ID#, Pay_Class ↛ Department
Department ↛ E_ID#, Department ↛ Pay_Class

If we know the E_ID# of an employee is 9138 we are able to infer that her name is "Sue Tibbots," her Pay_Class is A, and she is assigned to the Assembly department. We simply read across the appropriate row of the table to pick up all the attributes of the one unique occurrence of the employee entity whose E_ID# is 9138.

IDENTIFICATION OF ENTITY OCCURRENCES—THE PRIMARY KEY

Primary key
An attribute (or combination of attributes) that uniquely identifies an occurrence of an entity.

If the value of an attribute uniquely identifies an occurrence of an entity, that attribute can serve as the **primary key** of the entity. To serve as a primary key an attribute must be unique. It must be the case that no two occurrences do or can have the same value for the primary key attribute.

Based on our sample data in Figure 2.5, E_Name also uniquely identifies an occurrence of the employee entity. However, we cannot guarantee that there will never be two employees with identical names. Thus, E_Name is not a good candidate to serve as the primary key to the employee table.

When an entity does not have a single attribute that uniquely identifies its occurrences, a combination of attributes may be used for identification purposes. This type of primary key is called a **concatenated key.**

Note that it is possible to have an entity class that does not have a primary key. However, for several reasons we like to identify a primary key for each entity class. A specific occurrence of an entity class can be directly accessed only if it has a primary key whose value can be specified by a user to identify the desired occurrence. In addition, the relational model uses primary keys as the mechanism to link related entity classes together. Finally, examination of the relationship of attributes to the primary key of a table is an important part of "normalization" of a database. Normalization helps ensure that entity classes have been defined appropriately and that the boundaries between entity classes have been correctly drawn. Normalization will be discussed in detail in Chapter 3.

Concatenated key
A primary key consisting of two or more attributes that *together* uniquely identify an occurrence of an entity.

ASSOCIATIONS BETWEEN ENTITY CLASSES

In addition to associations among the attributes of an entity, associations exist between occurrences of different entity classes. For example, when a customer of Apex Products places an order, an occurrence of the order entity is created that is obviously associated with the customer who placed it. What is the nature of this association? In this case the association from customer to order is a many association. A given customer can place any number of orders, and identifying the customer does not allow us to uniquely identify a particular order occurrence. But what about the reverse association? There is a one association from order to customer. Each order is assigned to only one customer. If I can identify an order occurrence, I am able to infer the identity of the customer placing that order.

In describing the associations among entity classes, it is customary to consider the associations in both directions and to refer to them as relationships. There are two basic types of association from one item to another, one or many, and the same two possibilities apply to the reverse association from the second item to the first. Thus,

		Forward Association	
		One	**Many**
Reverse Association	**One**	One to One Relationship	One to Many Relationship
	Many	Many to One Relationship	Many to Many Relationship

FIGURE 2.6
A Pair of Associations Between Two Items Forms a Relationship

FIGURE 2.7

Examples of One to Many Relationships

Customer-Order Relationship

Advising Relationship

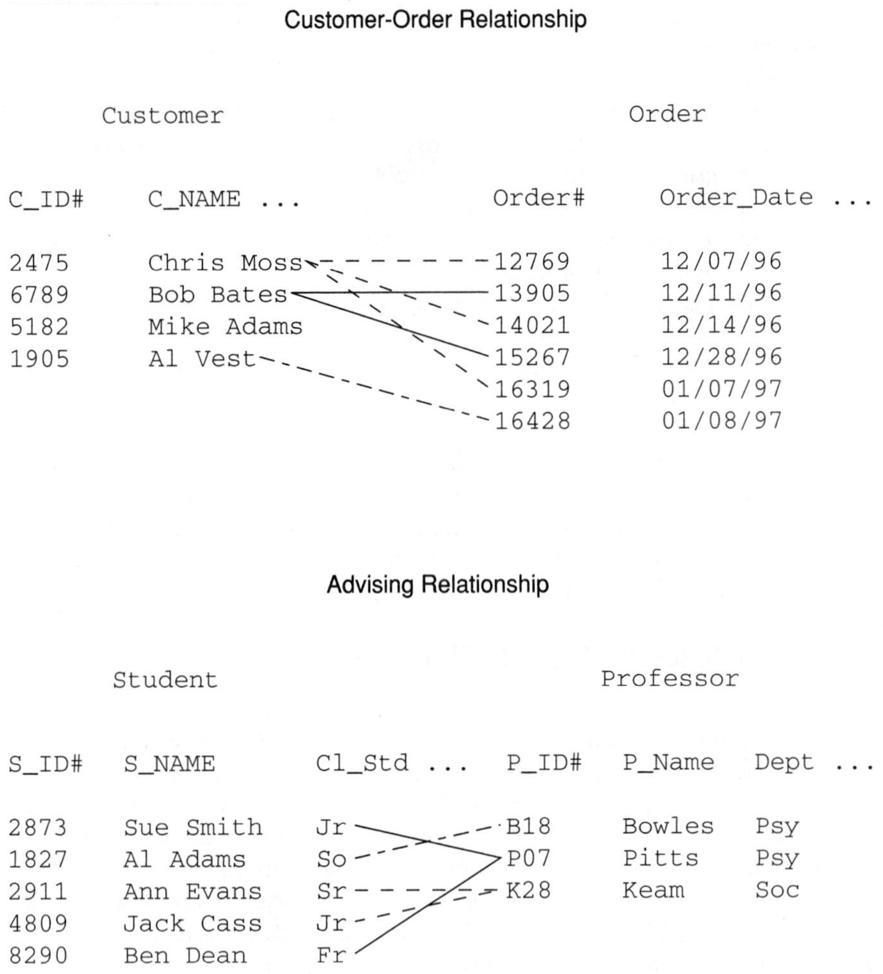

Relationship
A relationship between any two entities is defined by the pair of associations that exists between them. The types of relationships that can exist are *one to one, one to many,* and *many to many.*

as Figure 2.6 indicates, there are three possible types of **relationship** between two items: a one to one relationship, a one to many relationship, or a many to many relationship. The relationship between customers and orders is called *one to many.*

One to Many Relationships

Figure 2.7 shows two examples of one to many relationships. Looking first at the Customer–Order relationship, a customer occurrence can be associated with many order occurrences, but each order occurrence is associated with only one customer. Using values of the primary key attributes, C_ID# and Order#, to identify specific occurrences of each entity, the following inferences can be drawn. Knowing the value of Order# allows me to functionally determine the value of Customer. I can infer that the order with Order# 13905 was placed by the customer whose ID number is 6789, and whose name is Bob Bates.

Working in the opposite direction, knowing the value of C_ID# does not allow one to uniquely identify an occurrence of the order entity. Instead, each C_ID# is associated with a set of order occurrences, each of which is associated only with the identified customer. I know that order number 13905 placed on 12/11/96, and order number 15267 placed on 12/28/96, were placed by the one customer whose C_ID# is 6789, whose name is Bob Bates, and so on.

The second example in Figure 2.7 shows an advising relationship that might exist between students and professors at a university. If each student is allowed to have only one advisor, the relationship might look like the one shown in the figure. Each professor may advise many students, but each student can have only one advisor. Identifying a Student occurrence allows us to determine a single associated

FIGURE 2.8
Examples of Many to Many Relationships

Student-Organization Relationship

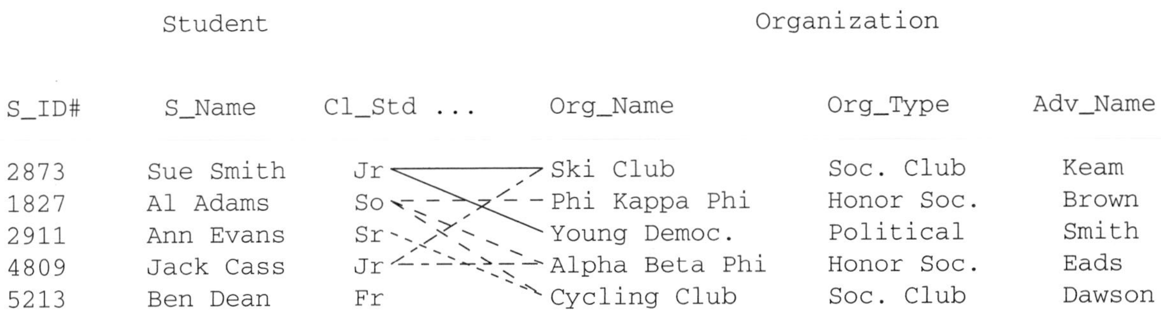

Order-Product Relationship

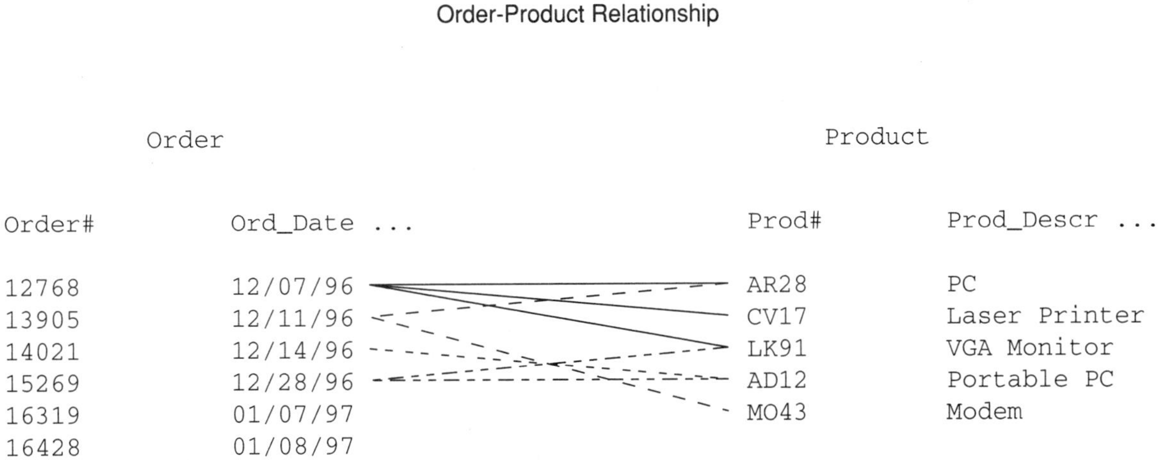

FIGURE 2.9
The Student-Org
Intersection Entity

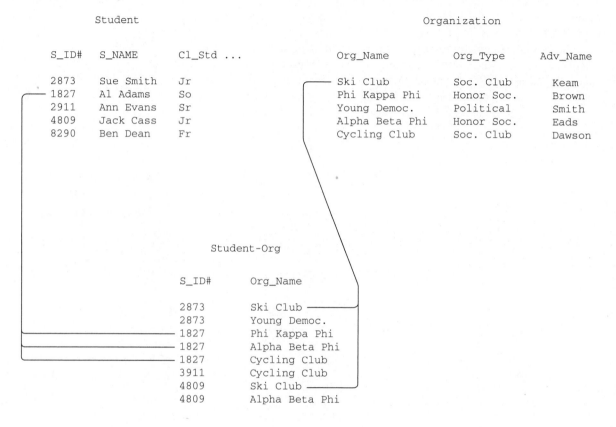

Professor occurrence. Identifying a Professor occurrence allows us to find a set of associated Student occurrences.

Many to Many Relationships

Now let's look at some examples of many to many relationships. Figure 2.8 gives a sample of the associations that might exist between students and organizations, and between orders and products. Looking first at the student–organization relationship, we see that a student can belong to many organizations—the student whose S_ID# is 1827 belongs to Phi Kappa Phi, Alpha Beta Psi, and the Cycling Club. Each organization has many members — S_ID#s 2873 and 4809 both belong to the Ski Club.

Can we functionally determine values of attributes in one of these entity classes based on the value of the primary key of the other entity class? For each student number, there may be a set of associated organization occurrences, and for each organizational name, there may be a set of associated students. Only a one association, however, allows the value of one item to functionally determine the value of another

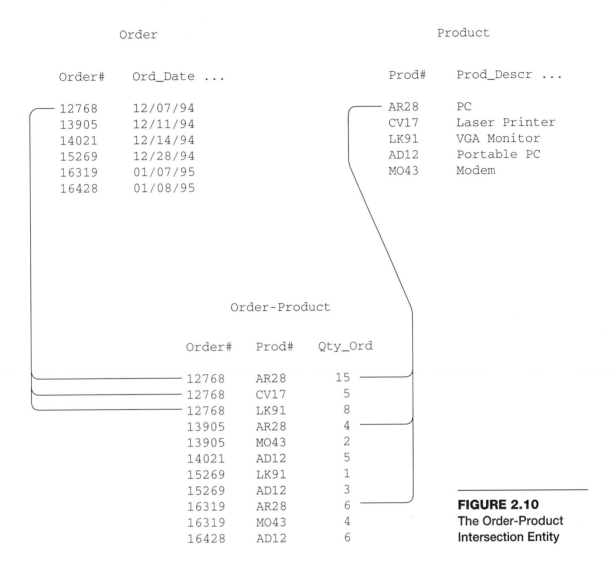

FIGURE 2.10
The Order-Product
Intersection Entity

item. Thus, many to many relationships donot allow us to extend a chain of inferences across the related entity classes to tie their data together.

The methods used for actual storage and retrieval of data in database management systems require that one be able to establish a chain of inferences, based on values functionally determining other values, to tie together all related data. Thus, many to many relationships cannot be directly implemented in the physical design of a database. They remain a valid conceptual structure, but something must be done if they are to be represented physically.

A many to many relationship can be converted to a pair of one to many relationships by creating an **intersection entity** class that contains one occurrence for each related pair of occurrences of the original entities. In the case of students and

Intersection entity
An intersection entity resolves a many to many relationship between two other entities. It appears on the many side of a one to many relationship.

organizations, the intersection entity class might be called Student–Org. As shown in Figure 2.9, the Student–Org entity class has three occurrences related to student number 1827, one for each of the organizations to which the student belongs. Similarly there is one occurrence of the Student–Org entity for each student belonging to a particular organization, such as the Ski Club. The chain of inferences is restored—each student number is tied to a set of Student–Org occurrences, each of

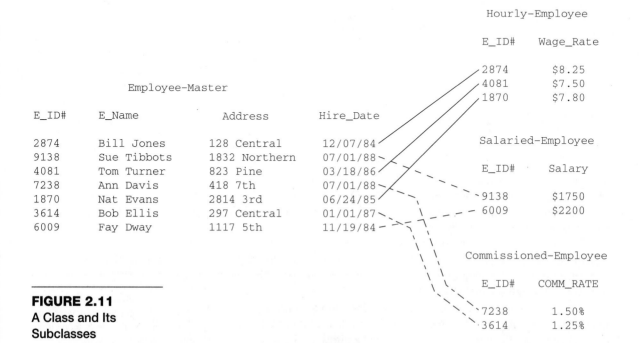

Employee

E_ID#	E_Name	Address	Hire_Date	Wage_Rate	Salary	Comm_Rate
2874	Bill Jones	128 Central	12/07/84	$8.25		
9138	Sue Tibbots	1832 Northern	07/01/88		$1750	
4081	Tom Turner	823 Pine	03/18/86	$7.50		
7238	Ann Davis	418 7th	07/01/88			1.50%
1870	Nat Evans	2814 3rd	06/24/85	$7.80		
3614	Bob Ellis	297 Central	01/01/87			1.25%
6009	Fay Dway	1117 5th	11/19/84		$2200	

Hourly-Employee

E_ID#	Wage_Rate
2874	$8.25
4081	$7.50
1870	$7.80

Employee-Master

E_ID#	E_Name	Address	Hire_Date
2874	Bill Jones	128 Central	12/07/84
9138	Sue Tibbots	1832 Northern	07/01/88
4081	Tom Turner	823 Pine	03/18/86
7238	Ann Davis	418 7th	07/01/88
1870	Nat Evans	2814 3rd	06/24/85
3614	Bob Ellis	297 Central	01/01/87
6009	Fay Dway	1117 5th	11/19/84

Salaried-Employee

E_ID#	Salary
9138	$1750
6009	$2200

Commissioned-Employee

E_ID#	COMM_RATE
7238	1.50%
3614	1.25%

FIGURE 2.11
A Class and Its
Subclasses

which is tied to that student alone, and each of those Student–Org occurrences is tied to one unique organization occurrence.

Notice that the Student–Org entity class does not contain any new data. All the data values it contains were in either the Student entity or the Organization entity. This intersection entity class is created strictly for the purpose of representing the many to many relationship that exists between students and organizations.

The Order–Product relationship shown as the second example in Figure 2.8 is slightly different. Because each order can request several different products and each product can be requested on many different orders, a many to many relationship exists and an intersection entity class must be created to physically represent this relationship. Figure 2.10 shows this relationship with the addition of an intersection entity class called Order–Product.

In a typical order entry system, multiple, and different, quantities may be specified for each product ordered. Thus Order# 13905 may request four units of the product AR28, but only two units of the product MO43. There is clearly a quantity ordered attribute. But where should this attribute be stored? Is it a characteristic of Order? For Order# 13905, the quantity ordered is both four and two, which violates the restriction that the primary key must have a one association with all other attributes of an entity. A similar problem would occur if we tried to place quantity ordered as an attribute of product—the quantity of product AR28 may be different on each order that requested it.

Quantity ordered is really an attribute of the Order–Product intersection entity. Its value can be identified only if we know both which order and which product are referenced. Thus Qty_Ord is shown as an attribute of the intersection entity class Order–Product.

Intersection entity classes often have one or more attributes of their own. When an intersection entity has its own data, it is likely to be recognized as an entity even early in the conceptual design of a database. Whether or not they are represented in conceptual modeling, intersection entity classes must be created to resolve many to many relationships prior to implementation, even if they have no independent attributes.

One to One Relationships

When a one to one relationship exists between two entity classes, knowledge of the value of either class is sufficient to uniquely identify an occurrence of the other class. Thus, it is very easy to establish a chain of inference across a one to one relationship. In fact, structures that can be represented by sets of entities with a one to one relationship to each other often can be represented as a single consolidated entity class.

One to one relationships among entity classes frequently occur within class/subclass structures. Figure 2.11 shows an example of a set of data about the employees of an organization. In the table at the top of the figure, Employee is treated as a single entity class. Notice that the last three attributes of this table have numerous blank, or *null,* values. This occurs because this organization really has three subclasses of employees, whose wages are computed by differing methods. Salaried employees receive a flat monthly amount, hourly employees are paid their wage rate times the number of hours they work, and commissioned employees are paid their commission rate times the value of the sales they make.

In the bottom half of Figure 2.11, this Employee entity class has been broken down into a set of subclasses. Some characteristics pertain to all employees and remain in an Employee–Master table. However, the information needed to determine earnings is now recorded in a subclass entity defined for each type of employee. Wage_Rate is a characteristic of the Hourly–Employee subclass and not a characteristic of all employees. Similarly, Salary is an attribute of the Salaried–Employee subclass, and Comm_Rate is an attribute of the Commissioned–Employee subclass. Each of these subclass entities has a one to one relationship with the overall Employee–Master entity class.

Figure 2.12 shows a set of employee data for a firm that keeps some information about the spouses of its employees. Once again this information could simply be represented as added attributes of the Employee entity class. The S_ID# and Spouse_Name attributes are treated as characteristics of the employee—he or she has a spouse with the given ID# and name. The rows with null values for S_ID# and Spouse_name correspond to employees who are not married. However, the S_ID# and Spouse_Name are actually characteristics of the employees' spouses. The spouses of the employees are certainly separate physical beings with attributes of their own. As the bottom portion of the figure shows, we could once again choose to create a separate entity class, in this case Emp_Spouse, to store this information about the spouses of the employees.

Conceptually, when subclasses with their own attributes or independent entities can be identified in the data used to represent an entity class, they should be treated as separate entities with a one to one relationship to the original entity class. In practice, if a very limited amount of information is needed about a related or subclass entity, it may be more expedient and efficient to treat these data as additional attributes of the original entity. However, if a substantial amount of data about a subclass or related entity is to be recorded, it is necessary to create a separate entity class for this data.

Optional and Mandatory Relationships

Optional relationship
A relationship is optional if it is not required that every occurrence of one entity be associated with an occurrence of the related entity.

You may have noticed in several of the previous figures that there were individual occurrences of one entity that were not associated with any of the occurrences of a related entity. For example, the C_ID# 5182 in Figure 2.7 is not associated with any order occurrences. Similarly, in Figure 2.8, S_ID# 5213 is not associated with any organization occurrences. These examples are perfectly valid. It is possible for a student to belong to many organizations, but it is also possible for a student to belong to no organizations at all. A customer may place many orders, but a new customer may not have placed any orders yet. Both of these are **optional relationships**—occurrences may have a relationship with occurrences in the related entity, but they are not required to.

Mandatory relationship
A relationship is mandatory if every occurrence in one entity class must be associated with at least one occurrence in the related class.

Not all relationships are optional, however. Could we have an order that was not associated with any customer? No! Every order must be placed by some customer. An order not associated with any customer would be meaningless. Such an order could never be filled because we wouldn't know where to ship it or whom to charge. The relationship between order and customer is a **mandatory relationship.**

Employee

E_ID#	E_Name	Address	Hire_Date	Sp_ID#	Spouse_Name
2874	Bill Jones	128 Central	12/07/84	6389	Sandra Jones
9138	Sue Tibbots	1832 Northern	07/01/88	4311	Adam Barnes
4081	Tom Turner	823 Pine	03/18/86	2613	Melissa Turner
7238	Ann Davis	418 7th	07/01/88		
1870	Nat Evans	2814 3rd	06/24/85	1923	Alice Smith
3614	Bob Ellis	297 Central	01/01/87		
6009	Fay Dway	1117 5th	11/19/84	3712	Joe Dway

Employee

E_ID#	E_Name	Address	Hire_Date
2874	Bill Jones	128 Central	12/07/84
9138	Sue Tibbots	1832 Northern	07/01/88
4081	Tom Turner	823 Pine	03/18/86
7238	Ann Davis	418 7th	07/01/88
1870	Nat Evans	2814 3rd	06/24/85
3614	Bob Ellis	297 Central	01/01/87
6009	Fay Dway	1117 5th	11/19/84

Emp-Spouse

E_ID#	Sp_ID#	Spouse_Name
2874	6389	Sandra Jones
9138	4311	Adam Barnes
4081	2613	Melissa Turner
1870	1923	Alice Smith
6009	3712	Joe Dway

FIGURE 2.12
Alternative Ways to
Present Employee
Spouse Data

We must ensure that an order occurrence can never be created unless it can be associated with a related customer occurrence.

Notice that a relationship can be mandatory in one direction and optional in the other. Every order must be associated with some customer occurrence, but there can be a customer who has not placed any orders.

A relationship should be considered mandatory only if we can think of no valid situation in which the relationship could fail to exist. For example, we might be tempted to say that all organizations must surely have at least one member and, therefore, the relationship from organizations to students is mandatory. But what about a new organization that we are trying to establish? Might we not have data to record about the organization even though it does not yet have any members? What if an organization suspends operation due to lack of interest, or for other reasons? If we expect the organization to be revived in the future, we might want to retain our data about the organization even though it has no members currently.

A further distinction can be drawn between relationships that are *fixed* and relationships that are mandatory but not fixed in nature. With a mandatory relationship each occurrence of one entity must be tied to some occurrence of the related entity but the occurrence it is tied to may change. For example, if every student is required to have an advisor, this would be a mandatory relationship—each student must be related to one professor for advisement. If students are allowed to change advisors, the professor occurrence can change.

With a **fixed relationship,** once an occurrence of the entity is associated with a given occurrence of the second entity, it must remain associated with that specific occurrence. The relationship of orders to customers is logically of this fixed type. The order is placed by a specific customer and logically must always be related to that customer. If we correctly associate an order with a customer, the order must continue to be associated with that customer for as long as we retain it.

Intra-Table Relationships

Relationships similar to those we have just described can exist within a table to tie related occurrences of that entity together. These are called **intra-table relationships**. For example, suppose that some of the students at a university are married to other students. We want to have a separate occurrence in our student table for each student,

Fixed relationship
A fixed relationship exists if, once an occurrence in an entity class is associated with a given occurrence of a related entity, it must remain associated with that specific occurrence.

Intra-table relationship
A relationship between occurrences of the same entity class.

FIGURE 2.13
Intra-Table Relationships of the Student Table

Student

S_ID#	S_NAME	Cl_Std
2873	Sue Smith	Jr
1827	Al Adams	So
3911	Ann Evans	Sr
4809	Jack Cass	Jr
5213	Ben Dean	Fr
6096	Sam Smith	Fr
6092	Jan Jones	So

A. Marital Relationship

Student

S_ID#	S_NAME	Cl_Std
2873	Sue Smith	Jr
1827	Al Adams	So
2911	Ann Evans	Sr
4809	Jack Cass	Jr
5213	Ben Dean	Fr
6096	Sam Smith	Fr
6092	Jan Jones	So

B. Mentorship Relationship

but we would also like to link the records for married couples. Logically, there is an optional one to one relationship between some of the occurrences of the student table. An association diagram for this relationship is shown in part A of Figure 2.13. Because the relationship is one to one, identifying either spouse allows us to uniquely identify the related spouse. S_ID# 6092 is married only to S_ID# 1827 and, conversely, S_ID# 1827 is married only to S_ID# 6092.

Suppose a mentorship program at the university allows junior or senior students to serve as volunteer mentors to one or more freshman or sophomore students. This mentorship program establishes an optional one to many relationship among occurrences of the student table. No student can have more than one mentor, but each mentor can have more than one student. Association diagrams for this relationship are shown in part B of Figure 2.13. Knowing the S_ID# of a student being mentored allows us to uniquely identify that student's mentor; for example, the mentor of S_ID# 1827 is S_ID# 4809. Knowing the mentor's S_ID# allows us to identify a set of students related only to that mentor: S_ID# 4809 is mentor to S_D# 1827 and 5213.

Figure 2.14 describes a somewhat more complex example. Suppose that some of the employees of Apex Products are supervisors. Each supervisor can supervise several employees, but each employee can have only one supervisor. In our example, E_ID#s 2874, 7238, and 1870 are supervisors. Each of them is associated with a set of employees that they supervise, but each employee has only one supervisor. Notice, however, that an employee can both have a supervisor and be a supervisor of others: E_ID# 2874 is supervised by E_ID# 1870, and, in turn, supervises E_ID#s 6009 and 9138. This intra-entity relationship is called a *recursive relationship*. Capturing this structure would allow us to identify all of the employees directly or indirectly supervised by E_ID# 1870 by first identifying the set of employees he directly supervises and then identifying the set of employees supervised by each of those employees. This chain could be followed recursively through several levels if necessary.

Could there be many to many relationships among the occurrences of a table? Such a relationship would exist if Apex Products assigned project teams to do particular tasks. Each employee might participate in several different project teams

EMPLOYEE

E_Id#	E_Name	Address	Hire_Date
2874	Bill Jones	128 Central	12/07/84
9138	Sue Tibbots	1832 Northern	07/01/88
4081	Tom Turner	823 Pine	03/18/86
7238	Ann Davis	418 7th	07/01/88
1870	Nat Evans	2814 3rd	06/24/85
3614	Bob Ellis	297 Central	01/01/87
6009	Fay Dway	1117 5th	11/19/84

FIGURE 2.14
The Supervision Relationship among Employees—
A Recursive Intra-Table Relationship

with a different supervisor for each team. As was the case for many to many relationships between different tables, this type of relationship can be implemented in a database only by creating an intersection entity class. In this case the intersection entity would link different occurrences of the same employee table, and one record in the intersection table would be needed for each employee assignment to each work group supervisor.

MODELING PROCESSES

Thus far we have largely ignored processes. In our discussion of entity classes, we indicated that an order could be thought of either as an event or as a process. As an event, an order is an entity class. But how are processes treated in database models? For instance, how do we represent the processes of selling and distributing a product?

Because processes are actions (verbs) rather than things (nouns), we cannot directly represent a process as an entity. However, processes cause changes in the status of the entities involved in those processes. For example, the sales process must cause changes to the values of some of the attributes of occurrences of the CUSTOMER and PRODUCT entities. When the purchase process is complete, the *Quantity-on-Hand* attribute for the products that were purchased must be reduced by the number of units that were received by the customer, and the *Account–Balance* attribute for the customer who placed the order must be increased by the amount that the customer was charged for this purchase until payment is received.

How are these changes accomplished? Programs must be written that execute these changes to the data. When physical processes change the status of entities (for example, the physical movement of products from a warehouse to a customer), computer processing activities must be executed to cause parallel changes in the data used to describe those entities. Thus, rather than being represented as entities, physical processes that the organization performs are essentially modeled by computer programs that perform similar *processes* upon the organization's data. Designing these processes is an important part of the development of the information systems that use a database, but they are not directly incorporated in our data models.

In many cases, however, we may feel that the changes to entities caused by a process do not provide enough information about the process to allow it to be effectively managed or controlled. We may create entities to store characteristics of the processes that are being performed. The Order and Order-Product entities discussed earlier in this chapter provide information about a process to be performed. This order data is used to ensure that the appropriate products are sent to the appropriate customer. Shipping clerks access data for occurrences of the Order and Order-Product entities to ensure that they send the correct products to the correct customers in the correct amounts.

When the items ordered have been pulled from the warehouse and are ready to be shipped, additional data about the order, such as the date of shipment, the quantity shipped (and quantity back ordered if any), the amount charged for each item, and the total amount that the customer owes, will be recorded. When payment is received from the customer, data indicating at least the amount of the payment received and the date of its receipt will be recorded. This additional data will be maintained either as additional attributes of the order or, more likely, as occurrences of other entities such as Invoices and Payment-Histories.

The use of entities that describe processes allows us to coordinate and control those processes more effectively. With the data described above, we can determine if orders are being shipped in a timely fashion, if payments are being received promptly, and if we have excessive back orders of some products.

CONCEPTUAL AND PHYSICAL DESIGN

Data models are our mechanism for representing data structures. A number of data models are available to support the conceptual and physical design processes.

The process of designing a database focuses on how data will be represented and how units and blocks of data will be organized and interconnected rather than on specifying the values of specific data items. The design process builds a structure that can be used to store and process data and is analogous to designing and building a factory to produce physical products. Just as the factory must be designed and built before the products can be produced, the database structure must be designed and implemented before actual data items can be stored and processed.

In designing a database, we first create a **conceptual data model** that describes the structure of the data to be stored in the database without specifying how and where it will be physically stored or the physical methods used to retrieve it. Once a conceptual design has been developed and analyzed, we move on to the *physical* design stage. Here, alternative methods of physically implementing the structures specified in the conceptual design are examined and an appropriate method is selected and implemented. This produces a database that supports the structures for storage and retrieval developed in the conceptual design phase. These steps are roughly equivalent to first designing a factory layout on paper, and then physically building the structure and installing the equipment.

The data model most commonly used to support the conceptual design stage is the **entity-relationship (E-R) model.** Some form of the E-R model is used for the conceptual design of most current database development projects regardless of the data model that will be used for physical design and implementation.

Data models supporting the physical design stage include the hierarchical model, the network model, the relational model, and the object-oriented model. Because we will be using the relational model throughout most of this textbook, physical storage and retrieval methods used under the relational model will be briefly summarized in the following section. Discussion of characteristics of the other models will be deferred to later chapters.

Conceptual data model
A conceptual data model provides representations of the structure of a database in a form that is independent of the physical structures required for implementation.

Entity-relationship model
(E-R) The entity-relationship model is a popular conceptual data model designed to provide a description of a database in visual form.

Represents an entity

Represents an attribute

Represents a relationship

Class–subclass relationships are represented by a square with rounded corners.

CONCEPTUAL DESIGN—THE ENTITY-RELATIONSHIP MODEL

Fundamentally, a model for conceptual design of a database must consist of mechanisms for representing the metadata structures that data can take on. The conceptual

FIGURE 2.15
E-R Diagram of the
Customer Entity

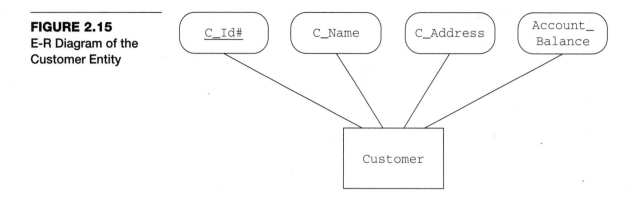

FIGURE 2.16
E-R Diagram of a One
to Many Relationship
between Entities

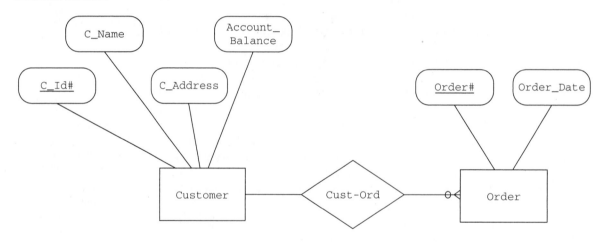

model must be able to represent entities and their attributes and the relationships that exist between those entities. The entity-relationship model was among one of the first methodologies developed for conceptual design of databases. It has become by far the most widely used model for conceptual database design.

The entity-relationship, or E-R, model was developed by Peter Chen (1976) and it has undergone substantial modification and refinement through the years (e.g., Teory, Yang, and Fry, 1986). No uniformly accepted set of notation exists for the elements of the E-R model. We will use a set of notation designed to represent the concepts of this model as simply and directly as possible.

Entities are represented as rectangles and attributes are represented as elliptical shapes with lines connecting them to the entity to which they belong. The name of each element is written inside its symbol. Figure 2.15 shows an example of this notation for the Customer entity class at Apex Products, which was described in tabular form in 2.2. Note that the attribute C_ID# is underlined. This indicates that this attribute is the primary key of the Customer entity.

Relationships between entities are represented by diamond-shaped symbols with lines connecting them to the related entities. Each relationship is given a name, written inside the diamond symbol. In Figure 2.16, the relationship between customer and order based on the sample data presented in Figure 2.7 is shown. Recall that this is a one to many relationship. The nature of the relationship is captured by showing a single line linking the Cust-Ord relationship to the Customer entity and a branched line, or *crow's foot,* next to the Order entity, indicating that many orders can be linked to a given customer through this relationship. Each customer may place many orders, but each order belongs to only one customer. The circle on the line between the Cust-Ord relationship and the Order entity indicates that the relationship is optional in this direction. It is possible that no orders exist for a given customer. A customer occurrence must be associated with each order occurrence, so there is no circle across the line from Cust-Ord to Customer.

Part A of Figure 2.17 shows an example of a many to many relationship that has been represented in E-R diagram form without creating an intersection entity class. This example is based on the order and product data described in Figure 2.8. Recall that many products can be requested on each order, and each product can be requested on many different orders. Thus we have a many to many relationship as depicted by the crows' feet on both sides of the Ord-Prod relationship symbol. The circle next to the order entity indicates that it is possible to have a product occurrence that has no orders related to it. However, each order must contain a request for at least one product, so no circle appears on the line next to the Product entity.

What about the quantity ordered, Qty_Ord? Recall that this is an attribute of a product for a specific order. It is uniquely identified only by the combination of Order# and Prod#; therefore, it can be shown as an attribute of the Ord-Prod relationship. This is a valid method of representing this type of data structure in E-R diagramming. However, this type of representation is not generally recommended.

Whenever data are associated with a many to many relationship, we will normally create an intersection entity type, like Ord-Line in part B of Figure 2.17. The creation of this intersection entity class converts the many to many relationship between orders and products into two one to many relationships. Qty_Ord is now an attribute of this new intersection entity class.

Whenever intersection entity classes are used, a combination, or concatenation, of the primary keys of each of the original entities will be required to uniquely identify occurrences in the intersect entity class unless it has a unique identifying attribute of its own. In our example, we have included the Order# and Prod# attributes in the Ord-Prod entity to serve as the primary key.

Special notation is frequently used to represent relationships among the components of a class–subclass structure. Figure 2.18 shows the E-R diagram for the employee class structure described in Figure 2.11. The relationship between the employee class and each of its subclasses is represented by a square with rounded corners instead of the diamond used for other relationships. Notice also that the

Entity

Attribute

Relationship

A. A Many to Many Relationship without an Intersection Entity

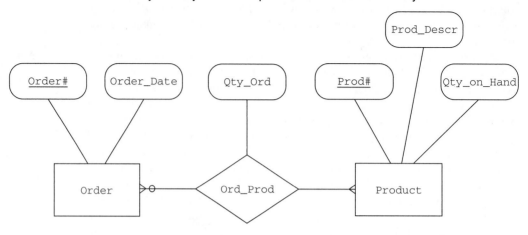

B. A Many to Many Relationship with an Intersection Entity

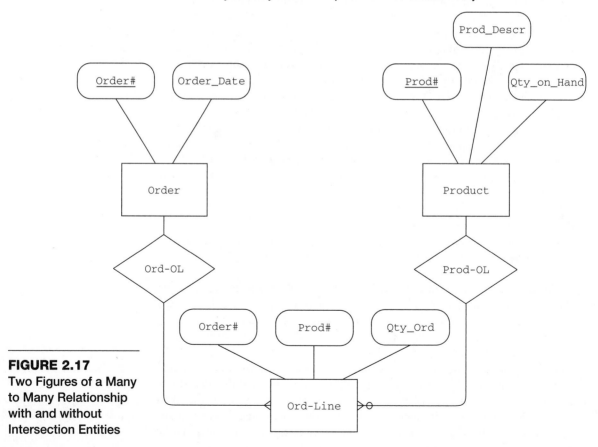

FIGURE 2.17
Two Figures of a Many
to Many Relationship
with and without
Intersection Entities

association from Employee to each of its subclasses is voluntary—not all employees are hourly employees. However, the association from each subclass back to the Employee entity class is mandatory—every hourly employee must be an employee.

Intra-entity relationships can be represented in E-R diagrams by a diamond relationship symbol connecting an entity with itself. Figure 2.19 shows how the intra-table relationships described in Figures 2.13 and 2.14 might be represented in E-R diagrams.

Of course these E-R diagram components are designed to be combined to provide a complete representation of the data model that is being constructed. Figure 2.20 shows such a diagram for the Apex Products example we have been using. All the relationships shown have been discussed earlier except the Salesp-Order relationship between Commissioned-Employee and Order. This relationship assumes that each order is processed by an employee who receives a commission for each sale processed.

Notice that the attributes of each entity are not identified in this diagram. Attributes are frequently omitted from E-R diagrams when complex structures involving several entities must be represented. You can imagine how cluttered Figure 2.20 would become if we added attribute bubbles.

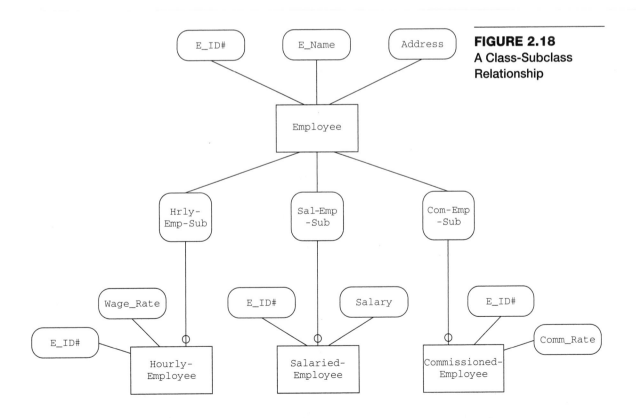

FIGURE 2.18
A Class-Subclass Relationship

FIGURE 2.19
E-R Model
Representation of
Intra-Table
Relationships

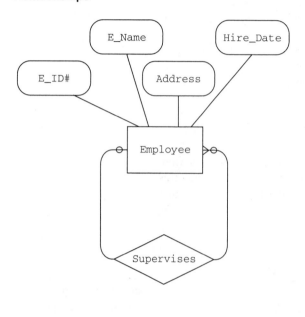

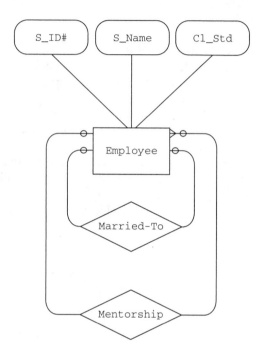

An alternative E-R diagram for the Apex Products example is shown in Figure 2.21. Notice that in this diagram many of the relationship diamonds do not have names. Also, a 1 is shown next to entities on the one side of a relationship and an M is shown next to entities on the many side of a relationship. Thus, the 1 next to Customer on the relationship linking Customer and Order indicates that one and only one customer is associated with each order. The M next to Order indicates that there can be many orders associated with one customer.

Under this representation, relationships are given names only if they are needed to avoid confusion. For example, the nature of the relationship between Customer and Order is clear from the names of the entities it connects. Thus, this relationship is not named in Figure 2.21. In the case of the intra-table relationship in the Employee table (Figure 2.20), confusion is quite possible. A number of relationships might exist here, such as *is married to, carpools with,* or *supervises.* Thus, we clarify the relationship with the name Supervises.

A single class–subclass relationship symbol is used to connect the Employee entity to all its subclasses, and the name ISA further indicates a class–subclass

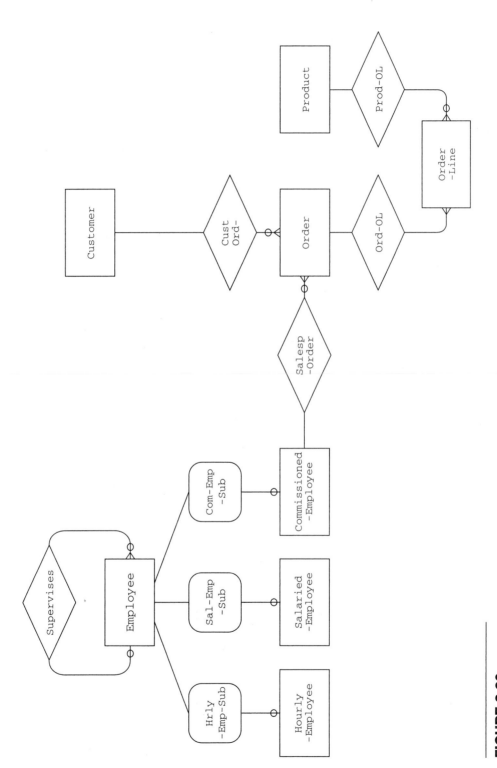

FIGURE 2.20
An E-R Diagram
for Apex Products

FIGURE 2.21
An Alternative E-R
Diagram for Apex
Products

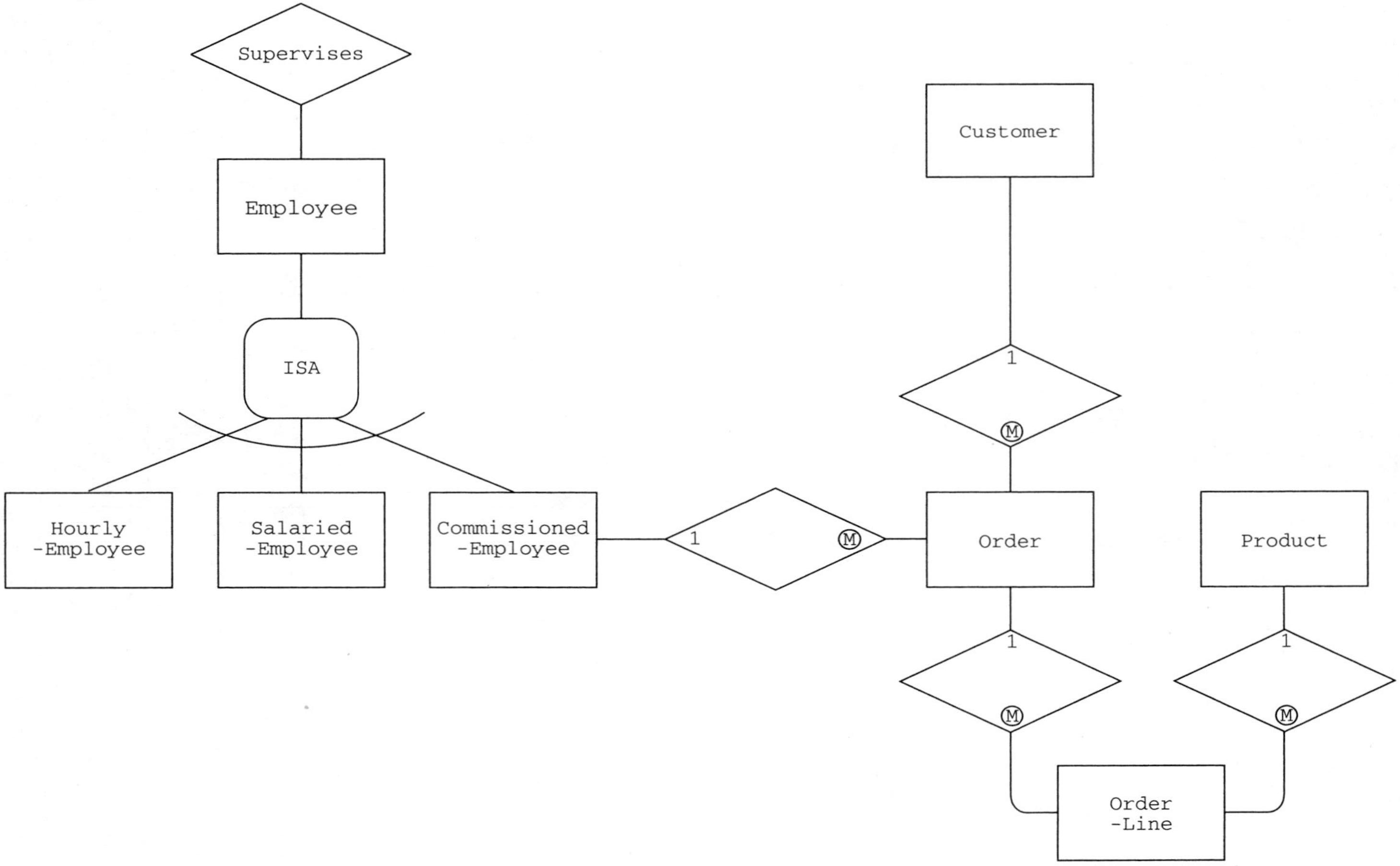

relationship. The arc drawn across the lines pointing to the three subclass entities indicates that they are *mutually exclusive.* This symbol provides a slightly richer representation of the relationship than do the symbols used in Figure 2.20, because we have now conveyed the idea that each individual employee can belong to only one of the subclass entities.

The choice of which E-R diagramming technique to employ is largely a matter of taste. In this textbook we will use methodology like that shown in Figure 2.21.

IMPLEMENTING CONCEPTUAL DESIGNS IN THE RELATIONAL DATABASE MODEL

To physically implement a conceptual database design we must have physical structures that allow us to store and retrieve logically related units of data both within entities and across related entity classes. In other words, we must be able to create physically implementable structures that correspond to all the logical structures represented in our conceptual designs.

The attribute, entity occurrence, and entity class structures within entity classes correspond to the field, record, and file structures of file-oriented processing. In relational databases, the terms *column, row,* and *table* are commonly used to describe these units. A field or column name identifies a specific attribute of interest, and the value of the primary key attribute identifies a specific occurrence—the row of the table identified by the primary key value. The entire set of data for an entity class is stored in a table. The relational model requires that all tables be flat files with records of a fixed size.

Relationships among entity types are represented in the relational model by repeating identifying data to link related tables. The relational model requires that all data structures be represented by sets of tables (entities) that can have only one to one or one to many relationships with each other. In addition, each table must have a primary key. All other attributes of a table must be functionally determined by the primary key. As you will recall, a process called normalization is used to ensure that these conditions are met. We will discuss normalization in detail in a later chapter.

A data structure diagram can be used to describe the structure of each table. For instance, the data structure diagram for the customer table might look like this: Customer(C_ID#, C_Name, C_Account, Acct_Bal).

Customer identifies the name of the table, while the items in parentheses are a list of the attributes or columns of the table. C_ID# is underlined to indicate that it is the primary key of this table.

Relationships between tables are shown by lines connecting the related tables. Thus, data structure diagrams visually represent the relational data model. Figure 2.22 presents a set of data structure diagrams of a portion of the Apex Products example relating to customers, orders, and products. Each entity is described by an appropriate table structure, and these tables are interconnected by lines representing the relationships that exist between them. For example, the line between the Customer and Order tables shows that the relationship is one customer to many orders and that

FIGURE 2.22
A Set of Data Structure
Diagrams for Apex
Products

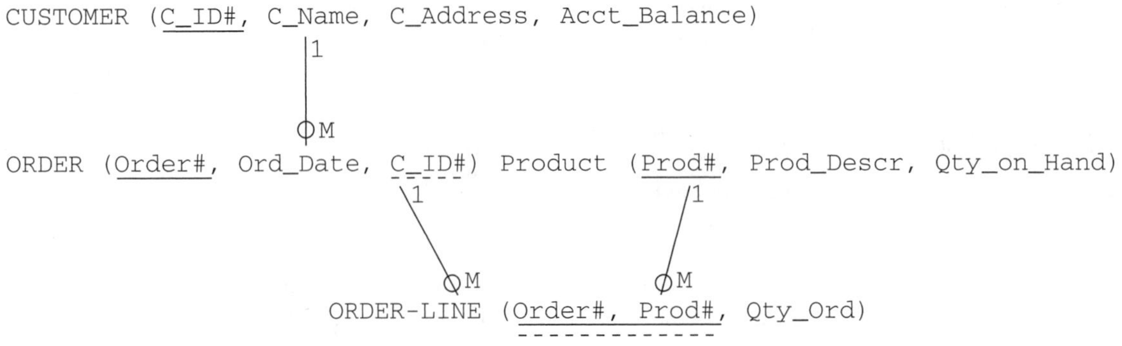

```
CUSTOMER (C_ID#, C_Name, C_Address, Acct_Balance)
                       │1
                       │
                       │
                       ◯M
ORDER (Order#, Ord_Date, C_ID#)  Product (Prod#, Prod_Descr, Qty_on_Hand)
                       \1                      /1
                        \                     /
                         \                   /
                          ◯M              ◯M
             ORDER-LINE (Order#,  Prod#, Qty_Ord)
```

each order must be related to a customer, but customer records are not required to have related order records. The underlined attributes are primary keys. Note that both Order# and Prod# are underlined for the Order_Line entity. This indicates that values for both of these fields are required to uniquely identify an occurrence of the Order_Line entity.

One added feature is shown in Figure 2.22. The attributes underlined with dotted lines are called *foreign keys*. When a one-to-many relationship exists between two tables, the primary key of the table on the one side is repeated in the table on the many side of the relationship, and that attribute in the many side table is called a foreign key.

The primary key that is copied must come from the table on the one side of the relationship. Thus, the primary key of Customer, C_ID#, was included as an attribute of the Order table to link these two tables. We could not have copied the Order# into the Customer table to establish this linkage, because that would violate fundamental rules for relational table structures. Each customer occurrence could potentially be related to many Order#s. Thus, with Order# included as an attribute of the Customer table, C_ID# would no longer functionally determine the value of all the table's attributes. Also, a variable length customer record, which is not allowed by the relational model, would be required.

This repetition of the primary key field is what implicitly links tables and allows us to retrieve related sets of data from multiple tables. We simply identify an occurrence on one of the tables and then use the value for the common, or linking, attribute to search the other table for an occurrence or a set of occurrences with a matching value. For example, in figure 2.23, if we want to know the name and address of the customer who placed Order# 15269, we simply use the order table to find the value of C_ID# for that order, 6789, then search the Customer table for the one occurrence with a matching C_ID#. The name of that customer is Bob Bates and his address is 382 Locust Street.

CUSTOMER			
C_ID#	C_Name	C_Address	Acct_Balance
2475	Chris Moss	147 Dale Tr.	$72.34
6789	Bob Bates	382 Locust St.	$286.54
5182	Mike Adams	286 Front St.	$0.00
1905	Al Vest	1701 Market St.	$1826.54

ORDER-LINE		
Order#	Prod#	Qty_Ord
12768	CV17	5
12768	AR28	15
12768	LK91	8
14021	AD12	5
13905	AR28	4
13905	MO43	2
15269	LK91	1
15269	AD12	3
16319	AR28	6
16319	MO43	4
16428	CV17	8

PRODUCT		
Prod#	Prod_Descr	Qty_on_Hand
AR28	PC	3850
CV17	Laser Printer	1725
LK91	VGA Monitor	2217
AD12	Portable PC	958
MO43	Modem	1364

ORDER		
Order#	Ord_Date	C_ID#
12768	12/07/96	2475
13905	12/11/96	6789
14021	12/14/96	2475
15269	12/28/96	6789
16319	01/07/96	2475
16428	01/08/96	5182

FIGURE 2.23
A Set of Relational Tables

Similarly, we can use a known value of a customer occurrence to identify all the orders placed by that customer. If we want to know the order number and date of all orders placed by the customer whose C_ID# is 6789, we search the Order table for the set of orders whose C_ID# attribute is 6789—Order# 13905 placed on 12/11/96 and Order# 15269 placed on 12/28/96.

This mechanism can be used to identify sets of logically related data in any tables that can be linked even if this linkage is indirect. For instance, suppose we need to know the names of all customers who have ordered Portable PCs from Apex Products. To answer this question, a query language statement would be written that would cause the system to follow a search path from the Product table to the Order-Line table to the Order table and finally to the Customer table. The Prod# for this product in the Product table is AD12. The Order-Line table is searched for matching values of Prod#. Two rows of the Order-Line table have matching values for Prod#: Order#s 14021 and 15269. From the Order table we find that Order# 14021 belongs to the customer whose C_ID# is 2475, and Order# 15269 was placed by C_ID# 6789. Finally, we search the Customer table and find that the names of these customers are Chris Moss and Bob Bates. This process could be extended to relate data in any sets of tables so long as a path of related tables can be followed to connect them. This type of retrieval could be executed through a single query language statement, albeit a rather complex one. We will examine the language used for these retrievals in Chapter 6.

In the relational model, we must always be able to link related tables without referencing any information outside the tables themselves. Of course, the process of searching a large table to find matching values of the key attributes can be quite time consuming. Thus, for practical performance reasons, sorted indexes on these key attribute values are normally established and used to speed the process of linking data in related tables.

SUMMARY

Metadata is data about the structure of data. Fundamental metadata units are: entities—persons, places, things, or events—and attributes—characteristics of entities. The set of all instances of a particular entity type is called an entity class. An individual member of an entity class is called an entity occurrence. Other types of metadata include relationships between entity classes, restrictions on the domain of values that an attribute can take on, and other restrictions on the form of data based on business rules.

If there is a one association from unit X to unit Y, we can infer that knowing the value of X allows us to uniquely identify the value of Y. This type of inferencing is used to establish data structures both within an entity class and between entity classes. An attribute, or a combination of attributes, can serve as a primary key to any entity class if, and only if, knowledge of the value of the primary key allows you to uniquely identify the values of all other attributes of that entity class. Entity classes can be related to one another in one of three ways: a one to one relationship, a one to many relationship, or a many to many relationship. A one association on either side of the relationship allows data from the two entity classes to be linked. If a many to many relationship exists between entity classes, an intersection entity must be created before the relationship can be implemented in a database.

The entity-relationship (E-R) model is the data model most commonly used in the conceptual design process. It provides mechanisms for depicting the key metadata structures of a set of data during the conceptual design process. In the E-R model, entities are represented by rectangles, attributes by ellipses, and relationships by diamond symbols.

Databases may be implemented using any of the data models discussed in Chapter 1. The relational model stores entity classes as tables whose rows are entity occurrences and whose columns are attributes. The relational model implements relationships among entity types by repeating the primary key attribute from the one side entity as an attribute of the entity class on the many side of the relationship. Related data are linked by searching for matches in the value of the repeated attribute.

REVIEW QUIZ

_____ A set of data describing an instance of an entity.

_____ The set of all allowed values of an attribute.

_____ Data about data.

_____ Resolves a many to many relationship.

_____ Represented by a diamond in an E–R diagram.

_____ A relationship between occurrences of the same entity class.

_____ Representation of the structure of a database that is independent of the physical structure used for implementation.

_____ Uniquely identifies an occurrence of an entity.

_____ The set of all occurrences of an entity type.

_____ There is only one possible value of Y associated with each value of X.

_____ An individual characteristic or property of an entity.

_____ Represented by a rectangle in an E-R diagram.

_____ Tool for representing conceptual data models in visual form.

1. Conceptual data model
2. Primary key
3. Entity
4. Entity class
5. Entity occurrence
6. Relationship
7. Domain
8. Metadata
9. Functional determination
10. Entity-relationship model
11. Intra-table relationship
12. Attribute
13. Intersection entity

REVIEW QUESTIONS AND EXERCISES

1. Describe the relationship between the metadata units attribute, entity occurrence, and entity class.

2. Which units in the standard file structure and the relational table structure correspond to the attribute, the entity occurrence, and the entity class?

3. How are many to many relationships handled in database implementations? Give an example of a many to many relationship and describe how it would be represented in a database.

4. How are one to many and one to one relationships normally handled in database systems? Give examples of each type of relationship.

5. What is functional determination, and why is it important?

6. Distinguish between a mandatory relationship, a fixed relationship, and an optional relationship. Give an example of each type of relationship.

7. How is the idea of a primary key related to the concept of functional determination?

8. How are processes handled in data modeling?

9. Give an example of an intra-table relationship and a recursive intra-table relationship.

10. Distinguish between conceptual and physical design.

11. How does the E-R model represent the following?

    a. Entities

    b. Attributes

    c. Relationships

    d. Class-subclass relationships

    e. The cardinality of relationships

    f. Mandatory versus optional status of relationships`

12. Use the accompanying car and driver tables to complete the following:

    a. Give an example of an attribute, an entity occurrence, and an entity class.

    b. Based on the sample data shown, what type of association exists from Lic_# to Address? From Address to Lic_#? From State to Make? From Make to State?

DRIVER				
LIC#	Name	Address	Age	Sex
F3607	Dan Davis	28 Pine St.	42	M
E2791	Ann Jones	361 Birch Ave.	18	F
L3070	Rex Renn	1021 1st St.	27	M
F4213	Jane Law	28 Pine St.	39	F
E9711	Sue Sales	632 Oak St.	18	F

CAR				
Plate_#	St.	Make	Model	Yr.
AZY 213	CA	Ford	Escort	91
ZFN 311	CA	Buick	LeSabre	88
LMN 214	AZ	Ford	Tempo	94
AZY 213	AZ	Buick	Regal	90
CSF 337	CA	Honda	Civic	93

c. What attribute or attributes would you select as the primary key to each table?

d. Assume that the data shown are intended to be samples of entities in an insurance company's database. Each driver in the database must be associated with at least one car and may be associated with several cars. Draw an E-R diagram describing this set of data. Draw a set of (relational) table structure diagrams for this set of data.

13. Based on the sample data shown, what items functionally determine other items? (Include indirect functional determinance, for example, A —> B and B —> C implies that A —> C.)

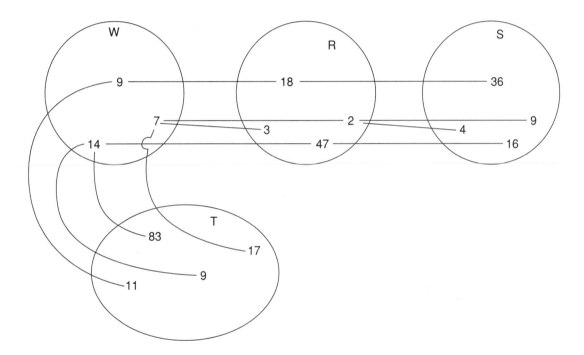

14. D.E. Fitness Company, a health club, offers a number of exercise classes for its members. A member can participate in several exercise classes or none at all. Each exercise class has one employee assigned as its instructor. Each instructor teaches at least one class and may teach several classes. Each exercise class is taught in a specified room, on a specified date and time.

a. Suppose we want to establish a database to be used to schedule exercise classes, to allow members to register for them, and to allow instructors to retrieve a list of the members in each class. What entities would be involved? What attributes might be included in each entity? What field or fields would you identify as the primary key for each entity?

b. Draw an E-R diagram for the set of data described in part a.

  c. Draw a set of relational data structure diagrams for the set of data described in part a.

15. Students at a university can have only one major and are assigned to one advisor. All students must have a major, but they may choose not to have an advisor. A professor may have many students to advise or may have none.

  a. Which of the associations described are mandatory? Which are optional?

  b. What entities are described in this exercise?

  c. Describe some attributes that you feel would need to be maintained for each of the entities. What attribute would you select as a primary key for each entity?

  d. Draw an appropriate E-R diagram for the data described in this exercise.

16. Suppose you were manager of a video rental store. Describe some of the entities you would expect to deal with. Describe some appropriate attributes for each of these entities. Think of at least one pair of entities with a many to many relationship between them. How would you resolve this relationship? Draw an E-R diagram showing at least four of the entities you thought of and the relationships between them.

TOOLS AND METHODS FOR CONCEPTUAL DESIGN

LEARNING OBJECTIVES

After completing this chapter, you should be able to

- Identify the various normal forms from first normal form through fourth normal form.

- Describe the insertion, modification, and deletion anomalies associated with tables that are not fully normalized.

- Identify any violations of normalization rules in a table and propose an appropriate modified structure that is in at least third normal form.

- Describe appropriate methods for dealing with derived attributes.

- Identify situations in which a time history of an attribute or set of attributes should be maintained and propose appropriate methods for storing history data.

- Describe the domain of an attribute appropriately, including the specification of any types of domain restrictions that might apply.

One of the most important tools used in conceptual design, the E-R or Entity-Relationship model, was described in Chapter 2. Generation of pictorial representations of the table and relationship structure of user views, and ultimately the database as a whole, is a key element of conceptual design. E-R diagrams are the most commonly used methods of providing those pictorial representations.

In this chapter, we will discuss additional tools and methods that must be applied in order to produce a complete and effective conceptual model of a database. We need to ensure that the table and relationship structures created will allow data to be stored efficiently with no unnecessary data redundancy and with minimal risk of inconsistent data. Normalization of data structures, an important element of conceptual design, can help to ensure that these goals are met. In addition, some special characteristics commonly found in business-related organizational data pose special challenges in the design of databases. In particular, computed and summary data and attributes whose values change over time require special attention in the conceptual design process. Finally, there is a need to describe individual attributes in greater detail than is provided by the E-R model or data structure diagrams. In particular, the domain of each attribute needs to be fully described so that all restrictions on valid values of attributes are captured during conceptual design. In the sections that follow, we will describe methods for normalization of data structures, discuss the treatment of summary data and attributes whose values change over time, and describe a method for recording domain descriptions of attributes.

NORMALIZATION

Normalization assists in the process of finding the most appropriate structure for data. Database systems can operate using data that has not been fully normalized. However, normalized data structures possess some powerful advantages. Normalization helps to ensure that data are stored in structures that do not cause unnecessary redundancy. Normalized data structures also help to assure that units of data can be represented in the database as soon as their values are known, that the value of a unit of data in a database can be accurately and efficiently modified, and that meaningful data will not be accidentally deleted from a database. Because of these advantages, database designers attempt to ensure that the data structures they use are normalized unless there are compelling reasons for accepting an unnormalized structure.

Normalization is most closely associated with the relational data model. However, normalization rules are used to evaluate and improve conceptual designs regardless of the data model to be used for implementation. When applying normalization rules, we think of the entities of our design in relational terms, as two-dimensional tables, or **relations.**

A relation is a two-dimensional array—a table—that meets the following restrictions: each cell of the array must contain a single-valued entry, no duplicate rows may exist, and each column must have the same meaning across all rows. Recall that each column in a relational table represents an attribute and each row represents an occurrence of an entity. Thus, we would expect that the meaning of each column would be identical across all rows of a relational table. The restriction that there be no duplicate rows means that there cannot be two completely identical entity occurrences in our table. Finally, the requirement that all cells be single-valued means that for any given entity occurrence (row), there can be only one value for each attribute (column). A table meeting these conditions can be described as a relation, and all tables used in a relational data model must be relations.

The Customer table in Figure 3.1 is an example of a table that is not fully normalized. Normalization seeks to identify and correct data structures that are subject to **anomalies** when new data are added or existing data are modified or deleted. An insertion anomaly occurs if there are data items that are available and whose values should be recorded in a database, but that cannot be added to the database until the values of some other data element or elements are known. If a new salesperson named Adams is to be assigned the Salesperson number 2300 and given an initial commission rate of 1.5 percent, we cannot enter this data until at least one customer has been assigned to this salesperson. A modification anomaly occurs if a change to the value of a data item must be recorded in more than one location in a database. For example, if the commission rate for Salesperson number 1425 changes to 2.3 percent, this value must be corrected in five records of the table. A deletion anomaly occurs if the deletion of a data item in a database causes other, still valid data to be deleted as well. If the only customer assigned to the salesperson Jones is deleted, we lose the fact that salesperson Jones is assigned the salesperson number 1872 and is paid commission at the rate of 2.0 percent of sales.

Normalization
A process of evaluating table structures and reorganizing them as necessary to produce a set of stable, well-structured relations.

Relation
A two-dimensional array that has a single-valued entry in each cell, has no duplicate rows, and has columns whose meaning is identical across all rows.

Anomaly
A condition that may prevent the storage or retention of relevant data or may create the potential for inconsistent data. Anomalies may arise in the process of creating, modifying, or deleting a table. There are three types of anomalies: insertion, modification, and deletion.

CUSTOMER

Customer Number	Customer Name	Credit Limit	Salesperson Number	Salesperson Name	Commission Rate
13728	A. Andrews	$2500	1425	Barnes	1.8%
71687	L. Morris	$1000	1872	Jones	2.0%
32763	G. Gates	$1500	1425	Barnes	1.8%
61395	V. Bass	$1000	1763	Hansen	2.2%
20698	H. Fain	$2000	1425	Barnes	1.8%
49217	R. Pate	$1500	1425	Barnes	1.8%
50387	L. Knowles	$1250	1763	Hansen	2.2%
36103	P. Dalh	$2000	1138	Roberts	2.2%
23076	H. Bain	$1750	1425	Barnes	1.8%

FIGURE 3.1
A Table with Anomalies

The fundamental problem with Figure 3.1 is that it contains data about two different things, two different entities. Salesperson Number, Salesperson Name, and Commission Rate are all characteristics of salespersons, while Customer Number, Customer Name, and Credit Limit are characteristics of customers. Normalization seeks to ensure that each table describes only one thing, one entity.

Different degrees or levels of normalization exist. We can speak of a table being **unnormalized,** being in first normal form, being in second normal form, and so on. Higher orders of normalization require that a table meet an ever more restrictive set of rules. Figure 3.2 illustrates this point. We begin with a set of possible tables. At the bottom of the figure no degree of normalization has been achieved. The **first normal form (1NF)** imposes the restriction that tables must contain no repeating groups of fields. For a table to be in second normal form (2NF) it must be in first normal form, and it must also meet the additional restriction of having no **partial dependencies**. For a table to be in third normal form (3NF), it must be in second normal form and meet the additional restriction of having no transitive dependencies. Ever more restrictive conditions are imposed as we move to higher level normal forms until, theoretically, we arrive at conditions that assure a fully normalized relation—a table—with no anomalies. First, second, and third normal forms were first defined by E. F. Codd (1970). Since that time, additional higher levels have been discovered.

The ideal of fully normalized relations that eliminate all anomalies may be unachievable and is probably impractical. Database theorists periodically discover new sources of anomalies and develop higher degree normal forms to eliminate them. However, these very high order normal forms tend to involve rather obscure anomalies that are unlikely to occur in practice and that would be difficult to detect and correct. In the remainder of this section, we will describe normalization down to the fourth normal form. In practice, database designers are usually satisfied if their data structures achieve third normal form.

Unnormalized table
An unnormalized table is one that does not meet the definition of a relation. A table containing rows with multiple values for an attribute or containing duplicate rows is an unnormalized table.

First normal form (1NF)
A table is in first normal form if it contains no repeating groups of attributes.

Partial dependency
A dependency in which the value of a nonkey attribute can be uniquely identified (functionally determined) using only part of a concatenated primary key.

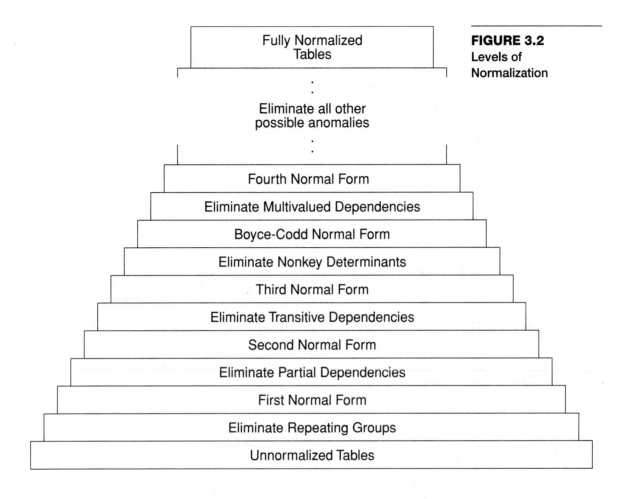

FIGURE 3.2
Levels of
Normalization

Fully Normalized
Tables

.
.
Eliminate all other
possible anomalies
.
.

Fourth Normal Form

Eliminate Multivalued Dependencies

Boyce-Codd Normal Form

Eliminate Nonkey Determinants

Third Normal Form

Eliminate Transitive Dependencies

Second Normal Form

Eliminate Partial Dependencies

First Normal Form

Eliminate Repeating Groups

Unnormalized Tables

FIRST NORMAL FORM—ELIMINATING REPEATING GROUPS

A table that meets the definition of a relation is said to be in first normal form. This means that the table can have no duplicate rows and must have a single-valued entry for each cell. The set of all possible table structures includes structures that have rows, or records, of unequal length. The Parts table shown in part A of Figure 3.3 provides an example of this. This table contains a set of fields that can store the names of up to five different suppliers of the specified part. If a part is available from only one or two suppliers, such as Part Number B2738, the storage space for the additional part numbers and quantities is wasted: The file structure does not allow variable length records. A further problem occurs if there are six or seven available suppliers for a part. To accommodate this situation, the file would have to be reorganized to allow for additional occurrences of the repeating field.

Logically, Supplier Name is a single attribute that can have multiple values for each part, as suggested in part B of Figure 3.3. Thus, Part Number cannot serve as the primary key for the table in its present configuration. Recall that the primary key must

PARTS

Part Number	Part Description	Ware-house	Supplier Name–1	Supplier Name–2	Supplier Name–3	Supplier Name–4	Supplier Name–5
W2792	1/4" washer	B	ABC Parts	Boyd Metal	Metfab Inc.		
B2738	3/8" X 2" lug bolt	D	Boyd Metal				
B7618	1/4" X 4" bolt	A	Metfab Inc.	Parts R Us	ABC Parts	Bay Bolts	Boyd Metal

FIGURE 3.3a
An Unnormalized
Parts Table
Represented with Variable
Length Rows (Records)

PARTS

Part Number	Part Description	Warehouse	Supplier Name
W2792	1/4" washer	B	ABC Parts
			Boyd Metal
			Metfab Inc.
B2738	3/8" X 2" lug bolt	D	Boyd Metal
B7618	1/4" X 4" bolt	A	Metfab Inc.
			Parts R Us
			ABC Parts
			Bay Bolts
			Boyd Metal

FIGURE 3.3b
An Unnormalized
Parts Table
An Alternative
Representation

functionally determine all other attributes in a table. In our example, Part Number functionally determines Part Description and Warehouse, but it does not functionally determine Supplier Name. If the Part Number is W2792, the Supplier Name may be ABC Parts, Boyd Metal, or Metfab.

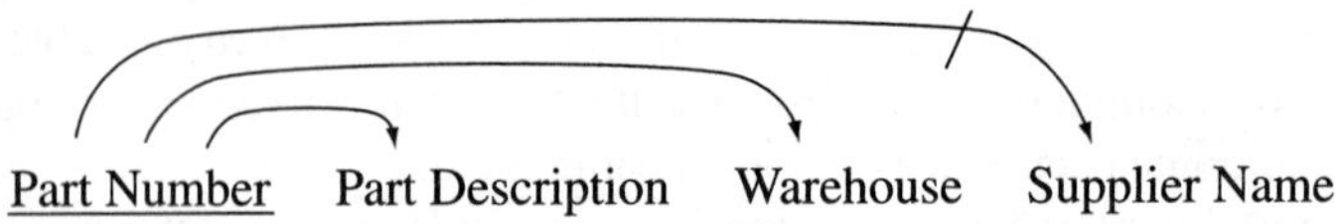

Part Number   Part Description   Warehouse   Supplier Name

This problem of repeating group data applies only to the relational model. Some languages, most notably COBOL, have very effective methods for handling

PARTS
PART–SUPPLIER

Part Number	Part Description	Warehouse
W3792	1/4" washer	B
B2738	3/8" X 2" lug bolt	D
B7618	1/4" X 4" bolt	A

Part Number	Supplier Name
W3792	ABC Parts
W3792	Boyd Metal
W3792	Metfab Inc.
B2738	Boyd Metal
B7618	Metfab Inc.
B7618	Parts R Us
B7618	ABC Parts
B7618	Bay Bolts
B7618	Boyd Metal

Data Structure Diagram

PARTS (<u>Part number</u>, Part description, Warehouse)

PART–SUPPLIER (<u>Part number</u>, <u>Supplier name</u>)

FIGURE 3.4
Parts of Data Stored
in Tables of at Least
First Normal Form

repeating group data through the use of variable length records, and some network and hierarchical DBMSs allow them.

When an existing data structure does not meet a normalization standard, it needs to be reorganized to produce a conforming structure. The Parts table in Figure 3.3 can be transformed into a set of two related tables that are in first normal form. Figure 3.4 shows the table structures and an E-R diagram for this set of data after reorganization. Here the repeating field, Supplier Name, is stored in a separate Part–Supplier table. Part Number, the primary key[1] of the Parts table, is included as a field in this new table. It serves as a *foreign key*—a key to link two separate tables—in the Part–Supplier table referencing the Parts table. The dashed line indicates that it is a foreign key. There is one row in the Part-Supplier table for each

[1]The copying of a primary key attribute as a foreign key in a new related table applies only to relational implementation. We will describe the necessary primary to foreign key linkages in our examples, because they help to illustrate how the anomaly problems are being addressed. You should remember that the use of foreign key attributes applies only to the relational data model.

supplier of each part, and the two fields together, Part Number and Supplier Name, form a concatenated key to this table. As the accompanying data structure diagram in the figure indicates, a one to many relationship exists between the Parts table and the Part–Supplier table. If we need to identify all the suppliers of 1/4" x 4" bolts, we can pick up the Part Number, B7618, in the Parts table and use it to identify all the rows in the Part–Supplier table belonging to suppliers of that part. We have not changed the meaning of the data, but our two new tables are in at least first normal form. *In general, unnormalized tables are converted to first normal form by placing any repeating groups of fields in a separate table that includes the primary key field of the original table in each row along with a single occurrence of the repeating field.*

SECOND NORMAL FORM—
ELIMINATING PARTIAL DEPENDENCIES

The Part–Supplier table in Figure 3.5 shows an example of a table that is in first normal form but is not in second normal form. For this table we have information about the number of the part, the name of the supplier of the part, the wholesale price charged *by that supplier,* and the supplier's address. The table requires a concatenated key consisting of Part Number and Supplier Name. Though the table does not contain any repeating groups of fields and, thus, is in first normal form, it does have anomalies. Suppose we have data about the name and address of a new supplier and want to add that data to our database. We cannot record this data until we know the part number and price of at least one part that will be supplied by this supplier. Suppose the address for ABC Parts changes. We must record this change in three places in our sample table, once for each part supplied by ABC Parts. Finally,

FIGURE 3.5
A Table with a
Partial Dependency

PART–SUPPLIER

Part Number	Supplier Name	Supplier Address	Wholesale Price
W3792	ABC Parts	270 N. Market St.	.025
B2738	Boyd Metal	1432 E. Park Ln.	.175
B7618	Metfab Inc.	307 West Ash St.	.250
W3792	Boyd Metal	1432 E. Part Ln.	.023
B7618	Parts R Us	12 West 1st St.	.225
B7618	ABC Parts	270 N. Market St.	.240
W3792	Metfab Inc.	307 West Ash St.	.024
B7618	Bay Bolts	1211 S. Ocean St.	.225
B7618	Boyd Metal	1432 E. Park Ln.	.235

suppose we delete the record for Part Number B7618 supplied by Parts R Us. Because that is the only record in the table for that supplier, our table could no longer record the fact that the address of Parts R Us is 12 West 1st Street, although this is still valid and useful data. The Part–Supplier table has insertion, modification, and deletion anomalies.

These anomalies occur because this table contains data about two different things. Wholesale depends upon both the part sold and the supplier who provides it. Price is a characteristic of a part. However, Supplier Address is a characteristic of the supplier only and is completely unrelated to the Part Number. The Supplier Address is functionally determined by only half of the concatenated key of the Part–Supplier table. In order for a table to be in second normal form, all of its nonkey attributes

FIGURE 3.6
Conversion into
Tables in at Least
Second Normal Form

PART–SUPPLIER

Part Number	Supplier Name	Unit Price
W3792	ABC Parts	.025
B2738	Boyd Metal	.175
B7618	Metfab Inc.	.250
W3792	Boyd Metal	.023
B7618	Parts R Us	.225
B7618	ABC Parts	.240
W3792	Metfab Inc.	.024
B7618	Bay Bolts	.225
B7618	Boyd Metal	.235

SUPPLIER

Supplier Name	Supplier Address
ABC Parts	270 N. Market St.
Boyd Metal	1432 E. Park Ln.
Metfab Inc.	307 West Ash St.
Parts R Us	12 West 1st St.
Bay Bolts	1211 S. Ocean St.

Data Structure Diagram

SUPPLIER (<u>Supplier Name</u>, Supplier Address)
1 |
m ⌀
PART-SUPPLIER (<u>Part number</u>, <u>Supplier name</u>, Unit Price)

must be functionally determined only by use of the full primary key and not by just a portion of the primary key.

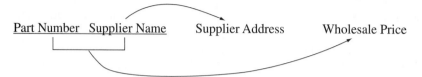

Part Number   Supplier Name   Supplier Address   Wholesale Price

Figure 3.6 shows how the Part–Supplier table can be converted to a pair of tables that are in second normal form. The Supplier Address is simply moved to a new table called Supplier, which has only Supplier Name as its key. Now each supplier address appears only once in the database, so modifications are recorded only once. In addition, supplier name and address information can now exist independently of parts supplied by that supplier. Violations of second normal form can occur only in tables having a concatenated primary key. *In general, tables that contain partial dependencies can be converted into sets of tables in second normal form by placing fields that depend on only a portion of the key in separate tables, whose primary key contains only the portion of the original primary key needed to identify those fields.*

THIRD NORMAL FORM—ELIMINATING TRANSITIVE DEPENDENCIES

Second normal form (2NF)
A table is in second normal form if it is in first normal form and has no partial dependencies.

The Customer table in Figure 3.7, the same table that was presented in Figure 3.1, is in **second normal form.** It contains no repeating groups of fields, and, because it does not have a concatenated primary key, it cannot contain any partial dependencies. However, this table does have insertion, modification, and deletion anomalies: Salesperson information cannot be recorded in the database until a salesperson has

FIGURE 3.7
A Table with Transitive Dependencies

CUSTOMER

Customer Number	Customer Name	Credit Limit	Salesperson Number	Salesperson Name	Commission Rate
13728	A. Andrews	$2500	1425	Barnes	1.8%
71687	L. Morris	$1000	1872	Jones	2.0%
32763	G. Gates	$1500	1425	Barnes	1.8%
61395	V. Bass	$1000	1763	Hansen	2.2%
20698	H. Fain	$2000	1425	Barnes	1.8%
49217	R. Pate	$1500	1425	Barnes	1.8%
50387	L. Knowles	$1250	1763	Hansen	2.2%
36103	P. Dalh	$2000	1138	Roberts	2.2%
23076	H. Bain	$1750	1425	Barnes	1.8%

at least one customer, changes to salesperson information must be recorded in multiple rows of the table, and salesperson information is lost if the last row for a customer assigned to the salesperson is deleted.

This table has a **transitive dependency;** that is, the values of some of its fields are actually functionally determined by a nonkey field whose value in turn is functionally determined by the primary key field. The Salesperson Number, Salesperson Name, and Commission Rate are all characteristics of salespersons. If we know the Salesperson Number, we can uniquely identify the name and Commission Rate of that salesperson. Thus, Salesperson Number could serve as the primary key for the Salesperson Name and Commission Rate attributes although it is a nonkey field in the Customer table. Customer Number does uniquely identify values of these two attributes but only in an indirect, or transitive, manner. Customer Number uniquely identifies Salesperson Number, which, in turn, uniquely identifies Salesperson Name and Commission Rate.

Transitive dependency
A dependency in which the value of one nonkey attribute is functionally determined by another non-key attribute.

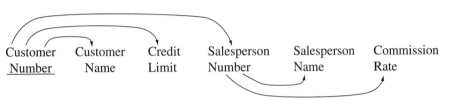

Third normal form (3NF)
A table is in third normal form if it is in second normal form and has no transitive dependencies.

Figure 3.8 shows how the transitive dependency can be eliminated to produce a set of tables in **third normal form.** Salesperson Name and Commission Rate are placed in a Salesperson table that has Salesperson Number as its primary key (Salesperson Name is also a **candidate key** for this table). As the data structure diagram in Figure 3.8 shows, there is a one to many relationship between the Salesperson and Customer tables. Salesperson Number continues to appear as an attribute of the Customer table, so that all data about a salesperson can still be linked to any customer assigned to that salesperson. *In general, transitive dependencies can be eliminated by placing any attributes that are determined by nonkey attributes in a separate table with the determining field serving as the primary key of this new table.*

Candidate key
An attribute or combination of attributes that can uniquely identify an occurrence of a table. A candidate key can serve as the primary key of a table. If a table has multiple candidate keys one of them is selected to serve as the primary key.

BOYCE-CODD NORMAL FORM—ELIMINATING NONKEY DETERMINANTS

Even when third normal form has been achieved, anomalies can remain (Codd, 1974). Suppose that Apex Products has service representatives who specialize in servicing PCs, printers, or LANs and are not allowed to service more than one product line. Further suppose that each customer is assigned a different service representative for each product line purchased from Apex. The Service–Assignment table in Figure 3.9 represents these assignments. Clearly none of the three fields can serve alone as the primary key. However, the combination of either Customer Number and Product Type or Customer Number and Service Rep. can serve as a concatenated key. In this instance, the combination of Customer Number and Product Type has been chosen to serve as the key.

You should be able to verify that this table is in third normal form. It has no repeating groups and no partial or transitive dependencies. However, anomalies still

CUSTOMER

Customer Number	Customer Name	Credit Limit	Sales Person Number
13728	A. Andrews	$2500	1425
71687	L. Morris	$1000	1872
32763	G. Gates	$1500	1425
61395	V. Bass	$1000	1763
20698	H. Fain	$2000	1425
49217	R. Pate	$1500	1425
50387	L. Knowles	$1250	1763
36103	P. Dalh	$2000	1138
23076	H. Bain	$1750	1425

SALESPERSON

Sales Person Number	Sales Person Name	Commission Rate
1425	Barnes	1.8%
1872	Jones	2.0%
1763	Hansen	2.2%
1138	Roberts	2.2%

Data Structure Diagram

SALES PERSON (<u>Salesperson Number</u>, Salesperson Name, Commission Rate)

```
                                1 |
                                m ⌽
```

CUSTOMER (<u>Customer Number</u>, Customer Name, Credit Limit, <u>Saleperson Number</u>)

FIGURE 3.8
Tables in Third
Normal Form

exist. Suppose a new service representative has been hired to service PCs. We cannot record the name of this new service representative or the type of equipment she repairs until at least one customer has been assigned to her. Suppose the service representative J. Jackson is seriously injured and unable to work for several months. We might need to reassign all of his customers to a different representative. However, if we remove all assignments of customers to this service representative, we also lose the fact that the product line serviced by J. Jackson is PCs.

The source of this anomaly is the fact that a nonkey attribute (Service Rep.) is actually a determinant of an attribute that is part of the concatenated primary key (Product Type). Service Rep. functionally determines the value of Product Type, since each service representative can service only one product line. The anomalies

SERVICE–ASSIGNMENT

Customer Number	Product Type	Service Rep.
13728	PC	J. Jackson
32763	Printer	M. Mays
13728	LAN	A. Ames
61395	PC	J. Jackson
20698	PC	F. Files
61395	Printer	M. Mays
23076	Printer	M. Mays
50387	PC	F. Files
20698	LAN	A. Ames

FIGURE 3.9
A Table with a
Nonkey Determinant

can be corrected by creating a second table called Service–Specialization with Service Rep. as the primary key and Product Type as a nonkey attribute (see Figure 3.10). Product Type no longer appears in the Service–Assignment table. Customer Number and Service Rep. do appear and are used as a concatenated key.

Boyce-Codd normal form is really an extension of the idea behind third normal form. To achieve third normal form we eliminated instances where a nonkey attribute functionally determines another nonkey attribute. Boyce-Codd normal form extends this by eliminating instances where a nonkey attribute functionally determines an attribute that is part of the primary key of a table. *In general, we can say that a table is in Boyce-Codd normal form if it is in third normal form and no determinants exist that are not either the primary key or a candidate key for the table.*

Boyce-Codd normal form (BCNF)
A table is in Boyce-Codd normal form if it is in third normal form and contains no nonkey determinants. By key, we mean both the actual primary key and any alternative candidate keys.

FOURTH NORMAL FORM—ELIMINATING MULTIVALUED DEPENDENCIES

Multivalued dependencies can occur when two or more multivalued attributes are associated with some entity. For example, suppose a company provides training on computer software internationally. Before we assign an employee to conduct a seminar on word processing in Spain, we must know that the employee has word-processing skills and can speak Spanish. Individual employees may be proficient in more than one type of software and may also be proficient in more than one language. We might try to capture data about these skills in the Employee–Skills table shown in Figure 3.11. Note that the combination of all three fields of this table is needed to uniquely determine an occurrence. If you examine this table, you can determine that no single field or combination of two of the three fields is sufficient to serve as the primary key.

This table certainly meets the requirements for all normal forms down through Boyce-Codd normal form. It has no repeating groups, no partial dependencies, and,

Multivalued dependency
A dependency in which an attribute has an independent relationship with two or more other attributes. For each value of the first attribute there is an associated set of values for each of the other attributes, but the sets of values for these other attributes are independent of each other.

FIGURE 3.10
Tables in Boyce-Codd
Normal Form

SERVICE–ASSIGNMENT

Customer Number	Service Rep.
13728	J. Jackson
32763	M. Mays
13728	A. Ames
61395	J. Jackson
20698	F. Files
61395	M. Mays
23076	M. Mays
50387	F. Files
20698	A. Ames

SERVICE–SPECIALIZATION

Service Rep.	Product Type
J. Jackson	PC
M. Mays	Printer
A. Ames	LAN
F. Files	PC

Data Structure Diagram

SERVICE–SPECIALIZATION (Service Rep, Product Type)

1
m

SERVICE ASSIGNMENT (Customer Number, Service Rep)

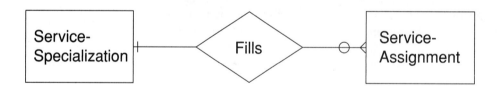

since it has no nonkey attributes to serve as determinants, it cannot violate the third or Boyce-Codd normal forms. There are problems with the structure of this table, however. There is a great deal of data redundancy. Employee Number 1267 knows Word Processing and both French and German, which results in two different records. Additionally, two records are needed for Spreadsheets because of this employee's language skills. Now suppose that employee 1267 learns to speak Russian. We will need to add two new records: one to show that employee 1267 has both Russian and Word Processing skills, and one showing the combination of Russian and Spreadsheet skills.

The problem is that data about two independent multivalued attributes is being recorded in a single table. The computer software skills of employees are unrelated to their language skills. When there are two unrelated multivalued attributes of an

EMPLOYEE–SKILLS

Employee Number	Computer Skills	Language Skills
1267	Word Processing	French
1267	Word Processing	German
1345	Spreadsheets	Spanish
1267	Spreadsheets	French
1267	Spreadsheets	German
1345	COBOL	Spanish
1193	Word Processing	French

FIGURE 3.11
A Table with Multivalued Dependencies

entity, they should be placed in separate tables (see Figure 3.12). Separate Software–Skills and Language–Skills tables are created to ensure that each skill is recorded only once for each employee possessing that skill, thus eliminating the data redundancy and anomaly problems.

It is worth noting that the problem of multivalued dependencies is related to the first normal form problem of repeating groups. The computer skills and language skills originally identified in Figure 3.11 are both attributes of employees and might be dealt with as shown in Figure 3.13. Here we are assuming that we are trying to model the Employee entity and begin to list the attributes of employees: ID numbers, names, hire dates, and so on. Eventually we note that not only can employees have computer and language skills but each employee can also have several different types of these skills. Both computer skills and language skills are multivalued attributes and are expressed as repeating groups. Thus, the Employee table is unnormalized and must have its repeating groups removed to achieve first normal form. If, at this point, we note that computer skills and language skills are independent multivalued attributes and place them in separate tables, the multivalued dependency shown in Figure 3.11 will never occur. *Violations of fourth normal form are unlikely to occur if we amend the process used to achieve first normal form to include a requirement that independent multivalued attributes will be placed in separate tables when eliminating repeating groups.*

BEYOND FOURTH NORMAL FORM

Each time we have introduced a higher order normal form, we have examined tables meeting the requirements of the normal forms preceding it and found remaining anomalies that could be identified and resolved. Anomalies have been found in tables that are in **fourth normal form (4NF)** and yet another level of normalization, fifth

Fourth normal form (4NF)
A table is in fourth normal form if it is in third normal form and contains no multi-valued dependencies.

FIGURE 3.12
Tables in Fourth
Normal Form

SOFTWARE–SKILLS

Employee Number	Computer Skills
1267	Word Processing
1267	Spreadsheets
1345	Spreadsheets
1345	COBOL
1193	Word Processing

LANGUAGE–SKILLS

Employee Number	Language Skills
1267	French
1267	German
1345	Spanish
1193	French

Data Structure Diagram

SOFTWARE-SKILLS (<u>Employee Number</u>, <u>Computer Skills</u>)

LANGUAGE-SKILLS (<u>Employee Number</u>, <u>Language Skills</u>)

Each on many side of a relationship to employee

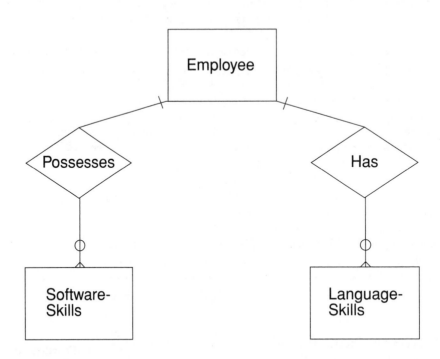

normal form, has been identified. This normal form corrects some rather obscure situations in which relations can be divided into subrelations but those subrelations cannot be used to recreate the original relation. For a thorough treatment of normalization, including mathematical proofs, see Date (1992).

EMPLOYEE

Employee Number	Employee Name	Hire ... Date	Computer Skill-1	Computer ... Skill-2	Language Skill-1	Language ... Skill-2
1267	P. Smith	10/02/88	Word Processing	Spreadsheets	French	German
1345	L. Walker	01/24/93	Spreadsheets	COBOL	Spanish	
1193	R. Gale	07/01/94	Word Processing		French	

FIGURE 3.13
An Initial View of
Employees' Skills

It should be clear that this process can never guarantee that all possible anomalies have been eliminated. We are able to find problems, but we are never able to be certain that no further problems exist. However, we can take comfort in the fact that the violations of normal forms beyond third normal form often seem to take on a contrived look. Although the anomalies they address may occasionally creep into databases, most practicing database designers are satisfied with attempting to build databases that are in at least third normal form.

DOMAIN/KEY NORMAL FORM

Fagin (1981) decided to take a different approach to normalization. He asked this question: Are there conditions that, if met by a set of tables, will guarantee that no anomalies can exist? Instead of trying to identify bad structure, he sought to identify the rules for "good" structure. Fagin identified a new normal form called **Domain/Key normal form (DKNF),** and he was able to prove that tables that are in Domain/Key normal form cannot have modification anomalies.

Domain/Key normal form can be defined as follows: A table is in Domain/Key normal form if every logical restriction on the attributes of the table is a result of the definition of keys and domains. The keys (primary and candidate) of the table should be the only fields that functionally determine attributes in the table. The domains of attributes encompass all additional rules that restrict the values the attribute can take on. These rules may include restrictions on the value of one attribute based on the value of some other attribute in the same or a different relation, as long as these restrictions do not functionally determine the attribute. For example, we may have a rule in a student database that courses whose number is greater than 300 can be taken only by students who have completed 60 or more hours of course work. These types of domain restrictions are not addressed in the other normal forms. We will treat the topic of domain specifications and processing rules in more detail later in this chapter.

One difficulty in applying Domain/Key normal form is we are not sure when we have achieved it. In fact, we cannot be sure that all types of the logical restrictions on the structure of data can be expressed exclusively in the form of key and domain definitions. Domain/Key normal form lacks the step-by-step rules provided by the levels of normalization, but it does focus on what the normalization process should

Domain/Key normal form (DKNF)
A table is in domain/key normal form if every logical restriction on the value of attributes in the relation is a result of the definition of keys and domains. A table that is in domain/key normal form cannot contain anomalies.

Examine each table of the proposed structure and perform the following operations:

1. Remove any repeating groups of attributes (multivalued attributes) to a separate table. If there are independent sets of multivalued attributes, place each set in a separate table.

2. Remove any attributes that are functionally determined by only a portion of a concatenated key to a separate table.

3. Remove any attributes that are functionally determined by a nonkey attribute to a separate table.

FIGURE 3.14

A Proposed Normalization Process for Database Designers

be attempting to achieve: tables whose attributes are functionally determined only by their keys and whose other restrictions are fully specified in domain definitions.

A SUGGESTED PROCESS FOR NORMALIZATION

It is desirable to summarize normalization rules in terms of some simple rules of thumb that provide a systematic process for the normalization of a set of tables. One very abbreviated method of expressing the requirements for normalization is the following statement. "All attributes in every table must be determined by *the key, the whole key,* and *nothing but the key.*" This statement provides a good memory aid and a handy summarization of the first three normal forms.

Figure 3.14 describes a set of steps that can be used to achieve normalization down to at least third normal form. These steps are essentially a restatement of the requirements to achieve first, second, and third normal forms, respectively. However, the steps described have been expanded, so that following those steps will typically result in data structures that are in fourth normal form.

The first step of the process is designed to ensure that tables are in first normal form and to prevent the creation of table structures that may violate fourth normal form. It states simply that we should search each table in a proposed data structure for repeating fields or groups of fields. If a repeating group is found, it should be removed to a separate table. If two or more independent sets of repeating groups are found, each set should be placed in its own table. In most cases, this should prevent violations of fourth normal form from developing. The primary key of the original table must be repeated as a foreign key in each new table that is created, and it may also serve as a portion of a concatenated primary key for a newly created table.

The second step in the process is simply the procedure used to convert tables in first normal form into tables that are in second normal form. We simply place any attribute that is functionally determined by only a portion of the primary key into a separate table. The portion of the original concatenated key that identifies the attribute is also placed in the new table and serves as its primary key. Multiple new tables may be created if there are attributes that are determined by different components of the primary key.

The third step in the process addresses third and Boyce-Codd normal forms. Tables are searched for any attributes that are functionally determined by a nonkey

EMPLOYEE

Employee SS#	Employee Name	Hire Date	Department Name	Supervisor	Optional Insurance Memberships	Dependent SS#	Dependent Name	Dependent Birth Date
476321845	B. Jones	01/12/88	Sales	R. Phillips	Extended Medical Dental			
385152309	L. Adams	04/03/82	Production	J. Martin	Dental	593602913	J. Adams	03/19/84
						603913817	R. Adams	08/03/86
						642184193	B. Adams	06/26/89
483119807	S. Davis	11/22/91	Sales	R. Phillips	Eye Care Dental Disability	492613815	V. Davis	09/03/87

FIGURE 3.15
Employee Data in an Unnormalized Table Structure

attribute (or a combination of nonkey attributes). Attributes that are determined by a nonkey attribute are removed to a separate table with the determining attribute serving as the primary key of this new table.

EXAMPLES OF THE NORMALIZATION PROCESS

Each of the examples presented earlier in this section was designed to show violations of a specific normal form. In a typical design process, information received from a user may contain no violations of normal forms or it may contain several different normal form violations.

Figure 3.15 shows a set of data about the employees of a company. The top portion of this figure shows how the user of this data might describe it to a database designer. "Data we keep include each employee's social security number, his or her name, the date he or she was hired, the department name, and the name of their supervisor. We also record the names of the optional insurance plans that each employee has enrolled in. We have an extended medical plan, a dental plan, an eye care plan, and several other insurance plans, all of which are optional. Employees can sign up for none, for all of them, or for any number they choose. Also we record the social security number, name, and birth date of each of the employee's dependents." The designer might ask for some sample data for a few employees, or a printed report showing the data that has been described.

How should we proceed to normalize this data? Following the normalization process described in Figure 3.14, we would first look for multivalued attributes. Several multivalued attributes are present in this table. The Optional Insurance Memberships, Dependent SS#, Dependent Name, and Dependent Birth Date attributes are all multivalued. However, there are only two independent sets of multivalued attributes in the table. The Dependent SS#, Dependent Name, and Dependent Birth Date attributes are obviously related. In fact, Dependent Name and

EMPLOYEE

Employee SS#	Employee Name	Hire Date	Department
476321845	B. Jones	01/12/88	Sales
385152309	L. Adams	04/93/82	Production
483119807	S. Davis	11/22/91	Sales

DEPARTMENT

Department Name	Supervisor
Sales	R. Phillips
Production	J. Martin

EMPLOYEE–INSURANCE

Employee SS#	Insurance Type
476321845	Extended Medical
476321845	Dental
385152309	Dental
483119807	Eye Care
483119807	Dental
483119807	Disability

EMPLOYEE–DEPENDENT

Dependent SS#	Dependent Name	Dependent Birth Date	Employee SS#
593602913	J. Adams	03/19/84	385152309
603913817	R. Adams	08/03/86	385152309
642184193	B. Adams	06/26/89	385152309
492613815	V. Davis	09/03/87	483119807

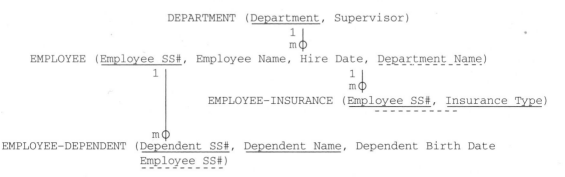

Data Structure Diagram

```
             DEPARTMENT (Department, Supervisor)
                              1 |
                              m ⏀
    EMPLOYEE (Employee SS#, Employee Name, Hire Date, Department_Name)
                  1 |                              1 |
                    |                              m ⏀
                           EMPLOYEE-INSURANCE (Employee SS#, Insurance Type)
                                                  ----------
                  m ⏀
    EMPLOYEE-DEPENDENT (Dependent SS#, Dependent Name, Dependent Birth Date
                        Employee SS#)
                        ----------
```

FIGURE 3.16
Conversion to a Set of
Normalized Tables

Dependent Birth Date are both determined by the nonkey field Dependent SS#, so this set of repeating fields violates third normal form as well as first normal form. The obvious solution is to place these three attributes in a new table with Dependent SS# as its primary key. We might call this table Employee–Dependent (see Figure 3.16). Employee SS# is also included as a foreign key to tie the new table to the Employee table. The Optional Insurance Memberships attribute appears to be unrelated to the dependent characteristics, so it should be placed in another new table. The Employee

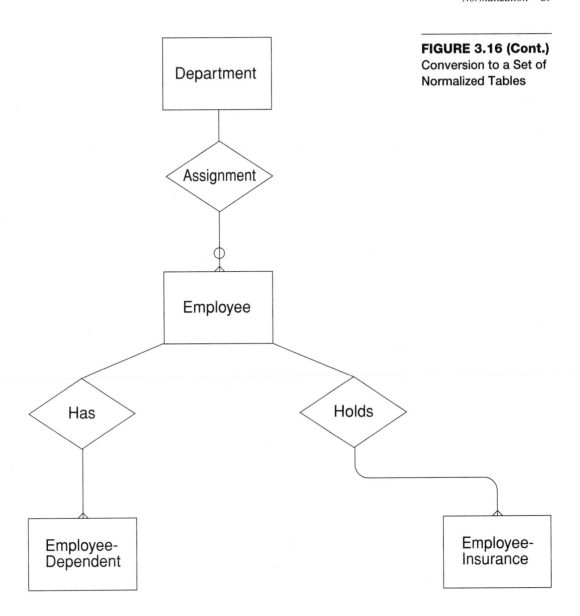

FIGURE 3.16 (Cont.)
Conversion to a Set of
Normalized Tables

SS# and the Insurance Type form a concatenated key for the new table called Employee–Insurance. Once again Employee SS# also serves as a foreign key to link this table to the Employee table. With these changes there are no remaining repeating groups, so the first step of our normalization process is complete—the Employee table is in first normal form.

The second step of the normalization process is to find and eliminate any partial dependencies. Because the Employee table has a single attribute as its primary key, there can be no partial dependencies for this table.

Next we look for any attributes of the Employee table that are functionally determined by a nonkey attribute. One pair of attributes appears to have this characteristic: Department_Name allows us to determine an employee's Supervisor and vice versa. This would be verified by asking the user. Suppose that it is true that each employee's supervisor is the head of the department in which he or she works. In this case, Department_Name functionally determines the name of the Supervisor, so the Supervisor attribute should be placed in a separate Department table with Department_Name as its primary key. The Department_Name attribute is also retained in the Employee table where it serves as a foreign key. In this case the relationship between Department_Name and Supervisor is one to one, so either of these two fields could have been selected as the primary key. However, supervisors are likely to be reassigned more frequently than departments will change their names. Thus, Department is a better choice as a primary key.

At this point we have completed the normalization process for the Employee table. However, while normalizing the Employee table, we created three new tables—Department, Employee–Dependent, and Employee–Insurance, which could potentially violate normalization rules. Check these tables and verify for yourself that they do not require modification.

Figure 3.17 shows a set of data from a user who schedules planes for flights. She determines the type of plane to be used each day for each flight, and can change the type of plane assigned if necessary. She indicates that she needs to work with a set of data that looks like the table shown. She must be provided with the Flight#, Date, Destination, Scheduled Departure Time, and Seats Reserved data. She then assigns a type of plane for the flight for that date, records the capacity of the plane, and subtracts the number of Seats Reserved from Capacity to compute the number of seats that are still available.

In examining this data we would first observe that one attribute can be mathematically calculated from a combination of two other attributes. Seats Available is always equal to Capacity minus Seats Reserved. Thus, Seats Available does not really provide any new data, and we do not need to include it as an attribute in the

FIGURE 3.17
A User's View of Plane Scheduling Data

Flight #	Date	Destination	Scheduled Departure Time	Assigned Plane Type	Capacity	Seats Reserved	Seats Available
102	11/12/94	Memphis	9:00AM	Boeing 727	165	124	41
329	11/12/94	Los Angeles	9:10PM	DC9	248	260	-12
507	11/12/94	Chicago	12:45PM	Boeing 747	440	372	68
102	11/14/94	Memphis	9:00AM	DC9	248	188	60
329	11/15/94	Los Angeles	9:10PM	DC9	248	230	18
507	11/15/94	Chicago	12:45PM	DC9	248	157	91
329	11/16/94	Los Angeles	9:10PM	Boeing 727	165	131	34

database. Actually, any two of the three attributes Capacity, Seats Available, and Seats Reserved can be used to compute the third. In this case, we choose to retain Capacity and Seats Reserved.

Next, we would begin the normalization process for this table by looking for repeating groups of attributes. In this case there are none, so we would proceed to the second step of the normalization process—finding and eliminating partial dependencies. Both Destination and Scheduled Departure Time are determined by Flight# alone. Flight 102 goes to Memphis regardless of the date and Flight 507 is always scheduled to depart at 12:45 P.M. regardless of the date. These two attributes must be placed in a separate table with just Flight# as its primary key. Once this modification has been made, no other partial dependencies remain, so we move on to the third step of the normalization process. We search for attributes that are functionally determined by nonkey attributes. From the sample data, it appears that Capacity is functionally determined by the Assigned Plane Type. If the user verifies this, we would remove Capacity to a separate, Plane–Type table with Plane Type as its primary key. Assigned Plane Type would remain in the Flight–Schedule table serving as a foreign key linking to the new Plane–Type table. At this point the normalization process for the Flight–Schedule table is complete. Figure 3.18 shows the normalized set of tables for this data. A quick look at the Flight and Plane–Type tables we created shows that they are already in at least third normal form, so no further changes to the data structure are required.

Initial conceptual database designs are generally laid out based on the designer's "feel" for the set of things (entities) that underlie a process or a set of data and the characteristics (attributes) of those things. The normalization processes described here are then used to test the accuracy and completeness of those initial specifications. However, experienced designers often have a feel for appropriate data structures that allows them to avoid most data structure problems that would violate normalization rules. For example, attributes with partial or transitive dependencies are almost always actually attributes of some other identifiable entity. An experienced designer would likely look at the data described in Figure 3.17 and quickly see that three entities are being described: flights, plane types, and the daily scheduling of flights. Such a designer would probably initially record the data for this application in a form very close to that shown in Figure 3.18 without formally working through the steps of the normalization process. This "feel" for good structure comes, in part, from experience in formally applying normalization rules to tables. Thus, it is good practice for beginning database designers to formally consider normalization issues each time they specify an Entity-Relationship or table structure diagram.

ISSUES IN THE PRACTICE OF DESIGNING TABLE STRUCTURES

LIMITATIONS OF NORMALIZATION

Anomalies in data structures make the maintenance of a database more cumbersome and time consuming and can make it more difficult to ensure data integrity. As we

FLIGHT–SCHEDULE

Flight#	Date	Assigned Plane Type	Seats Reserved
102	11/12/94	Boeing 727	124
329	11/12/94	DC9	260
507	11/12/94	Boeing 747	372
102	11/14/94	DC9	188
329	11/15/94	DC9	230
507	11/15/94	DC9	157
329	11/16/94	Boeing 727	131

FLIGHT

Flight #	Destination	Schedule Departure Time
102	Memphis	9:00AM
329	Los Angeles	9:10PM
507	Chicago	12:45PM

PLANE–TYPE

Plane Type	Capacity
Boeing 727	165
DC9	248
Boeing 747	440

Data Structure Diagram

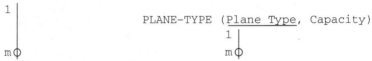

```
FLIGHT (Flight#, Destination, Scheduled Departure Time)
              1 |
                            PLANE-TYPE (Plane Type, Capacity)
                                          1 |
              m ⌀                         m ⌀
FLIGHT-SCHEDULE (Flight#, Date, Assigned Plane Type, Seats Reserved)
                ------          ----------------
```

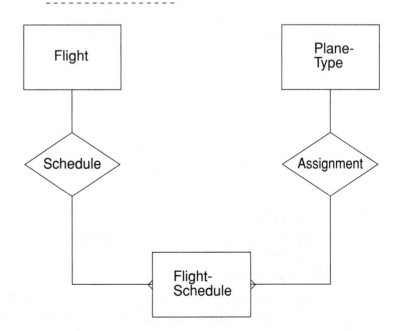

FIGURE 3.18
A User's View of Plane
Scheduling Data

have seen, normalization is a powerful tool that can help us identify and eliminate serious anomalies in databases. Thus, there is a very strong presumption that the structure of a database should be fully normalized. However, there are situations where judgment is required to determine whether an apparent violation of normalization should be corrected. Situations exist in which business reasons compel us to deliberately maintain a table in less than fully normalized form.

Figure 3.19 shows an example of a table requiring a judgmental normalization decision. Each row of the table shows the hours worked by one employee for each day of a specified week. The Employee SS# and the beginning date of the Week serve as a concatenated key. At issue in this table is whether the hours columns for

FIGURE 3.19
Employee Hours Data Recorded on a Weekly Occurrence Basis

EMPLOYEE–WEEKLY–HOURS

Employee SS#	Week of (Monday)	Monday Hours	Tuesday Hours	Wednesday Hours	Thursday Hours	Friday Hours	Saturday Hours
476321845	9/18/95	8	8	8	8	8	0
385152309	9/18/95	8	8	8	8	8	8
483119807	9/18/85	8	8	4	0	8	0
385152309	9/25/95	8	8	8	8	0	0
483119807	9/25/95	8	8	8	8	8	4
476321845	10/02/95	8	8	8	8	8	0
385152309	10/02/95	0	0	8	8	8	0

FIGURE 3.20
Hours Data Recorded on a Daily Occurrence Basis

EMPLOYEE–DAILY–HOURS

Employee SS#	Date	Hours
476321845	9/18/95	8
385152309	9/18/95	8
483119807	9/18/95	8
476321845	9/19/95	8
385152309	9/19/95	8
483119807	9/19/95	8
476321845	9/20/95	8
385152309	9/20/95	8
483119807	9/20/95	4
476321845	9/21/95	8

the six workdays constitute a repeating group of fields. If we assume that the day of the week when a set of hours were worked is irrelevant, then the six hours columns do constitute a repeating group. Under this interpretation, the data should be normalized by rewriting the table as shown in Figure 3.20, where each day's hours are treated as a separate row identified by the Employee SS# and the Date.

On the other hand, if we assume that the day of the week is important, that Monday hours are different from Wednesday hours, the six hours columns can be interpreted as representing six separate attributes. Under this assumption, the Employee–Weekly–Hours table is fully normalized.

In practice, the choice of structure will be based on how the data will be used. Suppose hours data are converted to computerized form only on a weekly basis. Further suppose that all reporting of hours data occurs over weekly or larger units of time, and that managers frequently use a weekly report that compares absenteeism across the days of the week. The Employee–Weekly–Hours table would seem to provide an efficient structure for storing data used in this fashion.

On the other hand, suppose a company records hours data in computerized form daily and produces several hours reports on a daily basis. A firm using hours data in this way would almost surely require the structure shown in the Employee–Daily–Hours table.

Figure 3.21 presents a Customer table that violates third normal form. Can you find its transitive dependencies? It would appear from the data that both City and State are functionally determined by Zip Code. In fact, U.S. Postal Service rules for ZIP code numbers ensure that this is the case. Each ZIP code is assigned to only one city, or a portion of a city, in only one state.

The Customer and Zip–Address tables shown in Figure 3.22 could be used to represent this data in fully normalized form. We might question the appropriateness of normalization in this case, however. We do not think of City and State as being attributes of a ZIP code. In fact, we almost always use the entire address as if it were a single attribute. Let's examine the anomalies in the original Customer table. We

FIGURE 3.21
A Customer Table
with Address Data

CUSTOMER

Customer Number	Customer Name	Credit Limit	Street Address	City	State	Zip Code
13728	A. Andrews	$2500	914 E. Fir	Phoenix	AZ	85023
71687	L. Morris	$1000	702 N. 3rd	Buckeye	AZ	85312
32763	G. Gates	$1500	1107 W. Ash	Gallup	NM	84874
61395	V. Bass	$1000	318 W. Grant	Phoenix	AZ	85017
20698	H. Fain	$2000	232 S. Main	Buckeye	AZ	85312
49217	R. Pate	$1500	1104 E. Grove	Phoenix	AZ	85022

CUSTOMER

Customer Number	Customer Name	Credit Limit	Street Address	Zip Code
13728	A. Andrews	$2500	914 E. Fir	85023
71687	L. Morris	$1000	702 N. 3rd	85312
32763	G. Gates	$1500	1107 W. Ash	84874
61395	V. Bass	$1000	318 W. Grant	85017
20698	H. Fain	$2000	232 S. Main	85312
49217	R. Pate	$1500	1104 E. Grove	85022

ZIP–ADDRESS

Zip Code	City	State
85023	Phoenix	AZ
85312	Buckeye	AZ
84874	Gallup	NM
85017	Phoenix	AZ

FIGURE 3.22

A Customer Table with Address Data

```
Data Structure Diagram

ZIP-ADDRESS (Zip Code, City, State)
           1 |
           m φ
CUSTOMER (Customer Number, Customer Name, Credit Limit, Street Address, Zip Code)
```

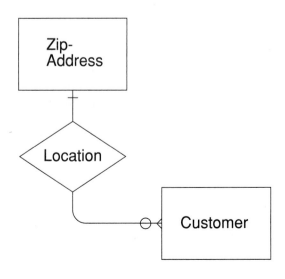

cannot record the fact that the ZIP code 65201 is assigned to Columbia, Missouri, until we have at least one customer from that city. However, this ZIP code assignment information is meaningless to the organization until such a customer exists. Many thousands of ZIP codes exist, and we would not want to clutter up our database with information about ZIP codes for cities where we have no customers. The same logic would apply to deletion anomalies. If we no longer have any customers in a ZIP code, we no longer need to know the city and state to which that ZIP code is assigned. Now let's consider modification anomalies. If the name of the city or state to which a ZIP code is assigned changes, we must change that data on every record having that ZIP code. But how likely is such a change? City, state, and ZIP code assignments are extremely stable, so it is highly unlikely that modification will be required.

Data redundancy is another issue. Suppose a company has a thousand customers in Zip Code 85023. The fact that ZIP code 85023 serves Phoenix, Arizona will be recorded a thousand times. The repeated copies will take up significant storage space. More important, repetitive entry of the same data will be required, which will present a thousand opportunities for errors to occur in the spelling of the city name and state code.

There can be some strong processing advantages to having all the customer address data in a single table. The full address will be needed each time address data is requested, and performing join operations on large tables can slow response time significantly. This data provides an example of a situation in which the anomalies caused by unnormalized tables are of minimal significance and there may be strong processing advantages to retaining a structure that is not fully normalized.

Even in this case the choice is a difficult one. Although leaving City, State, and ZIP code in the Customer table may significantly speed access to addresses, it does raise the possibility of inconsistencies in the data. The fact that the structure shown in Figure 3.22 will not make intuitive sense to users is not a major problem because they can access this data through a view that makes it look like the Customer table of Figure 3.21.

A possible compromise would be to use a Customer table like the one in Figure 3.21 along with the Zip–Address table shown in Figure 3.22. At data entry, the ZIP code would be typed in by a clerk, but the City and State for that ZIP code would be retrieved, if available, from the Zip–Address table. This would eliminate redundant data entry and potential errors. The data would still be stored redundantly, but this redundant storage would allow quicker access to address data and would present address data in a manner that is more logical to users.

Denormalization
The intentional maintenance of a database table (or tables) in less than fully normalized form. The purpose of denormalization is to enhance performance. Denormalization of tables creates the potential for anomalies that must be prevented by careful control of update procedures.

It should be clear from these examples that strong arguments exist for normalization of data structures and that intentional **denormalization** of tables should be considered only when there are substantial processing advantages to be gained. Even then, the consequences of the proposed structure should be carefully considered and appropriate measures should be taken to protect against any negative impacts of such structures on the integrity of the data. For a discussion of issues in the application of normalization in practice, see Christoff (1990) and Holt (1995).

TREATMENT OF COMPUTED AND SUMMARY DATA

In Figure 3.17, we eliminated the Seats Available column from a set of flight schedule data on the grounds that the number of available seats could always be determined by subtracting the number of seats reserved from the capacity for a flight schedule occurrence. Seats Available is an example of a **derived attribute**—an attribute whose value can always be determined by calculations based on the values of other data already stored in the database. In principle, this applies to all computed and summary data. If a value can be derived by performing mathematical computations on existing data, it provides no new information; hence, storing it as an attribute constitutes data redundancy. If a value for Seats Available is stored as well as values for Seats Reserved and Capacity, then every time the number of Seats Reserved or the Capacity of a flight is changed, the number of Seats Available must also change. In essence, a form of modification anomaly exists. When one piece of data, the number of Seats Reserved, changes, two data values must be changed in the database— the number of Seats Reserved and the number of Seats Available.

Derived attribute
An attribute whose value can always be determined by performing some calculation on values of other attributes in the database. Derived attributes are not normally stored in a database.

The exclusion of summary data from a database may, however, have serious performance implications. The Seats Reserved attribute in Figure 3.18 is itself logically a summary field. Presumably the number of seats reserved on a particular flight on a particular date could be obtained by counting the occurrences for that Flight# and Date from a Reservation table (see Figure 3.23). Since the Seats Reserved value can be obtained from existing reservations data, we could, in principle, exclude Seats Reserved from the Flight–Schedule table. If we do this, we will have to search a very large Reservation table to get a count of reservations for a particular Flight# and Date each time we need to know the number of Seats Available. Customers will want to know whether seats are available each time a reservation is made, perhaps hundreds of times per hour. The processing required to perform such a search so frequently could seriously degrade the performance of a reservation system.

Now let's compare this to what happens if we retain Seats Reserved as an attribute of the Flight–Schedule table. We can see whether seats are available for a flight on a given day by finding the one occurrence of the Flight-Schedule table that

RESERVATION

Flight #	Date	Passenger Name	Seat Assigned
102	11/12/94	Bob Barnes	D 7
102	11/12/94	Al Adams	F 14
102	11/12/94	Joe Jones	A 9
329	11/12/94	Bob Barnes	B 11
329	11/12/94	Fred Lewis	C 11
102	11/13/94	Dan Dawson	A 9
•	•	•	•
•	•	•	•
•	•	•	•

FIGURE 3.23
A Reservation Table

retains the needed data. When reservations are made, we add a new Reservation occurrence and update the Seats Reserved attribute on the corresponding occurrence of the Flight–Schedule table. We must make sure that all processes that add, delete, or modify reservations data also make appropriate corresponding changes to the Flight–Schedule table. We do have a form of data redundancy and a risk of data inconsistency. However, the processing time required is drastically reduced. For a high volume real-time system, this is often the only viable alternative.

Often the summary data needed by users does not have to be continuously updated. For example, a manager may need to have daily summary data about sales by product line before the start of the next business day. The simplest way to provide this information would be through a daily report generated from detailed data tables and provided to the manager. Such a summary report would not require the creation of a database table containing summary data. However, this report would provide only a predefined set of information, and would not allow the manager to interrogate the summary data to answer ad hoc questions.

When users need to manipulate and interrogate summary data, tables containing summary data must be generated from tables containing the detailed operational data. Views may be created in which summary data is automatically generated from the detailed data tables when requested by the user. In other cases, a separate managerial database, or a set of databases, containing summary data can periodically be generated from the detailed operational database. This type of operation is often

FIGURE 3.24
Supplying Data for
Payroll Reporting

```
PAY STUB REPORT

Check#: 3723817
Employee ID.: 136279843          Employee Name: J. Adams

Pay Period:        9/25/95 - 9/30/95
                                    Gross Pay: $580.00
                                             •
                                             •
                                             •
```

EMPLOYEE

Employee ID	Employee Name ...	Salary	Department ...	Job Title
•	•	•	•	•
•	•	•	•	•
•	•	•	•	•
136279843	J. Adams	$580.00	Shipping	Shipping Clerk
287463192	S. Norris	$975.00	Paint	Assistant Manager

referred to as a *data warehouse* and will be described in Chapter 4. Such databases are frequently used to support decision support systems and executive information systems. This type of database can also be referred to as a *snapshot,* or *replica,* database. Managers use a copy (replica) of the database, which provides a picture (snapshot) of the state of the database at a particular point in time. With either of these two processes, data are never directly entered into the summary database tables. The values in the summary tables are instead generated from detailed data, thus avoiding the data consistency problems encountered when summary tables must be continually updated.

As we have seen, there are numerous instances where users either need continuous access to updated summary data or need to be able to manipulate and interrogate data in summary form. When this is the case, appropriate table structures for the summary data are specified during the conceptual design process, and methods of supplying data to such tables without compromising data integrity must be found.

CAPTURING THE EFFECTS OF TIME

Variables whose values change over time present a particular problem for most current database management systems. Such time varying values must be identified and appropriately modeled in the design of a database. However, the identification of time varying variables can be difficult, and methods for implementing them are awkward in most current DBMSs.

Look at the example shown in Figure 3.24. Here, a set of employee salary data is used to produce paychecks and a Pay Stub Report on a weekly basis. This report has been greatly simplified by excluding taxes and other deductions. We are assuming that all the employees are salaried workers and that their Gross Pay amount is simply determined by their salary level.

At first glance, the Employee table seems to provide sufficient data to produce the Pay Stub Report. The Salary attribute for a given Employee occurrence is simply used to produce the Gross Pay amount for that employee.

Let's suppose that on October 1, 1995, Employee# 136279843 is given a raise in salary to $605. We would update the Employee table by changing the Salary value for this worker to $605. Now suppose that we need to reproduce the Gross Pay information for the week of 9/25/95 in the Pay Stub Report. The data in the Employee table now produces a salary value of $605. However, the Gross Pay value is invalid because it uses a Salary that was not in effect at the time the work was performed. Transactions occurring before October 1, 1995, should validly use the previous value of Salary, while transactions occurring after that date should have the new value applied to them.

This type of change is very different from a correction to the Salary due to the discovery of an error. When an error is detected, all data and reports generated from the affected data should be adjusted to reflect the corrected value. However, a change made to a valid data value should not affect historical data or reports generated for periods prior to the change.

How can the tables in Figure 3.24 be modified to correct this problem? Figure 3.25 shows one approach. A field has been added to the Employee table called Effective Date, containing the date that the current Salary became effective. A

EMPLOYEE

Employee ID	Employee Name	Current Salary	Effective Date	Department	Job Title
136279843	J. Adams	$580.00	10/01/95	Shipping	Shipping Clerk
287463192	S. Norris	$975.00	10/01/95	Paint	Assistant Manager

SALARY–HISTORY

Employee ID	Effective Date	Terminal Date	Salary
•			
•			
•			
136279843	10/01/94	09/30/95	$580
•			
•			
136279843	10/01/92	09/30/94	$550
287463192	10/01/92	09/30/95	$975

PAY–HISTORY

Check Number	Employee ID	Gross Pay	Pay Period Beginning
•			
•			
•			
8637419	136279843	$580.00	09/25/95
8637418	287463192	$975.00	09/25/95
•			
•			
8216911	136279843	$580.00	09/18/95
•			
•			
•			

FIGURE 3.25
A Set of Tables to
Support Payroll
History Reporting

Salary–History table has also been created. This table stores a history of previous Salary amounts for each employee and includes the Employee ID#, Salary, Effective Date, and Terminal Date. When an employee is assigned a new Current Salary, the existing Current Salary and Effective Date for the employee in the Employee table are used to create a new occurrence in the Salary–History table. The value assigned to the Terminal Date attribute is one day prior to the date on which the new salary takes effect. Once this history record has been created, the new salary and its effective date replace the existing values in the Employee table.

Alternatively, we could have removed salary entirely from the Employee table, placing current as well as historic salary values in the Salary–History table. Under this treatment, current salaries could be specifically detected because of their lack of a Terminal Date. A disadvantage of this treatment is that the Salary–History table would have to be searched for the current salary of each employee each time paychecks are issued. Because it is likely that the current salary will be requested more frequently than historic salary data, the structure placing the Current Salary in the Employee table is more efficient.

Note that a Pay–History table is created even though its data seems redundant. With the Salary–History table in place, the appropriate Salary can reproduce historic Gross Pay values. However, each paycheck is itself an entity of importance and its attributes should be recorded in the database. Corrections or modifications to data used to determine check amounts will have no effect upon prior checks issued. Such corrections must be handled through adjusting entries which affect future checks. For example, this week's check might be increased by $50 to compensate for a $50 error found in a previous period's pay calculations. In general, any lookup, calculated, or summary values that document financial transactions or trigger actions by an organization must be documented in history records.

It is not always necessary that history data like that in the Pay–History and Salary–History tables be maintained within the database. If transactions using noncurrent data for these attributes occur only rarely, this type of history data may be saved in independent archival files or may even be maintained only in paper documents. However, if a substantial amount of processing of history data is expected to occur, it is imperative that it be maintained within the database.

There are many attributes whose values vary over time. Within the Employee table of Figure 3.24, both the Department and Job Title attributes may vary over time for a given employee. Does a history file for these attributes need to be maintained? For most larger organizations, this type of information and a variety of other personnel-related data will be maintained in some manner in computerized form. Another employee attribute not shown in Figure 3.24, but which is subject to change over time, is the employee's address. Does a history of employee addresses need to be maintained in computerized form? In most cases, it would not seem to be necessary to provide for rapid computerized access to the former addresses of employees.

Essentially, for all attributes whose values are time dependent, a determination must be made about the extent to which access to noncurrent values of the attribute will be needed. When historic information will be processed frequently, this information should be stored in database tables to assure rapid and flexible access. Less frequently accessed data may be stored in archival files separate from the database or may be maintained only in paper form.

Many types of business data have the following usage pattern. Current data values for an attribute will be accessed and used very frequently. Recent historical values also will be accessed relatively frequently, but the rate of use of historic data will decline consistently with the age of the data. Efficient handling of data with this type of usage pattern may involve a three-tiered storage pattern. One table may contain only current values. This keeps the table relatively small and thus speeds up the large volume of processing that is based on the most recent data values. Recent historic values that are expected to be used relatively frequently might be maintained in a separate history table. This allows quick access to historic data without slowing down processing of current data. Finally, historic data that have reached an age where it is felt that they will rarely be accessed might be migrated to archival files outside the database structure.

During the conceptual design process, tables should be created for any history data that is expected to be maintained in computerized form. Decisions about database versus archival file storage of history tables are normally made later in the design process as the design is implemented.

Lack of effective treatment of time varying data is a serious limitation of many DBMSs in use today. As we have seen, the designer must normally explicitly create and maintain tables of historic data. Prototype DBMSs are available that automatically create and maintain historic data by producing *versions* of tables (Kim, 1991; Frank, 1995). If an attribute is defined as "versionable," when it is modified the former values are automatically saved as versions of the attribute. Time stamping is used to determine the effective and terminal dates for each version. Requests for data can indicate a historic point in time. The time stamps on the requested attributes are then examined and, if appropriate, an older version of the attribute will be retrieved.

Although systems with enhanced capabilities to manage the effects of time are an interesting and promising area of database research, these capabilities are not currently obtainable in commercially available DBMSs. The database designer must plan for the treatment of attributes whose values change over time and must create any additional table structures needed to store historic data.

DEFINING AND DESCRIBING ATTRIBUTE DOMAINS

Domain
The domain of an attribute is the set of all values that can validly be assigned to that attribute.

The discussion of Domain/Key normal form earlier in this chapter illustrated the importance of domain restrictions in the process of defining the structure of data. However, up to this point, we have not discussed **domain** definitions in detail, nor have we described a method for recording domain descriptions during the conceptual design. Data structure diagrams, at most, list the names of attributes and identify those attributes that serve as keys. Entity-Relationship diagrams often give no information at all about the attributes of an entity. The information about attributes that needs to be recorded is the sort of information that will appear in the data dictionary of the completed database. We are, in essence, creating a preliminary data dictionary that will eventually be extended and transformed into the data dictionary for the database. We will use the term Domain Description for these preliminary specifications of attributes and their domains that have not yet been implemented.

Domain Restrictions

Figure 3.26 shows an example of what a domain description might look like for the Flight–Schedule table in Figure 3.18. The name of the table is identified, and then several characteristics of each attribute are described, including the attribute's name, and information about allowable values and how the attribute will be used. The data type, domain, and nulls status actually define the domain of the attribute in its broadest sense.

The data type restricts the domain to values consistent with the specified type. Specification of Seats Reserved as an Integer variable excludes such values as Bob, AZ28, and 23.75 from the domain of possible values for Seats Reserved.

The Domain characteristic allows more specific restrictions to be applied. In the case of the Flight# attribute, we define the data type as alphanumeric, because flight numbers will not be used mathematically, but also restrict the domain further to allow only numeric digits equal to or greater than 100 and equal to or less than 699. In the case of the Seats Reserved variable, the Data Type specification restricts the domain to include only integers, while the Domain specification further restricts this variable to values between 0 and 600. It makes no sense to have a negative number of seats reserved and 600 seats is well beyond the capacity of the largest available plane. Restricting the domain to disallow values for Seats Reserved greater than 600 will help prevent unreasonable values from being erroneously entered into the table.

Disallowing a null value for an attribute is, in a sense, a further restriction on the domain of a variable. However, the decision about whether to allow or disallow null values for an attribute is also closely related to the key status of an attribute. If we say that nulls are not allowed for an attribute, we are saying that a value for this attribute is required to define an occurrence of the entity, and unless a value for this variable is known, we don't have a meaningful set of data to include in the database. Attributes that are a part of the primary key of a table obviously meet this criterion. The primary key is used to identify occurrences and to link them to related tables.

FIGURE 3.26
Domain Description for the Flight–Schedule Table

TABLE: FLIGHT–SCHEDULE

Attribute Name	Data Type	Domain	Nulls Allowed	Key Status
Flight#	Alphanumeric 3 digits	100 thru 699	No	Concatenated Key with Date Foreign Key referencing FLIGHT table
Date	Date 8 dights	Dates after January 1, 1982	No	Concatenated Key with Flight#
Assigned Plane Type	Alphanumeric up to 5 digits		Yes	Foreign Key referencing PLANE–TYPE table
Seats Reserved	Integer	0 thru 600	Yes	

An occurrence with a null value for its primary key would be lost. Thus nulls are never allowed for attributes that are part of the primary key.

An attribute whose key status is primary key must have a unique value for each occurrence. For concatenated keys, the combination of values for the key attributes must be unique. This uniqueness characteristic was part of our definition of a primary key, and it can be thought of as a type of domain restriction—the domain of the primary key for this occurrence cannot include the values of the primary key attribute for other occurrences.

Nulls can be allowed or disallowed for attributes that serve as foreign keys. If nulls are disallowed, the relationship of this table to the table referenced by the foreign key is mandatory. In the case of our Flight–Schedule table, Flight# is a foreign key referencing the Flight table and this relationship is mandatory. It makes no sense to create daily flight schedule information for a flight that does not exist. Flight–Schedule occurrences cannot exist unless they can be tied to a row in the Flight table.

The designation of an attribute as a foreign key is another special form of domain restriction. The domain of Flight#s in the Flight–Schedule table is restricted to the set of values for Flight# that are used in the Flight table. A Flight# value in the Flight–Schedule table should be accepted only if it is equal to the Flight# of one of the occurrences of the Flight table.

Nulls are allowed for foreign key attributes that establish optional relationships to some parent table. For example, the Assigned Plane Type attribute in the Flight–Schedule table (see Figure 3.18) is a foreign key referencing the Plane–Type table. In this case, the relationship should be optional. We can identify a Flight schedule occurrence and begin to record data about it before a type of plane has been assigned to it. At the same time, when a plane type is assigned to a Flight schedule occurrence, we want to make sure that the Assigned Plane Type value that is entered is valid and exists in the Plane–Type table. The combination of nulls allowed and the attribute's foreign key status gives us this type of domain for Assigned Plane Type. The domain of the Assigned Plane Type attribute is restricted to a null value or a value assigned to some occurrence of plane type found in the Plane–Type table.

Attributes that are not primary or foreign keys are allowed to have null values unless a good organizational reason exists for disallowing nulls. For example, in a customer table whose primary key is Customer Number, a mail order company might want to disallow null values for the Customer Name and Customer Address attributes. Name and address information should be available at the time that a new customer occurrence is added, and a customer occurrence is not meaningful to this type of organization without name and address information. Products must be shipped and bills sent to a named customer at that customer's mailing address.

Secondary keys can also be noted in the key status column of the Domain Description. This indicates that we expect to sort a table based on the values of the specified attribute and, therefore, want to have a nonunique index created for that attribute. In Figure 3.18, the Destination attribute of the Flight table is designated as a secondary key. We expect that users may frequently want to get a listing of flights sorted by destination or get a listing of just those flights going to a specified destination. Therefore, we want to create an index to speed this type of processing.

Cross-Attribute Domain Restrictions

In some instances, the domain of one attribute is restricted based on the value of another attribute in the same or a different table. In fact, foreign keys are a type of cross-table domain restriction. However, there can be many other restrictions on the domain of one attribute based on values of another attribute within a table.

Figure 3.27 provides an example of a Domain Description containing this type of restriction. The attribute Product# in a Product table is defined as an alphanumeric field of five characters. A picture or mask is used to describe further domain restrictions. Only values beginning with a single alphabetic character and followed by four numeric digits are allowed. The product numbers A1697 or B0389 could be valid, but BA214 could not. A further domain restriction placed on the Product# is dependent on the value of the Product Line variable for this occurrence. If the Product Line is PC, the product number must begin with an A. If the Product Line is Printer, the Product# must begin with a B, and so on.

Figure 3.28 shows an example of a domain restriction that involves data from multiple tables. One of the processing rules used by a university is that students may not enroll for a course on a pass-fail basis if that course is in their major. This restriction is shown for the Pass–Fail attribute of the Registration table. Note that this restriction requires that a portion of the Course–No attribute of the Registration table be compared to the value of the Major field in the Student table. If these two values are equal, the value of the Pass–Fail attribute can only be No.

Many important instances of organizational policies exist that restrict domains in a manner similar to these examples. The domain of a Credit–Limit attribute might vary depending on how long a firm has been a customer of our company, with higher credit limits being allowed for long-term customers. The domain for the total dollar value of purchases on an order might be restricted to amounts greater than or equal to zero and less than or equal to the customers' credit limit minus their outstanding balance. At a medical clinic, the domain of care givers authorized to provide treatment to a patient might be restricted based on the patient's type of illness. All these are examples of instances where the domain of one attribute is restricted

Attribute Name	Data Type	Domain
Table: **PRODUCT**		
Product #	Alphanumeric 5 characters	Picture X9999 First Character A if Product Line is PC B if Product Line is Printer C for all other Product Lines
Product Line	Alphanumeric 10 characters	List (PC, Printer, LAN)

FIGURE 3.27
A Domain Description Containing a Cross-Attribute Restriction

FIGURE 3.28
Domain Description
Showing a Cross-
Domain Restriction

Attribute Name	Data Type	Domain
Table: STUDENT		
Student #	Alphanumeric 9 characters	Picture 999999999
Student Name	Alphanumeric 20 characters	
Major	Alphabetic 3 characters	Picture XXX
Credit–Hrs	Integer	$\geq 0, \leq 300$
Table: REGISTRATION		
Student #	Alphanumeric 9 characters	Picture 999999999
Course–No	Alphanumeric 6 characters	Picture XXX999
Pass–Fail	Alphabetic 3 characters	Picture XXX List (Yes, No) Value must be No if 1st 3 digits of Course–No = Major of student

based on values of other attributes. In some cases, values of several attributes in multiple tables may be combined to form a domain restriction. These forms of domain restrictions cannot always be built directly into the structure of the database when it is implemented. However, these types of restrictions need to be recorded in the domain descriptions used in conceptual design of databases. Any restrictions that cannot be directly imposed in the structure of the database should be recalled and used during the design of applications so that the applications can enforce these restrictions.

SUMMARY

Normalization seeks to produce data structures that facilitate efficient and error-free storage and processing. A series of normal forms have been discovered that assure certain types of anomalies are not present in tables. A table that has no repeating groups of fields is said to be in first normal form. A table that is in first normal form and has no partial dependencies is said to be in second normal form. A table that is in second normal form and has no transitive dependencies is said to be in third normal form. Although other, more restrictive, normal forms have been discovered, most database designers are satisfied with achieving third normal form.

Domain/key normal form provides an ideal of the state that tables should achieve, but does not provide practical rules of thumb for achieving that state. A table is in domain/key normal form if all restrictions on it are a logical consequence of the key of the table or the domain restrictions on its attributes. Tables in domain key normal form cannot have anomalies.

Databases are sometimes intentionally denormalized in order to improve processing efficiency. However, when a denormalized structure is used, anomalies can result and special measures must be taken to maintain data integrity of such structures.

Calculated and summary values are, in the strictest sense, redundant data, since their values can be derived from combinations of other data elements in a database. However, maintenance of calculated and summary values in tables or views can often greatly improve processing efficiency and can provide users with more convenient access to data. Thus, calculated and summary attributes are often included in tables developed during conceptual design.

Attributes whose values change over time require special treatment in database management systems. If historic as well as current values of an attribute will be used frequently in processing, tables must be maintained showing the values of the attribute and the applicable time period when a given value was in effect.

Domain descriptions provide detailed information about attributes that is not provided by E-R models or data structure diagrams. These descriptions serve as a preliminary data dictionary during conceptual design. Domain descriptions typically provide the following kinds of information about each attribute: the attribute's name, its data type, its domain, whether it is allowed to have a null value, and its key status. These features, in combination, encompass all possible restrictions on the domains of attributes.

REVIEW QUIZ

_____ A condition in which a meaningful unit of data cannot be stored until related data becomes available.

_____ The value of a nonkey attribute can be uniquely identified using only part of a concatenated primary key.

_____ Every logical restriction on attributes is a result of the definition of keys and domains.

_____ The set of all values that can validly be assigned to an attribute.

_____ A two-dimensional array with a single-valued entry in each cell and no duplicate rows.

_____ A table containing no repeating groups of attributes.

_____ The value of one nonkey attribute is functionally determined by another non-key attribute.

_____ When the value of an attribute is updated, it must be updated in several places in the database.

_____ A table that is in 3NF and has no nonkey determinants.

_____ A table containing duplicate rows or rows with multivalued attributes.

_____ The allowed values of one attribute are restricted based upon the value of another attribute in the same or a related table.

_____ An attribute whose value can be determined by adding together the values of two other attributes.

_____ A table that is in Boyce-Codd normal form and contains no multivalued dependencies.

_____ Integer, date, numeric, alphabetic.

_____ State of an attribute that indicates no value has yet been assigned to it.

_____ The intentional maintenance of a table or tables in less than fully normalized form.

_____ Meaningful data may be removed from the database when a related set of data is deleted.

1. Relation
2. Insertion anomaly
3. Modification anomaly
4. Deletion anomaly
5. Unnormalized table
6. First normal form
7. Partial dependency
8. Transitive dependency
9. Boyce-Codd normal form
10. Fourth normal form
11. Domain/Key normal form
12. Denormalization
13. Derived attribute

14. Domain

15. Data type

16. Null

17. Cross-attribute domain restriction

---

1. Distinguish between a table and a relation. What conditions must a table meet in order to be a valid relation?

2. Describe the anomaly problem. Describe and distinguish among insertion, modification, and deletion anomalies. How does normalization attempt to limit anomalies?

3. Describe and distinguish among the following normal forms: first normal form, second normal form, third normal form, Boyce-Codd normal form, and fourth normal form.

4. Can a table be in third normal form without being in second normal form? Why or why not?

5. What is a repeating group? Give an example of a table containing a repeating group and indicate how you would eliminate the repeating group problem. What normal form is a table in if it contains a repeating group?

6. Describe and give an example of a partial dependency. How would you restructure the data to correct a partial dependency problem?

7. Describe and give an example of a transitive dependency. How would you restructure the data to correct a transitive dependency?

8. Describe Boyce-Codd normal form and the problem of nonkey determinants. Give an example of a table that is in third normal form but not in Boyce-Codd normal form.

9. What is a multivalued dependency? Give an example of a table containing a multivalued dependency.

10. Define Domain/Key normal form. What are the advantages and limitations of this alternative approach to normalization?

11. Discuss denormalization. What advantages might be realized by denormalizing a table? What disadvantages must be addressed?

12. What do we mean by a derived attribute? Under what circumstances would you consider recording a derived attribute in a database?

13. How does an update to reflect a change in the value of an attribute differ from an update that corrects an erroneous value?

14. When and why is it necessary to maintain tables containing historical data?

15. Historic data can be maintained in a variety of forms. Describe and assess alternative methods of storing historic data.

16. What is the meaning of the domain of an attribute?

17. What is a data type and how does it restrict the domain of an attribute?

18. How does disallowing null values restrict the domain of an attribute? What types of attributes must always have nulls disallowed?

19. What is a cross-attribute domain restriction? Give two or more examples of different types of cross-attribute domain restrictions.

The first six exercises that follow present tables with sample data that are not fully normalized. The primary key for each table is underlined. Based on the sample data provided for each of these tables:

a. Indicate which normal form(s) is (are) violated by the table in its current form.

b. Give an example of insertion, deletion, and modification anomalies (if any) associated with the table in its present form.

c. Present a data structure diagram showing a reorganized table structure that is in at least third normal form.

20. A public library keeps the following table of data about its patrons:

Patron Name	Home Phone #	Library Card #	Books Checked Out					
			ID#	Due Date	ID#	Due Date	ID#	Due Date
J. Smith	3-7285	L19673	L282.9	09/23/95	HC12.1	9/23/95		
A. Ault	2-1793	L84361						
S. Davis	3-1983	L24639	LV302	09/25/95	Q17.50	9/28/95	BA81.3	10/01/95
R. Jones	2-1846	L41925	HA1.25	10/13/95				
R. Ault	2-1793	L82630	BC12/3	09/22/95				

21. A school keeps the following table of data about its students:

ID #	Name	Advisor's Name	Class Standing	GPA	Advisor's Office #
12637	Carol Coats	B. Jones	Freshman	2.85	B 117
14392	Al Evans	T. Turner	Sophomore	2.17	E 283
26701	Ed Davis	L. Lewis	Freshman	3.40	B 213
19306	Lynn Peal	T. Turner	Junior	2.17	E 283
23907	Dan Mead	B. Jones	Senior	3.82	B 117
20639	Pam Sneva	G. Court	Junior	2.84	B 213

22. A company keeps the following table of data about orders:

Order #	Product #	Quantity Ordered	Unit Price	Product Description	Customer #
1001	102	3	$75	Widget	104
1001	107	6	$110	Gadget	104
1002	102	2	$75	Widget	101
1003	107	4	$110	Gadget	103
1003	104	1	$155	Dealie	103
1004	107	2	$110	Gadget	104

23. A company keeps the following table of information about employees:

ID #	Employee Name	Wage Class	Wage Rate	Department Name	Department Head	Birth Date
46823	Jan Jones	B	$8.50	Packing	L. Davis	08/06/57
37910	Al Evans	A	$7.25	Shipping	S. Smith	01/04/51
52907	Sam Smith	C	$9.75	Shipping	S. Smith	02/23/44
63015	Ann Adams	A	$7.25	Packing	L. Davis	09/27/59
29414	Tom Bates	B	$8.50	Sales	J. Kerns	11/03/64
40174	Fay Moss	C	$9.75	Shipping	S. Smith	04/15/42

24. A university keeps the following table of information about course offerings:

Course Number	Section Number	Course Description	Instructor	Room Number	Room Capacity
CIS 120	01	Intro. to CIS	Morgan	108	50
CIS 120	02	Intro. to CIS	Lorents	205	60
CIS 220	01	Programming I	Bosse	108	50
ACC 255	01	Intro. to Acc.	Evans	204	50
ACC 255	02	Intro. to Acc.	Smith	205	60

25. A university keeps the following file of information about employees and students and their automobiles:

ID Number	Name	# of Autos Registered	Auto Lic. # 1	Sticker Type	Auto Lic. # 2	Sticker Type	Auto Lic. # 3	Sticker Type
F23078	L. Lewis	2	CBR 268	Red	BZY 890	Blue		
E39019	J. Adams	1	ZFA 960	Blue				
F38074	A. Eads	3	MNY 009	Blue	CPR 705	Red	TVP 376	Red
F84906	L. Bates	1	DZA 259	Red				

26. A company maintains the following set of data about employees. Are there any derived attributes in this table? If you found a derived attribute, how would you recommend that it be treated in terms of database storage? Are there any attributes that change over time and whose history should be maintained? Identify these attributes and suggest how they should be treated in terms of database storage.

ID #	Employee Name	Wage Rate	Department Name	Job Title	Birth Date	Age
46823	Jan Jones	$8.50	Packing	Asst. Mgr.	08/06/57	38
37910	Al Evans	$7.25	Shipping	Clerk	01/04/51	44
52907	Sam Smith	$9.75	Shipping	Manager	02/23/44	51
63015	Ann Adams	$7.25	Packing	Laborer	09/27/59	36
29414	Tom Bates	$8.50	Sales	Salesperson	11/03/64	31
40174	Fay Moss	$9.75	Shipping	Asst. Mgr.	04/15/42	53

27. Generate a set of domain descriptions for the employee table in exercise 26. You may assume that ID # is to serve as the primary key of this table. Every employee must have an assigned wage rate at all times. The value of the Department Name attribute must reference a valid value of Department Name in the Department table (not shown here). However, some employees may not be assigned to any department.

28. The following table is a proposed product table for a company. Quantity on Hand refers to the quantity of the product that is currently in inventory. Quantity

Encumbered refers to the number of units of the product that have been ordered by customers but have not yet been shipped. Quantity Available refers to the number of units of the product that are on hand and not encumbered by existing orders. All product numbers consist of two alpha characters and two numeric digits. For computers, the first character of the product number is always an A, while it is a C for all other products.

a. Identify any derived attributes and any attributes that require maintenance of a time history.

b. Describe how you would handle these attributes in creating a database storage structure.

c. Generate a set of domain descriptions for this table.

PRODUCT

Product#	Product Description	Unit Price	Quantity on Hand	Quantity Encumbered	Quantity Available
AR28	Personal Computer	$1,125	3850	612	3,238
CV17	Laser Printer	$895	1725	422	1,303
CK91	VGA Monitor	$275	2217	582	1,635
AD12	Portable PC	$1,450	958	980	-22
CO43	Modem	$95	1364	344	1,020

THE PROCESS OF
DATABASE PLANNING
AND DEVELOPMENT

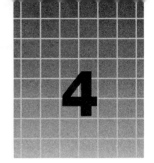

LEARNING OBJECTIVES

After completing this chapter you should be able to

- Explain the fundamentals of alternative data planning methods.
- Construct simple data planning documents utilizing hierarchies or lists and matrices.
- Understand the role of CASE tools in IS planning and systems development, and be familiar with the CASE tools most frequently used for data modeling.
- Understand the data-oriented steps involved in a traditional systems development process and how they relate to the overall systems development process.
- Understand the concept of the Three Schema Architecture and its implications for database development.
- Explain what is meant by an I-CASE product and understand how such a product can serve as a systems repository.

Organizations use planning and development processes to assure that organizational databases are developed in the most effective manner. Such organizations must determine the appropriate size and scope of each database that is developed and prioritize projects scheduled for development. As each database is developed, its requirements must be determined and decisions must be made about the structure of the data, how processes will create, maintain, and manipulate the data of the system, and where various elements of the database system will be placed.

Chapters 2 and 3 have focused on the organization of data—the logical structures and relationships that exist in data and techniques for modeling data. In this chapter we examine how data and databases fit in the overall process of developing and maintaining an organization's information systems.

METHODOLOGIES FOR INFORMATION SYSTEMS DEVELOPMENT

A number of models relating to information systems development methods have an impact upon data planning and development issues. A few of the more important models and methodologies are reviewed here.

THE WHAT, HOW, AND WHERE DIMENSIONS OF INFORMATION SYSTEMS

Zachman (1987) has suggested that information systems can be thought of as having three fundamental dimensions, or components. The *what dimension* refers to the data of a system; the *how dimension* refers to the processes of a system, and the *where dimension* refers to the network elements of a system. An organization's **information systems architecture**, its overall plan for the structure of information systems, can be described in terms of these three major elements. The organization must plan for the acquisition and implementation of hardware and software resources required to provide the needed types of data, processing, and network capabilities, and must assure that appropriately skilled personnel are available.

Any information system must address all three of these dimensions. The data modeling methods discussed in Chapters 2 and 3 serve only to describe the structure of the data in a system. Data are created, maintained, and manipulated by processes— the *how dimension* of the architecture. Also, physical system resources must reside at some location, so the question of where system activities take place must be addressed. However, the data component *(what dimension)* generally needs to be addressed in greater detail than the other two dimensions at early stages of the development cycle. The structure of the data in an information system must be determined before designing the processes that will use that data, and the physical structure of the database must be in place before applications that will process the database can be developed. With respect to the *where dimension,* it will always be a goal to provide systems that make services available to the user as if the system itself resided on his or her personal workstation. Thus, decisions about the placement of resources within the network should not affect the conceptual design of our systems. Information about the locations where system services are needed will be gathered throughout the planning and development cycle, but will interact with the data and process elements only at the level of physical design and implementation.

Detailed treatment of methods for developing complete information systems is outside the scope of this textbook. We will focus on those elements in the planning and development of information systems that emphasize data and databases or that relate to the location of system resources and activities. However, it is important that we have a basic understanding of how database planning and development techniques fit into broader information systems development methodologies. Thus, we next present a brief summary of three commonly used information system development methodologies.

THE SYSTEMS DEVELOPMENT
LIFE CYCLE METHODOLOGY

Early databases were developed using the **systems development life cycle (SDLC)** approach, which had been designed to support the development of systems using file-oriented processing. This approach divides the development process for information systems into five components, as illustrated in Figure 4.1. These steps, or phases, are designed to be undertaken in sequential order.

First, in the systems investigation phase, the economic and technical feasibility of a proposed system is evaluated. If the system is determined to be feasible, a project team is formulated and a management plan for the project is presented. If approval is obtained, the project moves forward to the systems analysis phase, in which the information requirements of end users are explored in detail. These requirements are then consolidated into a set of functional requirements for the

Information systems architecture
An overall plan for the structure of information systems in an organization described in terms of data, process, and network elements.

Systems development life cycle (SDLC)
A methodology for the development of information systems that divides the process into five stages: investigation, analysis, design, implementation, and maintenance.

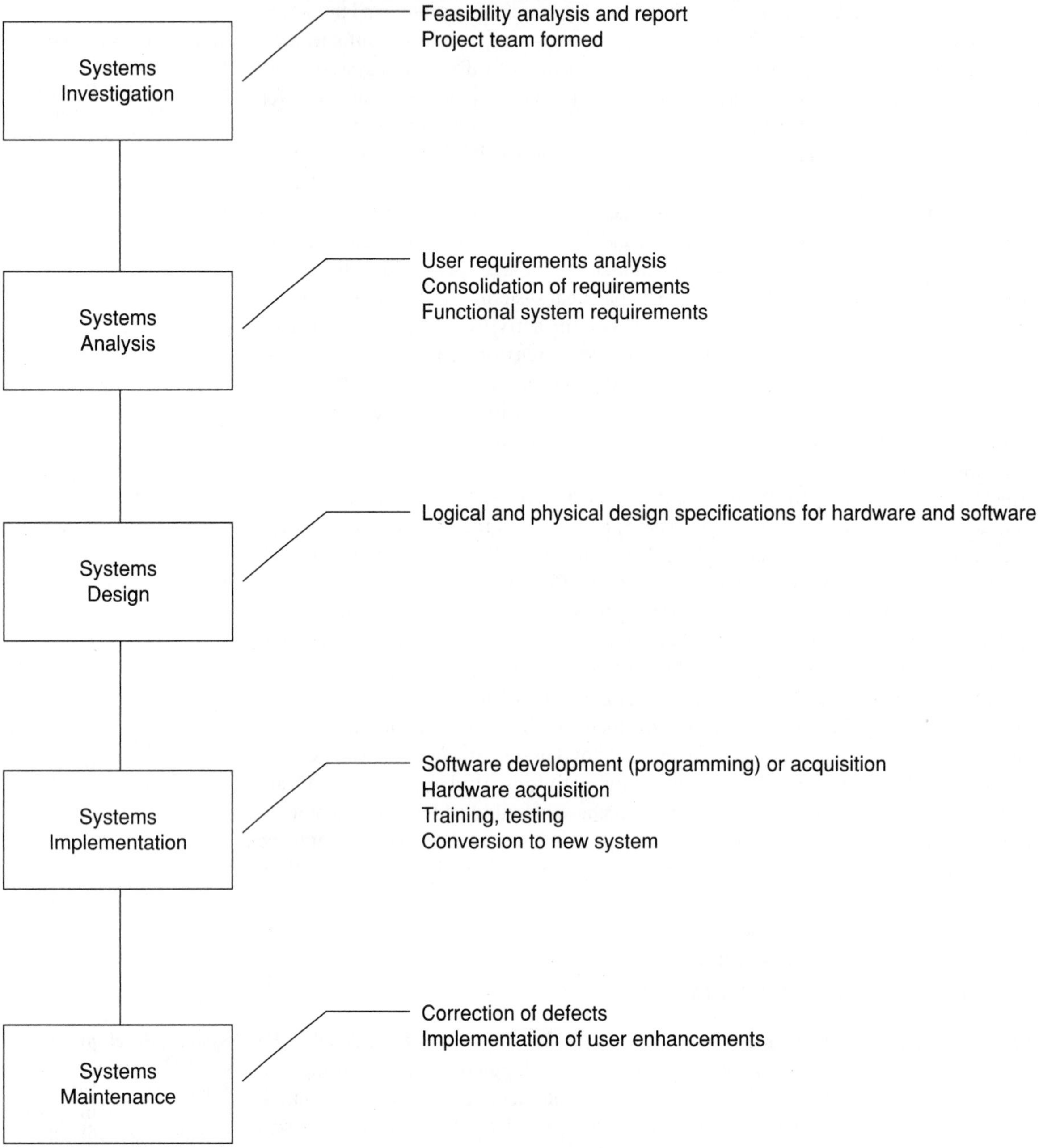

```
┌──────────────────┐ ──────── Feasibility analysis and report
│                  │          Project team formed
│    Systems       │
│  Investigation   │
│                  │
└──────────────────┘


┌──────────────────┐ ──────── User requirements analysis
│                  │          Consolidation of requirements
│    Systems       │          Functional system requirements
│    Analysis      │
│                  │
└──────────────────┘


┌──────────────────┐ ──────── Logical and physical design specifications for hardware and software
│                  │
│    Systems       │
│    Design        │
│                  │
└──────────────────┘


┌──────────────────┐ ──────── Software development (programming) or acquisition
│                  │          Hardware acquisition
│    Systems       │          Training, testing
│  Implementation  │          Conversion to new system
│                  │
└──────────────────┘


┌──────────────────┐ ──────── Correction of defects
│                  │          Implementation of user enhancements
│    Systems       │
│   Maintenance    │
│                  │
└──────────────────┘
```

FIGURE 4.1
The Systems
Development
Life Cycle

system. The systems design phase encompasses development of the hardware and software specifications. Once the design phase is completed, the system must be implemented. It is here that any new hardware is acquired and the needed software is either purchased or developed. In this phase, the programming of applications occurs. Training the users of the system and converting to operation of the new system round out the systems implementation phase. The systems maintenance phase begins as soon as implementation has been completed. Modifications to correct errors and implement enhancements are made throughout the operational life of the system.

This methodology is still widely used. However, the traditional SDLC methodology contains a number of limitations that have caused many organizations to either modify it or adopt other methodologies.

SDLC focuses on an individual information system development project. It does not provide for a systematic planning process or any mechanism for establishing priorities for alternative development projects. Nor can it provide methods for determining the appropriate scope of a system or establishing appropriate boundaries between related systems.

Traditionally, the SDLC methodology has tended to focus principally on processes to be performed rather than on the data of a system. Traditional SDLC methods often need to be modified somewhat to provide an appropriate focus on data and data modeling in database-oriented information systems.

Finally, the traditional SDLC methodology was developed prior to the availability of computerized tools to assist the design process. The development of systems was a lengthy and complex process, and it was very difficult to maintain the interest and involvement of the system's users. Due to the costs, both in time and money, of revising specifications, the results of each phase of the development process could not normally be adjusted once one moved on to the next development phase.

Over the years, substantial progress has been made in addressing these limitations. A number of alternative information systems development methodologies have been formulated and the SDLC methodology has been adapted and expanded to accommodate changing development needs. SDLC methods can now support a strong emphasis on data modeling and the use of computerized design tools. **Computer Assisted Software Engineering (CASE) tools** have been developed to provide computerized support for various phases of the development process. In addition, the need for data planning to support the strategic plans of the organization is widely recognized. A number of alternative methodologies and computerized tools to support data planning are now available.

Computer assisted software engineering (CASE) tools
Software products designed to support one or more phases of the planning and/or development of information systems.

THE INFORMATION ENGINEERING DEVELOPMENT CYCLE

Information engineering (IE) is an information systems development methodology that incorporates planning into the development cycle and makes full use of CASE tools. This methodology was pioneered by James Martin (1990). As Figure 4.2 indicates, this methodology has four phases: planning, analysis, design, and implementation.

Under the IE approach, a planning phase identifies business areas for analysis and development of information systems (IS). The scope of the planning phase is the entire organization. The planning phase is linked to organizational planning and is designed to identify all the information systems needed to support the organization's plans. Interrelationships between systems as well as some high-level specifications for each business area are identified. The systems investigation phase that was

Information engineering (IE)
An information systems development methodology whose phases are: planning, analysis, design, and implementation. The IE methodology calls for computer generation of applications based on conceptual level specifications. It requires the use of I-CASE tools.

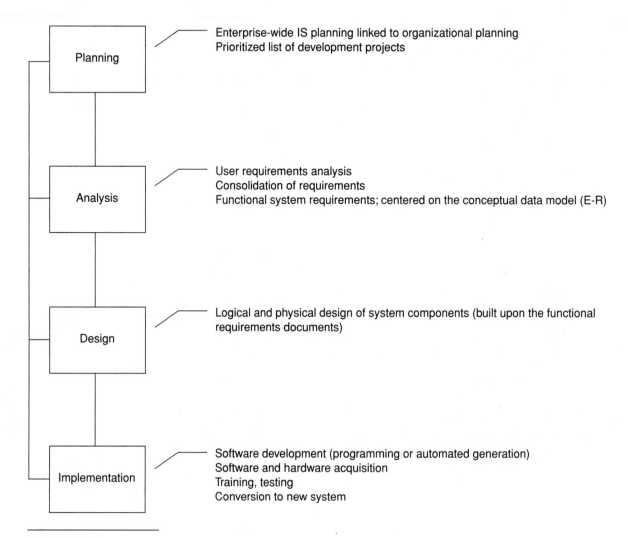

FIGURE 4.2
The Information
Engineering
Development Model

used in the SDLC is no longer needed because the planning phase will result in a prioritized set of projects to be carried forward to the analysis phase.

The analysis, design, and implementation phases that follow are similar in scope to the corresponding phases of the SDLC. However, there are some notable differences in the manner in which these activities are completed. Under the IE approach, specifications of system requirements are defined by system designers at the conceptual level. The conversion of these conceptual or logical specifications into operational applications is viewed as a predominantly mechanical process that can best be performed by computerized CASE tools. Full implementation of the IE methodology requires the use of an integrated set of CASE tools, where the results of each step of the development process are stored in a CASE document that is linked to and provides structure for the next phase of development. This integrated set of CASE tools is called an **Integrated CASE (I-CASE) product.**

Another aspect of the IE methodology is its strong emphasis on data modeling. Under the IE methodology, the data model is to be developed prior to the modeling of processes, and the data model (as represented in the E-R diagram) tends to be the central representation of a system around which other elements are organized. This contrasts with the SDLC in which the data flow diagram, which focuses primarily on processes, has traditionally been seen as the central element.

THE PROTOTYPING DEVELOPMENT CYCLE

The **prototyping development cycle,** sometimes referred to as *rapid application prototyping* (**RAP**), focuses on rapid development of systems and a high degree of end-user involvement in the development process. As Figure 4.3 illustrates, there is no planning or investigation phase. It is assumed that the decision to develop the system has already been made. The heart of the prototyping cycle is an iterative set of analysis, design, and implementation methods wherein user information requirements are analyzed. Systems meeting these requirements are designed, and working models (prototypes) of the resulting implementation are rapidly developed and presented to users for their review. User feedback about the functioning of the system is gathered, which initiates a new iteration of the cycle. Suggested modifications to the system become revised user requirements that feed into a revised design and a revised prototype implementation. The iterations continue until the user is satisfied with the system.

Once the system has been accepted by users, it is converted into a fully implemented system by adding any functionality not included in the prototype system. This may involve relatively minor adjustments or may require extensive reprogramming of elements that were not fully implemented in the prototype.

Prototyping is designed to provide rapid development with strong user involvement. In the initial requirements analysis, only a preliminary look at the user's requirements is sought. As designs are prototyped based upon the initial specifications, the reactions of users to these implementations serve to refine the system until the user feels comfortable that his or her requirements have been met.

Increasing pressures to deliver information systems quickly are causing prototyping methods to be used more and more extensively in information systems. The major limitation of prototyping methods is the difficulty of providing the rapid turnaround required to keep users actively involved in development. For large, highly interrelated systems with many users, it may be impossible to develop a working model of the full system in a sufficiently timely fashion to keep users actively involved. This is true of most large-scale organizational database systems. However, prototyping methods may still be used to develop key parts of the system. Development teams work with users of each key element of the system to prototype their portion of the system. The prototypes developed by the teams must then be integrated into the overall system. Thus, prototyping methods may be integrated into projects whose overall development process follows the SDLC or IE methodology.

Organizations may use one or more of these methodologies or an adaption from each of them in developing their database-oriented information systems. In the

Integrated CASE (I-CASE) products
Products that provide an integrated set of tools supporting all stages of the planning and development of information systems from data and IS planning through automated generation of programs to implement applications.

Prototyping development cycle (RAP)
An information systems development methodology that incorporates rapid, iterative processes of gathering requirements and designing and implementing a prototype.

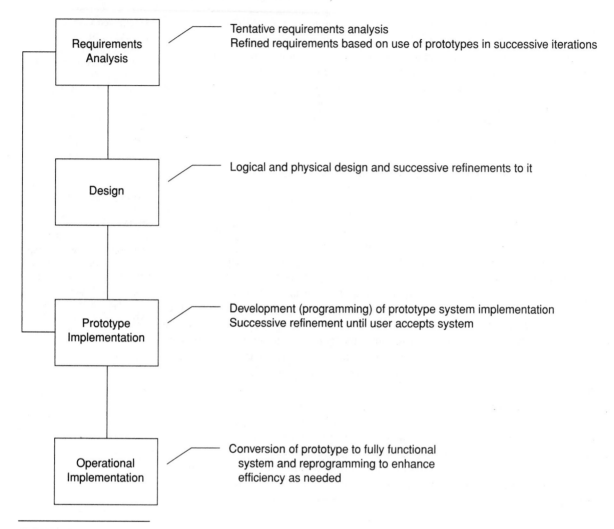

FIGURE 4.3
The Prototyping
Development Cycle

remainder of this chapter, we focus on the important data-oriented elements of the information system development process.

First, we will discuss data planning methodologies. Although planning is treated as an explicit stage only in the Information Engineering development methodology, a separate planning process, which serves to establish the scope and initial priorities for systems to be developed, is often used in conjunction with SDLC and RAP development methodologies.

Next, we will describe the data- and database-oriented elements of the Analysis, Design, and Implementation phases. These phases are common to each of the development methodologies described earlier. Our description of these development phases takes the data-centered approach most closely associated with the IE methodology, but is consistent with any of the three development methods.

We will also provide examples of the use of CASE tools in the information system development process. In particular, we will focus on the role of CASE tools in data planning and database development.

DATA PLANNING

INFORMATION AS A RESOURCE

Information can be viewed as an organizational resource. This view, called **information resource management,** holds that information can provide a strategic advantage to the organization (Guimares, 1985). Strategic advantage is achieved when someone in the organization finds an innovative way to use information to enhance products or services or to reduce costs. For example, information about customers and the products they have purchased from an appliance company is helpful in targeting specific customers: Information about a sale on servicing dishwashers can be mailed only to those customers who purchased a dishwasher from the company. To support this type of use, sufficient information must be recorded in the database by the order entry process, and the resulting data must be maintained in accessible form. Of course, the marketing staff must be aware that this data exists.

Another highly visible example of the strategic use of information systems is the just-in-time inventory system. This type of system requires real-time linking of production planning, inventory control, and procurement information. Its goal is to reduce the level of inventories needed to support production. The strategic use of information as a resource is much broader than these examples of organizational systems. Information is used as a strategic resource whenever a manager is able to access a set of data and is able to use it in an innovative way to improve his or her decision making.

To achieve this strategic advantage, information systems must be attuned to the strategic plans of the organization. The information in databases must be designed to support current and future needs of the organization's management. Ready access to data resources also is necessary to achieve maximum benefit from the information resource. This means that access rights to data should be spread as broadly as possible while maintaining adequate protection of sensitive data. It also means that access to data resources should be made as simple as possible and that users should be trained in methods needed to access, understand, and utilize data resources.

Information resource management
A concept that views information as a resource that can be used to strategic advantage. To achieve this, the information resource must be effectively planned and readily accessible to users throughout the organization.

THE DATA PLANNING PROCESS

At first blush, it may be tempting to think in terms of placing all an organization's data into a single, immense database. However, for most organizations, it would require many years to design and implement such a system. Also, such a system would be so complex that it would be impossible to maintain it while responding to changing needs in a timely manner. In addition, the cost associated with potential failures of such a system would be enormous. At some point these negative effects of increasing the size of databases outweigh the benefits.

The data required by an organization can normally be organized into clusters of entities that are highly interrelated and that have relatively few relationships with

Data planning
A process used to identify information needed to support strategic plans of the organization. Data planning identifies basic entities that need to be represented in databases and helps to define the scope of business area or subject area databases to be developed.

Subject area database
A database containing data that is needed to support a set of related processes within an organization. The set of data within a subject area database should be highly interrelated but as independent as possible of data in other subject area databases.

entities in different clusters. All the data in a given cluster should be stored in the same database. However, data from different clusters would normally be stored in different databases.

Data planning should provide the information required to determine the appropriate scope for individual databases. In data planning terminology, the individual databases are commonly referred to as **subject area databases.** The data planning process helps to clarify where the boundary lines between subject area databases should be drawn and to identify the types of interfaces that will be needed to link data across different databases.

The data planning process also ties database development to strategic planning processes within an organization and helps to ensure that the databases developed support future as well as current needs of the organization. The long time horizon and broad (organization-wide) focus make the data planning process the ideal mechanism for ensuring that the strategic data needs of the organization are supported by the databases that are developed.

Figure 4.4 provides a broad outline of the data planning process and illustrates how it fits into individual database development projects. As the figure indicates, data planning ties into and begins with organizational strategic planning. For effective use in data planning, the organization's strategic planning process should include the development of an enterprise model. An *enterprise model* describes the organization by beginning with broad business functions and then breaking down these functions into more detailed processes and activities that must be accomplished for the organization to meet its current and future goals. This process is similar to the idea of viewing the organization as a system and breaking down that system into more and more detailed subsystems. The enterprise model should allow us to gain a good understanding of the organization's systems and subsystems, the processes they perform, and the entities that are involved in, and important to, those processes. The enterprise model should also allow us to evaluate the degree to which entities are interrelated. In other words, the enterprise model is designed to provide a description of the physical processes of importance to the firm and the physical entities that are involved in those processes.

Based on the enterprise model, we identify the key entities associated with each process about which management will need information. If the planning process producing the enterprise model has been thorough enough, we should be able not only to identify the set of entities that need to be modeled in databases, but also to identify those processes and those managers or departments that use each of these entities. This information allows us to see which entities are highly interrelated, and which entities are relatively independent.

If the pattern of relationships between entities and processes shows that a group of entities are involved in many of the same processes, those entities should be a part of the same database. Groups of entities that are identified as relatively independent of each other should be placed in different databases. The relationship between entities and processes is examined to identify clusters of related entities. This clustering of entities along with other organizational considerations is used to define subject area databases.

Once a set of subject area databases has been defined, priorities for the development of these databases must be established. Such factors as the adequacy of

Data Planning   **Database Development**

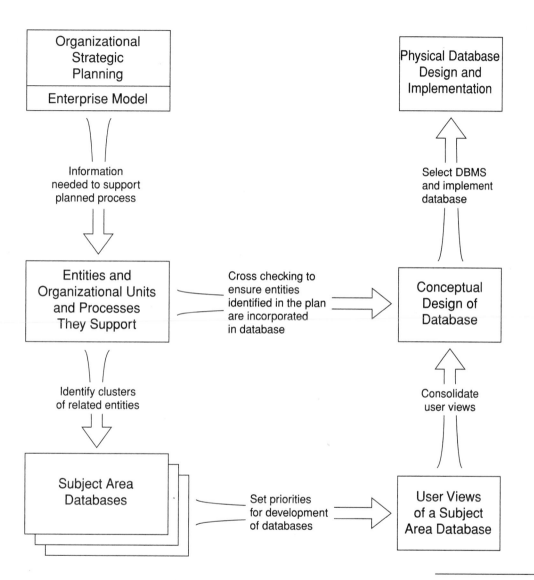

FIGURE 4.4
Data Planning and
Its Relationship
to Database
Development

existing systems, the perceived importance of each system, and the availability of
resources to develop each potential decision will be considered.

Figure 4.4 indicates that the data planning process affects the design and development of individual databases in several important ways. The priorities assigned to
various database projects determine which databases will be developed first. The
scope of each database, as defined by the set of entities it is to include, has also
been determined, at least in preliminary form, by the data planning process. This

information can be used to help identify the set of users to be contacted and to establish the boundaries of what is, and is not, to be included in the database. Finally, and perhaps most important, the entities belonging to the database that were identified during the data planning process can be used as a cross-check to ensure that the conceptual design is a complete one.

Developing the data model for a subject area database, as summarized on the right side of Figure 4.4, is essentially a bottom-up approach in which each user's requirements are gathered and incorporated into an overall conceptual model. A frequent criticism of the approach is that it focuses on current requirements and ignores future needs. The sets of entities identified in the data planning process should be future oriented since they are tied to the organization's strategic plans. Thus, the link to data planning should help to assure that the databases developed provide the data needed to support future strategic thrusts as well as existing needs.

CASE TOOLS FOR DATA PLANNING

Support for data planning is available in several CASE software packages. The PRISM software package by Index Technology is designed specifically to support data planning. A number of computer-supported planning products incorporate data planning elements along with other features designed to support other aspects of strategic planning. In addition, some CASE products are designed to provide integrated support for planning and development of information systems. Composer by Texas Instruments (1995) and ADW by Knowledgeware are two prominent examples of this type of product.

CASE tools for the data planning process normally include components supporting varied enterprise modeling approaches. The tools provide the ability to identify and record multiple hierarchical and nonhierachical lists of objects. The company's organization chart would be recorded as a hierarchy. A hierarchy could be used to identify and record the business functions, processes, and activities discussed earlier. Managers would also be asked to identify the entities they deal with and need information about.

Figure 4.5 shows an example of a hierarchy of functions and processes produced by Composer. From interviews with managers, we have identified four high-level functions: marketing, assembly and servicing, warehousing, and human resources. Each of these functions is made up of a number of lower level functions.

The figure, however, does not provide a fully detailed set of functions and processes because it lacks one or more levels of processes for each of the lowest level functions. For example, the procurement function might include the processes of vendor selection, generation of a purchase order, and check-in of received goods. Some of these processes might, in turn, have subprocesses, and so on. Processes or activities can be broken down to an elementary level process or activity, carried out by a specific individual at a specific place and time and having only one outcome.

In Figure 4.6, a list of entities have been identified for Apex Products. At this point, neither relationships among the entities nor the attributes of the entities have been defined. The managers have been asked to specify the things that they work with and need information about. The entity list shown does not represent a fully detailed list of the entities that will ultimately appear in databases. It is simply a list of key

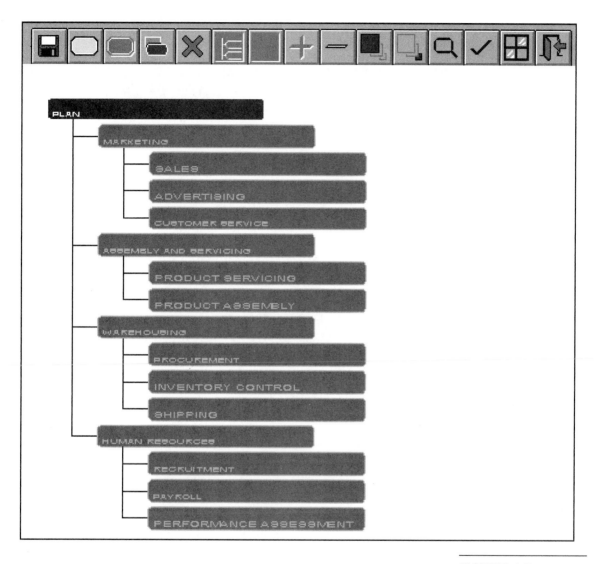

FIGURE 4.5
A Hierarchy of
Functions and
Processes Identified
for Apex Products

or base entities that must be represented. For example, the employee entity may ultimately be broken into subclasses of production workers, salespersons, and so forth. In addition, a dependent entity may be created to store information about the dependents of employees. At this stage, however, this set of information is represented by the base entity Employee.

Once an appropriate set of hierarchies and lists has been developed, relationships between these lists can be explored using matrices. A matrix allows examination of relationships among two lists. One list is placed on the vertical axis and the other on the horizontal. A grid of cells is produced that represents relationships between items in the two lists.

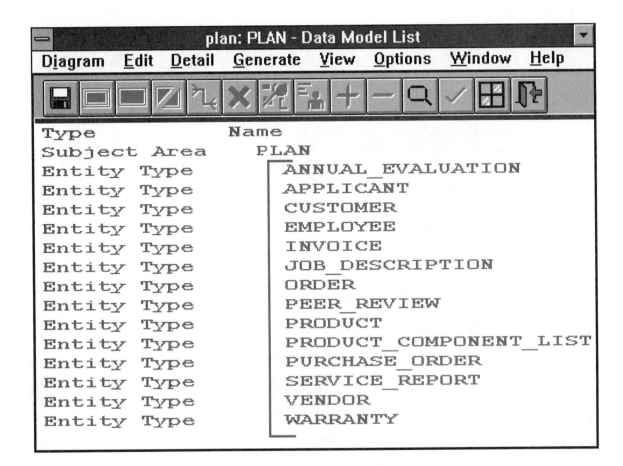

FIGURE 4.6
A List of Entries
Identified for Apex
Products

Figure 4.7 shows a matrix relating the list of functions and the list of entities identified for Apex Products. Only the lowest level functions are displayed on the matrix. In each cell of the matrix, the user identifies the relationship that exists between the row and column items for that cell. In our example, the types of relationships that can exist are entities that can be created, updated, deleted, or read by various functions. Thus, the C in the cell relating the entity job description and the function performance assessment means that the entity Job Description is created by the Performance Assessment function. The matrix is filled out based on information that has been gathered from managers. Once a matrix has been completed, *clustering* is performed. Most CASE products include a function that will automatically perform clustering. Clustering reorders rows and columns of a matrix by identifing sets (clusters) of closely related items from the two lists. This has been done for the data shown in Figure 4.7.

The clusters of relationships that appear in matrices are a very important aid in identifying appropriate boundaries for subject area databases. In our example,

```
Model :APEX
Subset:ALL

Cell Values:

  = Not referenced

C = Create

D = Delete

U = Update

R = Read only
```

Function \ Entity Type	PRODUCT	ORDER	CUSTOMER	EMPLOYEE	APPLICANT	JOB DESCRIPTION	PEER REVIEW	ANNUAL EVALUATION	PURCHASE ORDER	VENDOR	SERVICE REPORT	WARRANTY	PRODUCT COMPONENT LIST	INVOICE
PERFORMANCE ASSESSMENT				U		C	C	C						
RECRUITMENT				C	C	R								
PAYROLL				U										
SALES	U	C	C	U										
SHIPPING	U	U												C
INVENTORY CONTROL	C	R	R						R	R				
PROCUREMENT	U								C	C				
PRODUCT ASSEMBLY	U												C	
PRODUCT SERVICING		R	R								C	U	U	
CUSTOMER SERVICE	R	R	R								R	C		R
ADVERTISING		R	R											

FIGURE 4.7
Affinity Matrix Entities vs. Functions for Apex Products

Product, Order, and Customer appear to be widely used by all functions except those in the Human Resources area. Employee, Applicant, Job Description, Peer Review, and Annual Evaluation form another cluster that is used primarily by Human Resources functions. The Service Report, Warranty, and Product Component List form a third cluster used by the Product Assembly, Product Servicing, and Customer Service functions. Purchase Order and Vendor form a very small fourth cluster, while Invoice seems not to fit into any cluster. This type of pattern is typical. Some entities fit very cleanly into a cluster, while others either do not fit a cluster or participate in more than one cluster (for example, the Employee entity).

This same technique can be applied to any combination of the lists that have been developed. For example, the relationship between entities and organizational units in the hierarchy chart could be examined, or the relationship between functions and organizational units could be examined.

Matrix analysis can also be used to examine relationships between different items in the same list. Figure 4.8 shows this type of matrix for the Apex Products functions list. The list of functions is shown on each axis. A ranking ranging from one to nine can be assigned to cells with nine representing the highest degree of association and one the lowest. Cells are left blank if there is no association. The judgment of the planner based on the interviews with management is normally used to determine appropriate cell entries. The matrix function in the Composer tool set is also able to automatically generate a set of numbers for this type of matrix from the relationships specified in other matrices. The values shown in Figure 4.8 are the relationships among functions that the Composer matrix tool inferred from the degree to which various functions interact with a common set of entities.

Planning-related CASE tools have the ability to develop a wide variety of hierarchies, lists, and diagrams that support alternative planning methods. Users can select a set that they feel will identify the key features of the organization that need to be represented in its data models. For instance, we might have developed lists recording goals, objectives, and standards measuring the achievement of objectives. We could then examine the information needed to measure performance against those objectives and use that to help determine the list of appropriate entities.

The tools we have described provide support for decisions about boundaries, establish priorities for the development of subject area databases, and furnish preliminary lists of entities and other characteristics that can be used in the development of individual subject area systems. Decisions about content and priorities for the development of subject area databases are based upon the evaluation of numerous lists and matrices plus a substantial amount of judgment on the part of the decision maker. Pertinent information from the data planning process is to be passed forward to the development teams for each subject area database system. This information may be passed forward in the form of paper documents, which can be cross-checked during the database development process. However, a number of CASE products now support both data planning and database development processes. When these products are used, specifications from the data planning process become the initial high-level specifications for the database development process.

Business process reengineering
A methodology or approach to data planning and IS development that requires the reorganization and streamlining of business processes as a part of the implementation of the information system.

BUSINESS PROCESS REENGINEERING

Besides identifying subject area boundaries for databases, the tools we have described can be used to evaluate the manner in which business functions and processes are organized. If irrational patterns of associations are uncovered, business functions and processes may be reorganized. The term **business process reengineering** is often used to describe information systems development processes that are intended to cause reorganization of business processes.

Model :APEX Subset:ALL	PERFORMANCE ASSESSMENT	RECRUITMENT	PAYROLL	SALES	SHIPPING	INVENTORY CONTROL	PROCUREMENT	PRODUCT ASSEMBLY	PRODUCT SERVICING	CUSTOMER SERVICE	ADVERTISING
PERFORMANCE ASSESSMENT	9	2	2	2							
RECRUITMENT	2	9	4	4							
PAYROLL	2	4	9								
SALES	2	4		9	5	4	3	3	1	2	1
SHIPPING				5	9	5	4	4	1	3	1
INVENTORY CONTROL				4	5	9	9	8	6	8	6
PROCUREMENT				3	4	9	9	3			
PRODUCT ASSEMBLY				3	4	8	3	9	8	2	
PRODUCT SERVICING				1	1	6		8	9	8	3
CUSTOMER SERVICE				2	3	8		2	8	9	6
ADVERTISING				1	1	6			3	6	9

Cell Values:

1	2	3
4	5	6
7	8	9

FIGURE 4.8
Affinity Matrix for Apex Products Functions

Our simple example shows some areas where reorganization might be appropriate. By comparing Figures 4.5 and 4.8, we can see that the three subfunctions of the Marketing function in the first figure appear rather fragmented in the second. Sales is most closely associated with the Shipping and Inventory Control subfunctions of Warehousing, while Customer Service is most closely related to Product Servicing. Advertising does not have a strong relationship with any other subfunction. In this case, the observed pattern is primarily a result of the very incomplete nature of our example. However, if the information in Figure 4.8 was considered to be complete and accurate, a reorganization of the set of functions might be appropriate.

The same type of analysis could be performed on hierarchy chart data to examine relationships between the various divisions and departments of an organization and possibly suggest reorganization of the departmental structure or reassignment of the activities of departments. This potential to serve as a catalyst for the reorganization of the way in which processes are organized is a powerful aspect of the data planning process. Benefits from improving the efficiency of business processes may be greater than the direct benefits of the information systems themselves. In fact, the investment of time, effort, and money required to complete a thorough data planning exercise is normally justified only if the organization expects it to lead to the streamlining of processes and is prepared to make the necessary changes. However, changes of the type required by business process reengineering can be very threatening to system users and can make it very difficult to obtain the level of support and involvement needed to effectively conduct data planning.

DATA PLANNING AND DATA WAREHOUSING

Most IS theorists and practitioners would agree that data planning can add important value to database systems. However, many organizations have not implemented a formal data planning process. Many firms are too busy "draining the information systems swamp" to devote major resources to long-term planning. These firms often face a substantial waiting list of operational and information database projects that are very important, high priority projects. The diversion of resources to long-term planning under such circumstances is difficult to accomplish. Other firms may be unwilling to devote the substantial amount of management resources required to successfully accomplish data planning.

Data warehouse
A database or set of databases distinct from operational databases that contains historical, summarized data from broad sectors of the organization needed to support decision making.

Data warehousing gives firms the opportunity to gain many of the information-as-a-resource benefits of the data planning process without delaying implementation of key operational databases. Under the data warehousing concept, data to support management decision making are placed in one or more databases that are separate from the operational databases of the organization.

Operational databases retain only the relatively current data required to support ongoing operations. The scope of these operational databases can also be relatively limited because operational processes tend to focus on rather narrow subject areas.

The data warehouse database(s) contain data extracted from the operational databases. Because the data warehouse is designed to support management, it will contain historical data to support analysis of trends, data may be in summary rather than fully detailed form, and the scope or subject area covered by a single data warehouse database will be broader than that of a single operational database. Also, the data warehousing database will be used only for retrieval—its data will not be created, updated, or deleted by users.

Where data warehousing databases are maintained, they will be developed using processes significantly different from those described in this chapter. Data warehousing databases are discussed in greater detail in Chapter 12. However, it is important to note at this point that data warehousing may significantly affect an organization's approach to data planning. Where data warehousing is to be used, data planning activities may be tied primarily to the data warehouse database(s). Operational databases could be developed as needed to support operational priorities, while the data warehouse database(s) would be developed starting from a data planning process like the one we have described here.

DATABASE DEVELOPMENT

DATABASE DEVELOPMENT AND SYSTEMS DEVELOPMENT

Database development commonly occurs as a part of a systems development project that includes the design of a fundamental set of applications (processes) using the database as well as the design of the database itself. The design of such systems can take either a process-centered or a data-centered approach. The processes used by organizations tend to change quite rapidly over time. Thus, systems designed using a process orientation require frequent modifications and quickly become obsolete. In contrast, the sets of entities organizations deal with and the key characteristics of those entities are relatively stable. With occasional updates to the sets of attributes that are recorded, data representing such entities as employees, customers, products, parts, and departments are likely to be used as long as an organization exists. In addition, databases storing data about these entities may be used by many different applications representing a variety of organizational processes. Data about these entities are often used by processes that weren't even conceived of when the databases containing them were developed.

> **Database development**
> The analysis, design, and implementation of a database system.

Based on these observations, systems development projects that involve the development of databases should utilize a data-centered methodology. This means fully developing the data model early in the development process and making the data model the central integrating element of the system. In the section that follows, we describe a partial development methodology employing this data-centered approach. Our model focuses on data- and database-oriented activities and covers the Analysis, Design, and Implementation phases of system development that are common to all three of the popular development methodologies.

A MODEL OF DATABASE DEVELOPMENT IN A SYSTEMS DEVELOPMENT CONTEXT

Figure 4.9 presents our systems development model, which corresponds rather closely to the traditional SDLC at the Analysis stage. At the stages of Design and Implementation, however, this model calls for both conceptual design and physical design and implementation of the database to occur before attention is turned to the application systems or processes utilizing the database.

Systems Analysis

Systems analysis identifies the requirements that a system must meet to satisfy the needs of end-users. The goal of this stage in the traditional systems development life cycle is to define the input, processing, storage, output, and control requirements of the proposed system. What input data is or can be provided by each end-user? What output reports and documents does each end-user require or desire? What data need to be stored to meet these input and output requirements? What processing will be required to record and store input data and to produce the required outputs? What controls are necessary to enforce business rules and to ensure the integrity and security of the system? All these questions are addressed by requirements analysis.

FIGURE 4.9
A Database-Oriented
Systems Development
Model

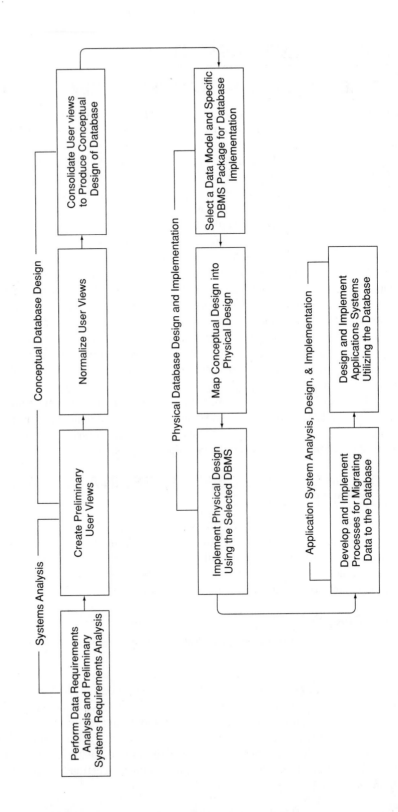

Figure 4.9 suggests a change in the focus of requirements analysis for database-oriented systems development projects. Here, requirements analysis emphasizes the need to determine of the data requirements of a system. Other system requirements may be determined only on a preliminary basis. Analysis of these system requirements may be revisited as application systems are designed and implemented after database design and implementation have been completed. However, requirements for other systems components should be specified in sufficient detail to allow determination of the database access requirements of high-volume use.

Methods used to secure systems requirements include examination of existing systems and interviews, surveys, and observations of end-users. For database-oriented systems, a data requirements thrust is needed. An existing system would be examined first to determine what entities are represented in it, how those entities are related, and what attributes of those entities are recorded by the system. Similarly, as end-users are interviewed or surveyed, the focus is on determining entities, attributes, and relationships. Users are initially asked to describe their information needs in a form with which they are comfortable. Typically, a user might describe the type of output reports or graphic displays she or he would like to have available and the type of forms she or he would like to work with in supplying input data to the system. The interviewer would then develop layout forms or mock-ups of the input and output documents described by the user. These forms provide preliminary documentation of requirements for the applications that will produce them, but they also provide a framework for describing the data requirements of the system. What are the things, or entities, that you work with? What characteristics of these things do you need information about? What are the relationships among the entities with which you work? What restrictions are there on the values that attributes can take on? What data are sensitive and what controls on access and data modification are needed? These are the sorts of questions that need to be asked in determining a user's data requirements.

The layout form in Figure 4.10 might be produced in an interview with a user who is responsible for making student advisement assignments at a college. Based on this layout form, the interviewer would identify the entities that are represented—in this case, a Student entity and a Professor entity. The user would then be asked for other characteristics of the identified entities that she or he would like to have available and would also be asked about the nature of the relationships among the identified entities.

In our example, the interview might proceed as follows:

Interviewer: Is there any additional information about students that you would like to have available to you to support activities you are currently performing or to support things you would like to do in the future?

User: Well, I'd like to start mailing a notice of the advisor assignment to each student each semester, but to do this I'd need the student's local address. Also, professors often request grade point average information about their advisees. It would be nice to be able to provide this, but it is sensitive information. Professors should have access only to the GPAs of students they advise.

Interviewer: I expect that each professor typically advises several students, but I'm wondering, can a student be assigned to more than one advisor?

User: Yes, professors usually have several advisees, about 12 to 15 on average. We do have students with dual majors, but those students must select one major as their primary one for advisement purposes. They are assigned only one formal advisor, although they are encouraged to see someone in their second major on an informal basis.

As you can see, these questions have identified some additional attributes to be added to the Student entity—Local Address and GPA. The relationship between the entities has also been clarified. One professor can have many student advisees, but each student is assigned to only one professor for advisement. There is also an indication that access to one of the attributes, GPA, should be restricted.

Questions now become more detailed. For example, the following questions might be asked about the Professor Code attribute:

Interviewer: Who assigns the professor code?

User: I assign a professor code to each professor as soon as he or she is hired.

Interviewer: Are there other users who should be allowed to assign or modify Professor Codes?

User: No, I can easily handle those assignments myself. It is my responsibility and for control purposes I don't want anyone else to be able to make changes.

Interviewer: Are there any restrictions on who should be allowed to see a Professor Code?

User: No, this is public information.

Interviewer: Is there some rule that is used in assigning Professor Code values?

User: Yes, all the codes are five characters long. The first digit of the code is always the first letter of the professor's last name.

FIGURE 4.10
A Sample Layout Form

Commonwealth College

Advisor Assignments 19 __–__ Academic Year

Student Id#	Student Name	Cred. Hrs. Earned	Student Major	Professor Code	Professor Name	Office Number	Department
362754189	Evans, Ann	57	Biology	B86	Brown, Bill	PS322	Biology
491378526	Jones, John	24	Undeclared	L22	Lutz, Jane	SS218	Sociology
683152497	Powell, Amy	103	Mathematics	R34	Rice, Arthur	MS234	Mathematics
•		•		•			
•		•		•			
•		•		•			

The answers to these questions help determine the domains of attributes and describe organizational rules that need to be enforced on the data. Rules with respect to who should be able to access data and who should be allowed to create, modify, or delete it are an important element of the data requirements of a database. These rules help to ensure the integrity and privacy of data.

In Figure 4.9, the step of generating user views was shown as being on the boundary between Systems Analysis and Conceptual Database Design. This occurs because the development of representations of user views is the first step of conceptual database design, but such representations are usually initiated while data requirements are being developed and refined. As the entity and relationship structure of the data to support a user becomes known, tentative E-R diagrams, as discussed in Chapter 2, are developed. Further, as domain restrictions on attributes and organizational rules affecting data use become known, this information starts to be recorded in an organized form that can be maintained throughout the design process. Methods for storing this type of information were discussed in Chapter 3.

When CASE tools are used to support database design, this information is immediately recorded in computerized form . The visual modeling provided by E-R or data structure diagrams is tied to the more detailed information about attribute domains and other restrictive business rules. Part a of Figure 4.11 provides an example of an E-R diagram, while part b shows attribute specifications for an entity and detailed domain specifications for an attribute generated by the IEF CASE product. These types of diagrams and lists provide data dictionary information for use during database and application design.

Conceptual Database Design

Development of models (such as E-R diagrams, data structure diagrams, and domain descriptions) to represent the structure of the data needed to meet a user's requirements carries us into the conceptual database design process. When a user's data requirements have been fully specified and modeled, a preliminary user view results. This process of gathering data requirements and modeling user views from them is repeated for each user.

Before the user views are consolidated, each user view is examined to determine whether its data structures will promote efficient and error-free database operation. The normalization process, described in Chapter 3, is often applied at this point to evaluate the entity and relationship structures that have been specified. You will recall that normalization seeks to identify and correct entity and relationship structures that are inappropriate and may cause unnecessary data duplication and/or increase the risk of data inconsistencies. If structures are found that violate normalization rules, these structures are corrected and revised user views are generated.

Although normalization generally improves the accuracy and efficiency of a database, it may make it more difficult for the user to understand and use the database. When this is the case, a normalized version of the user's view is still developed and used in the overall conceptual design of the database. However, the version of the user view with which the user is comfortable will also be maintained, and procedures will be implemented, if possible, that allow the user to

FIGURE 4.11
(a) E-R Diagram
(b) Specifications
Generated by the IEF
CASE Products

(a)

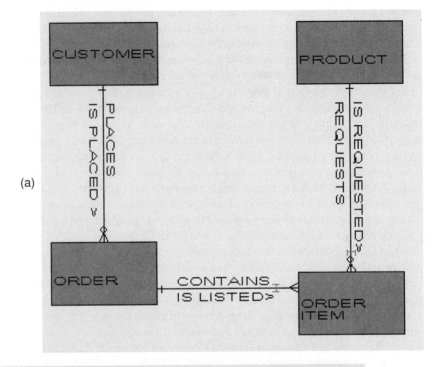

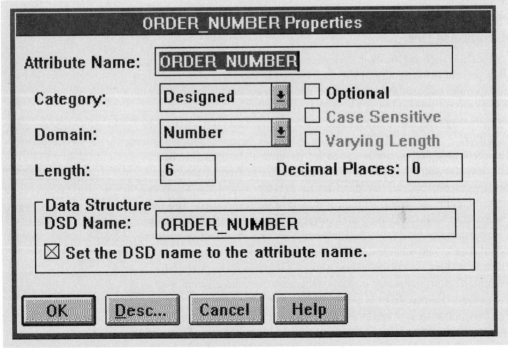

(b)

access the data based on that version. The data structures that users or specific applications see are called external models, or external schemas. Any individual external model of a database will normally contain only a subset of the full database, and may contain structures that have been modified to meet the needs of a particular user or application.

As Figure 4.9 indicates, once user views have been generated and normalized, they must be consolidated to produce the conceptual design for the database as a whole. This design is also called the conceptual model, or conceptual schema of the database. Every data structure that appears in any user view must be incorporated into the conceptual model of the database. As user views are consolidated, some entities will be encountered that appear in only one user view. Those entities are simply included in the conceptual design for the database as a whole. More frequently, however, we will find that a given entity appears in more than one user view. Some attributes of the entity may appear in only one of the user views, while others may appear in several different user views. During consolidation, every attribute that appears in at least one user view must be included in the conceptual database design. A variety of complications may be discovered during this consolidation process. We may find that different users have different names for the same attribute, that different users use the same name for different attributes, or even that different users differ in their understanding of the business rules to be applied to certain data elements. These conflicts must be resolved during the consolidation of user views. An extended example of the process of gathering and consolidating user views is provided in Chapter 5.

Physical Database Design and Implementation

The first step in physical database design is to select a data model and specific DBMS package for implementation, if this has not already been done. Three data models (the hierarchical, network, and relational models) are widely available for systems being implemented today. Several competing DBMS packages are available utilizing each of these data models. There are distinct advantages and disadvantages for each of the data models. The relative effectiveness of the alternative models depends upon the nature of the database being developed and, most important, upon how the database is expected to be used. As we noted in Chapter 2, the relational model is by far the most prevalent in systems developed today.

Theoretically, the data model and specific DBMS package to be used for a database development project should be selected only after conceptual design has been completed. The conceptual design provides vital information about how the database will be used, which can help the development team make an informed choice about the types of data model to be used. When multiple DBMS packages using the same data model are available, the package selection decision should be based on the strengths and weaknesses of the available packages in the context of the uses required to support the database that is being developed. However, numerous situations may arise in which there is no effective choice. The organization may have made a commitment that all new database systems developed will use the relational model. The organization may have only one DBMS package available and may feel that it is unable to support a new package. Even if multiple DBMS packages are supported, the scope and data volume of an application may dictate the DBMS package to be used.

Once the data model and DBMS package have been selected, the conceptual design is mapped into a physical design that can be implemented by the selected data model. Then the data definition language (DDL) of the selected DBMS package is used to implement the design. The physical design is also called the internal data model, or internal schema of the database. This internal schema is data model and DBMS product specific. Tuning of the physical storage structures to optimize performance based on expected usage patterns occurs as a part of the mapping to physical design.

As we saw in Chapter 1, the alternative data models differ substantially in the physical storage structures they provide. Therefore, the process of mapping to a physical design and implementing that physical design varies substantially across data models. This process will be described for the relational model in Chapter 7. Physical design concepts relating to the hierarchical and network models will be described in Chapters 14 and 15, respectively.

Implementation of appropriate access controls on system users is another element of the physical design. The controls should assure that users have access to all needed data while, at the same time, assuring the privacy of sensitive data and the validity of all data. Access control measures are described in Chapter 10.

Application System Analysis, Design, and Implementation

Once physical database design and implementation have been completed, we have built a structure that will hold the data. However, we have not yet developed processes to populate that structure with data or to use data that might be stored in that structure. Often a database will incorporate existing historic data that must be migrated into the database before the database can process new transactions. In such cases, procedures for migrating the historic data must be developed for one-time execution prior to the database going on-line for the processing of transactions. In other instances, most notably data warehouse databases, some or all of the data in a database may be extracted from other databases. When this type of data is to be used, procedures for summarization and extraction must be written and then executed on a scheduled basis to provide the data for the summary databases.

With the exception of procedures for the migration of stored data to a database, processes that manipulate data stored in a database or produce reports based on database data are similar to applications that work with file-oriented data. The types of analysis, design, and implementation tools and procedures commonly described in systems analysis texts are applied to develop such applications systems, and these tools and procedures will not be described in detail here.

As we noted earlier, preliminary specifications of the requirements of major applications using a database will have been gathered at the time that the data requirements analysis was performed. However, in most cases, it will be necessary to revisit the requirements analysis stage in order to gather more detailed specifications of the requirements associated with specific applications. Once the requirements have been fully specified, these systems will be designed and implemented. The actual coding of applications does take advantage of DBMS software. For applications that are developed using traditional programming languages, host language interface software is available in most DBMSs. This allows the data handling portions of a program to be written in the form of embedded DBMS language statements that can be executed and converted to a form that is understood and utilized by a programming language. Statements to process the data are written in the host programming language. Other applications may be implemented in fourth generation languages (4GLs). Many DBMSs have rather extensive 4GL features built into them that provide for the development of such common types of applications as forms, reports, and menus. Application development using 4GL features of DBMSs is discussed in Chapter 8, and application coding using database language statements embedded in a host language is discussed in Chapter 9.

THE THREE SCHEMA ARCHITECTURE

Database architecture can be thought of as having three levels, or schemas. This architecture, commonly referred to as the ANSI/SPARC **three schema architecture,** is illustrated in Figure 4.12. Each individual user has an external model (or user view) of the database. This **external model** is like a window that allows the user to see a portion of the conceptual design of the database as a whole. Only the portion needed by a user is revealed and it may include transformations of some of the structures in the **conceptual model** that have been made to better meet the user's needs. An application can be thought of as a user with an external model as well. The application's external model includes only the portion of the database that that particular application needs to access.

Beneath these external models lies the conceptual model, or conceptual schema of the database as a whole. This conceptual model contains all the logical data structures supported by the database. However, it describes these structures in generic form that is independent of the mechanisms used for physical storage of data.

Beneath the conceptual model lies the **internal model.** The internal model is DBMS and sometimes hardware specific. It maps the logical structures described in the conceptual model into actual physical storage of database data in structures supported by the specific DBMS package that is being used.

The three schema architecture insulates users and applications, as far as possible, from changes in the database. Users and applications interface only with external models. The external models are commonly referred to as subschemas in network and hierarchical systems and views of the database in relational systems. These external models, in turn, interface only with the conceptual model, and the conceptual model interfaces with the internal model to actually store and retrieve data.

Suppose we need to physically move the database to new hardware or to retune portions of the physical storage structures to reflect changing access patterns. This should not affect any users or applications. We simply need to modify the internal model that is used to map the existing conceptual model into physical storage structures. Since the conceptual model does not change, and all users and applications access the internal model through the conceptual model, none of the user views or applications need to be modified.

Three schema architecture
An architecture for databases developed by ANSI/SPARC that identifies three levels of models: the external model, the conceptual model, and the internal model. It is designed to insulate users and applications from changes in the internal and conceptual models.

External model
The model of a database from the perspective of an individual user or group of users; a user view.

Conceptual model
The model of a database that fully describes the logical structure of the entire database in a manner that is independant of the methods used for implementation.

Internal model
The model that describes how data are physically stored in a database system.

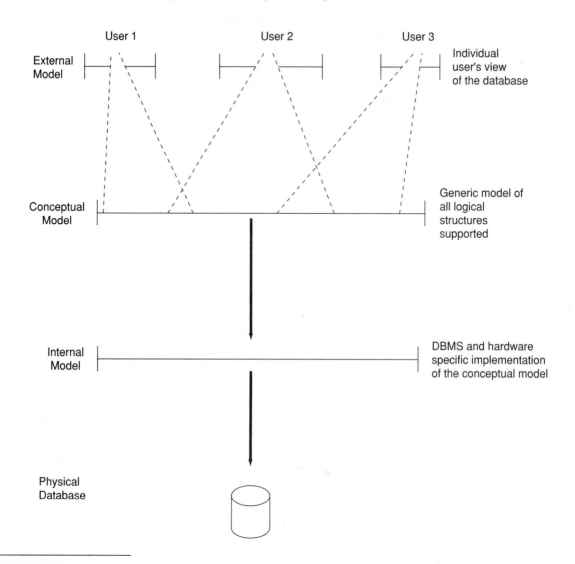

FIGURE 4.12
Three Levels of
Models or Schemas

Now suppose we need to make a modification to the conceptual model. A new entity, which is related to two existing entities, is to be added to the database, or new attributes will be added to an existing entity, or the domain or structure of existing attributes needs to be changed. Any of these changes would require modification to the conceptual model. To map the modified conceptual model to physical storage, the internal model would also need to be modified, but how about the external models? Only those external models that see (use) the affected portion of the conceptual model need to be modified. If a user or an application does not utilize the affected portion of the conceptual model, then that user or application is unaffected by the changes in the conceptual model.

Real-world DBMS packages fall short of fully providing these three independent schema levels. However, modern DBMS packages do provide most of the practical data independence features of the three schema architecture that we have described.

CASE TOOLS AND THE DEVELOPMENT PROCESS

The availability of CASE tools has had a substantial effect on the process of information systems development. Modern CASE tools can provide rapid, user-friendly methods to record system specifications. When an integrated set of CASE tools is provided, they play a vital role in coordinating the systems development process. The availability of integrated CASE tools has caused substantial changes to the process of developing information systems.

CASE AND I-CASE

The term *I-CASE* (Integrated Computer Assisted Software Engineering) is used to describe software products that provide an integrated set of CASE tools designed to support all stages of development from planning to implementation. The set of tools provided should allow specifications for the planning stage to be rolled forward into analysis. In the analysis stage, detail is added and additional types of tools are introduced. Those specifications are in turn rolled forward into the design stage where more detail and more tools are added. In addition, the sets of tools throughout the process are connected to each other in a way that assures that they form a consistent whole. When a fully detailed design has been completed, the I-CASE tool set should be able to automatically generate the set of DBMS and programming language statements required to implement a system.

Integrated support for the entire planning and development process is provided by only a few I-CASE tools. However, a number of other CASE products provide an integrated set of tools for analysis and design and support some elements of implementation—most frequently the generation of a set of Data Definition Language commands to create a database based on conceptual data model specifications.

To achieve integration, elements of the CASE tool set are created as objects that can be related to a virtually unlimited number of other objects to form a complex of **hyper-diagrams.** Each entity, for instance, can be linked to other entities to form an E-R diagram, but it also may be linked to the process or processes that utilize it and perhaps to the organizational units that create and maintain it. What is created is an interrelated set of diagrams and lists that document the relationships among the various components of the design. The linkage among components can also be used to provide automatic checking of the consistency and completeness of design components. For example, the system could check to see that, for any entity that is referenced in a process, a corresponding entity exists in the data model. Capabilities to interlink elements of the tool set vary substantially across different CASE tools.

Hyper-diagrams
Sets of interconnected diagrams produced by a CASE or I-CASE tool. Hyper-diagrams allow a virtually unlimited number of objects to be interconnected, thus supporting the complex interrelationships among design components.

THE CASE TOOL SET AS A SYSTEMS REPOSITORY

Systems repository
A collection containing all forms of information required to develop information systems, including: planning information, business rules, and data and processing requirements.

An integrated set of CASE tools can serve as a **systems repository,** or systems encyclopedia. A systems repository contains all forms of information required to develop information systems. It records data planning information, business rules, data model specifications, and the specifications of processes and user interfaces. If a full I-CASE tool is available, there will be a single systems repository recording data planning specifications and the analysis, design, and implementation specifications for all systems developed from the plan.

The systems repository coordinates the work of project teams as they develop new systems and enforces consistency. Portions of the model stored in the repository are checked out whenever a member of the team starts to work on a design element. As soon as that team member has completed a component and checked it back into the repository, it becomes available for use by the rest of the development team. The repository thus maintains an updated version of the model for use by all team members. Access to the systems repository, or portions of it, can also be made available to system end-users.

One of the greatest benefits of the systems repository is in systems maintenance. Maintenance programmers can use the systems repository to gain an understanding of an installed system and to identify the portions of it that need to be modified. The systems repository is also to be updated each time changes are made by a maintenance operation. If this procedure is followed, systems should be maintainable for longer periods of time.

SUMMARY

Database planning and development take place in the context of broader organizational planning and systems development processes. Data planning is a broad, long-range function that is an element of organizational strategic planning and should establish the scope and timing of database projects to be implemented. Database development, on the other hand, addresses the more detailed process by which specific databases are implemented.

Information can be viewed as a resource that can produce strategic advantages for an organization. This can be achieved only if data planning is closely tied to the strategic planning process of the organization.

Data planning as practiced by organizations typically utilizes Computer-Assisted Software Engineering (CASE). In the data planning process, hierarchies and lists of objects of importance to the organization (such as functions and processes, critical success factors, and basic data entities) are developed. The relationships among these sets of objects are then explored using affinity matrices to determine the scope of various subject area database systems and establish priorities for development.

Database development commonly occurs as an element of a systems development process, which also includes the development of a set of applications using the database. Organizations' data requirements are typically more stable processing requirements. Therefore, systems development projects involving the creation of databases should focus first on data. This causes some modification to the traditional systems development life cycle. Initially, requirements analysis focuses on data requirements of the system, while other requirements are defined only in preliminary form. Users' data requirements are then converted into user views and these are normalized and consolidated to create the conceptual design of the database. The conceptual design is next converted to a physical design and implemented using an appropriate DBMS software package. After the database structure has been designed and physically created, requirements for applications using the database are further analyzed and then designed and implemented.

A three schema architecture consisting of external models, a conceptual model, and an internal model has been proposed by ANSI/SPARC and is reflected, to some extent, in modern DBMSs. External models are essentially user views of the database and each external model includes only the portion of the database needed by the particular user. The conceptual model describes the entire database in a generic form that can be used by any DBMS package. The internal model maps the conceptual model to physical storage locations using DBMS specific structures and commands. The three schema architecture maximizes program–data independence by insulating users and applications from changes to database structures that do not directly affect the data they are using.

Integrated CASE products are software tool sets designed to provide integrated support for the entire spectrum of information systems planning and development activities. Elements of an I-CASE tool set are organized into interconnected hyperdiagrams that document and enforce the connections between various components. I-CASE products can serve as a systems repository documenting all forms of information system specifications, including data, processes, and business rules. I-CASE tools can also support the Information Engineering (IE) methodology. The IE methodology encompasses both IS planning and IS development.

REVIEW QUIZ

_____ The analysis, design, and implementation of a database system.

_____ Consists of external models, conceptual models, and internal models.

_____ Uses rapid iterations of analysis, design, and implementation activities to develop a system.

_____ Sets of interconnected diagrams produced by an I-CASE product.

_____ Software product providing an integrated set of tools supporting stages of IS planning and development.

_____ Identifies scope and basic entities to be represented in various organizational databases.

_____ Includes the stages of investigation, analysis, design, implementation, and maintenance.

_____ Software product designed to support one or more phases of IS planning and/or development.

_____ Views information as a resource that can be used to strategic advantage.

_____ A collection of all forms of information needed to develop information systems.

_____ A database containing the data that are needed to support a set of related processes within an organization.

_____ Model of a database that corresponds to a user view.

_____ Methodology requiring the reorganization and streamlining of business processes as a part of implementing an IS.

_____ Model that describes how data are physically stored.

1. Data planning
2. Subject area database
3. Database development
4. Systems development life cycle
5. Information resource management
6. Business process reengineering
7. CASE tools
8. Integrated CASE products
9. Prototyping development cycle
10. Three schema architecture
11. External model
12. Internal model
13. Hyper-diagrams
14. Systems repository

REVIEW QUESTIONS AND EXERCISES

1. Describe the role of data planning. How does it relate to strategic planning? What outputs are expected from the data planning process?

2. What is meant by a subject area database? What criteria are used in determining the appropriate boundaries for subject areas?

3. Contrast the planning phase of the IE development methodology with the investigation phase of the SDLC.

4. What does the term *information resource management* mean? What are its implications with respect to the data planning process?

5. Why is data planning described as a top-down process and database development sometimes described as a bottom-up process?

6. Compare and contrast the systems development, information engineering, and
prototyping methodologies.

7. Describe and distinguish between CASE and I-CASE products. What additional capabilities are provided by I-CASE products?

8. Briefly describe the stages of the database-oriented systems development cycle
presented in this chapter.

9. What is meant by a three schema architecture? Describe how this architecture
insulates users from changes to the internal and conceptual models.

10. What is a user view? What does consolidating user views mean?

11. Describe the term *systems repository.* What are the major functions of a systems repository?

12. Describe the information engineering methodology. Why is an I-CASE product
necessary to fully implement the IE methodology?

13. What types of hierarchies or lists are normally developed in the data planning
process? Can you think of lists other than those described in the text that would
be useful? Identify at least three other hierarchies or lists that might be used.

14. Using an organization you are familiar with, perform a simple data planning
exercise in which you compile at least three hierarchies or lists and construct at
least two matrices. Be sure to fully analyze and describe your work.

15. Identify an organization that utilizes a CASE or I-CASE product and interview
a user of that product. Report on how the product is used and the perceived
advantages and disadvantages of the product.

16. Gather information about two different CASE and/or I-CASE products.
Compare and contrast the products in terms of the types of tools provided, stage
of development supported, and so on.

THE AIRLINE DATABASE: A CONCEPTUAL DESIGN CASE

5

LEARNING OBJECTIVES

After completing this chapter, you should be able to

- Formulate a set of questions that could be used in an interview to elicit a user's data requirements.

- Generate an appropriate E-R diagram to support a user view based upon descriptions of a user's data requirements.

- Define a set of attribute domain descriptions to support a user view based upon the user's data requirements.

- Consolidate a set of user views to produce a conceptual data model.

- Check the entities of a user view or a conceptual model for normalization and perform any modifications needed to put the model in at least third normal form.

- Describe how the use of CASE tools affects the process of creating a conceptual data model.

In this chapter we will present a hypothetical conceptual design process for an airline database. Our example deals with a set of data that might constitute a subject area database covering reservations and scheduling for a small airline. We will call our airline Air West.

The example we will be using is intended to be as realistic as possible with respect to the database design processes used. However, it must be noted that some simplifying assumptions will be made to reduce the scope of our database. A moderate-sized, real-world database might contain several dozen related tables and some of those tables might contain as many as 50 to 100 or more columns. Dealing with that level of complexity and detail is beyond the scope of an introductory database textbook.

Our focus will be on how data requirements are gathered during the requirements analysis phase of systems development and on how those requirements are converted to user views and the conceptual database model. Preliminary analysis and design of the transactions processing applications associated with the airline database would logically be performed in parallel with the conceptual database design steps described here.

We will assume that all data of the database reside on a single computer. Our database will use either a teleprocessing approach—remote access but all processing on a centralized computer—or a client/server approach. We will examine a possible distributed database configuration for our Air West database in a later chapter.

The design documents we will be describing can be generated manually, or they can be produced using CASE tools. Because CASE tools are not always available, manual methods will be assumed in describing this case. However, some of the CASE tools that can be used for this process will be briefly described.

In the following sections, we will first describe the setting in which our database is to be developed. Next we will present a set of vignettes describing interviews conducted with users to obtain data requirements and derive user views of the database. Then we will describe the process used to move from a set of user views to a conceptual design for the database as a whole. A final section gives an example of the use of CASE tools for this type of design process.

AIR WEST AIRLINES

Air West Airlines is a regional carrier that operates primarily in the southwestern United States. It operates out of a hub in Phoenix with flights to other major cities in the Southwest, including Los Angeles, San Francisco, Las Vegas, and San Diego. It also services Tucson and Flagstaff and has three round trips a day to Minneapolis to bring the snowbirds from the upper Midwest to Phoenix. Air West is a young, rapidly growing company whose information systems face accelerating demands with limited staffing and funds to support improvements.

Air West operates its own reservation information system. To simplify our analysis, we will assume that all reservations on Air West flights are placed through Air West employees. Flights are not booked through travel agents and Air West does not participate in industry-wide reservation services such as the SABRE system. All flights can be viewed as nonstop flights from an origin to a destination. If the same plane flys from Flagstaff to Phoenix and then from Phoenix to Los Angeles, this is treated as two separate flights. Each is assigned a unique flight number and has its own set of flight characteristics. Reservation information is currently processed by a set of file-oriented application programs. However, the current system is viewed as antiquated and inadequate.

A number of scheduling operations at Air West are closely related to the reservation system. First, Air West's schedule of flights is determined by the vice-president of Marketing. The flight schedule is adjusted as needed to accommodate changes in consumer demand. The fare for each flight is set as a part of the flight schedule, and there is a single prescribed fare for a given flight at any point in time. Any discounts are applied as adjustments to the unique fare assigned to a flight. The flight schedule is currently distributed to other departments in the form of a printed list. When adjustments are made, a revised list is sent showing any changes and their effective dates.

The flight schedule information that we have just described applies to each daily occurrence of a particular flight. However, reservations are issued for a specific flight *on a specific date*. To avoid confusion, we will use the term *flight-day* to refer to the occurrence of a flight on a specific day and the term *flight-schedule* to refer to flight data that applies to all occurrences of a flight.

A plane must be scheduled for each flight-day. Air West flies a number of different planes with differing capacities. Because the larger planes expend more fuel and require larger crews, it is wasteful to assign a plane with a large passenger capacity to a flight-day having few passengers. On the other hand, Air West obviously loses money if it must turn away passengers because a flight-day is assigned a plane with too small a capacity. Air West attempts to optimize the scheduling of its aircraft by making assignments of planes to flight-days only 10 days in advance of the departure date. The director of Flight Operations makes the assignment of planes to flight-days. In making these assignments, the director examines summary reservations data to help estimate the capacity that is likely to be required. Once a plane assignment has been made for a flight on a specific departure date, this information is passed on to the reservation information system for use in scheduling seats. Until a plane has been assigned to a flight-day, passengers making reservations cannot be given assigned seats.

Shortly after the plane assignment for a flight-day is made, a crew assignment must be produced. Union contracts require that employees be informed of their work schedule at least one week in advance. Any changes after that time are subject to the employee's consent and typically require the payment of a wage premium. Crew assignments are made by the director of Flight Personnel. Both the type of plane and the number of passengers booked on a flight-day affect the size and composition of the crew assigned to that flight-day. Summary reports showing the type of plane assigned and number of reservations for a flight-day are examined when making crew assignments. Reservations are also monitored after the initial crew assignments to determine if additional crew members are needed for a flight-day.

A number of other systems at Air West interact with the systems we have just described. Work schedules must be established for ground crews and airport counter staff. However, these schedules are determined by managers in the individual airports served by Air West. These managers do receive summary reservation information and use it in establishing their schedules. However, the schedules they produce do not directly impact the reservation and scheduling systems described earlier. Also, Air West must keep maintenance histories on its aircraft. Information about the flight history of an aircraft is used in scheduling aircraft maintenance. However, we will assume that aircraft maintenance records are kept in manual form. Also, the Air West reservation system described here is assumed to operate more or less independently of the customer billings and payments system. We will assume that Air West handles customer billings through a separate vendor-provided information system.

After going through a rather abbreviated and informal data planning process, Air West officials have determined that they have an immediate need to develop a database system to handle reservations and the scheduling of flights, aircraft, and flight crews. Approval has been received to proceed immediately with the development of this system, and a project team has been formed.

CONCEPTUAL DESIGN OF THE AIRLINE DATABASE

User requirements are determined through interviews with the major users of a proposed system. When this development project was approved, a project steering committee including two users was formed. One of the first tasks of the project steering committee is to determine who are the major users of the system so that arrangements can be made for interviews with each user. In this case, the major users and user groups that have been identified are: the Reservations Department, which generates and manipulates reservation data; the vice-president of Marketing, who establishes the flight schedules; the director of Flight Operations, who handles the scheduling of planes to flight-days; and the director of Flight Personnel, who schedules flight crews. Because reservations are a key element of the proposed database and will involve many users, two users from the Reservations Department will be interviewed: a senior reservations clerk and the director of the Reservations Department. Summaries describing the interviews conducted with these users and the process of developing user views are presented in the following sections.

USER VIEW 1: VICE-PRESIDENT OF MARKETING

Bob Smith has been assigned to interview the vice-president of Marketing, Suzanne Santee. As the interview begins, Bob asks Ms. Santee how she plans to use the proposed database. She indicates that she expects to interact with the proposed database in two ways. First, she produces Flight Schedules, which are used in reservations and scheduling operations. Second, she reviews summary reservations information periodically to help her determine what modifications might be needed to scheduled flights.

Ms. Santee hands Bob a copy of a printed Flight Schedule table that is distributed to customers and provides summary information about all of Air West's flights. This table is presented in Figure 5.1. She indicates that this is the same type of information that she provides to other departments within Air West. As Bob examines the printed Flight Schedule table, he quickly begins to see that at least two distinct entities are described: Flights and the Airports that serve as their origin and destination points. A third possible entity is Meals, where the single-character meal code and the full meal description would be the attributes. However, Bob suspects that storing the meal descriptions is unnecessary. Ms. Santee confirms this.

Bob begins to ask further clarifying questions. As he gathers more and more information, he begins to sketch, in crude handwritten form, both an entity-relationship (E-R) diagram and a set of domain descriptions of attributes. These preliminary designs are shown in Figure 5.2.

Dialogue samples can help to illustrate how Bob gathered the information needed to sketch the E-R diagram and note the domain descriptions.

> *Bob:* Does each flight have a single departure airport code and arrival airport code?
>
> *Ms. Santee:* Yes.

Thus the relationships from Airport to Flight are one to many. However, there is a departure airport and an arrival airport for each flight, so there are two separate one to many relationships between these entities.

> *Bob:* Are flight numbers always three digits and numeric?
>
> *Ms. Santee:* Flight numbers are always numeric. Values for flight number can range from 1 to 799.

Flight number is an integer and its domain is restricted to integers between 1 and 799.

Flight Number	Departure Airport[1]	Time[2]	Arrival Airport	Time	Meal Served[3]	Ticket Price[4]
101	FLG	7:00 AM	PHX	8:05 AM	S	$48.50
102	PHX	9:00 AM	MPS	1:00 PM	L	$156.00
103	MPS	5:00 PM	PHX	7:15 PM	D	$156.99
104	PHX	8:30 PM	FLG	9:15 PM	S	$48.50
15	PHX	7:00 AM	LAX	8:20 AM	B	$49.00
•						
•						
•						
1260	SFO	5:58 PM	PHX	7:51 PM	D	$109.00

[1]Air West serves the cities shown below. For local Air West information call the phone number shown.

Airport Code	City	Elevation	Local Phone Number
FLG	Flagstaff, AZ	6920	(602) 774-1897
PHX	Phoenix, AZ	1257	(602) 583-1971
LAX	Los Angeles, CA	37	(310) 273-1846
SFO	San Francisco, CA	78	(415) 839-9273
MPS	Minneapolis, MN	862	(612) 378-2910

[2]All times shown are local.

[3]B—breakfast, L—lunch, D—dinner, S—snack

[4]Prices and flight times subject to change without notice. Contact your travel agent or one of our airport offices for current information.

FIGURE 5.1
Air West Airlines Flight Schedule Table

Bob: Is each flight assigned a unique flight number?

Ms. Santee: Yes, and the flight number is used to identify the flight.

Flight number must be unique and can serve as a primary key for the flight entity.

Bob: Are all airport codes three characters long and are they unique?

Ms. Santee: Yes, the FAA assigns a unique three-character code to each airport and it must be used by all airlines.

Airport codes are three characters long and can serve as the primary key of the airport entity.

Bob: Are there restrictions on the amount of the base fare?

Ms. Santee: Yes, it is unreasonable that we would ever have a flight whose base fare is less than $10 or more than $1,000 dollars.

The domain of price can be restricted to values between $10 and $1,000.

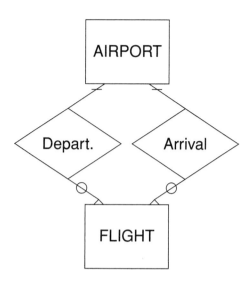

Attribute List

AIRPORT Entity	FLIGHT Entity
☐ Code	☐ Flight_No
Location	Dep_Time
Elevation	Arr_Time
Phone	Meal
	Base_Fare

Based on the preceding dialogue and additional questions in the same vein, Bob begins to feel that he has a good sense of the structure of the data underlying the Flight Schedule table. Now he turns to the second element of Ms. Santee's interaction with the proposed database—her use of summary reservation information. Here Bob finds that she is very dissatisfied with the current system. She says that she currently receives monthly summary reports showing the count of passengers for each flight on each departure date and an average passenger count for the month for each flight number. Ms. Santee indicates that this information is not sufficiently up-to-date to be of much use. She would prefer to have a set of summary data that is completely up-to-date, including reservation counts for future flights as well as counts of passengers for flights that have already occurred. She would like to be able to access this data herself using a query language so that she can organize in her own way to meet ad hoc needs. She indicates that she has Microsoft Access software on the PC in her office and is familiar with its query language. She feels that she could use Access, or any other software package with a similar visual query language, with only minimal additional training.

Bob asks her what information she feels she needs as the basis for her queries. Ms. Santee indicates that the required information is really extremely simple. She draws a sketch of what this table should look like (see Figure 5.3). For each flight on each departure date, Ms. Santee would like to know the airport from which the flight departs and its departure time, the arrival airport and time, and the number of passengers.

Bob can see that much of this information is already a part of the Flight entity. However, the departure date and passenger count are new items. He sees that the date of a flight could be considered a multivalued attribute of the flight itself—this flight occurs on each of the following days. However, such a representation would be unnormalized and, in addition, the count of the number of passengers appears to be an attribute of a flight on a specific departure date. Flight 101 can have a different passenger count for each date that it operates. Bob tentatively adds a new entity called Flight-Day to his E-R sketch and asks for further information about the passenger count.

In response to this, Ms. Santee says, "I suppose what I am asking for is a count of the number of tickets or reservations for a flight on a given date. I am not interested in seeing any information about individual reservations, though. I just need the count of actual passengers flying or the number of reservations made for upcoming flights."

The passenger count poses an interesting problem. It seems to be a computed value derived from other areas of the database that are outside Ms. Santee's purview. For now, Bob decides to list the passenger count as an attribute of Flight-Day with a notation that this data may be derived from elsewhere in the database.

Bob notes that users are likely to use the term *flight* to describe both schedule information pertaining to all days when the flight operates and information pertaining

FIGURE 5.3
Vice-President of
Marketing's View of
Reservation Data

		Departure		Arrival		
Flight #	Date	Airport	Time	Airport	Time	Passengers
101	09/28/97	FLG	7:00	PHX	8:05	172
101	09/29/97	FLG	7:00	PHX	8:05	156
101	09/30/97	FLG	7:00	PHX	8:05	191
101	10/01/97	FLG	7:00	PHX	8:05	137
•						
102	09/28/97	PHX	9:00	MPS	13:00	252
102	09/29/97	PHX	9:00	MPS	13:00	240
102	09/23/97	PHX	9:00	MPS	13:00	227
102	10/01/97	PHX	9:00	MPS	13:00	249
•						
•						
•						

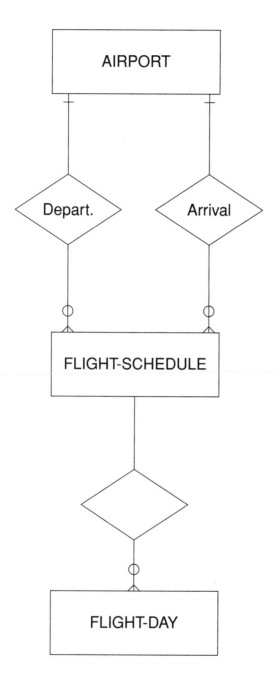

FIGURE 5.4
Tentative E-R Diagram
of the Vice-President
of Marketing's User
View

to the operation of a flight on a particular date. To reduce ambiguity, he changes the
name of the Flight entity he had sketched in Figure 5.2 to Flight–Schedule. By qualifying the names of both entities containing flight-related data, Bob hopes to increase
user awareness of the distinction between the two entity types.

Attribute Name	Data Type	Description/Domain	Nulls Allowed	Key Status
TABLE: AIRPORT				
Code	Char 3	Valid codes for airports served	No	Primary key
Location	Char 20	City name, State abbreviation	No	
Elevation	Integer	Altitude in feet of the Airport	Yes	
Phone	Char 12	Local Air West Phone # 999 999-9999	Yes	
TABLE: FLIGHT_SCHEDULE				
Flight_No	Integer	Unique 3 digit number > = 1 and < = 799	No	Primary key
Dep_Time	Time	Time of scheduled departure 0:00–24:00	No	
Arr_Time	Time	Time of scheduled arrival 0:00–24:00	No	
Meal	Char 1	Code for type of meal B, L, D, or S	Yes	
Base_Fare	Money	Base ticket price $10.00–$999.99	Yes	
TABLE: FLIGHT_DAY				
Flight_No	Integer	Valid 3 digit flight number	No	Concatenated primary key with Flight_Date. Foreign key to FLIGHT
Depart_Date	Date	Date of flight departure must be = > 01/01/87	No	Concatenated primary key with Flight_No.
Pass_Cnt	Integer	Passenger count = count of tickets for Flight-Day* 0 to 580	No	

*May be derivable from other database data

FIGURE 5.5
Domain Descriptions for the Vice-President of Marketing's User View

At this point, Bob feels that he has a reasonably strong feel for Ms. Santee's data requirements. He reviews and revises his E-R diagram and domain descriptions, producing the tentative documents shown in Figures 5.4 and 5.5.

A NOTE ON THE TREATMENT OF FOREIGN KEY ATTRIBUTES

The domain descriptions defined for each entity do not normally include foreign key attributes. For instance, the airport Code is the primary key of the Airport table. Thus, in a relational implementation, the airport Codes of the arrival and destination airports would be included in the Flight–Schedule table as foreign key attributes. However, there would be no need to include these attributes in the Flight–Schedule table if the database is implemented using the hierarchical or network model. The conceptual model is designed to be implementation independent; thus, foreign key attributes are not normally included in the attribute list for an entity. However, there are exceptions. Flight_No is shown as an attribute of the FLIGHT–DAY table even though it is a foreign key attribute that can be used to reference the FLIGHT–SCHEDULE table. In this case, Flight_No also serves as a part of the concatenated primary key of the FLIGHT–DAY table. Although it is possible to implement a network or hierarchical database in which Flight_No is not an attribute of the FLIGHT–DAY table, such a table would have no primary key, and specific FLIGHT–DAY records could not be directly accessed. If rapid access to FLIGHT–DAY occurrences is important, Flight_No would be included as an attribute of the FLIGHT–DAY table even under a network or hierarchical implementation. In the set of domain descriptions presented here, foreign key attributes will be included when they also serve as a part of the primary key, but otherwise will be excluded from attribute lists.

FIGURE 5.6
Reservation Booking
Form—Current System

```
Passenger Name:     Pete Peterson
Phone Number:       602 779-3829
Itinerary Number:   16732
Reservation Date:   09/27/97
```

Flight Number	Depart. Date	Departure Location	Departure Time	Arrival Location	Arrival Time	Assigned Seat
101	09/30/97	FLG	7:00	PHX	8:05	14 B
102	09/30/97	PHX	9:00	MPS	13:00	15 C
103	10/06/97	MPS	17:00	PHX	19:15	18 F

```
AVAILABLE FLIGHTS

From:              PHX
To:                FLG
Departing After:   20:00
```

Flight Number	Departure Time	Arrival Time
104	20:30	21:15

USER VIEW 2: RESERVATIONS DEPARTMENT

Ann Adams has been assigned to interview users in the Reservations Department. She plans to talk initially with Sandra Annandale, a reservations clerk in Phoenix with many years of experience. She will later interview Alan Bond, the director of the Reservations Department.

Ann has asked Sandra to demonstrate how she uses the current reservation information system and then critique it. The reservation system is an online system, so Ann calls up the reservation system on a computer terminal. A sample of the type of screen display that reservation clerks see is shown in Figure 5.6.

Sandra describes how she uses the form.

Sandra: First I ask for the passenger's name and phone number and key those in. Then an assigned itinerary number is generated by the computer and displayed on the screen. This number is very important. When I am finished generating the reservation information, I make sure the customer writes down the itinerary number because it is the only quick way she can check on her reservation later. Next the reservation date is entered. After the date is entered, the cursor moves down to just below the Flight number heading in the section that goes across the screen. The form is set up this way so that several flights can be booked on a single form. I ask the customer if she knows the flight number of the flight she wants to take. Most customers don't know the number of the flight they want. In that case, I ask where they are flying from and where they want to fly to and when they want to leave. Based on that information, I use our flight schedule data to help them find the best flight.

Ann: Is the flight schedule displayed on the screen, too?

Sandra: I can display selected parts of the flight schedule on the screen by pressing a function key. This puts an overlay on the screen. I have to enter the departure and arrival airport codes and a time representing the earliest possible departure flight. This last item is most helpful when I am scheduling a multi-leg trip. For example, if you are scheduled to get into Phoenix at 9:20 in the morning, I'll add 45 minutes to that and look only for flights leaving Phoenix after 10:05 for the next leg. That 45 minutes gives time for luggage to be transferred and allows a little slack for late flights.

Once the customer has decided which flight number she wants, I enter that flight number and the date she wants to fly on the booking screen. Once that information is entered, the computer looks up the departure and arrival locations and times and displays them on the screen. This helps to confirm that the flight number we picked is correct. Finally, there is a column for a seat assignment. Seat assignments can only be made if a plane has been assigned to a particular flight for the chosen date. This usually happens about a week before the date of the flight. If a plane has been chosen, we are given a printed seating chart for that plane with the flight and date indicated at the top. Customers can choose the seat they want and we draw an X through that seat on the chart. Of course, if they change their mind we have to erase the mark. It's a real mess and it's hard to keep those sheets clean and avoid errors.

That pretty much describes how a form is filled out. Of course, passengers can book a multi-leg trip. If they do, all the flight information is simply repeated for each flight they want to book. Once all the information is completed, I double-check with the customer to make sure it's right, and I make sure she has recorded her itinerary number. If everything is okay, I save the reservation. We book about 70 percent of all reservations from the central reservations office here in Phoenix. The other 30 percent are booked, using this same system, by agents at the check-in counters in the airports we serve.

Ann: What changes would you like to see in the system?

Sandra notes two major problems: the awkward system for handling seat reservations that was described earlier and a problem with the itinerary numbers.

Sandra: Often a customer calls up and wants to book a set of flights for several people, maybe a family of four. With our system, the customer has to record four itinerary numbers in order to check on the reservation later. Also, if there is a problem with one of the tickets, we call the phone number we've recorded and ask for the passenger listed on that ticket. But that could be somebody's 3-year-old kid. It's really embarrassing. It seems like we need another layer where one person can reserve tickets on multiple flights for multiple people and be given a single number for future reference. Also, that person's name and phone number should be associated with all the tickets he reserved. That way, if anything goes wrong we call the person who knows about the reservations.

Ann asks Sandra to tell her more about the printed seating charts.

Sandra says that the director of the Reservations Department distributes them after he receives "some sort of report showing what plane has been assigned to a flight for a particular departure date." Sandra thinks that all planes of a given type, for example, all Boeing 727s, have the same seating configuration, but she is not sure.

At this point, Ann feels that she needs to speak with the director of the Reservations Department before proceeding to get more detailed information from Sandra. She arranges a second meeting with Sandra. Although Ann has not yet gotten all the details of Sandra's user view, she does have a good feel for the entities involved and their attributes. She sketches a tentative E-R diagram to show the entities and relationships, and identifies the names of the attributes that will be defined for each entity. **Before looking at Ann's results, try drawing your own E-R diagram and list the names of the attributes of each entity. Once you have completed this, read the following descriptions and compare your model with Ann's.**

Ann sees three basic entities (Passenger, Flight–Schedule, and Ticket) in the system that is currently in use. Each passenger can reserve one or more tickets on a given itinerary. Each ticket is for a specific flight on a specific day. Obviously, many different passengers can reserve tickets on the same flight on the same date.

Ann mentally applies normalization rules to the attributes listed across the columns of the booking form in Figure 5.6. She can see that the departure and arrival locations and times depend only on flight number and, therefore, are attributes of the Flight–Schedule entity. On the other hand, a seat is assigned to a specific passenger on a specific flight departing on a specific date. It is an attribute of the Ticket

FIGURE 5.7
Preliminary Notes on
the Reservation Clerk's
User View

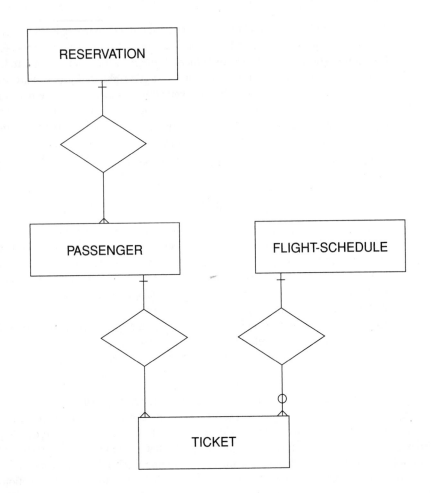

Attribute List

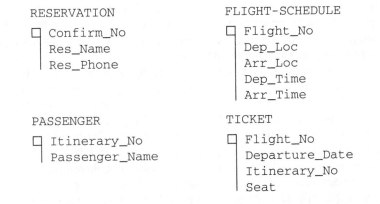

RESERVATION

☐ Confirm_No
│ Res_Name
│ Res_Phone

PASSENGER

☐ Itinerary_No
│ Passenger_Name

FLIGHT-SCHEDULE

☐ Flight_No
│ Dep_Loc
│ Arr_Loc
│ Dep_Time
│ Arr_Time

TICKET

☐ Flight_No
│ Departure_Date
│ Itinerary_No
│ Seat

entity. The combination of the flight number, the departure date, and the itinerary number is required to serve as the primary key uniquely identifying a Ticket occurrence. Itinerary number is used here rather than the passenger's name because one passenger may have several different bookings with Air West. The itinerary number identifies the tickets associated with a specific booking or trip. Ann's E-R diagram and attribute lists are shown in Figure 5.7. Ann decides to tentatively add an entity called Reservation that will create a single number, Confirm_No, which can be used to identify all tickets booked by a given customer at a given time. The name and phone number of the person making the reservation and the date the reservation was made are attributes of this new entity. A reservation can have one or more passengers related to it with an itinerary number assigned to each of them. In turn, the itinerary for each passenger can include tickets for several flights. The relationships should allow the system to identify the person who actually made the reservation associated with any ticket.

Ann focuses her interview with Alan Bond, the director of the Reservations Department, on two areas. She wants to get Alan's reaction to the proposed addition of a confirmation number to connect all related tickets. In addition, she wants to get further information about the process by which seat assignments are made.

Alan likes the idea of the confirmation number. He suggests one addition. "Often one person may have made numerous reservations with us. It would be helpful if the flight number and date of the first flight associated with a particular reservation could be stored in the Reservation table. That way, if the customer can't remember his confirmation number, we can look up all the reservations under his name and use the first flight to help identify the reservation he is interested in."

Ann makes a note of this. She can see that this information will be redundant if it is placed in the Reservation table. The first flight could always be found in ticket records associated with a given reservation. However, placement of this data in the Reservation table might speed processing. For now she decides to add attributes called Res_Flight_No and Res_Depart_Date to the Reservation table.

Now the interview moves on to the discussion of seat assignments. Alan indicates that the seating configuration is the same for all planes of a given type that Air West operates, and that he has a printed seating chart template for each plane type. Alan receives an Equipment Assignment Report from the director of Flight Operations three times a week. Alan shows Ann a copy of this report (see Figure 5.8). The report lists all new assignments of planes to departure dates. As soon as he receives this information, Alan makes a copy of the seating chart template for that type of plane, as shown in the bottom portion of Figure 5.8. He writes the flight number, departure date, and the number of the assigned plane on the seating chart and turns it over to his reservations staff.

Alan is very enthusiastic about the prospects of computerizing seat assignments. He feels that the existing system produces too many errors and that those errors sometimes alienate customers. He cautions that a seat reservation system must be able to guarantee that the seat number recorded on a ticket is both a valid seat number for the type of plane that is being flown and a seat number that has not been assigned to another customer.

Equipment Assignment Report

Flight	Date	Number	Plane Type	Seats
101	09/29/97	1368	DC 7	282
103	09/29/97	1257	BO 707	312
17	09/29/97	1194	DC 7	282
103	09/30/97	1026	BO 727	188
600	09/30/97	1368	DC 7	282
•				
•				
•				

DC7 Seating Chart

Flight # *101*   Date *9/29*   Equip. # *1368*

Row

1   A B C   D E F

2   X̶ X̶ C   D E X̶

3   A B C   D E F

4   X̶ X̶ X̶   D X̶ X̶

5   A B C   D E X̶

6   X̶ X̶ C   D E F

7   A B C   D E F

8   X̶ B C   X̶ X̶ X̶

          •

          •

FIGURE 5.8
Sample Document
Used by the
Reservations Director

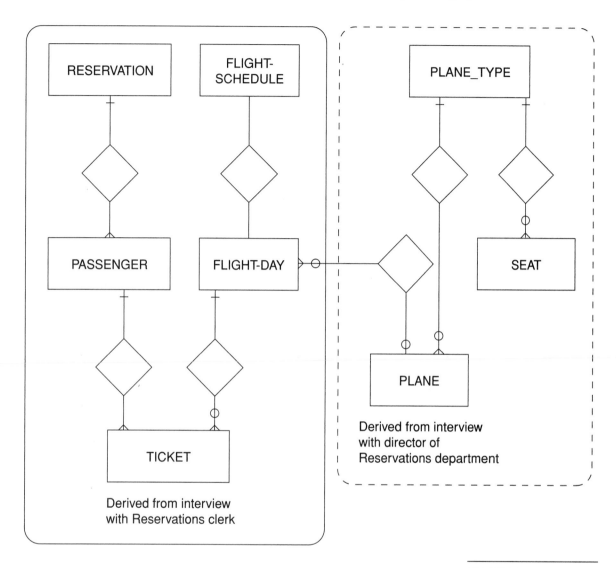

Derived from interview
with director of
Reservations department

Derived from interview
with Reservations clerk

FIGURE 5.9
E-R Diagram for the
Reservation
Department User View

Ann begins to add these features to her picture of the database. **Before examining the diagrams Ann produced, you should once again produce your own E-R diagram and list of attributes for each entity. The diagrams you produce should incorporate the requirements of both Sandra and Alan. Compare your results with those described in the following paragraphs.**

Ann's E-R diagram is shown in Figure 5.9. As Ann looks at the Equipment Assignment Report, she quickly identifies two new entities: Plane and Plane_Type. Each of Air West's planes is identified by a unique plane number, and has as an attribute its plane type. At the same time, the number of seats depends only on the plane type. Thus, Plane_Type should be established as a separate entity containing the number of seats as an attribute.

Customer Name:	Pete Peterson
Phone Number:	602 779-3829
Confirmation #:	6835
Reservation Date:	09/29/97

Passenger Name	Itin. Number	Flt. No.	Depart. Date	Departure Loc.	Departure Time	Arrival Loc.	Arrival Time	Seat
Pete Peterson	16732	101	9/30/97	FLG	7:00	PHX	8:05	14 B
		102	9/30/97	PHX	9:00	MPS	13:00	15 C
Sue Peterson	16733	101	9/30/97	FLG	7:00	PHX	8:05	14 C
		102	9/30/97	PHX	9:00	MPS	13:00	15 B
Jay Peterson	16734	101	9/30/97	FLG	7:00	PHX	8:05	14 A
				PHX	9:00	MPS	13:00	15 A

SEATS AVAILABLE

ROW	SEAT
1	A B C D E F
2	B C E
3	C D E F
4	A B E
5	B C D
6	
7	A B C
8	D
9	A B
10	D E F

← Seats Available Overlay

Available Flights Overlay ↓

AVAILABLE FLIGHTS

From: PHX
To: FLG
Departing After: 20:00

Flight Number	Departure Time	Arrival Time
104	20:30	21:15

FIGURE 5.10
Reservation Booking Form—Proposed System

It seems to Ann that seat numbers are a multivalued attribute of Plane_Type. That is, if the plane is a DC7, there are 282 valid seat numbers associated with that equipment type and those numbers are the same for all DC7s. Of course, if Seat_Number were added as an attribute of Plane_Type, it would be a repeating group, and Plane_Type would be unnormalized. Thus, Ann adds a new entity called Seat. Seat occurrences will have an equipment type attribute and a Seat_No attribute. The two attributes combine to form the primary key. There will be 282 Seat occurrences for the equipment type DC7, 312 occurrences for equipment type BO707, and so on.

Finally, Ann notes that a particular plane has been assigned to a flight on a particular date. This connection must be reflected in the database. If Ann adds Plane_No to the Ticket table, it will have to be stored redundantly in the occurrence for every ticket issued for that flight on that day. At the same time, Plane_No cannot be added to the Flight–Schedule table. Different planes may be assigned to the same flight on different days. Ann now sees that there is an intervening entity between Flight-Schedule and Ticket. She names this entity Flight-Day. Plane_No will be an attribute of Flight-Day, along with Flight_No and Flight_Date, which serve as its concatenated key.

At a follow-up interview, Ann is able to show the users a mock-up of what she expects their new booking form to look like. This mock-up, shown in Figure 5.10, includes the information for the new reservation entity and an overlay that can display the seats that are available for a given flight number and departure date. Ann works with the users to ensure that this form will meet their needs.

Ann also asks detailed questions in order to construct a set of domain descriptions. The questioning would be very similar to that described for the first user view, so we will not present the process in detail here. Ann's domain description results are shown in Figure 5.11. Note particularly the domain description for seats. The Seat assigned to a ticket must be a valid seat number for the type of plane used for the Flight-Day to which the ticket belongs. The Seat also must not be the same as the seat number assigned to any other ticket for the same Flight-Day. This restriction will be difficult to implement, but it is important that it is described at this stage of the design process.

USER VIEW 3: DIRECTOR OF FLIGHT OPERATIONS

While Ann Adams has been working with users in the Reservations Department, Bob Smith has been working with Darrel Barnes, Air West's director of Flight Operations. Air West's Flight Operations Department is located in Minneapolis. As Bob and Darrel begin to talk, it becomes clear that Darrel Barnes is apprehensive about the new system. He indicates that he has a spreadsheet program, in Microsoft Excel, that he uses for scheduling planes and tracking and evaluating performance. He indicates that he built the system himself and says he does a lot of very important analysis using this spreadsheet program. Darrel also indicates that much of his analysis is ad hoc in nature, so that he needs to get at the data himself.

Bob tries to reassure Darrel. "The intent of the new database is to make it easier for users to get at data, not harder. We hope the new database can give better

Attribute Name	Data Type	Description/Domain	Nulls Allowed	Key Status
TABLE: FLIGHT-SCHEDULE				
Flight_No	Integer	Unique 3 digit number	No	Primary key of FLIGHT
Dep_Loc	Char 3	Valid Airport codes	No	
Arr_Loc	Char 3	Valid Airport codes	No	
Dep_Time	Time	Time of scheduled departure 0:00–24:00	No	
Arr_Time	Time	Time of scheduled arrival 0:00–24:00	No	
TABLE: FLIGHT-DAY				
Flight_No	Integer	Valid 3 digit flight number	No	Concatenated primary key with Flight_Date. Foreign key to FLIGHT
Depart_Date	Date	Date of flight departure must be = > 01/01/87	No	Concatenated primary key with Flight_No.
TABLE: TICKET				
Itinerary_No	Integer	Valid 5 digit itinerary code	No	Concatenated primary key with Flight_No. and Flight_Date. Foreign key to PASSENGER
Flight_No	Integer	Valid 3 digit flight number	No	Concatenated primary key with Flight_Date and Itinerary_No. Foreign key to FLIGHT_DAY with Flight_Date
Depart_Date	Date	Date of flight must be = > 01/01/87	No	Concatenated primary key with Flight_No. and Itinerary_No. Foreign key to FLIGHT_DAY with Flight_No.
Seat	Char 3	Assigned seat number. Must be a valid seat # for the type plane assigned and must not be assigned to any other ticket for the flight day.		

FIGURE 5.11

Domain Descriptions for the Reservations Department User View

protection for your data and reduce the time you spend entering data, but it should definitely allow you to retrieve the same set of data you're working with now, and put it in spreadsheet form if you so desire."

With this reassurance, Darrel Barnes began to feel more comfortable about the new system. Bob asked to see his spreadsheet program, and Darrel brought it up on his PC. A sample of the layout of this spreadsheet is shown in Figure 5.12.

Attribute Name	Data Type	Description/Domain	Nulls Allowed	Key Status
TABLE: RESERVATION				
Confirm_No	Integer	Confirmation number. A unique 4 digit assigned code.	No	Primary key
Res_Name	Char 20	Name of customer placing reservations.	No	
Res_Date	Date	Date the reservations are placed > = 1/1/97	No	
Res_Phone	Char 12	Phone number for person making reservations	Yes	
Res_Flight_No	Integer	Flight_No for the first ticket on this reservation	No	
Res_Dep_Date	Date	Date of the first ticket on this reservation	No	
TABLE: PASSENGER				
Pass_Name	Char 20	Name of passenger	No	
Itinerary_No	Integer	Itinerary number. A unique 5 digit assigned code.	No	Primary key
TABLE: PLANE_TYPE				
Plane_Type	Char 6	Unique valid plane type description	No	Primary key
Seats	Integer	Seating capacity of this plane type. > 0, < 999	Yes	
TABLE: PLANE				
Plane_No	Integer	Unique 4 digit plane number	No	Primary key
TABLE: SEAT				
Plane_Type	Char 6	Valid plane type description	No	Concatenated primary key with Seat_No. Foreign key to Equip_Type
Seat_No	Char 3	Valid seat number for the associated plane type	No	Concatenated primary key with Equip_Type

FIGURE 5.11 (Cont.)
Domain Descriptions for the Reservations Department User View

Darrel began to explain his spreadsheet.

> *Darrel:* What you see here is the spreadsheet I use to store all the data I use. When I need to do some analysis on just a part of this data, I use the data commands in the spreadsheet package to retrieve the data I need.
>
> The first set of columns, from flight number over to passenger count, are values I get from the reservations people. About 12 days before the date of a

FIGURE 5.12
Spreadsheet
Maintained by Director
of Flight Operations

Flight Number	Depart. Date	Depart.	Sched. Time	Arrival	Sched. Time	Pass. Cnt.	Equip. No.	Equip. Type	Seating Capacity	Fuel Capacity	Depart. Time	Arrival Time	Fuel Used	Notes
101	08/30/97	FLG	7:00	PHX	8:05	96	1026	BO 727	188	1882	7:08	8:09	160	
102	08/30/97	PHX	9:00	MSP	13:00	146	1026	BO 727	188	1882	9:03	14:07	1340	Landing Delay at MSP
107	08/30/97	PHX	8:20	LAX	9:20	214	1194	DC 7	282	2340	8:22	9:18	295	
165	08/30/97	PHX	20:20	LAX	21:40	157	1080	BO 727	188	1882	21:15	22:20	308	Equip. probs. at PHX
600	08/30/97	PHX	17:45	SFO	18:36	236	1368	DC 7	282	2340	17:51	18:40	570	
.														
.														
.														
101	10/07/97	FLG	7:00	PHX	8:05	59	1081	BO 727	188	1882				
107	10/07/97	PHX	8:20	LAX	9:20	142	1368	DC 7	282	2340				

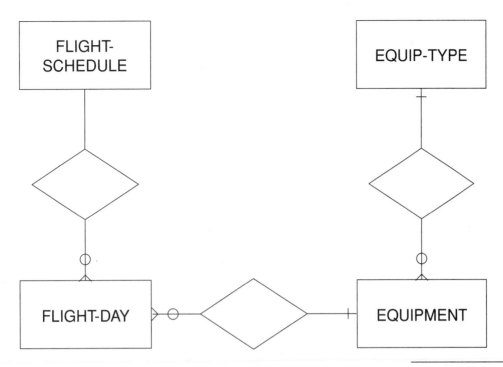

FIGURE 5.13
E-R Diagram for the
Director of Flight
Operations' User View

flight, they send me over a report with those items on it. The main thing I'm looking for is the passenger count. Of course, additional reservations will come in before the actual date of the flight, but I have a pretty good feel for that, so I can use the passenger count to decide what type of plane to assign to a flight. This is an area where your database can save me some time. Right now I have to enter all of that data on my spreadsheet.

The next set of columns, from equipment number over to fuel capacity, contains data I enter when I schedule the plane for a departure date. Of course, to schedule a plane I have to know which planes will be located at the departure airport for the flight I'm scheduling on the departure date. I have a macro command that will look up the arrival airport of the most recently scheduled flight for each plane, and show me which planes are expected to be available at the departure airport for the flight I'm working on. To be available, a plane must have arrived at least two hours before it is scheduled to depart on this new flight. That allows servicing time and a little slack for late arrivals.

Based on the set of available planes shown and the passenger count information, I select the most appropriate plane for the flight on that date. Then I simply record the equipment number of the plane and the additional characteristics that you see.

Bob: Do all planes of the same type have the same seating capacity and fuel capacity?

> *Darrel:* Yes.
>
> *Bob:* Then we should be able to save you some data entry there as well. We can build the system so that the computer will pop the equipment type, seating capacity, and fuel type onto the screen as soon as you enter the equipment number.

Darrel next notes that some of the information from this plane scheduling operation is put into a report that he sends to the Reservations Department three times a week. He shows Bob a copy of that report, which is identical to the one shown in Figure 5.8. Darrel notes that he uses the terms *plane number* and *plane type* in this report. However, he says that in the operations area, these items are called *equipment number* and *equipment type.* This terminology is used because many other kinds of equipment must be tracked within other systems and all are assigned numbers in the same numbering sequence.

Darrel goes on to explain the remainder of his spreadsheet.

> *Darrel:* The last four columns are for data that is entered after the completion of the flight. I get a report of the actual departure and actual arrival times and the amount of fuel we used. If the flight is significantly late or there were any problems with the flight, I put a description of the problem in the notes column. At this time I also get a count of the number of passengers actually flying and use it to update the passenger count.

Bob then asks Darrel to describe the kinds of ad hoc uses he makes of his spreadsheet. Darrel indicates that he uses it in a wide variety of ways, but some of the most common might be to analyze the performance of a particular plane or type of plane; to look up trends in passengers carried, on-time performance, or fuel consumption for a particular flight; or to examine scheduled and actual departure times from a particular airport.

Before examining the design documents that Bob created from this interview, sketch your own E-R diagram and produce a list of the attributes that should be defined for each entity.

Based on this information, Bob sketches a tentative E-R diagram for Darrel's user view (see Figure 5.13). He identifies four entities. An Equip_Type entity contains information that is defined for a particular type of plane, such as the seating and fuel capacities. An Equipment entity identifies a specific plane and its characteristics. Darrel's user view also includes the Flight-Day entity that Bob had identified in his first interview. Darrel assigns a Plane to each Flight-Day. Finally, Darrel's user view includes the Flight-Schedule entity. Darrel uses the origin and destination locations and times of a flight to make his plane assignments.

After some additional questions relating to the specifics of attribute domains and relationships, Bob is able to produce the set of domain descriptions shown in Figure 5.14. Notice that there are no entries for the Flight-Schedule table. When Bob asked about the data in that table, Darrel indicated that there was very little he could say. He simply used the information as he received it. Bob decided not to question Darrel any further about it, since he already had domain descriptions for this data from his interview with the vice-president of Marketing, the individual most responsible for Flight data.

USER VIEW 4: DIRECTOR OF FLIGHT PERSONNEL

Barbara Gordon, Air West's director of Flight Personnel, is located at the corporate headquarters in Phoenix. She has been one of the main supporters of the database project from its inception. She greets Ann Adams enthusiastically when their interview begins. She tells Ann that she has been making up flight crew schedules largely by hand and is badly in need of computer support for her scheduling operations. She indicates that she has little background in computer use but is eager to learn because she sees computer skills as a key to performing her job well in the future.

When Ann and Barbara get down to specifics, Barbara indicates that she currently makes out her crew schedules using manual forms. She shows Ann the form she uses (see Figure 5.15) and begins to describe it.

FIGURE 5.14
Domain Descriptions of Flight Operations' User View

Attribute Name	Data Type	Description/Domain	Nulls Allowed	Key Status
TABLE: EQUIP_TYPE				
Equip_Type	Char 6	Unique valid equipment type description	No	Primary key
Seats	Integer	Seating capacity of this plane type. > 0, < 999	No	
Mfg	Char 3	Abbreviation for manufacturer name		
Fuel_Cap	Integer	Fuel capacity of plane in gallons > 0, < 10000	No	
TABLE: EQUIPMENT				
Equip_No	Integer	Unique 4 digit equipment number	No	Primary key
Equip_Date	Date	Date this plane was received by Air West	Yes	
TABLE: FLIGHT_DAY				
Flight_No	Integer	Valid 3 digit flight number	No	Concatenated primary key with Flight_Date. Foreign key to FLIGHT
Depart_Date	Date	Date of flight departure must be = > 01/01/87	No	Concatenated primary key with Flight_No.
Pass_Cnt	Integer	Number of passengers	Yes	
Depart_Time	Time	Time of actual departure	Yes	
Arrive_Time	Time	Time of actual arrival	Yes	
Fuel_Used	Integer	Fuel expended < = fuel capacity of assigned plane	Yes	
Status_Note	Char 80	Text note describing any unusual occurrences	Yes	

Departure Date   *09/29/97*

Flight Number	Departure Loc.	Departure Time	Arrival Loc.	Arrival Time	Pass Count	Plane Number	Plane Type	Crew Assigned
101	FLG	7:00	PHX	8:05	70	1081	BO737	J. Smith, A. Cole, T. Turner
102	PHX	9:00	MPS	13:00				J. Smith, A. Cole, L. Coyle
• •								
17	PHX	7:00	LAX	8:05	183	1368	DC7	A. Erhardt, R. Ferris, L. Kay
• • •								
60	PHX	17:45	SFO	18:36	173	1194	DC7	E. Barne, D. Boyle, L. Lewis

FIGURE 5.15
Crew Scheduling Form

Barbara: I make up copies with the flight schedule information printed on them. Whenever the flight schedule changes, which isn't too often, I have to modify my form. When it's time to schedule a day's flight crews, I pull out a fresh form and write the departure date on it. Then I add the information on passenger count and the number and type of plane assigned. I get that information from reports coming from the Reservations Department and the Flight Operations Department and write it on my form. At that point I am ready to begin scheduling crew members for flights.

Now scheduling crews requires a lot of judgment. I use the passenger count and type of plane assigned to help determine the size of crew that will be needed. Also we try to give our senior employees the types of schedules they want. Many of them like to fly the same sets of flights all the time, which makes things a little easier. I usually fill in the slots for the senior people first and then add other crew as needed to fill out the schedule. I schedule a full week's crews at a time, so I end up with seven forms like this.

Once I have a tentative crew schedule for the week, I go through and check the number of hours assigned to each staff member. I also check to be sure that everyone has two days off sometime during the week, and I have to make sure that the flights I have scheduled people for are compatible. That is, I have to be sure that I don't have someone scheduled on the crew of two different planes flying at the same time. More commonly, I might have the problem of a crew member scheduled on a flight departing at Los Angeles when she will actually be in Phoenix at the time that flight leaves. Currently I check all these things manually, but as our operations keep expanding, it is getting more and more difficult to avoid errors. I don't expect you to be able to create a program to do the scheduling automatically, and I wouldn't want one. There are just too many decisions that require my judgment.

I've been thinking a lot lately about how your database might be able to help me, and I have some fairly specific ideas. I'd like to be able to have a program that will show me a list of the employees who will be available at a particular city at the time a flight is scheduled to depart. If possible, the program should also show a running total of each employee's scheduled work hours for the week. It would also be really helpful to have a program that could show the work schedules and days off for all employees once a full week's schedule has been produced. I want to be able to look at that summary, go back and make changes, and then look at the summary again to see how it changed.

Ann told Barbara that the programs she wanted could probably be produced, but that Ann needed a little more information for clarification.

Ann: First of all, surely there is some more information that needs to be recorded about your flight staff members. Only their names appear on your form.

Barbara: Of course, we have a mass of data about our employees in our files, but I only need a little bit of that for scheduling. Obviously, we should have the staff member's name and ID number. Beyond that, we need to know the type of staff they are—pilot, navigator, or steward—and the date they were hired.

Then I guess there is some information that would be good to have that pertains only to certain types of employees. For pilots and navigators, we need to keep track of when they had their last physical and when they last had their certification renewed. I can't schedule them if they aren't current on those dates. For stewards those dates don't apply, but it would be helpful to know whether a steward has an advanced CPR certification. Also, we have a program for new stewards called Sponsorship. For the first year, each new steward is assigned a senior steward to serve as her sponsor—sort of like a mentorship program. Whenever possible, I try to schedule these new stewards on the same flight as their sponsor.

At this point Ann asked if a senior steward could be the sponsor for more than one of the new stewards.

Barbara: Yes. Typically a senior steward will be sponsor to two or three of the new stewards. But it is a voluntary program so some of them don't sponsor anyone.

Ann: How are scheduled hours determined?

Barbara: It isn't just departure time to arrival time, of course. The pilot normally logs in one and one-half hours before a flight is scheduled to depart and logs out a half hour after it arrives. Most of the rest of the crew logs in an hour before departure and off a half hour after arrival. However, this can vary. For instance, suppose a staff member is scheduled for two connecting flights with a layover of less than three hours between them. Then that crew member stays on duty throughout the layover. The layover time should be split between the two flights. I'd like to be able to enter the number of scheduled hours for a staff member when I assign that person to a crew. With that information, the computer should be able to keep a running tab on the hours of each employee.

Based on the preceding information, sketch an E-R diagram of Barbara Gordon's user view of the database and list the attributes that should be defined for each entity. Then compare your results with the ones described in the following paragraphs.

Ann was beginning to get a picture of the needed data. She sketched an E-R diagram for Barbara's user view like the one shown in Figure 5.16. The personnel

FIGURE 5.16
E-R Diagram of
Director of Flight
Personnel's User View

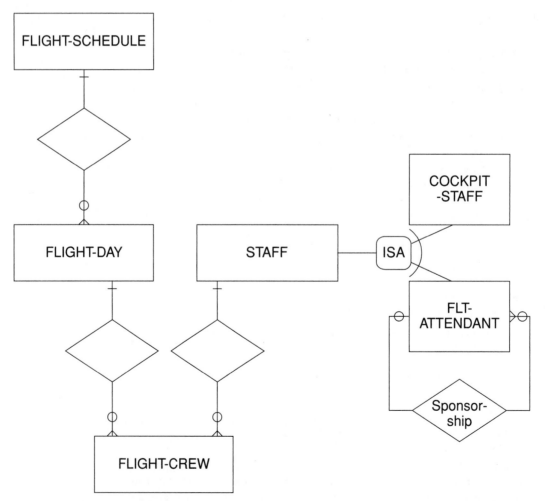

user view would need to include some common data about the flight staff, such as their names, ID numbers, and hire dates. However, there seemed to be a need to create entity subclasses here as well. Some data needed for the cockpit staff, pilots, and navigators is not relevant for the flight attendant staff and vice versa. The sponsorship also called for special treatment. As she analyzed it, Ann saw that this was a one to many intra-entity relationship among different occurrences of the Flight Attendant

FIGURE 5.17
Domain Descriptions for the Director of Flight Personnel's User View

Attribute Name	Data Type	Description/Domain	Nulls Allowed	Key Status
TABLE: STAFF				
Staff_No	Char 11	Social security number of employee: format 999-99-9999	No	Primary key
Staff_Name	Char 20	Name of employee	No	
Staff_Type	Char 2	Two character code for job type Allowed values (s1, s2, s3, n1, n2, p1, p2, p3)	No	
Staff_Date	Date	The date this staff member was hired	Yes	
TABLE: COCKPIT_STAFF				
Staff_No	Char 11	Social security number of employee: format 999-99-9999	No	Primary key
Phys_Date	Date	Date of last physical	Yes	
Certif_Date	Date	Date of last licensing certification	Yes	
TABLE: FLT_ATTENDANT				
Staff_No	Char 11	Social security number of employee: format 999-99-9999	No	Primary key
CPR_Cert	Char 3	Certified in advanced CPR techniques	Yes	
Sponsor_No	Char 11	Social security number of employee's sponsor	No	Intra-Table Linking attrib.
TABLE: FLIGHT_CREW				
Flight_No	Integer	Valid 3 digit flight number	No	Concatenated primary key with Flight_Date ad Staff_No. Foreign key to FLIGHT_DAY with Flight_Date
Depart_Date	Date	Date of flight departure must be = > 01/01/87	No	Concatenated primary key with Staff_No and Flight_No. Foreign key to FLIGHT_DAY with Flight_No.
Staff_No	Char 11	Staff ID number (social security number)	No	Concatenated primary key with Flight_No. and Flight_Date. Foreign key to STAFF
Work_Hrs	Num. (4.1)	Scheduled work hours for this worker on this flight date	Yes	

entity subclass. Each new flight attendant would be sponsored by one senior flight attendant, while each senior flight attendant could be the sponsor of one or more new flight attendants.

The staff members would be assigned as crews for various Flight_Days. The Flight_Crew entity in Figure 5.16 captures this relationship. For each Flight_Day, a crew of several staff members may be assigned and, of course, over time each staff member will be assigned to many different Flight_Crews. The Flight and Flight_Day entities are identical to those defined in earlier user views. Nothing in this user view will change those entities. Their presence simply reflects the fact that Barbara uses a report based on these entities to help her determine crew assignments.

After some additional questioning, Ann Adams was able to put together the domain descriptions shown in Figure 5.17. The contents of the Staff and Flight_Crew entities and the Cockpit_Staff and Flt_Attendant subclasses of the Flight entity reflect Barbara's data needs as described earlier. The Flight and Flight_Day tables are not included in these domain descriptions because Barbara works with them only in the form of printed reports produced by other departments, and she feels she knows very little about them.

CONSOLIDATING USER VIEWS

Once the four user views described in the preceding sections were collected, it was time to consolidate them into a conceptual design for the database as a whole.

Before you look at the results presented here, you should once again try the process for yourself. Based upon the E-R diagrams and domain descriptions of the four user views, produce a consolidated user E-R diagram and set of domain descriptions for the database as a whole. In consolidating this information, you should ensure that the overall model supports all the user views.

The consolidated design that Ann and Bob produced is presented in Figure 5.18, which shows an E-R diagram for the database as a whole, and Figure 5.19, which lists the domain descriptions for the entire database.

Because the Reservations Department user view appears to cover a wider portion of the database than the other user views, Bob and Ann used it as a starting point. They then took each of the other user views and considered their contributions one at a time. For example, when the vice-president of Marketing's user view was considered, the Airport entity needed to be added to the set of entities in the conceptual model. Also, additional attributes for the Flight_Schedule entity—Meal and Base_Fare—needed to be added to the domain descriptions. Further, there were some differences in the domain descriptions for common attributes across the two views. The Reservations Department listed the domain for Flight_No as any three-digit numeric value, while the user view of the vice-president of Marketing restricted it to values between 1 and 799. Since the vice-president of Marketing generates this data, her domain definition was used for the conceptual model.

The user view of the director of Flight Operations was considered next using the same technique. Here we see a conflict in table and attribute names. What the Reservations staff call Plane and Plane_Type are referred to as Equipment and

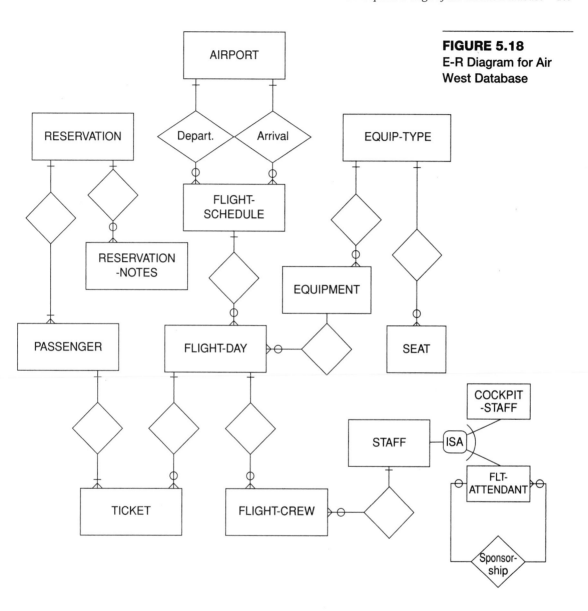

FIGURE 5.18
E-R Diagram for Air
West Database

Equip_Type by the director of Flight Operations. Because these tables are generated by the director of Flight Operations, it is decided to use his terminology in the conceptual model. If necessary, alias names can be created to allow other users to access the tables using terms they are familiar with. The director of Flight Operations' user view also includes several new attributes that needed to be added to the domain descriptions of the Flight_Day table.

Finally, the user view of the director of Flight Personnel was considered. Its effect on the database was quite straightforward. Two new entities, Staff and

Attribute Name	Data Type	Description/Domain	Nulls Allowed	Key Status
TABLE: AIRPORT				
Code	Char 3	Valid codes for airports served	No	Primary key
Location	Char 20	City name, State abbreviation	No	
Elevation	Integer	Altitude in feet of the Airport	Yes	
Phone	Char 12	Local Air West Phone # 999-999-9999	Yes	
TABLE: FLIGHT-SCHEDULE				
Flight_No	Integer	Unique 3 digit number > =1 and < =799	No	Primary key
Dep_Time	Time	Time of scheduled departure 0:00–24:00	No	
Arr_Time	Time	Time of scheduled arrival 0:00–24:00	No	
Meal	Char 1	Code for type of meal B, L, D, or S	Yes	
Base_Fare	Money	Base ticket price $10.00–$999.99	Yes	
TABLE: FLIGHT-DAY				
Flight_No	Integer	Valid 3 digit flight number	No	Concatenated primary key with Depart_Date. Foreign key to FLIGHT_SCHEDULE
Depart_Date	Date	Date of flight departure must be = > 01/01/87	No	Concatenated primary key with Flight_No.
Pass_Cnt	Integer	Number of passengers	Yes	
Depart_Time	Time	Time of actual departure	Yes	
Arrive_Time	Time	Time of actual arrival	Yes	
Fuel_Used	Integer	Fuel expended < = fuel capacity of assigned plane	Yes	
Status_Note	Char 80	Text note describing any unusual occurrences	Yes	
TABLE: TICKET				
Itinerary_No	Integer	Valid 5 digit itinerary code	No	Concatenated primary key with Flight_No. and Flight_Date. Foreign key to PASSENGER

FIGURE 5.19
Domain Descriptions for the Air West Database

Flight_Crew, and their attributes were added to the model. This user view did not cause any changes to previous entities or their domain descriptions.

At some point during the consolidation process, Alan Bond calls to say that he would like to see one more thing added to the database. He indicates that sometimes a need arises to record a note about special handling requirements for a particular reservation. For instance, a wheelchair might be required or small children might be traveling and need special services. Alan indicates that the best time to capture this information is when the reservation is made. There could be more than one note for a given reservation, but only about one reservation in 50 would require

Attribute Name	Data Type	Description/Domain	Nulls Allowed	Key Status
TABLE: TICKET				
Flight_No	Integer	Valid 3 digit flight number	No	Concatenated primary key with Flight_Date and Itinerary_No. Foreign key to FLIGHT_DAY with Flight_Date
Depart_Date	Date	Date of flight departure must be = > 01/01/87	No	Concatenated primary key with Flight_No. and Itinerary_No. Foreign key to FLIGHT_DAY with Flight_No.
Seat_No	Char 3	Assigned seat number. Must be a valid seat # for the type plane assigned and must not be assigned to any other ticket for the flight day	Yes	
TABLE: RESERVATION				
Confirm_No	Integer	Confirmation number. A unique 4 digit assigned code	No	Primary key
Res_Name	Char 20	Name of customer placing reservations	No	
Res_Date	Date	Date the reservations are placed. > = 1/1/97	No	
Res_Phone	Char 12	Phone number for person making reservations	Yes	
Res_Flight_No	Integer	Flight_No for the first ticket on this reservation	No	
Res_Depart_Date	Date	Date of the first ticket on this reservation	No	
TABLE: RESERVATION NOTES				
Confirm_No	Integer	4 digit confirmation number	No	Primary key and foreign key to RESERVATION
Note	Memo	Text description of special instructions related to a reservation	No	
TABLE: PASSENGER				
Pass_Name	Char 20	Name of passenger	No	
Itinerary_No	Integer	Itinerary number. A unique 5 digit assigned code	No	Primary key
TABLE: EQUIP_TYPE				
Equip_Type	Char 6	Unique valid equipment type description	No	Primary key
Seats	Integer	Seating capacity of this plane type. > 0, < 999	No	
Mfg	Char 3	Abbreviation for manufacturer name	No	
Fuel_Cap	Integer	Fuel capacity of plane in gallons > 0, < 10000	No	

FIGURE 5.19 (Cont.)
Domain Descriptions for the Air West Database

a note at all. However, fairly lengthy notes, up to several hundred characters, should be allowed. After considering these requirements, the designers decide that this note is a multivalued attribute of Reservation. Because this data cannot be stored in the Reservation table without violating first normal form, the designers decide to add a

Attribute Name	Data Type	Description/Domain	Nulls Allowed	Key Status
TABLE: EQUIPMENT				
Equip_No	Integer	Unique 4 digit equipment number	No	Primary key
Equip_Date	Date	Date this plane was received by Air West	Yes	
TABLE: SEAT				
Equip_Type	Char 6	Valid equipment type description	No	Concatenated primary key with Seat_No. Foreign key to Equip_Type
Seat_No	Char 3	Valid seat number for the associated plane type	No	Concatenated primary key with Equip_Type
TABLE: STAFF				
Staff_No	Char 11	Social security number of employee format 999-99-9999	No	Primary key
Staff_Name	Char 20	Name of employee	No	
Staff_Type	Char 2	Two character code for job type. Allowed values (s1, s2, s3, n1, n2, p1, p2, p3)	No	
Staff_Date	Date	The date this staff member was hired	Yes	
TABLE: COCKPIT_STAFF				
Staff_No	Char 11	Social security number of employee format 999-99-9999	No	Primary key
Phys_Date	Date	Date of last physical	Yes	
Certif_Date	Date	Date of last licensing certification	Yes	

FIGURE 5.19 (Cont.)
Domain Descriptions for the Air West Database

new entity called Reservation_Notes. This entity will have a one to many relationship with the Reservation entity and, of course, the relationship will be optional. This allows lengthy notes to be stored without slowing down the processing of the 98 percent of reservations that do not have notes.

CHECKING THE CONCEPTUAL MODEL FOR NORMALIZATION

Once consolidation of user views was completed, it was time to check the conceptual model for conformity to normalization rules. You should have noticed that Ann and Bob considered normalization issues both implicitly and explicitly while developing the models of the individual user views. Because they did their work well and the scope of this database is relatively small, it appears that no normalization problems remain. At least Ann and Bob have not been able to find any. After this final

Attribute Name	Data Type	Description/Domain	Nulls Allowed	Key Status
TABLE: FLT_ATTENDANT				
Staff_No	Char 11	Social security number of employee format 999-99-9999	No	Primary key
CPR_Cert	Char 3	Certified in advanced CPR techniques. Values (Yes or No)	Yes	
Sponsor_No	Char 11	Social security number of employee's sponsor	No	Intra-Table Linking attrib.
TABLE: FLIGHT_CREW				
Flight_No	Integer	Valid 3 digit flight number	No	Concatenated primary key with Depart_Date and Staff_No. Foreign key to FLIGHT_DAY with Flight_Date.
Depart_Date	Date	Date of flight departure must be = > 01/01/87	No	Concatenated primary key with Staff_No. and Flight_No. Foreign key to FLIGHT_DAY with Flight_No.
Staff_No	Char 11	Staff ID number (social security number)	No	Concatenated primary key with Flight_No. and Flight_Date. Foreign key to STAFF
Work_Hrs	Num. (4.1)	Scheduled work hours for this worker on this flight date		

FIGURE 5.19 (Cont.)
Domain Descriptions for the Air West Database

check, the structure of the conceptual model was approved by the steering committee. It was now time to move the project forward to the stage of creating and implementing the physical database model.

USE OF CASE TOOLS

As we noted earlier, CASE tools are often used in the process of gathering and consolidating user views of a database. Virtually all CASE software includes some form of E-R diagramming tool. Typically, a visual point-and-click interface is provided. The designer can create and manipulate entity and relationship objects to produce an E-R diagram. Figure 5.20 shows an E-R diagram for the Airline database that was produced using the integrated CASE tool IEF. To produce more detailed specifications of the attributes of an entity, the user simply selects the desired entity—usually by moving the cursor on to the entity and clicking on its image. Options for specifying detailed information for the entity then appear. The user might then specify the name of each attribute of the entity. Figure 5.21 illustrates this for the IEF tool.

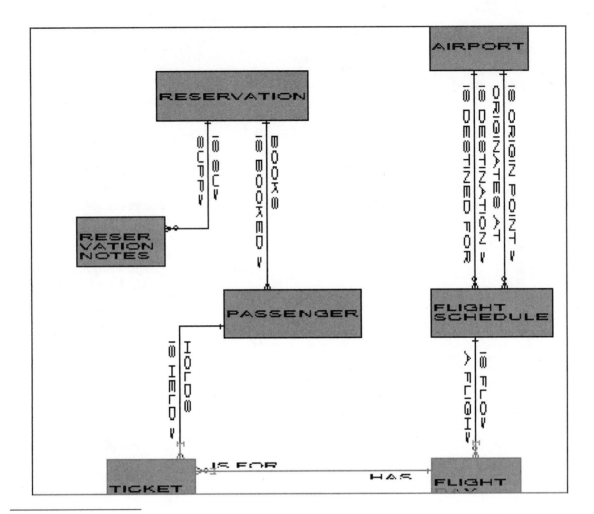

FIGURE 5.20
E-R Diagram of the Air
West Airline Database
Developed Using a
CASE Tool

Information about each attribute, such as its data type or a list of allowed values, might be added by moving to a still greater level of detail. The user would select the desired attribute and options for specifying detailed information about that attribute would appear (see Figure 5.22).

The same sort of process can be used to retrieve stored specifications. A user can begin by looking at an E-R diagram for the entire database. The user then can click on a particular entity he or she is interested in and see additional details. If a user wants still more detailed information about an attribute, he or she can click on it. These sets of related diagrams are called *hyper-diagrams* and are a key feature of CASE tools. These hyper-diagrams greatly facilitate the coordination of large-scale design projects, because related diagrams are automatically linked. The tools often contain consistency checks that can be used to ensure that all the pieces fit together.

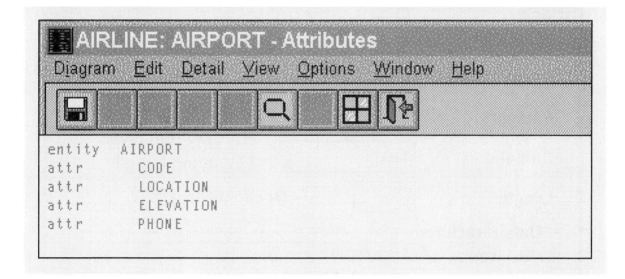

FIGURE 5.21
Attribute List Screen
for the AIRPORT Entity
Developed Using a
CASE Tool

CASE tools normally do not support the development of independent views and consolidation of those views. Rather, they support the development of a single, overall conceptual model. Designers may continue to sketch information about individual user views in manual form and introduce the CASE tool at the stage of producing the consolidated conceptual model. More often, however, the CASE tool will be used throughout the requirement gathering process. The user group considered most central to the project (probably the Reservations Department in our case) would be interviewed first. Their view of the database would be recorded in the CASE tool. Then, as other groups were interviewed, incremental changes to the model would be made as needed to arrive at the overall conceptual model.

Use of CASE tools from the beginning of the conceptual design process allows the designer to gain the full benefit of the tools' ability to coordinate the process. However, something is lost in using this process. User view specifications are important to the data administrator when it is time to specify access rights for users. Also, the perspective involved in producing individual user views and then consolidating them is different from that involved in folding each user view into an existing tentative conceptual model.

The various CASE tools represent E-R diagrams and attribute domain specifications in slightly different ways. For example, IEF does not use the diamond symbol for relationships. Any line connecting two entities specifies a relationship, and the relationship must be named in both directions. Also, IEF absolutely prohibits the specification of foreign key attributes in the attribute list for an entity. This occurs because IEF automatically generates the data definition language commands to implement the database once its design is completed. If the DBMS selected is a relational one, foreign key attributes are automatically added by IEF.

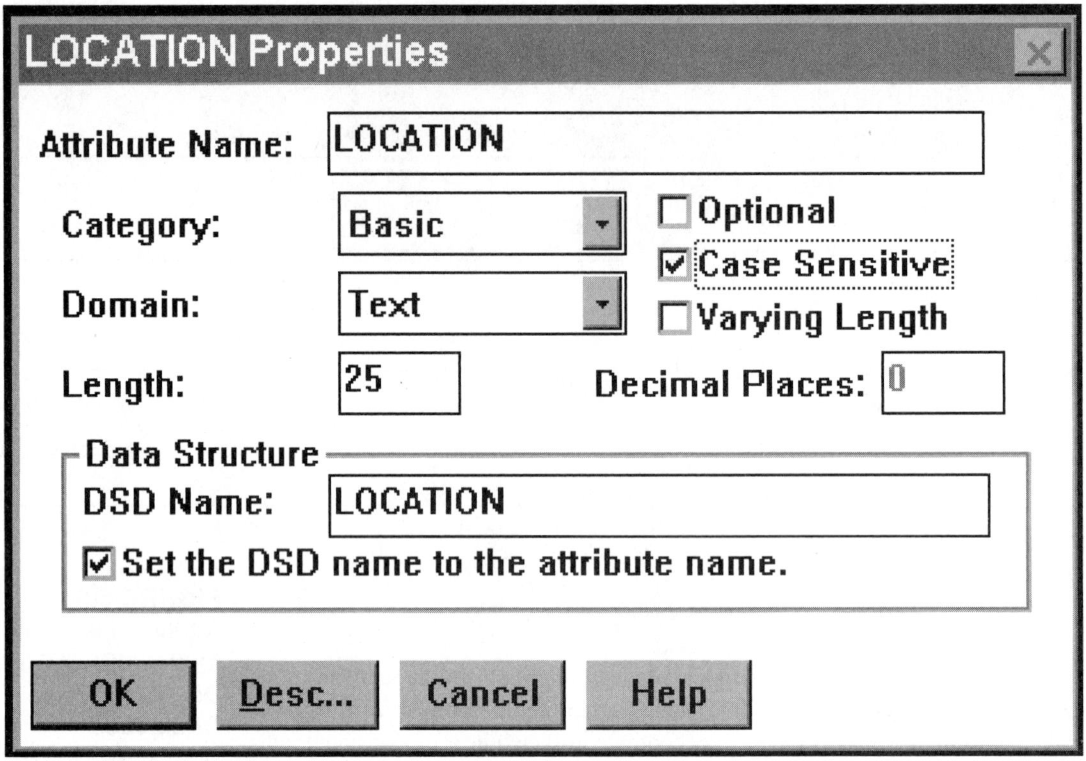

FIGURE 5.22
Detailed Specifications
for the LOCATION
Attribute Developed
Using a CASE Tool

CLIENT/SERVER OPTIONS FOR THE AIR WEST DATABASE

As we indicated in Chapter 4, conceptual database design is unaffected by issues of where data or applications are to reside. The conceptual design simply indicates what data are required and the logical relationships among data elements. However, information from the users of the system is very important in determining where various system resources should be placed, and this information is normally gathered at the same time that information requirements are generated.

As we gathered requirements from Air West's users, we also collected information about the nature of the processes performed by these users and the locations where those processes were performed. For example, we found that the vice-president of Marketing performs processes that require ad hoc access to data. Her processes are unique and are needed only at a single location, the PC in her office. She is familiar with the Access database package. Access can readily support her application needs, but is not designed to operate as the database server for a multiuser system of the magnitude required by the Air West database. Thus, her processing needs are a good candidate for implementation as a client-side application, using Access, in a client-server system.

The processing requirements of the director of Flight Operations are similar to those of the vice-president of Marketing. Again, processes are required at only a single site and a good interface is needed for ad hoc querying. Access is again a good candidate to provide client-side applications to meet this user's needs. The user's desire to continue to perform certain types of analysis on a spreadsheet could easily be accommodated via the interfaces Access provides to common spreadsheet packages.[1]

The processes required by the director of Flight Scheduling are needed only at a single site, her office. She does not have any familiarity with a database package nor does she have any special needs for ad hoc querying of the database. Her processes could be supported by applications residing either on the server or on her client station, and any of a great variety of database or application generator software packages could be used to develop the applications she requires.

The reservation handling processes of the Air West database are the most crucial to its efficient operation. Reservation processes need to be performed from each airport Air West serves. The processing required is routine and identical across all sites. These processing requirements could be supported by applications residing either on the server or on client computers. If reservation applications are to reside on client systems, those applications and the supporting software will need to be maintained on numerous machines in a variety of locations. Accordingly, because this is clearly the highest volume application in the Air West database, locating the reservation applications on client machines would substantially reduce the load on the database server.

Issues beyond user requirements will be crucial in the decision of where to place the reservation applications. If these applications are placed on client systems, how much money will be saved on the purchase and operating cost of the server, and how much additional expense will be incurred in purchasing and operating the client systems? How much expertise does the IS staff need to support each type of system? How will system performance be affected by alternative placements of this high-volume application? All these issues should be addressed in determining where to place the reservation applications.

Because 70 percent of all reservations are handled at the corporate offices, Phoenix is a likely location for the database server and the reservation applications. The DBMS package used for the server might be Oracle, DB2, or any of a number of similar DBMSs.

SUMMARY

In this chapter we have described the conceptual design process as it might have been performed for a small-scale Airline database. The intent of this example case was to describe the processes used. Our database was deliberately oversimplified. In

---

[1]Similar capabilities could be provided through most PC database packages; Access was chosen here because the users have some familiarity with it or with related products.

addition, we did not describe all aspects of the design process that were occurring. Our focus was on the database-oriented aspects of the design.

Our case illustrated the major steps of conceptual database design. User views were collected through interviews with the principal users of the database. The questions asked were designed to elicit the basic entity, attribute, and relationship structures in each user's data and to ascertain the logical restrictions on the domains of attributes. The designers applied normalization concepts as they assembled the set of entities and relationships reflecting each user's view. Once all the user views had been collected and modeled, the designers consolidated them. They started with the user view having the broadest scope and then folded-in successive user views, making additions and changes as needed and resolving any conflicts found among user views. When the consolidation was complete, they checked their conceptual model for normalization before accepting it as final.

CASE tools are frequently used in the conceptual design process. The connected hyper-diagrams produced by CASE tools can be a great aid in coordination of the design process. Where CASE tools are used, the conceptual design is often developed incrementally, beginning with specifications for a key user.

Because this chapter deals with the application of concepts described earlier, many of the following terms were defined in earlier chapters.

REVIEW QUIZ

_____ Two or more attributes that together uniquely identify an occurrence of a table.

_____ Sets of interconnected diagrams produced by a CASE tool.

_____ There must be at least one PASSENGER associated with each RESERVATION.

_____ A set of specifications that defines an individual's perception of a database.

_____ An entity that resolves a many to many relationship between two other entities.

_____ A model representing the structure of a database in a form that is independent of physical structures required for implementation.

_____ A process that adjusts data structures to minimize the risk of anomalies.

_____ Character, integer, date.

_____ The process of gathering information from users describing the information they need from a database system.

_____ For each FLIGHT-DAY there may be many TICKETS, but each TICKET is associated with only one FLIGHT-DAY.

_____ Indicates that an attribute has not yet been assigned a value.

_____ The range of values that can validly be assigned to an attribute.

_____ An attribute whose value can be determined from the values of other attributes.

_____ The process of integrating user views into an overall conceptual data model.

1. Intersection entity
2. Null
3. Concatenated key
4. Normalization
5. Hyper-diagrams
6. Consolidation
7. Domain
8. User view
9. Derived attribute
10. Requirements analysis
11. Mandatory relationship
12. Conceptual model
13. One to many relationship
14. Data type

1. Identify an example of each of the following in the specifications of the Airline database:
   a. A mandatory relationship
   b. An optional relationship
   c. A one to many relationship
   d. A one to one relationship

REVIEW QUESTIONS AND EXERCISES

2. In the chapter, it was noted that the attribute Passenger_Cnt is actually a derived attribute. What does this mean? Describe the alternative ways in which passenger count information might be provided to users.

3. Describe the role of normalization in the process of developing a conceptual model. Cite examples where normalization rules were explicitly or implicitly used in developing the conceptual model of the Airline database.

4. What determines whether an attribute should be allowed to have a null value? Use examples from the Airline database to illustrate when nulls should be allowed and when they should not.

5. Why are foreign key attributes normally not included in the lists of attributes of entities during conceptual modeling? When might you want to include a foreign key attribute?

6. Briefly describe the process of consolidating user views.

7. When would an attribute that appears in some user's view of a database not appear in the conceptual model of the database?

8. What do we mean by the term *hyper-diagram?* How do CASE tools utilize hyper-diagrams and what advantages do they provide to designers and users?

9. How does the use of CASE tools affect the process of requirements analysis and conceptual data model creation?

10. What is the purpose of a user view?

11. Suppose you have been assigned to perform a data requirements analysis and are preparing to conduct an interview with a user. Prepare a list of questions that you would ask in the interview.

12. The following set of data represents a sample of the types of data used by a clerk in a library. The clerk also indicates that there can be borrowers who do not have a book checked out and books that have not yet been checked out. All other relationships are mandatory. Draw an E-R diagram and a set of domain descriptions for this user view.

CHECK OUT

Borrower Number	Borrower Name	Book Number	Out Date	Book Title	Book Returned	Author's Name	Author Living
3652	Smith	HG18	9/12/97	Clouds	Yes	D. Drone	Yes
2854	Jones	LB87	9/15/97	I See C	Yes	C. Clay	No
4723	Brown	XR22	9/18/97	Birds	No	D. Drone	Yes
3652	Smith	HG18	9/23/97	Clouds	No	D. Drone	Yes
4723	Brown	LA07	9/25/97	Zen	Yes	M. Bush	Yes
3113	Jones	LB87	9/28/97	I See C	No	C. Clay	No

13. Based on the following document and description, create an appropriate E-R diagram and set of domain descriptions for the data of this user view.

> ***Registration clerk:*** I produce the class schedule report you see here. Each student is sent a copy of his/her class schedule. Some restrictions that may not be obvious from the sample data should be noted. The advisor assigned to a student must be a professor in the department in which the student is majoring (a CIS major must be advised by a CIS professor). Course numbers consist of a three-digit alphabetic prefix followed by three numeric digits. The alphabetic prefix must correspond to a valid department code.

```
ABC UNIVERSITY CLASS SCHEDULE
      Student Name: Joe Smith                       Major: CIS
      Student ID#: 468351212                        Advisor: Dr. Brown
                                              Advisor's Office #: CBA 234
```

Course #	Section #	Description	Time	Room
CIS345	01	Data Base 1	2:20 TTH	CBA 203
CIS360	01	Mgt. Info. Sys.	8:00 TTH	CBA 205
ACC255	02	Intro. to Acc.	9:35 TTH	CBA 103

```
      Student Name: Jack Jones                      Major: MGT
      Student ID#: 413828164                        Advisor: Dr. Jarrett
                                              Advisor's Office #: CBA 253
```

Course #	Section #	Description	Time	Room
CIS360	02	Mgt. Info. Sys.	9:35 TTH	CBA 206
ACC255	01	Intro. to Acc.	8:00 TTH	CBA 104

```
      Student Name: Al Evans                        Major: CIS
      Student ID#: 153229831                        Advisor: Dr. Brown
                                              Advisor's Office #: CBA 234
```

Course #	Section #	Description	Time	Room
CIS345	01	Data Base 1	2:20 TTH	CBA 203
CIS360	01	Mgt. Info. Sys.	8:00 TTH	CBA 205

14. The assistant dean at ABC University has been using a spreadsheet to maintain information for class scheduling. A portion of the spreadsheet follows. Based on the sample data shown, create an appropriate E-R diagram and set of domain descriptions for the assistant dean's user view.

Course No.	Course Description	Sect. No.	Time	Professor's Name	Office#	Room No.	Room Capacity	Equipment
CIS120	Intro. to CIS	01	TTH 8:00	Eirich	CBA272	CBA200	190	PC, VDT, Proj.
CIS120	Intro. to CIS	02	MWF 8:00	Eirich	CBA272	CBA200	190	PC, VDT, Proj.
CIS120	Intro. to CIS	03	TTH 9:35	Bosse	CBA260	CBA205	60	VDT, Proj.
CIS221	COBOL	01	MWF 8:00	Bosse	CBA260	CBA104	40	Proj.
CIS221	COBOL	02	MWF 11:10	Neal	CBA228	CBA204	60	PC, VDT
CIS345	Data Base I	01	TTH 9:35	Morgan	CBA218	CBA206	35	Proj.
CIS345	Data Base I	02	TTH 4:00	Morgan	CBA218	CBA204	60	PC, VDT

15. Consolidate the user views of registration data at ABC University presented in the two previous questions, generating a conceptual model including an E-R diagram and a set of domain descriptions.

16. Three user views of XYZ Company personnel data follow. Based on the documents and descriptions provided (a) draw an appropriate E-R diagram and set of domain descriptions for each user view (making sure that your entities are in at least third normal form) and (b) consolidate the user views to create a conceptual model (E-R diagram and domain descriptions) for XYZ Company's personnel database.

View One

Payroll clerk: Data for hours worked are taken from daily time sheets and recorded in computerized form on a weekly basis. Wage rates are uniform for each employee class and are set by management. I produce the following report each week:

XYZ COMPANY PAY REPORT
Week of: 9/21/97

Emp. #	Emp. Name	Hours Worked	Emp. Class	Wage Rate	Gross Pay
110	Jones	40	2	6.00	240.00
120	Smith	48	1	5.00	260.00
130	Alda	40	2	6.00	240.00
140	Bates	40	1	5.00	200.00
150	Adams	32	3	7.00	224.00

View Two

Production manager: I would like to be able to have a report showing the hours worked by each employee and total hours worked for each department on a daily basis, for example:

```
DAILY WORK REPORT
9/18/97
        Dept.              Emp.              Hours
                           Name              Worked
       ─────────────────────────────────────────────
        Processing         Bates               8
                           Jones               6
                           Alda                8

        Dept. Total                            22


        Packing            Smith               8
                           Adams               6

        Dept. Total                            14


        Grand Total                            36
```

View Three

Department supervisor: All department supervisors use the following form for annual evaluations. This data should be maintained in the database.

```
XYZ COMPANY EMPLOYEE
Annual Evaluation, 1996
Department: Packing
Supervisor #: 150
Supervisor Name: Jones

Effectiveness Rating

        Category                  Rating
       ───────────────────────────────────
        Reliability                 G
        Attention to deadline       O
        Sensitivity                 O
        Creativity                  A
```

17. Identify an individual who is a user of an information system. Interview that person and create an E-R diagram and set of domain descriptions for the data required by your user.

INTRODUCTION TO RELATIONAL TABLES AND SQL RETRIEVAL

6

RELATIONAL TABLES AND SQL

LEARNING OBJECTIVES

After completing this chapter, you should be able to

- Construct SQL SELECT statements to select data from relational tables using the following constructs:

  a. using simple relational operators such as =, <, and >.

  b. using special operators such as "like," and "between."

  c. using compound conditions to select data from selected rows.

  d. selecting data using joins.

  e. summarized data using group by operations.

  f. sequencing the output.

  g. using functions to calculate data.

  h. using functions to do data arithmetic.

  i. using functions to do string manipulations.

  j. create views.

  k. using simple subselects.

INTRODUCTION

The ability to access and retrieve selected data from a file or a set of related files is a central function of database management systems. Most database management systems developed today are relational. A common language used for data retrieval is **SQL (Structured Query Language).** Relational database management systems consist of related files called *tables*. The tables are related by primary key values. For example, a row of data in one table can be connected to a row of data in another table if both rows have the same social security number. In this chapter we will look at the fundamental elements of using SQL to retrieve data. The chapter is organized into two parts. The first section covers the structure of tables in any relational database system and discusses examples of introductory SQL. The second section includes examples of advanced SQL. The sections are designed so they can be used at any point in the database course. The first section can be used early in the course so you can work with database tables as you learn database design. The second section can be used in parts with other chapters as they are needed to build more advanced applications.

SQL (Structured Query Language)
A language that is used in relational databases to build and query tables.

Introductory SQL is easy to learn. However, SQL can become complex when you start to structure real-world questions for a database. It is important for you to think about real questions that support the day-to-day needs of a database. What information would various users at different levels of the organization need from the database in order to effectively do their jobs? You need to put yourself in the shoes of a manager or the operations person who deals with the customers, and pose real-world requests in a language they understand (English). Develop a list of various questions and requests for information from the database, and then work on converting these requests into SQL. The purpose of this chapter is to help you develop SQL queries that will support information requests by giving you various examples.

RELATIONAL DATABASE SYSTEMS

SQL is the query language used by most relational database management systems (DBMSs). We will emphasize the relational model in this chapter and throughout the majority of this book for three reasons: (1) The relational model is generally easier for beginning students to grasp, (2) many concepts associated with the relational model are often closely tied to general database design concepts, and (3) the relational model is the database structure that organizations are using to develop client-server applications into the next century.

DB2
A relational database system that is supplied by IBM and is used on various IBM platforms, including the large mainframes, OS/2 servers, and UNIX-based platforms.

Examples of relational database systems that run on large IBM mainframes are IBM's DB2 and SQL/DS. **DB2** and SQL/DS (recently renamed by IBM to DB2 for VSE and VM) are basically the same, except that they run under different operation systems. Digital Equipment Corporation (DEC) has a relational database called Rdb/VMS that runs on their VAX systems. Other popular relational database systems that run on various computer platforms are Oracle, Sybase, Ingres, and Informix.

XDB
A relational database system that has the look and feel of DB2 and that was originally built to support application development on the PC platform for applications that run on mainframe platforms using DB2.

The personal computer (PC) environment has had relational-oriented (table-based) databases for several years. Examples include the dBASE and Paradox products from Borland International, and the R:Base products from Microrim. The power of the PC workstation today makes it possible to run powerful relational databases that have all the functionality of those that run on the mainframe. Examples include Informix, Ingres, Oracle, Sybase, and XDB. **XDB** was originally developed as a DB2 clone to support PC-based workstation development of COBOL/DB2 applications that are run on IBM mainframes. The SQL illustrations used in this chapter were developed using XDB and will be referred to as DB2/XDB. These SQL illustrations show variations, when necessary, between Access, DB2/XDB, and Oracle. Many extensions to ANSI SQL will be illustrated because ANSI SQL is minimal, and most implementations of SQL go beyond ANSI SQL. DB2/XDB SQL has become a de facto standard.

HISTORY OF RELATIONAL DATABASE DEVELOPMENT

Relational database activity began with an article by Dr. E. F. "Ted" Codd titled "A Relational Model of Data for Large Shared Data Banks" in *Communications of the*

Association for Computing Machinery (1970). Dr. Codd worked in the IBM research laboratories. This work was a catalyst for projects to develop relational-type databases at a number of companies. IBM began with a project called System/R, which spawned a query language called SEQUEL (Structured English Query Language). IBM allowed customer sites to experiment with the database engine and the query language starting in 1978. **ORACLE** introduced their first relational database product in 1979, and Ingres was introduced in 1981. IBM delivered SQL/DS for VM/CMS operating systems in 1982 and DB2 for MVS operating systems in 1983. Oracle and Ingres were the first commercial systems working on mini-computers. DB2 was the first commercial database system to work on IBM mainframes. **Sybase** introduced their database system in 1986. One advantage of these database systems was the ability to have users construct ad hoc queries using the SQL language. The **ANSI** SQL standards committee was formed in 1982, and the first standard for SQL was set in 1986. SQL-86 was superseded by SQL-89 and later by SQL-92. [ANSI x3.135–1992] There tends to be some variation from the standard in all the leading database systems. DB2 tends to be a leading force in the industry and somewhat of a de facto standard for SQL. The main variations from the standard are in the definition of data types and the ways other software interacts with SQL.

ORACLE
A relational database system supplied by Oracle that runs on various platforms, including IBM mainframes, UNIX platforms, and various PC-based servers running OS/2, NT, and Windows.

Sybase
A relational database system supplied by Sybase that runs on IBM mainframes, UNIX platforms, and various PC-based servers.

ANSI (American National Standards Institute)
A U.S. government organization that defines standards used in all professions.

RELATIONAL DATABASE STRUCTURE

Relational databases are made up of data tables, index tables, and dictionary tables, which are often referred to as *database objects.* Other objects such as form definitions, report definitions, and query language definitions are also stored in tables and can be a part of the database management system. Most database management systems use database tables to store the definitions of the database, forms, reports, and queries. Let's look at some of these objects in more detail.

DATA TABLES

Two-dimensional data tables are the storage mechanism of a relational database system. All other tables are in the database to support the definition, storage, maintenance, and retrieval of the data stored in these two-dimensional tables. The two dimensions of the table are referred to as *rows* and *columns.* The rows of the table are equivalent to records, and the columns of the table are equivalent to fields. Tables are also referred to as files, or **relations.** The relational terminology equivalent to *table* is *relation, row* is **tuple** and *column* is **attribute.** A table consists of a table name, a unique column name for each column, and a data definition for each column. Data definitions specify data type and length when not predefined by the data type.

Relation
Relational terminology that means the same as *table.*

Tuple
Relational terminology for a row in a table.

Attribute
Relational terminology for a column of a table.

Related Terminology

1. File	Table	Relation
2. Record	Row	Tuple
3. Field	Column	Attribute

ANSI DATA TYPES

The ANSI data types include character for text data; integer and small integer for whole numbers; numeric or decimal for decimal data; and real, float, or double precision for scientific numeric data. The specific ANSI standard format is shown in the following table:

ANSI Data Types

TEXT DATA
      CHAR(len)
      CHARACTER(len)
WHOLE NUMBERS
      INTEGER or INT
      SMALLINT
PRECISE DECIMAL DATA
      NUMERIC(precision,scale)
      DECIMAL(precision,scale) OR DEC(precision,scale)
SCIENTIFIC DATA
      FLOAT(precision)
      REAL
      DOUBLE PRECISION

DATA TYPE VARIATIONS

Common variations from these standard data types include DATE and TIME, MONEY or CURRENCY, VARCHAR, LONG VARCHAR, and LOGICAL. The table below and at the bottom of page 201 shows data type variations between DB2, Oracle, and Access. XDB is a DB2 clone that runs on PC platforms. All the illustrations for DB2 in this chapter were done using XDB, and all references will be shown as DB2/XDB.

Data Type Variations

DATA TYPE	DB2/XDB	ORACLE	ACCESS
Character(fixed)	CHARACTER(n)	CHAR(n)	TEXT
Character(variable)	VARCHAR(n)	VARCHAR(n)	
Long Text	LONG VARCHAR	LONG	MEMO
		LONG VARCHAR	
Integer	SMALLINT	SMALLINT	
	INTEGER	INTEGER	INTEGER
		LONG	LONG INTEGER
Decimal	DECIMAL(p,s)	DECIMAL(p,s)	CURRENCY
Money		NUMBER(p,s)	
Floating Point	FLOAT(n)FLOAT(n)	NUMBER(p,s)	SINGLE

DATABASE NAMES

The ANSI SQL standard specifies names for tables, columns, and users. Specific implementations of SQL include names for other objects such as primary key and foreign key relationships, stored procedures, forms, and reports. The ANSI SQL standard name is one to eighteen characters, with no special punctuation characters. The first character must be a letter. Qualification names are separated by a dot or period. USER10.FLIGHT.FLIGHT_NO would refer to the FLIGHT_NO column in the FLIGHT table owned by user USER10. Database names are normally not case sensitive to database installations. The names for tables and columns are often shown using the following notation:

> flight (<u>flight_no,</u> orig, dest, orig_time, dest_time, meal, fare)

where flight is the name of the table and the names in parentheses are the column names. We will refer to this structure as a *relational diagram,* or *relational notation.* Multi-word names cannot be separated by a blank and are normally separated by an underscore. The underlined column or columns identify the primary key for the table. In this example, flight_no is a unique value in each row of the table. A graphical representation of this table would be as follows:

flight

flight_no	orig	dest	orig_time	dest_time	meal	fare

The graphical representation is often used by database systems to allow users to interact with the database system to view table contents. Users can select the columns desired along with selection criteria. This is referred to as Query by Example (QBE) and is discussed later in this chapter.

DATA TABLE EXAMPLE

A table of flight data as defined above would have a row for each flight flown by a particular airline. A flight is normally defined as a trip from an origination airport to a destination airport. The data in each row would be the flight number, origination airport, origination time, destination airport, destination time, a meal code designation,

	Data Type Variations (continued)		
DATA TYPE	**DB2/XDB**	**ORACLE**	**ACCESS**
	REAL	REAL	
	DOUBLE PRECISION		DOUBLE
Date/Time	DATE	DATE	DATE/TIME
	TIME		
	TIMESTAMP		
Logical			YES/NO
Binary		RAW	OLE Object
		LONG RAW	

FIGURE 6.1
Flight Data Table

Definition: flight (<u>flight_no</u>, orig, dest, orig_time, dest_time, meal, fare)
Table Data:

FLIGHT_NO	ORIG	DEST	ORIG_TIME	DEST_TIME	MEAL	FARE
101	FLG	PHX	07:00:00	08:05:00	S	48.50
102	PHX	MSP	09:00:00	01:00:00	L	156.00
103	MSP	PHX	17:00:00	19:15:00	D	156.00
104	PHX	FLG	20:30:00	21:15:00	S	48.50
15	PHX	LAX	07:00:00	08:20:00	B	49.00
17	PHX	LAX	08:20:00	09:20:00	B	79.00
31	PHX	LAX	17:55:00	19:10:00	S	49.00
33	PHX	LAX	18:55:00	19:15:00	S	49.00
35	PHX	LAX	20:20:00	21:40:00	S	49.00
329	LAX	PHX	21:10:00	23:59:00		49.00
40	PHX	LAX	22:25:00	23:42:00		49.00
694	LAX	PHX	07:40:00	08:55:00		79.00
434	LAX	PHX	08:50:00	10:44:00		49.00
400	LAX	PHX	10:10:00	11:26:00		49.00
600	PHX	SFO	06:46:00	08:50:00	B	109.00
604	PHX	SFO	08:33:00	10:43:00	B	109.00
606	PHX	SFO	11:45:00	13:50:00	L	109.00
60	PHX	SFO	17:45:00	18:36:00	S	139.00
202	SFO	PHX	07:00:00	08:55:00	B	79.00
691	SFO	PHX	11:25:00	13:24:00		109.00
518	SFO	PHX	14:23:00	16:16:00		109.00
1260	SFO	PHX	17:58:00	19:51:00	D	109.00

and the fares for that flight. An example of the table definition and some sample data for this table are shown above in Figure 6.1.

CONSTANTS

Constants in SQL statements include numeric, string, date, and time. Numeric constants are digits with the decimal point and sign or floating point format with the exponent notation of E.

Numeric Examples:

45
5.6
–3.5
1.7E5
–1.53789   –E8

String constants are enclosed in single quotes. The string can include any characters, including a single quote. The single quote is included by inserting a single quote twice at the point of the quote or apostrophe. The word 'don't' in quotes requires two quotes between the 'n' and the 't'.

String Examples:

'Apple 123'
'12–23–94'
'don''t'

DATE and TIME constants are not covered by a SQL standard and vary considerably among database implementations. In most implementations, the format can be selected at installation as American, European, Japanese, or ISO. The American date format is 12/23/2001 and the American time format is 10:40 AM. There is also a timestamp format that includes both the date and the time down to nanoseconds in descending sequence, such as 2001-12-23-13.51.09.123456.

NULLS

A **null value** is represented by a special character stored in any column of any row where no data has ever been entered. This means that there is a difference between no data and blank data (i.e., spaces for character fields and zeros for numeric fields). In SQL you can select the rows with a null value in a specific column as follows:

```
SELECT * FROM flight where meal is NULL
```

Also, SQL will skip rows with NULL values when you are doing averages on a particular column. A null value will not figure into the average, whereas a zero value will.

Null value, null character A special character representation in the database that represents a null value to all operations in that database system.

INDEXES

Index tables are used to speed up the process of looking for specific rows in the data tables. Indexes serve the same purpose as indexes in books. For example, the FLIGHT table would typically be indexed on FLIGHT_NO to speed up the process of finding data on a specific flight. FLIGHT could also be indexed on ORIG to increase the speed of finding all flights originating from a specific airport. FLIGHT_NO is referred to as a *primary index* because FLIGHT_NO is a unique identifier of a row. This means no two rows in the table contain the same FLIGHT_NO value. The index on ORIG is referred to as a *secondary index* because one or more rows in the table can have the same origination airport. A table can have one primary index and multiple secondary indexes.

DICTIONARY TABLES

Dictionary tables are used to store the definitions of all the other tables in the database. For example, the SYSCOLS table is used by XDB and DB2 to store the column names and their related table names for all the columns that have been defined in that database system. The table names used for the storage of dictionary tables varies substantially across alternative relational DBMS packages. However, with the exception of a few PC-based products, all relational DBMSs do use dictionary tables to store data dictionary information.

KEYS

Keys are identifiers that locate specific rows in a table. An identifier can be made up of one or more columns (fields). A primary key is a unique identifier meaning that no two rows in the table can have the same value in the column(s) designated as the primary key. A secondary key is an identifier (one or more columns) that may or may not be unique within a table. Secondary keys can be used to relate rows of one table to another table. In this case they are referred to as foreign keys.

Key Example: The FLIGHT_NO is a unique identifier of each row in the FLIGHT table (Figure 6.1). It can be used as the primary key. Airport CODE could be a primary key for an AIRPORT table containing data about that airport, such as the airport name, city, elevation, phone number, and other airport-related data. An example of the AIRPORT table is shown in Figure 6.2.

ORIG, which is the origination airport code in the FLIGHT table can be set up as a foreign key index to make it easy to link data in the FLIGHT table with data in the AIRPORT table. This would make the ORIG airport code a foreign key in the

FIGURE 6.2
Airport Data Table

Definition: airport (<u>code</u>, location, elevation, phone)
Table Data:

Code	Location	Elevation	Phone
FLG	Flagstaff, AZ	6920	602-774-1897
PHX	Phoenix, AZ	1257	602-583-1971
MSP	Minneapolis, MN	862	612-378-2910
LAX	Los Angeles, CA	37	310-273-1846
SFO	San Francisco, CA	78	415-839-9237

FIGURE 6.3
Table Structure
Diagrams for the
Airport Sample
Database

• flight (<u>flight_no</u>, orig, dest, orig_time, dest_time, meal, fare)

ticket (<u>itinerary_no</u>, flight_no, flight_date, seat)

passenger (pass_name, itinerary_no, fare, <u>confirm_no</u>)

airport (<u>code</u>, location, elevation, phone)

FLIGHT table linked to airport CODE as a primary key in the AIRPORT table. The DEST airport code in the FLIGHT table is also a foreign key linked to the airport CODE in the AIRPORT table. ORIG, DEST, and CODE all have the same range of values, which is referred to as the domain for these attributes.

A SIMPLE AIRLINE DATABASE EXAMPLE

The airline industry provides many interesting applications for developing database examples. Most of you have had some experience with using airlines and should be able to identify with these examples. We will be using a very simple database design for most of the examples in this chapter. The design of the complete airline database is presented in Chapter 5, and is used throughout the succeeding chapters. For now we will be working with a very simple database consisting of only four tables: FLIGHT, TICKET, PASSENGER, and AIRPORT. We have already discussed the FLIGHT and AIRPORT tables. All four tables are described in the table structure diagrams and data dictionary reports in Figures 6.3 and 6.4.

FIGURE 6.4
Data Dictionary Report

TABLE NAME:	FLIGHT		TABLE SIZE:	1026 bytes
RECORD OVERHEAD:	13 bytes		LAST UPDATE:	01/30/97
RECORD LENGTH:	38 bytes		NO. OF FIELDS:	7
TABLE TYPE:	Regular		CREATOR:	PUBLIC
FIELD NAME	DATE TYPE	NULL?	INDEX	UNIQUE
FLIGHT_NO	smallint	no	FIDX	yes
ORIG	char (3)	no	origx	no
DEST	char (3)	no	destx	no
ORIG_TIME	time	yes		
DEST-TIME	time	yes		
MEAL	char (1)	yes		
FARE	money	def		

TABLE NAME:	TICKET		TABLE SIZE:	432 bytes
RECORD OVERHEAD:	9 bytes		LAST UPDATE:	01/12/97
RECORD LENGTH:	24 bytes		NO. OF FIELDS:	4
TABLE TYPE:	Regular		CREATOR:	PUBLIC
FIELD NAME	DATA TYPE	NULL?	INDEX	
ITINERARY_NO	integer	no		
FLIGHT_NO	smallint	no		
FLIGHT_DATE	date	no		
SEAT	char (3)	yes		

TABLE NAME:	PASSENGER	TABLE SIZE:	1360 bytes
RECORD OVERHEAD:	10 bytes	LAST UPDATE:	06/02/97
RECORD LENGTH:	46 bytes	NO. OF FIELDS:	4
TABLE TYPE:	Regular	CREATOR:	PUBLIC

FIELD NAME	DATA TYPE	NULL?	INDEX	UNIQUE
pass_name	var char (20)	yes		
itinerary_no	integer	no	itinpkey	yes
fare	money	yes		
confirm_no	integer	no	confmfk	no

TABLE NAME:	AIRPORT	TABLE SIZE:	230 bytes	
RECORD OVERHEAD:	9 bytes	LAST UPDATE:	07/07/1997	
RECORD LENGTH:	46 bytes	NO. OF FIELDS:	4	
TABLE TYPE:	Regular	CREATOR:	PUBLIC CHECK OPTION:	no

FIELD NAME	DATA TYPE	NULL?	INDEX	UNIQUE
code	char (3)	no	codekey	yes
location	char (20)	yes		
elevation	smallint	yes		
phone	char (12)	yes		

FIGURE 6.4 (Cont.)
Data Dictionary Report

Figure 6.5 is a diagram of the relationships between the tables. As we have seen, the values of CODE in the AIRPORT table correspond to values in both the ORIG and DEST columns in the FLIGHT table. Each FLIGHT record has only one origination airport and one destination airport. However, each airport can be the origination and destination point for many other flights. Access shows the AIRPORT table twice in the relationship diagram to reflect the two relationships to airport CODE. The table is in the database only once.

For each FLIGHT there can be many associated tickets. Flight_no is the primary key of the FLIGHT table and is repeated as a foreign key in the TICKET table to allow the two tables to be linked. Similarly, each passenger can hold many tickets, while each ticket belongs to only one passenger. Itinerary number is the repeated field that allows these two tables to be linked.

SELECTING DATA FROM A RELATIONAL DATABASE

Data can be retrieved from relational databases through the use of a query language. As we noted earlier, the most common language is SQL, pronounced *see-quel* or *S-Q-L*. The acronym stands for Structured Query Language. SQL is easy to use

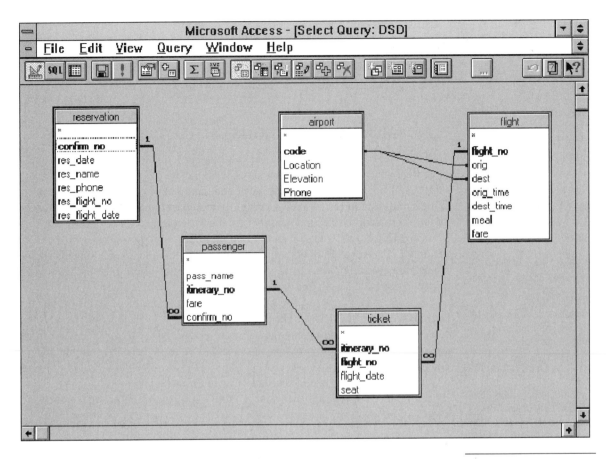

FIGURE 6.5
Air West Entity
Relationship Diagram

to obtain basic information from one or more tables. However, SQL can be quite complex when taking advantage of its real fourth generation language (4GL) power. The power of SQL will be explored further in the advanced section later in this chapter. As you will recall, SQL began in the 1970s with the relational database work of E. F. Codd at IBM. An ANSI standard for SQL was adopted in 1986 and revised in 1989 and again in 1992. However, the parallel development of SQL by various companies before this time resulted in various dialects of the language. This textbook will follow the ANSI standard and show the more important extensions used by some of the primary implementations (DB2, Oracle, Access). SQL is used to retrieve a basic subset of data (rows and columns) from a database. This subset of data is referred to as a SQL result table. Once this subset of data is retrieved, it can be used in a variety of ways:

1. Stored in a file for future processing
2. Stored in a temporary table for further work using SQL
3. As a means of transferring data from one database to another

4. Displayed on a screen

5. Printed as a report on a printer

6. Used as input to a report generator

7. Stored in a file for use in spreadsheets or word processing

FUNDAMENTAL OPERATIONS ON RELATIONAL TABLES

There is a set of operations that can be performed on relational tables. These operations were adapted from the mathematics of set theory. In practice, three fundamental types of operations (projection, selection, and join) can be used to retrieve the subsets of data required for the vast majority of applications. The fundamental operations of projection, selection, and join are illustrated in Figure 6.6.

PROJECTION creates a subset of a table that contains all rows of the table, but only a chosen subset of columns. Since the columns correspond to fields and are named, the column name is used to choose the set of columns to be included in the projection of the table (in this case ORIG, DEST, and ORIG_TIME).

SELECTION creates a subset of a table that contains all columns of the table but only a chosen set of rows. The rows of a table are not named. Rows must be chosen on the basis of conditions—the values of one or more columns (fields) for that row. In our example in Figure 6.6, rows are chosen if the value of column ORIG is equal to PHX.

The **JOIN** operation chooses data from multiple tables creating one result column for each column in either source table. This operation produces a row for each combination of the rows of the source tables that meet some conditional test. A variety of conditions can be applied to produce a join and, in fact, tables can even be joined unconditionally. However, the most common type of join is called an equijoin.

The **equijoin** combines tables that have at least one column of data in common. It creates rows for the SQL **result table** only for combinations of the source tables that have the same value for the common column. In the example in Figure 6.6, two tables are joined based on the value of column CODE in the AIRPORT table with the column ORIG in the FLIGHT table. One row in the SQL result table is created for each combination of the source tables (AIRPORT) and (FLIGHT) having equal values for CODE in AIRPORT and ORIG in FLIGHT. The value of column CODE for the first row of table AIRPORT (FLG) would be compared to the value of column ORIG for each row of the FLIGHT table. A row is created in the SQL result table for each instance of a match. PHX in the second row of the AIRPORT table will match many times with the FLIGHT table. If there is no match for an airport, a row for that airport will not be created in the SQL result table. Variations of this are called outer, left, and right joins and will be discussed later in the chapter.

The first relational data retrieval languages were called **relational algebra** systems. They used a separate statement for each of the operations described here. If you wanted to retrieve a subset of rows over a subset of columns meeting some condition, two statements were required. You could first project off the columns you wanted and

PROJECTION
A result table that consists of some subset of attributes from another table or tables.

SELECTION
A result table that consists of some subset of rows from another table.

JOIN
A relational operation that combines attributes from two or more tables to create another table or table result.

Equijoin
Same as inner join.

Result table
A table that is the result of a query. The result table is a temporary table that exists only during the time the query is in use.

Relational algebra
The operations on tables using relational operators such as union, difference, intersection, product, projection, selection, and join.

The FLIGHT Table in the AIRLINE Database

FLIGHT_NO	ORIG	DEST	ORIG_TIME	DEST_TIME	MEAL	FARE
101	FLG	PHX	07:00:00	08:05:00	S	48.50
102	PHX	MSP	09:00:00	01:00:00	L	156.00
103	MSP	PHX	17:00:00	19:15:00	D	156.00
104	PHX	FLG	20:30:00	21:15:00	S	48.50
15	PHX	LAX	07:00:00	08:20:00	B	49.00
17	PHX	LAX	08:20:00	09:20:00	B	79.00
31	PHX	LAX	17:55:00	19:10:00	S	49.00
33	PHX	LAX	18:55:00	19:15:00	S	49.00
35	PHX	LAX	20:20:00	21:40:00	S	49.00
329	LAX	PHX	21:10:00	23:59:00		49.00
40	PHX	LAX	22:25:00	23:42:00		49.00

The AIRPORT Table in the Airline Database

CODE	LOCATION	ELEVATION	PHONE
FLG	Flagstaff, AZ	6920	602-774-1897
PHX	Phoenix, AZ	1257	602-583-1971
MSP	Minneapolis, MN	862	612-378-2910
LAX	Los Angeles, CA	37	310-273-1846
SFO	San Francisco, CA	78	415-839-9237

A PROJECTION of the flight_no, orig, dest, and orig_time Columns from the FLIGHT Table

```
SELECT flight_no, orig, dest, orig_time FROM flight
```

SQL RESULT TABLE

FLIGHT_NO	ORIG	DEST	ORIG_TIME
101	FLG	PHX	07:00:00
102	PHX	MSP	09:00:00
103	MSP	PHX	17:00:00
104	PHX	FLG	20:30:00
15	PHX	LAX	07:00:00
17	PHX	LAX	08:20:00
31	PHX	LAX	17:55:00
33	PHX	LAX	18:55:00
35	PHX	LAX	20:20:00
329	LAX	PHX	21:10:00
40	PHX	LAX	22:25:00

FIGURE 6.6

A SELECTION of All PHX Origination Data from the FLIGHT Table

```
SELECT * FROM flight WHERE orig = 'PHX'
```

SQL RESULT TABLE

FLIGHT_NO	ORIG	DEST	ORIG_TIME	DEST_TIME	MEAL	FARE
102	PHX	MSP	09:00:00	01:00:00	L	156.00
104	PHX	FLG	20:30:00	21:15:00	S	48.50
15	PHX	LAX	07:00:00	08:20:00	B	49.00
17	PHX	LAX	08:20:00	09:20:00	B	79.00
31	PHX	LAX	17:55:00	19:10:00	S	49.00
33	PHX	LAX	18:55:00	19:15:00	S	49.00
35	PHX	LAX	20:20:00	21:40:00	S	49.00
40	PHX	LAX	22:25:00	23:42:00		49.00

A JOIN Result of the AIRPORT and FLIGHT Tables Using the Origination Airport from FLIGHT

```
SELECT * FROM airport, flight where flight.orig = airport.code
```

SQL RESULT TABLE

FLIGHT_NO	ORIG	DEST	ORIG_TIME	DEST_TIME	MEAL	FARE	CITY	ELEVATION	PHONE
101	FLG	PHX	07:00:00	08:05:00	S	48.50	Flagstaff, AZ	6920	602-772-1897
102	PHX	MSP	09:00:00	01:00:00	L	156.00	Phoenix, AZ	1257	602-583-1971
103	MSP	PHX	17:00:00	19:15:00	D	156.00	Minneapolis, MN	862	612-378-2910
104	PHX	FLG	20:30:00	21:15:00	S	48.50	Phoenix, AZ	1257	602-583-1971
15	PHX	LAX	07:00:00	08:20:00	B	49.00	Phoenix, AZ	1257	602-583-1971
17	PHX	LAX	08:20:00	09:20:00	B	79.00	Phoenix, AZ	1257	602-583-1971
31	PHX	LAX	17:55:00	19:10:00	S	49.00	Phoenix, AZ	1257	602-583-1971
33	PHX	LAX	18:55:00	19:15:00	S	49.00	Phoenix, AZ	1257	602-583-1971
35	PHX	LAX	20:20:00	21:40:00	S	49.00	Phoenix, AZ	1257	602-583-1971
329	LAX	PHX	21:10:00	23:59:00		49.00	Los Angeles, CA	37	310-273-1846
40	PHX	LAX	22:25:00	23:42:00		49.00	Phoenix, AZ	1257	602-583-1971

FIGURE 6.6 (Cont.)

Relational calculus
A complex, nonprocedural language based on predicate calculus that is rarely used in commercial implementations of relational databases.

save the SQL result table. Then a select operation was performed on that first SQL result table to produce the final desired SQL result table.

SQL data retrieval allows a single statement to perform multiple combinations of the projection, selection, and join operations. Some of the concepts that led to the development of SQL came from **relational calculus** systems. Relational calculus is a rather complex, nonprocedural language that is based on predicate calculus. Both

SQL and QBE have some of the nonprocedural language features that were precipitated by the relational calculus ideas.

BASIC FORMAT FOR SQL DATA RETRIEVAL

In SQL the basic statement used for data retrieval is the select statement. The select statement is very powerful and complex, because a single select statement must be able to perform multiple combinations of relational operations. In addition, the select statement has optional clauses that can be used to organize data for presentation in user-friendly form. An abbreviated form of the format for a SQL select data retrieval statement follows:

```
SELECT   data_element1[,data_element2...]
         *

FROM     table_name1[,table_name2...]
[WHERE   condition [AND/OR condition]]
[optional clauses for grouping or organizing results, e.g.
    ORDER BY data_element1, data_element2...]
```

Reserved words that must always be used are shown in all capital letters. Components of the statement that are optional are shown in brackets [ ]. When multiple data elements (columns) are named, they are separated by commas. An asterisk (star) can be used instead of listing individual data elements to select all data elements in the tables selected. Multiple tables can be specified to obtain related data items that are stored in separate tables. The conditions in the WHERE clause can be simple or compound using AND and OR with the operators shown in Figure 6.7. The operands in the conditions can be column names or constants. Constants that are compared to column names must adhere to the same data type definitions as the column data type definitions. For example, you cannot compare a date field to a string constant.

A number of optional clauses can be used to group and organize the data to be presented in a SQL result table. In this chapter, we will show only one example of this—the ORDER BY clause.

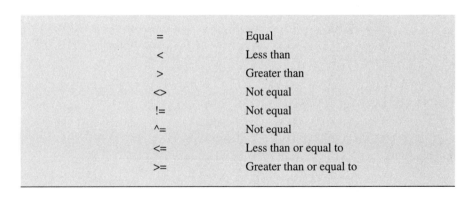

=	Equal
<	Less than
>	Greater than
<>	Not equal
!=	Not equal
^=	Not equal
<=	Less than or equal to
>=	Greater than or equal to

FIGURE 6.7
Conditional Operators

USER INTERFACE TO BUILD AND RUN SQL

Access
A relational database system, supplied by Microsoft, that runs primarily on local workstations. The database can be on a server and shared within a workgroup environment.

Most relational database systems have front-end application software that supports the process of building and testing SQL statements. DB2 SPUFI (SQL Processor Using File Input), XDB, Oracle, and **Access** have menu driven and graphical user interface windows (GUI) that bring up the different functions supported by the database system. You can refer to the appendix at the Dryden website or Appendix A at the end of this book for an introduction to the software that is supported in your lab.

FIGURE 6.8
A Query on a Single Table with No Qualifiers

```
    Access:  SELECT * FROM flight
 DB2/XDB:  SELECT * FROM flight
  ORACLE:  SELECT * FROM flight
```

SQL RESULT TABLE

FLIGHT_NO	ORIG	DEST	ORIG_TIME	DEST_TIME	MEAL	FARE
101	FLG	PHX	07:00:00	08:05:00	S	48.50
102	PHX	MSP	09:00:00	01:00:00	L	156.00
103	MSP	PHX	17:00:00	19:15:00	D	156.00
104	PHX	FLG	20:30:00	21:15:00	S	48.50
15	PHX	LAX	07:00:00	08:20:00	B	49.00
17	PHX	LAX	08:20:00	09:20:00	B	79.00
31	PHX	LAX	17:55:00	19:10:00	S	49.00
33	PHX	LAX	18:55:00	19:15:00	S	49.00
35	PHX	LAX	20:20:00	21:40:00	S	49.00
329	LAX	PHX	21:10:00	23:59:00		49.00
40	PHX	LAX	22:25:00	23:42:00		49.00
694	LAX	PHX	07:40:00	08:55:00		79.00
434	LAX	PHX	08:50:00	10:44:00		49.00
400	LAX	PHX	10:10:00	11:26:00		49.00
600	PHX	SFO	06:46:00	08:50:00	B	109.00
604	PHX	SFO	08:33:00	10:43:00	B	109.00
606	PHX	SFO	11:45:00	13:50:00	L	109.00
60	PHX	SFO	17:45:00	18:36:00	S	139.00
202	SFO	PHX	07:00:00	08:55:00	B	79.00
691	SFO	PHX	11:25:00	13:24:00		109.00
518	SFO	PHX	14:23:00	16:16:00		109.00
1260	SFO	PHX	17:58:00	19:51:00	D	109.00

Access: SELECT orig, dest, meal FROM flight	**FIGURE 6.9**
DB2/XDB: SELECT orig, dest, meal FROM flight	A Projection of
ORACLE: SELECT orig, dest, meal FROM flight	Selected Columns
	from the FLIGHT table

SQL RESULT TABLE

ORIG	DEST	MEAL
FLG	PHX	S
PHX	MSP	L
MSP	PHX	D
PHX	FLG	S
PHX	LAX	B
PHX	LAX	B
PHX	LAX	S
PHX	LAX	S
PHX	LAX	S
LAX	PHX	
PHX	LAX	
LAX	PHX	
LAX	PHX	
LAX	PHX	
PHX	SFO	B
PHX	SFO	B
PHX	SFO	L
PHX	SFO	S
SFO	PHX	B
SFO	PHX	
SFO	PHX	
SFO	PHX	D

SAMPLE SQL QUERIES FROM A SINGLE TABLE

Queries from a single table can use projection and/or selection operations. In the context of the select statement, the list of data element or column names following the word SELECT supports the projection operation. If a list of column names is entered, only those columns will appear in the SQL result table. The selection operation is supported by using conditions in the WHERE clause that create conditional tests on the values of one or more data items. Only rows passing the test are included in the SQL result table.

The simplest form of the SQL select statement is to select all columns from a single table. The asterisk (*) is used to specify all columns of a table in the order they appear in the table. The example in Figure 6.8 selects all data from the FLIGHT table. This query could be used by a database administrator (Rosie Begay) or an application developer (Tony Baca) at Air West to view all the data in a table when testing an application. There is no qualification on rows or columns.

The SQL result table for Oracle will show dates instead of times because Oracle uses one data type to store both dates and times. The time is not formatted when using the * as a selection parameter. Extracting just the time portion of the data is shown in Figure 6.10.

The next example illustrates a projection operation (Figure 6.9). Only the origination [ORIG], destination [DEST], and MEAL columns are chosen. Because there is no WHERE clause (no selection), all rows are included in the SQL result table for this query. This query might be useful to an analyst (Sandra OneFeather) in the meal management area of Air West for auditing the FLIGHT table for meal code accuracy.

Figure 6.10 shows a select statement that combines projection and selection operations. A reservation agent (Lena Olestad), may need to pull up more information on a specific flight number. Only the origination and destination data is shown for the row where the flight number is equal to 14. Because flight number is a primary (unique) key for the FLIGHT table, only one row can satisfy this selection.

As we have noted, the selection of rows is based on conditions specified in the WHERE clause. Figure 6.11 presents several examples of queries with alternative WHERE clause specifications. Query 1 in Figure 6.11 is just like the query in Figure 6.10 except it has no qualification on the columns. It does qualify the rows to those having a flight number of 14, and only one row satisfies this condition. A TO_CHAR function, as shown in Figure 6.10, would be added to the queries in Figure 6.11 to

FIGURE 6.10
A Query Combining
Projection and
Selection

```
    Access: SELECT orig, orig_time, dest, dest_time
            FROM flight
            WHERE flight_no = 14
  DB2/XDB: Same as Access
   ORACLE: SELECT orig, to_char (orig_time 'HH24:MM:SS'),
            dest, to_char (dest_time 'HH24:MM:SS')
            FROM flight
            WHERE flight_no = 14
```

SQL RESULT TABLE

orig	orig_time	dest	dest_time
PHX	05:55:00	LAX	07:11:00

```
1. SELECT * FROM flight WHERE flight_no = 14
```

FIGURE 6.11
Queries Using Various
WHERE Clauses to
Select Rows

SQL RESULT TABLE

FLIGHT_NO	ORIG	DEST	ORIG_TIME	DEST_TIME	MEAL	FARE
14	PHX	LAX	05:55:00	07:11:00		49.00

```
2. SELECT * FROM flight WHERE orig = 'PHX'
```

SQL RESULT TABLE

FLIGHT_NO	ORIG	DEST	ORIG_TIME	DEST_TIME	MEAL	FARE
102	PHX	MSP	09:00:00	01:00:00	L	156.00
104	PHX	FLG	20:30:00	21:15:00	S	48.50
15	PHX	LAX	07:00:00	08:20:00	B	49.00
17	PHX	LAX	08:20:00	09:20:00	B	79.00
31	PHX	LAX	17:55:00	19:10:00	S	49.00
33	PHX	LAX	18:55:00	19:15:00	S	49.00
35	PHX	LAX	20:20:00	21:40:00	S	49.00
40	PHX	LAX	22:25:00	23:42:00		49.00
600	PHX	SFO	06:46:00	08:50:00	B	109.00
604	PHX	SFO	08:33:00	10:43:00	B	109.00
606	PHX	SFO	11:45:00	13:50:00	L	109.00
60	PHX	SFO	17:45:00	18:36:00	S	139.00

```
3. SELECT * FROM flight WHERE orig = 'PHX'
                        AND dest = 'LAX'
```

SQL RESULT TABLE

FLIGHT_NO	ORIG	DEST	ORIG_TIME	DEST_TIME	MEAL	FARE
15	PHX	LAX	07:00:00	08:20:00	B	49.00
17	PHX	LAX	08:20:00	09:20:00	B	79.00
31	PHX	LAX	17:55:00	19:10:00	S	49.00
33	PHX	LAX	18:55:00	19:15:00	S	49.00
35	PHX	LAX	20:20:00	21:40:00	S	49.00
40	PHX	LAX	22:25:00	23:42:00		49.00

extract the time format when using Oracle. Query 2 in Figure 6.11 could be used by an Air West terminal manager in Phoenix to bring up all flight information on flights originating in Phoenix. Query 3 in Figure 6.11 might be used by a reservation agent who is trying to arrange an itinerary for a passenger who plans to fly from Phoenix to Los Angeles. Query 3 displays information on all the flights that are possible.

The selection criteria on rows can be such that a number of rows meet the criteria. The example shown in query 2 of Figure 6.11 can be used to bring up a list of all flights originating in Phoenix. Because there is no qualification on columns, all data in each row of the table meeting the row qualification criteria will be displayed.

Compound selection criteria are constructed by using ANDs and ORs. Rows that meet all conditions for AND logic and rows meeting either condition for OR logic are selected. SQL statements with multiple criteria can be difficult to read. Normally, SQL statements can be broken up into multiple lines (free format) with any editor. It is best to put multiple selection criteria on different lines for better readability. The example in query 3 of Figure 6.11 selects only those flights that originate in Phoenix with destinations to Los Angeles.

ANSI SQL does not define date and time data. Various dialects of SQL have built-in time and date intelligence, meaning that they can do date and time arithmetic

FIGURE 6.12
A Query Using Data
and Time Functions

```
Access:  SELECT * FROM flight
         WHERE flight.orig = 'PHX'
         AND flight.dest = 'LAX'
         AND flight.orig_time >  #10:10:00 AM#;
DB2/XDB: SELECT * FROM flight
         WHERE orig = 'PHX'
         AND dest = 'LAX'
         AND orig_time >  10:00:00
ORACLE:  SELECT flight_no, orig, dest,
         TO_CHAR (orig_time, 'HH24:MM:SS'),
         TO_CHAR (dest_time, 'HH24:MM:SS')
         FROM flight
         WHERE orig = 'PHX'
         AND dest = 'LAX'
         AND TO_CHAR (orig_time,
         'HH24:MM:SS') >  '10:00:00';
```

SQL RESULT TABLE

FLIGHT_NO	ORIG	DEST	ORIG_TIME	DEST_TIME	MEAL	FARE
31	PHX	LAX	17:55:00	19:10:00	S	49.00
33	PHX	LAX	18:55:00	19:15:00	S	49.00
35	PHX	LAX	20:20:00	21:40:00	S	49.00
40	PHX	LAX	22:25:00	23:42:00		49.00

as well as date and time comparisons. The SQL engines know that there are 60 seconds in a minute and 60 minutes in an hour, and the engines also know the calendar days, month by month, for every year. The example shown in Figure 6.12 uses comparison logic on time data to obtain flights leaving after 10:00 A.M. The use of a 24-hour clock or a 12-hour clock with A.M. or P.M. depends on the installation. Figure 6.12 illustrates the syntax for different implementations of a query that Lena (reservation agent) might use for limiting the selection of flights to a time frame.

Notice the difference in the use of delimiters for the time constants. Also, observe that the Access Sample illustrates the use of table qualification with a dot between the table name and the attribute name. This is not necessary in this example because only one table is involved. Access and DB2 use the same format except for the delimiters around the time constant.

See the World Wide Web page at **www.dryden.com/ infosys/lorents** for a complete program that includes the code samples from this chapter.

Suppose Lena wants to see a list of flights that leave after 10:00 A.M. but before 8:00 P.M. The selection of flights departing between a range of times can be done two different ways. AND logic can be used to meet both the conditions on the origination time. However, some SQL dialects will also support the use of the operator BETWEEN. The selection of flights leaving Phoenix for Los Angeles at or after 10:00 A.M. and at or before 8:00 P.M. can be accomplished by either of the two statements shown in Figure 6.13. The BETWEEN predicate is inclusive, meaning the two values are included in the range.

Data are not maintained in the tables in any specific order. Normally, the order of data in the tables is more a result of the order in which the data were put into the table. Also, the order of the data in a source table does not guarantee any order of that data coming from a SELECT statement. SELECTs that produce output for a window, data for reports, and advanced SELECTs that require grouped data often need to specify that the data be in some order.

Data in a SQL result table can be organized in a desired order by adding the ORDER BY clause to a select statement. Generally, data is presented in ascending sequence on a specific field or column. The order can also be specified on multiple columns where the first column listed is the primary sequence, and the second column is secondary. For example, if the columns ORIG and DEST were listed in that order in an ORDER BY clause, the data would be in destination sequence within origination. The parameters ASC and DESC can be added to specify either ascending or descending. The default is ascending order. For example, the clause

```
ORDER BY orig ASC, dest DESC
```

might be used to sort flight data in ascending order by origination, and descending order on destination for all flights with the same origination. The sample query in Figure 6.14 will always give Lena the flights listed in order by origination time. Because no ascending/descending parameter is specified, the list is in default (ascending) order.

JOINING DATA FROM MULTIPLE TABLES

As we noted in Chapter 1, databases maintain data in a form that is designed to minimize redundant data storage and to eliminate the problems of data integrity and

FIGURE 6.13
Queries Using Data
Ranges and the
BETWEEN Operator

```
Query 1
DB2/XDB: SELECT * FROM flight
        WHERE orig = 'PHX'
        AND dest = 'LAX'
        AND orig_time > = 10:00:00
        AND orig_time <= 20:000:000
ORACLE: SELECT flight_no, orig, dest,
        TO_CHAR (orig_time, 'HH24:MM:SS'),
        TO_CHAR (dest_time, 'HH24:MM:SS'),
        meal, fare
        FROM flight
        WHERE orig = 'PHX'
        AND dest = 'LAX'
        AND TO_CHAR (orig_time,
        'HH24:MM:SS') > = '10:00:00'
        AND TO_CHAR (orig_time,
        'HH24:MM:SS') < = '20:00:00'
Query 2
DB2/XDB: SELECT * FROM flight WHERE orig = 'PHX'
        AND dest = 'LAX'
        AND orig_time
        BETWEEN 10:00:00 AND 20:00:00
ORACLE: SELECT flight_no, orig, dest
        TO_CHAR (orig_time, 'HH24:MM:SS'),
        TO_CHAR (dest_time, 'HH24:MM:SS'),
        meal, fare
        FROM flight
        WHERE orig='PHX'
        AND dest='LAX'
        AND TO_CHAR (orig_time > 'HH24:MM:SS')
        BETWEEN '10:00:00' AND '20:00:00';
```

SQL RESULT TABLE

FLIGHT_NO	ORIG	DEST	ORIG_TIME	DEST_TIME	MEAL	FARE
31	PHX	LAX	17:55:00	19:10:00	S	49.00
33	PHX	LAX	18:55:00	19:15:00	S	49.00

update anomalies. This means that related data items are often split into multiple tables in the database. For example, much of the data about each flight (origination, destination, and scheduled times) is not repeated on each ticket for that flight. SQL has the ability to pull together related data from multiple tables through the join

```
   Access: SELECT * FROM flight
           WHERE ((flight.orig='PHX')
           AND (flight.dest='LAX')
           AND (flight.orig_time>#10:10:00 AM#))
           ORDER BY flight.orig_time;
DB2/XDB: SELECT * FROM flight
           WHERE orig='PHX'
           AND dest='LAX'
           AND orig_time >  10:00:00
           ORDER BY orig_time.
 ORACLE: SELECT flight_no, orig, dest,
           TO_CHAR (orig_time, 'HH24:MM:SS'),
           TO_CHAR (dest_time, 'HH24:MM:SS'),
           meal, price
           FROM flight
           WHERE orig = 'PHX'
           AND dest = 'LAX'
           AND TO_CHAR (orig_time,
           'HH24:MM:SS') >  '10:00:00'
           ORDER BY TO_CHAR (Orig_Time,
           'HH24:MM:SS');
```

FIGURE 6.14
A Query with an
ORDER BY Clause

SQL RESULT TABLE

FLIGHT_NO	ORIG	DEST	ORIG_TIME	DEST_TIME	MEAL	FARE
31	PHX	LAX	17:55:00	19:10:00	S	49.00
33	PHX	LAX	18:55:00	19:15:00	S	49.00
35	PHX	LAX	20:20:00	21:40:00	S	49.00
40	PHX	LAX	22:25:00	23:42:00		49.00

operation. Joins require you to list the names of the tables to be joined in the select statement after the keyword FROM separated by commas. Joins also use a join condition in the WHERE clause to interconnect the tables.

Let's use an example where we are obtaining data from the PASSENGER table and the TICKET table. The contents of these tables are shown in Figure 6.15.

Security wants to obtain a list of all passengers flying on July 15, 1997. To do this we would join the passenger name from the PASSENGER table with the flight date, flight number, and seat from the TICKET table for all passengers flying on 7/15/97. The join condition uses the itinerary number because it is the link between the two tables. All ticket rows with a specific itinerary number will be joined or connected with the one passenger row that has the same itinerary number. This will be done for all ticket rows that have the date 7/15/97. This is done to

FIGURE 6.15
Contents of the
PASSENGER and
TICKET Tables
Passenger Table

PASS_NAME	ITINERARY_NO	FARE	CONFIRM_NO
OLE OLSON	1	98.00	1
LENA OLSON	2	98.00	1
PETE PETERSON	3	409.00	2
HAZEL PETERSON	4	409.00	2
DAVID PETERSON	5	409.00	2
SWEN SWENSON	6	315.00	3
OLGA SWENSON	7	315.00	3
PETE SWENSON	8	315.00	3
ANDY ANDERSON	9	218.00	4
GLORIA ANDERSON	10	218.00	4
TORGIE TORGESON	11	218.00	5
ANDY ANDERSON	12	312.00	6
GLORIA ANDERSON	13	312.00	6

pick up the passenger's name for each ticket. The passenger name is not stored in the TICKET table. This type of join is referred to as the equijoin because it requires a column in one table to be equal to (have the same value as) a column in another table.

To facilitate the qualification of column names, since the same column name is used in multiple tables, the table name is used to prefix the column name. If the table names are long, it is easier to use an alias. The aliases are specified right after each respective table name in the SELECT statement. Figure 6.16 uses the alias 'p' for passenger and 't' for ticket.

Note that the select statement in Figure 6.16 performs selection, projection, and join operations. The PASSENGER and TICKET tables are joined, but only a chosen list of columns from the two tables is reported in the SQL result table. In addition, the WHERE clause contains not only the join condition *p.itinerary_no =t.itinerary_no,* but an additional condition selecting only rows whose flight_date is 7/15/97.

QUERIES WITH ARITHMETIC EXPRESSIONS

The list of data items selected in a SELECT clause can include arithmetic expressions. An arithmetic expression consists of any combination of numeric column names and constants separated by arithmetic operators. The arithmetic operators defined by ANSI SQL are:

+	Addition	–	Subtraction
*	Multiplication	/	Division

ITINERARY_NO	FLIGHT_NO	FLIGHT_DATE	SEAT
1	15	02/01/1997	10D
1	329	02/02/1997	12D
2	15	02/01/1997	10E
2	329	02/02/1997	12E
3	101	07/15/1997	3D
3	104	08/21/1997	4D
3	102	07/15/1997	10D
3	103	08/21/1997	15A
4	101	07/15/1997	3C
4	104	08/21/1997	4C
4	102	07/15/1997	10C
4	103	08/21/1997	15B
5	101	07/15/1997	3B
5	104	08/21/1997	4B
5	102	07/15/1997	10B
6	101	08/18/1997	10A
6	104	08/21/1997	8B
6	604	08/18/1997	13A
6	1260	08/21/1997	22A
7	101	08/18/1997	10B
7	104	08/21/1997	8C
7	604	08/18/1997	13B
7	1260	08/21/1997	22B
8	101	08/18/1997	10C
8	104	08/21/1997	8D
8	604	08/18/1997	13C
8	1260	08/21/1997	22C
9	606	02/20/1997	12B
9	518	02/21/1997	8C
10	606	02/20/1997	12C
10	518	02/21/1997	8B
11	606	03/17/1997	12B
11	691	03/18/1997	13B
12	102	02/18/1997	
12	103	02/19/1997	
13	102	02/18/1997	
13	103	02/20/1997	

FIGURE 6.15
Contents of the
PASSENGER and
TICKET Tables
Ticket Table

FIGURE 6.16

A Query Joining the PASSENGER and TICKET Tables for a Selected Flight Date

```
Access: SELECT pass_name, flight_date, flight_no, seat
        FROM passenger p, ticket t
        WHERE p.itinerary_no = t.itinerary_no
        AND flight_date = #07/15/97#
DB2/XDB: same except flight_date = 7/15/97 or '7/15/97'
ORACLE: same except flight_date = '7/15/97'
```

SQL RESULT TABLE

pass_name	flight_date	flight_no	seat
PETE PETERSON	07/15/1997	101	3D
PETE PETERSON	07/15/1997	102	10D
HAZEL PETERSON	07/15/1997	101	3C
HAZEL PETERSON	07/15/1997	102	10C
DAVID PETERSON	07/15/1997	101	3B
DAVID PETERSON	07/15/1997	102	10B

Expressions are evaluated according to the rules you are familiar with in algebra and computer languages. Expressions are evaluated left to right, with the execution of multiplication and division before addition and subtraction. This order can be altered through the use of parentheses. Operations within parentheses or sets of parentheses are executed from the inside to the outside.

Figure 6.17 shows queries containing arithmetic expressions, in projection lists. Lena could use query 1 to display fare options if customers are to be given a 15 percent discount for 7-day advanced purchases and a 40 percent discount for 14-day advanced purchases. Query 2 produces a revised fare schedule in which the new fare is one-half the old fare plus a $25 surcharge for all flights whose original fare is greater than $50. Finally, query 3 would be used if the surcharge is to be added before the 50 percent discount is applied.

Extensions to ANSI SQL allow arithmetic expressions that include date and time. These expressions can contain duration labels like YEARS, MONTHS, DAYS, HOURS, MINUTES, SECONDS, and MICROSECONDS. Ninety days can be added to a date by the expression FLIGHT_DATE + 90 DAYS. ORIG_TIME + 45 MINUTES will add 45 minutes to the origination time. Some examples with date and time arithmetic are shown in Figure 6.18. Lena could use these queries to assist the process of scheduling connecting flights and to determine flight duration times.

The first example, query 1 in Figure 6.18, shows the use of a column containing the origination time plus 45 minutes. The second, query 2, shows the computation of the flight time, the interval between the origination and destination times, in hours. Note that the time calculations vary. DB2 is done in seconds, making it necessary to divide by 3600 to convert to hours. Access is done in minutes, and Oracle does the internal calculation and converts it to the specified output format. Be mindful that the SQL result table contains the heading *column5* for the calculated column, rather

1. A list of fares at 7-day and 14-day advance purchase

                  Access: SELECT orig, dest, fare, fare * .85, fare * .60
                              FROM flight
                              WHERE fare > 50;

DB2/XDB and ORACLE: Same as Access

SQL RESULT TABLE

orig	dest	fare	fare*.85	fare*.60
PHX	MSP	156.00	132.60	93.60
MSP	PHX	156.00	132.60	93.60
PHX	LAX	79.00	67.15	47.40
LAX	PHX	79.00	67.15	47.40
PHX	SFO	109.00	92.65	65.40
PHX	SFO	109.00	92.65	65.40
PHX	SFO	109.00	92.65	65.40
PHX	SFO	139.00	118.15	83.40
SFO	PHX	79.00	67.15	47.40
SFO	PHX	109.00	92.65	65.40
SFO	PHX	109.00	92.65	65.40
SFO	PHX	109.00	92.65	65.40

2. Fares during the half-price fare wars with a $25 surcharge

                  Access: SELECT orig, dest, fare, fare/2+25 AS [Half Fare]
                              FROM flight
                              WHERE fare>50
            DB2/XDB: SELECT orig, dest, fare, fare/2 + 25
                              FROM flight
                              WHERE fare > 50
                ORACLE: Same as DB2

3. Fares with the $25 surcharge added before the half-price sale

                  Access: SELECT orig, dest, fare, (fare + 25) / 2
                              FROM flight
                              WHERE fare > 50

DB2/XDB and ORACLE: Same as Access

FIGURE 6.17
Queries Using Column Lists Containing Arithmetic Expressions

than its arithmetic formula. If the expression is too large, the SQL engine gives the column a name relative to the column position. Because this is the fifth column, it gives it the name column5.

    Query 3 retrieves instances from the TICKET table where a return flight date is more than one day later than the origination flight date for flights with the same

```
Q1 List of origination times and origination time + 45 minutes.
   Access: SELECT orig, orig_time, dateadd ('N',45,orig_time)
           FROM flight
           WHERE orig_time > #16:00:00#;
   DB2/XDB: SELECT orig, orig_time, orig_time + 45 MINUTES
           FROM flight
           WHERE orig_time >  16:00:00
   ORACLE: SELECT orig, to_char (orig_time, 'HH24:MI'),
           to_char (orig_time + (.75/24), 'HH24:MI')
           FROM flight
           WHERE to_char (orig_time, 'HH24:MI:SS') >  16:00:00
Q2 Origination and destination times with the interval of time between
in hours.
   Access: SELECT orig, orig_time, dest, dest_time,
           datediff ('n', orig_time, dest_time) / 60
           FROM flight
   DB2/XDB: SELECT orig, orig_time, dest, dest_time,
           (dest_time - orig_time) / 3600
           FROM flight
   ORACLE: SELECT orig, to_char (orig_time, 'HH24:MI'),
           dest, to_char (dest_time, 'HH24:MI'),
           to_char ((dest_time - orig_time), 'HH24:MI')
           FROM flight
```

SQL RESULT TABLE

orig	orig_time	dest	dest_time	column5
FLG	07:00:00	PHX	08:05:00	1.08
PHX	09:00:00	MSP	13:00:00	4.00
MSP	17:00:00	PHX	19:15:00	3.25
PHX	20:30:00	FLG	21:15:00	0.75
PHX	07:00:00	LAX	08:20:00	1.33
PHX	08:20:00	LAX	09:20:00	1.00
PHX	17:55:00	LAX	19:10:00	1.25
PHX	18:55:00	LAX	19:15:00	0.33
PHX	20:20:00	LAX	21:40:00	1.33

FIGURE 6.18
Queries with Column
Lists Using Data and
Time Arithmetic

Self join
A join of a table with itself.

itinerary number. This query uses the keyword DISTINCT to eliminate duplicate rows from the SQL result table (itinerary_no can book multiple passengers on the same set of flights). This query also joins a table with itself and is sometimes referred to as a **self join.** Each row is compared with every other row in the same table on the basis of itinerary_no. The row that is being compared is referred to with the alias *o* for outbound. The row being compared to is referred to with the alias *r* for return.

```
Q3 Query showing outbound and return flight dates and the number of
days between these dates on flights that return more than one day later
than the outbound flight.
   Access: SELECT DISTINCT o.itinerary_no, o.flight_date,
           r.flight_date,
           datediff ('d',o.flight_date, r.flight_date)
           FROM ticket AS o, ticket AS r
           WHERE o.itinerary_no = r.itinerary_no
           AND r.flight_date >  dateadd ('d',1,o.flight_date);
DB2/XDB: SELECT DISTINCT o.itinerary_no, o.flight_date,
           r.flight_date, r.flight_date - o.flight_date
           FROM ticket o, ticket r
           WHERE o.itinerary_no = r.itinerary_no
           AND r.flight_date >  (o.flight_date + 1 DAY)
  ORACLE: SELECT DISTINCT o.itinerary_no,
           to_char (o.flight_date, 'HH24:MI')
           to_char ((r.flight_date - o.flight_date), 'HH24:MI')
           From ticket o, ticket r
           WHERE o. itinerary_no = r.itinerary_no
           AND r.flight_date >  (o.flight_date + 1)
```

SQL RESULT TABLE

itinerary_no	o.flight_date	r.flight_date	column4
3	07/15/1997	08/21/1997	37
4	07/15/1997	08/21/1997	37
5	07/15/1997	08/21/1997	37
6	08/18/1997	08/21/1997	3
7	08/18/1997	08/21/1997	3
8	08/18/1997	08/21/1997	3
13	02/18/1997	02/20/1997	2

FIGURE 6.18 (Cont.) Queries with Column Lists Using Data and Time Arithmetic

We are interested in comparing the outbound date with the return date for each itinerary. Comparing data with data in the same table is called a *correlated query*. We will discuss this concept further in the advanced section of this chapter.

USING CONSTANTS IN A COLUMN LIST

Alphanumeric literals can be included in the column list of a query to enhance the display. SELECT r.flight_date - o.flight_date, "days" would put the label *days* on each row after the number of days between outgoing and return flight dates. Punctuation and dollar signs ($) can be included the same way.

QUERY BY EXAMPLE

QBE (Query by Example)
A graphical software tool used by many products to assist end-users in building queries. The tool allows users to build SQL using a graphical view of the database tables and a graphical view of the result table without having to know SQL.

Although the SQL data retrieval language is relatively easy for individuals with programming experience, it can be difficult for end-users with little experience or time to devote to learning data retrieval methods. To provide easier access to data retrieval commands for novice users, a variety of visual interfaces for database retrieval have been developed. The first and most widely used of these is **Query by Example (QBE).** QBE is supported in many relational or relational-like database systems. Some database systems, like Access and Paradox, use QBE as the interface for the user to build SQL commands. The name QBE comes from the process of the user giving an example or illustration of information desired from the database.

In a typical QBE implementation, a table or tables can be selected from a list box. Once a table is selected, a row of blank columns (example row) is displayed on the window. The user can select columns from the tables in any order to fill the example row of columns to be used in the query. The example row has multiple dimensions to allow the user to specify sort sequence, selection criteria, display control, and summary control. Logical operators, such as =, >, and <, along with constants are used in the criteria dimension to limit the rows to a specific domain range for that column. For example, entering >50 in the fare column would cause only flights whose fare is greater than $50 to be included in the SQL result table. This is the same as the WHERE clause in SQL. Check boxes are turned off or on to specify whether a column is displayed or not. The sort dimension can be turned on by clicking on that dimension under any column and specifying ascending or descending.

QBE also supports the joining of multiple tables. To perform a join, you call up multiple tables from the menu, and then link the tables together by dragging the link field of one table to a position over a link field in another table. The link field must be primary and foreign keys in the tables that are related. This relationship may have been defined previously by the database definitions. In Access, this can be done by going to edit relationships. The following example in Figure 6.19 joins the AIRPORT and FLIGHT tables by using the link field Code in AIRPORT and the link field Orig column in FLIGHT. The columns used in the query can be selected from the two tables by double-clicking the fields in the diagram or by using the drop down list in the QBE cell matrix. The condition > 1000 entered in the Elevation column of AIRPORT causes this selection criteria to be applied to the elevation values in the airport table. The SQL result table will be sorted first on airport and then on origination time of each flight. Airport is sorted first because it was the first sort criteria defined.

Figure 6.20 on page 228 shows an example of including a summary dimension. Access includes a total line in the example row by selecting the Sigma (Sum) icon. Users can select from a drop down list a type of total or aggregate function they want for a specific column in the example row. Note that the Elevation column has been turned off in the display dimension, so it will not show in the result table. The result table, the small window to the right, shows a count of the number of originating flights for each airport with an elevation over 1,000 feet.

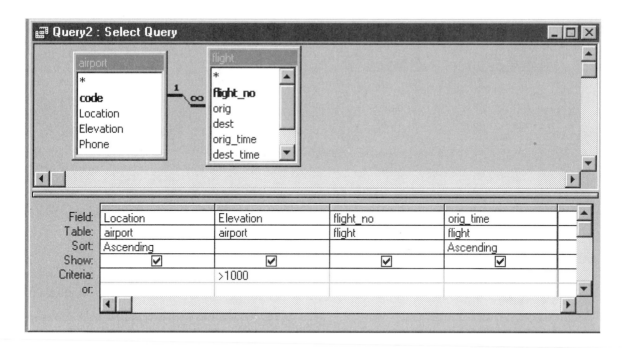

FIGURE 6.19
QBE Example

SUMMARY

Structured Query Language or SQL is a language that, with some dialect variations, is used in virtually all relational DBMSs. The SELECT statement in SQL is the primary statement used for data retrieval. The SELECT statement has a variety of clauses that allow it to perform multiple relational operations to produce desired subsets of data in SQL result tables. It also has optional clauses that can group and organize data presented in SQL result tables, such as the ORDER BY clause, which can sort the rows of a SQL Result table in either ASCending or DESCending order on one or more columns of data.

Three of the most fundamental relational operations are projection, selection, and join. In SQL, combinations of all these operations can be performed using a single select statement. Projection chooses columns (fields) of data from a source table to be included in a SQL result table. Within the select statement, the list of column names following the word SELECT performs the projection operation. The column list of a select statement can also include arithmetic computations and literals. Arithmetic computations within column lists can combine data columns, numeric constants, and/or built-in functions such as date and time functions.

Selection chooses rows from a source table to be included in a SQL result table on the basis of the value of one or more columns. Within the select statement, conditions specified in the WHERE clause can be used to perform the selection

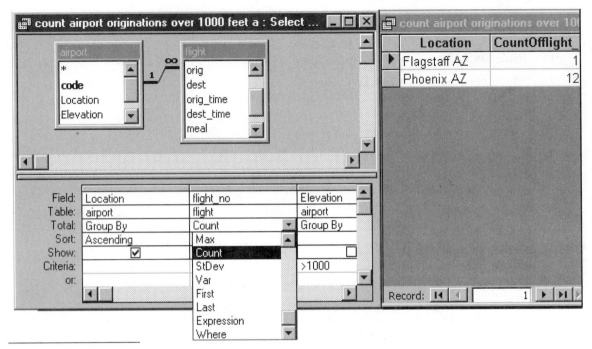

FIGURE 6.20
QBE Example with
Summary Dimension

operation. Conditions on the values of columns are specified in the WHERE clause, and rows are placed in the SQL result table only if those conditions are true. The operators AND and OR can be used, with their usual meaning, to create compound conditions.

The joining of tables produces a SQL result table with one column for every column in each of the source tables. Normally, a column is repeated in two source tables and the value of that column is required to be equal across both source tables before a result row is created. This type of join is called an equijoin. All combinations of rows in the source tables are checked and a result row is created for each combination having an equal value for the common field. Within the SQL select statement, an equijoin is executed by listing all the source table names after the keyword FROM and including a WHERE clause requiring that the value of the repeated column be equal in both source tables.

_____ Credited with starting the first work on relational database activity.

_____ IBM started letting customers experiment with a relational database in this year.

_____ Oracle introduced a relational database in this year.

_____ First commercial relational databases working on mini-computers.

_____ Relational term for a file.

_____ Relational term for a record.

_____ Relational term for a field.

_____ A relational data type for text data.

_____ A relational data type for numeric data.

_____ The character used to separate table names from attribute names in qualified names.

_____ The term used to refer to a value that does not exist.

_____ The characters used to delimit a text literal.

_____ The term given to a unique identifier in a table.

_____ The term given to an identifier in a table that references another table.

_____ A set of tables used to store the definitions of a database designed by a user.

_____ The relational operation that selects a subset of rows from a table or set of tables.

_____ The relational operation that selects a subset of columns from a table or set of tables.

_____ The relational operation that matches rows in one table with rows in another table.

_____ The term used to refer to a table name that is defined in the SQL statement and used instead of the table name in the dictionary.

_____ The clause used in a SQL statement to control row selection.

_____ The clause used in a SQL statement to specify sequence of the result table.

_____ A date function used in Oracle to convert dates.

_____ A date function used in Access to do date arithmetic.

_____ The character used to delimit dates in Access.

1. #
2. Quotes
3. Period
4. Plus
5. WHERE
6. FROM
7. ORDER BY
8. SELECT
9. Alias
10. JOIN
11. PROJECTION
12. SELECTION
13. to_char
14. dateadd
15. datediff
16. Codd
17. Date
18. 1978
19. 1979
20. 1981
21. Oracle and Sybase
22. Oracle and Ingres
23. Primary key
24. Foreign key
25. Null
26. Relation
27. Attribute
28. Tuple

29. Character

30. Money

31. Data dictionary

32. DB2 and XDB

When passengers are trying to arrange a trip, they typically want to find out times and routes to particular destinations. For example, if a passenger wants to fly from Flagstaff to Los Angeles, there are two legs to the trip because it is not a direct flight. The passenger must change planes in Phoenix. There is one flight from Flagstaff to Phoenix and one flight from Phoenix to Los Angeles. The passenger also has the option of driving to Phoenix and flying the second leg of the trip. Write some SQL queries to help the reservation agent assist this passenger in deciding which flights to schedule.

REVIEW QUESTIONS AND EXERCISES

1. What are the possible flights from Flagstaff to Phoenix?

2. What flights originating in Phoenix serve some type of meal (B, S, L, or D)?

3. What are the possible flights from Phoenix to Los Angeles?

4. What flights leave Phoenix for Los Angeles after 3 P.M.?

5. What flights leave Phoenix for Los Angeles before 3 P.M.?

6. What flights leave Los Angeles for Phoenix between 8 A.M. and 12 noon?

7. What flights leave Phoenix for Los Angeles between 3 P.M. and midnight?

8. What flights originating in Phoenix do not serve dinner?

9. List all passenger information available for passengers whose last name is Swenson.

10. List the itinerary number, seat, flight number, and flight date for all tickets held by the passenger Andy Anderson.

11. List the itinerary number, seat, flight number, flight date, origin airport code, and flight time for all tickets held by the passenger Andy Anderson.

12. What are the fares from Phoenix to Los Angeles if Air West is running a 20 percent discount special off the fares currently in the system?

13. List the flights with the new times assuming a change to daylight saving time on the first of May.

14. Obtain a passenger list for a flight on a specific date.

15. Obtain a list of all the flights booked for a specific passenger.

16. Assume a database for Apex products that was defined in Chapter 3. Set up some sample questions that users of that database would typically ask, and then set up the SQL to answer those questions.

17. Assume a database for a small car rental company that includes three entities: cars, customers, and rental contracts. The rental contract contains the car identification (license number) and the customer number (phone number): Add other appropriate attributes to the entities. Set up a number of questions that the users of this database would typically ask, and then set up the SQL to solve those questions.

18. Assume a database for maintaining a state's car registrations that includes three entities: vehicle, owner, and registration. Registration contains the vehicle identification (license number) and the owner identification (social security number). Add other appropriate attributes to the entities. Set up a number of questions that the users of this database would typically ask, and then set up the SQL to solve those questions.

ADVANCED APPLICATIONS USING SQL

LEARNING OBJECTIVES

After completing this chapter, you should be able to

- Develop advanced queries that select data using the following features:
  - **a.** Multiple table joins.
  - **b.** Selection with multiple subselects.
  - **c.** Selection of data from a table based on a subselect from the same table.
  - **d.** Joining a table with itself.
  - **e.** Selection using subselects with group by operations.
  - **f.** Selection with the use of predicates such as any, all, exists, not exists.
  - **g.** Create and use views to support typical use of relational databases.

ADVANCED SQL FORMATS

The basic principles of using SQL were covered in Section I. Using SQL to extract information from one table or multiple tables using joins is the easier part of understanding how to use SQL. SQL has a lot of power as a fourth generation language. However, learning how to use that power is somewhat more complex. This section will explore some of the power of SQL with various examples illustrating its use to solve complex queries. JOIN gives SQL the capability to put related data from multiple tables together using the primary key in one table with related foreign keys in another table. More examples of JOIN will be shown in this chapter. SQL also has the ability to put data together in other ways by manipulating subsets of data and data aggregates called groups.

Section 1 of this chapter illustrated a small portion of the SELECT structure. The complete format of the SELECT statement is as follows:

```
SELECT  [DISTINCT | ALL] {* | column_list}
  FROM [owner.]table_name [alias] [,[owner.]table_name [alias]]...
  [WHERE    condition]
  [GROUP BY column_list]
  [HAVING   condition]
  [ORDER BY column_list];
```

Remember the syntax from previous discussions: brackets [ ] mean optional or optional choice if the vertical bar I is present; braces { } mean a required choice of one; and all words outside the brackets or braces are required. A column list means that you are to name the specific columns in the desired order for the SQL result table. An asterisk * means to select all columns from the tables specified in the order they appear in the tables. An alias is an abbreviated name for a table that can be used later in the SELECT statement to qualify table names when the same name appears in multiple tables. The semicolon used to end the SQL statement is optional on most SQL dialects. However, the semicolon is necessary when executing multiple SQL statements in a script or procedure file. The table name can be prefixed in most relational database systems with the owner's (user's) ID or account number.

THE AIRLINE DATABASE REVISITED

This section illustrates the advanced query (SELECT) capabilities in SQL. Refer to the airline database entity-relationship (E-R) diagram (Figure 6.21) and database tables (Figure 6.22).

MULTIPLE TABLE JOINS REVISITED

SQL can support the selection of data from multiple tables in the database at the same time. Section I illustrated joining two tables together. The basic principle of the join

FIGURE 6.21
Air West Entity-
Relationship Diagram

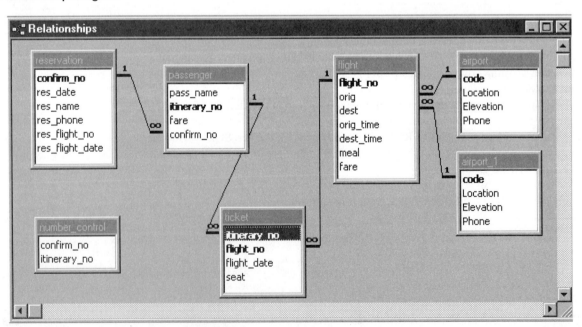

CONTENT: Data on all flights flown in the system.

FLIGHT_NO	ORIG	DEST	ORIG_TIME	DEST_TIME	MEAL	FARE
101	FLG	PHX	07:00:00	08:05:00	S	48.50
102	PHX	MSP	09:00:00	01:00:00	L	156.00
103	MSP	PHX	17:00:00	19:15:00	D	156.00
104	PHX	FLG	20:30:00	21:15:00	S	48.50
15	PHX	LAX	07:00:00	08:20:00	B	49.00
17	PHX	LAX	08:20:00	09:20:00	B	79.00
31	PHX	LAX	17:55:00	19:10:00	S	49.00
33	PHX	LAX	18:55:00	19:15:00	S	49.00
35	PHX	LAX	20:20:00	21:40:00	S	49.00
329	LAX	PHX	21:10:00	23:59:00		49.00
40	PHX	LAX	22:25:00	23:42:00		49.00
694	LAX	PHX	07:40:00	08:55:00		79.00
434	LAX	PHX	08:50:00	10:44:00		49.00
400	LAX	PHX	10:10:00	11:26:00		49.00
600	PHX	SFO	06:46:00	08:50:00	B	109.00
604	PHX	SFO	08:33:00	10:43:00	B	109.00
606	PHX	SFO	11:45:00	13:50:00	L	109.00
60	PHX	SFO	17:45:00	18:36:00	S	139.00
202	SFO	PHX	07:00:00	08:55:00	B	79.00
691	SFO	PHX	11:25:00	13:24:00		109.00
518	SFO	PHX	14:23:00	16:16:00		109.00
1260	SFO	PHX	17:58:00	19:51:00	D	109.00

FIGURE 6.22
Database Tables for
Air West
FLIGHT Table

is to put related data in one table together with data in another. It is necessary to specify the join condition for each table relationship. The join condition is a logical expression that consists of data elements (normally primary and foreign keys) that are compared by logical operators (normally equal). The purpose is to recreate complete sets of related data for display or report purposes from the normalized one to many structures in the database.

OBTAINING DATA FROM FOUR TABLES

In airline reservation systems, one individual can make a reservation for a group of people. The group is traveling together. The reservation table contains data on who made the reservation, the originating flight number, and the date. The passenger table

CONTENT: Data on the individual who made the reservation.

CONFIRM_NO	RES_DATE	RES_NAME	RES_PHONE	RES_FLIGHT_NO	RES_FLIGHT_DATE
1	02/01/1997	OLE OLSON	218-694-2221	15	02/01/1997
2	02/01/1997	PETE PETERSON	218-694-3000	101	07/15/1997
3	02/01/1997	SWEN SWENSON	218-694-8822	101	08/18/1997
4	02/10/1997	ANDY ANDERSON	602-523-3510	606	02/20/1997
5	02/17/1997	TORGIE TORGESON	208-222-3333	606	03/17/1997
6	02/17/1997	ANDY ANDERSON	602-523-3510	102	02/18/1997

FIGURE 6.22 (Cont.)
Database Tables for
Air West
RESERVATION Table

CONTENT: Data on each passenger holding space on a flight.

PASS_NAME	ITINERARY_NO	FARE	CONFIRM_NO
OLE OLSON	1	98.00	1
LENA OLSON	2	98.00	1
PETE PETERSON	3	409.00	2
HAZEL PETERSON	4	409.00	2
DAVID PETERSON	5	409.00	2
SWEN SWENSON	6	315.00	3
OLGA SWENSON	7	315.00	3
PETE SWENSON	8	315.00	3
ANDY ANDERSON	9	218.00	4
GLORIA ANDERSON	10	218.00	4
TORGIE TORGESON	11	218.00	5
ANDY ANDERSON	12	312.00	6
GLORIA ANDERSON	13	312.00	6

FIGURE 6.22 (Cont.)
Database Tables for
Air West
PASSENGER Table

CONTENT: Data on each ticket. There is a ticket for each passenger/flight combination. Normally, a trip is a round trip and consists of at least two tickets. Note that not all tickets have seat assignments.

ITINERARY_NO	FLIGHT_NO	FLIGHT_DATE	SEAT
1	15	02/01/1997	10D
1	329	02/02/1997	12D
2	15	02/01/1997	10E
2	329	02/02/1997	12E
3	101	07/15/1997	3D
3	104	08/21/1997	4D
3	102	07/15/1997	10D
3	103	08/21/1997	15A
4	101	07/15/1997	3C
4	104	08/21/1997	4C
4	102	07/15/1997	10C
4	103	08/21/1997	15B
5	101	07/15/1997	3B
5	104	08/21/1997	4B
5	102	07/15/1997	10B
6	101	08/18/1997	10A
6	104	08/21/1997	8B
6	604	08/18/1997	13A
6	1260	08/21/1997	22A
7	101	08/18/1997	10B
7	104	08/21/1997	8C
7	604	08/18/1997	13B
7	1260	08/21/1997	22B
8	101	08/18/1997	10C
8	104	08/21/1997	8D
8	604	08/18/1997	13C
8	1260	08/21/1997	22C
9	606	02/20/1997	12B

FIGURE 6.22 (Cont.)
Database Tables for
Air West
TICKET Table

CONTENT: Data on each ticket. There is a ticket for each passenger/flight combination. Normally, a trip is a round trip and consists of at least two tickets. Note that not all tickets have seat assignments.

ITINERARY_NO	FLIGHT_NO	FLIGHT_DATE	SEAT
9	518	02/21/1997	8C
10	606	02/20/1997	12C
10	518	02/21/1997	8B
11	606	03/17/1997	12B
11	691	03/18/1997	13B
12	102	02/18/1997	
12	103	02/19/1997	
13	102	02/18/1997	
13	103	02/20/1997	

**FIGURE 6.22
(Concluded)
Database Tables for
Air West**
TICKET Table

contains data on each passenger flying on a particular trip. Most often, the person making the reservation is also one of the passengers.

In the following example, Lena (reservation agent) wants to bring up on the screen the flight information (origination, destination, and times) on all passengers who are flying under a reservation made by Pete Peterson. Pete has called in to confirm his record. In this query the passenger name is coming from the PASSENGER table, the flight data is coming from the TICKET table, and the remaining data is coming from the FLIGHT table. The RESERVATION table is used as the basis for selecting Pete Peterson. The following SELECT uses all four tables (Figure 6.23).

The linkage between the RESERVATION and PASSENGER tables is confirmation number, between the PASSENGER and TICKET tables is itinerary number, and between the TICKET and FLIGHT tables is flight number. There is a unique confirmation number for each reservation, a unique itinerary number for each passenger per trip (where a trip can have one or more flights), and a unique flight number for each flight. Notice the need to have three join conditions when you are joining four tables. The fourth condition is in the SELECT to isolate the data attached to the reservation for Pete Peterson. The alias names of r for reservation, p for passenger, f for flight, and t for ticket are there to eliminate having to use full names as qualifiers in the remainder of the SQL statement. The alias names are temporary and are meaningful only for the SQL statement in which they are used.

Inner join
A join that includes the matching rows of all tables within the join operation. All attributes of the result table derive their values from their respective tables.

OUTER AND INNER JOINS

Most SQL join operations used support only the **inner join.** An inner join creates a SQL result table that is made up of rows that satisfy all the join comparison

```
Four-Table Join
   Access: SELECT p.pass_name, t.flight_date, f.orig,
          f.orig_time,
          f.dest, f.dest_time
          FROM reservation r, passenger p, flight f, ticket t
          WHERE r.confirm_no = p.confirm_no
          AND p.itinerary_no = t.itinerary_no
          AND f.flight_no = t.flight_no
          AND r.res_name = 'Pete Peterson'
DB2/XDB: Same as Access
 ORACLE: Same except for to_char function on time data.
```

SQL RESULT TABLE

pass_name	flight_date	orig	orig_time	dest	dest_time
PETE PETERSON	07/15/1997	FLG	07:00:00	PHX	08:05:00
PETE PETERSON	07/15/1997	PHX	09:00:00	MSP	01:00:00
PETE PETERSON	08/21/1997	MSP	17:00:00	PHX	19:15:00
PETE PETERSON	08/21/1997	PHX	20:30:00	FLG	21:15:00
HAZEL PETERSON	07/15/1997	FLG	07:00:00	PHX	08:05:00
HAZEL PETERSON	07/15/1997	PHX	09:00:00	MSP	01:00:00
HAZEL PETERSON	08/21/1997	MSP	17:00:00	PHX	19:15:00
HAZEL PETERSON	08/21/1997	PHX	20:30:00	FLG	21:15:00
DAVID PETERSON	07/15/1997	FLG	07:00:00	PHX	08:05:00
DAVID PETERSON	07/15/1997	PHX	09:00:00	MSP	01:00:00
DAVID PETERSON	08/21/1997	PHX	20:30:00	FLG	21:15:00

FIGURE 6.23
Flight Data for All Passengers Booked under Reservation "Pete Peterson"

constraints. For example, if we joined the TICKET table with the seat table using "seat," we would get a SQL result table of all tickets with assigned seats. The tickets that have not been assigned seats are not a part of the SQL result table. An **outer join** includes all the results of an inner join plus the tickets that did not have a seat assigned. The seat would show up as a null in the SQL result table; however, the row would still be accounted for. Other data that was requested from the matching table (SEAT) would also be null. For example, some seats may have special needs associated, such as an exit seat or a bulkhead seat, and we may want to match to obtain that data. The outer join is not supported by ANSI/OSI SQL or DB2. However, other implementations such as Oracle and SQL server support the outer join. The (+) is used by Oracle to request an outer join.

The outer join supports unmatched rows from both tables in the join. Consequently, the outer join of the ticket table with the seat table would also list all rows of the seat table that did not match with a ticket holding that seat. There is also

Outer join
A join that includes the nonmatching rows of the various tables included in the join. The attributes from the nonmatching tables are set to null in the result table.

Left outer join
A special form of the outer join used on two tables where the nonmatches from the first table (left table) are included in the result table.

Right outer join
A special form of the outer join used on two tables where the nonmatches from the second table (right table) are included in the result table.

a **left outer join** and a **right outer join.** The left outer join includes unmatched rows from the first table, but not unmatched rows from the second table. A right outer join would include unmatched rows from the second table, but not unmatched rows from the first. The notation and support for multiple tables beyond two tables make the support for outer joins complex.

USE OF ALL OR DISTINCT

The SQL result table will often contain duplicate rows as a result of a SELECT. If we look at selecting fares from the FLIGHT table for flights going from Phoenix to Los Angeles, we will get multiple rows with the same fare (Figure 6.24).

The default is SELECT ALL, so SELECT and SELECT ALL mean the same thing. If we want to eliminate the duplicates, we use the SELECT DISTINCT, which would produce the table in Figure 6.25.

USING SQL TO SUMMARIZE AND GROUP DATA

Five functions in SQL are referred to as aggregate functions: AVG for the average value of a column range, COUNT for the number of values in a column range, MIN for the minimum value in a column range, MAX for the maximum value in a column range, and SUM for the total of all values in a column range. Remember SQL selects the column by the column name, and the range of rows is determined by the WHERE clause. The following SELECTs show an example of using the column TEST1 in a table called GRADEBOOK.

FIGURE 6.24
SELECT and
SELECT ALL

```
          Access: SELECT fare FROM flight
                  WHERE orig = "PHX" and dest = "LAX"
DB2/XDB and ORACLE: Same as Access
```

SQL RESULT TABLE

```
fare
79.00
49.00
49.00
49.00
49.00
49.00
```

```
Access:  SELECT DISTINCT fare FROM flight
         WHERE orig = "PHX" and dest = "LAX'
DB2/XDB: Same as Access
```

FIGURE 6.25
Using DISTINCT

SQL RESULT TABLE

```
                    fare
                    79.00
                    49.00
```

```
Access:  SELECT COUNT (*) FROM flight
DB2/XDB: Same as Access
```

FIGURE 6.26
Counting All Rows in
the Table

SQL RESULT TABLE

```
                    Count (*)
                    22
```

Column TEST1 values (90, 80, 76, 84, 96)

```
A:  SELECT COUNT(test1)   FROM gradebook.  Result = 5
B:  SELECT COUNT(*)       FROM gradebook.  Result = 5
C:  SELECT MIN(test1)     FROM gradebook.  Result = 76
D:  SELECT MAX(test1)     FROM gradebook.  Result = 96
E:  SELECT SUM(test1)     FROM gradebook.  Result = 426
F:  SELECT AVG(test1)     FROM gradebook.  Result = 85.1
```

Only the count function can be performed on character columns. All the other aggregate functions are for use only with numeric columns of a table. Aggregate functions cannot be intermixed with nonaggregate columns in one select statement.

The SELECT statement

```
SELECT ORIG AVG(FARE) FROM FLIGHT
```

would produce an error because the first column specified requires a row for each row in the SQL result table while the second requires only a single, aggregate value. Nonaggregate columns may be specified along with aggregates if they are used to group data for subtotaling (summarization), as we will see later in this chapter.

In the airline application, the database administrator might want to know how many flights are currently in the FLIGHT table. This could be obtained with a simple SELECT, using the function count (Figure 6.26).

If we wanted to know the number of flights from Phoenix to Los Angeles, we would add a WHERE clause specifying this constraint (Figure 6.27).

> **Access:** SELECT COUNT (*) FROM flight
> WHERE orig = "PHX" AND dest = "LAX"
> **DB2/XDB and ORACLE:** Same as Access

SQL RESULT TABLE

Count (*)
6

FIGURE 6.27
Counting a Subset of
Rows

> **Access:** SELECT MIN (fare), MAX (fare), AVG (fare)
> FROM flight
> WHERE orig = "PHX" AND dest = "LAX"
> **DB2/XDB and ORACLE:** Same as Access

SQL RESULT TABLE

MIN (fare)	MAX (fare)	AVG (fare)
49.00	79.00	54.00

FIGURE 6.28
Sample of MIN, MAX,
and AVG

If Lena wants to know the average fare for these flights to Los Angeles, she would SELECT AVG (fare). She can get the lowest, highest, and average fares with the same SELECT (Figure 6.28).

USING SQL TO SUMMARIZE DATA WITH THE GROUP BY OPTION

The GROUP BY option is traditionally referred to as *control break logic* in report writing and COBOL programming. It allows one to obtain totals on each subset of data determined by the columns specified by the GROUP BY clause. The SQL engine groups the data internally and calculates a summary value on each group of data. The sequence of the output is not guaranteed unless an ORDER BY statement is used to control sequencing. The ordering of column names in the GROUP BY and ORDER BY clauses for multiple columns is also important. The first column name is the major key; the second, the intermediate key; and the third, the minor key. This means that output is in sequence by the first column specified. If there are duplicate data values in the first column, and a second column is specified, then the output is in sequence by the second column until the data in the first column changes.

The manager of flight operations, Russell Lomakema, wants to know on a regular basis the passenger counts on flights as the airline approaches each flight day. Figure 6.29 illustrates a query obtaining a passenger count for each flight that is currently in the TICKET table. Flight_no and flight_date isolate the data for a specific flight on a specific date. The columns could have been specified in either order in the GROUP BY phrase to obtain the same result. The ORDER BY phrase specifies the order for displaying the result. In this example, the result will be displayed in flight_no sequence within flight_date. Note that the ordering of the columns on the display is very dependent on the sequence of the columns named in the ORDER BY clause.

We were allowed to include the nonaggregate columns flight_no and flight_date in the select statement because those columns are used in grouping the data. Only

FIGURE 6.29
Passenger Count on Each Flight

```
Access: SELECT flight_no, flight_date, count (itinerary_no)
        FROM ticket
        GROUP BY flight_no, flight_date
        ORDER BY flight_date, flight_no
DB2/XDB and ORACLE: Same as Access
```

SQL RESULT TABLE

flight_no	flight_date	count (itinerary_no)
15	02/01/1997	2
329	02/02/1997	2
102	02/18/1997	2
103	02/19/1997	1
103	02/20/1997	1
606	02/20/1997	2
518	02/21/1997	2
606	03/17/1997	1
691	03/18/1997	1
101	07/15/1997	3
102	07/15/1997	3
101	08/18/1997	3
604	08/18/1997	3
103	08/21/1997	2
104	08/21/1997	6
1260	08/21/1997	3

```
         Access: SELECT flight_no, flight_date, COUNT (itinerary_no)
                 FROM ticket
                 GROUP BY flight_no, flight_date
                 HAVING COUNT (itinerary_no) >  2
                 ORDER BY flight_date, flight_no
DB2/XDB and ORACLE: Same as Access
```

SQL RESULT TABLE

flight_no	flight_date	COUNT (itinerary_no)
101	07/15/1997	3
102	07/15/1997	3
101	08/18/1997	3
604	08/18/1997	3
104	08/21/1997	6
1260	08/21/1997	3

FIGURE 6.30
Using COUNT on a
Specific Column

```
         Access: SELECT flight_no, flight_date, COUNT (itinerary_no)
                 FROM ticket
                 WHERE month (flight_date) = 7
                 GROUP BY flight_no, flight_date
                 HAVING COUNT (itinerary_no) >  2
                 ORDER BY flight_date, flight_no
DB2/XDB and ORACLE: Same as Access
```

SQL RESULT TABLE

flight_no	flight_date	COUNT (itinerary_no)
101	07/15/1997	3
102	07/15/1997	3

FIGURE 6.31
Select All Flights for
July with a Passenger
Count > 2

columns appearing in a GROUP BY clause can appear in the select list together with the aggregate function columns.

The resulting rows of a GROUP BY phrase can be limited to a subset through the use of the HAVING clause. The resulting rows are selected based on satisfying the conditions specified in the HAVING clause. The HAVING clause operates on

```
           Access: SELECT flight_no, flight_date, orig, dest,
                   COUNT (itinerary_no)
                   FROM ticket t, flight f
                   WHERE month (flight_date) = 7
                   AND t.flight_no = f.flight_no
                   AND Orig = 'PHX'
                   GROUP BY flight_no, flight_date, orig, dest
                   HAVING COUNT (itinerary_no) > 2
                   ORDER BY flight_date, flight_no
DB2/XDB and ORACLE: Same as Access
/*note that orig and dest must be in the GROUP BY phrase because they
are a part of the result list in the select clause */
```

SQL RESULT TABLE

flight_no	flight_date	orig	dest	COUNT (itinerary_no)
102	07/15/1997	PHX	MSP	3

FIGURE 6.32
GROUP BY Columns
in the SELECT

summarized or grouped data in the same way that the WHERE clause operates on data stored in a table. The following example adds a HAVING condition to the preceding SQL SELECT, restricting the resulting rows to those flights with a passenger count greater than two (Figure 6.30). Note that the COUNT function can be applied to rows in a table in general by using the * or to a specific column such as itinerary_no. The result is the same unless itinerary_no is null in some rows. Nulls will not be counted if the count relates to a specific column. COUNT (*) does not relate to a specific column so it includes rows with nulls.

SQL SELECTs can have WHERE and HAVING in the same statement. The WHERE clause is placed first in the statement to screen out the rows that are to be included in the GROUP BY operation. The HAVING clause screens the results of the GROUP BY operation that are to be included in the final output. Russell can use the query in Figure 6.31 to limit the analysis of load to a specific month and to those flights with a passenger count either above or below some limit. This query illustrates both constraints by selecting only the flights for the month of July, and then printing only those with passenger counts greater than two. The SELECT uses the month function to extract the month (using a month number parameter) from the flight date.

The GROUP BY clause can be used with SELECT statements that join multiple tables. For example, if Russell wants to see the origination and destination as part of the output, this could be done by joining the ticket data table with the flight data table. The query in Figure 6.32 extends the previous examples farther by doing a join to obtain origination and destination data, and uses a WHERE to limit the flights to those originating in Phoenix for the month of July. The addition of the new data, origination and destination, requires that these columns be added to the GROUP

BY phrase. As we have already noted, every column listed without an aggregate function in the SELECT statement must also be in the GROUP BY phrase. This is not required for the logic of the GROUP BY, but for the GROUP BY to maintain these columns so that they are available for the SELECT in the final result. This query emphasizes this point with a comment placed in the SQL statement. Comments begin with the characters /* (slash and asterisk) in columns one and two and end with an */. Comments can also be placed at the end of any line after two successive hyphens. Comments are not supported in Access.

ADVANCED FORMS OF CONDITIONS IN THE WHERE CLAUSE

Section I covered the simple and more common forms of conditions such as equal, greater than, less than, and combinations of these using AND and OR. SQL supports other forms of conditions that can be useful depending on the application.

USE OF LIKE

Predicate
A predicate is a search condition in a query such as logical operators, range tests, null test, and pattern match using LIKE, IN, EXIST, or BETWEEN.

The SQL LIKE **predicate** is useful to obtain rows of data that are close to the value desired. LIKE is also useful in selecting data where the spelling of a name may be difficult. There are various combinations of setting up the search string using the wild card characters of % (percent) and _ (underscore). The % specifies any number of characters with any value, and the _ specifies a single character of any value.

1. SWEN% means any string beginning with SWEN.
2. %SWEN means any string ending with SWEN.
3. %SWEN% means any string with SWEN in it somewhere.
4. %A_C% means any string with the letters A and C separated by some character.

FIGURE 6.33
Using LIKE to
Obtain Data

Lena (reservation agent) could use the query in Figure 6.33 to find all reservations made by individuals with SWEN somewhere in their name. This is convenient

```
   Access: SELECT * FROM RESERVATION
           WHERE RES_NAME LIKE '*SWEN*';
DB2/XDB: Use % in the constant instead of * '%SWEN%'
  ORACLE: Same as DB2
```

SQL RESULT TABLE

CONFIRM_ NO	RES_ DATE	RES_ NAME	RES_ PHONE	RES_FLIGHT_ NO	RES_FLIGHT_ DATE
3	02/01/97	SWEN SWENSON	218-694-8822	101	08/18/1997

when customers call in and do not remember their confirmation number. The system can look for the number knowing only part of the name.

USE OF IN

The predicate IN can be used on WHERE conditions when we want to select rows of a table whose value for some column is IN a list of desired values. For example, suppose Russell (flight operations manager) wants to get a listing of all the flight data for flights that originate in either FLG, PHX, or LAX. This could be accomplished by a compound WHERE clause using OR, such as:

```
SELECT * FROM flight
  WHERE orig = 'FLG'
  OR  orig = 'PHX'
  OR  orig = 'LAX'
```

Alternatively, we could produce the same result with the following SELECT statement using the IN predicate:

```
SELECT * FROM flight
  WHERE orig IN ('FLG', 'PHX', 'LAX')
```

The IN predicate is particularly useful when a long list of specified values is to be used for selection. IN is also used where the list of values is generated by another select clause. This will be illustrated later in the chapter.

COMPARING FOR NULL CHARACTERS

A null character is a special character in database systems that represents an empty field. No value has been stored in that position. It is different from a blank or a zero because blanks and zeros are values. Nulls are treated by SQL and the database system as though the row did not exist for that particular column function. For example, count (seat) would count only the rows where a seat value had been entered, and AVG (pay) would obtain an average over the rows that contained a pay value even if the

```
          Access: SELECT * FROM ticket
                  WHERE seat IS NULL
DB2/XDB and ORACLE: Same as Access
```

FIGURE 6.34
Selecting Rows
with Null Data

SQL RESULT TABLE

ITINERARY_NO	FLIGHT_NO	FLIGHT_DATE	SEAT
12	102	02/18/1997	
12	103	02/19/1997	
13	102	02/18/1997	
13	103	02/20/1997	

value were zero, but would not include null rows in the average calculation. The query in Figure 6.34 would give Lena a list of tickets where a seat has not been assigned.

SUBQUERIES

Much of the power of SQL comes in its ability to process subqueries or nested queries within a query. A subquery is an inner query within an outer query that can have most of the properties of the outer query. The inner query can process data from any number of tables, or from the same table as the outer query. The simplest form of the subquery is to select data from a table in the outer select based on a value obtained from the inner select. The following example would display the origination and destination data for all tickets held by Pete Peterson.

```
SELECT * FROM flight
   WHERE flight_no IN
      (SELECT flight_no FROM ticket
        WHERE itinerary_no IN
           (SELECT itinerary_no FROM passenger
              WHERE pass_name = 'Pete Peterson'))
```

Implicit join
Attributes used in the 'Where' clause implicitly reference tables used in the preceding 'From' clause.

Explicit join
Attributes used in the 'Where' clause explicitly reference tables used in the preceding or higher level 'From' clauses.

The use of IN here is a way of comparing a value for a column in one table to a set of values for the same column retrieved from a different table. If the value is in the list, then the WHERE statement is satisfied. The innermost subquery selects a list of itinerary numbers. The outer subquery selects a list of flight numbers based on the itinerary number of each ticket being in the list of itinerary numbers selected by the inner query.

This type of subquery is sometimes called an **implicit join.** The attributes used in the WHERE clause are implicitly qualified by the table referenced in the preceding FROM clause. In effect, the FLIGHT, TICKET, and PASSENGER tables have been joined to find the data for the SQL result table, although only data from the FLIGHT table are displayed. The following **explicit join** will produce the same SQL result table as the preceding implicit join. The attributes in the 'Where' clause make explicit references to tables referenced in the 'From' clause.

```
SELECT flight_no, orig, dest, orig_time, dest_time, meal, fare
   FROM flight f, ticket t, passenger p
   WHERE t.flight_no = f.flight_no
   AND p.itinerary_no = t.itinerary_no
   AND pass_name = 'Pete Peterson'
```

Subqueries can also be used to obtain an aggregate value, such as a minimum, maximum, or average, with the outer query selecting data based on that aggregate value. For example, if Lena wants to obtain the lowest-cost flights in the system, she could SELECT all flights with a fare equal to the lowest fare (MIN) of all flights in the system (Figure 6.35).

A more typical use of this example would occur when a passenger wants to obtain the lowest fare from one destination to another. Lena can use the query in

FIGURE 6.35
Selecting Data Based
on an Aggregate Value

```
   Access: SELECT * FROM flight
           WHERE fare =
           (SELECT MIN (fare) FROM flight)
DB2/XDB and ORACLE: Same as Access
```

SQL RESULT TABLE

FLIGHT_NO	ORIG	DEST	ORIG_TIME	DEST_TIME	MEAL	FARE
101	FLG	PHX	07:00:00	08:05:00	S	48.50
104	PHX	FLG	20:30:00	21:15:00	S	48.50

FIGURE 6.36
A Correlated Subquery

```
 Access: SELECT * FROM flight f1
         WHERE orig = 'phx'
         AND dest = 'lax'
         AND fare =
         (SELECT MIN (fare) FROM flight f2
         WHERE f1.orig = f2.orig
         AND f1.dest = f2.dest)
DB2/XDB: Same as Access
ORACLE: Use to_char function for times.
```

SQL RESULT TABLE

FLIGHT_NO	ORIG	DEST	ORIG_TIME	DEST_TIME	MEAL	FARE
24	PHX	LAX	13:05:00	14:25:00	S	49.00
23	PHX	LAX	11:55:00	13:15:00	S	49.00
20	PHX	LAX	10:45:00	12:05:00	S	49.00
19	PHX	LAX	09:31:00	10:50:00	S	49.00
17	PHX	LAX	08:20:00	09:20:00		49.00
35	PHX	LAX	20:20:00	21:40:00		49.00
33	PHX	LAX	18:55:00	19:15:00		49.00
31	PHX	LAX	17:55:00	19:10:00		49.00
30	PHX	LAX	16:35:00	17:55:00		49.00
29	PHX	LAX	15:25:00	16:45:00		49.00
15	PHX	LAX	07:00:00	08:20:00		49.00
39	PHX	LAX	21:20:00	22:40:00		49.00
14	PHX	LAX	21:00:00	22:20:00	S	49.00
40	PHX	LAX	22:25:00	23:42:00		49.00

Figure 6.36 to obtain all flights equal to the lowest fare from Phoenix to Los Angeles. This is done by adding a comparison on origination and destination in both the query and the subquery. The subquery is used to obtain the lowest fare for that specific route. The query is used to list the flights whose fare is equal to the lowest fare found in the subquery for that same route. Two different aliases (*f1* and *f2*) are used for the FLIGHT table so that it can be compared to itself in this subquery. This is referred to as a **correlated subquery.** This means that there is a subquery that contains an outer reference to the main query. The SQL engine has to process the subquery over and over again, once for each row in the outer query.

Correlated subquery
A subquery that refers to the same table used in the main query.

SUBQUERIES WITH GROUP BY AND HAVING

Subqueries can have all the characteristics of queries except for the ORDER BY clause. Consequently, the subqueries can include table joins and summary data using GROUP BY, with both WHERE and HAVING clauses to control the inclusion of rows. The query in Figure 6.37 illustrates how Lena can obtain the names and phone numbers of persons who have reservations on flights leaving Phoenix on March 17, for each flight booked with fewer than three passengers. The airline has decided to cancel these flights, and Lena needs to contact these customers to reschedule them. There are joins in both the query and the subquery. The subquery joins flight and ticket data and obtains the flight numbers for flights with fewer than three tickets on

FIGURE 6.37
Subqueries with
GROUP BY and
HAVING

```
Access:  SELECT Res_name, Pass_name, Res_phone, itinerary_no
         FROM Reservation AS r, Passenger AS p
         WHERE r.confirm_no = p.confirm_no
         AND res_flight_date = #3/17/97#
         AND res_flight_no IN
         (SELECT t.flight_no
         FROM ticket t, flight f
         WHERE flight_date = #3/17/97#
         AND t.flight_no = f.flight_no
         AND Orig = 'PHX'
         GROUP BY t.flight_no, flight_date
         HAVING COUNT (itinerary_no) < 3);
DB2/XDB: Same as Access except leave off the # delimiters on date.
ORACLE:  Same as Access except use ' instead of # for delimiters
         on date.
```

SQL RESULT TABLE

Res_name	Pass_name	Res_phone	itinerary_no
TORGIE TORGESON	TORGIE TORGESON	208-222-3333	11

the 17th of March. The query joins passenger and reservation data to obtain the names and phone numbers of passengers who have space on those flights for that day.

EXISTENCE AND NONEXISTENCE OF ROWS IN SUBQUERIES

EXISTS and NOT EXISTS are predicates used in SQL to test the existence of rows selected in subqueries. If one or more rows are selected in the subquery, EXISTS is a true condition. If no rows are selected, NOT EXISTS is a true condition and EXISTS is a false condition. The EXISTS predicate is rather complex to use and it is not used frequently. However, some requests for information are difficult to solve without its use.

USING NOT EXISTS TO TEST FOR MULTIPLES

The first example (Figure 6.38) shows flights with only one passenger. This has been done using a correlated subquery, meaning that the subquery depends on a variable supplied by the outer query. This means that the inner query must be evaluated for each row selected by the outer query. In this case, row one of the TICKET table will be compared with rows two through n of the same table. If there is an equal on flight number, date, and itinerary number, then EXISTS is true. This would mean that there are at least two tickets for that flight on that date in the TICKET table with different itinerary numbers. If no equal occurs, meaning NOT EXISTS is true, then there is only one row in the TICKET table with that flight number, date, and itinerary number.

FIGURE 6.38
Using NOT EXISTS to Test for Multiples

```
Access:  SELECT * FROM ticket AS t1
         WHERE not exists
         (select * from ticket t2
         where t1.flight_no = t2.flight_no
         and t1.flight_date = t2.flight_date
         and t1.itinerary_no <> t2.itinerary_no);
DB2/XDB: Use ! = for not equal instead of <>
ORACLE:  Same as Access
```

SQL RESULT TABLE

ITINERARY_NO	FLIGHT_NO	FLIGHT_DATE	SEAT
11	606	03/17/1997	12B
11	691	03/18/1997	13B
12	103	02/19/1997	
13	103	02/20/1997	

MULTIVALUED SUBQUERIES

A subquery that returns multiple rows is referred to as a *multivalued subquery*. Simple comparisons of a value cannot be done against multiple rows without using special predicates that have been set up in SQL. These predicates are ANY or SOME, and ALL. Although ANY and SOME are synonyms and can be used interchangeably, SOME is the more current and preferred usage. Any of the typical logical operators =, >, <, <=, >=, <>, and != can be used in conjunction with SOME or ALL. When a comparison is made using SOME, the condition is true when the condition is met on any one row. If no rows meet the condition, then the condition is false. The query in Figure 6.39 lists all the flights in the FLIGHT where the origination time is later than SOME flight going from Minneapolis to Phoenix. SOME flight means a comparison with a flight (ANY single flight) with the earliest origination time from Minneapolis to Phoenix. This means that flights selected may have an origination time earlier than many of the MSP/PHX flights, but must have an origination time later than at least one of the MSP/PHX flights.

FIGURE 6.39
Using ANY or SOME

```
    Access: SELECT * from flight
            WHERE orig_time >  SOME
            (SELECT orig_time FROM flight
            WHERE orig = 'MSP'
            AND dest = 'PHX')
  DB2/XDB: Same as Access
   ORACLE: Use TO_CHAR function to extract the time.
```

SQL RESULT TABLE

FLIGHT_NO	ORIG	DEST	ORIG_TIME	DEST_TIME	MEAL	FARE
104	PHX	FLG	20:30:00	21:15:00	S	48.50
31	PHX	LAX	17:55:00	19:10:00		49.00
33	PHX	LAX	18:55:00	19:15:00		49.00
35	PHX	LAX	20:20:00	21:40:00		49.00
329	LAX	PHX	21:10:00	23:59:00		49.00
399	LAX	PHX	21:20:00	22:40:00		49.00
39	PHX	LAX	21:20:00	22:40:00		49.00
301	LAX	PHX	22:20:00	01:22:00		49.00
40	PHX	LAX	22:25:00	23:42:00		49.00
198	LAX	PHX	23:20:00	02:53:00		49.00
60	PHX	SFO	17:45:00	18:36:00	S	109.00
1260	SFO	PHX	17:58:00	19:51:00		109.00
14	PHX	LAX	21:00:00	22:20:00	S	49.00
903	SFO	PHX	17:58:00	19:51:00		109.00

The query in Figure 6.40 shows the use of the ALL predicate. In this example, we are listing all flights that leave later than all flights going from Phoenix to Los Angeles. In order for ALL to be true, the origination time of each flight selected must be later than every flight from Phoenix to Los Angeles. Each row in the outer query must be true for every row in the subquery in order for the outer query row to be selected. If the subquery returns an empty SQL result table, then all conditions are false and no rows will be selected by the outer query.

SELECTING DATA FROM VIEWS

A **view** is some subset of data from the database that can be put together with any Select statement. A view is a virtual table that operates the same as a table with some exceptions.

VIEW EXCEPTIONS

1. A view does not take up any space in the database other than the space needed to define it.

2. A view is regenerated each time it is called for. The SQL engine actually substitutes the SELECT definition of the view into the SELECT referencing the view.

3. There are restrictions on updating and deleting data in a view if that view is the result of any GROUP BY operations.

4. Views can slow processing time because they are regenerated each time they are referenced.

View
A view is the same as a result table. It is the result of a SQL select that can be used by other features of the database system to build queries, reports, and forms. The definition of the view is saved in the database like any other query. The data represented by the view comes from the respective tables referenced in the view at the time a view is referenced by another operation in the database system.

CREATING AND USING VIEWS

The SELECT for a view can join data from multiple tables and multiple views. Views can make it easier to develop complex SELECT statements. Multiple views can

```
  Access: SELECT * FROM flight
          WHERE orig_time >  ALL
          (SELECT orig_time FROM flight
          WHERE orig = 'PHX'
          AND dest = 'LAX')
DB2/XDB: Same as Access
 ORACLE: Use TO_CHAR function to extract the time.
```

FIGURE 6.40
Using ALL

SQL RESULT TABLE

FLIGHT_NO	ORIG	DEST	ORIG_TIME	DEST_TIME	MEAL	FARE
198	LAX	PHX	23:20:00	02:53:00		49.00

define different constraints, and the production view (used by the application user) can employ a combination of these multiple views. A simple view could be to define Phoenix to Los Angeles flights (Figure 6.41).

Another view might be to define flights after 12:00 noon (Figure 6.42).

We can now define a view that consists of a particular combination of the precdeing views. Suppose Lena is interested in afternoon flights from Phoenix to Los Angeles that arrive before 6:00 P.M., or 18:00 hours. Note that this example selects data from two views to create a new view (Figure 6.43).

Data can be retrieved from views in the same way that data can be retrieved from tables. In the airline application, we might set up a procedure to query the number of seats left on a specific flight. Assuming we had a view of that specific flight labeled Seats_Left, we could query the view to give us a count of the seats remaining on that flight. Imagine a SEAT table that consists of all the seat numbers in a column named Seat for the aircraft used on a specific flight. A view has been set up by the following CREATE VIEW command (Figure 6.44).

The SEAT table has a list of all the seats that are available for assignment on the type of aircraft used for Flight 101. It is the seat inventory. The view, Seats_Left, is the

FIGURE 6.41
Creating a View of
Phoenix to Los
Angeles Flights

```
DB2/XDB: CREATE VIEW phx_lax AS
         SELECT * FROM flights
         WHERE orig = 'PHX' and dest = 'LAX'
ORACLE: Same as DB2
  Access: SELECT * FROM flights
         WHERE orig = 'PHX' and dest = 'LAX'
In Access, a view is created by defining a normal
query and saving the query with a name like
'phx_lax'. This query can be used like any other
table in other queries.
```

FIGURE 6.42
Creating a View of
All P.M. Flights

```
CREATE VIEW pm_flights AS
    SELECT * FROM flights
    WHERE orig_time >  12:00:00
```

FIGURE 6.43
A View Created by
Using Two Other Views

```
CREATE VIEW phx_lax_pm AS
    SELECT * from phx_lax
    WHERE flight_no IN
         (Select flight_no FROM pm_flights
              WHERE dest_time < 18:00:00)
```

difference between seats available and seats taken. The subquery obtains the seats taken or assigned, and the outer query obtains a SQL result table of all seats in the inventory that are not in the SQL result table of the seats taken. It is the same as subtracting the Seats_Taken SQL result table from the original inventory, which is the SEAT table.

We can now select information from the view, Seats_Left. Lena can use the query in Figure 6.45 to obtain a count of the rows in the view, which gives her the number of seats still available for assignment. Because some tickets in the TICKET table may not have seat assignments, the result is not a count of the seats remaining to be sold.

A view changes when any table used by that view changes. As soon as Lena sells another ticket on this specific flight with a seat assignment, the next access of that view will reflect that change. The specific seat that was assigned will not show up in the view as being available for assignment the next time the view is accessed.

SUMMARY

Section II has covered a variety of functions, conditions, operators, and optional clauses that give the SQL SELECT statement great power and flexibility. We will briefly review these options here.

A select statement beginning with SELECT DISTINCT will report a row only once if that row is exactly duplicated in a requested retrieval. SELECT ALL, or just SELECT, will cause duplicates to appear in the SQL result table.

The aggregate functions COUNT, MIN (for minimum), MAX (for maximum), SUM, and AVE (for average) can be used in the column list to produce summary results. The function chosen is followed by the column name in parentheses, for example, MIN (fare). Aggregate functions cannot be combined with nonaggregate

```
CREATE VIEW seats_left As
     SELECT seat FROM seat
  WHERE seat NOT IN
          (SELECT seat FROM ticket
              WHERE flight_no = 101
              AND flight_date = 8/18/97)
```

FIGURE 6.44
View of Seats
Remaining on a
Specific Flight

```
SELECT count(*) FROM seats_left;
```

FIGURE 6.45
Using a Complex View
as a Simple Table

SQL RESULT TABLE

count(*)
82

column specifications in the same SELECT statement. Each column named in an aggregate SELECT statement must be qualified by an aggregate function or must also appear in a GROUP BY clause.

The GROUP BY clause applies control break logic to the SELECT statement. It is designed to be combined with the use of aggregate functions and causes the functions specified to be calculated as subtotals over each value of the grouping variables.

The ORDER BY clause can be added to a SELECT statement to produce results in sorted order. It can be used in conjunction with a GROUP BY clause or with a nonaggregate SELECT. In either case, the ORDER BY clause causes the SQL result table to be sorted in order on the column(s) specified. If more than one column is specified in either an ORDER BY or GROUP BY clause, the first column named is the primary sort, or grouping, field.

The HAVING clause allows conditions to be applied to the results of GROUP BY clauses. Only those summary results meeting the specifications of the HAVING clause are placed in the SQL result table.

A number of conditions increase the flexibility of the WHERE clause. The % character is a wild card matching any value for any number of characters. The predicate NULL can test whether the value for some column exists. The predicate EXISTS can test for the existence of a row meeting some condition. The underscore character is a wild card matching a single character of any value. The predicate BETWEEN can describe a range of acceptable values (this range is inclusive of the limits specified). The predicate IN, followed by a set of values in parentheses, can specify a list of values that are to be accepted as meeting the WHERE clause.

The list for an IN clause may be generated by a subquery whose result is a single set of values instead of a list of literals. The result of the inner query produces a set of result values that are used by the IN condition of the outer query.

Not all subqueries use the IN condition. A subquery that produces a single value as its result can be used wherever such a value can appear in a WHERE clause. Also, the predicates SOME and ALL can be used with subqueries that produce multiple result rows. If SOME is used, the condition will be met if it is met for one or more of the subquery result rows. If ALL is used, each subquery result row must meet the condition.

Subqueries may be nested to any level of depth required. Sometimes there is a need to qualify values in the innerquery, or subquery, based on a value from the outer query. This type of operation is called a correlated subquery.

Select statements may be used to create views. A view does not take up space in the database, but is instead regenerated each time it is requested. A view can contain a subset of data from a table or multiple related tables. Most SQL operations can be performed on views just as if they were tables, but the use of views can slow processing time.

The following SQL features were covered in this section.

1. Joins of multiple tables using a WHERE clause to specify the join condition on each table.

2. Using DISTINCT to eliminate duplicate rows of data.

3. Functions to obtain counts, averages, minimum values, and maximum values.

4. Grouping data into groups with the GROUP BY option to obtain aggregate summaries on the group.

5. Ordering the output data using the ORDER BY option.

6. Selection on rows with the WHERE clause and selection on grouped data with the HAVING clause in the same statement.

7. Selection from a list using the IN feature.

8. Subqueries as a means of creating lists to select from.

9. Setting up subqueries with aggregate and GROUP BY processing.

10. Using ANY, ALL, and EXISTS to process multivalued subqueries.

11. Setting up and selecting data from views.

A number of good references on building SQL are listed in the Reference section at the back of this text. Specifically, Groff and Koch provide a number of good examples that are beyond the scope of this text.

REVIEW QUIZ

_____ Two or more tables used together to obtain a result table.

_____ Selection of some subset of rows from one or more tables.

_____ Selection of some subset of columns from one or more tables.

_____ Nonmatches from each table in a two-table join are included in the result table.

_____ Nonmatches from the first table are included in the result table.

_____ Only matches from each of two tables are included in the result table.

_____ A value treated by the database system as having no value.

_____ A relational database system that was developed by IBM.

_____ A subquery that includes a table in the main query.

_____ A query that can be defined and used later in the definition of other queries.

_____ A command used in SQL to sequence the result table.

_____ A command used in SQL to summarize the result table.

_____ A command used in SQL to specify selection criteria on rows.

_____ A command used in SQL to specify selection criteria on summary results.

_____ A command used in SQL to specify the table names.

_____ The method used in SQL to control projection.

_____ The graphical interface that allows a user to create a query.

_____ A database system that was developed to assist designers to test DB2 systems on a PC workstation.

_____ A predicate used in SQL to control selection using wild card characters.

_____ A predicate used in SQL to control selection over a range of values.

1. View
2. SQL
3. QBE
4. XDB
5. DB2
6. Oracle
7. Sybase
8. Outer join
9. Inner join
10. Left outer join
11. Right outer join
12. Selection
13. Projection
14. Join
15. WHERE
16. HAVING
17. From
18. Column names or *
19. GROUP BY
20. ORDER BY
21. Null character
22. Space
23. LIKE
24. BETWEEN
25. Correlated subquery

REVIEW QUESTIONS AND EXERCISES

Passengers who have made reservations often call in to verify their reservations, or to make changes to their reservations. Also, the airline may need to know certain information for passengers flying on specific flights. An example of a specific flight would be Flight 101 on August 1, 1997. Remember the same flight number is used to schedule the same flight every day it flies. It is made unique by the date of that flight, which is stored in the ticket. The airline also needs to request information to help manage flight schedules and operations in the future.

Refer to the E-R diagram in Figure 6.5, which supports the development of these queries. Note that in Access the AIRPORT table is repeated on the diagram to show multiple relationships to the same column. The table does not exist twice in the database.

Write the appropriate SQL statements to address the following requests:

1. Andy Anderson calls in to see if he has a reservation.
2. The airline wants to know the flight number, date, origin, destination, and related time data for all tickets related to passenger Pete Peterson.
3. The airline wants to know the total of the fares for all tickets related to Pete Peterson.
4. The airline wants to know the total of the fares by flight number for each specific date.
5. The airline wants to know which flights have no passengers scheduled on 8/21/97.
6. A passenger calls to ask for schedule information (flight number, departure, and arrival times) for all flights from Phoenix to San Francisco whose fare is at the lowest rate available for such flights.
7. The airline wants to know the passenger count by day for each flight that has more than one passenger scheduled.
8. The airline wants to know the flight numbers of all flights from Phoenix to Los Angeles whose flight duration (destination time minus origination time) is less than the average duration of flights from Phoenix to Los Angeles.
9. A passenger wants to fly from Phoenix to Los Angeles and back in a single day. He needs at least five hours in Los Angeles to get to and from the airport and conduct his business. List the flight numbers, origin times, and destination times of the sets of flights that will accommodate his schedule.
10. David Peterson wants to know if he is scheduled on any of the same flights on the same day with Olga Swenson. (Note that airlines are not allowed to give out this kind of information.)
11. Andy Anderson wants to know the passenger and ticket information on all passengers he has made reservations for.
12. What flights from Flagstaff to Phoenix have connecting flights in Phoenix going on to Los Angeles? Allow 40 minutes for a connection.
13. The airline wants to know the total maximum fare for flights between each origin and destination airport (Phoenix to Los Angeles, Phoenix to Flagstaff, Phoenix to San Francisco, etc.).
14. The airline wants to know the number of tickets sold for each flight across all dates.
15. The airline wants to know the total of the fares collected for each of its flights on each date. (Assume all tickets were sold at full fare.)
16. List the flight number, origin and destination codes, and origin elevation sorted from the highest to the lowest origin elevation.
17. The airline wants to produce a list showing the flight number, origin and destination, and airport names and phone numbers, along with the origin and destination times for all flights.

18. What is the maximum fare for flights originating at each airport?

19. List the maximum fare for flights originating at each airport if that fare is greater than $100.

20. What is the lowest fare on a flight from Phoenix to Los Angeles?

21. What are the lowest fare flights from Phoenix to Los Angeles?

22. What is the highest fare on a flight from Phoenix to Los Angeles?

23. What is the average fare for flights from Phoenix to Los Angeles?

IMPLEMENTING A RELATIONAL DATABASE

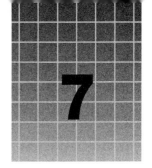

LEARNING OBJECTIVES

After completing this chapter, you should be able to

- Map conceptual data model E-R diagrams and domain descriptions into appropriate data structure diagrams.
- Create a database space and a set of tables to implement structures specified by data structure diagrams.
- Implement primary and foreign key restrictions on tables to ensure referential integrity.
- Use a variety of features of the data definition language to implement appropriate restrictions on the domains of attributes.
- Create unique and nonunique indexes and use them appropriately.
- Create views and use them appropriately.
- Use the INSERT, UPDATE, and DELETE commands to enter and maintain data in a database.

The process of moving from a conceptual design to an implemented database system requires conversion of the conceptual model to a set of structures supported by the type of database model that will be used for implementation. The data definition language of the DBMS is then used to physically implement these structures. The structures used will vary depending on the database model that is used. This chapter will concentrate on converting the conceptual design to a relational model. Other chapters will look at the hierarchical model and the network model.

A number of references can be useful in obtaining both broader and in-depth coverage of the topics in this chapter. Depending on the software you are using, you can refer to the Oracle, DB2, Access, and Sybase references at the end of this textbook. Groff (1990) and Koch (1994) are excellent references on SQL data description language examples. Date (1995) and Codd (1990) are excellent examples on the concepts and theory.

MAPPING THE CONCEPTUAL DESIGN TO THE RELATIONAL MODEL

E-R diagrams and the supporting domain description information gathered during conceptual design are intentionally generic in nature, so that they are compatible with implementation using any database model. This generic conceptual design information is then translated into a form compatible with implementation in the particular database model that is to be used.

For databases that are to be implemented using the relational model, data structure diagrams (introduced in Chapter 2) are used to create a visual relational data model design. The information from E-R diagrams and domain descriptions is used to generate a set of table structure diagrams in a form fully compatible with relational implementation. The data structure diagrams identify all the data tables that are to be created in order to implement the database, as well as the relationships among those tables. These diagrams also identify all the **attributes** (columns) of each table that must be created along with the identification of the primary and foreign key attributes.

Attribute
A column or field in a table.

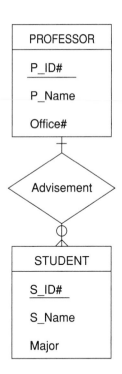

E-R Diagram

FIGURE 7.1
Mapping a One to Many Relationship to Data Structure Diagrams

Data Structure Diagram

PROFESSOR(P_ID#, P_Name, Office#)

STUDENT(S_ID#, S_Name, Major, P_ID#)

MAPPING RELATIONSHIPS TO DATA STRUCTURE DIAGRAMS

Figure 7.1 provides a very simple example of corresponding E-R and data structure diagrams for two related entities, PROFESSOR and STUDENT. The first step in mapping from E-R diagrams to data structure diagrams is very straightforward. Each entity in the E-R diagram, PROFESSOR and STUDENT in our example, corresponds to a table to be represented in the data structure diagram. Each attribute identified in the E-R diagram or supporting domain description translates into an attribute or column name of a table in the data structure diagram (P_ID#, P_Name, and Office# in the PROFESSOR table and S_ID#, S_Name, and Major in the STUDENT table). In addition, the primary key attribute for each table is underlined in our data structure diagrams. Note that the data structure diagram for the STUDENT table also includes a P_ID# column that was not shown as an attribute of the STUDENT entity in the E-R model.

Primary key
A unique identifier of a row in a table. Unique means that no other row can have the same data value for the attribute that is selected as primary key.

Foreign key
An attribute in one table that is the primary key or refers to the primary key of another table. It is a way of linking one table to another.

P_ID# is the **primary key** attribute of the PROFESSOR entity. Recall that the relational model implements relationships implicitly. The primary key attribute of the entity on the one side of a one to many relationship is repeated as a **foreign key** attribute in the data of the table on the many side. Foreign key attributes are not normally included in E-R diagramming, but they must be included in our data structure diagrams. Thus, each time there is a one to many relationship in an E-R diagram, we will add a foreign key column to the table on the many side of the relationship when creating the data structure diagram (for example, P_ID# in the STUDENT table). Foreign key columns are designated by a dashed underline in the data structure diagram.

Data structure diagrams also commonly show lines connecting related tables, and use symbols similar to those of the E-R model to visually represent relationships. However, it is the replication of corresponding identifying data in the primary and foreign keys that actually links tables in the relational model.

The mapping procedure is very similar for entities that have a one to one relationship. When this type of relationship exists in an E-R model, it almost always represents a class-subclass relationship. There is a base entity type that is mandatory in the relationship, and a subclass entity type that is optional. Figure 7.2 illustrates this type of relationship. STUDENT is the base entity type and GRAD-STUDENT is a subclass of STUDENT. All grad students are students, but not all students are grad students.

For this type of relationship, the same attribute (S_ID#) will serve as the primary key in both tables, but this attribute will also serve as the foreign key attribute in the table that is on the optional side of the relationship. Thus, the S_ID# in the GRAD-STUDENT table serves both as its primary key and as a foreign key linking each GRAD-STUDENT to the related row of the master STUDENT table.

MAPPING MANY TO MANY RELATIONSHIPS TO DATA STRUCTURE DIAGRAMS

As we noted in Chapter 2, many to many relationships cannot be directly implemented in a relational database. Many to many relationships are to be resolved by creating an

E-R Diagram

FIGURE 7.2
Mapping a One to One
Relationship to Data
Structure Diagrams

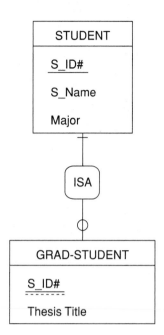

Data Structure Diagram

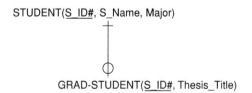

intersection entity type. Often this will have been done at the conceptual modeling stage. However, E-R diagrams may retain many to many relationships if there is no data associated with the intersection entity type.

Figure 7.3 shows this type of relationship for students and clubs. Each student may be in many clubs and each club has many students as members. Where there are many to many relationships in the E-R diagram, an intersection table must be created when mapping to data structure diagrams. Because the intersection table carries no data of its own, its column names or attributes are simply a pair of foreign keys linking to the respective primary key attributes of the parent tables (S_ID# and Club_Name in our example). The concatenation of the two foreign key attributes also serves as the primary key for the intersection table.

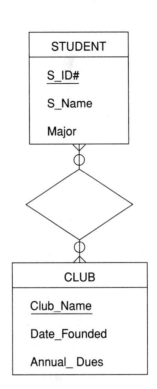

E-R Diagram

Data Structure Diagram

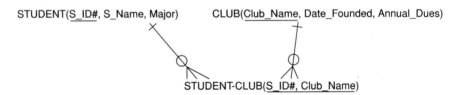

INTRA-TABLE RELATIONSHIPS

Intra-table relationship
A relationship between two
different instances of the
same entity or table.

Relationships between different record occurrences of the same entity type also
require special treatment when we map from E-R diagrams to relational data structure diagrams. In E-R diagrams, **intra-table relationships** are simply represented
by a relationship connecting a table to itself.

Figure 7.4 illustrates how a mentorship relationship between students would be
represented in an E-R diagram and shows how this relationship is mapped into a
data structure diagram. We are assuming that a school has a program that allows

E-R Diagram

FIGURE 7.4
Mapping a One to
Many Intra-Table
Relationship to Data
Structure Diagrams

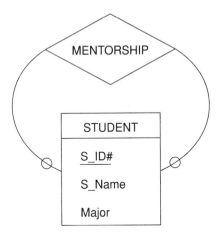

Data Structure Diagram

STUDENT(S_ID#, S_Name, Major, Mentor_ID#)

1234	Adams	ACC	2345
2345	Davis	CIS	
3456	Jones	HIS	5678
4567	Lewis	ECO	2345
5678	Travis	ACC	

students to serve as mentors for other students. A student can serve as mentor to many students. However, each student can be mentored by, at most, one other student.

In this situation, the STUDENT entity has a one to many relationship with itself. In one to many relationships between tables, the primary key from the table on the one side was repeated as a foreign key in the many side table. To achieve a similar linkage between rows of the same table, we add a new attribute identical in type to the primary key attribute, Mentor_ID#. This attribute is used like a foreign key to link each row on the many side of the relationship to the corresponding row on the one side. The value of the primary key attribute from the row on the one side of the relationship is placed in this linking attribute column for each corresponding row on the many side. In our example, each student who is mentored has the S-ID# of his or her mentor in the S_ID# column.

Intra-table relationships may also be many to many. Product assemblies provide a good example of this. Suppose a company sells assembled PCs and also sells components, such as memory chips and mother boards. Figure 7.5 illustrates this relationship. The E-R diagram indicates that one or more rows in the Product entity class may serve as components of one or more other product occurrences. That is, a component product, such as a memory chip, may appear in more than one type of

FIGURE 7.5

FIGURE 7.5

Mapping a Many to
Many Intra-Table
Relationship to Data
Structure Diagrams

E-R Diagram

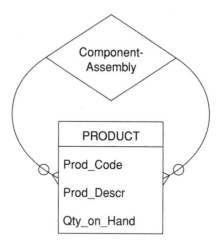

Data Structure Diagram

PRODUCT(Prod_Code, Prod_Descr, Qty_on_Hand)

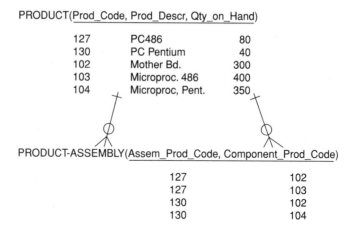

127	PC486	80
130	PC Pentium	40
102	Mother Bd.	300
103	Microproc. 486	400
104	Microproc, Pent.	350

PRODUCT-ASSEMBLY(Assem_Prod_Code, Component_Prod_Code)

127	102
127	103
130	102
130	104

assembled PC. At the same time, each assembled product may contain many different components—memory chips, mother boards, a keyboard, and so on.

Because many to many relationships cannot be represented in the relational model, we will need to create an intersection table, just as we did for inter-table relationships. In this case, the intersection table links pairs of rows from the same table. Two columns are created in the intersection table to store the values of the primary key attributes from each side of the relationship for each pair of rows that is to be linked together. These values act like foreign keys. In our example, each row

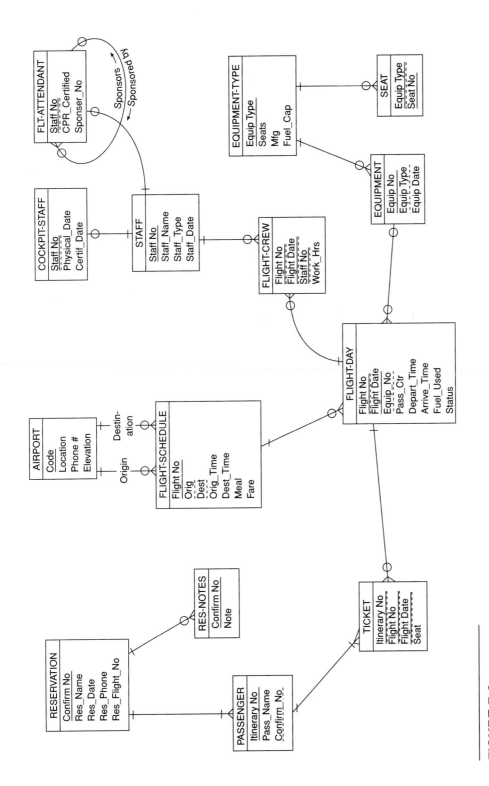

FIGURE 7.6
Data Structure
Diagram for Air West
Database

of the PRODUCT-ASSEMBLY intersection table links a row in the PRODUCT table for a component product to a row representing an assembled product of which it is a component. We can see that product 102 is a component of both product 127 and product 130, and product 130 has both products 102 and 104 as components.

OTHER MAPPING ISSUES

Other changes to the conceptual model representation of a database may be made at this point as well. There may be some tables that are to be denormalized for performance reasons, or the conceptual model may contain derived attributes whose values should be computed as needed rather than being stored as an attribute of a table in the database. If these sorts of changes are needed, they will be made in the process of mapping from the conceptual model to the table structure diagrams. The set of table structures produced should correspond to the set of relational tables that will be implemented.

DATA STRUCTURE DIAGRAMS
FOR THE AIRLINE DATABASE

The conceptual design of the Airline database presented in Chapter 5 is sufficiently detailed to support mapping into a set of data structure diagrams. **Before you look at Figure 7.6 or read the following descriptions, refer to Figures 5.18 and 5.19 in Chapter 5. Using those figures and the supporting text, develop your own set of data structure diagrams for the Airline database.** Once you have completed your set of data structure diagrams, read the following descriptions and compare them with your results.

No unresolved many to many relationships are shown in the E-R diagram of the Airline database. Therefore, the set of tables can be mapped directly from the E-R diagram with one table being created for each entity. A set of data structure diagrams for the Airline database is shown in Figure 7.6. The domain descriptions for the entities that were presented in Figure 5.19 serve to identify the set of attributes for each table defined in Figure 7.6. Where foreign key attributes were not included in the domain descriptions of the conceptual model, they have been added to the data structure diagrams of Figure 7.6.

BUILDING THE PHYSICAL DATABASE

INTRODUCTION

Building the physical database involves reserving physical space using disk file concepts, and defining the layout of this space with the data description language (DDL). In DB2 and Oracle, the term *tablespace* refers to an area where tables can be stored. The tablespace is the unit of storage that is restorable in case of a database failure. Normally there will be multiple tablespaces for a large database. In DB2 the tablespace is one or more VSAM data sets, or files. In the DOS environment used by most PC-based DBMSs, each table is normally multiple DOS

SMALLINT	2 bytes, range –32,768 to 32,767. Fractional values are truncated.
INT[EGER]	4 bytes, range –2.147,483,468 to 2,147,483,647. Fractional values are truncated.
FLOAT	8 bytes, range –1.0E + 300 to 1.0E + 300 approx., 15 digits of precision.
DEC[IMAL] [(precision[,scale])]	1–8 bytes, range -10^{15} to 10^{15}. Precision is the total number of digits including decimal with a maximum of 15 and a default of 5. Scale defines decimal positions with a default of zero.
MONEY	8 bytes, range -10^{13} to 10^{13}. Displayed as decimal (15,2).
DATE	6 bytes, range 1/1/0001 to 12/31/9999. Format can be either mm/dd/yy or mm/dd/yyyy.
TIME	3 bytes, range 00:00:01 to 24:00:00. Format is noramlly hh:mm:ss using a 24 hour clock.
TIMESTAMP	12 bytes, range 0001–01–01–00.00.01 to 9999–12–31–24.00.00 Format is yyyy-mm-dd-hh.mm.ss.nnnnnn where n = microseconds.
CHAR(n)	n bytes, range 1 byte to 1500 bytes. n = length of field in number of characters.
VARCHAR(n)	<= n bytes, range 1 byte to 4056 bytes. n = maximum length of field in characters.
LONG VARCHAR	<= 4056 bytes, range 1 byte to 4056 bytes. Can be defined as FOR BIT DATA.
DOUBLE	Same as float.
NUMERIC	Same as decimal.
REAL	Same as float.

FIGURE 7.7
Typical Data Types for
Relational Databases

files. The process of defining each table with the DDL involves naming the table, creating column names, and defining the data type and size properties for each column. Data type definitions vary across different implementations of relational database software. See the table on data type variations on pages 200–201 in Chapter 6. Figure 7.7 shows most of the data types that are used across various relational database systems.

SQL LANGUAGE ELEMENTS

The language elements of SQL are made up of characters, tokens, and identifiers. The characters in most systems are divided into letters, digits, and special characters. The letters can include both upper and lower case. Tokens are constants, identifiers, keywords, operators, and some special characters used in the syntax of SQL. The operators include =, <, <=, >, >=, !=, and ^=. The symbols !> and ^= are used for *not equal.* Identifiers are names given to objects defined in the database system.

Names

The ANSI standard for all names is 18 characters starting with a letter, with no blank or special characters. Normally an underscore is used to separate multi-word names to improve readability. The dot is used to separate multiple objects in a name, such as user qualifiers of table names and table qualifiers of column names. Because many relational database software packages were developed prior to the ANSI standard, a fair amount of variation exists in what has been implemented. DB2, for instance, requires that database and index objects be given names that consist of 1 to 8 characters. Tables, columns, and views are given 1- to 18- character names. User names are 1 to 8 characters long and identify the user of the database system. User names are part of the security system and will be discussed further in Chapter 10. The naming rules given here are for DB2; however, they will work for most systems.

Constants

Constants are specific values that can be character strings, dates, times, or numeric. Character strings must be enclosed in quotes. Double or single quotes can be used, but must match. Quotes within quotes are permitted. "O'Brien", "6'3"" and '6"' are all legal constants. A double quote within a quote ("6'3"") signifies a quote character within a quote delimiter of the same type.

Null
A nonvalue. The attribute has never been given a value. It is not the same as a zero or a blank. Database systems implement this by giving the attribute a special value that denotes it as a null to all other operations of that database system.

Nulls

Any column in a table can have a **null** for its value unless NOT NULL has been specified in the definition of that column. A null is the same as no value and is not included in some SQL operations, such as statistical and count operations.

SQL DATA DEFINITION LANGUAGE (DDL)

The framework for building a relational database using SQL has now been established. The remainder of this chapter will illustrate the various SQL statements that can be used to define a relational database, load data into it, and do some data maintenance with updates and deletes. Defining the database includes statements to define the database space, the tables, indexes, views, foreign keys, and various constraints on the database. We will also describe how these **data definition language (DDL)** statements can be used to enforce referential and domain integrity for the database, and illustrate the content of the data dictionary and how the definitions are stored in the dictionary. The statements will be covered in a sequence that approximates that which would normally be used to set up a database.

Data definition language (DDL)
The set of statements used by a DBMS to define the structure of a database.

Creating the Database Space

The database in most organizations will be built by the database administration group. However, on many smaller PC-based systems, the database can be the responsibility

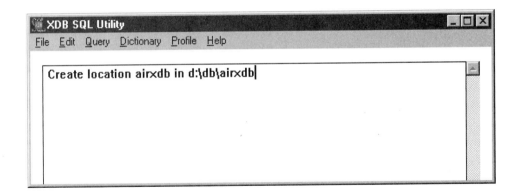

FIGURE 7.8

Database space
A physical space on a disk
(file) for storing database
tables and indexes.

of the application developer or the user. Creating the **database space** will vary depending on the hardware and software being used. The process used to create the database space is not a part of the SQL standard and thus varies significantly across implementations.

For example, the following process will create database space under XDB. The database space for XDB is normally created in its own subdirectory on a specific disk drive. The database is given a 1- to 8-character name. The instruction can be executed as part of interactive SQL. The command will create a number of skeleton files and a number of table files to store the database definitions as they are developed. The following command will create a database called airline1 in the airline1 subdirectory within the XDB directory on the D drive.

```
CREATE DATABASE airline1 IN d:\xdb\airline1
```

A skeleton database system of files and tables is created in airline1 as a data dictionary for all new objects to be created in that database. The tables include various system tables and special files to maintain information for XDB to operate on the database. The CREATE DATABASE command is fairly similar for other DBMSs, although the statement may contain additional parameter options that allow the creator to control the amount and type of space allocated to the database.

An XDB Lite that comes with Micro Focus Dialog Systems allows you to test Cobol and SQL on a PC workstation as though it were a DB2 application. This product does not support a Create Database command. Instead, the user must use a Create Location command (Figure 7.8):

```
CREATE LOCATION location-name IN location-path
   [SORT SEQUENCE {EBCDIC | INSENSITIVE | SENSITIVE | USER}]
   [FORWARD LOG forward-log-name]
   [XDB SYSTEM TABLES]
```

Creates a location in the specified directory. The SORT SEQUENCE keyword allows you to choose the sort sequence for the location. The FORWARD LOG keyword set the drive and path for the forward log. The XDB SYSTEM TABLES keyword causes a complete set of XDB Version 2.41 system tables and views to be created.

The Create Location command has the same purpose as the Create Database. It creates the files for maintaining information about the database and creates all the system tables that are similar to DB2. The following list shows most of these system tables:

SYSXDBMA TAB	2,640	03-28-96	9:37p
SYSTABLE TAB	18,224	03-28-96	9:37p
SYSCOLUM TAB	176,952	03-28-96	9:37p
SYSTABAU TAB	2,568	03-28-96	9:19p
SYSINDEX TAB	4,048	03-16-96	5:12p
15726231 TAB	14,168	03-16-96	5:12p
17684538 TAB	13,566	03-28-96	9:36p
SYSVIEWD TAB	0	03-16-96	5:12p
SYSDBRM TAB	0	03-16-96	5:12p
SYSSTMT TAB	0	03-16-96	5:12p
SYSDBAUT TAB	0	03-16-96	5:12p
SYSSTOGR TAB	66	03-16-96	5:12p
SYSVOLUM TAB	290	03-16-96	5:12p
SYSSYNON TAB	0	03-16-96	5:12p
13278014 TAB	3,024	03-28-96	9:26p
SYSDATAB TAB	222	03-16-96	5:12p
SYSUSERA TAB	0	03-16-96	5:12p
SYSKEYS TAB	4,096	03-16-96	5:12p
SYSREF TAB	0	03-16-96	5:12p
SYSRELS TAB	0	03-16-96	5:12p
SYSFOREI TAB	0	03-16-96	5:12p
SYSCHECK TAB	0	03-16-96	5:12p
SYSVIEWS TAB	0	03-16-96	5:12p
SYSCOLAU TAB	0	03-16-96	5:12p

Another way to look at this information is to execute a SQL query against the sysibm.systables table as shown in Figure 7.9.

Once the Location is created, you can go to Profile, Location, and Browse and pull up a window of different Locations to link to Figure 7.10. You want to be linked to the System Location when you execute the Create Location command. Once you switch to the Airline Location, then you can build tables within that database.

In most DBMSs designed to operate on mainframes or mini-computers, an intermediate structure called a *tablespace* can be created. A large database can

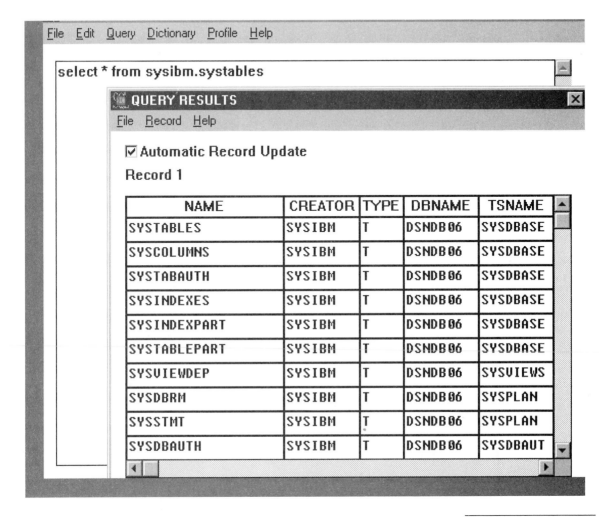

File Edit Query Dictionary Profile Help

select * from sysibm.systables

QUERY RESULTS

File Record Help

☑ **Automatic Record Update**

Record 1

NAME	CREATOR	TYPE	DBNAME	TSNAME
SYSTABLES	SYSIBM	T	DSNDB06	SYSDBASE
SYSCOLUMNS	SYSIBM	T	DSNDB06	SYSDBASE
SYSTABAUTH	SYSIBM	T	DSNDB06	SYSDBASE
SYSINDEXES	SYSIBM	T	DSNDB06	SYSDBASE
SYSINDEXPART	SYSIBM	T	DSNDB06	SYSDBASE
SYSTABLEPART	SYSIBM	T	DSNDB06	SYSDBASE
SYSVIEWDEP	SYSIBM	T	DSNDB06	SYSVIEWS
SYSDBRM	SYSIBM	T	DSNDB06	SYSPLAN
SYSSTMT	SYSIBM	T	DSNDB06	SYSPLAN
SYSDBAUTH	SYSIBM	T	DSNDB06	SYSDBAUT

FIGURE 7.9

have several defined tablespaces and individual tables can be assigned to specific tablespaces when they are created. Individual tablespaces can be backed up and taken on- and off-line independently. Managing the allocation of tables among these tablespaces effectively greatly improves the efficiency of a large database.

Database Space in DB2   DB2 has a database structure made up of tablespaces and index spaces. These are logical storage entities defined by CREATE DATABASE and CREATE TABLESPACE. Tablespaces and index spaces are assigned to a storage group, which is a physical entity that can be assigned to one or more VSAM files. Storage groups are defined with the CREATE STOGROUP statement. Tables can be assigned to specific tablespaces when they are created.

Database Space in Oracle   Oracle also uses a system of tablespaces. The database is created through a CREATE DATABASE statement, and one or more tablespaces

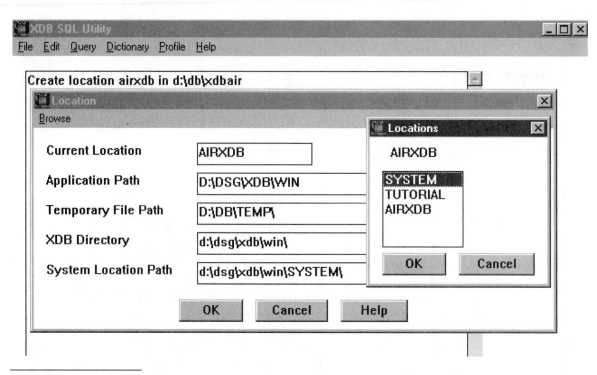

FIGURE 7.10

can be created for a database. Under Oracle it is recommended that all indexes be placed in a tablespace that is separate from the tablespaces used to store data tables.

Some database systems allow you to eliminate the database space with the DROP DATABASE command.

```
DROP DATABASE airline1
```

will erase the database files in the subdirectory and remove the database name from the system database maintained under the system subdirectory. Other database systems for the PC will have similar ways of dropping the database.

Creating Table Definitions

Tables can be defined to the database system as soon as a database space has been defined. Tables are created by the CREATE TABLE command. The basic syntax used to create a table is as follows:

```
CREATE TABLE table-name
( column-name data-type [(length)] [NOT NULL], . . .)
[ IN tablespace ]
```

Data type
A data property that defines an attribute as text, numeric, date, currency, or some other variation of text and numeric.

Defining the table includes giving the table a name, and giving each column in the table a name and a **data type**. Some data types will also require length specifications. The optional IN tablespace clause allows you to specify which tablespace that table will be placed in if you are using a DBMS that supports multiple tablespaces. The following example defines the flight table to the database. The column specifications (name, type, and size when needed) are in parentheses separated by commas. The

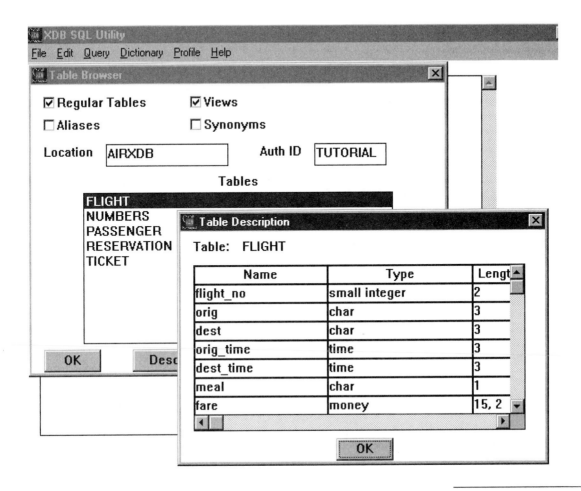

FIGURE 7.11

NOT NULL specification is a constraint for data entry that requires data in that field before the data record (row) can be inserted into the table.

```
CREATE TABLE flight
  (flight_no smallint NOT NULL,
  orig     char 3,
  dest     char 3,
  orig_time time,
  dest_time time,
  meal     char 3,
  fare     money)(Note that this column is sometimes referred to as Price)
```

The data dictionary will contain information that reflects the definition of this table after the execution of this SQL DDL command. In XDB, this information is available through the dictionary option under the main menu. You need to set the Location under Dictionary to Airline, and then go to Tables under Dictionary to bring up the Table Browser as shown. The Table Description window comes up by selecting a table and the Describe button (Figure 7.11).

Other DBMSs provide similar data dictionary information. In Oracle you can use the command *Describe Flight* to obtain the same information. The definitions are normally not case sensitive so table name flight is the same as table name FLIGHT.

The preceding example above shows a very simple table creation statement. The SQL supported by most DBMSs provides for a number of clauses that can be used to create tables in different ways or to impose referential integrity constraints on tables as they are created. The syntax of these clauses varies slightly across different DBMSs. We will use examples from XDB/DB2 for illustration purposes here. Oracle syntax for these statements is virtually identical, and is illustrated in a later section.

Creating Tables from Existing Table Structures   It is often convenient to be able to create a table based on specifications for some existing table. Two versions of this type of table creation are often offered. The first allows you to create a table based on the results of a select statement. The new table gets its table definition from the table on which the select statement is performed and is automatically populated with the data produced by the select statement. Under XDB/DB2, the following statement might be used to create a table to store just those flights originating in Phoenix:

```
CREATE TABLE flight_phx
SELECT * FROM flight WHERE orig = 'PHX'
```

The result table flight_phx will be created in the database as a real table. The flight_phx table will contain the same column definitions as the table flight. The content of the table will be only those rows from the table flight that have an origination code of 'PHX'.

Another example of creating a new table using SELECTs involves the use of the UNION. A UNION merges two tables into one table. Often, transaction data may exist in separate tables based on months. The month tables can be combined into one table consisting of all transactions to date or for a quarter.

```
CREATE TABLE qtr1_sales
   SELECT * FROM jan_sales
UNION
   SELECT * FROM feb_sales
UNION
   SELECT * FROM mar_sales
```

The qtr1_sales table will consist of all the rows in each of the month sales tables. The qtr1_sales table will have the same column definitions as the month sales tables. The UNION cannot be used unless the tables are union compatible, meaning the tables have compatible data types column by column.

Sometimes it is necessary to create an empty table whose definitions are identical to an existing table. XDB/DB2 provides a LIKE clause on the CREATE TABLE command that facilitates the creation of this type of table. The following example creates a flight1 table that has the same structure as the flight table. The new table will have no data in it. The CREATE LIKE does not carry forward any primary or foreign key definitions.

```
CREATE TABLE flight1 LIKE Flight
```

The full syntax of the CREATE TABLE command is as follows.

```
CREATE TABLE table-name
   {
        [(  column-name data-type [FOR BIT DATA]
            [NOT NULL [WITH DEFAULT]] [,...]
```

```
    )]
        [select command]
    | LIKE {table-name | view-name}
}
PRIMARY KEY [key-name] (column-list)
FOREIGN KEY [constraint-name] (column-list)
    REFERENCES referenced-table
    [ON DELETE
        {RESTRICT | CASCADE | SET NULL}]
```

The first part of the preceding syntax above shows the alternative ways to create a table that we have already discussed. The remaining clauses of the CREATE syntax allow you to define primary and foreign keys.

Adding Referential Integrity Restrictions   The primary and foreign clauses allow referential integrity constraints to be built into the definition of a table as it is created. **Referential integrity** constraints assure that required relationships between tables are established as data are added to the database, and assure that those relationships are accurately maintained as changes are made to data. The following samples of the CREATE TABLE set up the tables Airport and Flight with primary and foreign keys in the Airline database.

Referential integrity
Referential integrity is maintained by a DBMS if all logical relationships that exist between tables are implemented when data are added to tables and if these relationships are accurately maintained when data are modified or deleted.

Airport table:

```
CREATE TABLE airport
    (code CHAR (3) NOT NULL,
      location CHAR (20),
        elevation smallint,
          phone CHAR (12),
            PRIMARY KEY (code))
```

Flight table:

```
CREATE TABLE flight
    (flight_no SMALLINT NOT NULL,
      orig   CHAR 3 NOT NULL,
        dest   CHAR 3 NOT NULL,
          orig_time TIME,
            dest_time TIME,
              meal   CHAR 1,
                price  MONEY,
                  PRIMARY KEY (flight_no),
                    FOREIGN KEY orig_err (orig)
                      REFERENCES airport
                        ON DELETE RESTRICT,

FOREIGN KEY dest_err (dest)
    REFERENCES airport
      ON DELETE RESTRICT)
```

Unique index
An index that requires the values of the indexed column to be unique. Rows with duplicate values for the index column will not be allowed if a unique index has been defined.

PRIMARY KEY defines the column or columns that will be the unique identifier for each row in the table. Note that the NOT NULL is required for the columns designated as keys. Normally, you must create a UNIQUE index with the CREATE INDEX command for the primary key, which will be shown in the next section. The UNIQUE constraint is a part of the CREATE TABLE in some dialects of SQL. Once a primary key or **unique index** has been defined on a column, users will not be allowed to enter a row in the table whose value for the column duplicates the value for an existing row.

The foreign keys are the principal vehicle to enforce referential integrity. Once a foreign key has been established, the value of the foreign key column must correspond to a value for the primary key column of the referenced table. In our example, a FLIGHT (dependent table) cannot be entered with an origination or a destination airport that does not exist in the AIRPORT table (referenced table). If the relationship documented by the foreign key restriction is mandatory, the foreign key columns must be specified as NOT NULL. Note that this is the case for the foreign key columns of our example.

The RESTRICT option on the delete also enforces referential integrity. RESTRICT means that the Airport record in the AIRPORT table (parent) cannot be deleted if there are flights in the FLIGHT table (dependent) that originate or arrive at that airport. Other delete options include CASCADE and SET NULL. The CASCADE option will automatically trigger the delete of any flight (dependent) records in the FLIGHT table that originate at or are the destination of an airport (parent) that is being deleted. The SET NULL option will automatically set the origination and destination codes in the FLIGHT table to null and leave the flight records in the database. Only the airport record is deleted. The default for ON DELETE is the RESTRICT option if no ON DELETE is specified. The SET NULL option can be used only when the relationship documented by the foreign key is optional. For mandatory relationships, RESTRICT or CASCADE must be used to prevent the creation of orphan rows (rows in a child table that do not reference a valid row in a parent table) from being created.

Unique constraints on the primary key are a part of the CREATE TABLE in some SQL dialects. In DB2 the unique constraint is put into effect with the CREATE INDEX command. The following two CREATE INDEX commands are used to create unique indexes on airport code for the AIRPORT table and flight number for the FLIGHT table.

Unique index for the AIRPORT table:

```
CREATE UNIQUE INDEX codepkey ON airport (code)
```

Unique index for the FLIGHT table:

```
CREATE UNIQUE INDEX flytpkey ON flight (flight_no)
```

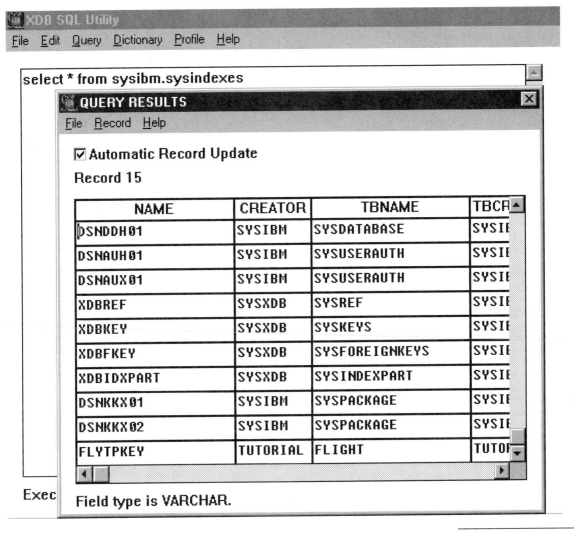

FIGURE 7.12

The data dictionary now reflects the index information for the primary and foreign keys. The flytpkey is shown as a unique primary index in the sysindexes table (Figure 7.12).

The foreign key constraint definitions have also been set up in tables with table names defined by the system. The remaining CREATE statements that set up the Airline database are as follows:

Flight day table (a flight on a specific day):

```
CREATE TABLE flight_day
      (flight_no   SMALLINT NOT NULL,
       flight_date DATE    NOT NULL,
       equip_no   SMALLINT,
       pass_ctr   SMALLINT,
       depart_time TIME,
       arrive_time TIME,
       fuel_used  INTEGER,
       status_note CHAR (20),
      PRIMARY KEY (flight_no, flight_date),
      FOREIGN KEY flt_err (flight_no)
              REFERENCES flight
              ON DELETE CASCADE)
```

Equipment table:

```
CREATE TABLE equipment
      (equip_no   SMALLINT NOT NULL,
       equip_type  CHAR (6),
       equip_date  date,
       PRIMARY KEY (equip_no))
```

Equipment type table:

```
CREATE TABLE equip_type
      (equip_type CHAR (6) NOT NULL,
       mfg    CHAR (3),
       seats   smallint,
       fuel_cap  integer,
       PRIMARY KEY (equip_type))
```

Seat table:

```
CREATE TABLE seat
      (equip_type CHAR (6) NOT NULL,
       seat    CHAR (3) NOT NULL,
       FOREIGN KEY Eqip_err (equip_type)
              REFERENCES equip_type
              ON DELETE CASCADE)
```

Reservation table:

```
CREATE TABLE reservation
      (confirm_no   INTEGER NOT NULL,
       res_date    DATE,
       res_name    VARCHAR (20),
```

Reservation table (continued):

```
        res_phone     CHAR (12),
        res_flight_no  INTEGER,
        res_flight_date date,
        PRIMARY KEY    (confirm_no))
```

Passenger table:

```
CREATE TABLE passenger
    (pass_name   VARCHAR (20),
     itinerary_no  integer NOT NULL,
     price      money,
     confirm_no  integer NOT NULL,
     PRIMARY KEY (itinerary_no),
     FOREIGN KEY conf_err (confirm_no)
            REFERENCES reservation
            ON DELETE CASCADE)
```

Ticket table:

```
CREATE TABLE ticket
    (itinerary_no INTEGER NOT NULL,
     flight_no  SMALLINT NOT NULL,
     flight_date date,
     seat    CHAR (3),
     PRIMARY KEY (itinery_no,
     flight_no,flight_date),
     FOREIGN KEY itin_err (itinerary_no)  Accs
            REFERENCES passenger (itincary_no)
            ON DELETE CASCADE,
     FOREIGN KEY flyt_err (flight_no)
            REFERENCES flight
            ON DELETE CASCADE)
```

Staff table:

```
CREATE TABLE staff
    (staff_no  CHAR (11) NOT NULL,
     staff_name CHAR (20),
     staff_type CHAR (2),
     staff_date date,
     PRIMARY KEY (staff_no))
```

Crew table:

```
CREATE TABLE flight_crew
    (flight_no  SMALLINT NOT NULL,
```

Crew table (continued):

```
                  flight_date DATE NOT NULL,
                  staff_no   CHAR (11) NOT NULL,
                  work_hrs   NUMERIC (4,1) NOT NULL
                  PRIMARY KEY (flight_no, flight_date,
                  staff_no),
                  FOREIGN KEY fli_err (flight_no, flight_date)
                          REFERENCES flight_day
                          ON DELETE CASCADE,
                  FOREIGN KEY stf_err (staff_no)
                          REFERENCES staff
                          ON DELETE RESTRICT)
```

Notes table:

```
CREATE TABLE notes
      (confirm_no  INTEGER NOT NULL,
       note   LONG VARCHAR NOT NULL WITH DEFAULT,
       PRIMARY KEY (confirm_no),
       FOREIGN KEY cfrm_err (confirm_no)
              REFERENCES reservation
              ON DELETE CASCADE)
```

Constant table called numbers:

```
CREATE TABLE numbers
      (ticket_no  INTEGER,
       confirm_no INTEGER,
       itinery_no INTEGER)
```

Note the differing ON DELETE clauses used. The CASCADE option is used where users might reasonably want to delete a parent and all its related children as a unit. Otherwise, RESTRICT is used. Because there are no instances where a child table has an optional relationship with a parent table in the Airline database, the SET NULL option does not appear.

Dropping Tables   Dropping tables is very easy to do as long as you are the owner or have authorization to do it. The DROP TABLE command specifies only the table name. The following command will remove the flight table from the database:

```
DROP TABLE flight
```

It may be tempting to remove a table in the DOS environment by deleting the DOS file that stores the table. This will not work because the relational system still has references to that table and its column names in various system tables. The DROP TABLE command removes all these definitions from the dictionary.

Altering the Definitions of Tables

Tables are often set up without the initial indexes and constraints. SQL allows you to add indexes and constraints any time after the table has been defined and data has been stored in the table. The SQL ALTER command allows you to change definitions, add and drop primary keys, add and drop foreign keys, drop keys, and add and drop data checks constraints. The ALTER command varies somewhat between database dialects. The syntax used in XDB and DB2 provides full capabilities for modifying the database definition. The general syntax follows:

```
ALTER TABLE table-name
{
    ADD column-name column-type[,...]
    | DELETE column-name[,...]
    | RENAME old-column-name new-column-name[,...]
    | MODIFY column-name column-type [FOR BIT DATA]
           [NOT NULL [WITH DEFAULT]] [,...]
    | UNIQUE KEY key-name (column-list)
    | PRIMARY KEY (column-list)
    | FOREIGN KEY [constraint-table] (column-list)
           REFERENCES referenced-table
           [ON DELETE
                  {RESTRICT | CASCADE | SET NULL}]
    | CHECK (search-condition)
    | DROP PRIMARY KEY
    | DROP FOREIGN KEY constraint-name
    | DROP KEY key-name
    | DROP CHECK
}
```

The following ALTER examples add and drop primary keys.

To add a primary key to the flight table:

```
ALTER TABLE flight
    PRIMARY KEY flytpkey (flight_no)
```

To drop the primary key from the flight table:

```
ALTER TABLE flight
    DROP PRIMARY KEY
```

To add a unique key to the ticket table:

```
ALTER TABLE ticket
    UNIQUE KEY tickpkey (itinerary_no,flight_no)
```

To drop a unique key from the ticket table:

```
ALTER TABLE ticket
    DROP KEY tickpkey
```

The following ALTER examples add and drop foreign key constraints from the database.

To add a foreign key on the ticket table referencing flight number in the flight table:

```
ALTER TABLE ticket
    FOREIGN KEY flt_err (flight_no)
    REFERENCES flight
```

To drop foreign key constraint on the ticket table:

```
ALTER TABLE ticket
    DROP FOREIGN KEY flt_err
```

To add a foreign key with delete constraint RESTRICT:

```
ALTER TABLE ticket
    FOREIGN KEY flt_err (flight_no) REFERENCES flight
    ON DELETE RESTRICT
```

The ALTER command can also be used to set up constraints on the domain of data entered in the columns. The domain refers to the range of values that are legal for that specific column. The following ALTER shows an example of putting a check domain constraint on a table:

```
ALTER TABLE ticket
    CHECK seat = SELECT seat FROM seat
```

Once this alter table statement has been executed, a row in the ticket table cannot be entered with a seat that is not in the seat table. Another form of CHECK restriction might be one to prevent price values greater than 999 from being entered:

```
ALTER TABLE flight
    CHECK price <= 999
```

Only one check statement is allowed per table, so if domain restrictions are needed for several columns, a single check with extensive compounding is used. The check statement helps to enforce the integrity of the data within the database.

Using Alter to MODIFY Table Definitions *Adding New Columns*: One or more new columns can be added to an existing table with the ADD option. The following example adds the column fuel_cap and fuel_usage to the equipment table:

```
ALTER TABLE airport
    ADD fuel_cap INTEGER, fuel_usage INTEGER
```

The two columns will be added after the existing columns for the table with null values for all existing rows. NOT NULL WITH DEFAULT can be used after each column definition. The default for an integer field is zero, which would fill these columns for all existing rows with zero instead of nulls. NOT NULL without default can only be used with the modify clause.

Modifying Existing Columns: The ALTER with modify can be used to change column types, sizes, and null permission.

```
ALTER TABLE equipment
     MODIFY equip_no integer, equip_type char (8) NOT NULL
```

Equipment number will be changed from small integer to integer, and equipment type from 6 characters to 8 characters. Equip_no will stay NOT NULL if it was defined not null originally, and equip_type will be changed to NOT NULL. If equipment type contains any nulls, an error message will alert you to that fact.

Renaming Existing Columns: A column can be renamed with the rename option after the table exists and has data in it.

```
ALTER TABLE equipment
     RENAME equip_type equip_model
```

The first name is the existing name and the second name is the new name. This option should not be used except when setting up a new system. Any SQL statements, forms, and reports that use the old name do not change to the new name.

Deleting Existing Columns: Columns can be removed from tables at any time even if they contain data. Deleting all columns of a table has the same effect as removing the table from the database.

```
ALTER TABLE equipment
     DELETE equip_date, fuel_cap, fuel_usage
```

Creating Indexes

Indexes are used in relational databases to enforce referential integrity and to speed the processing time. Indexes can be regular, unique, and compound. Unique and compound indexes basically serve the same purpose as the primary key and would be used if PRIMARY KEY were not a part of the CREATE TABLE command. A compound index uses multiple columns to create the field. Compound indexes can be regular or unique. Regular indexes are set up on columns in a table on which there will be frequent matching or lookup activity. If there is a lot of activity on social security number or name, indexes should be set up on these columns. This will speed the lookup process. Indexes are not free because they take up space in the database and require extra processing to maintain.

Index
A data structure that allows a table to be retrieved in sorted order based on some column or set of columns.

Once an index is set up, it is maintained automatically by the SQL engine when records are added to or deleted from the table that affects that index. Indexes can be set up or removed at any time. The general syntax is as follows:

```
CREATE [UNIQUE] INDEX index-name
     ON table-name (column [ASC | DESC] [,...])
```

where ASC refers to ascending and DESC refers to descending. ASC is the default if the order is not specified. The following examples illustrate some uses of setting up indexes. The first example creates a secondary index on origination airport for the flight table:

```
CREATE INDEX origx ON flight(orig)
```

Indexes on the origination and destination columns in the flight table will speed up matching data in the airport table with data in the flight table.

The next example creates a name index on the reservation table:

```
CREATE INDEX resnamx ON reservation (res_name)
```

An index on the name of the person requesting the reservation will accelerate the lookup process when that person does not know his or her confirmation number.

The next example creates a unique index on ticket:

```
CREATE UNIQUE INDEX tickpkey
    ON ticket (itinerary_no, flight_no)
```

Tickpkey is a primary key that is unique on itinerary number and flight number. An itinerary number is unique for a trip, and on any one trip (departure and return) a passenger cannot be on the same flight more than once.

Creating Views

View

A view is a subset of data from one or more tables of a database. Most commands that can be performed on tables can be performed on views. However, a view does not store data, but causes data meeting specified conditions to be retrieved whenever it is invoked.

A **view** is a subset of data from the database that is derived from one or more tables or views. The data can be a subset of data from a table, a combination of data from several tables, or calculated or summarized data based on aggregate functions. Views can be thought of as virtual tables. Views act and look like tables to SQL, but views don't actually exist in table form. Any operation that is performed against a view generates the view definition in SQL and executes the view definition as a part of its operation. This means that the data in a view definition automatically and instantaneously reflect any changes in the data tables from which the view is derived. Views are very important in the development of database applications. They simplify the look of the database (logical view) to the user. Each user can look at the database from different perspectives (views). Views can simplify the use of SQL by the user. The complex portions are predefined by the view. Views also screen and control the data users can access. Each view can be tailored to a specific user and only that user can access the view. The disadvantage of views is that they add performance overhead to the processing of data. All the operations necessary to produce the view are executed every time the view is accessed. The updating capability of views is limited to simple view structures.

The general syntax of the CREATE VIEW statement is as follows:

```
CREATE VIEW view-name
    [(view-col-name [,...])
    AS sql-query
    [WITH CHECK OPTION]
```

The view can contain its own column names, or use the column names from the tables in the view definition. The WITH CHECK OPTION is used on updatable views to enforce the WHERE clause of the SQL query on any data being added or updated. If the data being added or updated do not meet the WHERE clause, an error message is generated and the operation is aborted.

The typical restrictions for most SQL engines on a SQL query using a view are:

1. A view is not updatable (add, change, delete) if the SQL query contains any DISTINCT, expressions, functions, GROUP BY, ORDER BY, HAVING, or data from more than one table. If you create the view using the WITH CHECK OPTION, the SQL engine will notify you if it is not updatable.

2. If there are expressions in the SQL query, you must name all the columns of the view. These views are read only.

3. You must name all the columns of the view if there are duplicate names in the tables and views being joined to create the view. These views are read only.

4. Views containing GROUP BY and HAVING cannot be joined to other tables or views.

5. ORDER BY and UNION cannot be used.

View Examples   The following create view statements show some examples of setting up views for the Airline database. The first example creates a view called Phoenix flights that is updatable. This view could be given to personnel in Phoenix who have the responsibility for updating information on all flights originating in Phoenix. If they attempted to update or input data on flights originating from any other airport, the system would not allow the changes.

```
CREATE VIEW phx_flts
AS SELECT * FROM flight WHERE orig = 'PHX'
    WITH CHECK OPTION
```

The following example shows the use of joining two tables and doing some aggregate functions in the same view. The view flight summary is a summary of flights by flight number and flight date showing the number of passengers and the total revenue for each flight.

```
CREATE VIEW flt_sum
        (flight, flight_date, num_pass, tot_fare)
    AS SELECT
        flight_no, flight_date, count(*), sum(price)
    FROM ticket t, flight f
    WHERE t.flight_no = f.flight_no
    GROUP BY flight_no, flight_date
```

The following view uses a subselect within the select to create the view. In this example, the view obtains the difference between the original inventory of seats for a flight and the seats already assigned on the flight. Seats assigned come from the ticket table, and the original inventory is in the seat table. The difference between the two becomes a view called seats_left. The view will contain all the seat numbers that have not been assigned to any passengers.

```
CREATE VIEW seats_left
    AS
    SELECT seat FROM seat
    WHERE seat NOT IN
        (SELECT seat FROM ticket
        WHERE flight_no = 101
        AND flight_date = 08/18/92)
```

SQL FOR DATA ENTRY AND DATA MAINTENANCE

SQL supports the basic functions of adding, deleting, and updating data in a table. Because these statements add or manipulate data in a table, they are not DDL statements. They constitute the fundamental data manipulation statements required to insert and maintain data in tables. The SQL statements that support these functions are INSERT, UPDATE, and DELETE.

Insert: The INSERT statement can be used to insert single or multiple rows into a table. The general format of the INSERT is:

```
INSERT INTO table-name
    [(column-list)]
    {VALUES (value-list)
    | sql-query}
```

The column-list is the specific columns separated by commas that are in the table selected to receive the data. Columns not listed will receive a null or an appropriate default value depending on the column definition. If the column list is left out, the value list must account for every column. Each value in the value list is separated by commas, may contain the word NULL if there is no data for that column, and is bounded by quotes for character data. The first example illustrates adding data without specifying the column names.

Inserting data into the flight table:

```
INSERT INTO flight
    VALUES (1510,'MPS','LAX',8:00:00,10:00:00,'L',149)
```

Because flight contains the columns Flight_No, Orig, Dest, Orig_Time, Dest_Time, Meal, and Price in that order, the flight number will be 1510, the origination airport Minneapolis, the destination airport Los Angeles, and so on until all the columns for that row are filled. The meal code could have been ' ' for a blank or the word NULL for a null.

The next example uses the column list excluding the meal column. In this case, the meal values are not a part of the value list.

Inserting data into the flight table without the meal attribute:

```
INSERT into flight
    (flight_no, orig, dest, orig_time, dest_time, price)
    VALUES (1510,'MPS','LAX',8:00:00,10:00:00,149)
```

The insert can be used to add multiple rows of data to a table at one time. A good example of this is the need to archive data from one table into another. This next example shows how to take old ticket data in the ticket table and add it to an old_tickets table.

Inserting old tickets from the ticket table into the old_tickets table:

```
INSERT old_tickets
  SELECT * FROM ticket WHERE flight_date < 1/1/90
```

Delete: Deleting rows from a table can be done one at a time or as multiple rows across the table. The general syntax of the DELETE is as follows:

```
DELETE FROM table-name
  [WHERE search-condition]
```

If the WHERE clause is left off, all rows in the table will be deleted. Normally, the WHERE clause will locate the specific row to be deleted, such as:

```
DELETE FROM reservation WHERE confirm_no = 8
```

Remember from our earlier discussion of referential integrity that this will also delete all passengers associated with this reservation and their tickets if the foreign key constraints have been set up with ON DELETE CASCADE.

The next example of the delete removes a range of rows in the table:

```
DELETE FROM ticket WHERE flight_date < 1/1/90
```

This delete would remove all the tickets from the ticket table that we put into the old_tickets table (see INSERT above).

Updates: Data can be modified in tables row by row through the use of the SQL UPDATE. The general syntax of the UPDATE command is:

```
UPDATE table-name
  SET field-name = expression [,field-name = expression...]
  [WHERE search-condition]
```

The WHERE search condition operates in the same way as the WHERE condition on a DELETE. If the WHERE condition is not specified, all rows in the table will be updated. The SET statement assigns a value to the column(s) based on the expression in the SET statement. The following example increases the price on all flights from Phoenix to Los Angeles by 10 percent:

```
  UPDATE flight
  SET price = price * 1.10
      WHERE orig = 'PHX'
      AND  dest = 'LAX'
```

If we wanted to change the meal code on all flights to NULL, we would use the UPDATE without any WHERE clause. Every row in the flight table will be updated.

```
  UPDATE flight
      SET meal = NULL
```

SETTING UP AN ORACLE DATABASE

ORACLE SERVER

Oracle is available in a number of configurations for academic use at a very small cost per year under Oracle's Academic Grant Program. It can be installed on individual workstations (Personal Oracle 7 Enterprise Edition) or on a UNIX, OS/2, or NT server attached to a network such as Novell. Once the software is installed, the Oracle server is brought online by going into the SQLDBA software at an OS prompt on the server. The following commands are executed within SQLDBA: Connect internal/manager, and Startup. This loads and starts the Oracle database engine. Once the database engine is started, you exit SQLDBA and start the communication package that is configured for your network. An example would be to execute the command SPXSRV ORASRV at the operating system prompt. This is a listener package on the server to intercept all SPX/NETX Novell packets with the connect string of ORASRV.

The Oracle software comes with a demo database that you log into as Scott/Tiger. This database tests your communication to the server from workstations. Workstation software must be installed on each workstation that will be accessing the Oracle database. Once this software is installed, you can go into SQL*Plus and log in to the demo database SCOTT/TIGER. The first window that comes up after selecting SQL*Plus is the LOG ON window (Figure 7.13). Scott is the User name and Tiger is the Password. The connect string X:ORASRV (not case sensitive) links the communication channel to the Oracle server.

FIGURE 7.13

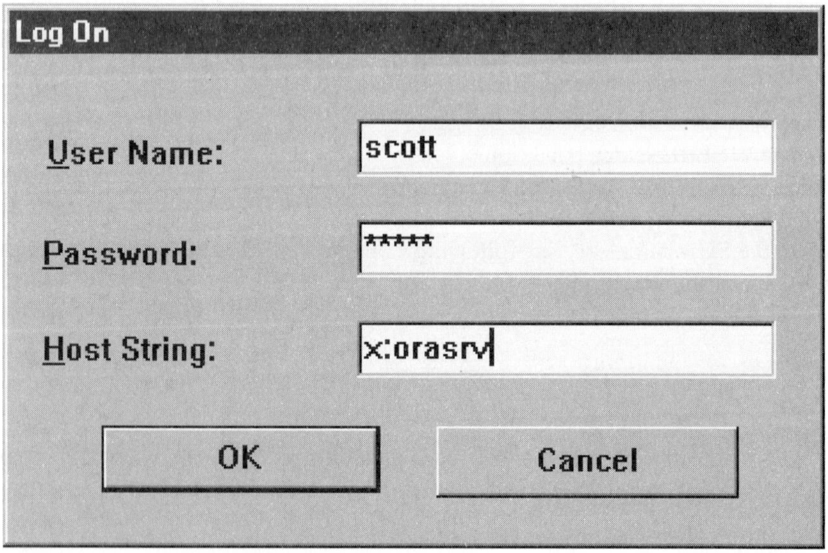

DATABASE SETUP

Once you have successfully logged in, you will be presented with the SQL*Plus window (Figure 7.14) to allow you to execute SQL instructions against the Scott/Tiger database.

Figure 7.15 shows an example of selecting data from the employee table within the Scott/Tiger database.

The next step in setting up an Oracle database is to set up new tablespace or expand the existing tablespace. Normally, it is best to set up a different tablespace for student projects.

```
CREATE   TABLESPACE   tabspace_2
         DATAFILE    'c:\tabspa_2.dat' SIZE 50M
```

Another step is to set up the users. Users can be set up with the command:

```
GRANT CONNECT TO cox IDENTIFIED BY charles
GRANT CONNECT RESOURCE TO cox IDENTIFIED BY charles
```

Using RESOURCE allows the users to have space to set up tables of their own. Space can also be allocated to users by specifying a quota in a specific tablespace, such as one megabyte:

```
GRANT RESOURCE (1M) ON tabspace_2 TO cox
```

Cox is now able to create tables within his own account. Tables can be created by copying a table from another user, as shown in the next SQL block. This is convenient for students who want to start working with SQL without modifying data in the master database.

FIGURE 7.14

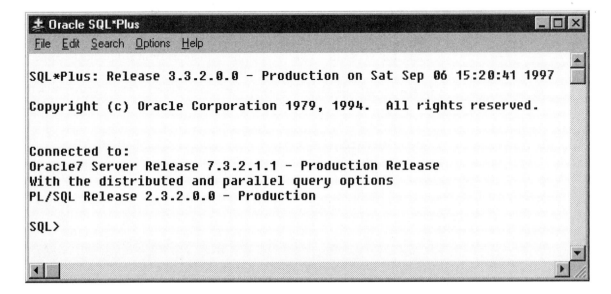

```
Oracle SQL*Plus                                              [_][□][X]
File  Edit  Search  Options  Help
SQL> select * from emp;

    EMPNO ENAME      JOB            MGR HIREDATE        SAL      COMM
--------- ---------- ---------- --------- --------- --------- ---------
     7369 SMITH      CLERK          7902 17-DEC-80       800
     7499 ALLEN      SALESMAN       7698 20-FEB-81      1600       300
     7521 WARD       SALESMAN       7698 22-FEB-81      1250       500
     7566 JONES      MANAGER        7839 02-APR-81      2975
     7654 MARTIN     SALESMAN       7698 28-SEP-81      1250      1400
     7698 BLAKE      MANAGER        7839 01-MAY-81      2850
     7782 CLARK      MANAGER        7839 09-JUN-81      2450
     7788 SCOTT      ANALYST        7566 19-APR-87      3000
     7839 KING       PRESIDENT           17-NOV-81      5000
     7844 TURNER     SALESMAN       7698 08-SEP-81      1500         0
     7876 ADAMS      CLERK          7788 23-MAY-87      1100
     7900 JAMES      CLERK          7698 03-DEC-81       950
     7902 FORD       ANALYST        7566 03-DEC-81      3000
     7934 MILLER     CLERK          7782 23-JAN-82      1300

14 rows selected.
```

FIGURE 7.15

```
Create Table Flight
as Select * from airline.flight;
```
The Create commands to set up the Air West database in Oracle are illustrated in SQL blocks at the end of this section. Most of these commands are close to what they would be for XDB/DB2. Oracle has some variations from DB2 when it comes to check constraints. The following SQL block shows the use of the constraint clause that sets up a check on Meal. The constraint is named check_meal, and the check that will be done by Oracle is to make sure that no value goes into Meal other than 'B', 'L', 'D', or 'S'.

```
/* CREATE FLIGHT */
/* drop table */
drop table FLIGHT;
/* create table */
create table FLIGHT
(
  flight_no integer not null PRIMARY KEY,
  orig    char (3),
  dest    char (3),
  orig_time date,
```

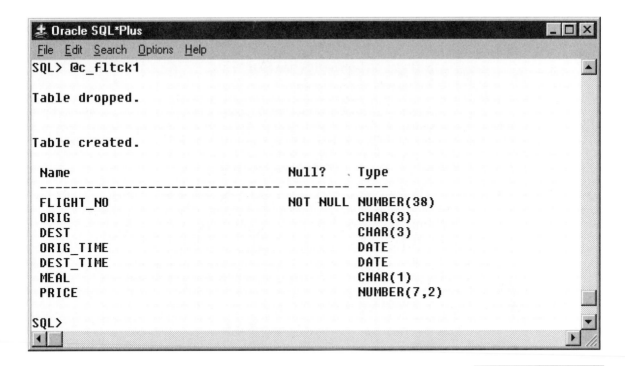

FIGURE 7.16

```
    dest_time date,
    meal      char (1)
        constraint check_meal
            check (meal in ('B', 'L', 'D', 'S')),
    price     number (7,2)
);
/* describe table */
desc flight;
```

Running a SQL batch file that has multiple SQL statements in it using SQL*Plus is done with the '@' symbol in front of the file name. The file name must have the extension .SQL and you must be in the directory where the file is stored. Any File Open or Save will allow you to select the directory in SQL*PLUS. Figure 7.16 is a sample of executing the Create statement with the check_meal constraint.

The check constraint can also be put in without specifying the constraint clause or the constraint name. In this case, Oracle builds its own name for the check constraint. A portion of the table definition is shown in the example below:

```
meal   char (1)
       check (meal in ('B', 'L', 'D', 'S')),
price  number (7,2)
```

The check statement can include such expressions as:

a. (eoq + qoh <= 500

b. (flight_no between 050 and 500)

c. (qty > 0)

Another difference is that Oracle supports multiple column constraints on the same column.

ORACLE DATA DICTIONARY TABLES

Many Oracle dictionary tables are useful for finding table names, column names, and information about the structure of the database as well as who has what rights. The following list of tables was obtained by selecting all columns from the DTAB table in Oracle. This list explains the content of all the dictionary tables that Oracle maintains.

Listing of Dictionary Tables Supported by Oracle

linesize 90
SELECT * FROM DTAB;

TNAME	REMARKS
Reference Date	ORACLE catalog as of 10-Oct-85, installed on 26-OCT-93 13:38:52.
AUDIT_ACCESS	Audit entries for accesses to user's tables/views (DBA sees all)
AUDIT_ACTIONS	Maps auditing action numbers to action names
AUDIT_CONNECT	Audit trail entries for user logon/logoff (DBA sees all users)
AUDIT_DBA	Audit trail entries for DBA activities—for DBA use only
AUDIT_EXISTS	Audit trail entries for objects which do NOT EXIST—DBA's only
AUDIT_TRAIL	Audit trail entries relevant to the user (DBA sees all)
CATALOG	Tables and views accessible to user (excluding data dictionary)
CLUSTERS	Clusters and their tables (either must be accessible to user)
CLUSTERCOLUMNS	Maps cluster columns to clustered table columns
COL	Specifications of columns in tables created by the user
COLUMNS	Columns in tables accessible to user (excluding data dictionary)
DBLINKS	Public and private links to external databases
DEFAULT_AUDIT	Default table auditing options
DTAB	Description of tables and views in Oracle Data Dictionary
EXTENTS	Data structure of extents within tables
INDEXES	Indexes created by user and indexes on tables created by user
FREESPACE	Free extents available in the system—for DBA use only

Listing of Dictionary Tables Supported by Oracle (continued)

TNAME	REMARKS
PRIVATESYN	Private synonyms created by the user
PUBLICSYN	Public synonyms
SEQUENCES	Sequences created by the user

TNAME	REMARKS
SESSIONS	Audit trail entries for the user's sessions (DBA sees all)
STORAGE	Data and Index storage allocation for user's own tables
SYNONYMS	Synonyms, private and public
SYSAUDIT_TRAIL	Synonym for sys.audit_trail—for DBA use only
SYSCATALOG	Profile of tables and views accessible to the user
SYSCOLAUTH	Directory of column update access granted by or to the user
SYSCOLUMNS	Specifications of columns in accessible tables and views
SYSDATABASE	Parameters of databases
SYSDBLINKS	All links to external databases-for DBA use only
SYSEXTENTS	Data structure of tables throughout system—for DBA use only
SYSFILES	Files allocation—for DBA use only
SYSINDEXES	List of indexes, underlying columns, creator, and options
SYSCONSTRAINTS	Constraint definitions
SYSCONSTRACOLS	Columns of primary keys, unique keys, and foreign keys
SYSSEQUENCES	List of accessible sequences
SYSSTORAGE	Summary of all database storage—for DBA use only
SYSTABALLOC	Data and index space allocations for all tables—for DBA's
SYSTABAUTH	Directory of access authorization granted by or to the user
SYSTABSPACES	Parameters of tablespaces—for DBA use only
SYSTSQUOTAS	Space privileges granted to users—for DBA use only
SYSTEM_AUDIT	System auditing options—for DBA use only

TNAME	REMARKS
SYSROLLBACKSEG	Rollback segments for tablespaces—for DBA use only
SYSUSERAUTH	Master list of Oracle users—for DBA use only
SYSUSERLIST	List of Oracle users
SYSVIEWS	List of accessible views
TAB	List of tables, views, clusters, and synonyms created by the user
TABALLOC	Data and index space allocations for all user's tables

Listing of Dictionary Tables Supported by Oracle (continued)

TNAME	REMARKS
TABQUOTAS	Table allocation (space) parameters for tables created by user
TABSPACES	Parameters of Tablespaces accessible by current user
TABLE_AUDIT	Auditing options of user's tables and views (DBA sees all)
TSQUOTAS	Space privileges granted to current user
VIEWS	Defining SQL statements for views created by the user

53 rows selected.

SQL>

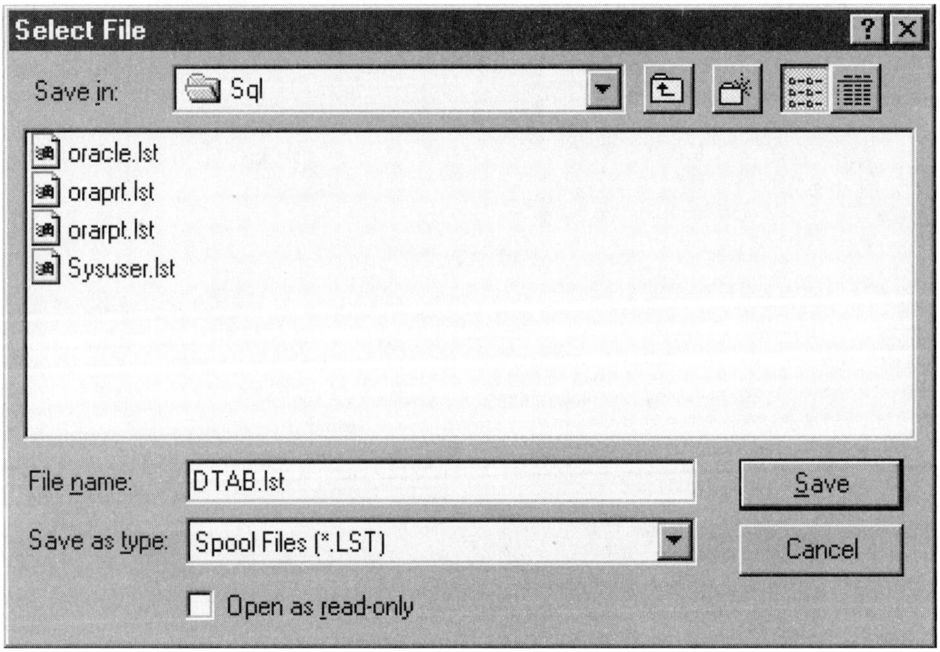

FIGURE 7.17

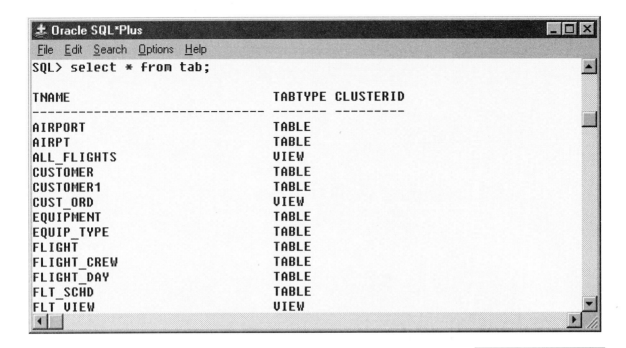

FIGURE 7.18

Listings can be captured in SQL*Plus by setting the File Spool to a file name, as shown in Figure 7.17. When all the output has been captured, you can set File Spool Off in the SQL*Plus window, open the file in Word, reset the fonts, and print the file to the printer, or put it in another Word document.

Figure 7.18 shows the table names that are available to this user.

The Create SQL Statements for the Air West Database in Oracle
```
/* CREATE AIRPORT */
/* drop table */
drop table AIRPORT;
/* create table */
create table AIRPORT
(
  air_code  char(3) not null PRIMARY KEY,
  air_location char(35),
  elevation number(4,0),
  air_phone char(12)
);
/* describe table */
desc airport;
/* CREATE EQUIPMENT */
```

```
/* drop table */
drop table equipment;
/* create table */
create table equipment
(
 equip_no  number(3,0) not null PRIMARY KEY,
 equip_type char(6),
 equip_date date
);
/* describe table */
desc equipment;
/* CREATE EQUIP_TYPE */
/* drop table */
drop table equip_type;
/* create table */
create table equip_type
(
 equip_type char(6) not null PRIMARY KEY,
 mfg        char(15),
 seats      number (3,0),
 fuel_cap   integer
);
/* describe table */
desc equip_type;
/* CREATE FLIGHT */
/* drop table */
drop table FLIGHT;
/* create table */
create table FLIGHT
(
 flight_no integer not null PRIMARY KEY,
 orig       char (3),
 dest       char (3),
 orig_time  date,
 dest_time  date,
 meal       char (1),
 price      number (7,2)
);
/* describe table */
desc flight;
/* CREATE FLIGHT_CREW */
/* drop table */
drop table flight_crew;
/* create table */
```

```
create table flight_crew
(
 flight_no     integer not null,
 flight_date   date not null,
 staff_no      char (11) not null,
 work_hrs      number (4,1) not null,
 PRIMARY KEY (flight_no, flight_date, staff_no),
 FOREIGN KEY (flight_no, flight_date)
    REFERENCES flight_day
    ON DELETE CASCADE,
 FOREIGN KEY (staff_no)
    REFERENCES staff
    ON DELETE CASCADE
 );
/* CREATE FLIGHT_DAY */
/* drop table */
drop table flight_day;
/* create table */
create table flight_day
(
 flight_no     integer not null,
 flight_date   date not null,
 equip_no      number(3,0),
 pass_ctr      integer,
 depart_time   date,
 arrive_time   date,
 fuel_used     integer,
 status_note   char(20),
 PRIMARY KEY  (flight_no, flight_date),
 FOREIGN KEY  (flight_no)
    REFERENCES flight
    ON DELETE CASCADE
);
/* describe table */
desc flight_day;
/* CREATE NOTES */
/* drop table */
drop table notes;
/* create table */
create table notes
(
 confirm_no integer not null PRIMARY KEY,
 note      char (50)  not null,
 FOREIGN KEY (confirm_no)
```

```
      REFERENCES reservation
        ON DELETE CASCADE
);
/* describe table */
desc notes;
/* CREATE PASSENGER */
/* drop table */
drop table passenger;
/* create table */
create table passenger
(
 pass_name   char(20) not null,
 itinery_no  integer not null PRIMARY KEY,
 price       number (6,2),
 confirm_no  integer not null
 REFERENCES RESERVATION(confirm_no)
   ON DELETE CASCADE
);
/* describe table */
desc passenger;
/* CREATE RESERVATION */
/* drop table */
drop table reservation;
/* create table */
create table reservation
(
 confirm_no integer not null,
 res_date    date,
 res_name   char(20),
 res_phone  char(12),
 res_flight_no integer,
 res_flight_date date,
 PRIMARY KEY (confirm_no)
);
/* describe table */
desc reservation;
/* CREATE SEAT */
/* drop table */
drop table seat;
/* create table */
create table seat
(
 equip_type char(6) not null,
 seat        char(3) not null,
```

```
  FOREIGN KEY (equip_type)
    REFERENCES equip_type
    ON DELETE CASCADE
 );
/* describe table */
desc seat;
/* CREATE STAFF */
/* drop table */
drop table staff;
/* create table */
create table staff
(
 staff_no       char (11) not null,
 staff_name     char (20),
 staff_type     char (20),
 staff_date     date,
 PRIMARY KEY (staff_no)
 );
/* describe table */
desc staff;
/* CREATE TICKET */
/* drop table */
drop table ticket;
/* create table */
create table ticket
(
 itinerary_no    integer not null,
 flight_no      integer not null,
 flight_date    date,
 seat           char(3),
 PRIMARY KEY (itinery_no, flight_no, flight_date),
 FOREIGN KEY (itinery_no)
   REFERENCES passenger
   ON DELETE CASCADE,
 FOREIGN KEY (flight_no)
   REFERENCES flight
   ON DELETE CASCADE
 );
/* describe table */
desc ticket;
```

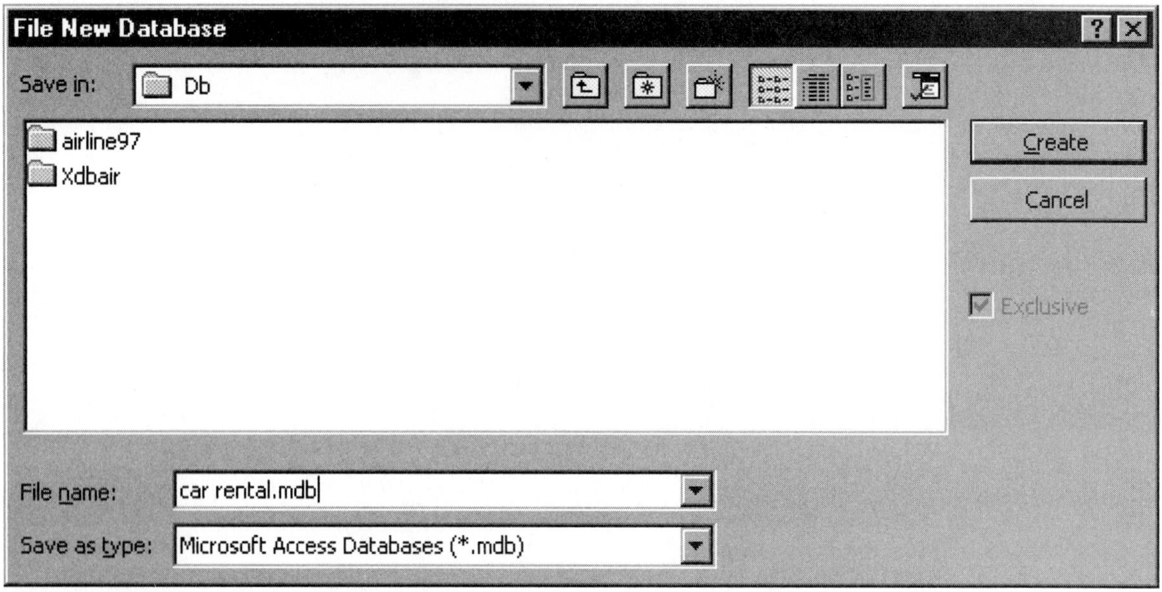

FIGURE 7.19

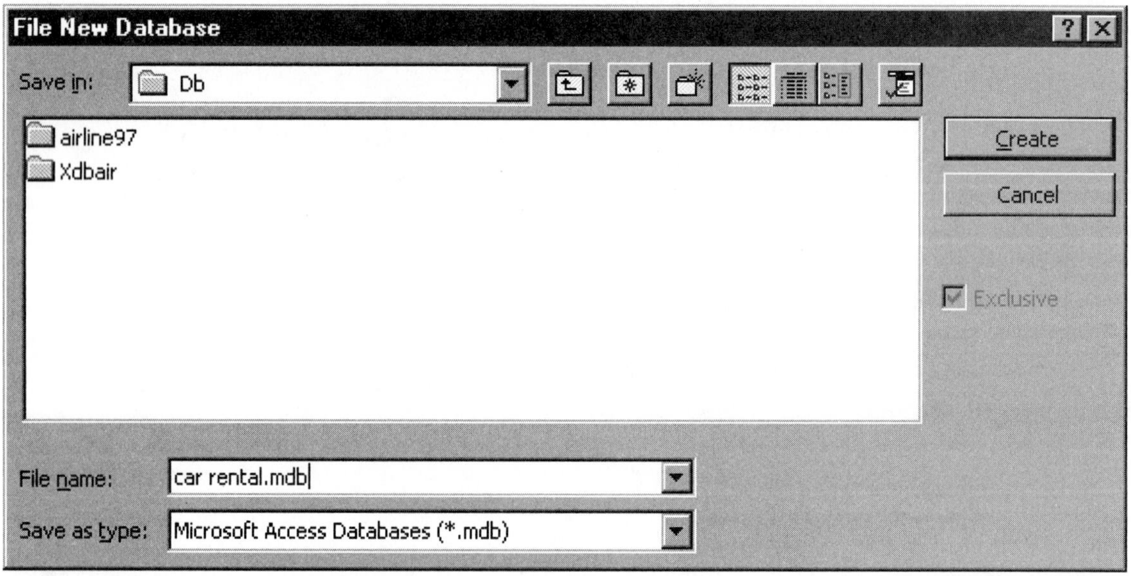

FIGURE 7.20

SETTING UP AN ACCESS DATABASE

Access has a user-friendly interface to allow developers and users to set up databases. A new database can be created by going to File New and selecting a blank database. Figure 7.19 is displayed, allowing the user or developer to select the name and location of the database.

The developer selects Create on the File New Database window, and the system generates all the files in the selected subdirectory to support a new database in Access. The developer is presented with a blank database window (Figure 7.20) with no tables, queries, forms, reports, menus, or modules, allowing the developer to begin the process of building these objects.

The developer can create a table by using the user interface, as shown in Figure 7.21. However, tables can also be created with the SQL interface, as shown in Figure 7.22. You can get to this interface by going to Query, New, and the SQL view within the view dropdown icon (upper left corner, Figure 7.22).

The CREATE statement in Access is very limited in terms of setting up keys, constraints, and relationships. The relationships view (structure icon, right side, Figure 7.20), is where all the relationship structures can be built. Figure 7.23 is an example of building some relationships for the Air West database. A relationship is created by dragging a key from the one side to a related key on the many side. The developer can select enforcement of referential integrity, cascade updates, and cascade deletes.

FIGURE 7.21

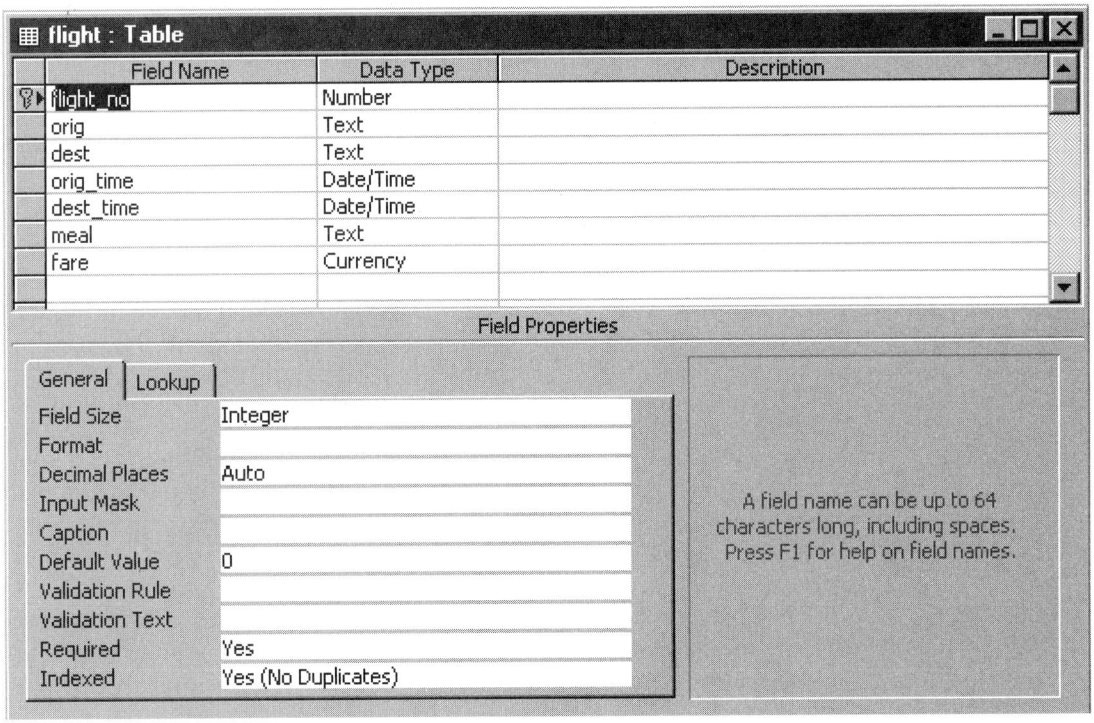

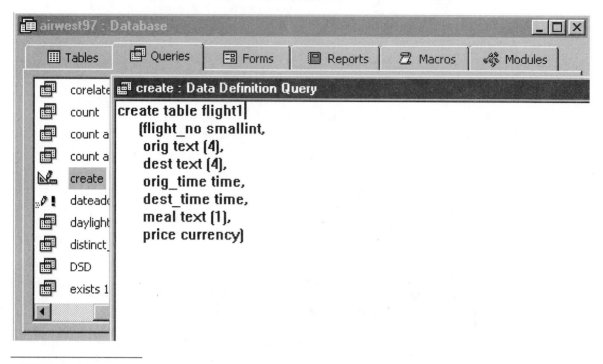

FIGURE 7.22

The developer can also specify the join conditions for joins that are done between the tables. Once the relationship has been built, Access can use this information to aid in building queries, forms, and reports.

SUMMARY

In the relational model, all data are stored in tables. Table structure diagrams are frequently used to provide a visual representation of the required set of tables. The table structure diagrams are derived from E-R diagrams and domain descriptions of the conceptual model. In mapping to table structure diagrams, intersection tables are added if any unresolved many to many relationships are represented in the E-R diagrams, and foreign key attributes are added wherever appropriate.

A relational database consists of various parts that include tablespaces, tables, indexes, and the relational database definitions that are stored in system tables. The tablespace, tables, and indexes are built using Create statements. The tables and indexes can be modified using Alter statements. Tables can also be built as a subset of other tables using the Select statement. The primary key definition is used to specify the unique identifier for each table. This is normally enforced by creating a unique index. Foreign keys are used to link a table with the primary keys in other

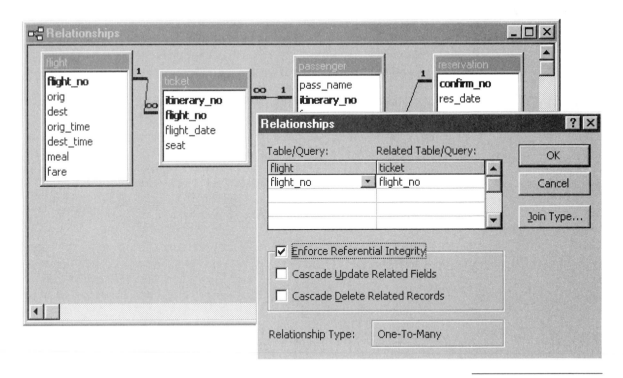

FIGURE 7.23

tables. Foreign keys enforce referential integrity between tables, meaning that rows in one table cannot be entered unless the foreign key exists as a primary key in another table. Delete constraints can also be set up such that when a parent is deleted the children can also be deleted, or the foreign keys can be set to null.

Relational databases support the definition of views. A view is a logical table that is defined with select statements. Views make it easier to set up select statements to process queries against the database. The definition of the view is added to any select statement executed against it when the select statement is submitted and the database engine reexecutes the view definition each time.

INSERT, UPDATE, and DELETE statements maintain the database data values. These statements are usually used with host languages or window-based systems. However, system developers often use these statements to put initial data into the databases for testing the applications.

REVIEW QUIZ

_____ Command that adds new rows to a table.

_____ A column in a table that is identical to the primary key column of a related table and is used to link the tables.

_____ Clause that can be used to enforce domain restrictions on a column of a table.

_____ Command that allocates space for a database and creates system files needed to manage it.

_____ Allows rows of a table to be retrieved in sorted order.

_____ Clause that does not allow a row from a parent table to be removed if it has related children.

_____ Statements that define the structure of a database.

_____ Command used to remove selected rows from a table.

_____ Ensures that logical relationships among tables are correctly implemented and maintained.

_____ Clause that causes related child rows to be deleted whenever a row from the parent table is deleted.

_____ Does not store data, but causes a selected set of data to be retrieved whenever it is invoked.

_____ Command used to change the structure of a table.

_____ Command used to remove a table from the database.

1. Referential integrity
2. DROP TABLE
3. Foreign key
4. INSERT
5. ON DELETE RESTRICT
6. ON DELETE CASCADE
7. ALTER TABLE
8. DELETE
9. Data definition language
10. Index
11. View
12. CREATE DATABASE
13. CHECK

1. We say that the relational model represents all data and relationships through tables. What does this mean?

2. Describe how E-R diagrams and domain descriptions from a conceptual model are mapped into table structure diagrams.

3. How are many to many relationships between entities that might exist in an E-R diagram treated in the relational model?

4. What does the CREATE DATABASE command create?

5. What is a tablespace? What is the function of a tablespace?

6. What does a FOREIGN KEY clause do and how does it serve to ensure referential integrity?

7. Describe the three options for the ON DELETE clause of foreign keys. When would each option appropriately be used?

8. Describe what happens when a table is created based on a select statement from another table.

9. Describe how the CHECK clause of the ALTER TABLE command works.

10. What is a view? How does a view differ from a table? How does it differ from a query?

11. What do we mean when we say that a view is updatable? What conditions must be met for a view to be updatable?

12. Describe and give examples of the three basic commands used to record and maintain data in a relation database.

Answer the first twelve questions based on the following example of an E-R diagram and attribute list for a car rental company.

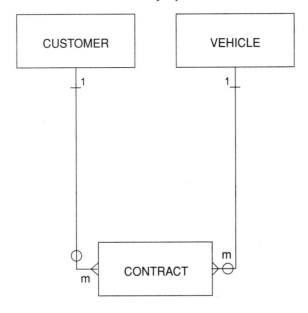

Attribute Lists		
CUSTOMER	**VEHICLE**	**CONTRACT**
Customer ID	Vehicle ID	Contract #
Address	Make	Date Out
City	Year	Date Due In
State	Type	Rate
Zip		Actual Date In
Phone		

13. How many tables would be set up in the database?

14. Which tables would have foreign keys and what would the foreign keys be?

15. Set up CREATE TABLE statements for the tables.

16. Set up ALTER TABLE statements to add the appropriate primary keys and the foreign key constraints for this database.

17. Set up an ALTER TABLE statement to add an attribute to the automobile table to carry the VIN attribute as (TEXT 20).

18. Set up an ALTER TABLE statement to drop the ZIP code attribute.

19. Set up a command to drop the VEHICLE table.

20. Assume a many to many relationship between Vehicle and a new entity called Maintenance in which each vehicle has regular maintenance checkups at certain mileage points. Set up the CREATE TABLE statement(s) needed to implement this new structure.

21. Create a table with all the 1998 vehicles in the table containing data from the VEHICLE table.

22. Create a view with the 1998 vehicles from the VEHICLE table.

23. Create a view of Vehicle, Customer, and Contract data consisting of name, license number, and actual return date.

24. Create a new table that consists of open contract data (a contract is open if the actual return date is null).

25. Set up an application for a small motel keeping track of rooms, reservations, and customers who rent the rooms. The application can be set up in phases: Phase one—reservation system; phase two—add actual rental of rooms; phase three—add billing and payments; phase four—add billing of other items such as telephone, restaurant, and bar.

Develop E-R diagrams and attribute lists for your application and use them to generate a set of table structure diagrams. Finally, write out the statements required to create the tables for your application, including appropriate primary and foreign key specifications.

26. Set up an application to maintain a national house-sharing system in which residents trade homes for vacations in different parts of the country. Participants can log in with their PC systems and enter their house, along with potential weeks and potential areas they are interested in. The areas are set up by zones across the United States. Participants can also scan the database to look at what has been entered.

Develop E-R diagrams and attribute lists for your application, and use them to generate a set of table structure diagrams. Finally, write out the statements required to create the tables for your application, including appropriate primary and foreign key specifications.

CLIENT-SERVER APPLICATION DEVELOPMENT

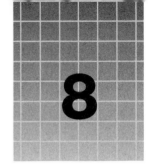

LEARNING OBJECTIVES

After completing this chapter, you should be able to

- Identify the components of a database application.
- Design a form using a software package that will update a database.
- Design a report using a software package that will select data from a database.
- Set up a menu system that will package an application that includes forms, reports, and queries.
- Identify and be able to explain the major components of forms, including GUI-based forms.
- Identify and be able to explain the major components of reports.
- Identify the components that are used to link applications together in client-server environments.

INTRODUCTION

A client-server application consists of various functions that operate together to accomplish the objectives of a business system. The various functions can be stored in an application library and executed individually, or they can be put together as a complete application through the use of menus. Menus give meaningful descriptions and structure to a system that consists of many different parts. Users can work through menus without having to remember cryptic procedure names and file names. A menu can be a simple list, a bar across the top, a pull down from a selected menu item, or command buttons, all of which are a part of most **graphical user interface (GUI)** features of a windows application.

Graphical user interface (GUI)
A windowing system with various window controls, such as buttons, check boxes, menu bars, and list boxes.

Database systems are designed to support the development of client-server applications using the data in the database. In particular, most transaction-oriented databases are designed to support fundamental transaction processing applications that store, maintain, and update data in the database. A client-server application typically involves forms, reports, queries, and menus designed to interact with a database to meet the data and information processing needs of a business system. The database normally resides on some central server or servers. The client software for the application can reside on the client or the server. It is easier to manage software upgrades if the client software resides on the server. The server software normally resides on some server.

The database system manages the data, and the database is the heart of the application. Database management systems (DBMSs) typically include both software to develop the database and software to develop many parts of the application. Applications may be developed using a built-in procedural or scripting language that is part of the DBMS software. Many PC-based relational DBMSs feature such a language. The command language of DBASE IV is a good example. However, these built-in languages are typically limited and are not normally used for the development of large applications. Windows-based front-end development can be done with tools like **Visual Basic**, **Powerbuilder**, and Access. These tools are very powerful and can be used to develop medium-sized applications. Access uses Visual Basic to allow the developer to build logic modules to process the data that is passed between the modules and the database.

Large-scale applications (enterprise-wide systems) are normally developed through programs written in a host language, such as COBOL. To build applications using a programming language external to the DBMS software, the DBMS's host language interface software must be used. This software component creates the interface allowing the database to supply data to and receive data from standard programs written in the host language. In SQL-based relational DBMSs, this software component is commonly called *embedded SQL.* The use of embedded SQL in application development is covered in Chapter 9.

In addition to a built-in programming language and host language interface software, many DBMSs also have software components supporting fourth generation language (4GL) applications development. Software for 4GL applications development commonly found in a DBMS include: a form generator, a report generator, and a query generator (SQL).

Overall, the applications development software components of client-server DBMSs typically provide the following capabilities:

1. Procedure or scripting language

2. Host language interface

3. Form and menu generation

4. Report generation

5. Query processing

This chapter covers menus, forms, and reports as an example of a user interface that interacts with the database. Normally the user interface starts with a menu displayed on a window. Each menu is attached to a logical function. Typical logical functions are: maintaining data, running reports, doing queries, and initiating simple to complex processing functions that may take minutes to hours to accomplish. The logical functions are accomplished with forms, reports, SQL queries, procedure language procedures, and host language procedures.

Visual Basic
A software system from Microsoft that is used to build GUI applications using procedural code that runs on the client.

Powerbuilder
A software system from Powersoft that is used to build applications with GUI and procedural code using SQL to database systems such as Oracle and Sybase.

DESIGNING AND BUILDING FORMS FOR CLIENT WORKSTATIONS

A form is used much the same way on a window as it is used manually. However, a Windows-based form can be programmed to be a smart form. The smart functions of a Windows-based form include format restrictions on the fields, domain or range restrictions, restrictions based on other data already in the database, and automatic loading of fields with data from the database related to data that was entered in the forms. Forms can be used to add, change, delete, and view data in the database. A form is normally set up as a user or application view of data. It is normally not a database view. The user view is how the user looks at a combination of data that represents the function or transaction. These views are sometimes referred to as *objects* or *object views.* A form is often related to many files or tables in the database. The execution of a form can add data to some parts of the database, change data in other parts, and remove data from parts of the database.

The implementation of forms on terminals in the past was done with software that supported character-based screens. The IBM 3270 terminal is a very common terminal used in these applications. The 3270 is referred to as a dumb terminal because it does not have processing capability. The software used to format the screen runs on the mainframe or server. Applications are still being built today to use these character-based 3270 terminals, because large organizations cannot afford to replace them with Windows-based personal computers (PCs). Normally, a form on a 3270 is referred to as a "screen" and a form on a Windows-based PC is referred to as character- or text-based because the terminal does not support graphics.

FORM CHARACTERISTICS

A form consists of two primary parts—fixed and variable. The fixed part is the form design that consists of characters, diagrams, lines, icons, buttons, colors, and shadings that normally remain constant and cannot be changed by the user. The variable portion of the form is that part the user fills in with data. Normally these are boxed, shaded, colored, or underlined areas that may or may not have data in them when the form is displayed. There are two types of data—control data and database data. The control data is used to tell the program what to do with the data in the form, and the database data is data stored in the database. Control data can come from a field on the form, be generated as a result of buttons or icons, or result from procedures that are executed when the form turns over control to the database processing software.

WINDOWS-BASED FORMS

A Windows-based form is a form that can run under Windows-based operating systems, and has all the functionality of typical windows found in any Windows-based product. This means the form can have icons, scroll bars, menu bars, drop down menus, buttons, check boxes, dialog boxes, and all the features supported by the windows operating system. It also means that a form can call another form so the user can be working with more than one form at the same time. Multiple form execution can be managed in different ways. In some cases the primary window calls another window that the user works on and then returns to the primary window. In other cases, a primary window will pass control to another primary window.

There are many parts to the design of windows. Some of the basic designs include the placement of data fields (**text box**) and their respective prompts or **labels.** The design of a data field includes the selection of length, the edit type (such as numeric and date), font type, font size, foreground color, background color, shading, borders,

Text box
A control on a window that is a field that accepts data from the user or displays data from other sources, such as databases, files, or calculations done by a procedure.

Label
A control on a window that displays the titles and text to identify other objects on the window.

Group box
A box with a label that is also referred to as an option group. Visually groups controls that are logically related to one another.

and the source of the data (entered from the keyboard or looked up in a table). The design of the prompt has many of the same selection considerations except that a prompt or label is filled with text. Other design considerations are the placement of all the data and prompts on the window, and the sequence of entering the data. Windows can have a number of special features that allow a user to easily select choices as a way of entering data. These include option buttons, command buttons, list boxes, **group boxes,** and check boxes. **Option buttons (radio buttons)** are mutually exclusive, meaning that you can have only one selected at any one time. Selecting another button cancels a previous one. **Check boxes** allow the user to select all choices that apply. A **list box** displays a list of rows in a separate box and allows the user to select a choice from that list. **Command buttons** allow the user to execute commands, or respond to YES/NO types of decisions. Typical command buttons include OPEN, NEW, UPDATE, DELETE, CLOSE, ADD, and CANCEL.

Another dimension of window design is setting up menus to allow the user to control the processing and sequencing of windows used in the application. The first window's sole purpose in an application can be a menu to select the applications or functions desired by the user. However, many windows-based applications use **menu bars** and icons across the top for this purpose. With this approach, the remainder of the window can be used to enter initial data to start the application. Menus can be designed into a menu bar, or they can be a set of icons, buttons, or some combination of these. Most data forms are designed with a menu bar at the top. This design allows the window to collect and display data, and also control the sequence of processing. A menu bar has the typical **drop down menu** lists that are common to windows-based applications.

Windows are often designed in multiples to represent the data structures. A primary window will correspond to the one side of a one to many relationship, and a secondary window, or subform window, will list the rows corresponding to the many side of the same relationship. This type of window design works well for common tree data structures, such as a passenger and the itinerary for that passenger. This structure can also be set up as an inverted structure in which the many side comes up first. The user can select from the list of many passengers and pop up a window with the detail data for the passenger selected. The itinerary window with all the flights for this passenger can also come up either automatically or on command. Each window can have its own set of commands for updating the database, such as NEW, UPDATE, and DELETE.

Various window behaviors can be built to support client-server application development.[1] One standard behavior, termed LIST behavior, is a window that displays a list of rows from a table or a query. The user can select a row and call upon other behaviors or actions relative to that row. Other behaviors include MODIFY, DELETE, and DETAILS, which are used to bring up additional data relative to a row that is selected. Another behavior is ADD, which is not relative to any row selected.

---

[1]For more information and examples of these behaviors, see Alden C. Lorents, Gregory Neal, and Deborah Codding, "Deployment of GUI Behavior Standards in an I-CASE Environment," Proceedings, International Association of Computer Information Systems, Toronto, October 1995.

Option button (radio button)
A control on a window that allows the user to select from a mutually exclusive group of options. Only one option can be selected within that group at any one time. Example: Sex: Male, Female.

Check box
A control on a window that allows the user to select from one or more selections in a group where the selections are not mutually exclusive. More than one selection can be selected at any one time. The control supports a Yes/No response to a selection. Example: Database Experience: Oracle, Sybase, DB2, Access.

List box
A control on a window that allows a user to view, select, and deselect various rows of data within a separate window or box.

Command button (push button)
A control on a window that allows the user to control the sequence of operations in an application by responding to major processing selections, such as Cancel, Add, Delete, Modify, OK, Yes, No.

Menu bar
Allows the user to control the sequence of processing events by selecting options; normally located at the top of the window.

Drop down menu
A menu on a window that drops down from a main menu when the main menu is accessed.

Each behavior normally has an associated standard window design. A LIST behavior that is combined with ADD, MODIFY, and DELETE is normally referred to as a LIST/UPDATE behavior.

A LIST window is often preceded with a SEARCH capability. SEARCH behavior allows the user to specify the domain of the list by putting boundaries around the list. An example might be to bring up a list of all open orders with a specific account. Another example might be to bring up all flight combinations between Phoenix and Dallas. Excessively large lists slow down response time and create more problems as the user scrolls through them.

A very common behavior is a two-list window referred to as AVAILABLE/ASSIGN. In this behavior the user selects rows from an available list and adds them to an assign list. Normally both lists are maintained as separate tables or queries in the database system. Selection causes the row to be removed from the available list and added to the assign list. However, this is not always the case. For example, a flight can be selected from an available list of flights and assigned to a passenger itinerary that is being built. In this case, the flight is still a part of the flight table. Another example would be a list of customers requesting tickets for a concert. As each customer is assigned a ticket with a specific seat, the customer would be moved from an order-to-be-processed status to an order-processed status. This may be just an update of a field within that same table. Once the field is updated, the row would not show up again on the order-to-be-processed list.

FIGURE 8.1
Selecting a Form
Type in Access

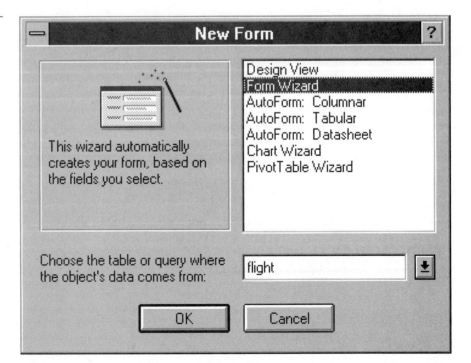

FORM EXAMPLES USING ACCESS

Access, Microsoft's database system, is included in a suite of products called *Microsoft Office.* The package combines a relational database engine with forms, reports, menus, **object linking and embedding (OLE)**, SQL, open database connectivity (ODBC) support, and Visual Basic. Access can be used to develop the front-end user interfaces to Microsoft SQL server on LANs, to Sybase on UNIX servers, and to Oracle databases running under UNIX, MVS, and NT.

Access supports a full range of application development tools, including forms, menus, reports, SQL, and procedural programming using Visual BASIC. The forms generator supports all the standard windows-based design objects. The design of a form can be initiated by selecting the form icon, specifying NEW, selecting a table, and using the form wizard (Figure 8.1). The first decision is to select a form type, such as single column, tabular, graph, or data sheet, or select the form wizard for

OLE (Object Linking and Embedding)
A protocol that allows the linking or embedding of objects, such as pictures, sounds, and graphs, into other objects, such as forms and reports.

FIGURE 8.2
Selecting the
Fields for the Form

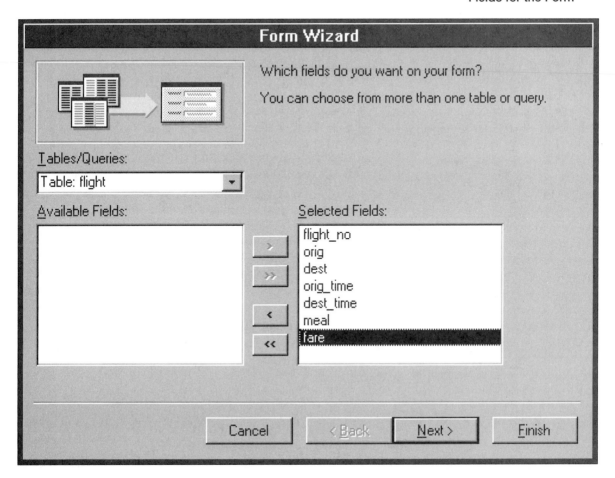

more complex forms, such as forms with subforms. The next step is to select the fields in that table or query corresponding to the type of form (Figure 8.2). Depending on the data and relationships that are in the query, the wizard will determine different options the developer can select for the form design. If it is a simple table, the options are columnar, tabular, or datasheet. If there are relationships, the form may include subforms.

Another step in the wizard process is to select the style and background for the form, as shown in Figure 8.3.

Figure 8.4 has been designed using Access. In this simple form, all the fields are coming from one table. This form can be used to display the existing data, modify the data, or enter new data to the flight table. It can be built by the form wizard using tabular format.

Another approach to form design uses the form design window called Design View, the first option in Figure 8.1 (see Figure 8.5a). The view can be used from the

FIGURE 8.3
Selecting a
Preformatted Style
for the Form

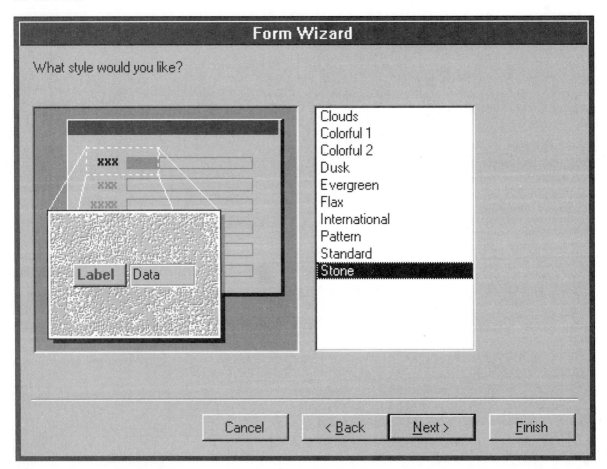

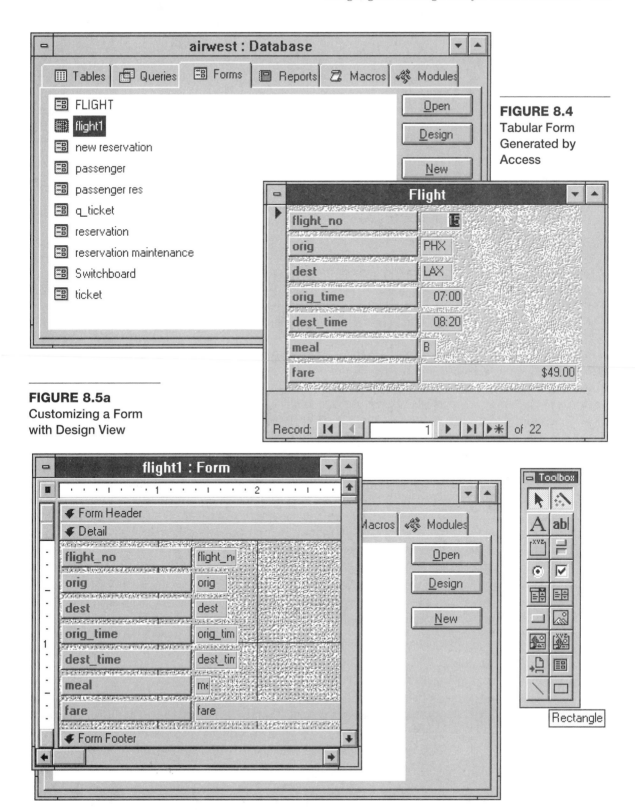

FIGURE 8.4
Tabular Form Generated by Access

FIGURE 8.5a
Customizing a Form with Design View

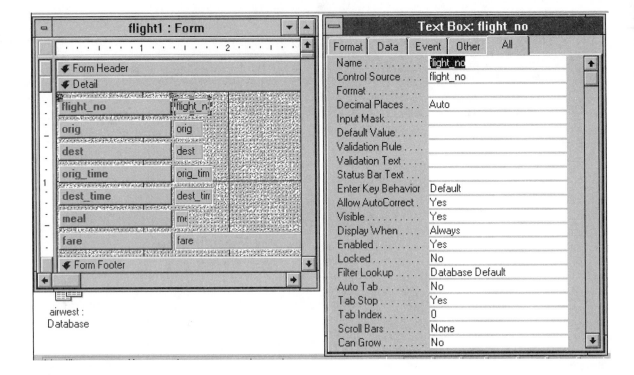

FIGURE 8.5b
Properties of the
Text Box Flight_No

Properties
The attributes, such as
color, font size, and position, of another object, such
as a field, form, query or
report.

Field properties
The attributes, such as type,
size, label, and format, that
describe the various characteristics of a field.

beginning of a new form, or a developer can start with the wizard and use the resulting design as a starting point for a customized form. Design View allows the designer
to size the window, set up horizontal and vertical scroll bars, and define the content
within headers, details, and footers. Design View also allows the developer to define
the attributes (color, fonts, size) and all the **properties** of all the specific objects. Note
that the **field properties** of the flight_no field are shown in Figure 8.5b. The developer can move the fields around on the form to any position desired. Other objects,
such as command buttons, option buttons, and list boxes, can be added to the form
using the tool bar on the right.

The control objects of the Access toolbox include the following (see the toolbox in Figure 8.6 on the next page):

Label: Used to create a frame for entering text, such as labels and instructions.

Text Box: Sets up a frame to display, enter, and edit data.

Option Group: Sets up a frame where you can put toggle buttons, option buttons,
or check boxes.

Toggle Button: Sets up a button that switches between on and off when clicked
with the mouse.

Option Button (Radio Button): Similar to a toggle button. It is used primarily in
option groups to select one option in a group.

Check Box: Similar to the option button. Normally used outside of option groups
so that you can select more than one option.

Select Objects		Control Wizards
Label		Text Box
Option Group		Toggle Button
Option Button		Check Box
List Box		Combo Box
Command Button		Image
Object Frame		Bound Object Frame
Page Break		Subform/Subreport
Line		Rectangle

FIGURE 8.6
Control Objects
Available from
the Toolbox

List Box: Sets up an area to list rows of data, allowing the user to select a row for entry into the assigned field.

Combo Box: A special list box that allows the user to enter a value in a text box or select one from the list.

Command Button: Allows the user to assign an Access routine to a button on the form.

SAMPLE APPLICATION USING ACCESS FORMS

The following application was set up using Access forms. The application supports the maintenance of airline reservations for Air West Airlines. The first window in the application (Figure 8.7, on the following page) is referred to as a Switchboard. A Switchboard window allows the user to switch between functions of the application by selecting buttons that are attached to different windows (forms), or generate reports, or execute other applications, or exit the application. The *Reservation* button activates the reservation subsystem. The *Flights* button allows the user to update flight data in the flight table, and the *All Fares* button displays a report showing all the tickets for each passenger for each reservation. When the user selects the reservation subsystem, a window (Figure 8.8) pops up, allowing the user to query a reservation based on a confirmation number entered by the user.

The example shows a query on confirmation number 3, which produces the data shown in Figure 8.9 on the reservation window. The user can modify data such as name and phone number on this figure. Changes can also be made to passenger data, including deleting and adding passengers. The reservation window is a typical main/subform application in which the top part of the form shows parent data and the bottom part of the form shows child data related to that parent.

FIGURE 8.7
Using a Form as the
Main Menu to an
Application

FIGURE 8.8
Entering Data on a
Form to Limit the
Domain of a Query

The user can highlight a specific passenger, then press the *Tickets* button to view another window (Figure 8.10 on the following page) that contains the ticket data for each passenger. It is like another subform, but it has been built as a separate window that is supported by a query of all tickets for a specific itinerary number. Data in this window can also be modified, including adding and deleting tickets.

USING ACCESS, ODBC, AND ORACLE

Client-server applications can be built by first using Access to develop the windows and then attaching the Oracle tables to access as though they are Access tables. This

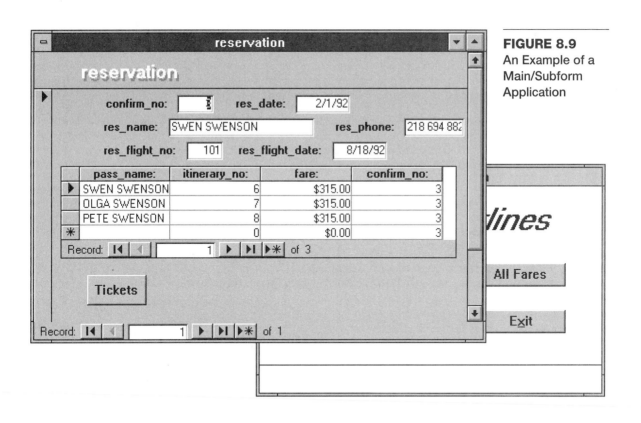

FIGURE 8.9
An Example of a Main/Subform Application

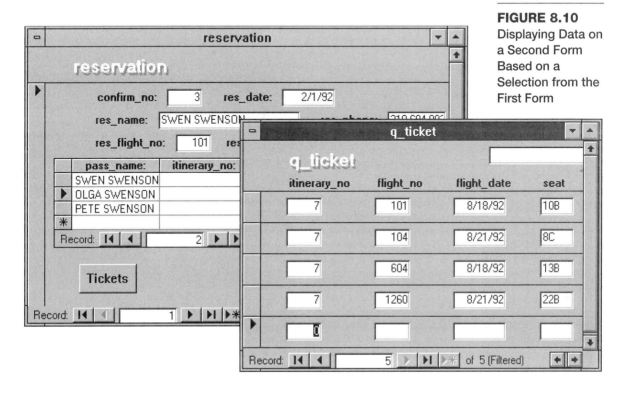

FIGURE 8.10
Displaying Data on a Second Form Based on a Selection from the First Form

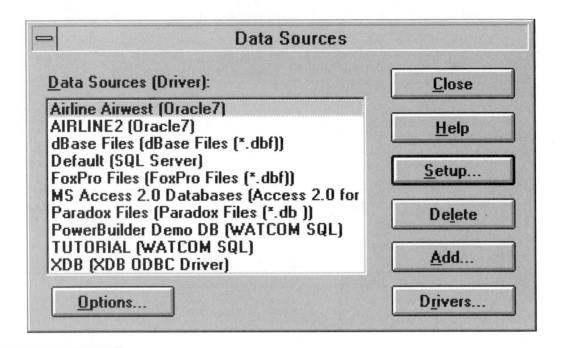

FIGURE 8.11
ODBC Data Sources

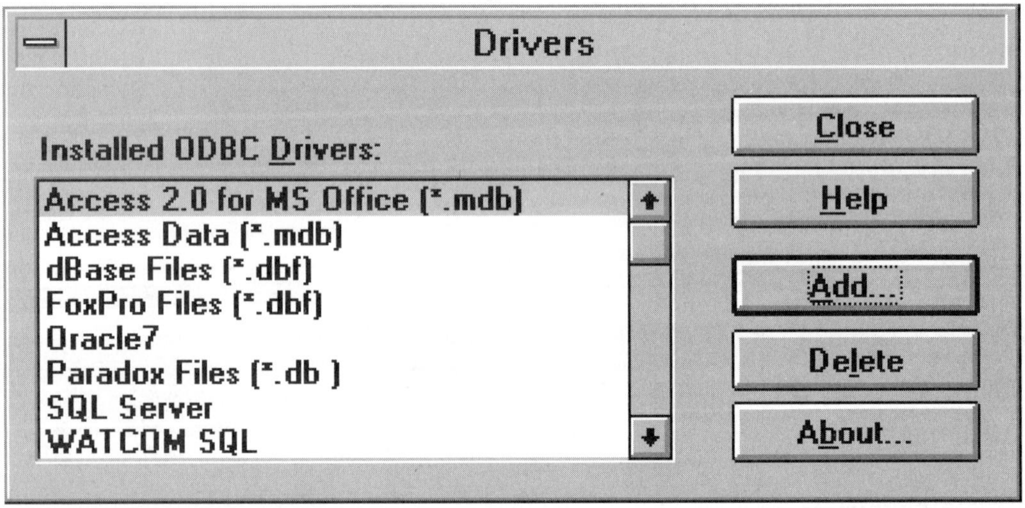

FIGURE 8.12
ODBC Drivers

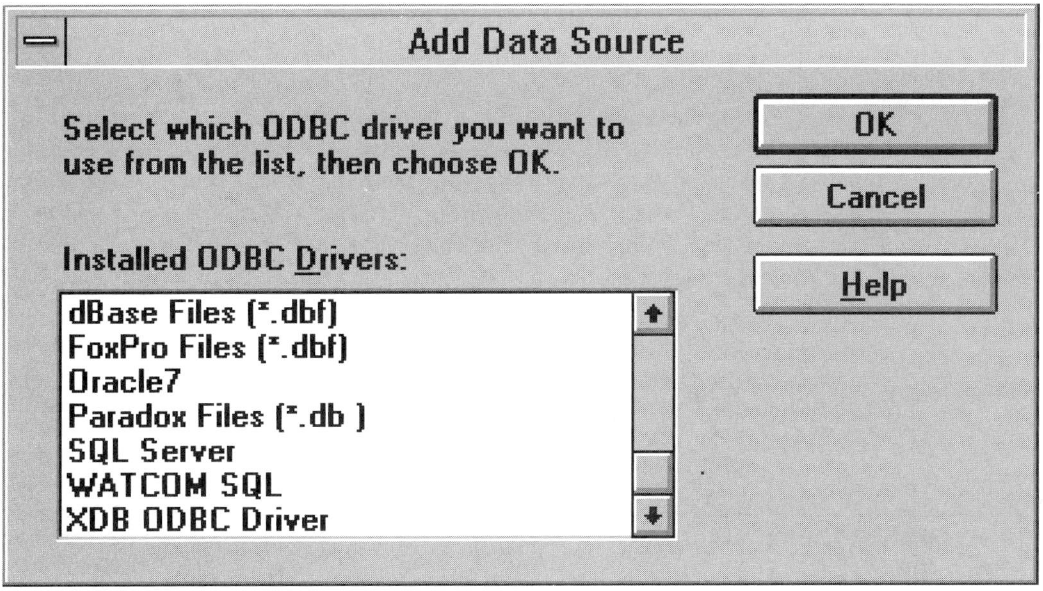

FIGURE 8.13
Selecting an ODBC
Driver to Match the
Database

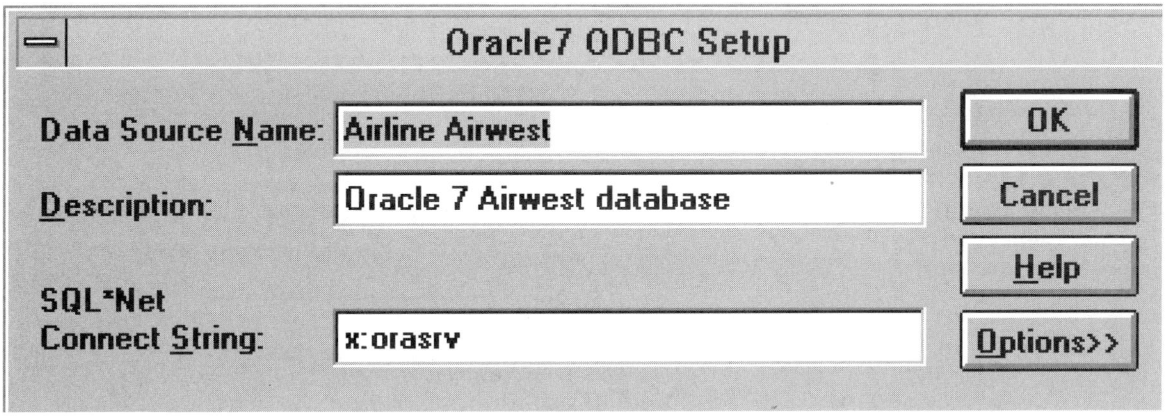

FIGURE 8.14
Setting Up the Data
Source Name and
Connect Location

ODBC (Open Database Connectivity)
Software that standardizes the interface to a database system to allow various application systems to access any database system. An ODBC interface allows Access to obtain data from Oracle.

is done through the **ODBC (Open Database Connectivity)** interface. An ODBC driver is obtained from Oracle and installed on your system. The driver is added to the set of ODBC drivers and can be used to set up a data source (Figure 8.11, page 326). The data sources available to an application on a workstation are managed by the Microsoft ODBC Administrator software. The list of drivers installed (Figure 8.12, page 326) is obtained by using the *Drivers* button on the Data Sources window. A data source is added by using the *Add* button. The driver is selected (Figure 8.13, page 327) and linked to the data source name specified in the data source setup (Figure 8.14, page 327). The data source setup window includes the data source name and the address (connect string) of the server that will work with the specified driver.

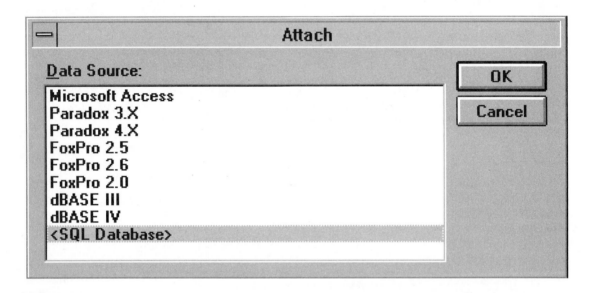

FIGURE 8.15
Attaching Access to Another Database

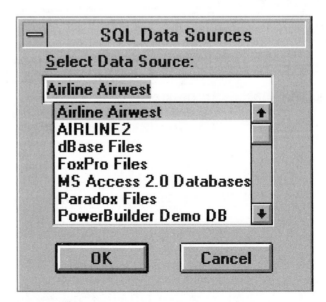

FIGURE 8.16
Selecting the Data Source for the Attachment

After the data source has been set up, Access can attach the tables at the server just like they are tables on the local workstation. The ATTACH command is part of the file menu under Access and brings up the Attach window (Figure 8.15, page 328), allowing the developer to select a particular database. In this example, we are attaching to an Oracle database, which is a SQL database based on this selection, another window (Figure 8.16, page 328) comes up to allow us to select a data source. We could have multiple databases that are Oracle, DB2, or Sybase to choose from. In this case we will choose the Airline Air West data source that was just defined in the preceding examples. As soon as we choose this data source, a window (Figure 8.17, below) pops up allowing us to log on to Oracle. It already knows the connect string, so it asks us for the user name and password.

Once we are connected to the Oracle database, a window comes up that lists all the tables in the database. The developer can choose the desired tables for this application, and these tables are now a part of an Access application just as though they were built in Access. The developer can go on to develop queries, forms, and reports using the tables or queries against the tables. Figures 8.18 (below) and 8.19 (page 330) show examples of a Customer Reservation window and a related Passenger (passenger selected on reservation) record along with the ticket itinerary. These forms are working directly with an Oracle database running on a network server.

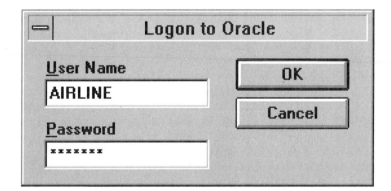

FIGURE 8.17
Logging On to the
Attached Database

FIGURE 8.18
Viewing Oracle
Reservation Data
with Access Forms

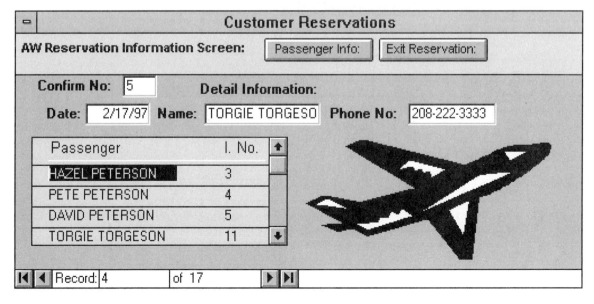

CLIENT-SERVER REPORT GENERATION

REPORT CHARACTERISTICS

Report layout
The process of designing the report format into various heading, detail, and footing sections.

Most database software systems provide some type of report generator. Typically a report is defined by specifying a **report layout** on the window similar to a form layout. This report definition can be used with a table or a query to produce a report. Reports can also be defined by selecting a set of data with a SQL command and customizing the layout. The simplest form of this is to produce a report based on the data from one table. Additional specifications can be added to obtain totals at breakpoints, calculate new columns, exclude columns, exclude the printing of detail data, and include report, page, and control break headers and footers. A more complex report can be developed using data from multiple tables. Normally the data selection is done with a SQL command, and the resulting table is handled by the report generator just as though it were a single table. Report specifications normally include the following:

1. Data selected to be in the report

2. Field placement, size, editing characteristics, and other properties of each field

FIGURE 8.19
Viewing Oracle Passenger Data with Access Forms

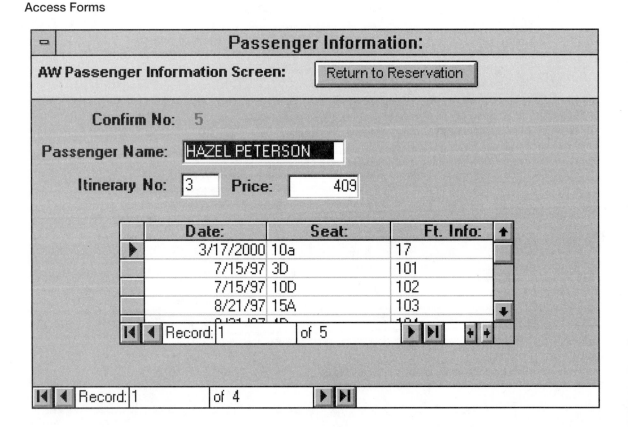

3. Report, page, and control break header and footer content (text and data fields)

4. Sequence of the report

5. Page control and numbering

6. Calculations

7. Detail and summary printing control

REPORTING WITH ACCESS

Designing reports in Access has many of the same features as designing forms. Basically, an Access report is a special kind of continuous form designed for printing. A report does not fit on a screen, so it really can't be used as a form. The report can be previewed on the screen during the design phase, so it can be tested. Reports cannot be used to accept data because they are designed to be output only. The designer can add sections to reports that include report **headers** and **footers** and page headers and footers. A report header includes one or more **heading lines** that label the content of the report. A page header includes one or more heading lines that label the content of a report page. Column labels and page numbers are typically included in page headers. Report and page footers are used to report totals for the page or the report. Page numbers can be placed in either the page footer or header. Group sections are similar to detail sections in forms. Group sections are referred to as *bands*. Normally a group header will have a title for the group, and a group footer will contain totals for that group. Access has built-in capability to design single column reports, group/total reports, and mail labels. The designer can begin with these and customize them as desired.

The following sequence of windows shows a group-level report built using a query. The first step in building a report is to build a query that contains all the data needed for that report. The following query has been modified from the originally generated QBE SQL to make it easier to read. The query selects all data in the database to obtain the total value of fares by reservation and by passenger. Typically this query would be limited by another query to select all reservations for a specific flight and specific date, or by some combination of flight and date.

Header
An area at the beginning of a section of a report to display heading lines and data that pertain to that section of the report.

Footer
An area at the end of a section of a report to display labels and data that pertain to that section.

Heading line
Line displayed on top of a section in a report or form that labels the content of that section.

```
SELECT DISTINCTROW  reservation.res_name, reservation.confirm_no,
                    passenger.pass_name, passenger.itinerary_no,
                    flight.flight_no, flight.fare
                    ticket.flight_date,
         FROM       reservation, passenger, flight
         WHERE      reservation.confirm_no = passenger.confirm_no
         AND        flight.flight_no = ticket.flight_no
         AND        passenger.itinerary_no = ticket.itinerary_no;
```

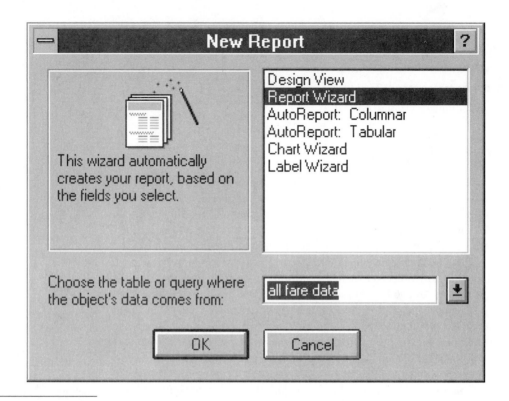

FIGURE 8.20
Selecting the
Report Type

Control break properties
Attributes that describe the
fields that control the combining of data into various
control groups, such as separate header, detail, and
footer sections in a report.

Once the query has been built, the report can be constructed using either the
Design View or various report wizards by going to New Report within Access
Reports (Figure 8.20). The first step is to select the report design similar to forms. The
developer can begin with a blank window by going to Design View, or use the wizard to begin and Design View to finish the report design. Simple reports can be generated with the columnar or tabular wizard. Group-level reports with **control breaks**
can be generated using the report wizard. The designer can then select the table or
query that supplies the data to the report.

The next step is to select the fields desired on the report. In most cases the SQL
query has been designed so that all fields can be selected for the report. Figure 8.21
shows that all fields except res_name will be used in the report.

In this report we want to obtain a total fare for each passenger for each trip
(itinerary number). We also want total fares for all passengers under a specific reservation. The total for a reservation is controlled by a change on confirmation number. Figure 8.22 (page 334) allows the developer to choose a report by reservation.
Because the relationships are already known to the database, the wizard is able to
structure the report using reservation data, passenger data under that reservation,
and ticket data under that passenger.

Figure 8.23 (page 335) allows the developer to select the sequence of the detail
data in the report. In this case the ticket data will be displayed in flight date order.

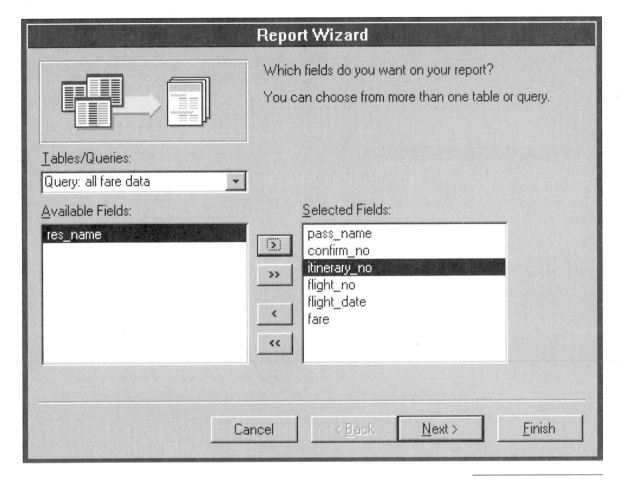

FIGURE 8.21
Selecting Fields
for the Report

Figure 8.24 (page 336) comes up by choosing *Summary Options* on Figure 8.21. It allows the developer to select the summary options for the report. In this case we want to sum the fare on each ticket for each passenger, and also sum the fare for each reservation. The selection of Detail and Summary under summary options will make this happen.

Figure 8.25 (page 337) allows the developer to choose the layout for the report and the orientation.

Access will control summary breaks when a portion of the value changes in the control field. Thus, if a developer wanted a new total each time the third digit changed, the developer would select the 100s value. This would be useful if we want a report on all 1XX courses, then all 2XX courses, and so on. This feature is shown in Figure 8.26 (page 337).

Once the report is defined, the developer can go to the Design View of the report and make modifications to it as though the report had been built from a blank report.

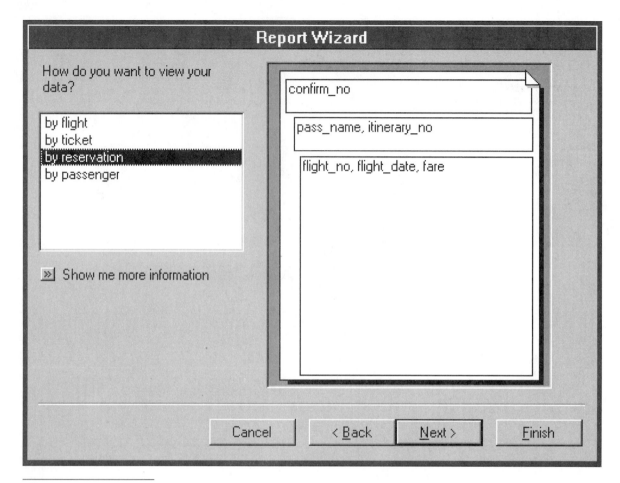

FIGURE 8.22
Selecting the Group-
Level Control Structure
for the Report

The Design View for this report is shown in Figure 8.27 (page 338). This report has been modified to reflect better column headings, and to remove some summary output in the confirmation and itinerary number footers. Note the various header and footer areas in this report. Note also that Figure 8.27 does not display the very top of the report, which shows the report header. The first line showing is the page header.

A partial listing of the actual report is shown in Figure 8.28 (page 339). The page header contains the report title, date, and page number along with column headings for the detail data in the report. The confirmation number control break header prints the confirmation number. The detail line prints each passenger name and related flight information for each leg of the trip. Notice that the passenger name and related itinerary number prints on the first line of an itinerary number group. Notice also that the itinerary number footer prints the total fare for a passenger for that trip, and that the confirmation number footer prints the total fare for all passengers under a reservation (unique confirmation number).

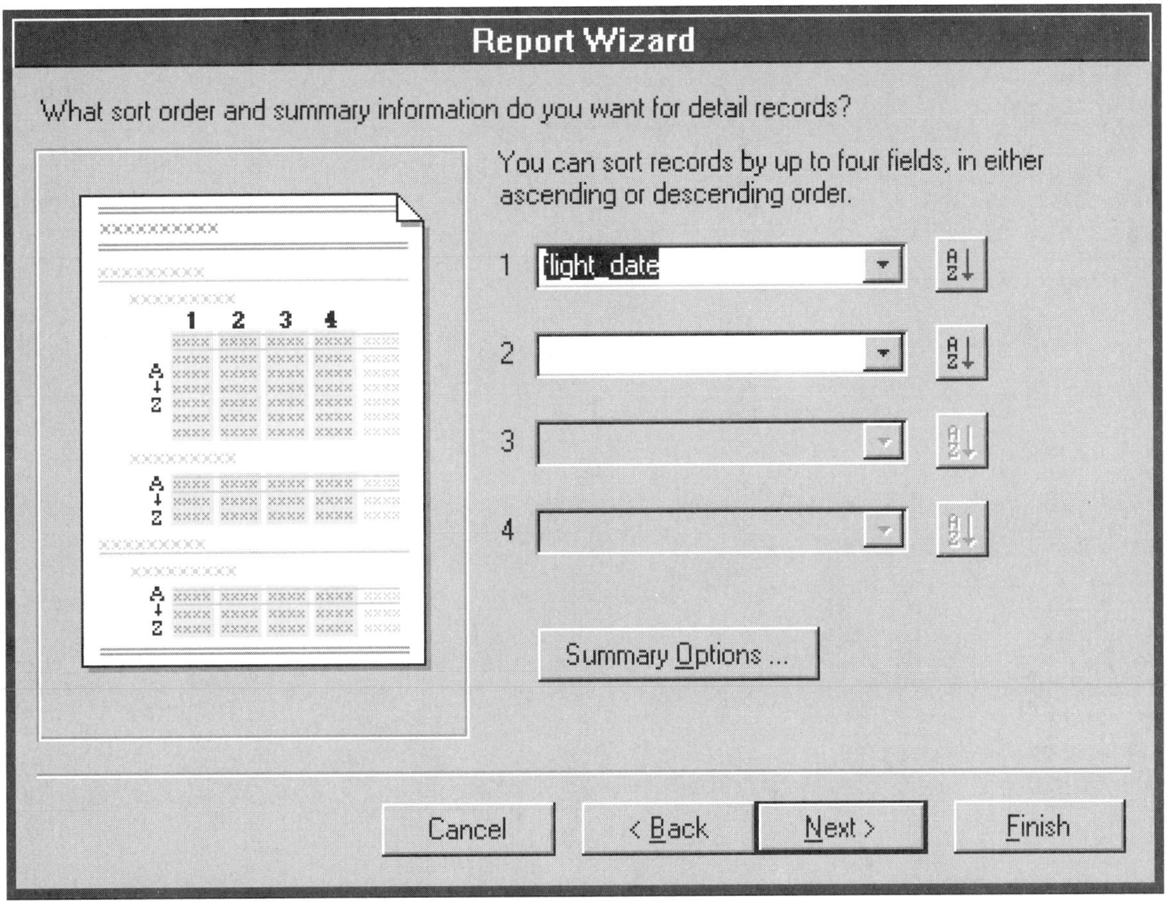

FIGURE 8.23
Selecting the Sort
Order for the Report

REPORTING WITH CRYSTAL REPORTS

Another widely used report generator is Crystal Reports. It is often used with Visual Basic applications and has also been used to support the reporting needs of applications built by Texas Instrument's Composer by IEF. Crystal Reports can support a wide variety of reporting needs. It also supports reporting in HTML format for World Wide Web applications. See the box about Crystal Reports on page 349.

CLIENT-SERVER MENU DEVELOPMENT

A client-server application is put together by linking various parts of the application into a common interface. The various parts include forms, reports, SQL, macros, and various client and server procedures. As stated in the introduction, menus can

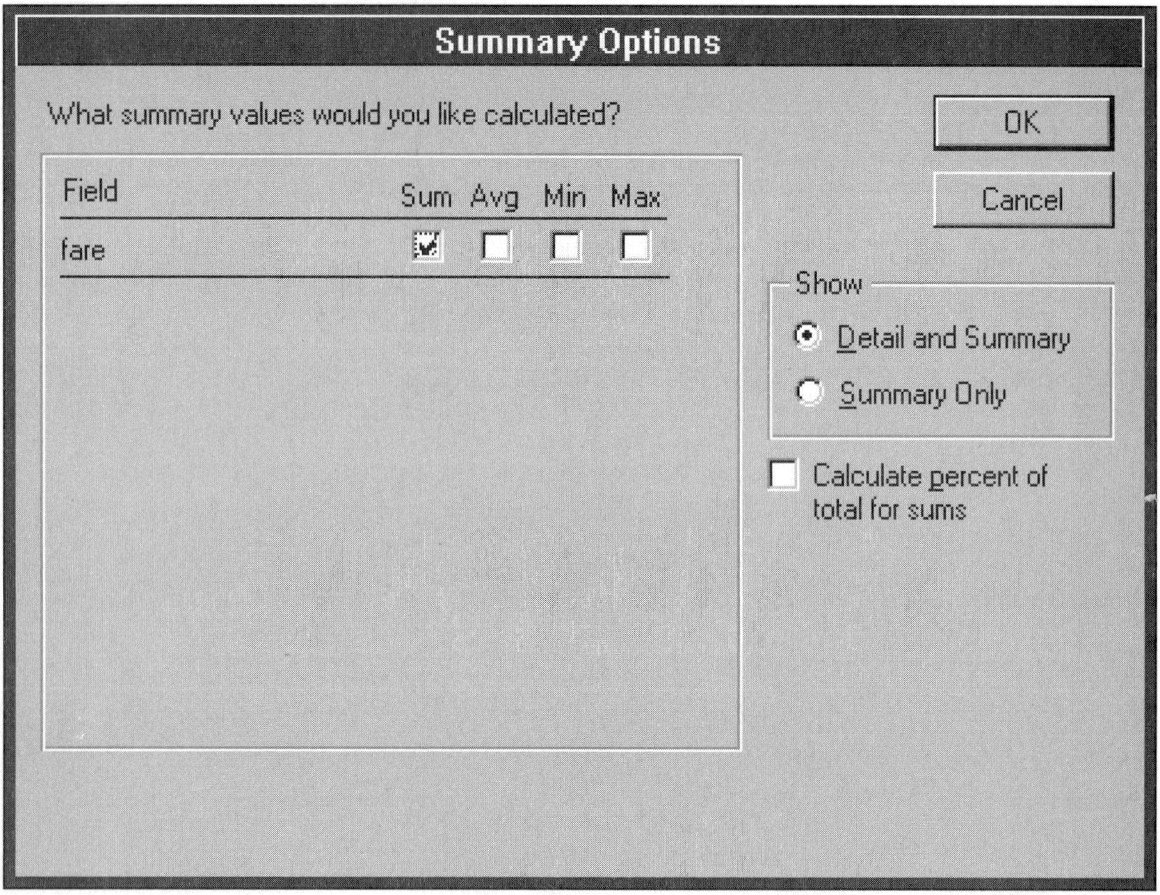

FIGURE 8.24
Selecting the Summary
Options for the
Summary Lines

be simple lists in character-based screens, or menu bars, buttons, and icons that are supported with all the graphical user interface (GUI) features of a windows application. The following example (Figure 8.29, page 340) shows the design of a simple window with buttons that are used to call different parts of the application. The window is called a switchboard because it plugs the user into different parts of the application. Each button is linked to a macro that calls a form and executes a report, a SQL query, or a procedure.

Figure 8.30 (page 341) shows the properties of the reservation button. The On Click event has been linked to the macro reservation within the macro switchboard.

Figure 8.31 (page 342) shows the macro switchboard, which consists of a number of submacros. The macro reservation opens the reservation form called *reservation maintenance*. Other buttons on the switchboard are linked to the same macro. *Flights* executes a SQL query. *All Fares* opens the report All Fares, and *Exit* closes the application. Notice that Figure 8.31 shows the detail of opening the form called *reservation maintenance*.

FIGURE 8.25
Selecting from Different Preformatted Report Layouts

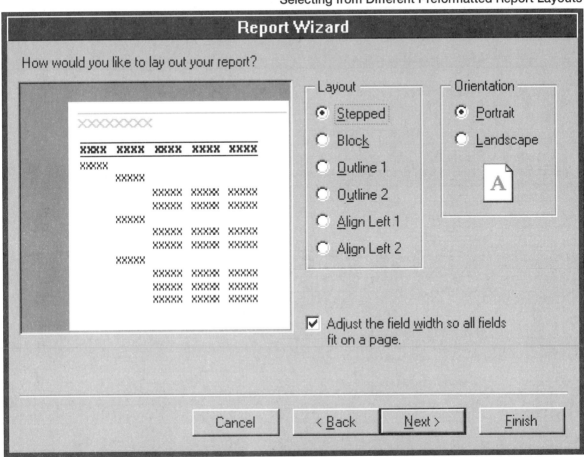

Report Wizard

How would you like to lay out your report?

Layout
- ⦿ Stepped
- ○ Block
- ○ Outline 1
- ○ Outline 2
- ○ Align Left 1
- ○ Align Left 2

Orientation
- ⦿ Portrait
- ○ Landscape

☑ Adjust the field width so all fields fit on a page.

Cancel   < Back   Next >   Finish

Grouping Intervals

What grouping intervals do you want for group-level fields?

OK

Cancel

Group-level fields:
itinerary_no

Grouping intervals:
Normal ▼

Normal
10s
50s
100s
500s
1000s
5000s

FIGURE 8.26
Selecting the Control on Group-Level Fields

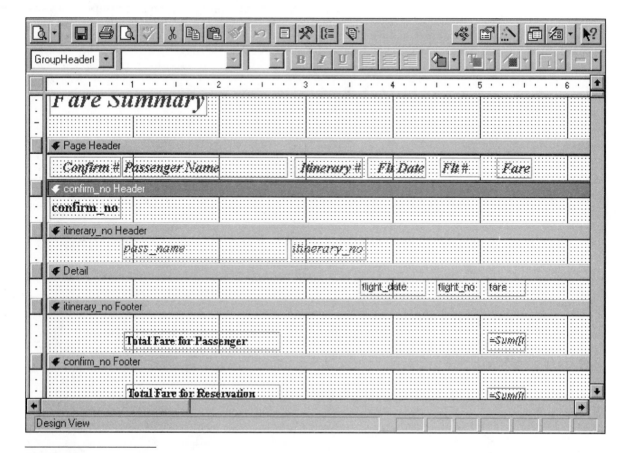

FIGURE 8.27
Report Design
View in Access

The application can be started from an application ICON within a windows group by setting up the properties of the ICON with the following line in the Command line:

```
c:\msoffice\access\msaccess.exe x/airwest.mdb mcrSwitchboard.mcrstartairline
```

Figure 8.32 (page 342) shows an example of the remaining properties of the application ICON. When the user selects this application ICON on the window, Access is started, and the Start Airline macro is initiated, which brings up the Switchboard window as the first window for the user.

Internet
Same as the World Wide
Web.

**World Wide Web
(WWW)**
Network of Web servers
around the world that can
be accessed by workstations
using a Web browser, such
as Netscape. Also referred
to as the Internet.

INTERNET AND INTRANET SERVER APPLICATIONS

INTERACTIVE HTML WINDOWS

Organizations are rapidly moving to setting up applications using both the Internet and Intranet as network and user interface tools. **Internet** is the **World Wide Web**

Confirm #	Passenger Name	Itinerary #	Flt Date	Flt #	Fare
1					
	OLE OLSON	1			
			2/1/92	15	$49.00
			2/2/92	329	$49.00
	Total Fare for Passenger				$98.00
	LENA OLSON	2			
			2/1/92	15	$49.00
			2/2/92	329	$49.00
	Total Fare for Passenger				$98.00
	Total Fare for Reservation				$196.00
2					
	PETE PETERSON	3			

FIGURE 8.28
Report Preview in Access

(WWW) that allows users anywhere in the world to access the application. **Intranet** refers to the same infrastructure, but access is normally limited to users within the organization. Instead of building the client front-ends with Access, Visual Basic, and Powerbuilder, the front-ends are built in an **HTML (Hyper Text Mark Up Language)** that can be used with browser software, such as Netscape. Application software that is stored on the Web server and executed on the client's server can be built with **JAVA** or COBOL to capture the data from the Netscape windows. JAVA is an object-oriented Internet development language developed by SUN Microsystems. The SQL data requests are sent to database servers and processed against any database system, including VSAM, IMS, IDMS, DB2, and Oracle. Data from the database systems can be fed back to the user via a Netscape window. The Web servers are part of the network architecture of the organization that support the intranet, and they can also be linked to the Internet.

An example of a form used by Northern Arizona University is shown in Figure 8.33 (page 343) and continued in Figure 8.34 (page 347). This form allows users to send change requests for telephone service to the office of Network and Telecommunication Services. The related HTML code is shown in the code block on page 346.

Insurance companies are setting up applications using the Internet to allow customers and potential customers to fill out forms relating to quotes on premiums. Customers can provide information on the cars they own along with information on drivers and driving records, and then receive quotes on the cost of insuring the vehicles.

Intranet
Use of WWW technology, JAVA applets, and a browser, such as Netscape, to develop internal networks to work with organizational databases. Similar to client-server using Web technology.

HTML (Hyper Text Mark Up Language)
Used to build window displays that can be used by browsers, such as Netscape.

JAVA
A language to build applications on servers and client stations to process data coming from the WWW or from internal databases using Web technology.

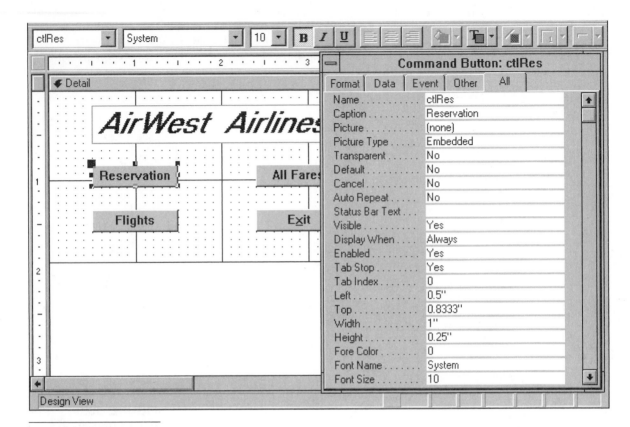

FIGURE 8.29
Menu Development
Using a Form

Federal Express is one of the leaders in allowing customers to come directly into database systems maintained by FedEx through the use of the Web. Whenever you ship a packet with Federal Express, the airbill number on the shipping form can be used to track the packet as it goes across the country. Figures 8.35 and 8.36 (page 348) show the results of a query on airbill 9178015803. The query tracked a packet that was picked up in Randolph, Massachusetts, at 20:17 on August 7 and delivered in Flagstaff, Arizona, the next morning. This particular packet was carrying a check that had to be deposited that day in order to close a piece of property. The FedEx customer in this example was able to track the packet on his home PC at different times during the night and early in the morning to ensure that it would arrive on time.

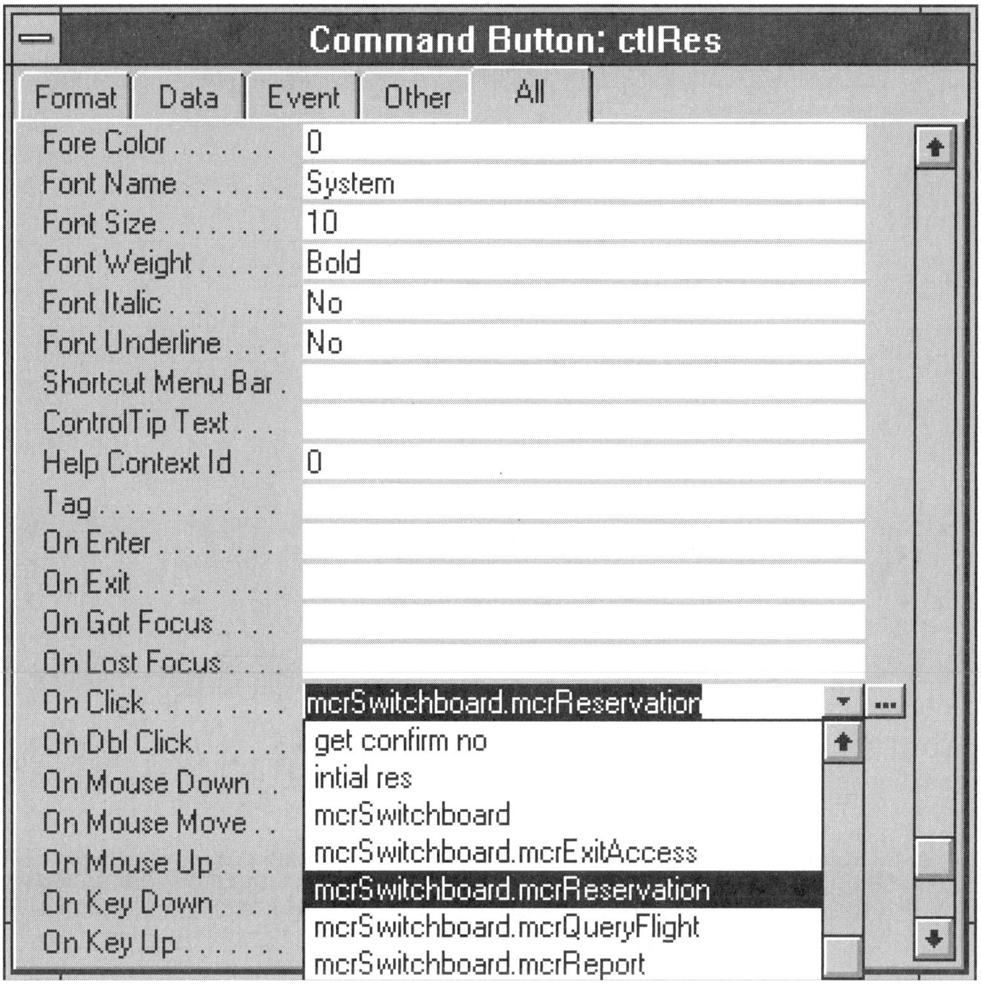

Command Button: ctlRes

| Format | Data | Event | Other | All |

Fore Color	0
Font Name	System
Font Size	10
Font Weight	Bold
Font Italic	No
Font Underline	No
Shortcut Menu Bar .	
ControlTip Text . . .	
Help Context Id	0
Tag	
On Enter	
On Exit	
On Got Focus	
On Lost Focus	
On Click	mcrSwitchboard.mcrReservation
On Dbl Click	get confirm no
On Mouse Down . .	intial res
On Mouse Move . .	mcrSwitchboard
On Mouse Up	mcrSwitchboard.mcrExitAccess
On Key Down	mcrSwitchboard.mcrReservation
On Key Up	mcrSwitchboard.mcrQueryFlight
	mcrSwitchboard.mcrReport

FIGURE 8.30
Properties of a
Command Button

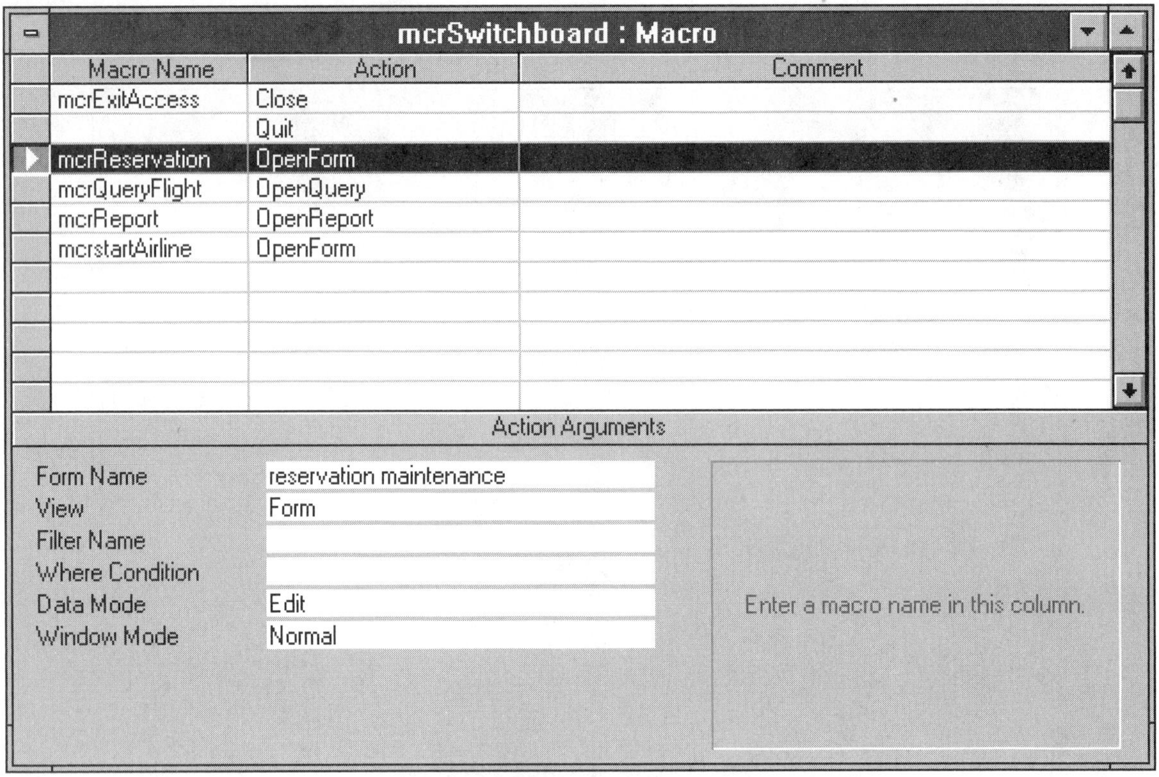

mcrSwitchboard : Macro

Macro Name	Action	Comment
mcrExitAccess	Close	
	Quit	
mcrReservation	OpenForm	
mcrQueryFlight	OpenQuery	
mcrReport	OpenReport	
mcrstartAirline	OpenForm	

Action Arguments

Form Name	reservation maintenance
View	Form
Filter Name	
Where Condition	
Data Mode	Edit
Window Mode	Normal

Enter a macro name in this column.

FIGURE 8.31
A Macro That Controls
Menu Actions

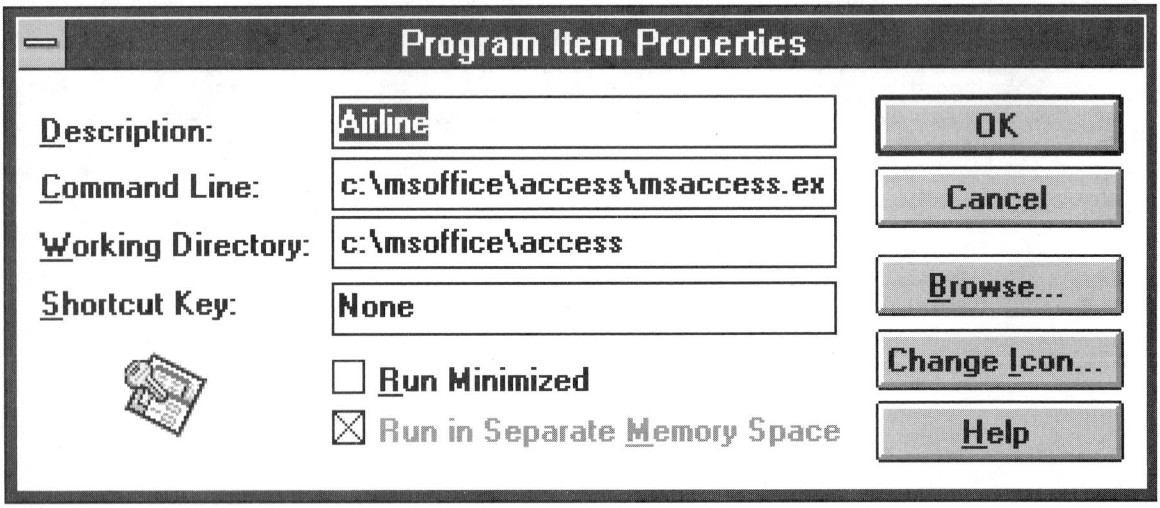

Program Item Properties

Description: Airline

Command Line: c:\msoffice\access\msaccess.ex

Working Directory: c:\msoffice\access

Shortcut Key: None

☐ Run Minimized
☒ Run in Separate Memory Space

OK
Cancel
Browse...
Change Icon...
Help

FIGURE 8.32
Setting Up an ICON in Windows to Run an Application

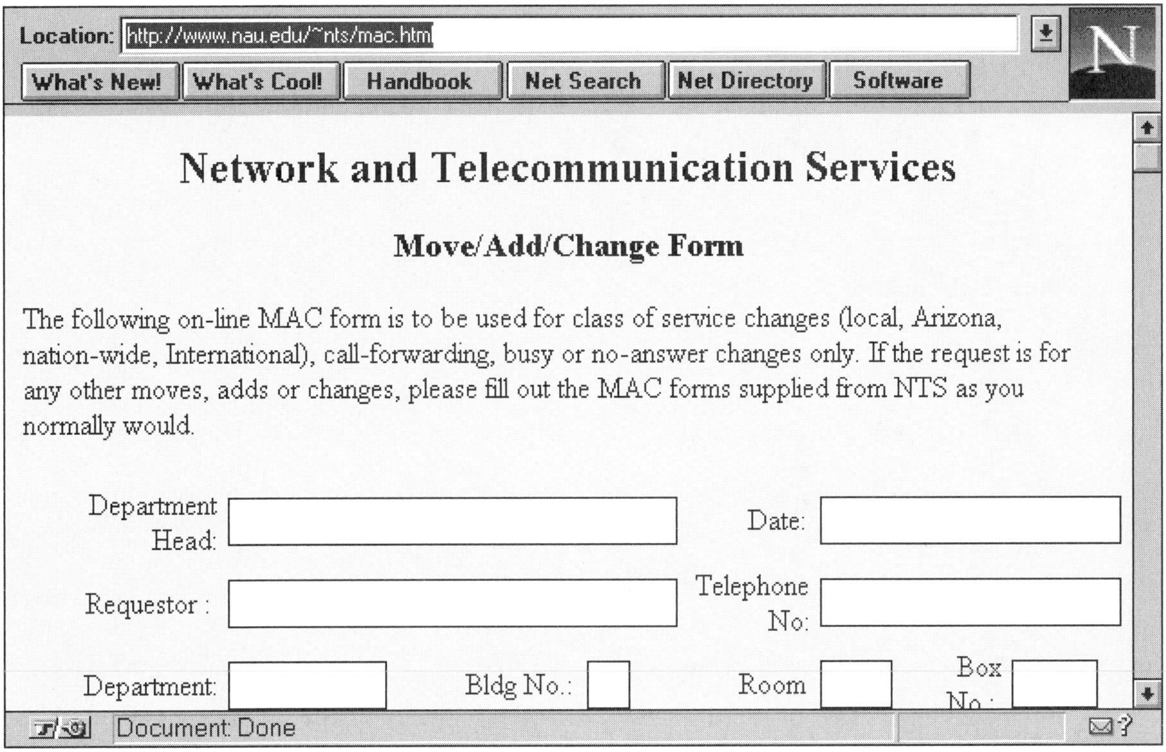

FIGURE 8.33
Collecting Data using an HTML Form: I

INTRANET AT JOHN DEERE

The following John Deere example shows one way companies are approaching Intranet applications. Many companies are starting to use the Internet infrastructure within the company to develop client applications that interface through client-side software using JAVA or COBOL. The client software sends database requests to various databases using SQL.

John Deere Harvests the Benefits of Information Integration with an Intranet

John Deere's Waterloo Works Division uses a Netscape-based Intranet to

- Access an on-line catalog of equipment that integrates data from multiple sources,
- Allow company-wide access to results from remote test sites,
- Provide technical documentation to employees,
- Offer a visual front-end to a parts database,
- Repurpose otherwise obsolete equipment as Web clients, and
- Integrate corporate information with agricultural data on the World Wide Web.

The company chose Netscape client and server technology because

- It's available on all major platforms,
- It incorporates Java, enabling distributed custom applications, and
- Netscape Commerce Server provides security features.

John Deere tractors are at work in farms and fields across the world. But it is the field of information that Deere views as critical to its continued success. Deere uses software from Netscape to integrate corporate data with Web-based agricultural information, provide access to remote test site results, enable employees to access on-line documentation and a parts database, and more.

AN ARCHITECTURE FOR INFORMATION

"A few years ago we started planning a systems architecture for information," says Phyllis Michaelides, head of the Methods, Architecture, and Data Team at John Deere's Waterloo Works Division, Waterloo, Iowa. The purpose of this architecture is to enable various Deere divisions to rapidly build custom applications that work alongside traditional desktop productivity applications, regardless of the platform.

Deere chose to build this architecture around an Intranet using software from Netscape. "One of the reasons Netscape is attractive to us is that we are in a mixed-platform environment," says Michaelides. "On the desktop, it's Macintosh and Windows. Our engineers use UNIX workstations. We have RS-6000, Hewlett-Packard, SGI, and Intel-based servers running Windows NT. But Netscape Navigator is ubiquitous—we've put it on all of our machines. It allows the viewing of design, product, marketing, and manufacturing data on all platforms."

But viewing information is only the beginning. "We need a front end that doesn't just view data, but manipulates it also," says Michaelides. "Netscape software enables us to control programs running on a server or mainframe using CGI scripts."

Deere will take this to the next level with Java, which is supported in Netscape Navigator 2.0. Java enables small programs called applets to be downloaded from the network and run on any client. "We're very excited about Java. In fact, we've already started experimentation and will definitely use it." For example, Deere plans to put a catalog of its tractors and equipment online. Rather than just browsing images of the tractors, Deere employees will be able to query various databases, and bring together a wide variety of product information, all in one place.

ACCESS TO REMOTE TEST SITE RESULTS

Deere is using its Intranet to distribute information from remote test sites, where new models of tractors and heavy equipment are put through their paces. Test results are more than just numbers. "They can also include pictures and sound. For example, you might want to listen to what an engine sounds like," says Michaelides. Given Netscape Navigator's multimedia capabilities, it's a natural fit.

continued

Distributing this information on the Web means that it will be available instantly to all authorized Deere employees. But because of its sensitive nature, the information must also be delivered securely. "We've purchased a Netscape Commerce Server, and plan to use it for our sensitive data," continues Michaelides. "The specific advantage of the Netscape Commerce Server is the Secure Sockets Layer (SSL) that enables us to encrypt sensitive data. The server will also position us to take advantage of online commerce in the future."

DYNAMIC, ON-LINE DOCUMENTATION

The company is finding a better way to distribute—and use—technical documentation by making it available over their Intranet. "We have a lot of technical documentation around the company. We're moving from a static, paper-based environment to a dynamic, on-line environment," says Michaelides. "We've begun to store computer systems documentation on a Web server and deliver it to people throughout the company. And this is just the beginning. New documentation is being added on an hourly basis."

AN INTEGRATED PARTS DATABASE

On-line documentation is only the first step. "We're even more excited about making the information dynamic," Michaelides continues. For example, Deere is in the process of implementing a parts database that employees can access via the Intranet. "It shows what the part looks like, and provides a detailed description—the part's size, bill of materials, assembly instructions, a list of operations that workers use to put it together, and timings of these operations," she explains.

The Web-based parts database will have many applications throughout Deere. "It will help the people in the purchasing department go out for quotes. For example, they could send a picture of a part to a vendor. The people on the shop floor will be able to call up information on how a part is put together. Our engineers will be able to automatically develop bills of materials for their designs," she says.

TURNING AGING EQUIPMENT INTO WEB CLIENTS

Deere has found a way to get more mileage out of its older computers by turning them into dedicated Web clients. Recently the Waterloo plant decided to convert several hundred six-year-old Macintosh IIcx computers to dedicated Web browsers running Netscape Navigator. "I don't think this is a return to the dumb terminal era. We need a smart desktop machine because we're using multimedia," she says. "It's a great way to continue to leverage our investment in equipment, while building a new information infrastructure. The network-centric model means we don't have to spend enormous amounts of money on desktop equipment. Your power is in the network."

INTEGRATING EXTERNAL AND INTERNAL INFORMATION

Deere's information architecture enables it to combine corporate knowledge with resources available on the World Wide Web. "There is a wealth of agricultural information on the Web, such as crop reports, weather reports, USDA information," she explains. "We can integrate this information with our rich store of internal information. With Netscape, we can deliver all of this very easily through a single interface."

The company sees tremendous benefits to their Netscape-based infrastructure. "It will enable us to bring applications up and get them running faster. It will help us to integrate a lot of information sources more easily. Because it is network-centric and cross-platform, we don't have to worry so much about desktop issues. And because it is a single front end, it's making support and maintenance less intensive," she concludes.

```
Source HTML Code for Figures 8.33 and 8.34
<HTML>
<HEAD>
<TITLE>MAC Form</TITLE>
</HEAD>
<body bgcolor="#F5F08B">
<center><h2>Network and Telecommunication Services<h2></center>
<center><h3>Move/Add/Change Form</h2></center>
<p>
<note role="NOTE" src"info.gif">
The following on-line MAC form is to be used for class of service changes
(local, Arizona, nation-wide, International), call-forwarding, busy or no-
answer changes only. If the request is for any other moves, adds or changes,
please fill out the MAC forms supplied from NTS as you normally would.
</note>
<p>
<form method=post action="/cts-cgi-bin/generic-mailer.pl">
<table>
<TR><TD ALIGN=RIGHT WIDTH=120>Department Head:<TD COLSPAN=3 ALIGN=LEFT><input
type="text" name="Dept Head" size="30"><TD ALIGN=RIGHT>Date:<TD COLSPAN=3
ALIGN=LEFT><input type="text" name="Date" size "8" MAXLENGTH="8"></TR>
<TR><TD ALIGN=RIGHT WIDTH=120>Requestor : <TD COLSPAN=3 ALIGN=LEFT><input
type="text" name"Requestor" size="30"><TD ALIGN=RIGHT>Telephone No:<TD
COLSPAN=3 ALIGN=LEFT><input type="text" name="Phone-No" size"8"></TR>
<TR><TD ALIGN=RIGHT WIDTH=120>Department:<TD ALIGN=LEFT><input type="text"
name="Department" size="10"><TD ALIGN=RIGHT>Bldg No.:<TD ALIGN=LEFT><input
type="text" name="Building" size="2"><TD ALIGN=RIGHT>Room<TD ALIGN=LEFT><input
type="text" name="Room-No" size="4"><TD ALIGN=RIGHT>Box No.: <TD
ALIGN=LEFT><input type="text" name="Box-No" size="5"></TR>
<TR><TD ALIGN=RIGHT WIDTH=120>e:mail address:<TD COLSPAN=3 ALIGN=LEFT><input
type="text" name="email-address" size="30"></tr>
</table>
<p>
Work Requested:<br>
<texarea name="Work-Requested" ROWS=5 cols=70></textarea></center>
<p>
<input type="hidden" value="Rose.Lopez@nau.edu" name="towho">
<input type="hidden" value="Network and Telecommunication Services"
name="recipient">
<input type="hidden" value="Move/Add/Change Form" name="mmsg">
<input type="submit" value="Submit"> or <input type="reset" value="Cancel">
</from.
<p>
If you have any questions, please e-mail us at <a href="mailto:nts@nau.edu">
NTS@nau.edu</a>.
<p><A HREF="http://www.nau.edu/~nts/index.html"</A><IMG align=left
SRC="images/back.gif"><br>
</body>
</html>
```

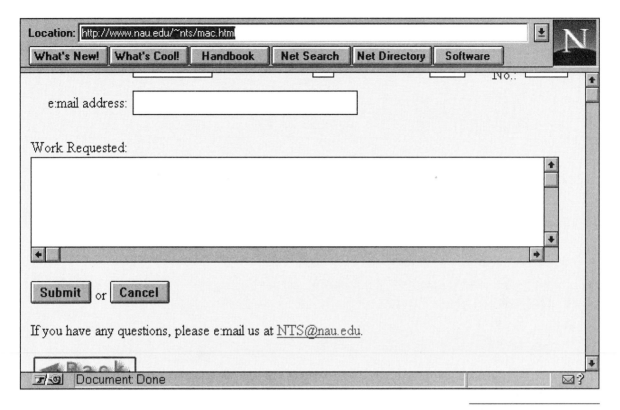

FIGURE 8.34
Collecting Data Using
an HTML Form: II

FIGURE 8.35
Querying a FedEx Database Using an HTML Form: I

||||||||||| Tracking

Airbill Number : 9178015803

- **Package has been Delivered!**

- **Delivered To : Recipient**

- **Delivery Time : 10:12**

- **Signed For By : A.LORENTS**

- Scan Activity :

    - Delivered FLAGSTAFF AZ 08/08 10:12

    - Delivered with Exception FLAGSTAFF AZ 08/08 10:12

    - Package on Van FLAGSTAFF AZ 08/08 09:02

    - Arrived at Destination FLAGSTAFF AZ 08/08 08:41

    - 24 PHOENIX AZ 08/08 05:26

    - Package Left Hub MEMPHIS TN 08/08 03:19

    - 22 EAST BOSTON MA 08/07 22:38

    - Left Origin Location RANDOLPH MA 08/07 20:17

FIGURE 8.36
Querying a FedEx Database Using an HTML Form: II

CRYSTAL REPORTS

The deployment of database information on the Internet can be done with **Crystal Reports.** The following block on "Database Information Deployment on the Internet" was taken from the Crystal Inc. home page on the Web. It describes taking information from databases and converting it to various reporting methods, such as summaries, charts, and graphs, in HTML format for display to the users using HTML formatted pages.

Crystal Reports
A report generator software package that runs under windows-based operating systems and can generate reports using SQL through ODBC connections to database systems, such as Oracle and Sybase.

Database Information Deployment on the Internet

Thank you for choosing Crystal Reports as your Web reporting tool. With Crystal Reports, information available from virtually any data source can now be instantly published on the World Wide Web in Presentation Quality. As Internet and World Wide Web standards continue to mature and evolve, more businesses will use this technology to build intranets as integral parts of their information systems. Being able to easily and quickly publish information from databases and other structured data sources on the Web will enable this growth to continue.

A new generation of Internet products now makes it possible to translate SQL query results directly into HTML pages. While certainly a step in the right direction, raw SQL queries don't provide all the functionality needed to tap the full potential of the information stored in databases. As is the case in existing client/server environments, a flexible and powerful analysis and reporting tool is required to convert complete, informative, and graphical information directly into HTML pages.

Crystal Reports is the #1 award-winning Windows database reporting tool, and provides you with a wide range of reporting and analysis features. Crystal continues to lead the way by adding a suite of simple and powerful tools to bring reporting to the Internet. The first of these tools is the addition of a function which allows reports to be exported directly to HTML for instant Web deployment. Crystal Reports Professional combines its powerful data access and report design features with this HTML export function to become a graphical database information authoring tool for the Internet. Exporting a report to HTML is as easy as printing the report on paper. Crystal Reports Professional generates HTML documents based on the HTML 3.0 standards draft; it also supports Netscape and Microsoft extensions to HTML—additional features and functionality can be added to any report.

Using the HTML exporting features of Crystal Reports provides a quick and easy way to publish static database reports, in .htm and .gif formats, on your Web Server for rapid access and viewing.

Crystal Reports© CRYSTAL A Seagate Software Company.

SUMMARY

QBE (Query by Example)
A window interface that allows users to define a query to a database by specifying the data to be included, any calculations, any summarization, and the order of the query result.

NT (New Technology)
A PC-based windows operating system from Microsoft; a multi-tasking operating system that supports various network architectures.

DBMSs commonly provide a number of software components in support of applications development. A DBMS may have a built-in programming language, a host language interface with one or more standard programming languages, and a number of 4GL application generators. Application generator components commonly found in DBMSs include form generators, report generators, SQL generators using a **QBE** interface, and procedural language support for event logic.

Most forms development today is done using windows-based forms to run under Windows, OS/2, or **NT.** This means that the form is designed as a window with all the common windows-based objects, such as buttons, check boxes, scroll bars, list boxes, menu bars, menu icons, and window management for multiple windows open at the same time.

Forms can be used for data entry, for updating and deleting existing table rows, and for displaying data currently stored in tables. It is often necessary for a single form to update multiple database tables. A good form generator should be able to support all these types of forms. The form generator must handle three major functions. First, it specifies the format that will be used to display labels and database data. Second, it provides a mapping between form data fields and the elements of the database to which they correspond. Finally, it provides instructions for database insertion, update, and delete operations to be performed when the form is executed. Form generator software normally allows form specifications to be entered by working through a set of windows driven by the generator.

Report generation software typically uses a window-driven approach similar to form generation in order to enter the various report specifications. A query based on one or more database tables supplies the set of data for the report. Report specifications include properties for each object on the report, formatting instructions for report and column headings, specifications on how to summarize and group data, and the layout of objects for each section of the report. The report's sections include report headers and footers, page headers and footers, grouping headers and footers, and the detail or body of the report.

When a report is saved, its specifications are generally saved in the form of commands in the DBMS's built-in programming language. This allows the report specifications to be customized by adding program language commands, as needed, to handle complex processing requirements. The generators normally produce specifications that are saved in tables in the DBMS's built-in programming language.

Menu design and generation provides the ability to link applications components of all types using a set of menus. Most menu design today uses graphical user interface (GUI) objects giving a user-friendly access to all application components. Menus can call other menus (drop downs or new windows), reports, forms, and various programs and objects created by the other tools and languages.

_____ Language used with Access to develop procedure modules.   **REVIEW QUIZ**

_____ Language used to develop medium-sized applications in client-server environments.

_____ Language used to develop queries in client-server environments.

_____ Language used to develop intranet applications.

_____ Control used on a window to select mutually exclusive options.

_____ Control used on a window to select multiple options from a group of options.

_____ Control used on a window to deliver commands to the procedures in the client-server application.

_____ Control used on a window to display a list of data.

_____ Control used on a window to display choices for processing options.

_____ Area in the design of a report for printing the detail data.

_____ Area in the design of a report for printing a control break summary.

_____ Area in the design of a report for printing column headings on the report.

_____ Area in the design of a report for printing report information once at the beginning of the report.

_____ Object used on a window to accept and display data.

_____ Object used on a window to identify fields on a window.

_____ Software that allows an application package to communicate with most database systems.

_____ Language that is normally used in large-scale client-server applications using mainframe servers.

_____ A property associated with a control break.

_____ A property associated with a field on a window.

_____ A property associated with list box control.

1. JAVA
2. COBOL
3. Visual Basic
4. SQL
5. Powerbuilder
6. Option button
7. Check box
8. List box
9. Text box
10. Label box
11. Command button
12. Report header
13. Control field header
14. Detail area
15. Control field footer
16. Page footer
17. ODBC
18. Access
19. Group box
20. Field name
21. Decimal places
22. Group level
23. Grouping interval

REVIEW QUESTIONS AND EXERCISES

1. What are the primary components of developing applications?
2. What are some of the different ways of setting up menus to control processing?
3. Define and give an illustration of each of the following:
   a. List box
   b. Command button (push button)
   c. Check box
   d. Option (radio) button
   e. Group box
   f. Text box
   g. Menu bar
   h. Menu icon
   i. Drop down menu

4. Design an example of a form with a master detail relationship.

5. Describe the design features and properties of a text field and a data entry field for a windows application.

6. Give an example of an application that has multiple primary windows with a primary window having multiple levels of dependent windows.

7. Explain some of the design features of reports.

8. What are some of the components of group/totals reports?

9. What objects can be used on windows-based forms to connect them to different actions against the database?

10. Define ODBC and explain its benefit to organizations.

11. Explain how Access can be used by organizations using Oracle.

12. Explain how application development is the same or different in the client-server world.

13. Explain why some organizations would still use character-based forms instead of Windows-based forms.

14. What are the components of an intranet infrastructure?

15. How do client-server and intranets blend together?

16. How do the Internet and organizational intranets blend together?

17. Bring up the Federal Express Web page (www.fedex.com) and print out the window that accepts the airbill number to obtain the latest status on the shipment.

18. Using the Web, do a report on an intranet application within a company.

19. Using the Web, do a report on how JAVA is used in an intranet application.

20. Reference the Web page www.dryden.com/infosys/lorents for updated information on this chapter.

EMBEDDED SQL PROGRAMMING FOR CLIENT-SERVER APPLICATIONS

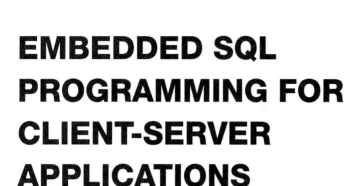

LEARNING OBJECTIVES

After completing this chapter, you should be able to

- Set up and execute the declaration generator (DCLGEN) to convert relational table definitions to COBOL data definitions.
- Set up the communication area in a COBOL program to communicate with a relational database engine.
- Set up and test SQL that will be embedded in a host program using a front-end processor.
- Write SQL statements that can be embedded into a host language like COBOL to interact with tables in a relational database.
- Set up cursor control to process a multiple row result in a host language like COBOL.
- Describe the concepts of dynamic SQL and explain how dynamic SQL is used in host languages.
- Describe the steps to build and process embedded SQL.

INTRODUCTION

Computer professionals entering the information systems field as system developers for larger organizations need to have a good grasp of client-server components in that environment. Client-server components for the larger enterprise-wide systems include: (1) GUI design, development, and management; (2) client processing logic; (3) server processing logic and database calls; and (4) database server design, processing, and stored procedures. Some of these components, such as database design and processing logic, have always been taught as a part of the traditional CIS curricula. The added components with client-server are: (1) GUI design and development, (2) the processing logic to support the GUI, (3) the division of processing logic between client and server, and (4) the interface to the database server.

A study done in October 1994 showed that 80 percent of the data in large, enterprise-wide systems was still in nonrelational database systems, such as VSAM, IMS, and IDMS. The move to relational has been slow, but is expected to pick up speed over the next 10 years. Organizations with these larger systems are migrating slowly to a client-server architecture, where the servers are the large IBM mainframes with DB2, Oracle, and other database systems, such as IMS and IDMS. "Neither object-oriented database technology nor distributed UNIX-based databases will replace mainframe database management systems anytime soon"[1] was the consensus of users at a 1995 DB2 users conference in Berlin. Conversion costs and the inability of UNIX-based

---

[1]Torsten Busse, "DB2 for MVS: Alive and Thriving," *ComputerWorld*, November 6, 1995.

systems to scale up to handle the volumes of these large systems are cited as reasons. Instead, organizations are opting to build new GUI front-ends, use tools like Powerbuilder and Visual Basic to do query and reporting, and install software to extract data from nonrelational databases into relational tables to support query and reporting. Other software is available to front-end the older databases with engines that convert SQL queries to database calls for the older databases. Almost all these existing large systems use COBOL as the **host language** to maintain these database systems. This will continue for the same reasons cited for staying with the mainframe databases. The use of embedded SQL in the estimated 2 billion lines of COBOL code today will continue to increase.

The main objective of this chapter is to give you experience with embedded SQL. COBOL is used as the host language in these examples because a large percentage of embedded SQL tends to reside in business systems that have been and continue to be maintained in COBOL. Examples will be shown in both DB2/XDB and **Oracle**, which account for a large portion of the relational database systems in large system environments in the corporate world. Note that **XDB** is a **DB2** clone for the PC workstation environment. XDB provides developers with the ability to develop and test DB2 applications on a workstation platform that are targeted for mainframe production. The illustrations in this chapter are based on the Air West database application using Micro Focus Workbench COBOL and Micro Focus Dialog System (GUI).

Relational database systems come with various tools to help developers build systems for users. One of the tools includes a **precompiler** that allows languages like COBOL, FORTRAN, and C to have embedded DML (Data Manipulation Language) calls to a relational database. The languages (COBOL, FORTRAN, and C) are referred to as HOST languages. A precompiler is used to convert all the SQL code into DML calls that a regular COBOL or C compiler can handle without any changes to the compiler. SQL can also be embedded in other procedural languages, such as the procedural language that comes with the relational database software.

AIRLINE DATABASE APPLICATION

The Samples in this chapter use the Reservation subsystem portion of the Air West Database System. The relationship of the tables used in the illustrations is shown in Figure 9.1. (See the World Wide Web page at **www.dryden.com/infosys/lorents** for a complete program that includes the code samples from this chapter.)

The Reservation subsystem allows a reservation to be made by one person for multiple passengers, each with his or her own itinerary. The primary key for Reservation is Confirmation Number, which links Reservation to Passenger. Each passenger can have an itinerary that consists of multiple legs for each trip, with a separate ticket for each leg. The primary key for Passenger is Itinerary Number, which links the passenger to tickets. If a traveler makes a reservation for two people to go from Flagstaff to Orlando round trip, there will be one reservation record, two passenger records, and eight ticket records (FLG to PHX, PHX to ORL, ORL to PHX, and PHX to FLG for each passenger). This sample project illustrates how reservations

Host language
Language used to write the main server procedures that contain the embedded SQL accessing the database systems.

Oracle   A relational database system capable of running on various platforms that is very popular in midrange client-server environments. Oracle supports a number of development tools, such as Forms, Reports, Browsers, and CASE tools, to develop midrange systems quickly without doing as much procedural language coding.

XDB   A relational database system used in conjunction with other development tools on PC platforms to develop, maintain, and test applications that run in a DB2 environment on mainframes. XDB is a DB2 lookalike that runs under Windows.

DB2   A relational database system that runs under most IBM platforms, including the PC (OS/2), the AS400, and the larger mainframes (MVS). It also runs on UNIX platforms from both IBM and other vendors. DB2 plays a major role in larger server-based systems because of its ability to handle large transaction volumes with optimum speed.

Precompiler   A processor used by developers to pre-compile the SQL code within a COBOL program before sending the source code to the COBOL compiler. Some COBOL compilers (Micro Focus) allow the user to specify the pre-compilation dialect (Oracle, DB2, XDB) as a part of the COBOL compilation.

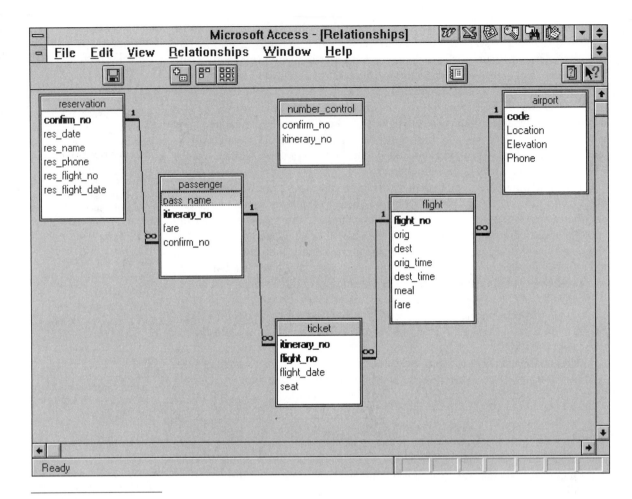

FIGURE 9.1
Air West Data
Structure Reservation
Subsystem

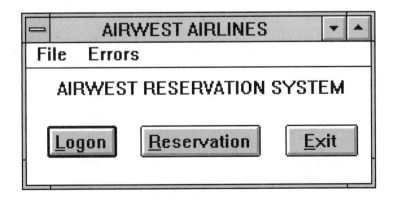

FIGURE 9.2
Main Menu

can be entered and maintained in this system with the application built in COBOL using embedded SQL to Oracle or DB2/XDB.

AIR WEST RESERVATION SUBSYSTEM—GUI PROTOTYPE

Each window in the Air West Reservation subsystem is shown in Figures 9.2 through 9.7. These windows were developed with Micro Focus Dialog System. The Dialog System windows will interface with COBOL, Powerbuilder, Visual Basic, and CICS, and directly with database systems, such as Oracle, Sybase, and DB2 through ODBC. The window design is compatible with any GUI builder. The first window (Figure 9.2) is displayed by the application as a main menu for the remainder of the application.

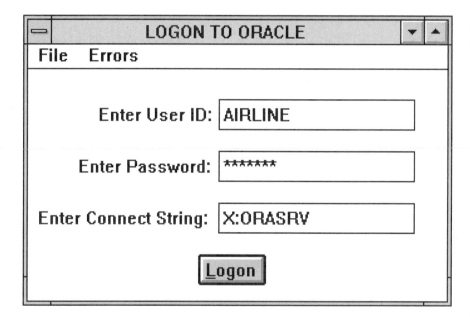

FIGURE 9.3
Log On

FIGURE 9.4
SQL Status

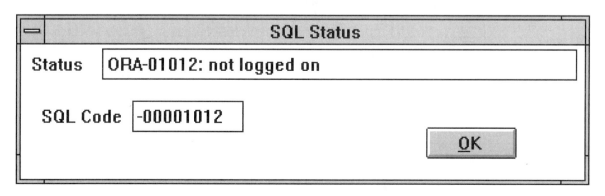

This menu window allows the user to select logon, reservation, or exit. In this project, only one application (the Reservation application) has been defined.

The log on window (Figure 9.3) is normally displayed with the connect string defaulted, and the user can fill in the user ID and password. The SQL status window (Figure 9.4) displays Oracle errors that are not normal to the application. This window is displayed based on script logic, or when a user selects "Errors" on the menu bar.

The remaining windows (Figures 9.5 through 9.7) illustrate an application that manages reservations for passengers. The reservation window allows the user to add, delete, and update reservation records. The passenger window allows the user to add and delete passenger records, and the ticket window allows the user to add and delete tickets to the itinerary of a specific passenger. The three windows operate as a unit, allowing the user to move from the reservation record to each passenger record and then to a set of tickets for each passenger.

To enter a reservation record, the user supplies the name and telephone number (Figure 9.5), the passenger name (Figure 9.6), and the itinerary (Flights Booked in Figure 9.7) for each passenger under that reservation. Confirmation numbers and itinerary numbers are generated by the system. The Flights Booked list box (Figure 9.7) manages the tickets for each passenger. The Flights Available list box (Figure 9.7) holds all flights from the Flight table. The data block (group view that supports the Flights Available list box) is populated from the Flight table when the user logs into the database. To add tickets to a passenger itinerary (Flights Booked), the user enters a date in the date field, selects a flight in the Flights Available list box (double-clicking), and selects the *Add* push button. The flight for that date is added to the Flights Booked list box.

FIGURE 9.5
Reservations

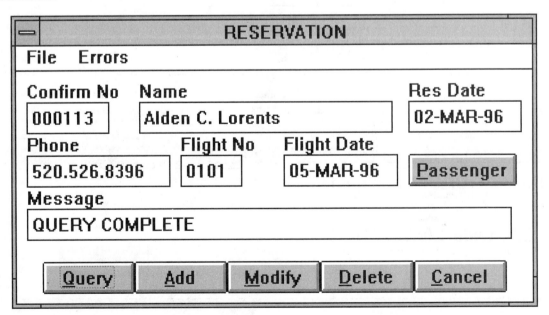

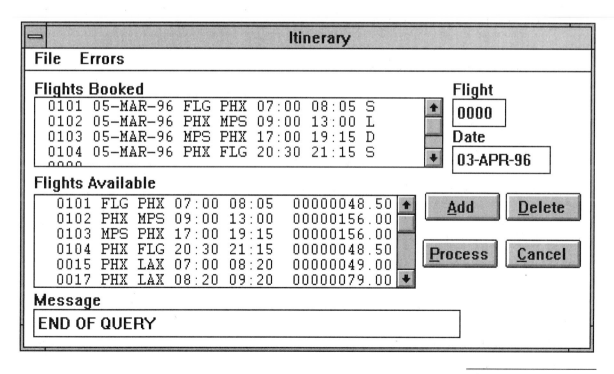

FIGURE 9.6
Passengers

FIGURE 9.7
Itinerary

This is a typical available/assign behavior used in many windows applications. Flights booked can also be removed by selecting the row in the list box (single click) and selecting the *Delete* push button. When Flights Booked is complete for a passenger, the user selects the *Process* push button. Control is returned to the COBOL program to add the flights that have been booked to the ticket table for that passenger. Flights Booked can be modified by doing a query on a reservation. A query on a reservation populates the reservation window, populates the passenger window for the first passenger, and populates all flights booked for that passenger under that reservation. The data for other passengers under the same reservation can be viewed by using the *Next* push button on the passenger window. Flights Booked (tickets) for any specific passenger can be modified at any time and reprocessed by using the *Process* push button. The ticket update logic in the COBOL program always deletes all existing tickets for a passenger itinerary before it adds the tickets currently held in the group view coming from the Flights Booked list box.

DATA DECLARATIONS FOR EMBEDDED SQL

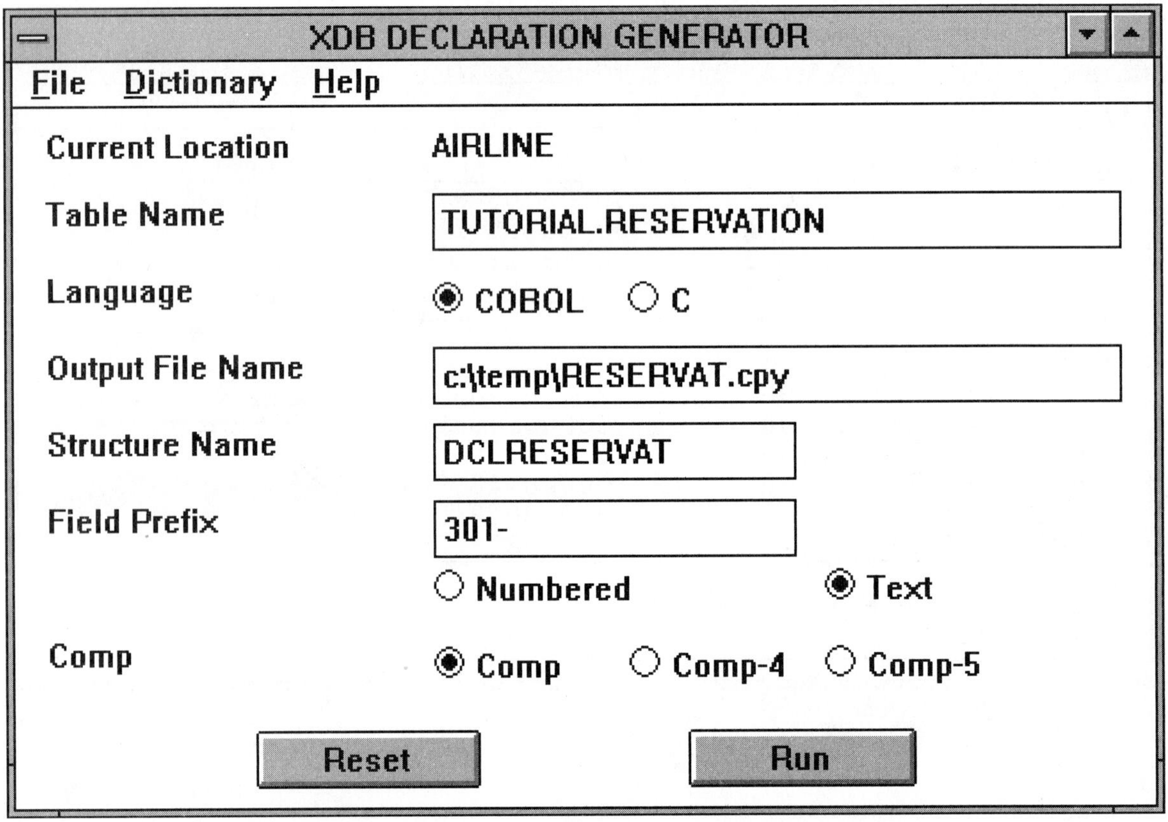

FIGURE 9.8
DCLGEN Generation
Setup

The COBOL program will require data definitions in COBOL format for each column definition of any table used by that program. A character definition of char(20) for a column in a database has to be converted to Pic X(20) for COBOL. Similar conversions are necessary for number, integer, and date columns. DB2 and XDB have a processor called a **declaration generator (DCLGEN)** that generates a file of COBOL formats for any table selected.

The database descriptions (relational table definitions) for each column in COBOL format are included (copied) into the program by the precompiler after they have been generated by the DCLGEN processor. The XDB DCLGEN process is executed by selecting the Declaration Generator Icon, which displays the window shown in Figure 9.8. The table name can be selected from a list box by going to Dictionary on the menu bar. The user selects the language (COBOL or C), the output file name for the COBOL copy file, the name for the 01 level in COBOL, a prefix if desired for the COBOL names, and *TEXT*, which will generate field names using the table names as opposed to field labels that are numbers. Figure 9.9 shows an example of an XDB DCLGEN output that is generated based on the values shown in Figure 9.8. Note the conversions that were made. Integer was converted to PIC S9(9) Comp and Date was converted to PIC X(10).

The same conversion process can be done in DB2. You will notice that SQL commands within a host program are set up within EXEC SQL and END-EXEC statements. All statements within these boundaries are processed by the SQL precompiler. Oracle does not have a DCLGEN processor to generate the COBOL variables. However, because the declarations are the same, you can use the DCLGEN from DB2 or XDB to declare the **host variables** for Oracle, or you can make the conversions manually.

The declaration of COBOL variables to the SQL precompiler is done so that these COBOL variables can be referenced by SQL statements. When they are referenced by SQL statements, they are preceded by a colon. When they are referenced by the

Declaration generator (DCLGEN)
A processor used by IBM and XDB to convert relational table definitions to COBOL data definitions for the COBOL program.

Host variable
A variable in a host language program that has to be defined to the precompiler so that it can be referenced both in SQL statements and by statements in the host language.

```
EXEC SQL DECLARE TUTORIAL.RESERVATION TABLE
    (
        301-CONFIRM_NO          INT,
        301-RES_DATE            DATE,
        301-RES_NAME            CHAR (20),
        301-RES_PHONE           CHAR (12),
        301-RES_FLIGHT_NO       INT,
        301-RES_FLIGHT_DATE     DATE
    )
    END-EXEC.
01  DCLRESERVAT.
    03 301-CONFIRM-NO           PIC S9(9) COMP.
    03 301-RES-DATE             PIC X(10).
    03 301-RES-NAME             PIC X(20).
    03 301-RES-PHONE            PIC X(12).
    03 301-RES-FLIGHT-NO        PIC S9(9) COMP.
    03 301-RES-FLIGHT-DATE      PIC X(10).
```

FIGURE 9.9
Sample Output from the DCLGEN Process

```
        EXEC SQL   Begin Declare Section   END-EXEC
01      DCLRESERVAT.
        03 301-CONFIRM-NO              PIC S9(9)    COMP.
        03 301-RES-DATE               PIC X(10).
        03 301-RES-NAME               PIC X(20).
        03 301-RES-PHONE              PIC X(12).
        03 301-RES-FLIGHT-NO          PIC S9(9)    COMP.
        03 301-RES-FLIGHT-DATE        PIC X(10).
        EXEC SQL End Declare Section END-EXEC.
```

FIGURE 9.10
Host Variables
Declared for Oracle

```
*       EXEC SQL
*       INCLUDE SQLCA
*       END-EXEC
01      SQLCA.                                      00000900
        05   SQLCAID          PIC X(8).             00001000
        05   SQLCABC          PIC S9(9) COMP-5.     00001100
        05   SQLCODE          PIC S9(9) COMP-5.     00001200
        05   SQLERRM.                               00001300
             49   SQLERRML    PIC S9(4) COMP-5.     00001400
             49   SQLERRMC    PIC X(70).            00001500
        05   SQLERRP          PIC X(8).             00001600
        05   SQLERRD OCCURS 6 TIMES                 00001700
                              PIC S9(9) COMP-5.     00001800
        05   SQLWARN.                               00001900
        -  10 SQLWARN0        PIC X(1).             00002000
           10 SQLWARN1        PIC X(1).             00002100
           10 SQLWARN2        PIC X(1).             00002200
           10 SQLWARN3        PIC X(1).             00002300
           10 SQLWARN4        PIC X(1).             00002400
           10 SQLWARN5        PIC X(1).             00002500
           10 SQLWARN6        PIC X(1).             00002600
           10 SQLWARN7        PIC X(1).             00002700
        05   SQLEXT           PIC X(8).             00002800
```

FIGURE 9.11
SQL Communication
Area

COBOL program, they are used without the colon. Figure 9.10 shows a sample of taking the conversions from the XDB DCLGEN process and placing them in a declare section for the Oracle precompiler.

SQL COMMUNICATION AREA

Another area in working storage is set up to communicate information between the relational database software (Database Engine) and the COBOL program. This area is called the SQLCA (SQL communication area). It is normally called with an INCLUDE statement as a part of the precompile process. An example of this area is shown in Figure 9.11.

SQLCA (SQL communication crea)
An area set aside in the host program to communicate various control data passed between the SQL engine and the program during the execution of SQL statements.

The SQLCA is used to communicate error conditions from the database engine to the application program. Various portions of the communication area are loaded depending on the type of error. Most of the warning codes relate to dynamic SQL, which will be introduced later in this chapter. A variable used most frequently by the application program is the **SQLCODE** that contains a value relating to the status of the last SQL execution. A negative value means there was an error in execution, a zero means the SQL statement executed successfully, and a positive value is a warning that an exception has occurred that may or may not be normal for the processing of the application. A typical warning is +100 (DB2/XDB) or 1403 (Oracle), meaning that no rows were found for the search condition. This code is used frequently in COBOL programs to check for a record not found. The general meaning of SQL codes is shown in Figure 9.12. There are more than 100 negative codes for each of the database systems. To obtain information on a specific error code, you need to reference the error code manual for the database system you are using. (See References at the end of this book.)

SQLCODE
A code within the SQLCA that communicates to the program the status of the last SQL statement executed by the SQL engine.

The typical functions done by SQL in host programs include inserts, updates, deletes, and selects. Relational database maintenance with COBOL is the same as maintaining any database with COBOL. The data normally come in from a screen/window, along with an action code that was generated by a function key or GUI push button. The data are moved to variables that have been declared to SQL so they can be used in the SQL statement. The record is either inserted, updated, or deleted. Records can be retrieved from the database in many different ways. This is where embedded SQL can be very powerful. SQL can be written to obtain one unique row in a table like we normally read flat files or other types of databases. SQL can

FIGURE 9.12
SQLCODE
Reference Table

SQL Status	DB2	XDB	Oracle
Successful Execution	000	000	0000
Row Not Found	+100	+100	+1403
Execution OK with Exception	+nnn	+nnn	+nnnn
Error in Execution	−nnn	−nnn	−nnnn

also be written with joins and subselects with all the power of SQL to retrieve a virtual table that is some subset of rows, attributes, and calculated fields from the entire database. This virtual table can be processed like a flat file within the COBOL program. The same search and match logic using COBOL statements against a number of flat files without SQL and relational tables could result in many lines of complex COBOL code.

The following examples demonstrate how a relational database is updated using COBOL. The examples were built with Micro Focus COBOL and the Oracle precompiler. The window interface uses the Micro Focus Dialog System. See the World Wide Web page at **www.dryden.com/infosys/lorents** for a complete example of this program implemented with Oracle.

FIGURE 9.13
INSERT Examples

```
720-READ-RESERVATION.
      EXEC SQL
            SELECT CONFIRM_NO, RES_DATE, RES_NAME, RES_PHONE,
                   RES_FLIGHT_NO, RES_FLIGHT_DATE
                  INTO :600-CONFIRM-NO, :600-RES-DATE,
                       :600-RES-NAME-TEXT,
                       :600-RES-PHONE, :600-RES-FLIGHT-NO,
                       :600-RES-FLIGHT-DATE
            FROM RESERVATION
            WHERE CONFIRM_NO = :600-CONFIRM-NO
      END-EXEC.
700-ADD-RES.
      PERFORM 850-GET-CONFIRMATION-NUMBER.
      MOVE CONFIRM-NO TO 301-RES-CONFIRM-NO.
      MOVE 301-RES-CONFIRM-NO       TO 600-CONFIRM-NO.
      MOVE 301-RES-DATE             TO 600-RES-DATE.
      MOVE 301-RES-NAME             TO 600-RES-NAME-TEXT.
      MOVE 301-RES-PHONE            TO 600-RES-PHONE.
      MOVE ZERO                     TO 600-RES-FLIGHT-NO.
      MOVE SPACE                    TO 600-RES-FLIGHT-DATE.
      EXEC SQL
            INSERT INTO RESERVATION
                  (CONFIRM_NO, RES_DATE, RES_NAME, RES_PHONE,
                  RES-FLIGHT_NO,
                  RES_FLIGHT_DATE)
            VALUES (:600-CONFIRM-NO, :600-RES-DATE,
                  :600-RES-NAME-TEXT, :600-RES-PHONE, :600-RES-FLIGHT-NO,
                  :600-RES-FLIGHT-DATE)
      END-EXEC.
```

RELATIONAL TABLE INSERTS

Adding data to a table in a database with a host program is normally done with the following steps:

1. The data are passed from the screen/window to a working storage area in the program.
2. The data are moved to host variables in working storage that were declared to the precompiler.
3. The record (row) is read from the relational table to see if it exists.
4. If the record (row) does not currently exist in the table, the record can be inserted from the data area in working storage.
5. [Alternate step to 3 and 4] Insert the record (row) without trying to read it first and check the SQLCODE to see if it already exits.

The routines in Figure 9.13 show how data can be read and inserted with embedded SQL. A read is used if we want to make sure the record does not exist before trying to insert it. If the record does not exist, the SQLCODE will come back as +100 (1403 Oracle). If the record does exist, the return code will come back as +000 along with the data from the tables for that row. It is not always necessary to read before you insert if you check the SQL code after the insert to see if it is a duplicate. In the Air West program, a read is not necessary, because each add generates a new confirmation number (primary key) for each new reservation.

FIGURE 9.14
SQL Update

```
710-UPDATE-RESERVATION.
        MOVE 301-RES-CONFIRM-NOTO 600-CONFIRM-NO.
        MOVE 301-RES-DATETO 600-RES-DATE.
        MOVE 301-RES-NAMETO 600-RES-NAME-TEXT.
        MOVE 301-RES-PHONETO 600-RES-PHONE.
        MOVE 301-RES-FLIGHT-NOTO 600-RES-FLIGHT-NO.
        MOVE 301-RES-FLIGHT-DATETO 600-RES-FLIGHT-DATE
        EXEC SQL
            UPDATE RESERVATION
                    SET CONFIRM_NO =    :600-CONFIRM-NO,
                        RES_DATE =      :600-RES-DATE,
                        RES_NAME =      :600-RES-NAME-TEXT,
                        RES_PHONE =     :600-RES-PHONE,
                     RES_FLIGHT_NO =    :600-RES-FLIGHT-NO,
                   RES_FLIGHT_DATE =    :600-RES-FLIGHT-DATE
                   WHERE CONFIRM_NO =   :600-CONFIRM-NO
        END-EXEC.
```

You should notice how the SQL read is constructed. SQL does reads with the SELECT statement. All embedded SQL is set up within EXEC SQL and END-EXEC statements. All host variables are noted to SQL with a colon. A host variable is a COBOL data name in the data division that has been declared to SQL.

The record area of host variables should be defined with the same definitions and field order as the attributes in the relational table. This is assured by using the definitions provided by the DCLGEN process. Order is mandatory if a SELECT statement is ever written using an * instead of specifying the fields. The selection in Figure 9.14 will retrieve only one row because confirmation number is a unique key. If more than one row is retrieved, the SQLCODE would contain a -811 (1427 Oracle) and the data passed to the fields in working storage are unpredictable. Move statements are necessary before the inserts and after reads to translate data between display formats on the window, and between integer and decimal formats in the table.

The 700-ADD-RES in Figure 9.13 moves (formats) the data that came from the window into integer and decimal formats used in the database. The **INSERT** command specifies the table name and the data list of data that is to be inserted. The second list specifies the host variable names in COBOL where the data values are coming from. These two lists must correspond in terms of order and data type. Rows can be inserted with a partial list of attributes. The missing attributes will be set to null or to the default specified by the database definitions. Normally it is best to control all variables from the COBOL program, leaving nothing to the defaults.

SQL INSERT
A SQL statement to add a row of data to a table.

RELATIONAL TABLE UPDATES

Updating data in a database with a host program is normally done with the following steps:

1. The data are passed from the screen/window to a working storage area in the program.
2. The data are moved to the host variables in working storage that were declared to the precompiler.
3. The record (row) is updated in the table.
4. Normally a query is done before the update process in order to verify existing data and populate the fields on the window so the user can make changes to existing data.

Updating a relational table is a process of changing existing values in columns in one or more rows of a table. Normally the process involves a query to bring the existing data to the window. The user can modify data on the window, such as an address or a phone number, and send the data back to the program with a command to update the database. The update command is communicated to the program with a code generated by a pull down menu, a push button, or a function key. An example of a SQL statement to update the table is shown in Figure 9.14.

SQL UPDATE
A SQL statement to modify data in a table.

The **UPDATE** command names the specific table to update. The columns to be updated are specified by the SET commands. Columns that are not specified retain their existing values. The WHERE clause specifies which rows to update. Since Confirmation Number is a unique number, only one row will be updated.

Another update example in the Air West reservation subsystem (Figure 9.15) updates the numbers table with the next itinerary number and confirmation number each time a number is used. The number is read from the table using a SQL FETCH command. **SQL OPEN, FETCH,** and **CLOSE** will be covered later in the chapter. The routine adds 1 to the number, uses the result for the current confirmation number, and then updates the table with this number.

In this example, the WHERE clause is missing. This means every row in the table will be updated. In this case, that is okay because there is only one row in the NUMBERS table. The itinerary number did not change so it is updated with the same value. Although this is unnecessary in our example, the 870-UPDATE-NUMBERS routine is used for updating either number.

DELETING ROWS IN A RELATIONAL TABLE

Deleting data in a database with a host program is normally done with the following steps:

1. The key is passed from the screen/window to a working storage area in the program.
2. The key is moved to the host variable in working storage that was declared to the precompiler.
3. The record (row) is deleted from the table.
4. Normally a query is done before the delete process in order to verify existing data.
5. A dialog box can be added to the window to verify "Do you really want to delete this record?" with YES/NO buttons.

The process of deleting a row is similar to that for updating a row. Normally the record to be deleted is retrieved and displayed on the window with a query. The

SQL OPEN
Executes a SQL statement that has been defined as a Cursor. Depending on implementation variations, the result table is set up with a pointer to the first row.

SQL FETCH
An embedded SQL statement to obtain a row of data from a result table that has been set up by the execution of an OPEN statement.

SQL CLOSE
An embedded SQL statement that terminates the setup of a result table that has been set up by the execution of an OPEN statement.

FIGURE 9.15
Sample Update for the Numbers Table

```
850-GET-CONFIRMATION-NUMBER.
    EXEC SQL OPEN NUM        END-EXEC.
    EXEC SQL FETCH NUM         INTO
                :TICKET-NO, :CONFIRM-NO, :ITINERARY-NO
                        END-EXEC.
    EXEC SQL CLOSE NUM      END-EXEC.
    ADD 1 TO CONFIRM-NO.
    PERFORM 870-UPDATE-NUMBERS.
870-UPDATE-NUMBERS.
    EXEC SQL
        UPDATE NUMBERS
            SET CONFIRM_NO = :CONFIRM-NO,
                ITINERARY_NO = :ITINERARY-NO
    END-EXEC.
```

SQL DELETE
A SQL statement to remove a row of data from a table.

sample in Figure 9.16 shows the passenger **DELETE** based on a unique itinerary number. The passenger is found based on a query of a reservation that the passenger is linked to via the confirmation number. The itinerary number for that passenger (stored in the passenger record) is used to delete the row in the passenger table.

The SQLCODE is checked to verify that the delete worked correctly. This check is not really necessary since the delete uses an itinerary number from the passenger table that was retrieved by the previous query. Note that the delete passenger routine also deletes the tickets for this same itinerary. Deleting tickets in the program depends on how the database was defined. If the database was set up to delete tickets when a passenger is deleted, then the program would not have to do the deleting.

The delete routine also shows a SQL statement to commit all work up to this point. A commit sets a check point so that any rollback of work done during this run will only roll back work to that check point. Commit should be executed after all work for any one transaction has been completed. This leaves the database in a consistent state if something should happen that requires a rollback of previous work.

PROCESSING MULTIPLE ROWS OF DATA

Cursor
A pointer system used to process SQL statements that result in a multiple row response from the SQL engine. The SQL statement is defined as a Cursor early in the host program, and then is executed with OPEN, FETCH, and CLOSE statements in the same way a sequential file would be processed.

Extracting data from tables for queries and reports requires COBOL to process a SQL SELECT statement that delivers multiple rows. This is done with a concept called a *Cursor*. A **Cursor** is really a pointer that points to one row of a multiple row result from a query. The SQL statement is defined in the beginning of the program and given a name. The SQL statement can be a combination of joins and subselects that would require a fair amount of code to do the same processing in COBOL. The SQL statement produces a temporary set of rows in a buffer that consists of some subset of rows and columns from any set of tables in the database when the Cursor is opened. This buffer file is processed by fetching rows from the buffer one at a time just like processing any file. When all processing is done, the Cursor is closed. This allows the program to reopen the SQL process again in the same execution of the program with different values in the selection criteria.

FIGURE 9.16
Sample Delete

```
410-DELETE-PASS.
      MOVE 302-PASS-ITIN-NO TO 610-ITINERARY-NO.
      EXEC SQL
            DELETE FROM PASSENGER
               WHERE ITINERARY_NO = :610-ITINERARY-NO
      END-EXEC
      IF SQLCODE = 0
            MOVE 410-RECORD-DELETED TO 301-MESSAGE
            PERFORM 500-DEL-TICKETS
            EXEC SQL COMMIT WORK END-EXEC
            perform u520-initialize-passenger
      ELSE
            MOVE 410-RECORD-NOT-FOUND TO 301-MESSAGE
      END-IF.
```

Figure 9.17 shows an example of using the Cursor in the Air West sample program. In this example, a request is made for all data on flights that a specific passenger is scheduled to take. The request obtains data from the PASSENGER table, TICKET table, and FLIGHT table. The PASSENGER table contains the name of the passenger, the TICKET table contains the dates and flight numbers, and the FLIGHT table contains the origination, destination, and fare data. A SQL statement is set up to join these three tables to select the data for a specific passenger. The Cursor has been given the name 'RES'. From this point, the program makes all references to the data in the RES buffer by opening, fetching, and closing the Cursor RES with OPEN, FETCH, and CLOSE SQL statements.

Figure 9.18 shows how this Cursor is used in processing. A window delivers data to the program with a request to query a reservation. The reservation is retrieved along with data for the first passenger under this reservation. The itinerary number of this passenger is loaded into the variable 610-ITINERARY-NO, which is used by the RES Cursor to obtain all the ticket data for that passenger. The result table in the buffer is ready to be processed. A FETCH statement delivers the first row of data into the 570 work area in working storage. The 570 data are moved to the window defined 305 group view area that supports a list box on the window. This process continues until either the list box fills, or SQL returns a code of +100 (1403 Oracle), meaning there are no more rows. The Cursor is closed so the process can be repeated with another passenger name when a new request is made.

An example of the window that accepts reservation data from the reservation agent was shown in Figure 9.5. The confirmation number is entered on the window, and the query button sends the reservation number to the program. The program obtains the reservation record based on the confirmation number and the first passenger record based on the same confirmation number in the passenger record. The passenger record has an itinerary number that links all the ticket records connected to a passenger for this trip. The program executes a SQL statement that obtains these ticket records along with related flight information in the flight records. These data

FIGURE 9.17
Sample Cursor Setup
for Reservation Data

```
T101-RESERVATION-CURSOR.
     EXEC SQL
          DECLARE RES      CURSOR FOR
          SELECT FLIGHT.FLIGHT_NO, FLIGHT.ORIG, FLIGHT.DEST,
               TO_CHAR (FLIGHT.ORIG_TIME, 'HH24:MI'),
               TO_CHAR (FLIGHT.DEST_TIME, 'HH24:MI'),
               FLIGHT.MEAL,
               FLIGHT.PRICE, PASSENGER.ITINERARY_NO,
               TICKET.FLIGHT_DATE, TICKET.SEAT
               FROM FLIGHT, TICKET, PASSENGER
          WHERE FLIGHT.FLIGHT_NO = TICKET.FLIGHT_NO
          AND PASSENGER.ITINERARY_NO = TICKET.ITINERARY_NO
          AND PASSENGER.ITINERARY_NO = :610-ITINERARY-NO
     END-EXEC.
```

```
780-GET-PASSENGER-TICKETS.
     EXEC SQL OPEN RES END-EXEC
     PERFORM VARYING I FROM 1 BY 1 UNTIL I >  8 OR SQLCODE <> 0
          EXEC SQL FETCH RES INTO  :570-FLIGHT-NO,
                                   :570-ORIG,
                                   :570-DEST,
                                   :570-ORIG-TIME,
                                   :570-DEST-TIME,
                                   :570-MEAL,
                                   :570-PRICE,
                                   :570-ITINERARY-NO,
                                   :570-FLIGHT-DATE,
                                   :570-SEAT
          END-EXEC
          IF SQLCODE < 0
               MOVE 410-DATABASE-PROBLEM TO 302-MESSAGE
          ELSE
               IF SQLCODE >  0
                    MOVE 410-END-QUERY TO 302-MESSAGE
          ELSE
               MOVE   570-FLIGHT-NO        TO 305-FLIGHT (I)
               MOVE   570-ORIG             TO 305-ORIG (I)
               MOVE   570-DEST             TO 305-DEST (I)
               MOVE   570-ORIG-TIME        TO 305-ORIG-TIME (I)
               MOVE   570-DEST-TIME        TO 305-DEST-TIME (I)
               MOVE   570-MEAL             TO 305-MEAL (I)
               MOVE   570-PRICE            TO 305-FARE (I)
               MOVE   570-FLIGHT-DATE        TO 305-DATE (I)
               MOVE   570-SEAT             TO 305-SEAT (I)
          END-IF
          END-IF
     END-PERFORM.
     EXEC SQL CLOSE RES END-EXEC.
```

FIGURE 9.18
Using a Cursor to
Process the
Reservation Data

are moved to successive lines defined in the group view that supports the list box
Flights Booked on the window. The program returns control to the window manager, which displays the windows to the user. A sample of this window and the list
box was shown in Figure 9.7.

COMPILING AND TESTING EMBEDDED SQL

Most COBOL compilers in the future will directly support embedded SQL without
going through a precompiler. Micro Focus Workbench COBOL already supports

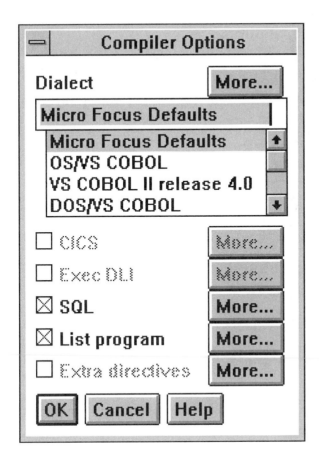

FIGURE 9.19
Setting Up Compiler
Options Using Micro
Focus Workbook

embedded SQL for XDB. The compiler options window (Figure 9.19) allows the user to select SQL, and the SQL options window (Figure 9.20) allows the developer to define the SQL engine. Once these parameters are set, the developer can compile and test COBOL programs with embedded SQL on the workstation the same way she or he would compile and test any COBOL program. DB2 and XDB require a compiler directive at the beginning of the program to log on to the database. The command for XDB is $XDB LOGON LOGOFF DEBUG with the $ starting in column seven. A similar command is used for DB2.

PRECOMPILERS

A precompiler from Oracle is used to process the COBOL source program that is used with Oracle. The COBOL source program is stored as a dot PCO file, and the precompiler generates the dot CBL file that is input into the Micro Focus COBOL compiler. The window in Figure 9.21 shows the interface to the Oracle precompiler. A project file is set up by defining the location of the dot PCO file and the location of the generated dot CBL file. Once the project file (dot PRE) has been defined, the

FIGURE 9.20
Setting Up SQL
Options for the
Precompiler Using
Micro Focus
Workbook

```
┌─────────────────────────────────────────────┐
│ ▬              SQL options                   │
├─────────────────────────────────────────────┤
│ ┌─Database engine──────────────────────────┐ │
│ │ ○ IBM  ○ MS  ○ IBM + HCO  ◉ XDB          │ │
│ └──────────────────────────────────────────┘ │
│ ┌─Database initialization──────────────────┐ │
│ │ ☒ Connect to database                     │ │
│ │ ◉ Shared mode   ○ Exclusive mode          │ │
│ │ ☒ Protect                                 │ │
│ └──────────────────────────────────────────┘ │
│ ┌─Database commit──────────────────────────┐ │
│ │ ○ Never                                    │ │
│ │ ◉ On STOP RUN                             │ │
│ │ ○ On STOP RUN and EXIT PROGRAM            │ │
│ │ ○ After every SQL statement               │ │
│ └──────────────────────────────────────────┘ │
│ Database            [                       ] │
│ ☐ Bind file         [                       ] │
│ Database password   [                       ] │
│ Remote server       [                       ] │
│ Extra preprocessor directives                 │
│ [                                           ] │
│ [ OK ]  [ Cancel ]  [ Help ]                  │
└─────────────────────────────────────────────┘
```

user does a FILE OPEN on the project file, displaying it in the window list. The user highlights the line and selects run, and the precompile process executes. A red X in the left column signifies that the precompile has errors. A yellow check mark signifies that there are warning messages, and a green check mark signifies that the

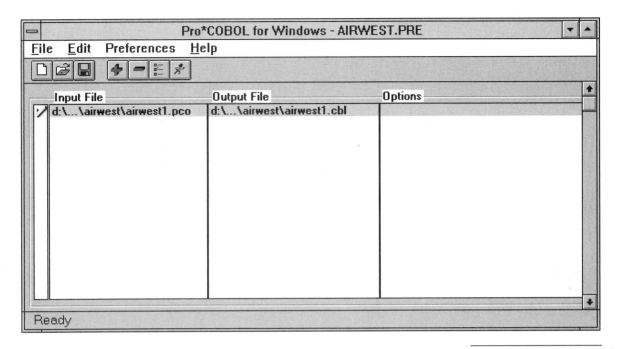

FIGURE 9.21
Setting Up the
Precompiler Options
for the Oracle
Precompiler

precompile is OK. The precompiler created a dot LIS file that contains the source listing and any errors. This file can be used to reference the errors, while the user makes corrections to the dot PCO file. Once all the errors have been corrected, the dot CBL file can be sent to the COBOL compiler. Errors in the COBOL compiled file need to be corrected in the dot PCO file, with the precompile and compile steps repeated until all the COBOL errors have been corrected.

EXECUTING THE PROGRAM

The program can be executed in the Micro Focus Workbench animator just like any other COBOL program. Using the animator, you can verify the data as they come into the program from the window, verify the data as they are passed on to the SQL statement, and view the status of the SQL statement. It is normally a good practice to put the SQLCODE variable in a monitored window so it can be watched constantly without having to query it each time a SQL statement is executed by the animator. The SQL-CODE holds the status of each call to the database engine. Figure 9.11 shows an example of animating the Air West program with the SQLCODE in monitored status. The SQLCODE is always checked by the program after each execution of a SQL statement, as you can see by the top line in the window. Debugging a program that has calls to a database is somewhat more complex because there are so many linkages and various calls to library routines. Some of these calls are shown at the bottom of Figure 9.22.

Most of the complexity of testing programs with embedded SQL lies with the SQL interface. The precompilers are not as powerful as compilers, so many errors are not caught until execution time. These errors show up in the SQLCODE.

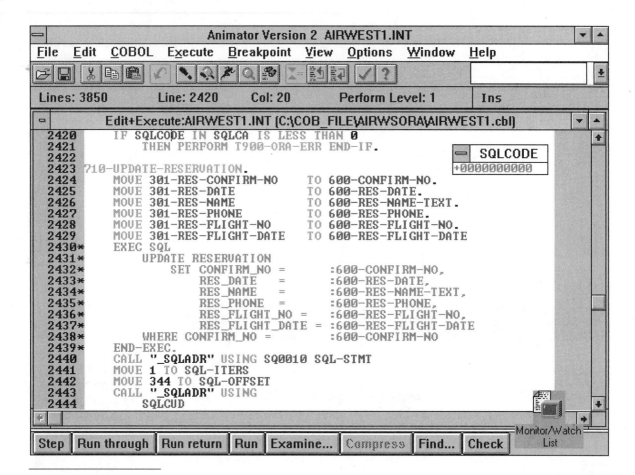

FIGURE 9.22
Monitoring the SQL-CODE When Testing the Program in Trace Mode

PRETESTING EMBEDDED SQL

It is much easier to test SQL directly against the tables using a SQL window before installing the SQL into the COBOL program. This can be done using the various SQL interface products that come with the database engines. These interface tools are also necessary to: (1) build the initial tables, (2) insert starting data in these tables for testing, and (3) view the results of the tables after testing has been done.

USING DB2 SPUFI TO PRETEST SQL

SPUFI (SQL Processor Using File Input)
A processor used by IBM to allow developers to test SQL against the database system before embedding the SQL in the COBOL program.

SPUFI (SQL Processor Using File Input) is a front-end processor developed by IBM to allow users to build and test SQL commands against the same DB2 tables they will use when they are in a COBOL program. SPUFI is accessed from the DB2I primary option menu shown in SPUFI Panel 1 in Figure 9.23. Normally, most installations access DB2I from the ISPF main menu screen when you log into a TSO environment.

SPUFI Panel 1

```
DB2I PRIMARY OPTION MENU
  COMMAND ===>
  DB2 subsystem id: DB2T
  Select one of the following DB2 functions and press ENTER.
  1  SPUFI                 (Process SQL statements)
  2  DCLGEN                (Generate SQL and source language declarations)
  3  PROGRAM PREPARATION   (Prepare a DB2 application program to run)
  4  PRECOMPILE            (Invoke DB2 precompiler)
  5  BIND/REBIND/FREE      (BIND, REBIND, or FREE plans or packages)
  6  RUN                   (RUN an SQL program)
  7  DB2 COMMANDS          (Issue DB2 commands)
  8  UTILITIES             (Invoke DB2 utilities)
  9  CATALOG VISIBILITY    (Invoke catalog dialogs)
  D  DB2I DEFAULTS         (Set global parameters)
  X  EXIT                  (Leave DB2I)
PRESS:                     END to exit        HELP for more information
                                   naumvs.ucc.nau.edu 14:03:40
```

FIGURE 9.23 SQL Processor Using File Input (SPUFI) Panels

The user sets up two data sets on the SPUFI panel, one to store the SQL and the other to store the results. Normally, the user will use options 5 through 7 shown in SPUFI Panel 2 in Figure 9.23 to set up the SQL statement and execute it. These options allow the user to enter a new SQL statement using the editor, execute the statement, and browse the results. Once the statement is tested, it can be taken from the data set and placed into the COBOL program between the EXEC SQL and END-EXEC statements. The statement is modified to include the host variables of the host program.

The example shown in Figure 9.23 is stored in the file member 'SPUFI2' in the CBA1ACL.LIB1.COB partitioned data set. The results of the executed SQL statement are saved in the sequential data set called CBA1ACL.LIB.DTA. Option 6 on Panel 2 brings the user into Panel 3, allowing the user to edit existing SQL, or to enter new SQL and save it as a new member in the data set. Panel 4 shows the results of the execution of the SQL. The execution is automatic when the user exits Panel 3 and option 7 on Panel 2 has been set to YES.

USING XDB TO PRETEST SQL

The XDB SQL window is brought up by going into interactive SQL. This window can be used to build, edit, save, open, and run any SQL against the XDB database. When the SQL is executed, another window displays the results (Figure 9.24). This figure shows the SQL window in the background with a SQL statement that was executed. The query results window, which is a result of executing the SQL, is shown in the foreground.

```
                              SPUFI Panel 2
SPUFI (Customized for NAU)
 ===>
 DB2 subsystem id: DB2T
 Enter the input data set name:  (Can be sequential or partitioned)
   1  DATA SET NAME  . .===> 'CBA1ACL.LIB1.COB(SPUFI2)'
   2  VOLUME SERIAL  . .===>      (Enter if not cataloged)
   3  DATA SET PASSWORD ===>      (Enter if password protected)

 Enter the output data set name: (Must be a sequential data set)
   4  DATA SET NAME  . .===> 'CBA1ACL.LIB.DTA'

 Specify processing options:
   5  CHANGE DEFAULTS  .===> NO   (Y/N - Display SPUFI defaults panel?)
   6  EDIT INPUT . . . .===> YES  (Y/N - Enter SQL statements?)
   7  EXECUTE  . . . . .===> YES  (Y/N - Execute SQL statements?)
   8  AUTOCOMMIT . . . .===> YES  (Y/N - Commit after successful run?)
   9  BROWSE OUTPUT  . .===> YES  (Y/N - Browse output data set?)

 For remote SQL processing:
  10  CONNECT LOCATION .===>

 PRESS: ENTER to process    END to exit    HELP for more information
                                    naumvs.ucc.nau.edu 14:28:58
```

```
                              SPUFI Panel 3
EDIT -- CBA1ACL.LIB1.COB(SPUFI2) - 01.00 ---------- COLUMNS 001 072
  COMMAND ===>                                      SCROLL ===> CSR
****** ********************TOP OF DATA*************************
 000100        SELECT * FROM
 000200                      GTPCBA3.TICKET T,
 000300                      GTPCBA3.FLIGHT F
 000400            WHERE T. FLIGHT_NO = F. FLIGHT_NO;
****** ********************BOTTOM OF DATA**********************
```

FIGURE 9.23 (Cont.)
SQL Processor
Using File Input
(SPUFI) Panels

USING ORACLE SQL PLUS TO PRETEST SQL

SQL Plus is a tool used by Oracle developers to test SQL before placing it in host language applications. SQL Plus is accessed from the Oracle group window. The user is presented with a log on window (USER ID, Password, and Connect String) and, after a successful log on, a window is presented to allow

FIGURE 9.23 (Cont.)   SQL Processor Using File Input (SPUFI) Panels

```
                              SPUFI Panel 4
BROWSE --- CBA1ACL.LIB.DTA ------------ LINE 00000000 COL 001 080
  COMMAND ===>                                  SCROLL ===> CSR
********************************TOP OF DATA****************************
---------+---------+---------+---------+---------+---------+---------+
        SELECT * FROM                                    00010000
                      GTPCBA3.TICKET T,                  00020000
                      GTPCBA3.FLIGHT F                   00030000
              WHERE T.FLIGHT_NO = F.FLIGHT_NO;           00040000
---------+---------+---------+---------+---------+---------+---------+
ITINERARY_NOFLIGHT_NO  FLIGHT_DATE  SEAT  FLIGHT_NO  ORIG DEST ORIG_TIME  DES
---------+---------+---------+---------+---------+---------+---------+
        3       101  2000-07-15  3D         101  FLG  PHX  07.00.00  08.
        4       101  2000-07-15  3C         101  FLG  PHX  07.00.00  08.
        5       101  2000-07-15  3B         101  FLG  PHX  07.00.00  08.
        6       101  2000-08-18  10A        101  FLG  PHX  07.00.00  08.
        7       101  2000-08-18  10B        101  FLG  PHX  07.00.00  08.
        8       101  2000-08-18  10C        101  FLG  PHX  07.00.00  08.
        3       102  2000-07-15  10D        102  PHX  MPS  09.00.00  01.
        4       102  2000-07-15  10C        102  PHX  MPS  09.00.00  01.
        5       102  2000-07-15  10B        102  PHX  MPS  09.00.00  01.
       12       102  2000-02-18             102  PHX  MPS  09.00.00  01.
       13       102  2000-02-18             102  PHX  MPS  09.00.00  01.
        3       103  2000-08-21  15A        103  MPS  PHX  17.00.00  19.
        4       103  2000-08-21  15B        103  MPS  PHX  17.00.00  19.
                              naumvs.ucc.nau.edu 14:33:41
```

the user to enter, edit, and run SQL (Figure 9.25). The Edit menu allows the user to define an editor, such as Windows Notepad. The SQL can be entered in Notepad, saved, and brought up by the File Open selection in the SQL Plus window. The SQL is executed by using File Run on the Oracle SQL Plus window menu bar. Figure 9.25 shows an example of opening a file that displays the SQL command on the window. When the SQL is run, the command is displayed again, and the results are displayed immediately after the command. The window is scrollable, so the results from various commands can be viewed by scrolling up and down.

CASE TOOL GENERATION OF EMBEDDED SQL

CASE tools, such as Texas Instrument's **Composer by IEF,** generate COBOL code with embedded SQL. The processing logic is written in PADs (process action diagrams), as shown in Figure 9.26. The **PAD logic** is converted by IEF into COBOL

CASE (Computer Aided Software Engineering)
A tool used to define systems using an information engineering methodology, in which business rules and data are defined and stored in a repository and the COBOL or C code is generated from the definitions.

Composer by IEF
A CASE tool marketed by Texas Instruments.

PAD (process action diagram) logic
An area in IEF in which program logic and database actions are defined and stored in the IEF repository.

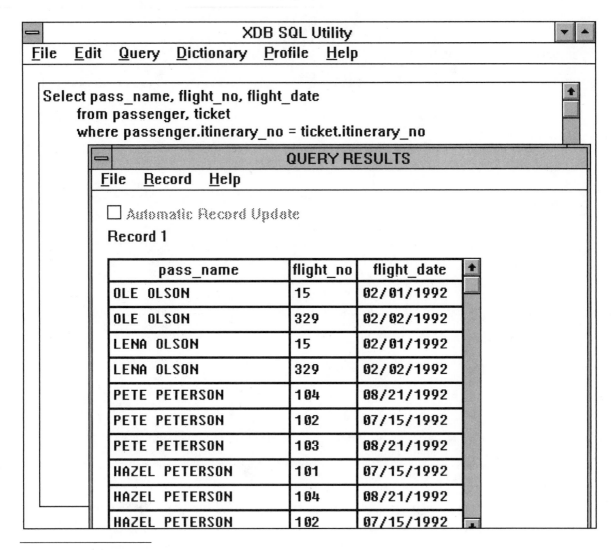

FIGURE 9.24
Sample of Testing
SQL Using XDB

SYBASE
A relational database system that runs on various platforms and is used in midrange client-server environments.

with embedded SQL. The result of this generation is shown in Figure 9.27. This action diagram supports the logic to read all the reservations based on a reservation date. The entity view export reservation is part of a group view that can hold up to 200 reservations. The read statement in IEF is translated into an embedded SQL Cursor structure, because the result table includes more than one row. The target environment for the generation of code was Oracle and C running under Windows 3.1. The only difference in the generated SQL is the semicolon used in C to end the EXEC SQL as opposed to END-EXEC to end the statement in COBOL.

IEF Composer supports the development of systems using such client-server database systems as Oracle, **SYBASE,** and DB2. All code that manages window displays resides in the client procedure, and all code that includes calls to the database resides in the server procedures. The server procedures can be generated in either

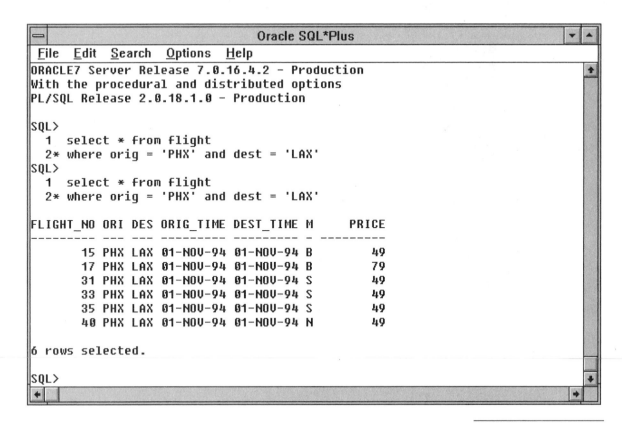

FIGURE 9.25
Testing SQL in Oracle Using SQL* Plus

COBOL or C with embedded SQL. These procedures can be packaged so that all the server procedures can run either on one server or on different servers. Typical servers include SUN and HP systems running UNIX with a database system such as Oracle or SYBASE. In a single-user or student environment, the client code and server code can run on the same workstation.

DYNAMIC SQL

Dynamic SQL, as the name implies, refers to a SQL statement that is put together during execution with input from the user. A skeleton statement will exist and various pieces will be added to make the SQL statement more flexible to address the needs of the user. Typical additions to the SQL statement include supplying table names, logical operators, attribute names, and host variable names.

The SQL statement can be put together with string commands using a shell and various variables that have been filled by the user. The resulting SQL statement will be stored in a COBOL variable such as SQL-STATEMENT that will be used in a PREPARE statement to bind the statement and prepare a plan. **Static SQL** is bound and a plan is prepared before execution. A *plan* is used by the database engine to map

Dynamic SQL
SQL statements that are partially built before the precompile process and then modified while the program is executing using input from the user. An example is to modify the conditions of the WHERE clause in the SQL statement.

Static SQL
SQL statements that are defined at compile time and do not change after the precompile process.

```
        Entity View export reservation (transient)
          confirmation_number
          name
          date
          phone_number
          1st_flight_date
          1st_flight_number
    LOCALS:
    ENTITY ACTIONS:
      Entity View reservation
        confirmation_number
        name
        date
        phone_number
        1st_flight_date
        1st_flight_number

  READ EACH reservation
          TARGETING group_export FROM THE BEGINNING UNTIL FULL
          SORTED BY ASCENDING reservation 1st_flight_date
          WHERE DESIRED reservation 1st_flight_date IS EQUAL TO
                in reservation 1st_flight_date
    MOVE reservation  TO export reservation
```

FIGURE 9.26

IEF Composer Process
Action Diagram

the database call to the correct tables and attributes in the most efficient way. Dynamic SQL cannot be mapped until the SQL statement is known. Preparing a plan is done with the following statement:

```
EXEC SQL PREPARE SQLPLAN FROM :SQL-STATEMENT  END-EXEC.
```

The SQL statement would be executed with the following statement in the COBOL program:

```
EXEC SQL EXECUTE SQLPLAN [USING] :PASSENGER-NAME END-EXEC.
```

The USING is optional depending on the SQL statement that was built. If the SQL statement requires variable data, such as the passenger name, coming in from the window, then the USING will be needed. Multiple parameters can be a part of the dynamic SQL statement by defining multiple parameter markers. A parameter marker is the (?). If the following SQL statement had been prepared:

```
SELECT * FROM PASSENGER WHERE
          PASSENGER_NAME = ? OR PASSENGER_NAME = ?
```

then the statement to execute it would be

```
EXEC SQL EXECUTE SQLPLAN USING :FIRST-PASS-NAME :SECOND-PASS-NAME
          END-EXEC.
```

Dynamic SQL requires the COBOL program to do extensive analysis of the SQL communication area due to the wide variety of errors that can be generated when

```
    EXEC SQL DECLARE CUR_0704908968_1 CURSOR FOR
        SELECT
            RESERVATION01.CONFIRMATION_NUMBER,
            RESERVATIONO1.NAME,
            TO_CHAR (RESERVATION01.DATE0,
                                'YYYY-MM-DD'),
            RESERVATION01.PHONE_NUMBER,
            TO_CHAR (RESERVATION01.A00185_54Z,
                                'YYYY-MM-DD'),
            RESERVATION01.A00152_54Z
    FROM
        RESERVATION                          RESERVATION01
    WHERE
        RESERVATION01.A00185_54Z =
            TO_DATE (:nst_flight_d_001tp,
        'YYYY-MM-DD')
    ORDER BY 5 ASC
    ;

EXEC SQL OPEN CUR_0704908968_1 ;

EXEC SQL FETCH CUR_0704908968_1 INTO
        :confirmation_001ef,
        :name_003ef,
        :date0_005ef,
        :phone_number_007ef :phone_number_007nf,
        :a00185_54z_009ef ,
        :a00152_54z_011ef

EXEC SQL CLOSE CUR_0704908968_1 ;
```

FIGURE 9.27
IEF Composer
Generated Embedded
SQL

the SQL statement is executed. It is possible for the user to request a table that does not exist or attribute names that don't exist. All of these errors must be interpreted by the COBOL program and sent back to the user on the window. Other problems are that the user can set up SQL that is too inefficient and complex for the COBOL program to handle, consuming too much computer time. For these reasons, dynamic SQL is not used in the development of COBOL applications.

SUMMARY

SQL is embedded in COBOL and other languages as a **data manipulation language (DML)** to update and obtain data from relational databases. The operations

DML (data manipulation languge)
The general language used in any database system to manage the data within that system. Typical DML statements include operations to add, modify, delete, connect, and disconnect data.

384 CHAPTER 9 *Embedded SQL Programming for Client-Server Applications*

done by the SQL are much the same as those done by any DML in a host language. The primary operations of adding, modifying, deleting, and retrieving are a part of all DMLs. SQL in COBOL, however, has the ability to deliver to the COBOL program data from a complex query. Complex processing of millions of rows can occur in the SQL engine, including joins, subselects, summarizing, and ordering, that the COBOL program does not have to do.

The process of setting up a COBOL program with SQL involves converting the relational database definitions (field types and names) to COBOL definitions and then including them in the COBOL program. There are processors (DCLGEN) or declaration generators that help automate the conversion process. Another step in the process is to include the database communication area. In this area, the status of all SQL calls to the database is communicated to the requesting program. Static SQL statements that deliver multiple rows of data to the program are defined early in the program as Cursors. These statements are executed when they are opened and processed like a flat file of data. The SQL Cursor can be closed and reopened multiple times in the execution of the program. These statements give SQL in COBOL much more processing power than the DML for other types of databases.

Some of the SQL in COBOL works much like other DMLs when it comes to adding, modifying, and erasing rows in a table. You can convert COBOL from IDMS to SQL by converting STORE statements to INSERT, MODIFY statements to UPDATE, and ERASE statements to DELETE. These are one for one translations. Reads are also one for one translations to a SQL SELECT. . . INTO statement.

Once the SQL statements are coded, the program is sent through the precompiler to translate all the EXEC SQL statements into call statements that call library routines. The COBOL compiler can then compile the entire program into an object program that can be linked to libraries and made executable. In the Micro Focus environment, testing can be done with the animator, using the XDB database engine or an Oracle server. The DB2 environment includes a bind process that creates what is called a *plan*. In this process, processors within the DB2 system determine the most direct paths by which to access the data. This plan is used at execution time to speed the data retrieval process.

REVIEW QUIZ

_____ A statement to obtain a row of data from multiple rows of data that are managed by a Cursor.

_____ Statements to delimit SQL statements in a host language.

_____ The process to translate SQL statements that are embedded in a host language.

_____ A database system that allows developers to test DB2 applications on PC development workstations.

_____ A statement to execute or initialize a SQL statement that has been defined as a Cursor.

_____ A statement to allow a Cursor-defined SQL statement to be initialized again within the same execution of an application.

_____ A work area that communicates status between the host language and the SQL engine.

_____ A code that carries the status of the last SQL operation.

_____ The action block logic area in IEF that can include embedded SQL.

_____ A SQL statement that is built at execution time.

_____ A SQL statement that is defined at compile time.

_____ A processor in DB2 that converts relational table definitions to COBOL data definitions.

_____ A variable defined in a host language that is used by a SQL statement.

_____ An area of the host program used to identify variables used by both the host language and by SQL statements within the same application.

_____ A processor in DB2 to test a SQL query before it is put into a host language.

1. Host language
2. DCLGEN processor
3. SPUFI processor
4. Precompiler
5. SQLCA
6. SQLCODE
7. Cursor control
8. OPEN
9. CASE
10. IEF
11. PAD logic
12. Dynamic SQL
13. DML
14. XDB
15. SYBASE
16. INSERT
17. UPDATE

18. DELETE

19. FETCH

20. CLOSE

21. Host variable

22. Static SQL

23. Dynamic SQL

24. EXEC SQL/END EXEC

25. Declaration area

REVIEW QUESTIONS AND EXERCISES

1. Explain the DCLGEN process. What are the inputs? What are the outputs?

2. How are the outputs of the DCLGEN process used in a program?

3. How are the outputs of the DCLGEN process put in the program?

4. What is the purpose of the SQLCA in the COBOL program?

5. What is one of the major fields used in the SQLCA?

6. What does a SQL error return of zero mean?

7. What does a SQL error return of +100 mean?

8. What does a negative SQL error return code mean?

9. What is SPUFI? What is its purpose?

10. Explain how the Cursor setup is used in COBOL?

11. Why is the Cursor setup necessary?

12. What does the precompile process do?

13. How does char (25) convert to a COBOL definition?

14. How does integer convert to a COBOL definition?

15. How does date convert to a COBOL definition?

16. Show an example of setting up in COBOL the Include of a table definition.

17. Show an example of defining a Cursor to obtain all flights from PHX to LAX.

18. Show an example of OPENING a Cursor.

19. Show an example in COBOL of processing the data in the PHX to LAX Cursor, where that data would be stored in a group view to support a list box on a window.

20. Show an example of inserting a new flight into the Flight table within a COBOL program.

21. Show an example of deleting all flights leaving PHX within a COBOL program.

22. Write a small COBOL program to maintain a table of airports. The program should allow the user to add, modify, and delete airports. Use a screen generator or a window builder, such as the Micro Focus Dialog Systems, to develop the user interface.

23. Write a COBOL program to maintain an automobile rental database that consists of an Auto table, a Customer table, and a Contract table where the Contract table is the associative entity between Auto and Customer. Design some of the typical attributes for each table. The program should be able to put in new contracts and produce such queries as what cars are currently rented to which customers.

24. Set up a DCLGEN process to convert relational tables in the automobile database from relational table definitions to COBOL definitions. Show the results of the conversion.

25. Set up some examples of using dynamic SQL for the airline database. What are some parts of the SQL statement that can be dynamic? How is a dynamic SQL statement processed by a program as opposed to a static SQL statement that is precompiled?

26. Set up an example of using Cursor control to process a query for the automobile rental company. Show the Define Cursor, Open Cursor, Fetch Cursor, and the close.

27. Use the Web to look up topics on embedded SQL and precompilers within Oracle, IBM, Sybase, Texas Instruments, and XDB. Write a summary report on your findings.

10

CONTROL AND ADMINISTRATION OF DATABASE SYSTEMS

LEARNING OBJECTIVES

After completing this chapter, you should be able to

- Describe and distinguish between database administration and data administration.
- Discuss the major responsibilities of the data administration function.
- Give examples of various types of standards that might be established by the data administration function.
- Use the GRANT and CREATE VIEW statements to establish appropriate access rights for a database user.
- Describe the concurrent update problem, the deadly embrace problem, and the methods used to deal with these problems.
- Describe various types of data locking used in database systems.
- Describe database recovery mechanisms and discuss how they could be used to recover a database from various types of disasters.

Most databases are designed to support the needs of multiple users. In fact, there may be hundreds of users of a database system and they may need to access the system at the same time (concurrently). To ensure that systems of this magnitude operate smoothly and meet the needs of all their users, important technical and managerial issues must be addressed. Organizations commonly create a Database Administration (DBA) or Data Administration (DA) unit to provide coordination control and technical administration of their database systems. These units have important responsibilities throughout the database planning, design, and implementation processes. In addition, DBA units have primary responsibility for control of databases once they become operational. Important elements of this responsibility include access control, concurrency control, and database recovery services.

Databases frequently contain sensitive and private data that should be available only to those individuals who need the information to perform their jobs. Even where data privacy is not an issue, the right to create or modify data should be restricted only to those users directly responsible for that unit of data. This type of restriction is necessary to preserve the integrity of the database and to ensure that users whose job success depends upon the accuracy of the database will have confidence in it. Thus, the DBMS needs to provide a mechanism for controlling the access of individual users to the database. Ideally this *access control* mechanism will control both what data can be accessed by a user and what types of actions the user can take with respect to data she or he has accessed.

When two or more users want to work with the same unit of data within the database at the same time (**concurrent access**), there is the potential for their actions to cause errors to occur. The integrity of the database could be compromised, for instance, if two or more users are allowed to make changes to the same unit of data at the same time. *Concurrency control* mechanisms are needed that will prevent this type of problem while still supporting multiple concurrent access to the database.

Despite all our best efforts, various types of failures will inevitably occur in our database systems. Because database systems frequently contain crucial organizational data affecting many users throughout the organization, it is particularly important that we have mechanisms and procedures that can provide rapid recovery from failures without loss of data. *Database recovery systems* are designed to provide this. A well-designed database recovery system should allow rapid and efficient recovery from small- or large-scale failures with no loss of data.

The first portion of this chapter provides a brief overview of the role of the DBA or DA unit in an organization. After that overview, we will shift our attention to issues relating to the operational control of multiple-user databases. We will discuss the problem of access control and describe the mechanisms for access control commonly provided by relational DBMSs. Next, we will provide a similar discussion of the concurrency control problem and mechanisms for solving it under relational DBMSs. Finally, we will discuss the various types of failures that can happen to database systems and examine the recovery methods provided by DBMSs along with the backup elements (hardware, software, and procedures) needed to support database recovery.

Concurrent access
Concurrent access occurs if multiple users access a database at the same time. Control measures must be taken to ensure that this multiple access does not compromise the integrity of the database.

DATA ADMINISTRATION

Early in the evolution of database systems, organizations found that they needed to establish units with responsibility for administering their databases. The management of databases involves a number of technical considerations requiring expert knowledge. Databases must be designed to provide efficient access to needed combinations of data, and physical storage structures need to be tuned to provide high-speed access for high-volume applications. Access to the database must be controlled effectively to ensure the broadest possible access to data without compromising the security and integrity of the database. Additional control services must also be provided to allow multiple users to access the database concurrently without interfering with each other and without compromising the accuracy of the database. Finally, backup and recovery services must be provided to protect against data loss.

The position of Database Administrator was created largely to provide the preceding technical functions. In larger organizations, a **Database Administration (DBA)** unit was established with a small staff headed by the Database Administrator.

Database administration (DBA)
An information systems function with responsibility for the technical management of an organization's databases.

DBA units were expected to oversee the conceptual design of databases, implement the physical database design, control user access to databases, provide appropriate controls for concurrent access, and provide effective backup and recovery services.

As organizations' experience with databases expanded, it soon became clear that the effective administration of databases would require strong managerial skills in addition to the technical skills described earlier. Problems with the implementation and operation of databases tended to center not on technical issues, but on managerial ones. User reluctance to surrender control over crucial data to the database administrator and problems in resolving conflicting needs and desires of different user groups limited the success of many database development projects. Clearly, effective database management would require someone with the managerial skill and political savvy to overcome these problems.

As data planning efforts become prevalent in more organizations, the database administrator's need for managerial skills becomes still more important. As we noted in Chapter 4, successful data planning must be closely tied to the organization's strategic planning process. The individual responsible for the development and administration of the data plan must, therefore, be a high-level manager who can work with those responsible for the organization's strategic management.

Data administration (DA)
An information systems function with responsibility for data planning and for the administrative and technical management of an organization's databases.

Organizational units that take on these managerial and planning functions as well as the technical administration functions are referred to as **Data Administration (DA)** units. The responsibility of DA is not confined to the technical management of the organization's databases. The DA units are also expected to work with user groups throughout the organization to ensure that the organization's existing data resources are utilized as effectively as possible, and to develop a data planning process that will allow the organization's information resources to support its strategic plan.

Figure 10.1 summarizes some of the major responsibilities that are often given to the DA function in an organization. The degree to which the DA function is involved

FIGURE 10.1
Major Responsibilities of the Data Administration Function

1. Serve as the focal point for data planning in the organization.
2. Establish the database development environment.
3. Perform data requirements analysis and conceptual database design in conjunction with the project development team.
4. Manage the data dictionary and/or systems repository.
5. Perform physical database design and implementation.
6. Design and implement control and backup methods and procedures.
7. Establish and enforce standards.
8. Conduct user training and provide support services to users.
9. Manage initial database loading.
10. Monitor database use and make modifications as needed.
11. Manage the development of data warehouse systems.

in and responsible for these activities varies substantially across organizations. In organizations with a strong data administration unit, major authority and responsibility for all these functions may rest with the Data Administrator and her or his staff. Other organizations may maintain a DBA unit focusing almost exclusively on the technical aspects of administering database systems. In those organizations, some of the functions described in Figure 10.1 are either not performed or are the responsibility of other units within the IS department.

The responsibilities described in Figure 10.1 fall into two groups in terms of their scope and time horizon. The first two items and the last one describe responsibilities that span multiple database development projects. They involve planning and organizing resources for the development of a portfolio of database development projects, and the consolidation of data from multiple databases in data warehousing operations. Logically, the first two sets of responsibilities should be performed prior to the development of any individual database projects and should be repeated over the organization's strategic planning horizon. The management of data warehousing operations, listed as the last item, is also linked to these planning steps, but implementation and management of data warehouse systems can occur only after the systems from which they draw data have been completed. The eight remaining responsibilities pertain to and would be performed for each individual database that is developed.

THE DA ROLE IN PLANNING

Serving as a Focal Point for Data Planning

As we noted in Chapter 4, data planning is a long-term, high-level planning activity designed to tie the development of information resources to the organizational strategic plan. The major steps in this data planning process are outlined in Figure 10.2. An enterprise model is developed describing crucial organizational processes. The enterprise model is used to determine information requirements to support those crucial processes. Analysis of these information requirements allows the identification of clusters of related entities that are candidates for development as subject area databases. Once candidate database development projects have been identified, preliminary feasibility analysis can be performed for each proposed database, leading to prioritization and tentative scheduling of projects.

The data administrator is a logical candidate to serve as the focal point for data planning activities. However, effective data planning requires substantial support from the highest levels of management. If the data administrator is not actively involved in strategic planning, someone else, such as the Chief Information Officer, might take the lead role in enterprise modeling. Once enterprise modeling has been completed, the DA staff takes the lead role in determining information requirements to support it, identifying clusters of related entities that are good candidates for database development, and assessing the feasibility of the candidate database projects. A high-level management steering committee is then called upon to prioritize the proposed projects.

Establishing the Database Development Environment

The DA function has primary responsibility for establishing and maintaining the database development environment. Key elements of this responsibility are outlined

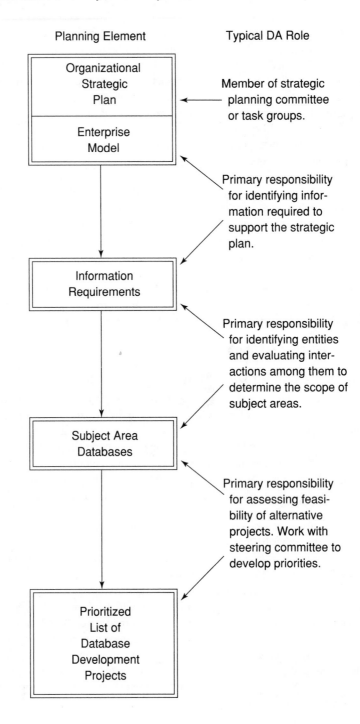

FIGURE 10.2
DA as a Focal Point
for Data Planning

1. Establish the DBMSs that will be maintained, supported, or both by the organization.
2. Determine the systems repository and/or CASE tools to be used.
3. Determine the general architecture of computing and communications hardware for the organization.
4. Determine the distribution of personnel responsibilities for database development activities.

FIGURE 10.3
Primary Elements
Involved in Establishing
the Database
Development
Environment

in Figure 10.3. One important element is the selection of appropriate hardware and software resources supporting database systems. Most crucial to the DA function is the selection of the DBMS software package or packages that will be utilized for organizational databases. Special needs associated with a specific database project may cause an organization to adopt a DBMS package to support that specific database. However, more commonly, DBMS selection decisions are based on the ability of alternative DBMS packages to support a portfolio of planned database development projects.

The degree to which client-server systems are to be used is also an important consideration, and plans for their implementation must be established. Which systems should be developed in the client-server environment? How extensive should the processing on client systems be? Which systems should be developed in, or converted to, the client-server environment first? How will the organization hire or develop the expertise required to implement client-server systems effectively? All these questions need to be addressed if a data administrator plans to move an organization's database systems into the client-server environment. In addition, the DA must decide which software products will be supported on both the client and server sides of systems.

The DA function should also be heavily involved in the process of selecting systems repository and CASE tool software. CASE, and particularly I-CASE, tool sets have the capability to serve as systems repositories. The DA function is ideally suited to serve as custodian of the systems repository. Systems repository information is maintained in a database, and access to it is managed in a manner similar to the management of database access. Because CASE and I-CASE tool sets are designed to support various aspects of database and application analysis, design, and development, the selection of a CASE or I-CASE tool set will not be the province of DA alone. However, the DA function should have appropriate input into the selection process.

The DA unit should also play an important role in decisions about the direction the organization will take with respect to its computer and communications hardware architecture. This clearly is not a decision to be made by DA alone. However, the DA function must be involved in these decisions because they substantially affect the database development environment.

These decisions about hardware and software elements of the database development environment may be revisited on a frequent, if not, almost continual, basis. The DA function will be expected to monitor and evaluate new technology that could effectively augment or replace existing hardware and software in the database development environment.

Determination of personnel responsibilities with respect to database development activities is also an important aspect of establishing the database development environment. The internal division of responsibilities among DA personnel must be established. However, this internal division of responsibilities is not sufficient. Database development projects are commonly undertaken within systems development projects leading to the implementation of applications systems. Thus, an appropriate division of authority and responsibility between the DA and applications development units must be established. DA staff may serve on systems analysis teams and take a lead role in data requirements definition and generation of user views. Alternatively, data requirements analysis and preliminary conceptual design may be undertaken by applications development staff with DA staff being involved in an oversight role—reviewing and critiquing preliminary designs and negotiating a final conceptual model. The distribution of responsibilities in this and other areas must be established through negotiations between the two departments. In practice, the degree of responsibility and authority taken on by the DA unit will depend upon the size and skill base of the DA staff and the political clout of the data administrator.

A final element of the personnel component of the database development environment is establishment of procedures that guarantee end-user involvement. For example, rules might be established prescribing minimum levels of end-user participation in steering and/or project management committees, which must be met by all projects.

THE DA ROLE IN ANALYSIS AND DESIGN

Data Requirements Analysis and Conceptual Database Design

As we noted in the preceding section, the degree of involvement by DA staff in data requirements analysis and in initial specification of the conceptual database model can vary considerably. DA staff may be actively involved as members of project teams that perform the requirements analysis leading to specification of data requirements and generation of user views. In other organizations, these functions, and initial specification of the conceptual model for the database, may be the responsibility of the applications development staff. At a minimum the DA staff will have responsibility for reviewing the proposed user views and conceptual database model and negotiating a final conceptual model and set of user views that is acceptable to DA staff, applications development staff, and the affected end-users.

Managing the Data Dictionary or Systems Repository

The data dictionary or systems repository is perhaps the most important tool supporting DA functions. With a reasonable level of training, users should be able to access the data dictionary to find the metadata—data about data—that they need to make full use of a database. Thus, a well-managed data dictionary becomes the users' window to databases, supporting and encouraging broader use. At the same time, the data dictionary or systems repository is a key vehicle for communicating data standards and for enforcing integrity constraints. As we saw in Chapter 7, many SQL-based DBMSs can enforce integrity constraints, such as the uniqueness of primary key values, the existence of values specified for foreign key attributes in the referenced table, and, in some cases, conformance of the value of any attribute to domain limits specified by a check statement.

In addition to these integrity constraints that may be automatically imposed by the DBMS, information about data standards and business rules that cannot be enforced by the DBMS is communicated to users through the data dictionary or systems repository. The completeness of the metadata descriptions varies with the scope of the data dictionary or systems repository that is used. In general, systems repositories provide a broader range of information than data dictionaries, including information about application files using a database. Repositories also generally support the design as well as the implementation and operation of a database, while data dictionaries are generally a component of DBMS software that is not created until the beginning of database implementation.

THE DA ROLE IN IMPLEMENTATION AND OPERATIONS

Physical Database Design and Implementation

The DA function is responsible for designing and implementing the internal model of the database—the structures that will be used to physically store database data. The internal model must capture the entities and relationships represented in the conceptual model and represent them through physical data structures. The CREATE TABLE command covered in Chapter 7 is the basic mechanism for database creation in SQL-based relational DBMSs. The internal model should be tuned to enhance operational performance. **Database tuning** consists of adjusting physical storage structures so that high-volume access paths are made as efficient as possible. Physical storage structures and tuning issues are discussed in Chapter 11. The database is initially tuned based on projected patterns of database use.

Integrity controls are normally imposed when the internal model is initially implemented. As we saw in Chapter 7, the ANSI SQL standard provides for the imposition of integrity constraints as a part of the CREATE TABLE command, and integrity constraint capabilities are available in most relational DBMSs in use today.

Database tuning
The adjustment of physical storage structures of a database to improve its operational efficiency.

FIGURE 10.4
Typical Control and Backup Procedures Implemented by the DA Function

1. Implementation of external models (user views) of a database to limit access to sensitive data through:
    A. Implementation of subschemas (network or hierarchical DBMSs).
    B. Creation of restrictive views of tables (relational DBMSs).
2. Control of access to the database system through:
    A. Passwords and/or physical access control systems.
    B. User identification controls granting access to subschemas or views only to identified users.
3. Control of concurrent access through locking.
4. Database backup and recovery procedures.

Control and Recovery Methods and Procedures

The DA function is responsible for controlling access to the database and for taking all necessary measures to preserve the integrity of the database. Figure 10.4 describes some of the more common control and recovery procedures. Database access is controlled by creating structures that give each user access *only* to the data in her or his external model or user view of the database. Passwords or other methods of verifying the identity of a user ensure that each user sees only the data that she or he is authorized to see. These procedures are discussed in detail later in this chapter.

Standards for Database Access and Use

As Figure 10.5 suggests, the DA function is responsible for establishing and maintaining a variety of standards and policies for database access and use. This includes the establishment and enforcement of testing procedures and standards. Also included are security and access policies—such as physical security standards, control of passwords, and standards for regular modification to passwords. Standards for application development are also very important. Standards must be established enforcing any integrity constraints that cannot be automatically enforced by the system. This would include business rules that are too complex to be enforced by the active data dictionary capabilities of the DBMS and referential integrity constraints if those are not enforced by the DBMS. Standards for locking and transaction control to preserve data integrity under concurrent processing are also defined. The concurrency control problem is discussed later in this chapter.

When client-server systems are to be supported, standards must be established specifying the types of applications that are to be developed on client systems and establishing appropriate testing procedures for them. In client-server systems, client processors often may secure a substantial volume of data and retain that data for a

FIGURE 10.5
Typical Types of Standards Established by the Data Administration Function

1. Naming conventions for data elements and other system components:

   All flag attributes will use the suffix _FLG (e.g., ORDER_FILLED_FLG).

   Process names should consist of a verb-noun combination in which the verb describes the action of the process and the noun describes the unit of data affected (e.g., CANCEL_ORDER).

2. Testing standards:

   All testing will be performed by a unit independent of the development team.

3. Data integrity, concurrency control, and other standards for applications:

   All transactions whose expected average duration is greater than 10 seconds must release locks acquired when data elements are read and must revalidate the values of any data elements that are to be modified.

4. Security/database access policies:

   Passwords must be changed on a monthly basis.

   Access privileges to personnel data must be approved by the director of personnel as well as the data administrator.

significant period of time while processing operations are performed. This type of use adds to the complexity of concurrent processing issues and may require modified standards.

Establishment of standards is of little use unless the users of the system understand and comply with those standards. It is vitally important that application developers and end-users understand the meaning and purpose of standards. Monitoring and enforcement measures must also be taken to ensure compliance with the established standards.

User Training and Support

Users should receive training that will allow them to make the fullest use of the database resources at their disposal. The DA unit is normally responsible for providing training, and should stress the importance of the control standards discussed earlier. Whenever possible, training should be provided in the use of query languages and application development tools that are suitable for use by end-users. Applications programmers may need training in the use of application development tools and host language interface features of the DBMS. Also, users will need training in how to use applications that are developed to process the database. These last two training elements may be the responsibility of either the applications development function or the DA unit.

Support services are a key mechanism for ensuring wide acceptance and utilization of databases. Strong user support encourages broader and more sophisticated use of the system and builds the goodwill in the user community that is necessary to enforce standards and secure user cooperation in the planning and design of databases.

Database Loading

Virtually all database projects involve the conversion of at least some data into a form that can be stored in the database and the loading of that data prior to operational use of the database. Data to be loaded typically represent needed history information and information about the current status of persistent entities, such as employees or products. The DA function is responsible for either performing this loading or at least supervising the operation to ensure that new data are not lost or damaged in conversion. The data administration function is also normally responsible for the migration of older history data from the database to other archival storage media.

Database Monitoring and Maintenance

Once a database becomes operational, the DA function must continually monitor the performance of the system. It may be necessary to adjust the tuning of the storage structures of the internal model to correct bottlenecks. A database may also need to be migrated to new hardware. Such a migration may be necessary because the transactions volume of the system outstrips the capabilities of existing resources, or migration may occur simply because better price–performance results can be achieved using newly available technology. With appropriate planning, it should be possible to make these types of changes with only minimal disruption to the operation of the database. If the principles of the three-schema architecture have been successfully implemented, these modifications should affect only the internal schema and should require no changes to user applications.

Insulating users from changes due to migration to new software resources is a more difficult problem. In the case of migration to a new DBMS, substantial redesign and recoding typically will be required.

The DA function is also responsible for correcting errors detected in the database and for supporting user-requested enhancements. Required changes can range from a simple modification of an attribute domain definition to addition of a whole set of interrelated entities that constitute an important subsystem to be added to the database. These changes cause modification of the conceptual model. Conceptual model changes will affect those users who access the modified elements of the conceptual model. Extensive conceptual model changes may seriously impact existing users and applications. Thus major system modifications should be implemented by going through a mini database development cycle to ensure the new specifications are correct and to determine the impact of the changes on existing users and applications.

Even simple changes may produce unanticipated problems. For example, if an attribute domain specification is changed, it may be necessary to check all existing data for violations of the new domain and correct those violations before modifying the domain specification.

THE DA ROLE IN MANAGING DATA WAREHOUSING

Data warehouse
A database system designed to support the query and reporting needs of management. A data warehouse typically contains summary data that have been extracted from one or more operational databases and organized to facilitate managerial analysis.

Data warehousing operations make data from various information systems across an organization available to managerial users. A **data warehouse** contains data from multiple operational databases organized in a form that makes it easy to link related data from throughout the organization as needed. The data warehouse stores historical data and will retain its data for a much longer period than will current operational databases. Data in the data warehouse are normally for retrieval only—users are not allowed to insert, modify, or delete warehouse data. The data stored in the warehouse may also be in aggregate or summary form and may be denormalized if this will simplify and improve the efficiency with which frequently required retrievals can be performed.

A data warehouse usually consists of one or more databases that is populated with data extracted from an organization's operational databases. Data from multiple operational databases may be combined in a single warehouse database. If multiple databases are used in the data warehouse, it is essential that they be compatible, and it must be easy for users to link related data from multiple databases.

The design and development of a data warehouse follows steps similar to those that have been described for other databases. However, the focus is substantially different. User requirements are in the form of types of data that managers feel they will need to support their decision making. The data warehouse information system may include a set of formal reports that can be provided to managers on demand. However, much of the focus will be on supporting ad hoc requests by supplying the types of data that managers feel they will need to address problems as they arise.

In addition to its normal responsibilities in the design and implementation of the database, the data administration function is responsible for loading all the data that appear in a data warehouse. Procedures must be established for the periodic copying of data from operational databases into the data warehouse database(s).

REQUIREMENTS FOR EFFECTIVE DATA ADMINISTRATION

The scope of the data administration function varies substantially across organizations. If an organization expects its data administration unit to take on the data planning role and other managerial roles described earlier, it is imperative that the position of data administrator be placed at a high level in the organization chart. With this role, the data administrator position is predominantly managerial. In other organizations, a largely technical role of database administrator may be used and the scope of DBA responsibility and authority is substantially reduced. The DBA may have only a limited role in data planning and only a review and approval role in requirements analysis and conceptual database design. The DA or DBA function may be a centralized unit in an organization or may be decentralized. In smaller organizations, a single individual may take on the entire DA or DBA responsibility, or an individual may even perform these duties on a part-time basis. In any organization, it is important that the staffing and organizational placement of the data administration function be consistent with the role that this unit is expected to play.

Our focus throughout this textbook has been on the design and development process for database systems. We have not dealt in detail with issues surrounding the operation of a database system. However, important operational issues must be addressed by any system. Controlling access to the database, managing concurrent use of the database, and ensuring efficient recovery from any failures that occur while the system is operating are key operational issues that constitute the very heart of the database administration function. We will focus on these issues in the remainder of this chapter.

ACCESS CONTROL

Effective database security requires that we be able to limit the portions of a database that certain users are allowed to access. We might want to severely limit access to employee salary information, for instance. We also need to limit the types of actions that users are allowed to perform on data. For example, we might want to allow a salesperson to retrieve a listing of information about orders placed by customers she or he serves, but we probably would not want to allow the salesperson to make changes to this data or to add or delete order records.

The way in which users are given authorization to access and perform operations on elements of a database varies substantially across the various types of DBMSs. In network and hierarchical DBMSs, a **subschema** is created that enumerates the portions of the database that a particular user or group of users are allowed to access. Users access the database through their subschema and thus would not even know of the existence of portions of the database that are not in their subschema. Subschemas will be described in more detail in the chapters covering the network and hierarchical models.

Relational DBMSs control a user's access to the database by GRANTing a set of authorizations to the user. Users can be granted the right to perform various types of

Subschema
A subset of a database that represents those components needed by a particular user or set of users. Users are able to access only the portion of a database that is included in their subschema.

actions on sets of tables or views within a database. The set of authorizations is stored in a special table of the database, and, each time a user attempts to perform some action on a set of data within the database, the authorization table is checked to determine whether the user has the right to perform the requested action.

For example, suppose that my user name is A12 and I issue an interactive SQL SELECT statement to retrieve some data based on a join of two tables, say CUSTOMER and ORDER. The system would check the authorization table and would process my request only if it found that user A12 had authorization to retrieve data from both the CUSTOMER and ORDER tables. The process for GRANTing authorization in relational DBMSs using SQL will be discussed in greater detail later in this chapter.

PASSWORDS AND DATABASE ACCESS

The task of verifying the identity of a user is normally assigned to the computer's operating system. The DBMS software specifies the access privileges that are to be given to a user by associating those access privileges with the user name of that user. The operating system is given the responsibility of ensuring that the user is correctly identified before it grants the user access to the DBMS. Most commonly a password may be assigned to each user or user group and that password must be entered during LOGIN to verify the user's identity. However, many alternative methods may be used. For instance, a terminal or PC unit located in a secure area might be assigned a user name, so that all log ins from that hardware unit would be automatically assigned that user name and granted appropriate access. Such a system might provide stronger security than a password system if physical access to the area containing the terminal or PC is sufficiently restricted. In addition, physical means of positively identifying an individual might be used, such as handwriting analysis or fingerprint identification.

Regardless of the mechanism used, it is the operating system that manages the verification of a user's identity in most mainframe-oriented systems. DBMSs designed to operate PCs typically provide their own user identification mechanism. Oracle and Access, for example, have user identification systems (based on passwords) as a part of their DBMS software. The access control capabilities of these alternative methods are discussed further later in this chapter. For client-server systems operating on a network, a combination of network and operating system software is used to verify the identity of users.

Regardless of whether the validation of a user's identity is handled by the DBMS, it is still a database administration responsibility. The database administration staff must determine appropriate user validation procedures and ensure that they are carried out effectively. The database administration staff is also responsible for educating and training users to understand the need for security measures and appropriate procedures to ensure that security systems are not breached.

GRANULARITY

Granularity is an important term associated with database security. The term *granularity* deals with the roughness or fineness with which access can be controlled. We can describe the **access granularity** of a database in terms of two aspects—the size of the unit of access and the scope of actions allowed on the data that have been accessed. The set of granularity options with respect to the size of the unit of access is illustrated in Figure 10.6.

The roughest conceivable granularity would be a system that lets all authorized users access all data in the database for all types of operations. At the other extreme, we could conceive of a system in which access to each atomic data element could be controlled. That is, authorization could be granted, or not granted, to each user to access a specific column (field) on a specific row (record) of a specified table (file).

The units of access shown in Figure 10.6 are in order from roughest to finest granularity and are described in the terminology of the relational model. Thus, a system allowing access to selected columns of a table by implication allows access to full tables or to the database as a whole. In relational terms, this column level of access allows users to be granted access to projections from a table without having access to the table as a whole. A system allowing access to selected rows of a table by implication also allows access to selected columns, as well as to tables or to the database as a whole. From the perspective of the relational model, these units of data can be seen as selections from database tables.

Most SQL-based relational DBMSs designed to support multiple users, including Oracle and DB2, allow access control down to the level of selected rows of a table. Users can be GRANTed access to enumerated tables and/or *views*. A user can be granted access to a view without having access to the table or tables on which the view is based. This provides the ability to limit access to selected columns and/or rows of a table, because a view can be created that contains a subset of a table based on projection or selection operations on that table. The use of the GRANT statement in conjunction with views will be discussed in greater detail later in the chapter.

In general, finer granularity in controlling the unit of access allows tighter and more complete data security. However, finer granularity comes at the expense of increased overhead. In the extreme case of access controlled at the level of atomic units of data, a tremendous volume of storage space would be required to store the access authorization information—potentially an entry for each user for each data

Access granularity
Refers to the degree of control over access to a database. Its dimensions are the size of the unit of data accessed and the scope of actions allowed on the data.

Level of Access Control Supported

Unit of Data Access					
Database	X				
Table		X			
Column			X		
Selected Rows				X	
Atomic Unit					X

FIGURE 10.6
A Hierarchy of Granularity with Respect to the Unit of Data Accessed

SELECT:	Allows use of the SELECT statement on the named tables and views.
INSERT:	Allows use of the INSERT statement on the named tables and views.
UPDATE:	Allows use of the UPDATE statement on the named tables and views.
DELETE:	Allows use of the DELETE statement on the named tables and views.
INDEX:	Allows use of the CREATE INDEX and DROP INDEX commands on the named tables and views.
ALTER:	Allows use of the ALTER TABLE command on the named tables.
ALL:	Allows use of all the statements listed above on all named tables and views.

FIGURE 10.7
Common Levels of
Access Privileges
Supported by SQL-
Based DBMSs

element in the database. Searching such a vast volume of information to verify access authorization for a transaction would cause unacceptable delays in processing.

Granularity with respect to the scope of actions a user is allowed to perform on a unit of data can be described as follows. A system with no granularity might simply grant all or nothing access to some unit of data. If you are allowed to access a table at all, you are allowed to do all possible operations on that table, including: reading or retrieving data; adding, deleting, and modifying data; and even changing the structure of the table. A system with fine granularity with respect to scope of actions would provide full control of the level of actions allowed. One user might be allowed to perform all possible operations, while another is allowed only to read the data. Between these extremes, there might be a user who is allowed to read the data and add new rows but is not allowed to change or delete existing data. Still another user might be allowed to read, add, modify, and delete, but not change the structure of the table.

Oracle, DB2, and most other SQL-based relational DBMSs designed to support multiple users allow full control of the scope of user actions that are allowed on a unit of data. The user may be granted, or not granted, the right to execute each individual SQL command involving the access and use of a table or view.

Between these extremes are network and hierarchical DBMSs, such as IMS and IDMS. These systems divide actions into two types—definition and manipulation. Definition actions create or modify the structure of a database, and manipulation actions read data or add, modify, or delete data in existing structures. Separate languages are provided for these two types of actions: the data definition language or DDL for definition actions, and the data manipulation or DML language for data manipulation. Access to the DDL is typically more tightly controlled than access to the DML.

ACCESS CONTROL UNDER SQL— THE GRANT AND REVOKE STATEMENTS

DBMSs using SQL provide access control through the GRANT and REVOKE statements. A user with database administration privileges can grant privileges to other users or revoke those privileges as needed. The basic syntax of the GRANT command is shown at the bottom of page 405:

Selected Tables

```
FLIGHT (Flight No, Orig, Dest, Orig_Time, Dest_Time, Meal, Price)
FLIGHT_DAY (Flight No, Flight Day, Equip_No, Pass_Ctr, Depart_Time,
Arrive_time, Fuel_Used, Status_Note)
    TICKET (Itinerary No, Flight No, flight date, Seat)
```

User Ids

V.P. of Marketing	VP_MKT
Reservations Staff	RES_STF
Reservations Shift Supervisor	RES_SUP
Director of Flight Operations	FLT_OP

Views Created for Access Control

```
CREATE VIEW FLT_DAY_RES AS
    SELECT Flight_No, Flight_Date, Pass_Ctr FROM FLIGHT_DAY
CREATE VIEW FLT_DAY_OPS AS
    SELECT Flight_No, Flight_Date, Equip_No, Depart_Time,
        Arrive_time, Fuel_Used, Status_Note FROM FLIGHT_DAY
```

Grant Statements

```
    GRANT SELECT
        ON FLIGHT, FLIGHT_DAY
            TO PUBLIC
    GRANT ALL
        ON FLIGHT
            TO VP_MKT
    GRANT SELECT, INSERT, UPDATE, DELETE
        ON FLT_DAY_RES
            TO RES_STF
    GRANT SELECT, INSERT, UPDATE, DELETE
        ON FLT_DAY_OPS
            TO FLT_OPS
    GRANT SELECT, INSERT
        ON TICKET
            TO RES_STF
    GRANT SELECT, INSERT, UPDATE, DELETE
        ON TICKET
            TO RES_SUP
```

FIGURE 10.8
Sample Access
Control Operations for
the Airline Database

```
GRANT list-of-privileges
ON table/view
TO {user-name(s) | PUBLIC }
```

The privileges in the list identify types of SQL commands that the identified
users are to be allowed to execute. Some of the more common levels of privileges are

listed in Figure 10.7. Access can be granted to one or more users to execute one or more types of SQL commands on a table or view through a single grant statement.

To illustrate how the GRANT statement can be used, let's consider some of the access control needs of the Airline database. We will consider only three tables, the FLIGHT, FLIGHT_DAY, and TICKET tables. Table structure diagrams for these three tables are reproduced in Figure 10.8, along with a listing of access control statements that might be used for these tables. Virtually all users need to be able to access and read the FLIGHT table contents, but only the vice president of marketing should be able to make any changes to the flight table. With respect to the FLIGHT_DAY table, again all users need to be able to have access to read all the data in this table. However, access to insert new rows or to update or delete existing rows should be more restricted. Only the director of flight operations should be allowed to insert or update the Equip_No, Depart_Time, Arrive_Time, Fuel_Used, and Status_Note columns in this table. Additionally, the reservations staff need to be able to update the Pass_Ctr column of the FLIGHT_DAY table each time a ticket is issued. Only the reservations staff need to access the TICKET table. They need to be able to insert new rows in the TICKET table and to read all existing ticket data. However, we might want to restrict modification or deletion of existing TICKET table rows. Perhaps only the reservations supervisor on each shift should be allowed to perform the update and delete operations.

The CREATE VIEW and GRANT statements in Figure 10.8 are designed to provide the levels of access we have just described. Because all users are to be allowed to read data from the FLIGHT and FLIGHT_DAY tables, we GRANT use of the SELECT statement to PUBLIC. Only the vice president of marketing is to perform other actions on the FLIGHT table and she is granted ALL privileges. Views on the FLIGHT_DAY table are created, because users are to be allowed to perform insertion or update operations only on selected columns of that table. We create views containing only the columns that each user is allowed to create or modify. However, the full key must be included in both views for identification purposes. On the TICKET table, all members of the reservations staff are allowed to execute SELECT and INSERT commands, but only shift supervisors are allowed to UPDATE or DELETE rows.

Users can also be granted privileges that apply to the database as a whole. The syntax for this type of GRANT statement is as follows:

```
GRANT list-of-privileges
ON DATABASE database-name
TO {user-name | PUBLIC}
```

The types of privileges that can be granted include database administration privileges—DBADM, the right to create new tables—CREATETAB, and the right to drop or delete the entire database—DROP.

When it is necessary to remove access privileges from a user, the REVOKE command is used. This statement is identical to the GRANT statement except that the word REVOKE indicates that the privileges are to be withdrawn from the user. The syntax of the REVOKE statement is as follows:

```
REVOKE list-of-privileges
ON table/view
FROM {user-name | PUBLIC}
```

Appropriate specification of access rights is a crucial element of the database administration function and one in which end-users have a vital interest. Users need to be assured of access to the data they need to perform their jobs effectively. At the same time, a user who has primary responsibility for a particular set of data must be assured that she or he has control over that set of data. Access to data, and particularly the ability to change data, must be adequately controlled by the database system.

To ensure adequate controls, the DBA might appoint data stewards for various sets of data in a database. A **data steward** is given responsibility for controlling access to a specific set of data. Data stewards can take some of the burden off the DA function. In addition, the method places control of access to data closer to the primary users of that data and can reduce user resistance to database systems and the DA function.

Data steward
An end-user of a database system who has the responsibility and authority to control the granting of access right to some portion of a database.

CONTROL OF CONCURRENT UPDATES

Most real-world databases are designed to support access by multiple users at the same time (concurrently). In the absence of appropriate controls, concurrent access to the same data element by multiple users can cause erroneous data to be used and stored in the database. A simple example based upon the Airline database will help us understand the problem.

THE CONCURRENT UPDATE PROBLEM

Let's consider the reservation process. This process requires that Flight and Flight_Day data be retrieved and requires insertion of new records into several tables, as well as requiring the updating of the FLIGHT_DAY table. To keep this analysis as simple as possible, we will consider only the portion of the reservation application affecting the FLIGHT_DAY table. Recall that the FLIGHT_DAY table includes a column called Seats_Res, which is to be used to keep a running total of the number of seats reserved. As a reservation is made, we must read the row for the Flight_Day that a customer is interested in and, if the customer books one or more tickets on that flight date, we must update the number of Seats_Res on that Flight_Day.

Now, suppose we have two reservations clerks, Adam and Barbara, working on different computer terminals in the reservations department at the same time. Figure 10.9 illustrates the type of problem that this concurrent use might cause. First, Adam takes a call from a customer who wants to book some tickets on Flight 101 on 10/11/97. Adam's application reads the appropriate row from the FLIGHT_DAY table containing data on this flight date occurrence, including a value of 18 for Seats_Res. Before Adam can complete the reservation transaction for his customer, Barbara gets a call from a customer who wants to book tickets on the same flight date. Because Adam's transaction has not yet changed the database, the value read for Seats_Res is 18, as shown in step 2 of Figure 10.9. Now, Adam proceeds to process the reservation information for his customer. Three tickets are booked for this Flight_Day in step 3, so the value of Seats_Res must be updated by adding 3 to the value that was read in step 1. The result, shown in step 4 of Figure 10.9, is written

USER A—Adam
1. Read Flight_Day   record -
Flt# Date Seats_Res 101 10/11/97 18

3. Create reservation
   records for 3 people
   on this Flight_Day

4. Write updated   Flight_Day record -
Flt# Date Seats_Res 101 10/11/97 21

Database
Flight_Day Table
Flt# Date Seats_Res
.   .   . 101 10/11/97 18 .   .   .
After Step 4 21 After Step 6 20

USER B—Barbara
2. Read Flight_Day   record -
Flt# Date Seats_Res 101 10/11/97 18

5. Create reservation
   records for 2 people
   on this Flight_Day

6. Write updated   Flight_Day record -
Flt# Date Seats_Res 101 10/11/97 20

FIGURE 10.9
The Concurrent
Update Problem

back to the database. Now Barbara processes the reservation information for her customer, who wants to reserve two tickets on this flight day. To complete her transaction, she updates the Flight_Day data read in step 2 to reflect the 2 additional reservations that have been made.

Notice that the result for Seats_Res is 20 and not 23! What has gone wrong? Because of the effects of another transaction, the value of 18 for Seats_Res, which was perfectly valid at the time it was read in step 2, was not valid when the update was performed in step 6. This is the concurrent update problem.

Because uncontrolled concurrent updates can lead to inaccurate results, we must find a way to control concurrent updates. This is done by allowing units of data to be locked. Suppose that a user is allowed to lock a row in a table for his or her exclusive use and then release the lock at the conclusion of that transaction. This could certainly prevent the problem shown in Figure 10.9. If step 1 placed a lock on the selected Flight_Day row in addition to reading its data, then step 2 would not occur. Barbara would be prevented from reading the data for that flight date until Adam's application was completed. Adam's transaction would be completed, including updating the value of Seats_Res to 21, before Barbara would be allowed to access the data. Barbara's transaction could be processed once Adam's transaction was completed, and it would now produce the correct result, because the updated value of 21 for Seats_Res would be read.

Deadlock
A deadlock occurs for a set of transactions if each transaction has requested access to data that has been locked by another transaction in the set. None of the transactions can complete and release its locks.

THE DEADLY EMBRACE

Although locking guarantees the integrity of the database under concurrent processing, it introduces a problem known as a **deadlock** or "deadly embrace." A deadly

User A—Adam	Database	User B—Barbara
1. Read and lock record for Flight 101 on 10/11/97	Flight_Day Table	2. Read and lock record for Flight 102 on 10/11/97
3. Seek to read and lock the record for Flight 102 on 10/11/97		4. Seek to read and lock the record for Flight 101 on 10/11/97

Flight_Day Table

Locks	Flt#	Date	Seats_Res
	.	.	.
User A	101	10/11/97	18
User B	102	10/11/97	14
	.	.	.

FIGURE 10.10
The Deadly Embrace Problem

embrace can occur when two or more transactions involving multiple units of data are processed concurrently. In such a situation, it is possible that two transactions each require data that have been locked by the other. In such a case, neither transaction can obtain locks on all the data it needs, and thus neither transaction can reach completion and release the locks it has already obtained. To illustrate this problem we will use another simple example based on the FLIGHT_DAY table of the Airline database.

Figure 10.10 shows what could happen if Adam and Barbara are each working on a reservation that involves both Flights 101 and 102 on the same date. Adam's customer begins by specifying that she wants to reserve tickets on Flight 101 on 10/11/97. In step 1 of Figure 10.10, Adam reads the data for this row of the FLIGHT_DAY table and acquires a lock on that row.[1] Now Barbara begins a transaction with a customer who indicates that she wants to reserve tickets on Flight 102 on 10/11/97. In step 2, Barbara reads the data for this row of the FLIGHT_DAY table and acquires a lock on it. Our problems begin in step 3, when Adam's customer next wants to reserve tickets on Flight 102 on this same date. Adam attempts to read this row and acquire a lock for it, but he cannot do so. Barbara's transaction has acquired a lock on that row of the FLIGHT_DAY table, so Adam's transaction must wait for Barbara's transaction to finish and release its lock. Now suppose that Barbara's customer wants to reserve tickets on Flight 101 for the date 10/11/97. Barbara's transaction cannot read the data for this Flight_Day row because of Adam's lock. Her transaction must wait for Adam's transaction to complete and release its lock.

These transactions have generated a deadlock or deadly embrace that could leave each transaction waiting forever for the other to complete its work and release its locks. The DBMS must have procedures to prevent or to detect and correct this problem.

---

[1]The lock data shown in Figure 10.10 are intended to represent the logical process and do not represent the literal means by which the lock is imposed.

Deadlock Avoidance

Deadlocks could be prevented if each transaction had to acquire all of the locks it needed at one instant of time. However, this method of dealing with deadlocks is impractical in most real-life databases. For example, customers want to schedule their itinerary one flight at a time. Customers may not be able to tell what flight they will want to take from Phoenix to Flagstaff until they know when some prior flight they are booking will arrive in Phoenix. In this and many other real-world situations, the value of the data retrieved in one part of a transaction affects the units of data that need to be acquired and locked in later parts of the transaction. Thus, deadlock prevention or avoidance is impractical.

Deadlock Detection and Correction

Most DBMSs provide a system for deadlock detection and correction. There are two common methods for detecting deadlocks.

One method requires that the DBMS maintain a matrix of resource usage showing which users are accessing which units of data at any time. By monitoring this matrix, the system can detect deadlocks. When a deadlock is detected, one of the deadlocked transactions is terminated.

A second method requires that transactions attempt to acquire the locks they need repeatedly. When a lock blocks a transaction from acquiring a needed unit of data, the transaction waits for a system-determined amount of time and then tries again. The DBMS software keeps track of how many times a transaction has attempted to access a unit of data. After a certain number of unsuccessful attempts, the DBMS software assumes that there is a deadlock and causes the transaction to terminate. Under either of these methods, the termination of a transaction requires that the portions of the transaction that were processed before its failure must be undone by means of a **rollback.** Rolling back a transaction restores the database to the state that it would have been in had the transaction never been initiated. The transaction can then be reprocessed in its entirety after the conflicting transaction has been completed.

Rollback
The rollback of a database transaction means that all portions of the transaction that have been completed are "undone." The database is restored to the state it would have been in had the transaction never occurred.

Let's see how this second method might work for the deadlock situation described earlier. Suppose the transaction for Adam's customer is detected as being in deadlock. It will be terminated and its effects rolled back. After Adam's transaction releases its lock, Barbara's transaction will succeed in accessing the data for Flight 101 on the date 10/11/97 on its next attempt. Now Barbara's transaction will be able to successfully complete its work. Once Barbara's transaction is finished, the transaction for Adam's customer can be reprocessed in its entirety. Methods for rolling back transactions will be covered in a later section.

What we want to avoid is a situation where Adam's and Barbara's transactions each decide that they are deadlocked at the same time. If this occurs, each would roll back and possibly be reprocessed over a concurrent period, causing a deadlock to occur again. To minimize the chances of this happening, systems with this type of deadlock handling normally allow each transaction a random number of attempts to access a unit of data before deciding that deadlock has occurred. This minimizes the probability that two or more deadlocked transactions will be simultaneously rolled back.

MANAGING DATA LOCKING

Lock Types—Shared versus Exclusive

From the preceding discussion, it is clear that data locking has introduced a new problem—deadlocks—while solving the problem of potentially inaccurate concurrent updates. If the volume of transactions accessing certain records is high, processing delays due to deadlocks may be extensive. Clearly we want to minimize deadlocks while ensuring the validity of our database. We want to lock out other transactions from accessing a unit of data only if their accessing the data poses a risk of inaccuracy.

The example transactions we have examined thus far have involved updating or modifying a unit of data. Suppose we have a pair of transactions that only read an existing unit of data, and have no intent to modify that unit of data. Is there any reason that one of the transactions should block the other from accessing such a unit of data? No! Because neither transaction expects to change the data, there is no danger of inaccurate updates nor is there a danger that either transaction will be using obsolete data. An example of this situation might be two concurrent transactions that are accessing data from the FLIGHT table for Flight 101 in order to print an itinerary report of destination and arrival times and cities. Neither transaction will change the set of data for Flight 101, so there is no need for these transactions to lock each other out. In this case, the volume of transactions needing to read the data for a particular flight is likely to be quite high. Thus, many unnecessary deadlocks will occur if one read transaction is allowed to lock out another read transaction.

Another combination of concurrent transactions that must be considered is having one transaction attempting to read a unit of data while another transaction seeks to update the same unit of data. In this situation there is no danger that inaccurate data will be stored in the database, because only one of the transactions will change the data. However, there is a danger that the reading transaction will produce results based on obsolete data—data that were accurate at the time they were read but that do not reflect the status of the database at the time the reading transaction is completed. In some circumstances this type of inaccuracy may be unimportant, but in other instances it may be of serious concern. Suppose, for instance, that one transaction is reading a record for a flight in order to schedule reservations while, at the same time, another transaction is being processed that might change the arrival and departure times for that flight. Booking passengers based on this obsolete data might cause important problems. Even more severe problems might occur if one transaction is deleting a record while another transaction is reading that record. In the absence of strong integrity constraints built into the DBMS, this situation could lead to creation of an orphan Flight_Day occurrence—a Flight_Day record that links to a flight that no longer exists.

To protect against problems associated with concurrent combinations of read and update operations, most DBMSs provide two levels of locking. A transaction can acquire a **shared lock** or an **exclusive lock.** If a shared lock has been issued to a user, another user can also access and acquire a shared lock on that same unit of data. However, a shared lock held on a unit of data by one user would prevent another user from acquiring an exclusive lock on that same unit of data. If a user acquires an exclusive lock on a unit of data, other users cannot acquire either a shared or an

Shared lock
A shared lock on a unit of data allows other transactions to read the locked data, but does not allow another transaction to modify the locked unit of data.

Exclusive lock
An exclusive lock completely prohibits other transactions from accessing the locked data.

exclusive lock on that unit of data. As Figure 10.11 indicates, under this locking scheme two transactions that are merely reading the same unit of data will not lock each other out—two or more transactions can each hold a shared lock on the same unit of data. However, transactions concurrently accessing a common unit of data where one or more of those transactions will change the data will not be allowed. One of the transactions will lock out the other until its work is finished.

As we noted earlier, for some read transactions we are not particularly concerned about the possibility that the data that were read will be modified by the time the transaction terminates. A type of read operation called a *dirty read* can be performed in these cases. A dirty read does not attempt to acquire any type of lock on the data that are read. Figure 10.12 expands the analysis of locking alternatives to include transactions accessing the database without requesting a lock of any type. This type of read will not lock out other transactions; thus, it cannot cause a deadlock situation. However, the system cannot guarantee that the results produced by a dirty read will reflect the status of the database as of the time that the transaction terminates. This type of read might be desirable for situations in which we are reading a large volume of data in order to produce summary statistics. If shared locks are acquired and retained until the transaction is completed, then such a transaction would lock out updates for a rather long time and would be likely to cause deadlock situations. At the same time, the effects of updates to individual records might produce only very minimal impacts on the summary data that the transaction is designed to produce.

Two phase locking
A locking protocol that requires that all locks needed for a transaction be acquired before any of its locks are relinquished. This locking protocol is designed to ensure that actions taken by a transaction are based on current data.

Two Phase Locking

The method used to guarantee that a transaction does not take an action based on erroneous or obsolete data is called a **two phase locking** protocol (Eswaren et al., 1976). Under this protocol, a growing phase is followed by a shrinking phase. During the growing phase, locks are acquired, but no locks can be relinquished. During the shrinking phase, locks are relinquished and no new locks can be acquired. In other

FIGURE 10.11
Effects of Shared and Exclusive Locks

Lock Held by User A	Type of Permitted Access by User B	
	Shared Lock	Exclusive Lock
Shared	Yes	No
Exclusive	No	No

FIGURE 10.12
Effects of Shared and Exclusive Locks and of Nonlocking (Dirty Read) Transactions

Lock Held by User A		Type of Permitted Access by User B	
	No Lock	Shared Lock	Exclusive Lock
None	Yes	Yes	Yes
Shared	Yes	Yes	No
Exclusive	Yes	No	No

words, no lock can be relinquished by a transaction until after all locks needed by that transaction have been acquired.

Suppose this procedure were not followed. The lock on one record of data, call it record A, could be released and, at some later time, the transaction could lock some other record, B, and modify it based on the value the transaction had read for record A. However, it is possible that some other transaction will have changed the value of record A in a way that makes the activities of our transaction inaccurate. The two phase locking protocol protects against this type of inaccuracy. The repeatable read isolation level, discussed in a later section, implements this two phase locking protocol.

Controlling Locking under SQL

Protocols for locking under relational DBMSs vary substantially across products. The treatment described here is based upon the methods used by DB2. Most systems issue locks on units of data down to the individual record (table row) level. However, locking at the individual record level is normally controlled by establishing a set of locking procedures to be used each time a record is accessed, rather than by having users issue locks on individual records. The SET ISOLATION command is used to establish locking procedures. The most exclusive **isolation level** is EU, which stands for *exclusive use.* With this isolation level setting, the entire database is locked for the exclusive use of the user issuing the command. This level would be used only by the database administrator to perform important clean-up or reorganization operations. At the other end of the spectrum, an isolation level of DR, which stands for *dirty read,* causes a user's commands to issue no locks and to ignore all locks imposed by other users.

The most frequently used isolation levels are RR, which stands for *repeatable read,* and CS, which stands for *cursor stability.* The RR isolation level assures that data read at any point during a transaction could be repeated later in the transaction and produce the same result. A shared lock on each record read is maintained until the end of the transaction, and an exclusive lock is acquired and maintained until the transactions end for all records that are modified. The CS isolation level locks items that are read only until the cursor moves on to another record. However, records that are modified acquire an exclusive lock that lasts until the transaction is committed.

The repeatable read isolation level ensures a user that data he or she has accessed will not be changed for the duration of the transaction. However, this assurance may come at the cost of numerous deadlocks and poor system performance. Take our reservations example. Suppose some passenger wants to book a complex set of flights where the booking might take 10 minutes to complete. As the transaction reads records from the FLIGHT_DAY table, a shared lock is acquired, preventing other transactions from updating this table. If another customer, with a much simpler transaction, wants to book tickets on the same flight on the same date, the booking agent will not be able to acquire the exclusive lock needed to update the FLIGHT_DAY record. A deadlock will occur and one of the transactions will roll back. If this type of deadlock occurs too frequently, a repeatable read isolation level may not be appropriate.

Isolation level
Refers to the degree of protection that each user of a database has from the effects of other users' transactions. A high isolation level protects data integrity very well, but may cause substantial deadlock problems.

If the cursor stability isolation level is used, we could delay updating the FLIGHT_DAY table until all segments of a reservation have been booked. Until that point, other transactions would be able to both read and *update* FLIGHT_DAY records that had previously been read by our transaction. This would greatly reduce the chances of deadlocks occurring. However, there is a risk that the contents of a FLIGHT_DAY record will have changed after we read it and before we update it. To protect against this we might *revalidate* the data by doing a second read just before we perform our update. XDB offers this type of locking scheme as one of the options in its form generator. The risk with this method is that the last available ticket for a flight date might be issued to another customer in the middle of our transaction. This risk would have to be balanced against the reduced performance that might be caused by a repeatable read isolation level.

The appropriate isolation level is influenced by the type of database system. For a client-server database system, we would expect transactions to be rather large with the client machine perhaps performing extensive manipulations on a block of data retrieved from the server. Under these circumstances it would be impractical to retain the locks required for the repeatable read isolation level until processing of the data by the client is completed. A cursor stability or dirty read isolation level is more likely to be used in client-server systems. This means, however, that values read by the client will have to be reverified prior to any updating of the server database from an application running on the client.

Locks can be explicitly requested at the table level. Thus, if a user needs guaranteed access to an entire table for an application that will read or modify a number of records, she or he can place a lock on the entire table. The syntax for this is as follows:

```
LOCK TABLE table-name IN {SHARE | EXCLUSIVE} MODE
```

To guarantee access to read any desired record of the FLIGHT table, a user could acquire the following lock:

```
LOCK TABLE FLIGHT IN SHARE MODE
```

If numerous records of the FLIGHT table need to be modified, the user could lock it in EXCLUSIVE mode. When a user has explicitly acquired a lock, that user must explicitly relinquish that lock when it is no longer needed. The UNLOCK TABLE command is used to relinquish a table lock, for example, UNLOCK TABLE FLIGHT.

Defining Transaction Boundaries—COMMIT and ROLLBACK

As we noted earlier, when two transactions cause a deadlock, one of them must be rolled back. When a transaction is rolled back, all the effects of that transaction must be negated so that the condition of the database is exactly as it would have been had the transaction never occurred. To be able to undo the effects of a transaction, the DBMS must be able to precisely define the boundaries of each transaction. To define these boundaries, a **COMMIT** statement is used. Once a transaction has successfully concluded all its operations, a COMMIT statement is issued for that transaction. If a rollback condition later occurs, actions are undone only back to the point where the last previous commit is encountered. The system can be sure that all actions before this commit point are related to transactions that were successfully completed. Thus, the boundaries of a **transaction** are from one commit point to the

COMMIT
A database language statement that makes permanent the changes to a database that have been made by a transaction. It serves as a transaction boundary. Once COMMITted, a transaction's effects cannot be rolled back.

Transaction
In the context of database processing, an interrelated set of actions affecting a database. During a transaction, the database may be in an inconsistent state. However, each transaction must return the database to a consistent state if it is successfully completed.

next commit point or from the initiation of the transaction to its first commit point.

Figure 10.13 shows an example of how the commit and rollback statements might be used for an application based on the Airline database. The application considered is one used by the director of flight operations to assign planes to Flight_Day occurrences. Pseudocode for the application is presented on the left side of this figure. We assume that the application is designed to allow the director of flight operations to retrieve the data for each Flight_Day occurrence for a given date and assign a plane (Equipment_No) to each Flight_Day record on that date. Once an equipment number has been selected, the application checks to make sure that the plane will be at the necessary location at the departure time. If the plane will not be at the

FIGURE 10.13
Commit and Rollback
Option for a Plane
Scheduling Application

Pseudocode for Plane Scheduling Application		Results COMMIT at Point 1
Read FLIGHT_DAY Record for 1st flight scheduled on this date.		Begin transaction record for flight 101 read
While valid FLIGHT_DAY record	1st trans.	Equip_No A7689 assigned record for flight 101
Assign an Equipment Number (a plane) to this flight date.		updated Equip_Valid = Yes record for flight 101 committed
Write modified FLIGHT-DAY record		mitted
Perform Equipment Validation		Record for flight 102 read
(Check to see if the		Equip_No E4293 assigned
assigned plane will be	2nd trans.	record for flight 102
available at the origin		updated Equip_Valid = No
airport at departure		transaction rolled back
time.)		**Results COMMIT at Point 2**
IF Equip_valid = No		Begin transaction record
ROLLBACK		for flight 101 read
End		Equip_No A7689 assigned
IF Equip_valid = Yes	1st trans.	record for flight 101
COMMIT 1		updated Equip_Valid = Yes
Read FLIGHT_DAY Record		Record for flight 102 read
for the next flight		Equip_No E4293 assigned
scheduled on this date.		Record for flight 102
WEND		updated Equip_Valid = No
COMMIT 2		transaction rolled back

FLIGHT_DAY Table status at end of Transaction

With COMMIT at Point 1			With COMMIT at Point 2		
Flight_No	**Flight_Date**	**Equip_No**	**Flight_No**	**Flight_Date**	**Equip_No**
101	10/12/97	A7689	101	10/12/97	Null
102	10/12/97	Null	102	10/12/97	Null

correct location, Equip_Valid is set to a value of No and the transaction is rolled back. If, on the other hand, Equip_Valid equals Yes, we can either commit the transaction at that point and read the next Flight_Day record or we can read the next Flight_Day record without committing. The COMMIT at point 1 in Figure 10.13 represents the former case, while the COMMIT at point 2 would cause the work to be committed only after planes had been assigned to all Flight_Day records for this date.

With the COMMIT at point 1, the update of each Flight_Day record is treated as a separate transaction. If the validation check is successful, the update of a Flight_Day record is committed before processing of the next Flight_Day record begins. When the COMMIT statement is read, the locks acquired for the transaction are released. Thus, the reading of the second Flight_Day record begins a new transaction. For the example shown in Figure 10.13, we are assuming that the plane whose Equipment_No is A7689 is assigned to Flight 101 on 10/12/97 and that the validation check for this assignment is correct. Then Flight 102 is assigned Equipment_No E4293, but the equipment validation for this assignment fails. Only the Equipment_No assignment for Flight 102 is rolled back in this case. The processing of the data for Flight 101 is a separate transaction whose work has been completed and committed.

With the COMMIT at point 2, we would get a very different result. Here we treat the assignment of planes to all records for a given date as a single transaction. The work is committed only after the last Flight_Day record is updated and we exit the loop. Thus, if a rollback condition is encountered in processing any of the Flight_Day records for this date, all the Flight_Day records will be rolled back.

We might use this latter approach if we feel that the equipment is highly interrelated. We would in effect be saying that we don't want to commit to the assignment of any plane to a Flight_Day record until we are able to successfully make assignments to all the records changed by this application. On the other hand, if we use commit point 1, we are saying that the assignments of planes to the various Flight_Day records can be treated as independent events.

DATABASE RECOVERY

Because no system is 100 percent reliable, it is necessary to provide mechanisms that allow a system to recover from any error or disaster. Because database systems encourage organizations to store large collections of related data together in a single integrated database, the potential loss due to the failure of a database is quite large. Therefore, it is particularly crucial that DBMSs provide a full range of features to support recovery from any type of error or failure—large or small. For an in-depth discussion of concurrency and database recovery issues, see Bernstein, Hadzilacos, and Goodman (1987).

COMMON DATABASE RECOVERY MECHANISMS

In order to provide recovery services, a DBMS must ensure that data sufficient to support recovery of the system are maintained. Then software must be provided that can operate on the recorded backup data to recover the database to its status at the time of the failure. Four major elements are required for a DBMS to provide database recovery services. These are:

Backup Copies of the Database

Backup copies of the database must be made on a regular basis. The frequency of backup varies with the scope and activity of the database, but typically a backup copy should be made at least once a day. The DBMS software must provide a mechanism for backing up the database in an efficient manner. The database administration staff must provide appropriate procedures to ensure that backup copies are made with appropriate frequency. They must also ensure that necessary measures are taken to minimize the chance of a single disaster destroying both the active and backup copies of the database. At a minimum the backup copy should be stored on a separate storage device. For crucial databases, the backup copy may be stored in a fireproof vault or transmitted to a different location for storage.

A Transactions Log

A log that records the effects of each transaction on the database is called a **transactions log.** This log might record all information needed to recreate the transaction. Alternatively, before and after images of each unit of data affected by a transaction may be written to the log. Most modern DBMSs use these before and after images for database recovery. This allows the effects of a transaction to be recreated without reprocessing it. If the effects of a successful transaction have been lost, we can simply write the log's *after image* of each unit of data affected by the transaction to the database. On the other hand, if we need to undo the effects of a failed transaction, we can simply write the log's *before images* for all data affected by the transaction to the database.

Sometimes the term *database status log* is used to refer to the log containing before and after images of data changed by transactions. Logging may actually occur in several different log files. For example, some systems separately store the before images in a *backward log* and the after images in a *forward log*. In addition, many systems may continue to operate a separate log containing information that is not needed for database recovery but is required for auditing purposes.

For our purposes, log information can be treated as if it were all placed in a single log file. Throughout the remainder of this section, we assume that all information about transactions is recorded in a single file that we will call the transactions log. To support recovery operations, this transactions log must record the before and after images of all units of data affected by each transaction. The transactions log must also record an entry each time a transaction is committed or rolled back and each time a checkpoint is issued. The commit and rollback commands were described earlier in the chapter. They define the boundaries and outcomes of transactions. The concept of checkpointing is described below.

Checkpoint Generation

To generate a **checkpoint,** the DBMS must guarantee that the database is in a stable state—no transactions are in process—at a particular instant of time. This is

Transactions log
A log that records the effects of each transaction on a database. This log normally records a before image and an after image of each unit of data that is changed by a transaction.

Checkpoint
A checkpoint is a point in time when no transactions on a database are in process. Checkpoints are used to limit the processing required for recovery from database failures.

accomplished by having the system periodically refuse to accept new transactions until all transactions in process are completed. A checkpoint is then issued and entered into the transactions log. Each entry in this log contains a time stamp.

Checkpoints are used when recovery operations need to be performed only on transactions that were in process at the time the system failed. Because, by definition, there were no transactions in process at the time a checkpoint was issued, the checkpoint can be used to simplify recovery. Entries whose time stamp is prior to the time that a checkpoint was issued do not need to be examined during recovery, because their transactions must have been completed at the time of the checkpoint and cannot have been in process at the time of the failure.

Recovery Management Software

Recovery management software is designed to operate on either the active or the backup copy of the database and the transactions log. Its goal is to recover the database to its status at the time a failure occurred. The recovery management software should be able to provide recovery services for a wide variety of both large and small failures. The specifics of recovery operations needed for some common types of failures will be discussed later in this section.

COMMON TYPES OF DATABASE FAILURES

Failures encountered in the operation of a database can be classified into the following three categories:

1. In-Process Transaction Failure: The failure of an individual transaction during its processing and before it has been committed.

2. System Failure: The operation of the computer system is interrupted for a period of time and the contents of volatile (primary) storage are lost but there is *no damage to nonvolatile (secondary) storage.*

3. Loss of Stored Data: A nonvolatile storage device holding the active copy of the database is damaged or destroyed.

The failures described here can occur in a variety of ways. Failure of a transaction can occur if the program processing that transaction encounters an error from which it cannot recover. Also, if the concurrency control system detects that a transaction is deadlocked, it may force the transaction to fail. A common source of system failure would be a loss of power to the system, causing the contents of volatile storage to be lost. A disk head crash is perhaps the most common type of problem affecting data stored on nonvolatile storage devices.

DBMS software typically provides mechanisms for automatic recovery from all these failures. We will take a look at the problems posed by each of these types of failures, using example transactions logs. The log entries shown in our example figures are not complete and do not correspond to the form of actual entries in a transactions log. They are designed to show how a transactions log is used for each type of recovery. In the first example (Figure 10.14), the important thing to note is the existence of both a transaction ID number and a log entry number. Each transaction typically causes several entries to be made—before and after images of each unit of data modified by the transaction and the commitment or rollback of the transaction. In addition, other events, such as the generation of a backup copy of the database or the issuing of a checkpoint, are entered in the transactions log.

In-Process Transaction Failure

Figure 10.14 shows a transactions log containing an in-process transaction failure. We will assume that transactions 167 and 168 are deadlocked. The deadlock detection software of the DBMS eventually detects this deadlock and causes one of the transactions to be rolled back. Log entry 333 indicates that transaction 167 is to be rolled back. We would like to simply wipe out all the effects of the failed transaction. To do this we would need to know what each unit of data that was modified by a transaction looked like before the transaction changed it. This picture of the status of a unit of data prior to modification by a transaction is called the *before image*. In our example, only one before image is associated with transaction 167. Log entry 326 provides this before image, and its value for the affected record is posted to the active database copy to execute the rollback operation. The lock on this unit of data is then released, so that transaction 168 can complete its processing and commit as shown in the *italicized* log entries *336* through *338*.

FIGURE 10.14
A Transactions Log Showing a Transaction Failure

Transactions Log

Entry No.	Trans. ID #	Type of Entry	Data Image
302	146	Before Image	102 10/11/97 . . 22
303	146	Before Image	103 10/11/97 . . 17
304	146	After Image	102 10/11/97 . . 25
305	146	After Image	103 10/11/97 . . 20
306	146	Commit	
.			
326	167	Before Image	102 10/11/97 . . 25
327	168	Before Image	101 10/11/97 . . 20
328	168	After Image	101 10/11/97 . . 22
329	167	After Image	102 10/11/97 . . 27
.			
333	167	Rollback	
.			
336	*168*	*Before Image*	*102 10/11/97 . . 25*
337	*168*	*After Image*	*102 10/11/97 . . 26*
338	*168*	*Commit*	

Transactions Log Postings for Recovery
Log entry 326 posted.

It should be noted that a transaction could be rolled back for reasons other than a deadlock. Typically, transactions processing programs are designed to terminate and roll back the database if certain types of error conditions are encountered. Also, hardware or communication link failures affecting a remote terminal that is being used to process a transaction could cause that transaction to fail and be rolled back.

The process we have described applies only to *in-process* transaction failures. It is also possible for a transaction to complete successfully but place erroneous data in the database. This type of problem is most frequently due to human error. Errors in data associated with transactions that have been completed and committed pose difficult recovery problems. If a significant amount of time has passed since the erroneous transaction was committed, numerous other transactions may have been processed that relied upon the erroneous data. To assure absolute integrity, all affected transactions would need to be undone and reprocessed after the correction of the erroneous transaction. Typically this is impractical. A common method to deal with this type of error is to make a special correcting transaction, but to allow other transactions, which may have used the erroneous data, to stand. Recovery from this type of error is not normally handled by built-in DBMS software.

System Failure

Suppose a system failure occurs after entry 357 is posted in the transactions log (see Figure 10.15). Perhaps power to the system is lost. When power is restored to the system, the active copy of the database in secondary storage has not been damaged. But can we be sure of the status of the database? The answer is no! We cannot be sure of the status of transactions that were in process at the time of the failure. Because computers execute instructions serially, it is impossible for a commit indicator to be written to the transactions log at exactly the same instant that the values of the data units updated by that transaction are written to the active copy of the database in secondary storage.

Look-ahead log
A transactions log that is always updated before the results of a transaction are actually recorded in the database.

Suppose that the commit entry is written to the log just before the database is actually updated. This type of log is sometimes called a **look-ahead log.** With this type of logging, it is possible that a failure will occur before all the results of the transaction are actually recorded in the database. The log will indicate that the transaction committed, but the after images of the transaction may not have actually been written to the database. To recover the system, we must ensure that all transactions having a commit in the transactions log have had their results posted to the database. We must *redo* transactions listed as committed in the log. This is accomplished by applying the *last* after image for each unit of data modified by a committed transaction occurring after the last checkpoint. We do not need to consider transactions occurring before the last checkpoint. The database was guaranteed to be in a stable state (no transactions in process) at the time the checkpoint was issued. Also, if a unit of data has been updated by more than one committed transaction, we need only to post the last update. In our example, the after image for entry 304 is not posted because a later after image exists for it, and entry 329 is not posted because its transaction was rolled back and not committed.

Transactions Log

Entry No.	Trans. ID #	Type of Entry	Data Image
114	079	Before Image	101 10/12/97 . . 12
115	079	Before Image	102 10/12/97 . . 16
116	079	After Image	101 10/12/97 . . 18
117	079	After Image	102 10/12/97 . . 15
118	080	Before Image	103 10/11/97 . . 15
119	079	Commit	
120	080	After Image	103 10/11/97 . . 17
121	080	Rollback	
.			
286	132	Checkpoint Issued	
.			
302	146	Before Image	102 10/11/97 . . 22
303	146	Before Image	103 10/11/97 . . 17
304	146	After Image	102 10/11/97 . . 25
305	146	After Image	103 10/11/97 . . 20
306	146	Commit	
.			
326	167	Before Image	102 10/11/97 . . 25
327	168	Before Image	101 10/11/97 . . 20
328	168	After Image	101 10/11/97 . . 22
329	167	After Image	102 10/11/97 . . 27
.			
333	167	Rollback	
.			
336	168	Before Image	102 10/11/97 . . 25
337	168	After Image	102 10/11/97 . . 26
338	168	Commit	
.			
351	176	Before Image	104 10/11/97 . . 22
352	177	Before Image	102 10/13/97 . . 16
353	176	After Image	104 10/11/97 . . 24
354	176	Before Image	103 10/11/97 . . 20
355	177	After Image	102 10/13/97 . . 19
356	176	After Image	103 10/11/97 . . 22
357	177	Commit	

System failure immediately after log entry 357

FIGURE 10.15
A Transactions Log Showing a System Failure

```
Transactions Log Postings for Recovery
Type of Recovery            Log Entries Posted
```

Type of Recovery	Log Entries Posted
Redo	305, 328, 337, 355
Undo	351, 354
Redo/Undo	305, 328, 337, 355, 351, 354

FIGURE 10.15 (Cont.)
A Transactions Log Showing a System Failure

In practice, the recovery software would search the transactions log and build a sorted list of the entries to be posted. This would allow the system to post only the last after image for each affected unit of data.

In our discussion thus far, we have assumed that the commit entry in the log occurred before the actual database update. What if the reverse were true? In this case we might have posted the changes associated with a transaction to the database, but had a system failure before the commit entry was written to the transactions log. On recovery, we must ensure that the status of the database corresponds to the status of the transactions log. To do this we could roll back, or *undo,* all transactions not having a commit entry in the log. The *undo* postings shown in Figure 10.15 represent this case. Before images of all transactions not committed in the log are posted. The checkpoint helps us once again, because we do not need to look at the log entries prior to the last checkpoint—they cannot contain any entries for uncommitted transactions. Finally, it is possible that the system we are using does not guarantee the order in which logging is done. If this is the case, we would post both sets of images to the database at recovery—undoing all noncommitted transactions and redoing the committed transactions.

Loss of Stored Data

A more serious form of disaster is one in which the active copy of the database is damaged or destroyed. If this occurs, the latest backup copy of the database must be made active and then the appropriate entries from the transactions log must be used to bring it up to date. Essentially we must redo all committed transactions occurring after the backup copy of the database was made. Figure 10.16 shows an example of this situation. A backup database copy was made as entry 114 on the log. All later entries in the transactions log are searched. The last after image for each unit of data updated by a committed transaction must be posted to the database. Once this is done the database will be returned to its status at the time of the disaster, and processing can continue.

Fault tolerant system
A system that contains redundant copies of crucial system elements and is designed to continue operating at or near normal capacity when certain common types of failures occur.

Where continuous system operation is crucial, backup hardware systems need to be available to minimize downtime due to computer system failures. Redundant hardware components can be used to provide **fault tolerant systems.** If the cost of system downtime is very high, a complete redundant facility with all the hardware necessary to recover and operate the database may be owned or leased. This type

Transactions Log

Entry No.	Trans. ID #	Type of Entry	Image Data
111	077	Before Image	102 10/11/97 . . 22
112	077	After Image	102 10/11/97 . . 23
113	077	Commit	
114	078	Database Backup Copy Made	
114	079	Before Image	101 10/12/97 . . 12
115	079	Before Image	102 10/12/97 . . 16
116	079	After Image	101 10/12/97 . . 18
117	079	After Image	102 10/12/97 . . 15
118	080	Before Image	103 10/11/97 . . 15
119	079	Commit	
120	080	After Image	103 10/11/97 . . 17
121	080	Rollback	
.			
286	132	Checkpoint Issued	
.			
302	146	Before Image	102 10/11/97 . . 22
303	146	Before Image	103 10/11/97 . . 17
304	146	After Image	102 10/11/97 . . 25
305	146	After Image	103 10/11/97 . . 20
306	146	Commit	
.			
326	167	Before Image	102 10/11/97 . . 25
327	168	Before Image	101 10/11/97 . . 20
328	168	After Image	101 10/11/97 . . 22
329	167	After Image	102 10/11/97 . . 27
.			
333	167	Rollback	
.			
336	168	Before Image	102 10/11/97 . . 25
337	168	After Image	102 10/11/97 . . 26
338	168	Commit	
.			
351	176	Before Image	104 10/11/97 . . 22
352	177	Before Image	102 10/13/97 . . 16
353	176	After Image	104 10/11/97 . . 24

FIGURE 10.16

A Transactions Log Showing Recovery When There Is a Loss of Stored Data

Entry No.	Trans. ID #	Type of Entry	Image Data
354	176	Before Image	103 10/11/97 . . 20
355	177	After Image	102 10/13/97 . . 19
356	176	After Image	103 10/11/97 . . 22
357	177	Commit	

Data loss occurs immediately after log entry 357

Transactions Log Postings for Recovery
Log entries 116, 117, 305, 328, 337, 355 posted

FIGURE 10.16 (Cont.)

A Transactions Log Showing Recovery When There Is a Loss of Stored Data

Cold site
A site that contains a duplicate copy of all of the hardware and software required to operate a database system; designed to be quickly brought on-line should a disaster damage or destroy an organization's data center.

Hot site
An alternate data center site operated to continuously maintain a redundant copy of a database to protect against damage or destruction of the organization's main data center.

of facility is called a **cold site.** For every crucial systems, a redundant copy of the database may be continuously maintained in real time at an alternate site called a **hot site.** The DA function plays a key role in determining the types of redundant hardware and facilities used by an organization.

SUMMARY

In this chapter, we have described the role of the database administration (DBA) or data administration (DA) unit and have discussed some of the key technical and managerial elements of the DA role. The DBA function is expected to fulfill a number of largely technical responsibilities. The DA function adds a substantial managerial and planning role to these responsibilities. The major responsibilities of the data administration function were summarized in Figure 10.1. These responsibilities relate to many of the planning, design, and development activities that have been described in earlier chapters. In addition, the DA or DBA unit has core responsibilities for the successful operation of systems once they are put on-line. Three key requirements for successful operation of multiuser database systems are access control, concurrency control, and recovery systems.

Access control is necessary to protect sensitive data from casual access. In addition, appropriate limitations on the range of users who are able to perform data creation, modification, and deletion operations are necessary to protect the integrity of all data. Access granularity is a measure of the fineness with which access to a database can be controlled. Access granularity has two dimensions—the size of the unit of data and the level of actions that can be performed.

Relational databases commonly allow control over the unit of access down to the level of selected rows and/or columns within a table. Actions allowed can be controlled down to the level of individual commands that a user is allowed or not allowed to execute. This control is exerted through the GRANT and REVOKE statements, which allow or deny users PRIVILEGES to execute specific commands on specified tables or views in the database.

Concurrency control is necessary to preserve the integrity of the database from threats posed by multiple users accessing, and potentially making conflicting changes to, the same unit of data at the same time. Locking is the method commonly used to protect against this problem. However, locking creates another problem—the deadly embrace. A deadly embrace occurs if each of two transactions holds a lock needed by the other transaction. In such a case neither transaction can ever acquire the locks it needs to complete successfully. Most DBMSs contain software designed to detect deadlocks and to cause one of the deadlocked transactions to roll back, allowing the remaining transaction to terminate successfully.

Most DBMSs provide for two levels of locking—a shared or *read* lock and an exclusive or *write* lock. Normal locking procedures follow a two phase locking protocol—no locks are released by a transaction until all necessary locks have been acquired. This assures that locks will not be released until we are sure that the transaction can be successfully completed. Adjustments to the type of lock acquired and the timing of lock acquisition can be used to tune system performance.

Procedures for user control of locking are not standard across relational DBMS products. Most relational DBMSs allow users to perform explicit locking at the table level through a LOCK TABLE command. However, record locking is normally automatically handled by the DBMS itself. In many systems the DBA can adjust the locking scheme used by the DBMS. Under XDB record-level locking, locking can be controlled by the SET ISOLATION LEVEL command. Stronger isolation provides better protection from the effects of other users, but this may come at the expense of lower system throughput.

Database backup and recovery procedures are designed to get the database back in operation without the loss or compromise of data in the face of any potential disaster. Four major elements are normally used to provide recovery services:

1. Backup copies are made on a regular basis and stored in a secure manner.

2. A transactions log is maintained. It contains before and after images of all units of data affected by transactions and other status information.

3. Checkpoints are generated by the system periodically and entered into the transactions log. Acceptance of new transactions is suspended until a point is reached at which no transactions are in process. At that instant, the checkpoint is issued.

4. DBMS recovery management software is used. It is designed to provide automatic recovery from a variety of disasters. Recovery is achieved by processing portions of the transactions log and backup copies of the database as needed.

DBMSs normally are designed to provide recovery for three basic types of disaster. The failure of a transaction while it is being processed is handled by rolling back that transaction. This requires that any before images in the transactions log associated with that transaction be posted to the database.

The second type of disaster is a system failure. When a system failure occurs, recovery requires examination of all entries in the transactions log occurring after the last checkpoint. A redo operation is performed by posting the last after image of all data modified by committed transactions occurring after the checkpoint. This would be done if the transactions log is a *look-ahead log* whose contents are posted before the changes are recorded in the database. If the database is updated before log postings are done, one would "undo" noncommitted transactions by posting their before images to the database. Both the redo and undo operations would be required if the order of transactions log writing versus database update is unknown.

The final type of disaster occurs when data are lost from the current copy of the database. Recovery from this type of disaster requires use of a backup copy of the database. The last after image for each unit of data modified since the backup copy was made is posted to the database to make it current.

REVIEW QUIZ

_____ Normally contains a before image and an after image.

_____ Occurs when there is a time overlap in the transactions of two or more users of a common database.

_____ Isolation level that ensures that the values of all data read during a transaction will not change prior to the conclusion of the transaction.

_____ Restores a database to the state it would have been in if the transaction had never occurred.

_____ A point of time during which no transactions in a database are in process.

_____ Occurs if each of two or more transactions has requested data that has been locked by another transaction in the set.

_____ Refers to the degree of control of access to a database with respect to, for instance, the size of the unit of data accessed.

_____ Isolation level that allows only the specified user to access the database while her or his application is operating.

_____ A lock that allows other transactions to read the locked data, but not modify them.

_____ Makes changes to a database that have been produced by a transaction permanent.

_____ A transactions log that is always updated before the results of a transaction are actually recorded in the database.

_____ A lock that completely prohibits other transactions from accessing the locked data.

_____ Isolation level that allows an application to run without acquiring any locks.

_____ An interrelated set of actions on a database that will return the database to a consistent state if all of the actions are executed successfully.

_____ All locks needed for a transaction must be acquired before any of the trans
action's locks are relinquished.

_____ A site that operates continuously and provides a redundant copy of a database
system.

_____ A database user who has been given responsibility and authority for
controlling access to a portion of a database.

_____ An IS function that is responsible only for the technical management of an
organization's databases.

_____ Adjustment of physical storage structures of a database to improve its
operational efficiency.

_____ Multiple users accessing the same database at the same time.

_____ DA responsibility that includes the determination of the DBMSs that will be
supported by an organization.

_____ DA responsibility that includes performance tuning of databases.

_____ The IS function that is responsible for data planning and administration of
databases as well as technical management of databases.

_____ A system containing redundant copies of key components designed to allow
the system to continue operating when some system elements have failed.

_____ A site containing all hardware and software required to operate a database
system, which is put into operation only if the data center is damaged or
destroyed.

1. Access granularity
2. Deadlock
3. Concurrent access
4. Rollback
5. Exclusive use isolation level
6. Repeatable read isolation level
7. Dirty read isolation level
8. Shared lock
9. Exclusive lock

10. Two phase locking

11. COMMIT

12. Transaction

13. Transactions log

14. Checkpoint

15. Look-ahead log

16. Fault tolerant system

17. Cold site

18. Hot site

19. Establishing the database development environment

20. Database administration

21. Data administration

22. Data steward

23. Subschema

24. Database tuning

25. Physical database design and implementation

REVIEW QUESTIONS AND EXERCISES

1. Describe and contrast the functions of database administration and data administration.

2. List the major responsibilities of the data administration function. Which are primarily technical in nature? Which require the greatest managerial skills?

3. Describe data administration's role in data planning.

4. Describe the principal elements involved in establishing the database development environment for an organization.

5. Describe the advantages and limitations associated with establishing a limited set of DBMSs to be supported by an organization as a part of the database development environment.

6. Discuss the DA involvement in requirements analysis and conceptual database design. How does this role vary across organizations? What is the minimum role that the DA function should be expected to play in this process?

7. Describe a systems repository. How does it differ from a data dictionary? Why would the management of a systems repository be assigned as a responsibility of the data administration function?

8. What is database tuning?

9. What is the role of a subschema in network and hierarchical databases? What elements fulfill a similar role under the relational model?

10. What is meant by the term *data steward?* Why would a data administrator appoint a data steward?

11. What is a fault tolerant system? A cold site? A hot site?

12. Describe and give examples of various types of standards that might be established and enforced by the data administration function.

13. One objective of the DA function in maintaining a database system is to insulate users, as much as possible, from the effects of system changes. What is meant by insulating users from changes and what features of DBMSs help to support this insulation?

14. Define the following terms:

    a. Granularity

    b. Deadlock

    c. Two phase locking

    d. Dirty read

    e. Repeatable read

    f. Checkpoint

    g. Transaction log

    h. Rollback

    i. Commit

    j. Before and after images

15. Discuss granularity of data access.

    a. Describe the two dimensions of data access granularity.

    b. Compare the granularity of data access control provided by major types of DBMSs as described in this chapter.

    c. Describe the data access control measures offered by a DBMS software package you are using in class or at work and assess the access granularity it offers.

16. Contrast the methods used to control database access in SQL-based relational DBMSs with those used by hierarchical and network DBMSs.

17. In this and previous chapters we have described several roles for the SQL VIEW statement. Briefly describe these roles.

18. Application of DBMS access control measures is not sufficient to fully control database access. What other elements are necessary to provide an effective system of data access control?

19. What is the nature of the concurrent access problem? When does concurrent access pose a threat to data integrity? What type of data integrity problems may occur if concurrent access remains uncontrolled?

20. Describe shared locks and exclusive locks. How does the level of locking and the timing of lock acquisition affect system performance? Database integrity?

21. How does two phase locking help to ensure data integrity? Describe how data integrity might be compromised if two phased locking procedures are not followed.

22. Describe and give an example of a pair of transactions that would generate a deadlock. Describe the measures commonly used by DBMSs to deal with the problem of transaction deadlocks. What procedures does the DBMS you are using have for dealing with deadlocks?

23. What is a "dirty read"? What are the advantages and risks associated with this type of read operation? When might a dirty read appropriately be used?

24. A number of types of failures that might occur during the operation of a database were discussed in this chapter. Describe and give an example of each major type of failure.

25. How and when are transactions log checkpoint entries used in database recovery operations?

26. When is it necessary to use a backup copy of the database for disaster recovery? A backup copy of the transactions log?

27. Suppose you are data administrator for the Air West Airline database (described in Chapter 5). Define at least five different standards that you might impose for this database system.

28. Suppose you are data administrator for the Air West database. Which user(s) would you select as data stewards? What data would you assign to each of your data stewards?

29. Interview a data administrator or member of a data administration staff in an organization in your community. Find out whether this person performs all the responsibilities described in Figure 10.1. What is her or his involvement in data planning? In conceptual database design? What type of backup and recovery facilities does she or he maintain? What types of standards does she or he impose?

30. Interview a user of a database system that does not have a formal data administrator. Are data administration functions being performed on his or her database systems? If so, which functions are performed and by whom? Are there any important data administration functions that are not being performed and that expose the system to risk?

31. Assume a company has a database with an EMPLOYEE table having the following structure:

EMPLOYEE (Emp_#, Emp_name, Home_addr, Department, Salary)

The following levels of user access to this table are required.

a. Personnel department clerks (User Pers_clk) need to be able to read all data for every employee and can insert or update all attributes except Salary.

b. The personnel director (User Pers_dir) must be able to read, insert, update, and delete all data for every employee. She is the only one allowed to insert or update a Salary value and to delete an Employee record.

c. The foreman of the shipping department (User Ship_for) needs to be able to read all data attributes for employees assigned to his department. This is the only access to the Employee table that he should be allowed to have.

d. The benefits coordinator (User Ben_coord) should be allowed read access to the average salary of all employees in each department. She is not to be given access to information about any individual employee.

What GRANT and VIEW statements would be necessary to create the set of access privileges described in *a* through *d*?

32. The Vitalife Health Club maintains a database that, in part, contains three tables called CUSTOMER, SERVICE, and CUST_SERVICE. The CUSTOMER table stores basic data about each club member. The SERVICE table stores descriptions and pricing information about each type of service offered by the club. The CUST_SERVICE table contains one record for each service ordered by a customer and is used for billing.

Sales clerks (Sls_clk) are allowed to read data from all tables and to insert new CUST_SERVICE records. They are not allowed to delete or update CUST_SER-VICE records. The membership director (Mem_dir) is the only user authorized to create, change, or delete CUSTOMER records. The operations manager (Op_mgr) is allowed to read all data. In addition, she is responsible for creating, updating, and deleting data in the SERVICE table as needed to reflect current services and prices. Finally, she is responsible for making changes to CUST_SERVICE records if errors are found and for deleting old CUST_SERVICE records when they are no longer needed.

a. What GRANT statements would be required to provide the necessary levels of access to the users Sls_clk, Mem_dir, and Op_mgr?

b. What difficulties would the access levels described here pose if it were decided that the CUSTOMER table should have an outstanding balance attribute that would be updated each time a new CUST_SERVICE record was created?

Refer to Chapter 5. Reread the description of the user view for the director of flight operations. What VIEW and GRANT statements would be required to provide the access this user needs to the Airline database?

33. Suppose a database containing product data allows concurrent access by multiple users, but does not provide locking. The value of quantity on hand (QOH) for a product is decreased each time the product is ordered and increased when shipments of the product are received. If an order requests more units of a product than are currently available, that order is refused. The customer placing the order is told that it cannot be filled, and the QOH is not adjusted. Suppose the following three transactions overlap, and each initially reads the same value, 35, for the QOH of product number PB783.

a. A customer orders 25 units of product PB783.

b. A second customer orders 20 units of product PB783.

c. A shipment of 1,000 units of product PB783 is received and must be added to the quantity on hand.

(1) What will be the database's value for the QOH of product PB783 if the transactions are completed in the order a, b, c?

(2) What will be the database's value for the QOH of product PB783 if the transactions are completed in the order a, c, b?

(3) What *should* be the value for the QOH of PB783 after all these transactions have been completed?

34. Based on the transactions described in question 33:

a. What kind of locking would you recommend for use with each transaction?

b. If your locking scheme were used and the transactions were executed in the order a, b, c, what would be the value for the QOH for product PB783 once all the transactions had been processed?

c. If your locking scheme were used and the transactions were executed in the order a, c, b, what would be the value for the QOH for product PB783 once all the transactions had been processed?

d. If your answer for part c is different than that for part b, why? Does this represent a loss of data integrity?

35. Assume that the activities of two users, A and B, who are accessing Customer records, have occurred as follows:

a. User A acquires a lock on the data for Customer 1063.

b. User B acquires a lock on the data for Customer 1185.

c. User A tries to get a lock on the data for Customer 1185.

d. User B tries to get a lock on the data for Customer 1063.

(1) Assume both users have acquired exclusive locks for the purpose of updating data. Is this a deadlock situation? If so, how would the deadlock be resolved by the DBMS you are using?

(2) Assume that user A is acquiring exclusive locks for the purpose of updating the database, while user B acquires only shared locks for the purpose of reading the data. Would the actions shown cause a deadlock situation?

(3) Assume that user B is acquiring shared locks only and user A is acquiring his locks in two phases. He acquires a read lock at step a, with the intention of later (after step d) converting it to an exclusive lock. Would the actions shown cause a deadlock situation? If not, which user's transaction would be completed first?

(4) How would the actions shown in steps a through d be changed if user B's transaction were processed as a dirty read?

36. Based on the transactions log data shown in Figure 10.17, what log entries would be posted to the database to roll back transaction 1053?

Entry No.	Trans. ID #	Type of Entry	Data	Image[a]
2857	1047	Before Image	PB647	102
2858	1048	Before Image	PA722	86
2859	1047	Before Image	PB652	55
2860	1048	After Image	PA722	79
2861	1047	After Image	PB647	94
2862	1048	Commit		
2863	1047	Rollback		
2864	1049	Database Backup Copy Made		
2865	1050	Before Image	CR237	29
2866	1051	Before Image	TY814	48
2867	1050	After Image	CR237	26
2868	1051	Before Image	SX622	72
2869	1051	After Image	TY814	43
2870	1050	Commit		
2871	1051	After Image	SX622	62
2872	1051	Commit		
2873	1052	Checkpoint Issued		
2874	1053	Before Image	PB783	59
2875	1054	Before Image	XS318	20
2876	1053	Before Image	CR237	72
2877	1054	After Image	XS318	120
2878	1053	After Image	PB783	44
2879	1054	Rollback		
2880	1053	After Image	CR237	62
2881	1055	Before Image	LN406	107
2882	1053	Commit		
2883	1055	Before Image	PB783	44
2884	1056	Before Image	XS208	85
2885	1055	After Image	LN406	92
2886	1055	After Image	PB783	37
2887	1056	After Image	XS208	75
2888	1055	Commit		

[a]For this example log, all entries are assumed to affect a **PRODUCT** table consisting of a product number, which serves as the primary key, and a value for the quantity on hand.

FIGURE 10.17
An Example
Transactions Log

37. Based on the transactions log data shown in Figure 10.17, what log entries would be posted to the database to recover from a system failure not involving damage to the active copy of the database and occurring after log entry 2888?

    a. If entries are written to the transactions log before they are posted to the database?

    b. If entries are written to the transactions log after they are posted to the database?

    c. If the order of postings to the transactions log and database is unknown?

38. Based on the transactions log data shown in Figure 10.17, what log entries would be posted and what recovery process would be required if damage to the active copy of the database occurred immediately after transaction log entry 2873?

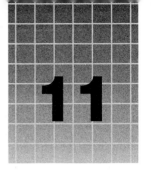

PHYSICAL DATA ORGANIZATION FOR DATABASE SYSTEMS

LEARNING OBJECTIVES

After completing this chapter, you should be able to

- Describe the process of physically retrieving data from a direct access storage device (DASD).
- Describe ISAM, VSAM, and B-Tree index structures.
- Demonstrate how data elements are retrieved using ISAM, VSAM or B-Tree index structures and show how each type of index is modified as data are added or deleted.
- Suggest appropriate indexing and "clustering" structures for a relational database to enhance performance.
- Describe the Hashing access method.
- Determine where a given record will be stored when Hashing is used.
- Describe Linked List structures and be able to indicate how pointer chains would be used/updated when data are retrieved, added, or deleted.
- Discuss the use of Hashing and Linked Lists in network DBMSs and be able to suggest appropriate use of these structures for a sample database.

In the preceding chapters of this text, we have largely ignored the issue of how database data are physically stored. We have been able to do this because the relational DBMSs that we have been describing insulate users from concerns about physical storage characteristics of their database. This is possible because relational DBMSs have been implemented to a substantial degree in the *three schema architecture* that was described in Chapter 3. End-users of a database, and even analysts and programmers who develop database applications, do not need to know how the data in the database are physically stored. They access the database through the conceptual model (schema) or, more properly, through their user view (subschema) of the conceptual model. Users employing SQL commands operate on a database as if it consisted of a set of flat rectangular files. All commands to manipulate and interconnect these tables are based on values of stored data without reference to storage or indexing structures. Beneath the level of the conceptual model lies the internal model, which specifies how data are physically stored and the mechanisms by which they may be accessed. Software of the relational DBMS must translate requests stated in conceptual model terms into requests to read from or write to an appropriate location on some storage device. The internal model includes indexes and other structures designed to speed the process of finding the data requested by users. The operational performance of a database system (the volume of transactions it can handle and the speed with which it can process them) is largely determined by how well the internal model has been designed. As we noted in Chapter 10, the design and implementation of physical storage structures is normally a responsibility of the data administration function.

The insulation of users from physical storage structures is a characteristic only of relational DBMSs. Under the hierarchical and network models, described in Chapters 14 and 15, users must understand and be able to manipulate the physical storage structures of the database in order to access its data. Under any data model, the design of physical data storage structures is crucial to the effective performance of database systems. In this chapter, we will review various data storage structures and illustrate the types of structures most commonly used to support hierarchical, network, and relational database systems.

PHYSICAL DATA STORAGE CHARACTERISTICS

In most database systems, the transfer of data between secondary storage and primary storage is the biggest potential bottleneck that can slow system performance. Thus, to be effective, physical data storage structures must be designed to minimize the number of transfers between secondary and primary memory required to accomplish database processing activities. To see why this is true, let us briefly review the characteristics of primary and secondary memory and the storage devices and media they commonly use.

Primary memory is a part of the central processing unit (CPU) of a computer. Only the contents of primary memory can be directly accessed and manipulated by the computer's processor unit(s). Thus, all instructions and data must be stored in primary memory at the time they are executed or operated upon by the computer.

Two major limitations of primary memory make it inappropriate for the long-term storage of data. First, most primary memory consists of random access memory (RAM) chips, which provide volatile storage. Volatile storage means that any data stored in a RAM chip will be lost if electric power to a computer unit is stopped, even for an instant. In addition, RAM is a relatively expensive storage medium.

Devices used for *secondary memory* must be nonvolatile, meaning that the data is recorded in a manner that all data is retained even when the power is shut off. Currently, magnetic disk systems are the predominant secondary storage device for database data. Data are recorded in the form of magnetized spots on the recording media and, once recorded, these magnetic dots are not affected by a loss of electric power. Magnetic disk storage has a number of additional desirable characteristics. It provides relatively low-cost storage and the ability to store and access a virtually unlimited amount of data. Magnetic disk storage also provides the ability to randomly access data. This is crucial for database storage because applications frequently require quick access to just a few selected records.

Based on these characteristics, it is clear that ongoing data, such as that of a database, must be stored on a nonvolatile secondary storage medium. At the same time, data must be in primary memory when processing of the data is performed. Thus, to change a unit of data, it must be transferred from secondary storage to primary memory before processing, and the new value must be transferred back to secondary storage when the processing to change its value has been completed. The length of time required to transfer data between secondary storage and primary memory is often 100 times as great as the time required to read data in primary memory.

Direct access storage device (DASD)
A storage device that allows data to be accessed in approximately the same amount of time no matter where it is stored on the medium and regardless of its logical ordering in a data structure. Magnetic disk is the most common DASD.

Track
A concentric circle on the surface of a disk platter. A read/write head will pass over the set of data for a track if the read/write head remains stationary while a disk makes one complete revolution.

Thus, the transfers of data between primary and secondary storage can create a major processing bottleneck. To see why this is the case, let's examine characteristics of Direct Access Storage Devices (DASD) and the process needed to transfer data from disk storage to primary memory.

PHYSICAL CHARACTERISTICS OF DISK DRIVES

Direct Access Storage Devices (DASD) are normally referred to as disk drives. Disk drives come as fixed drives (hard drives) or removable drives referred to as floppy drives or cartridge drives. Floppy drives have one platter whereas fixed drives are concealed units with multiple platters. The storage of data on a platter follows the same approach on most disk drives. Data are recorded on **tracks,** which are concentric circles on the surface of the platter. The tracks are only positions on the surface with no physical difference between a track and the surface between the tracks. The

An 8 Platter Disk Drive   A Single Platter Floppy Drive

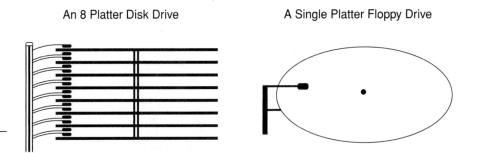

FIGURE 11.1

Storage Structure for a Multiple Platter Disk

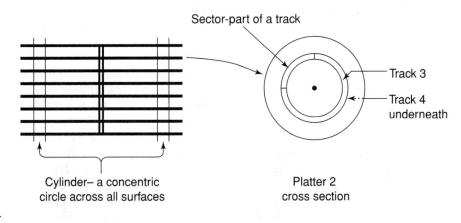

FIGURE 11.2   Side View

read/write heads record data on the surface without touching the surface. There is normally one set of read/write heads per surface. Consequently, a one-platter disk drive would have a set of read/write heads on the top surface and another set on the bottom surface. The two sets of heads operate on one arm that moves in and out across both surfaces so they can read and write data on any track or concentric circle they float across. Figure 11.1 shows a diagram of a platter and the read/write heads on the arm.

A multiple platter disk drive has a set of read/write heads for each platter. On most multiple platter drives, the read/write heads are positioned on the same concentric circle position on all surfaces at any one time. This occurs because the read/write heads are all connected to the same arm mechanism. The set of concentric circles, each on a separate surface one above the other, is referred to as a **cylinder.** When the arm moves, it goes from one cylinder to another. The storage structure of a multiple platter disk drive is illustrated in Figure 11.2.

Data are recorded on the tracks as a series of 1s and 0s to record the characters, digits, and numeric data in whatever format is being used. Tracks can be divided into fixed sectors or logical sectors. A fixed sector can hold a fixed number of bytes and will be the same for all sectors on that disk drive. Logical sector sizes are determined by the developer and can vary in size from one file to another on the same drive.

ACCESSING DATA ON DISK DRIVES

Finding and retrieving a unit of data stored at some random location on a disk drive involves three distinct time delays. Figure 11.3 illustrates this process.

First, the read/write head must be moved into position over the cylinder containing the data to be accessed. The time required to do this is referred to as the **seek time.** If the database we are accessing fully utilizes the disk device, the average seek time will be one half the time required to move the read/write heads from the outermost cylinder to the innermost cylinder.

Once the read/write heads are in position, there will be a delay until the data to be transferred rotate into position under the read/write heads. The time required for this is referred to as the **rotational delay** or *latency.* On average, the rotational delay is equal to one half of the time required for the disk to complete one revolution.

Finally, when the desired data are in position under the read/write heads, the data must be transferred to primary memory. The time required for this operation depends on the amount of data to be transferred and the speed at which data can be transferred—the **data transfer time.**

The computation at the bottom of Figure 11.3 shows the average time required to retrieve a block of 8,000 bytes using a common disk device found in mainframe DBMSs. Note that the seek and rotational delay times dominate. To date, innovations in disk technology have caused roughly proportional improvements in the three components of retrieval time. Because the seek and rotational delay times tend to dominate total retrieval time, the time required to retrieve data needed to support a database application can be minimized by retrieving relatively large blocks of highly related data at one time.

Read/write head
A device that can read or write magnetic spots on a disk surface. Multiple read/write heads are often attached to a common arm that can adjust their position over the disk surface.

Cylinder
A set of parallel tracks across all surfaces of a disk pack that can be assessed when the read/write arm is in a stationary position.

Seek time
The average time required for the read/write arm to be moved into position for the reading of a randomly selected record.

Rotational delay
The average wait time for the beginning of a set of data to be retrieved to rotate under the read/write head once it is in position.

Data transfer time
The time required to physically transfer a set of data from secondary to primary storage once the read/write head has been positioned over the beginning point of the requested data.

FIGURE 11.3
Access Time for
Magnetic Disk
Secondary Storage

Access Time = Seek Time + Rotational Delay + Data Transfer Time
AT   =   ST   +   RD   +   DTT

On Average:

Seek Time = Half the time required to move the read/write heads
from the outermost to the innermost cylinders
containing data for the file being accessed

Rotational Delay = Half the time required for the disk platter
to complete one revolution

Data Transfer Time = Proportional to the amount of data
transferred for a given access and
inversely proportional to the speed
at which the disk rotates

For an operation to retrieve one random 8,000-byte sector from a
3380 disk where the referenced file fills the entire disk, the access
time components might be approximately:

Seek Time = 16.7 milliseconds
Rotational Delay =   8.0 milliseconds = (1/2 rotation at 3600 RPM)
Data Transfer Time =   3.2 milliseconds
TOTAL ACCESS TIME = 27.9 milliseconds

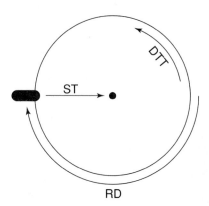

THE 3380 DISK DRIVE

One popular drive system used on IBM mainframes is the 3380, described in Figure
11.4. The 3380 comes in units with two drives per unit. Each drive consists of two
volumes for a total of four volumes in a unit. A volume has eight platters, giving it 15
surfaces. The very bottom surface is not used. Each surface has 885 concentric circles
on which to record data.

Volume 1	Volume 1	Volume 1	Volume 1
Volume 2	Volume 2	Volume 2	Volume 2

Drive 1

Volume 1	Volume 1	Volume 1	Volume 1
Volume 2	Volume 2	Volume 2	Volume 2

Drive 2

    1   2   3   4

Units

4 3380 units

2 drives per unit

2 volumes per drive

Total of 16 volumes

Volume = 885 Cylinders

Each Cylinder has 15 Tracks (15 Surfaces)

Track = 47,476 Bytes

Cylinder = 712,140 Bytes

Volume = 630 Megabytes

Drive = 1.26 Gigabytes

Unit = 2.52 Gigabytes

4 Units = 10 Gigabytes

Volume

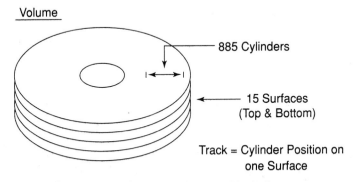

885 Cylinders

15 Surfaces
(Top & Bottom)

Track = Cylinder Position on
one Surface

Address= (Volume #, Cylinder #, Track #, Block #)

FIGURE 11.4
IBM 3380
Disk Format

The data recording on a track (one concentric circle on one surface) is variable, because the 3380 does not have fixed sectors. A track can hold up to 47,000 bytes. This would be the case if all the bytes were in one block. Normally, data are recorded in block sizes of about 8,000 bytes. Overhead data and gaps are used to break the track into multiple blocks. Figure 11.4 shows how the track is laid out given multiple 8,000-byte blocks. Each block starts with a count data area that holds the relative block number on the track (block address). The address holds the cylinder number, the head number (surface or track), the record (block) number, and the length of the key and length of the data block. The next data area is the key area, which stores the primary key of the last record in the block. The last data area is the data block itself, which consists of multiple logical records. If the block is 8,000 bytes and the record size is 400, we can store 20 records in the block. The gaps between each data area take up additional space on the track. There are roughly 1,000 bytes of overhead for each data block. The table in Figure 11.5 shows the number of blocks a track will hold given different block sizes.

The 3380 can hold up to 2.5 gigabytes per unit, depending on the block structure chosen. Using our example of five 8,000-byte blocks on a track, a volume could hold about 2.14 gigabytes. This calculation is shown in Figure 11.6. on page 444.

A disk format more familiar to most of you is the 1.4 megabyte 3.5 inch diskette. The disk has only one platter containing 80 cylinders. Both the top and bottom surfaces are used, giving it 80 tracks on each surface. A track is separated into 18 fixed sectors each holding 512 bytes. A track can hold 9,216 (18 x 512) bytes, and one cylinder holds 18,432 bytes. The 80 cylinders hold 1,474,560 (80 x 18,432) bytes.

Another common disk format used in hard drives on PC systems is the Winchester Drive format, shown in Figure 11.7 on page 444. The Winchester format is similar to the 3380 format; however, it uses fixed sector sizes. Multiple cylinder and platter combinations are used to get drives in the larger megabyte ranges.

FILE ORGANIZATION FOR RANDOM ACCESS

Sequential access
When sequential access methods are used, data must be retrieved in sequential order based upon some characteristic of the data.

Random access
When random access methods are used, all data items can be retrieved in approximately the same amount of time regardless of their position on the storage medium and regardless of any logical sequencing of records that might exist.

The processing demands on business databases often include requests requiring quick access to a small amount of selected data from the database. For example, suppose a company has 500,000 customers and operates a hot line that customers can call to request information about the status of their accounts. If account data are stored in a file that can only be accessed sequentially, the database must be searched from the first record until the record of the desired customer is found. On average, 250,000 records will be read to access the one record containing the needed data. Clearly, storage structures providing only **sequential access** to data are inadequate for database systems.

Some form of random access file structure is provided with all types of database systems. A **random access** structure provides a mechanism for quickly finding and retrieving a selected unit of data (record). Under a random access structure, each record within a file can be accessed in approximately the same amount of time, regardless of its location within the file. The random access structures most commonly used in database systems are *index* structures, pointer or *linked list* structures, and *hashing* access methods. Relational databases use index structures

Count-key Data Format		Blocks per Track
Data block (bytes)		
Min.	Max.	
23,221	47,220	1
15,221	23,220	2
11,221	15,220	3
8,821	11,220	4
7,221	8,820	5
6,101	7,220	6
5,237	6,100	7
4,565	5,236	8
4,021	4,564	9
3,605	4,020	10
3,221	3,604	11
2,933	3,220	12
2,677	2,932	13
2,421	2,676	14
2,229	2,420	15
2,069	2,228	16
1,909	2,068	17
1,749	1,908	18
1,621	1,746	19
1,525	1,620	20
1,429	1,524	21
1,333	1,428	22
1,237	1,332	23
1,141	1,236	24
1,077	1,140	25
1,013	1,076	26
949	1,012	27
885	948	28
820	894	29
789	520	30

FIGURE 11.5
3380 Block per Track Capacity

exclusively as their mechanism to provide random access. Hierarchical and network databases may use all three of these types of structures. In the sections that follow, we will first discuss index structures, culminating with an example of how these structures might typically be used by a relational DBMS. Hashing and linked list

FIGURE 11.6
3380 Capacity
per Unit Using
8K Byte Blocks

5 blocks per track

75 blocks per cylinder (5 x 15 surfaces)

66,375 blocks per volume (75 x 885 cylinders)

531,000 K bytes per volume (8K x 66,375 blocks)

4 volumes per unit = 2.124 gigabytes

FIGURE 11.7
Winchester Disk
Track Format

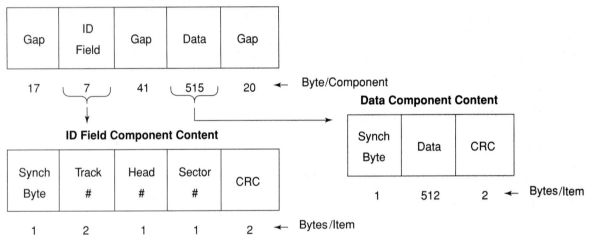

Sector Components

Gap	ID Field	Gap	Data	Gap
17	7	41	515	20	← Byte/Component

Data Component Content

Synch Byte	Data	CRC
1	512	2	← Bytes/Item

ID Field Component Content

Synch Byte	Track #	Head #	Sector #	CRC
1	2	1	1	2	← Bytes/Item

SAMPLE DRIVES

Western Digital AC 34000—4 Gigabytes

Cylinders	7752	Rotation 5200 RPM
Sectors	63	Ave Seek 11.5 ms
Bytes/Sector 512		

Seagate 2520—2.5 Gigabytes

Cylinders	4970	Rotation 5400 RPM
Sectors	63	Ave Seek 11 ms
Bytes/Sector 512		Latency 5.58 ms
		Transfer Rate 16.6 Megabytes/Sec

structures will then be described and an example will illustrate how they might be used in a network or hierarchical database.

INDEX STRUCTURES

An **index** is a list of identified items coupled with an indication of where those items can be found. For example, an index to a book is an alphabetized list of terms coupled with page numbers indicating the page or pages of the book where information about

Index
An ordered list of items coupled with an indication of where those items can be found.

FIGURE 11.8

Index on Customer Name

	Cust-Name	Storage Location
L30	Adams	L57
	Allen	L70
	Bates	L62
L31	Baxter	L53
	Bowers	L72
	Coles	L66
L32	Davis	L58
	Evans	L50
	Gates	L71
L33	Giles	L55
	Howard	L60
	Jones	L52
L34	Law	L65
	Lowell	L76
	Marx	L68
L35	Morris	L63
	Owens	L56
	Packard	L74
L36	Powell	L67
	Randall	L75
	Rice	L51
L37	Rooker	L59
	Smith	L73
	Stone	L54
L38	Tower	L64
	Vance	L61
	White	L69

Customer File

	Cust-ID#	Cust-Name	Cred-Lim ...
L50	8732	Evans	1000 ...
L51	1843	Rice	3000 ...
L52	7629	Jones	1000 ...
L53	3243	Baxter	500 ...
L54	5098	Stone	2000 ...
L55	2764	Giles	1000 ...
L56	7219	Owens	500 ...
L57	4811	Adams	2000 ...
L58	0926	Davis	500 ...
L59	6901	Rooker	3000 ...
L60	3423	Howard	5000 ...
L61	2610	Vance	1000 ...
L62	9802	Bates	500 ...
L63	3767	Morris	3000 ...
L64	7113	Tower	2000 ...
L65	6004	Law	500 ...
L66	8190	Coles	1000 ...
L67	2173	Powell	3000 ...
L68	4006	Marx	500 ...
L69	5811	White	1000 ...
L70	3297	Allen	5000 ...
L71	6829	Gates	500 ...
L72	5047	Bowers	2000 ...
L73	3928	Smith	1000 ...
L74	2488	Packard	500 ...
L75	0649	Randall	1000 ...
L76	9126	Lowell	1000 ...

1st Level Index

	Cust_Name	2nd Level Index Location
L10	Gates	L20
	Packard	L21
	White	L22

FIGURE 11.9
A Multilevel
Index Structure

2nd Level Index

	Cust_Name	3rd Level Index Location
L20	Bates	L30
	Coles	L31
	Gates	L32
L21	Jones	L33
	Marx	L34
	Packard	L35
L22	Rice	L36
	Stone	L37
	White	L38

3rd Level Index on Customer Name

	Cust_Name	Storage Location
L30	Adams	L57
	Allen	L70
	Bates	L62
L31	Baxter	L53
	Bowers	L72
	Coles	L66
L32	Davis	L58
	Evans	L50
	Gates	L71
L33	Giles	L55
	Howard	L60
	Jones	L52
L34	Law	L65
	Lowell	L76
	Marx	L68
L35	Morris	L63
	Owens	L56
	Packard	L74
L36	Powell	L67
	Randall	L75
	Rice	L51
L37	Rooker	L59
	Smith	L73
	Stone	L54
L38	Tower	L64
	Vance	L61
	White	L68

these terms can be found. An index to a file is a list of values for some key identifying attribute or attributes coupled with addresses indicating where records with the specified values for the identifying attribute(s) can be found. The address of a record is a physical location on a secondary storage device. This physical location can very quickly be determined if a record's relative location within its file is known; for example, the requested record begins at the 12,455th byte of storage allocated to the

Number of Levels	3 Entries/Range		5 Entries/Range		7 Entries/Range	
	Number of Items	Number of Items Read	Number of Items Stored	Number of Items Read	Number of Items Stored	Number of Items Read
1	3	2	5	3	7	4
2	9	4	25	6	49	8
3	27	6	125	9	343	12
4	81	8	625	12	2,401	16
5	243	10	3,125	15	16,807	20
6	729	12	15,625	18	117,649	24
7	2,187	14	78,125	21	823,543	28
8	6,561	16	390,625	24	5,764,801	32
9	19,683	18	1,953,125	27	40,353,607	36
10	59,049	20	9,765,625	30	282,475,249	40

FIGURE 11.10
Index Levels versus File Size

file. The address information in most modern indexes is in this file displacement form. However, for the purposes of this discussion, index and pointer addresses will be presented as numbers preceded by the letter L, so that the value L07 stands for storage location 07 on the secondary storage medium.

Figure 11.8 presents a simple index structure providing an index to a customer file based on the attribute Customer Name. The CUSTOMER file contains 27 records, which are stored at the locations indicated by the numbers in front of each record. They are not stored in order with respect to Customer Name or any other attribute. However, the index (left of Customer File) lists each customer name and the location where the data record for that customer can be found. The index is in alphabetical order on Customer Name. Thus, the index could be used to process CUSTOMER records in sorted order based on customer name. It can also be used to find the record for a specified customer whose name is known. Suppose we need to retrieve the CUSTOMER record for Ms. Law. Without an index, we would simply begin reading the records of the CUSTOMER file and continue until we found the record for Ms. Law. In this case, 16 CUSTOMER records would be read. With the index available, we first read just the index. In this case, we would read 13 entries to find Ms. Law. Her entry in the index would tell us where to find her CUSTOMER record—L65. Thus, we would need to read only one CUSTOMER record once the location of that record was found in the index.

This index can substantially reduce the amount of data to be read in order to find a given record. However, if there are a large number of records in a file, searching this type of index could still be quite time consuming. Performance can be improved substantially by using multilevel indexing. This type of indexing is shown in Figure 11.9. Suppose we break our index into ranges. The index is also stored on secondary storage and perhaps we can place three index entries in each index range beginning at a given storage location. We could then create a higher level index that contains the highest valued (latest in the alphabet) name appearing in a given range of the low-level index. For example, in Figure 11.9, the locations of the records for Adams, Allen, and Bates are shown in the 3rd level index range located at L30. Because Bates is the highest value associated with that range, the name Bates is entered in the 2nd level index along with the location L30. The next entry in this 2nd level index indicates that all customers whose names are after Bates alphabetically up to and including Coles will be found in the 3rd level index range at location L31. The 2nd level index is also organized into ranges of three entries each, and an additional index level provides indexing to the ranges of that 2nd level index. For example, all records later than Gates but up to and including Packard will be addressed by the 2nd level index range at L21.

To find Ms. Law's record under this index structure, we would read the first two entries of the 1st level index to determine that her record is addressed in the 2nd level index range at L21 (> Gates and =< Packard). We would then read the first two entries of the 2nd level index, determining that her record is in the 3rd level index range at location L34 (> Jones and <= Marx). Reading the first entry of the 3rd level index tells us that Ms. Law's record is at location L65. A total of 5 index entries were read as opposed to the 13 required with a single-level index.

As the number of records to be accessed grows, the need for multilevel indexing becomes more and more apparent. The number of items that can be indexed increases exponentially with the number of index levels. If each index range has 3 entries, a 2-level index could store 3x3 or 9 records, a 3-level index could store 3x3x3 or 27 records, and so on. The maximum number of records that can be indexed is equal to the number of entries per range times the number of index levels. An index that is 6 levels deep with 3 entries per index range could index up to 3 to the 6th power or 729 records. On average, half of each index range must be searched to process a given request. Thus, with a 6-level index and 3 entries per range, a typical retrieval would require reading 12 index entries (average 2 entries per level times 6 levels) and one data record. By contrast, an average of 365 data records (1/2 of 729) would be read without indexing.

Figure 11.10 indicates the number of levels of indexing required to accommodate various numbers of records given differing numbers of entries in each index range. Note that there is a trade-off between the number of levels of an index and its breadth (the number of entries per index range). Also note that up to several million records can be indexed with multilevel indexes, requiring on average less than 30 index entries to be read to find a given record.

In describing index structures thus far we have assumed that we were dealing with a stable set of data. In database processing this is seldom the case. That is, records are constantly being added to or removed from database files. The structure shown in Figure 11.9 cannot accommodate these changes. To be effective, an index structure must not only be able to provide efficient access, it must also be capable of being readily maintained as records are added to the indexed file. File indexing methods have changed substantially over time. The first type of indexed structure to be widely used was the indexed-sequential access method (ISAM) file structure. In later years, virtual sequential (VSAM) and balanced tree (B-Tree) structures have replaced ISAM structures. We will first discuss the ISAM structure and then examine the VSAM and B-Tree structures widely used in databases today.

Cylinder Index

Cylinder	Highest Key
1	1427
2	2273
3	3065
4	5290
•	

FIGURE 11.11
An Example of the
Indexed Sequential
File Organization

Track Index (Cylinder 1)

Track	Highest Key
1	114
2	263
3	304
•	
11	1427

Track Index (Cylinder 2) . . .

Track	Highest Key
1	1592
2	1634
3	1786
•	
11	2273

Cylinder 1

Track 1	19 Jones . . .	57 Davis . . .	114 Lewis . . .
Track 2	164 Allen . . .	199 Kelly . . .	263 Burns . . .
Track 3	288 Norris . . .	297 Tyler . . .	304 Ricks . . .
•			
Track 11	1359 Evans . . .	1411 Watts . . .	1427 Adams . . .
Track 12	Overflow track (initially empty)		

Cylinder 2

Track 1	1483 Morris . . .	1506 Owens . . .	1592 Gates . . .
Track 2	1609 Tsosie . . .	1622 Howard . . .	1634 Lynd . . .
•			

Indexed-Sequential (ISAM) File Structure

The indexed-sequential (ISAM) structure predates databases and has been widely used in file-oriented processing. When the ISAM structure was first developed, there was very little insulation of programming from the hardware used by a particular computer system. Thus, the index levels developed for the ISAM structure addressed physical units of storage. Figure 11.11 shows an example of an **ISAM file structure.** The lowest level of indexing referenced a track on the physical storage device, the next level of indexing addressed a cylinder, and higher levels addressed ranges of cylinders.

ISAM (Indexed-Sequential Access Method) file structure
Supports both random and sequential access by physically storing data in sequential order, but providing an index structure to allow random access. For ISAM files, the index ranges are fixed.

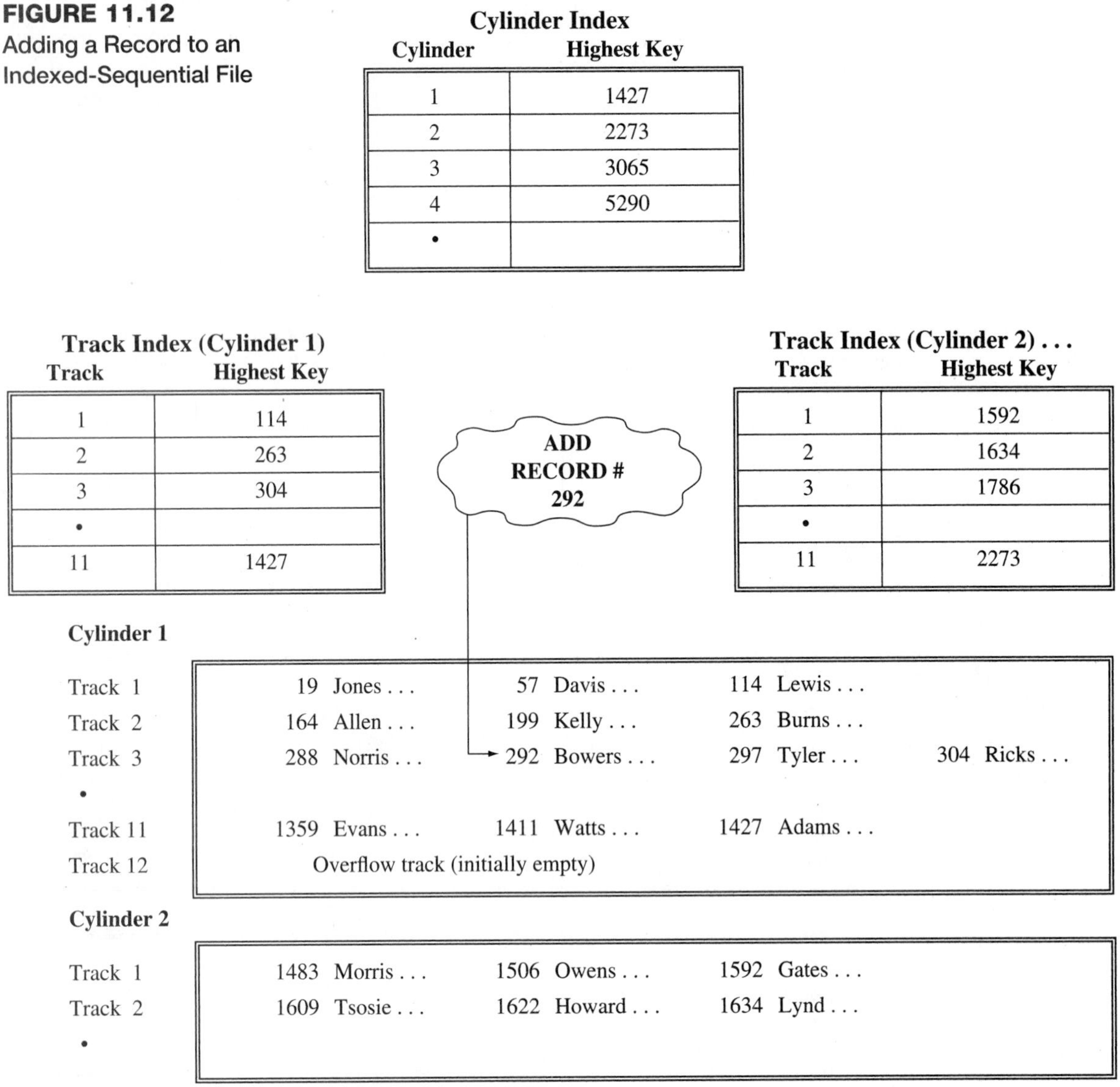

FIGURE 11.12

Adding a Record to an
Indexed-Sequential File

Cylinder Index

Cylinder	Highest Key
1	1427
2	2273
3	3065
4	5290
•	

Track Index (Cylinder 1)

Track	Highest Key
1	114
2	263
3	304
•	
11	1427

Track Index (Cylinder 2) . . .

Track	Highest Key
1	1592
2	1634
3	1786
•	
11	2273

ADD
RECORD #
292

Cylinder 1

Track 1	19 Jones . . .	57 Davis . . .	114 Lewis . . .	
Track 2	164 Allen . . .	199 Kelly . . .	263 Burns . . .	
Track 3	288 Norris . . .	292 Bowers . . .	297 Tyler . . .	304 Ricks . . .
•				
Track 11	1359 Evans . . .	1411 Watts . . .	1427 Adams . . .	
Track 12	Overflow track (initially empty)			

Cylinder 2

Track 1	1483 Morris . . .	1506 Owens . . .	1592 Gates . . .
Track 2	1609 Tsosie . . .	1622 Howard . . .	1634 Lynd . . .
•			

The actual data were stored in the tracks in sequential order, hence the term
indexed-sequential. A number of logical records would be stored on each track and
were kept in sequential order. In addition, the tracks were also maintained in sequence.
Maintaining this structure as records were added and deleted was a major challenge.
To accommodate changes, the ISAM file was initially built with excess space. In
our example, tracks have room for four records, but only three records are initially
stored in each track. This provides some room to add new records. The index structure (track and cylinder indexes) was created at the time the file was initially loaded,

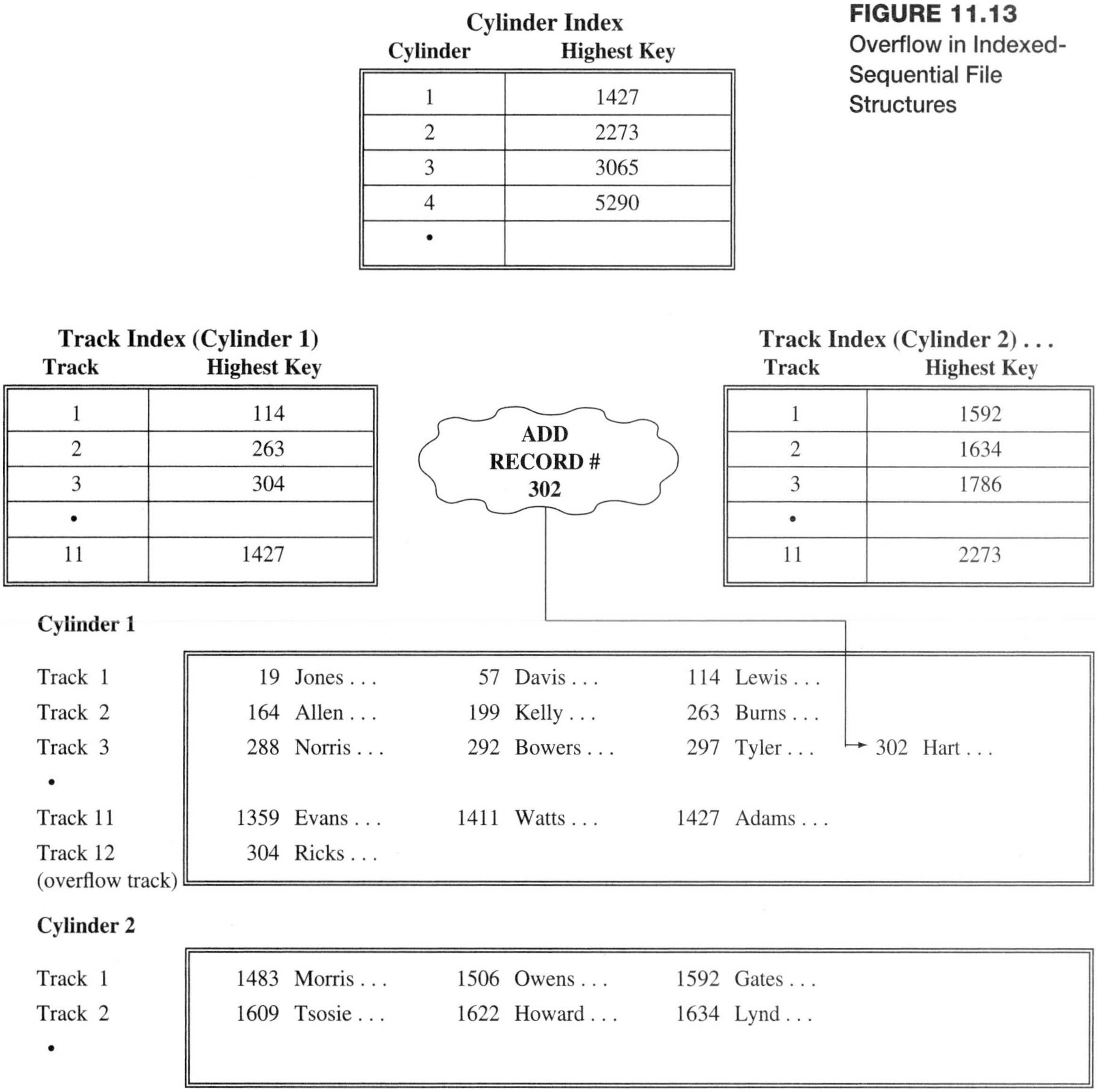

Cylinder Index

Cylinder	Highest Key
1	1427
2	2273
3	3065
4	5290
•	

FIGURE 11.13
Overflow in Indexed-
Sequential File
Structures

Track Index (Cylinder 1)

Track	Highest Key
1	114
2	263
3	304
•	
11	1427

ADD RECORD # 302

Track Index (Cylinder 2) . . .

Track	Highest Key
1	1592
2	1634
3	1786
•	
11	2273

Cylinder 1

Track 1   19 Jones . . .   57 Davis . . .   114 Lewis . . .

Track 2   164 Allen . . .   199 Kelly . . .   263 Burns . . .

Track 3   288 Norris . . .   292 Bowers . . .   297 Tyler . . .   302 Hart . . .

Track 11   1359 Evans . . .   1411 Watts . . .   1427 Adams . . .

Track 12
(overflow track)   304 Ricks . . .

Cylinder 2

Track 1   1483 Morris . . .   1506 Owens . . .   1592 Gates . . .

Track 2   1609 Tsosie . . .   1622 Howard . . .   1634 Lynd . . .

and this structure could not change. Thus, if track 1 indicates a high key of 114 and track 2 a high key of 263, all records whose key value is >114 and =< 263 will always be stored in track 2.

As records are added to the file, there is no particular problem as long as there is additional room in the track where the record is to be added. For example, if we need to add a record whose key value is 292, we would simply determine where this record is to be entered. From the cylinder index, its value is less than 1427, so it is in cylinder 1. From the track index, its value is between 263 and 304, so it belongs in track 3. Now we simply rewrite track 3 to place this record in its proper sequential order. The records for 287 and 304 are moved over and this track is now full. This procedure is illustrated in Figure 11.12.

Eventually, as data continue to be added to the file we will need to add a record to a track that is already full. For example, suppose we now need to add a record for customer number 302. From the cylinder and track index entries, we can see that this record belongs in track 3. However, track 3 is now full. Under ISAM structures, some tracks were always initially left empty as overflow areas. When a record was to be added to a full track, the overflow area was utilized. Records would be written in sequential order within the track and the record or records that didn't fit would be placed in the overflow area. In our case, the records from 288 through 302 fit in track 3 and record number 304 is placed in the overflow area (see Figure 11.13). To connect the record in the overflow area to the records in the original track, a pointer was placed at the end of the track indicating the location of the next record. If still more records were added to track 3, the track would be rewritten again and a chain of pointers would connect the first overflow record for track 3 with the second, and so on. Each overflow record was designed to serve a number of tracks.

Initially, records with this structure were very rapidly and efficiently accessed, but performance tended to deteriorate over time as the number of records in overflow areas increased. It was necessary to completely reorganize the ISAM file structure on a periodic basis in order to maintain reasonably efficient access. Also, any migration to a different storage device required complete file reorganization. Although the ISAM structure was the first to allow the combination of efficient sequential and random access, it has now been replaced by other structures that are independent of the physical storage device and that allow incremental reorganization of the index structure.

Virtual-Sequential (VSAM) File Structure

The Virtual-Sequential Access Method (VSAM) provides a structure that is very similar to the ISAM structure with some nice improvements. The improvements include the ability to expand the file size without much decrease in performance, the ability to maintain an efficient index structure for large file systems, and the ability to have multiple indexes. As the name implies, data records can be processed as if they were in sequential order. However, the blocks storing various sets of records need not be physically in sequence. Most **VSAM file structure** environments in the IBM world are maintained using Key-Sequenced Data Sets (KSDS). The KSDS structure sets up a tree index structure that indexes a sequence set that maintains the highest key stored in each data block. The data blocks are accessed using a relative byte address (RBA) relative to the beginning of the file.

Figure 11.14 presents a VSAM file using a KSDS structure. As with ISAM a number of data records are stored in a block in the data area, and the records in each block are maintained in sequence by the indexing attribute (Customer Number). A multilevel index structure is used to track the location of each record. However, the structures are no longer described in terms of physical units, such as

VSAM (Virtual Sequential Access Method) file structure
Supports both random and sequential access by storing data within sequence sets that can be processed sequentially, but providing an index structure to allow random access. For VSAM files, the index ranges can be modified as data are added to or removed from the file.

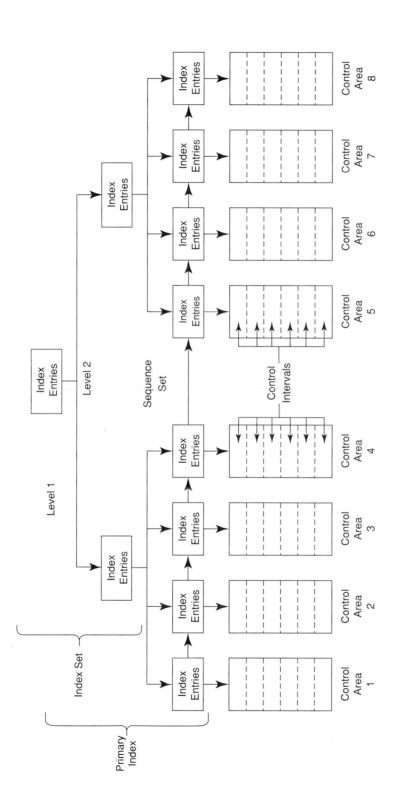

FIGURE 11.14
VSAM Using a
Key-Sequence Data
Set (KSDS) Structure

FIGURE 11.15
VSAM File Example
Using Customer
Numbers

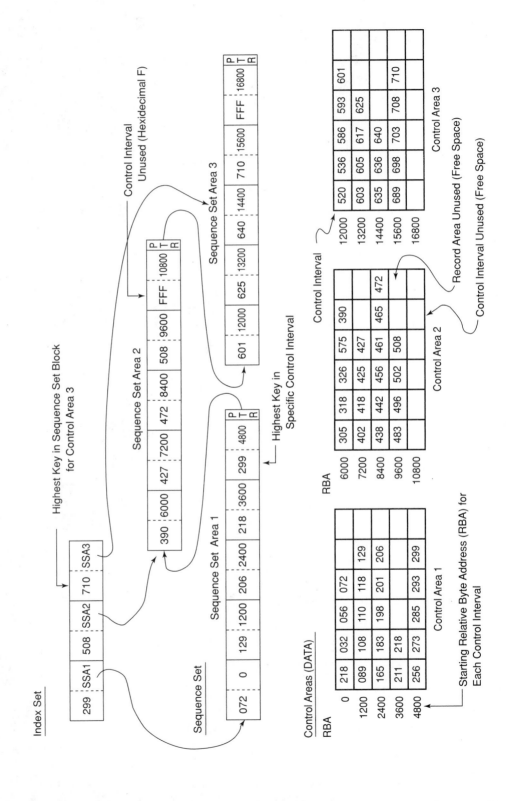

tracks and cylinders. Data records are stored in data blocks called *control intervals*. A control interval is similar to a track concept and can be the same size as a track. Control intervals are stored in an area referred to as a Control Area. A Control Area is similar in concept to a cylinder. The primary index area consists of two parts, an index set and a sequence set. The index set can be multiple levels as the file increases in size. Level 1 *index blocks* point to or index the level 2 index blocks, and level 2 index blocks will index the next level as the levels grow. The last level of index blocks (level 2 in this example) points to the sequence set blocks. One entry in the index set contains the highest key and a pointer to each sequence set block. A sequence set block maintains the highest key and the respective relative byte address (pointer) for each control interval that is part of a control area. The sequence set also maintains a pointer to the sequence set that follows it in logical order by the primary key (Customer Number). Processing a VSAM file in sequential order is done by processing the sequence set for that file, and following the pointers to each control interval within a control area. The control intervals within a control area are not always in logical sequence based on the key, nor are the control areas. It is the sequence set that maintains the logical sequence, allowing the file to be processed in sequence by customer number even though the customer numbers are not maintained strictly in physical sequence.

Processing a VSAM file with random or direct processing where you want to access a specific customer number is done by using the index, similar to ISAM. The difference is that the index structure points to a sequence set that contains a pointer to the data block containing the data. In Figure 11.15, data for customer numbers less than or equal to 299 are found by following the pointer associated with 299 to the sequence set SSA1. If the customer number is greater than 299, but less than or equal to 508, the associated pointer for 508 is used to go to the sequence set SSA2. The index entries in a sequence set are processed the same way as the index entries in an index set in order to locate the specific control interval that contains the data for that customer. The entire data block or control interval is read into memory to obtain the data for that customer. Each control interval maintains an index to all records within that control interval to locate a specific customer number. The index blocks for larger VSAM files will have multiple index levels, as shown in Figure 11.14. The first level will index the second level, and the second level will index a third level as the file grows to speed the process of getting to a specific sequence set that contains the pointer to the appropriate data block. The VSAM index structure is really a B+ -Tree structure, discussed later in this chapter.

One advantage of the VSAM file structure can be seen when new records are added to the file. Data blocks and index ranges are initially set up with some room for expansion, as is shown by the free space in the VSAM file example in Figure 11.15. Space to add new records is normally allowed in each control interval and in each control area when the file is initially built. If a new customer (Customer 60) is added to the example in Figure 11.15, the record would be added to the first control interval between Customers 56 and 72. Customer 72 would be moved to the free space to the right to make room for Customer 60.

VSAM manages file expansion very efficiently through control interval splits and control area splits.

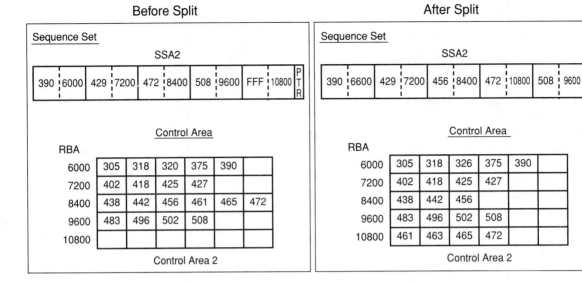

FIGURE 11.16
VSAM Split Interval
Example

Control Interval Split Note that the control interval at location 8400 is full, as shown in Figure 11.15. What will happen if a record belonging in this control interval is added? Suppose Customer 463 is added. The index is followed from the index set to the sequence set for area 2 (SSA2) to the control interval 8400. Because control interval 8400 has no additional room, the control interval will be split, as shown in Figure 11.16. The lowest three records (half the records) remain in the existing control interval 8400. The remaining records are moved to a control interval that is empty within the same control area (10800 in this example). Customer 463 is placed in this control interval because 463 goes between Customers 461 and 465.

The index sequence set for this control area must also be updated to reflect the change in keys for the control intervals. Note the changes in SSA2 (Figure 11.16) after the split. The highest customer number in control interval 8400 is now Customer 456 instead of Customer 472. Customers above 456 and less than or equal to 472 are now in control interval 10800. Note that the customer numbers are always in sequence within the index sequence set. However, the control interval addresses are not in sequence. When this control area is processed sequentially, control interval 10800 is processed after control interval 8400, and control interval 9600 is processed after control interval 10800. Remember that VSAM sequential processing is accomplished by using the index sequence sets to access the data in sequence by primary key.

Control Area Split What happens when there are no more unused control intervals within a control area? A VSAM structure can add new control areas with unused control intervals as the file expands. A control area with no more unused control intervals can be split the same way a control interval is split, moving half the

INDEX
SETS

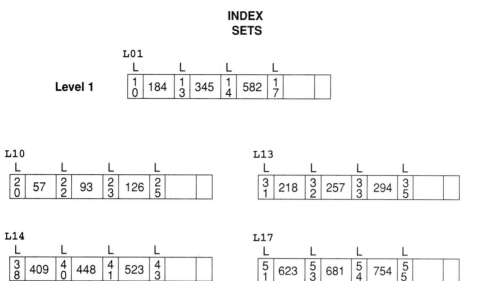

Level 1

L01

| L 1 0 | 184 | L 1 3 | 345 | L 1 4 | 582 | L 1 7 | | |

Level 2

L10

| L 2 0 | 57 | L 2 2 | 93 | L 2 3 | 126 | L 2 5 | | |

L13

| L 3 1 | 218 | L 3 2 | 257 | L 3 3 | 294 | L 3 5 | | |

L14

| L 3 8 | 409 | L 4 0 | 448 | L 4 1 | 523 | L 4 3 | | |

L17

| L 5 1 | 623 | L 5 3 | 681 | L 5 4 | 754 | L 5 5 | | |

SEQUENCE SET

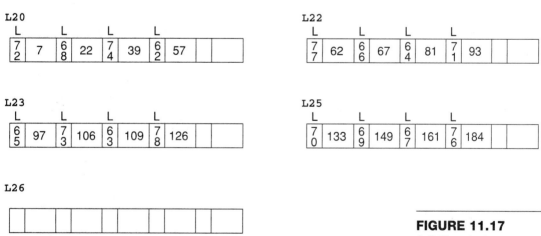

L20

| L 7 2 | 7 | L 6 8 | 22 | L 7 4 | 39 | L 6 2 | 57 | |

L22

| L 7 7 | 62 | L 6 6 | 67 | L 6 4 | 81 | L 7 1 | 93 | |

L23

| L 6 5 | 97 | L 7 3 | 106 | L 6 3 | 109 | L 7 8 | 126 | |

L25

| L 7 0 | 133 | L 6 9 | 149 | L 6 7 | 161 | L 7 6 | 184 | |

L26

FIGURE 11.17
A B-Tree Index
Structure

control intervals from the split control area to the new control area. The split control area now has unused control intervals that can be used for control interval splits. The pointer in the sequence set for the split control area is updated to point to the new control area, and the pointer in the sequence set for the new control area is set to the pointer that was originally in the sequence set of the split control area.

The actual physical implementation of VSAM structures varies for different platforms. Implementations in the IBM environment normally use a Key-Sequenced Data Set (KSDS) as discussed earlier. The index set is a hierarchical structure of keys that point to different blocks in a sequence set similar to a B-Tree structure, explained in the next section. The sequence set stores the values of the highest key for every data block in key sequence. The sequence set carries a pointer to the control interval, and a pointer to the next block in the sequence set allowing the sequence set to be processed sequentially. This is an extension of B-Tree structure that is referred to as a B+ Tree, also discussed later in this chapter. VSAM files can be processed sequentially or dynamically using the sequence set. Dynamic processing means that an application can enter a sequence set with a key at any point and process the data records sequentially from that point by following the sequence sets.

B-Tree Index Structures

A B-Tree is a balanced, multiway tree that has a specific set of characteristics. The B in B-Tree stands for *balanced*. This means that the number of index levels is the same for all data. As deletions and additions are made to the data that we are indexing, the processing algorithm of the **B-tree index structure** must reorganize the index structure as needed to maintain this balance.

B-tree index structure
An index structure that has an algorithm that incrementally adjusts the index structure to maintain a balanced depth of index ranges as data are added to or deleted from the database.

This structure is illustrated in Figure 11.17. The sequence set is the lowest level of the index. A range of the sequence set lists each individual Customer Number in its range, preceded by the storage location where that individual data record can be found. The Customer Number values in each sequence set range are maintained in sequential order. The actual data records can now be in any order on the disk. New records may simply be added to the end of the file, regardless of their Customer Number value (this is commonly done in PC-based relational DBMSs) or they may be in order based on some other attribute. The physical ordering of the data records no longer matters, because we have a sequence set of pointers to allow record-by-record retrieval in order by the attribute indexed in our B-Tree structure.

As records are added, the structure is adjusted similarly to VSAM. If a record is added to a sequence set that has additional room, the sequence set is simply rewritten to include the new item in its proper sequential order. Figure 11.18 illustrates this for records 88 and 72.

Suppose, however, a new record is to be added to a sequence set that is full. If the sequence set can be split without increasing the depth of the index structure, it is split in a manner very similar to that shown for VSAM files. Figure 11.19 shows the results of adding record 122. Now suppose a record to be added belongs in a sequence set that is full and the index set range that the sequence set belongs to is also full. In such cases, adjacent ranges in the index are searched for available space. If space is available in some sequence set, the index structure is reorganized as needed to accommodate the new data without increasing the depth of the index. This reorganization will include changes to one or more ranges in the index set, as necessary. After the reorganization, each range in the sequence set must remain in sequential order.

The depth (number of index levels) in a B-Tree index will be increased only if all ranges are full at its current depth and a new data item is to be added. At this point, ranges are split so that the index becomes one level deeper with a balanced amount of free space across all ranges of the index and sequence sets. Similarly, if sufficient deletions occur to allow the depth of the index to be reduced, the processing algorithm performs the required reorganization.

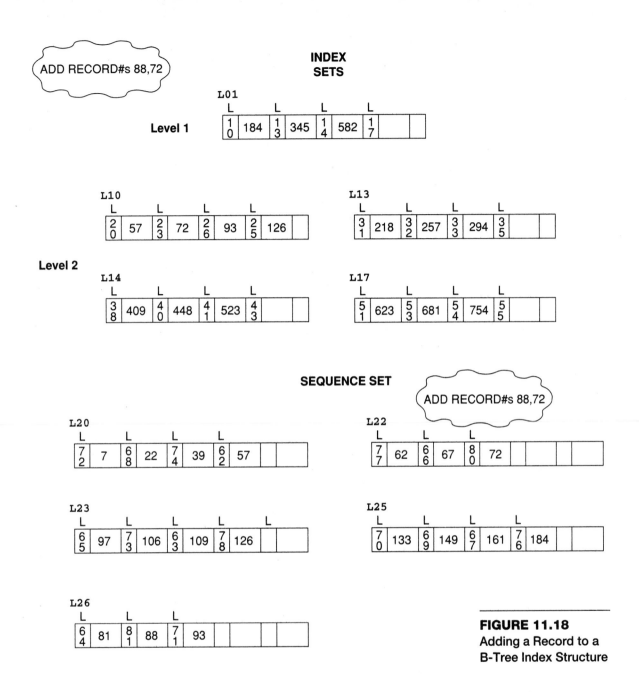

FIGURE 11.18
Adding a Record to a
B-Tree Index Structure

The complex processing algorithm used by B-Tree indexes causes them to be incrementally reorganized as changes to the indexed data occur. This incremental reorganization prevents the deterioration of performance that can occur in ISAM. With B-Tree indexes there is no need to periodically reorganize the index to improve performance.

The term B+ Tree (B Plus Tree) is used for a special type of B-Tree that has an extra pointer added to each range of its sequence set. That extra pointer points to the

B+ tree index structure
An index structure with all the properties of the B-Tree structure but with additional pointers in its sequence set that support sequential processing without reference to higher levels of the index.

INDEX SETS

Level 1

L01

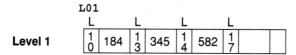

L		L		L		L		
10	184	13	345	14	582	17		

Level 2

L10

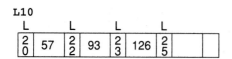

L		L		L		L		
20	57	22	93	23	126	25		

L13

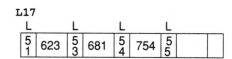

L		L		L		L		
31	218	32	257	33	294	35		

L14

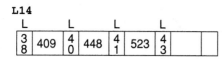

L		L		L		L		
38	409	40	448	41	523	43		

L17

L		L		L		L		
51	623	53	681	54	754	55		

SEQUENCE SET

L20

L		L		L		L		
72	7		22	74	39	62	57	

L22

L		L		L		L		
77	62	66	67	64	81	71	93	

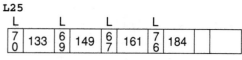

ADD RECORD# 122

L25

L		L		L		L		
70	133	69	149	67	161	76	184	

L23

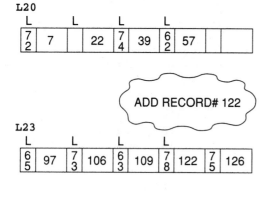

L		L		L		L		
65	97	73	106	63	109	78	122	75	126

L26

FIGURE 11.19
Splitting a Sequence
Set in a B-Tree
Index Structure

sequence set containing the next sequential range of values. With these pointers in place, a file can be processed sequentially without reference to its higher level indexes.

Clusters

In VSAM, a dataset (physical file space) is defined as a cluster. It is the physical file area that contains the indexes and data areas for the VSAM file. The IBM DEFINE CLUSTER command for a VSAM dataset defines the name of the dataset, the record size, the position and length of the key in the record, the volume (disk) where the dataset is to be stored, the primary and secondary allocation of tracks, and the names to be used for the data space and the index space. Secondary indexes in VSAM are referred to as *alternate indexes*. An alternate index in VSAM is another Key-Sequenced Data Set (KSDS). A KSDS groups all control areas within a dataset into a cluster. The data records make up the BASE cluster, the primary index is referred to as the PRIME INDEX cluster, and each alternate index is referred to as an ALTER-NATE INDEX cluster. The ALTERNATE INDEX cluster has the index ordered by alternate key. The data area of the ALTERNATE INDEX cluster consists of a matching pair that contains the alternate key and a corresponding primary key. This primary key is used to search the PRIME INDEX cluster for the actual record containing the information for the alternate key. The KSDS structure allows the processing of duplicates on the same key, because the index can be processed sequentially. If we were processing all records for a specific ZIP Code, we could get to the first occurrence using the index in the ALTERNATE INDEX cluster, and then process the alternate index sequence set sequentially on that ZIP Code because all the entries for a specific ZIP Code have been clustered together.

Clusters are also used to set up tables for relational database systems. A cluster can be set up to include multiple tables that have a close relationship to each other. In the Airwest Airline application we may want to put the PASSENGER table together with the TICKET table in the same physical space clustered on itinerary number. For example, the SQL statement CREATE CLUSTER passenger_ticket (cluster_key_itinerary number) would create a cluster space. Then the statements CREATE TABLE passenger (itinerary_no number, etc.) CLUSTER passenger_ticket (itinerary_no), and CREATE TABLE ticket (itinerary_no number, etc) CLUSTER passenger_ticket (itinerary_no) will be created in the same space with one itinerary number. Itinerary number can be set up as a clustered index with the CREATE INDEX ix_itinerary on CLUSTER passenger_ticket. Clustering can save disk space and improve the access time on data that are accessed frequently as a unit, such as a passenger and all related tickets.

Nonunique Indexes

The index structures we have shown thus far have assumed that the indexing variable uniquely identifies a single record in the file. However, nonunique indexes are often used to identify sets of related records. Foreign key attributes are an important example of a type of nonunique attribute that should be indexed to speed retrieval. The index structure for a nonunique index would be very similar to the B-Tree structure shown earlier except that at the lowest index level, each attribute value would be associated with a pointer to a location containing a list of pointers to all the data records having that value for the index variable.

Index Structures in Relational DBMSs

Relational DBMSs make extensive use of index structures to speed processing. Whenever a SQL retrieval is requested, a system file listing all available indexes is searched. Any available indexes that can speed processing of the request are used. If a condition is specified on an indexed field, the condition is tested on the index values and only qualifying data records are actually retrieved. Similarly, when joins of tables are required, the indexes are used and only the matching entries from the data tables are actually retrieved. Most PC-based relational DBMSs use B-Tree index structures exclusively for unique indexes. Data are actually always physically added to the end of the database tables, but maintained in order through B-Tree indexes.

Relational DBMSs that can be used on mini-computers and mainframes often support VSAM-like block structures as well as B-Trees. These structures can be used for only one sorting order for any given table. For example, we could request that all orders made by the same customer be placed in the same block of storage whenever possible. If retrievals frequently involve looking up a customer and then retrieving all his or her orders, this method could speed processing substantially. A single access to secondary storage might retrieve a data block containing all the orders for a particular customer. Where this type of ordering is possible, it is requested by adding a CLUSTER BY clause to the CREATE TABLE statement. In our example,

```
CREATE TABLE order . . . CLUSTER order_customer (c_id_number)
```

would be used to create the desired data storage blocks.

FIGURE 11.20

A Hashed File Structure

(11 Buckets, 3 Slots/Bucket)

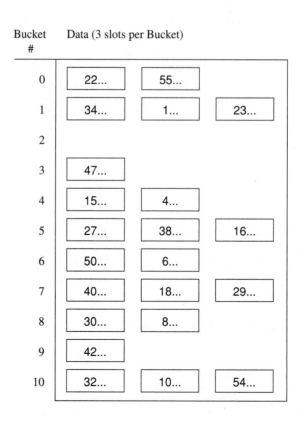

Bucket #	Data (3 slots per Bucket)		
0	22...	55...	
1	34...	1...	23...
2			
3	47...		
4	15...	4...	
5	27...	38...	16...
6	50...	6...	
7	40...	18...	29...
8	30...	8...	
9	42...		
10	32...	10...	54...

HASHING STRUCTURES

Hashing is a pure direct access storage method. It simply uses a mathematical algorithm performed on the value of some key attribute to determine the storage location of a record. This provides the fastest possible access to a random individual record. However, hashing methods do not support sequential access. Hashing will have to be supplemented by other organization methods if sequential access is needed.

Under hashing, data records are stored in blocks called *buckets,* and it is assumed that several logical data records can be stored in each bucket (physical record). Each logical record is called a *slot.*

A number of buckets is assigned to a file and the algorithm used for storage and retrieval assigns each record to a bucket. If more records are assigned to a bucket than the number of available slots, an overflow situation similar to that described for ISAM structures occurs. To limit overflows, a hashed file is never completely filled initially.

The hashing algorithm is designed to allocate records as randomly as possible across buckets in order to further reduce the probability of overflows. Typically, a prime number of buckets is chosen and the key value is then divided by that prime number with the remainder from that division determining the bucket in which the record will be stored. For example, suppose 19 buckets have been allocated for a file. A record whose key field value is 71 would be stored in bucket 14 ($71/19 = 3$ *remainder 14*).This algorithm will work because it is repeatable for the purposes of retrieval. To retrieve record 71 we simply repeat the computation producing the same result and go to bucket 14 to find our data. When an alphabetic field is used as the key for hashing, its characters are simply converted to numeric equivalents by ignoring their high-order bits. The ordering of characters in the key field can even be scrambled by the algorithm to further assure randomness. It is only necessary that whatever algorithm is used to store records be repeatable for the purpose of retrieval.

Figure 11.20 shows an example of a hashing structure with 11 buckets, each containing 3 slots. Notice that the buckets are numbered 0 through 10, corresponding to the possible remainder values when dividing by 11. Twenty-two records have been stored in this structure. You can verify for yourself that each record is in the correct slot. At this point, no buckets have overflowed, but some buckets are already full.

As records are added to and removed from the file, some buckets will inevitably overflow. Figure 11.21 illustrates how this problem is normally handled. Step A illustrates the effects of adding record number 36. In this case, the record hashes to 3 ($36/11 = 3$ *remainder 3*). There is an empty slot in bucket 3, so record 36 is simply added to its correct bucket.

Step B shows what happens if we attempt to add record 12. This record hashes to 1, but bucket 1 is full. At this point, record 12 could be placed in an overflow area and connected via a pointer in bucket 1. This method was used in some early hashing structures. However, most hashing structures in use today simply call for the overflowing record to be placed in the next available bucket. In our case, bucket 2 is empty, so record 12 is placed there.

This obviously changes the retrieval algorithm. If a record hashes to a bucket that is full, but the desired record can't be found in that bucket, we must search the next

Hashing
An access method that determines the storage location of a record based on a mathematical algorithm performed on some key attribute of that record. Hashing supports direct access, but not sequential access.

FIGURE 11.21

Handling Overflows in a Hashed File

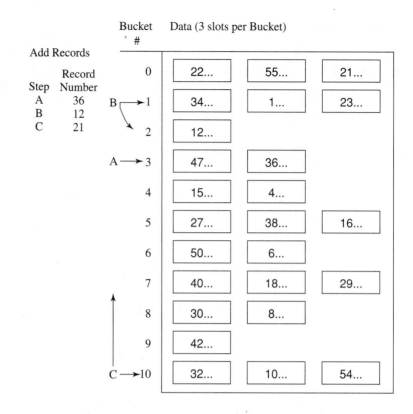

Add Records

Step	Record Number
A	36
B	12
C	21

sequential bucket. This process is repeated until the desired record is found or a bucket with empty slots is found. If a bucket with empty slots is found without finding the requested record, we can conclude that the record is not stored in the file. The algorithm for managing overflows must also make provision for moving displaced records back to their correct bucket if space becomes available.

Step C of Figure 11.21 illustrates how the overflow method is applied to records at the bottom of the file. Record 21 hashes to bucket 10, which is full. Because this is the last bucket, it rolls over to bucket 0 at the top of the file.

Now suppose we added record 5 to the file. This record obviously hashes to 5 and because bucket 5 is full, it would be stored in bucket 6. Now suppose we add record 17. This record hashes to 6 and would be placed there except that record 5 has filled the last available slot. This illustrates the concept of a *coalesced chain*. Record 17 belongs in slot 6 and could fit there except for the effects of another record (5) that does not really hash to bucket 6. Some systems have algorithms designed to find and correct coalesced chaining. Under such a system, record 17 would go into bucket 6 and record 5 would be moved to the next available slot (in bucket 8). This method minimizes the number of displaced records.

Linked list
A data structure in which each record in the linked set contains a pointer to the next record in the set. Thus, the set of related records can be retrieved using data stored with each record, without reference to a separate index.

POINTER (LINKED LIST) STRUCTURES

A **linked list** is essentially a structure that incorporates the concept of an index into the data records themselves. Instead of having a separate index structure containing pointers to related records, each record in a file has a field or fields that point to related records. When a record is processed, the values in its pointer fields are used to determine which record to access next.

Figure 11.22 illustrates this concept using a set of pointers designed to allow processing of a file of CREW records in alphabetical order by the crew member's name.

	ID#	Name	Job Title	Sequential Name Ptr.
		CREW		
L1	345	Lewis	Steward	L5
L2	218	Allen	Pilot	L4
L3	746	Jones	Navigator	L1
L4	531	Barnes	Steward	L3
L5	412	Smith	Pilot	*

FIGURE 11.22
A Linked List Structure
Head Name Ptr.: L2

	ID#	Name	Job Title	Sequential Name Ptr.	1st. Assmt. Pointer
		CREW			
L1	345	Lewis	Steward	L5	L13
L2	218	Allen	Pilot	L4	L12
L3	746	Jones	Navigator	L1	L11
L4	531	Barnes	Steward	L3	*
L5	412	Smith	Pilot	*	L14

	Date	Hours	Next Assmt. Pointer
	ASSIGNMENT		
L11	1/22/98	5	L17
L12	1/22/98	6	L16
L13	1/22/98	5	L15
L14	1/24/98	4	L5
L15	1/25/98	3	L18
L16	1/25/98	4	L19
L17	1/26/98	5	L3
L18	1/26/98	4	L20
L19	1/27/98	6	L2
L20	1/27/98	5	L1

FIGURE 11.23
A Linked List Structure Connecting Two Tables
Head Name Ptr.: L2

A head pointer record stores the first record in the list. In this case it indicates that the record located at L2, the record for Allen, should be read first. When the L2 record is processed, its pointer field contains the location of the next record that should be processed, L4 in this case. The L4 record in turn points to L3, which is to be retrieved next, and so on. When the last record in this linked list of pointers is processed, it contains a null pointer (an asterisk in Figure 11.22) which indicates that we have reached the end of the chain.

If we needed to process the CREW table in order by ID# as well as by Name, we would create a second set of pointers to process the records in order by the attribute ID#. Its head pointer would also point to L2 in this instance. However, that record would point to L1, which would point to L5. The L5 record would point to L4 and that record would point to L3. Any number of pointer sets can be created to facilitate processing based on various logical relationships that exist among data records.

Linked lists can also be created that link records across multiple files. It is this feature of linked list structures that has been used most extensively in database systems. Figure 11.23 illustrates a linked list of pointers across two files. An ASSIGNMENT file has been added to the CREW file that was shown in Figure 11.22. Each crew member may have one or more *assignments* to work a certain number of hours on a particular flight on a specified date. We want to establish a set of linked lists, one for each crew member, that will link the crew member to all his or her work assignment records. Note that there is a one to many relationship between CREW and ASSIGNMENT records. For this type of linked list, there is an owner record type—CREW—and a member record type—ASSIGNMENT. There is only one owner record in each list of pointers, but there may be several members.

In this structure there is no separate head pointer. The pointer in the owner file for a given record is the head pointer; it points to the first member record in a linked list of member records belonging to that owner record. For instance, the CREW record for Lewis, L1, contains a 1st Assmt. Pointer to the record at location L13 in the ASSIGNMENT file. It, in turn, contains a pointer to the record at L15, the next ASSIGNMENT record associated with the crew member Lewis. This record points to the ASSIGNMENT record at L18, which, in turn, points to the record at L20. The ASSIGNMENT record at L20 is the last assignment for Lewis. The last record in a linked list will either contain a null pointer or point back to the head of the list, creating a chain. For the name pointers, we used a null pointer to terminate the list. The assignment pointers, however, are shown as chains with the last member pointing back to the head of the list. Thus, the record at L20 points to L1, the location of the Lewis CREW record.

A similar chain of pointers exists for each of the CREW records, linking it to the set of ASSIGNMENT records belonging to that CREW record. To verify this, follow the pointer chains for the Allen and Jones CREW records. The crew member Barnes has no assignments and, thus, his CREW record contains a null value for the 1st Assmt. Pointer.

Because the assignment pointers have been formed into a complete chain or circle, they can be used either to retrieve the set of assignments for a given crew member or to find the crew member associated with a given assignment record. For example, suppose we need to know the name of the crew member to which ASSIGNMENT

Head Name Ptr.: L2

CREW

	ID#	Name	Job Title	Sequential Name Ptr.	1st. Assmt. Pointer	Last Assmt. Pointer
L1	345	Lewis	Steward	L5	L13	L20
L2	218	Allen	Pilot	L4	L12	L19
L3	746	Jones	Navigator	L1	L11	L17
L4	531	Barnes	Steward	L3	*	*
L5	412	Smith	Pilot	*	L14	L14

ASSIGNMENT

	Date	Hours	Next Assmt. Pointer	Prior Assmt. Pointer	Owner CREW Ptr.
L11	1/22/98	5	L17	L3	L3
L12	1/22/98	6	L16	L2	L2
L13	1/22/98	5	L15	L1	L1
L14	1/24/98	4	L5	L5	L5
L15	1/25/98	3	L18	L13	L1
L16	1/25/98	4	L19	L12	L2
L17	1/26/98	5	L3	L11	L3
L18	1/26/98	4	L20	L15	L1
L19	1/27/98	6	L2	L16	L2
L20	1/27/98	5	L1	L18	L1

FIGURE 11.24
A Linked List Structure with Prior and Owner Pointers
Head Name Ptr.: L2

record L16 belongs. Record L16 points to another ASSIGNMENT record at L19. However, the record at L19 points to L2, the CREW record for the crew member Allen.

Notice that the only thing linking a CREW record to its related ASSIGNMENT records is the ASSIGNMENT pointer chain. If the pointer value on any of the records in the chain becomes damaged, the chain is broken. Because this pointer chain is the only thing that identifies the crew member to whom assignments belong, potentially all the assignment records for a given CREW member could become lost if the chain is broken. Because of this risk, dual chains of pointers are often created. A set of *forward* pointers links the owner to the first member record and it to the next and so on until the last member points back to the owner. A set of *prior* pointers links the owner record to the last member record and it to the prior record and so on until the first member points back to the owner. Owner pointers can also be added to each member record so that each member points directly back to its owner record. This provides additional protection from lost data and speeds processing when there are long pointer chains. Figure 11.24 shows the CREW and ASSIGNMENT files with prior and owner pointers added.

ACCESS METHODS FOR THE NETWORK DATA MODEL

The network data model typically utilizes a combination of hashing and pointer structures. Hashing is used to establish an appropriate entry point to the database, and linked list pointer chains are used to find related data once an entry point is established.

Linked list pointer chains like the ones described earlier are used to implement intertable relationships in the network data model. For each relationship, a pointer chain is established. A table that has relationships with several other tables would participate in one set of pointers for each of its relationships.

Hashing is used in the network model to establish an entry point to the database. If users will want to access the database by directly supplying the value of a key attribute of a table, that table will be stored using hashing based on the value of the key attribute.

Once the entry point has been established through hashing, pointer chains can be followed to retrieve related data as needed. If our CREW and ASSIGNMENT tables were implemented in a network model, the CREW table would be stored using hashing on the ID# attribute with a linked list pointer chain (or a set of next, prior, and perhaps owner pointer chains) used to link each CREW record to a set of ASSIGNMENT records. To retrieve the assignments for an individual, the individual's ID# would be supplied by the user. This would be used to hash to the correct CREW record. Then the pointer chain for that CREW record would be followed to retrieve all the related ASSIGNMENT records.

The combination of hashing and pointers provides for very efficient retrieval of a selected set of data. Hashing establishes an entry point with just one access to secondary storage. Then each record retrieved contains the address of the next record that should be retrieved. No additional retrievals from secondary storage are needed to obtain external index information. Thus, only one access to secondary storage is required to retrieve each record that will be processed.

Data are normally stored in physical records or blocks large enough to hold several logical records. Methods similar to those discussed for the clustering of records under the relational model can be used under the network model to store several related logical records in the same physical block. Thus, one access to secondary storage can often retrieve several related records needed by an application.

SUMMARY

The movement of data between primary and secondary storage is an important potential bottleneck to the efficient operation of database systems. The time required to position a direct access storage device (DASD), such as a magnetic disk, for retrieval of a random set of data is largely relative to the time required to read or write data. Because of this, reading and writing is often done on physical records or blocks of data that are large enough to hold several logical records. When this is the case, it is important to attempt, whenever possible, to store highly related records together in the same physical storage block.

Indexes are ordered lists of items and the locations where those items can be found. One of the first index structures was the Indexed-Sequential Access Method (ISAM). This structure stores data sequentially on the basis of some key attribute, but adds an index that allows random access to a data block containing the desired record. Index ranges are fixed under ISAM. This means that overflow areas will be used and that performance will deteriorate over time, requiring periodic restructuring of the entire file. A Virtual-Sequential (VSAM) structure is very similar to the ISAM structure, except that the index ranges are managed as a B-Trees, and there can be multiple indexes. A B-Tree structure is a type of index designed to incrementally adjust the index structure in a way that assures that the depth of the index (the number of levels accessed to get to a data item) is the same for all items in the file. A B-Tree structure is completely separate from the data of a file. The bottom level of the B-Tree index is a sequence set, which lists each record in order by the indexing attribute and indicates the location of the data. Thus, the data need not be in order based on the indexing attribute, and multiple unique B-Tree indexes (for different attributes) can be established for the same file of data. Sequence sets that are implemented with a pointer to point to the next sequence set in sequential order is a variation called a B+ Tree. Relational databases make extensive use of B-Tree structures and many also utilize VSAM structures to improve the efficiency of storage and retrieval.

Hashing is an access method that uses the value of a key attribute to determine the storage location of a record. Specifically, the remainder from the process of dividing the key by the number of blocks is used to assign the storage location using a prime number. Hashing supports very rapid direct access, but does not support sequential access.

Many data records are stored in relative file systems using linked list systems. The records are linked together using pointers. A pointer is an address of the location of a specific record. Pointer chains are created by embedding a pointer to the next related record in the data of each record in the chain. A pointer chain linking an owner record with all the member records belonging to that owner can be used to implement one to many relationships between entities. This mechanism is used extensively by the network data model to implement intertable relationships. In the network model, hashing is used to establish an entry point to the database and then pointer chains are used to navigate the database.

_____ The element of a disk that is one concentric circle on a surface.

REVIEW QUIZ

_____ The smallest portion of a disk that contains data.

_____ The portion of a disk that consists of the same relative concentric circle on all surfaces.

_____ A file structure that can process records sequentially or in a direct (random) mode.

_____ A file structure that supports a primary index and multiple secondary indexes.

_____ The element of an ISAM file structure that supports direct processing of records.

_____ The time needed for one rotation of a disk.

_____ The time needed for the heads to move to another cylinder.

_____ The time needed for the data to move from a disk to a buffer in memory.

_____ An index system that supports leveling such that any key can be found with the same number of search levels in the hierarchy.

_____ An index system that supports the processing of records sequentially when the data blocks are not in sequence.

_____ A data structure that uses pointers to connect logically related records.

_____ A method to distribute logical records into physical records by using a mathematical algorithm.

_____ The address used to locate another record in the same file or another file.

_____ The number used to divide by in a hashing algorithm.

_____ Another name for a data block in VSAM.

_____ Adding pointers to a sequence set to point to the next sequence set in sequence.

_____ Typical structure used for VSAM files implemented in IBM environments.

_____ A sequence set indexes all the control intervals in a(n) _____.

_____ Processing a VSAM file sequentially starting at some point within the file.

_____ Method of adding records to a full block in VSAM.

1. Rotational delay
2. Seek time
3. Track
4. Sector
5. Cylinder

6. Surface
7. Block
8. VSAM
9. ISAM
10. B-tree
11. Prime
12. Pointer
13. Linked list
14. Transfer time
15. Index
16. Hashing
17. Control interval
18. Control area
19. B+ - tree
20. KSDS
21. Dynamic processing
22. Sequential processing
23. Split control interval

---

1. Why is the process of moving data between primary and secondary memory so crucial to the performance of database systems?
2. Describe the physical storage structures of magnetic disk storage—blocks, tracks, and cylinders.
3. What determines the "optimal size" of a physical storage block in secondary storage?
4. Describe the components of disk access time—seek time, rotational delay, and data transfer time.
5. Describe the ISAM file structure. What are its major advantages and limitations?
6. When using ISAM, a file was initially set up only 70–75 percent full and overflow areas were used. Why was this necessary?
7. Describe the VSAM file structure. What are the principal differences between VSAM and ISAM?
8. Describe the B-Tree index structure. What does the B in B-Tree stand for? What added feature does a B+ Tree have?
9. What is the role of the CLUSTER BY clause of a CREATE TABLE SQL statement? How can it be used to improve processing efficiency?
10. Describe the incremental adjustment to the index structure that is used by VSAM and B-Tree indexes. Why is this feature so important?

REVIEW QUESTIONS AND EXERCISES

11. Describe the hashing access method. Discuss how clashes (overflows) are commonly handled.

12. Describe how linked lists are used to implement one to many relationships among different entity types.

13. Why are dual (next and prior) and owner pointers commonly used in databases utilizing linked list access?

14. Describe how hashing and linked lists are combined under the network model to provide database access and manipulation.

15. Assume that a file has been stored on disk using hashing based on the remainder method. Data are stored in 113 buckets with 5 slots in each bucket. The field used for hashing is Order Number.

   a. In which bucket would Order Number 184 be placed? Order Number 342?

   b. What happens if an Order Number calculates to a bucket that is full?

   c. When can we conclude that an Order Number for which we are searching is not in the hash file?

16. Assume that the accompanying file (Figure 11.25) is stored using hashing based on the remainder method with 13 buckets and 4 slots per bucket.

   a. Indicate where each of the following records would be stored (assuming they are added to the file in the order indicated): 44, 31, 53, 135.

   b. Suppose we attempt to retrieve each of the following records: 139, 21, 54, 35. For each of these records, indicate which bucket(s) would be searched and whether the record would be found.

17. Based on the B-Tree index shown, indicate changes to the index required to add each of the following records: 450, 270, 510, 720, 530.

18. Assume an application of maintaining 30,000 student records with a master record on each student holding 400 bytes. Assume 8,000-byte blocks, a 3380 disk system, and 75 percent fill factors.

   a. How many cylinders would be needed to store the file assuming sequential storage?

   b. How many cylinders would be needed to store the data records assuming ISAM/VSAM?

   c. How many cylinders would be needed to store the data records assuming relative file structure?

   d. How many blocks would be used to store the data assuming relative file structure?

   e. Using a prime number or an odd number with a magnitude close to the number of blocks, in what block would the social security number 473826632 be stored?

19. Set up a linked list structure to store the student data using hashing on social security number to store the records, and using linked lists to store the data in social security number sequence.

Bucket
Data (4 Slots per Bucket)

FIGURE 11.25

Bucket #	Data (4 Slots per Bucket)			
0	26	13		
1	40	1	131	
2	28	41	2	67
3	3	54		
4	30			
5	18	70	5	
6	71	6	19	32
7	33	20	46	59
8	8			
9	48	22	9	74
10	62	36	23	139
11	50			
12	12	51	64	

20. Set up a sample index structure for ISAM and for VSAM and using a B-Tree to index the student data. Show sample social security numbers in a range from 100 to 999. Use Figures 11.10 through 11.16 as examples.

21. Use the Web to find the latest specifications on disk drives and compare the structures on three different drives. Western Digital is www.wdc.com and Seagate is www.seagate.com.

DISTRIBUTED DATABASE SYSTEMS

12

LEARNING OBJECTIVES

After completing this chapter, you should be able to

- Describe the transparency concept and identify the dimensions of transparency that are important for distributed systems.

- Distinguish between replication and partitioning of data and between vertical and horizontal partitioning, and be able to discuss the advantages and disadvantages of each method.

- Propose an appropriate distribution of a database across a set of nodes based on a description of how the database will be used.

- Describe the uses and limitations of linkages to external databases through Attached Tables or Create Database Link commands.

- Set up a Snapshot table to support a manager's requirements for periodic data for analysis.

- Describe the fundamental characteristics of Data Warehouse Databases.

A bank stores all the information about a customer's account on a computer at the branch where the customer does most of his or her banking. If a computer in one of the bank's branches fails or if some of the phone lines between bank branches fail, most of the bank's customers can continue to have their transactions processed using the equipment and communications lines that are still in operation.

A university has a database of survey information that is generated under a federal grant. Surveys are conducted and new data are added to the database on a monthly basis. The university is able to make this data available on-line to any other interested researchers around the world.

An organization is able to replace a mainframe computer requiring an operations staff with three microcomputer database server units located near the work groups that are the most extensive users of the data they will store. As the volume of data handled increases, any of the three microcomputer servers can be individually replaced or augmented as needed. These incremental changes can be made with minimal impact on the flow of work and the corporate computing budget.

A customer calls one of the branch offices of a company with a question about her bill. A service representative is able to have the last several months of order and billing information for the customer downloaded from a corporate database on a mainframe at the company's headquarters to the personal computer on his desk. From there the service representative is able to run predefined analysis reports that have been developed for him, but is also able to query the data in an ad hoc fashion to retrieve any information needed to respond to the customer. The queries are executed using a PC-based database product that the service representative is familiar with and feels comfortable using.

A company creates a *warehouse* database consisting of summary historical and current data extracted from other operational databases. Managers can execute ad hoc queries on the warehouse database to evaluate trends and investigate problems or opportunities without slowing the performance of high-volume operational systems.

The first three preceding scenarios involve the use of permanently distributed data managed as a single database system. The last two examples are not normally considered to be distributed database systems, but they still involve the use of distributed copies of database data. Until now, the data of our database systems have always been located at a central site. Although applications could be distributed through the use of client-server systems, we always insisted that the data, and its core management functions, be centralized in a single database server.

Now we want to examine systems that support the use of data whose storage is distributed over multiple computers (nodes). Ideally, when an integrated set of data is distributed across multiple nodes, it should still be managed as a unified whole. Distributed Database Management Systems (DDBMSs) are designed to allow users to retrieve any data in the system without knowing where they are stored or even being aware that the data are stored at remote locations.

Although commercial DBMS products with some of the DDBMS features are available, they are not yet in wide use. However, the capabilities of a distributed database system can, to some extent, be created without the use of a formal DDBMS. When this is done, much of the burden of managing the system to ensure its accuracy and consistency will fall on developers and users.

Data warehouses store data extracted from operational databases and external sources. A data warehouse would not normally be considered to be a distributed database system. However, data warehouse databases incorporate some of the key features of distributed database systems.

In this chapter, we will discuss the features of DDBMSs, assess some of their advantages and disadvantages, and provide examples of the types of distribution of data that can be provided by such systems. Additionally, we will discuss systems that provide access to distributed data without the use of a DDBMS. Features of client-server–oriented relational DBMSs that can be used to support data distribution will be described, using Access and Oracle as examples. Finally, we will discuss data warehouse databases and examine how distributed database concepts and techniques can be applied to them.

DISTRIBUTED DATABASE MANAGEMENT SYSTEMS

We have already described the basic characteristics of a **distributed database system.** Data are distributed across multiple locations, or nodes, of the database. Generally, sets of data are to be located where they are expected to be used most frequently. This type of distribution maximizes the amount of database processing that can be done locally. At the same time, users throughout the system should be able to get to any data they are authorized to see without specifying its location. This is illustrated in Figure 12.1.

Distributed Database Management Systems (DDBMSs) are designed to support these objectives while still maintaining data integrity and consistency standards. This can be a very complex task.

Distributed database system
A database system in which data are stored at multiple nodes (processors) of the system, but all data are accessible to any authorized user.

Distributed database management system (DDBMS)
A database management system that supports the distribution of data across multiple nodes while managing the database as an integrated whole. A DDBMS should allow users to access data throughout the system as if the data were all located on each user's computer.

FIGURE 12.1
A Distributed Database System

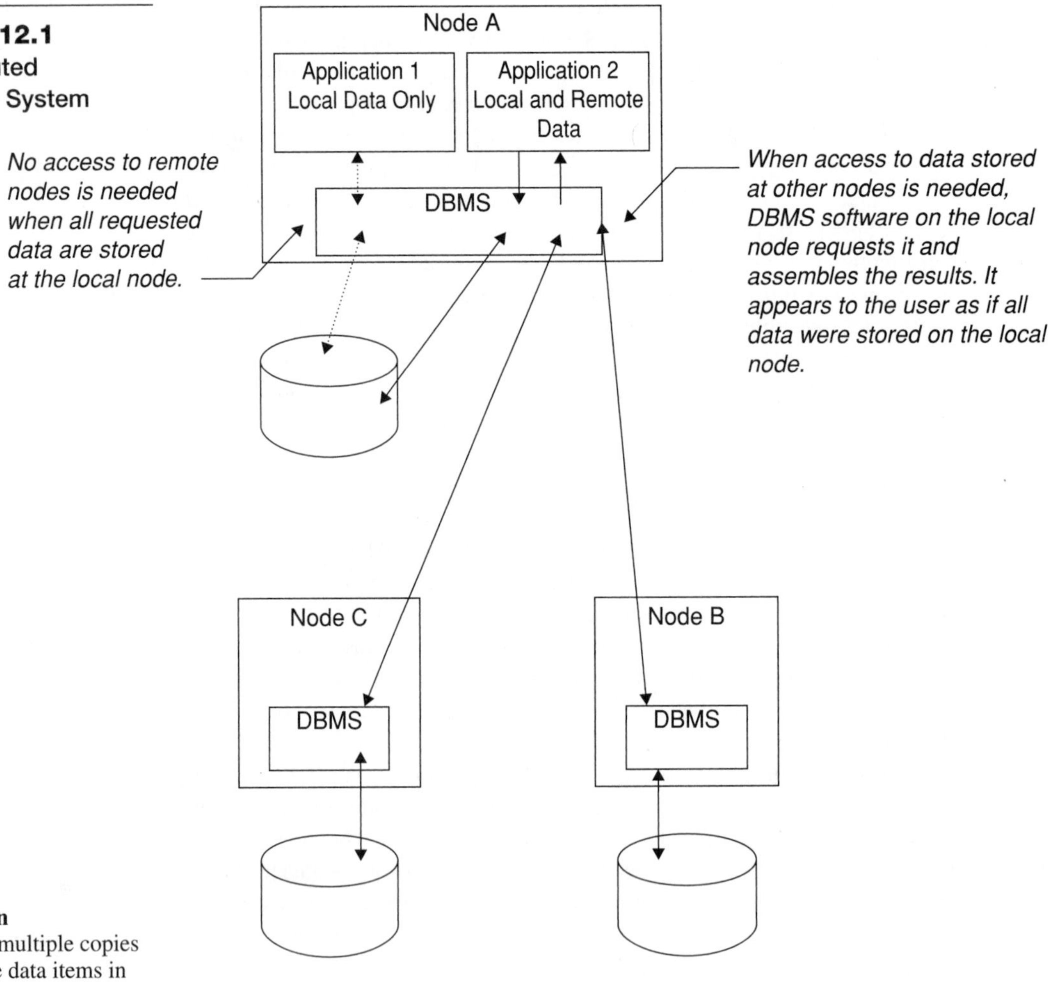
Node A
Application 1
Local Data Only
Application 2
Local and Remote
Data
DBMS
No access to remote nodes is needed when all requested data are stored at the local node.
When access to data stored at other nodes is needed, DBMS software on the local node requests it and assembles the results. It appears to the user as if all data were stored on the local node.
Node C
DBMS
Node B
DBMS

Replication
Storage of multiple copies of the same data items in different nodes of a distributed database. A data element is said to be *fully replicated* if a copy of it is kept at every node of a distributed database system.

Partitioning
Refers to a data distribution schema that splits tables, or rows or columns within tables, into "pieces" which are stored at different nodes of a distributed database system. Under a *fully partitioned* distribution scheme, each unit of data is stored at only one node.

The data of a distributed database can be distributed among alternative sites in two basic ways. First, data may be replicated—stored at multiple sites. Under **replication,** multiple copies of the same data elements are maintained at different nodes of the system. Alternatively, data may be partitioned—each data element stored at only one site. Under **partitioning,** different tables, or even different portions of a single table, may be stored at different nodes.

TRANSPARENCY IN DISTRIBUTED SYSTEMS

The goal of the DDBMS is to allow the data in a database to be distributed through replication, partitioning, or a combination of those methods, while allowing each user of the system to treat the database as if it were all located at her or his local node. The term **transparency** describes this capability. Data are actually distributed over a number of nodes, but the user never sees this distribution. The database appears to be a single whole located at each user's site.

Transparency has a number of dimensions (Traiger, Gray, Galtieri, and Lindsay, 1982). **Location transparency** means that users must be able to access data from throughout the database system without knowing its location. Queries specified under a DDBMS look just like standard queries—they do not need additional clauses identifying the storage location of the data. This is true even if the DDBMS must assemble the data needed to answer the query from fragments of tables located at different nodes. The term **Fragmentation transparency** is sometimes used to describe this capability. If the DDBMS allows some data to be replicated—multiple copies of the same unit of data maintained at different nodes—it should also provide **Replication transparency.** This means that the add, update, and delete operations performed by users are identical to the operations they would use for a centralized database with a single data copy. The DDBMS must have features that will automatically ensure that all copies are added, updated, or deleted appropriately and that the data stored are consistent across all nodes.

Two other elements of transparency apply equally to both DDBMSs and centralized DBMSs. After recovery from any type of failure has been completed, **Failure transparency** allows a user to execute transactions on a database as if the failure had never occurred. The DBMS must be able to recover the database to its exact state at the time of the failure. The commit and rollback procedures described in Chapter 10 were designed to provide failure transparency in centralized database systems. Similar measures are used in distributed systems, but added layers of complexity are involved. The last element of transparency that we will discuss is **Concurrency transparency,** which implies that each user can process a transaction as if she or he were the only user on the system. The DBMS will manage concurrent access to ensure that the actions of different concurrent users do not interfere with one another or cause the results of any user's transactions to be changed. The methods used to manage concurrent processing in a distributed environment are very similar to those used for centralized databases. However, coordinating locking operations across multiple nodes of a network can add substantially to the complexity of this problem, as we will see.

These elements of transparency should be present for all users engaged in all types of database manipulation activities. Programmers from the IS staff, as well as managerial end-users, can treat the database as if it were a single copy at a central site for all data manipulation operations.

DATA DISTRIBUTION IN A DDBMS

Although the location of data will be transparent to users once the design of the database has been put in place, the placement of data is an extremely important part of the design process for a distributed database. The goal is to arrange the location of data in the way that maximizes the amount of transactions that can be processed locally (Taylor, 1981). Thus, each unit of data should be located at the node where it is most frequently used.

Transparency
Refers to the ability of a user of a database system to process data in that system as if the data were stored, managed, and maintained on the user's own computer.

Location transparency
Ability of a user to process data in a distributed system without knowing where the data is located.

Fragmentation transparency
Ability of a user to retrieve data that are stored in fragments on multiple nodes without being aware that the data is fragmented.

Replication transparency
Ability of a user to retrieve, insert, modify, or delete data that are replicated across multiple nodes of the network without knowing that the data are replicated.

Failure transparency
Allows users to execute transactions after recovery from failure in a distributed system as if the failure had never occured.

Concurrency transparency
Allows each user of a distributed database to process transactions as if he or she were the only user of the system.

Vertical partitioning
Assigns different columns of a table or different tables in the database to be stored at different nodes.

Horizontal partitioning
Assigns different rows of a table to be stored at different nodes, but assigns all columns for a given row of the table to be stored at the same node.

As we noted earlier, there are two basic methods of distribution: Data may be replicated at multiple nodes or may be partitioned. Two alternative types of partitioning, vertical and horizontal, may be used. **Vertical partitioning** assigns various rows of a table, entity occurrences, to different sites. **Horizontal partitioning** assigns different tables or table fragments to different sites, but assigns all occurrences of a given table or table fragment to the same site (Date, 1993). These distribution schemes are not mutually exclusive. Portions of the data of a database may be replicated at multiple sites while other portions are partitioned vertically and still others partitioned horizontally.

A BANKING EXAMPLE

Let's use a banking industry example to see how these distribution methods work. Apex Bank has branches in three cities: Greenville, Springfield, and Ash Grove. For the sake of simplicity, let's assume that the only services provided by Apex Bank are checking accounts and loans. Customer account information is maintained by personnel at each branch and check processing is performed at each branch. However, credit analysis and loan processing are handled only by Apex Bank's Loan Office, located in a suburb of Greenville called Compton Heights.

Let's look at how a set of customer data for this bank might be distributed. Figure 12.2 presents the structure and a set of sample data for a CUSTOMER table as it might appear in a centralized database. This table begins with the typical attributes of customer ID number, name, and address. The Home Branch attribute identifies the branch where the customer does the majority of her or his banking. This would normally be the branch where the account was established. The attribute Mother's Maiden Name is to be used as a security measure. For example, a customer asking for account information over the phone might be asked to provide her or his mother's maiden name in order to verify her or his identity. The Contact_Date attribute records the date when the customer was last contacted by a service representative. Each customer is to be contacted periodically by a service representative from his or her home branch, and the Contact_Date attribute is used to manage these contacts. Finally, the

FIGURE 12.2
Apex Bank CUS-TOMER Table for a Centralized DBMS

Customer ID#	Customer Name	Customer Address	Phone Number	Home Branch	Mother's Maiden Name	Contact _Date	Credit _Rating	Credit _Eval._ Date
46732	Jones, J.	228 S. 1st	793-6812	Springfield	Bates	08/03/95	AA	06/01/92
49316	Davis, W.	1313 W. Pine	821-6346	Ash Grove	Lewis	01/06/95	AAA	06/21/94
50213	Norris, A.	140 E. Main	791-4371	Springfield	Jones	03/17/95	A	02/04/95
53802	Boyd, B.	2602 N. 7th	603-1702	Greenville	Adams	06/11/95	AAA	09/04/95
56071	West, J.	702 N. Ash	821-6119	Ash Grove	Aaron	07/19/95	AAA	07/19/95
59132	Evans, R.	2803 W. 3rd	601-3491	Greenville	Yates	05/02/95	AA	08/03/93
60613	Coles, D.	314 S. Elm	788-9208	Springfield	Downs	04/26/95	A	03/14/91

Credit_Rating and Credit_Eval_Date attributes are used by loan officers at the Compton Heights Loan Office to record results of credit checks and to determine whether credit ratings need to be updated.

How might this data be distributed? Let's look at several alternatives.

Replication

We might choose to replicate all customer data at all sites. If a copy of all the data in a database is available at each site, the database is said to be fully replicated. In our example, four copies of the complete CUSTOMER table, as shown in Figure 12.3, would be maintained—one at each bank branch location and one at the Compton Heights Loan Office.

Replication Advantages Replication of data has a number of advantages. Under this scheme it will never be necessary to communicate with a distant site in order to retrieve data about a customer. If B. Boyd applies for a loan, personnel at the Loan Office can retrieve her Credit_Rating and Credit_Eval_Date from the Compton

FIGURE 12.3
CUSTOMER Table Using a Fully Replicated Distribution Scheme

Springfield Branch Database

Customer ID#	Customer Name	Customer Address	Phone Number	Home Branch	Mother's Maiden Name	Contact _Date	Credit _Rating	Credit _Eval._ Date
46732	Jones, J.	228 S. 1st	793-6812	Springfield	Bates	08/03/95	AA	06/01/92
49316	Davis, W.	1313 W. Pine	821-6346	Ash Grove	Lewis	01/06/95	AAA	06/21/94
50213	Norris, A.	140 E. Main	791-4371	Springfield	Jones	03/17/95	A	02/04/95
53802	Boyd, B.	2602 N. 7th	603-1702	Greenville	Adams	06/11/95	AAA	09/04/95
56071	West, J.	702 N. Ash	821-6119	Ash Grove	Aaron	07/19/95	AAA	07/19/95
59132	Evans, R.	2803 W. 3rd	601-3491	Greenville	Yates	05/02/95	AA	08/03/93
60613	Coles, D.	314 S. Elm	788-9208	Springfield	Downs	04/26/95	A	03/14/91

Ash Grove Branch Database

Customer ID#	Customer Name	Customer Address	Phone Number	Home Branch	Mother's Maiden Name	Contact _Date	Credit _Rating	Credit _Eval._ Date
46732	Jones, J.	228 S. 1st	793-6812	Springfield	Bates	08/03/95	AA	06/01/92
49316	Davis, W.	1313 W. Pine	821-6346	Ash Grove	Lewis	01/06/95	AAA	06/21/94
50213	Norris, A.	140 E. Main	791-4371	Springfield	Jones	03/17/95	A	02/04/95
53802	Boyd, B.	2602 N. 7th	603-1702	Greenville	Adams	06/11/95	AAA	09/04/95
56071	West, J.	702 N. Ash	821-6119	Ash Grove	Aaron	07/19/95	AAA	07/19/95
59132	Evans, R.	2803 W. 3rd	601-3491	Greenville	Yates	05/02/95	AA	08/03/93
60613	Coles, D.	314 S. Elm	788-9208	Springfield	Downs	04/26/95	A	03/14/91

Greenville Branch Database

Customer ID#	Customer Name	Customer Address	Phone Number	Home Branch	Mother's Maiden Name	Contact _Date	Credit _Rating	Credit _Eval._ Date
46732	Jones, J.	228 S. 1st	793-6812	Springfield	Bates	08/03/95	AA	06/01/92
49316	Davis, W.	1313 W. Pine	821-6346	Ash Grove	Lewis	01/06/95	AAA	06/21/94
50213	Norris, A.	140 E. Main	791-4371	Springfield	Jones	03/17/95	A	02/04/95
53802	Boyd, B.	2602 N. 7th	603-1702	Greenville	Adams	06/11/95	AAA	09/04/95
56071	West, J.	702 N. Ash	821-6119	Ash Grove	Aaron	07/19/95	AAA	07/19/95
59132	Evans, R.	2803 W. 3rd	601-3491	Greenville	Yates	05/02/95	AA	08/03/93
60613	Coles, D.	314 S. Elm	788-9208	Springfield	Downs	04/26/95	A	03/14/91

Compton Heights Loan Office Database

Customer ID#	Customer Name	Customer Address	Phone Number	Home Branch	Mother's Maiden Name	Contact _Date	Credit _Rating	Credit _Eval._ Date
46732	Jones, J.	228 S. 1st	793-6812	Springfield	Bates	08/03/95	AA	06/01/92
49316	Davis, W.	1313 W. Pine	821-6346	Ash Grove	Lewis	01/06/95	AAA	06/21/94
50213	Norris, A.	140 E. Main	791-4371	Springfield	Jones	03/17/95	A	02/04/95
53802	Boyd, B.	2602 N. 7th	603-1702	Greenville	Adams	06/11/95	AAA	09/04/95
56071	West, J.	702 N. Ash	821-6119	Ash Grove	Aaron	07/19/95	AAA	07/19/95
59132	Evans, R.	2803 W. 3rd	601-3491	Greenville	Yates	05/02/95	AA	08/03/93
60613	Coles, D.	314 S. Elm	788-9208	Springfield	Downs	04/26/95	A	03/14/91

FIGURE 12.3 (Cont.)
CUSTOMER Table Using a Fully Replicated Distribution Scheme

Heights copy of the CUSTOMER table. Similarly, if any of the branch bank offices needs to retrieve data about B. Boyd, they can do so without communicating with a remote site. In addition, replication makes the database less susceptible to system failures. If the Greenville site goes down, transactions on all the customer data can continue to be processed at other sites. Depending on the nature of the failure, it may even be possible to route transactions originating at the Greenville site to other sites for processing. In addition, redundant copies of the database provide additional security against data loss. After a failure, it may be possible to recover a site by sending it a copy of the database data from a site that remained operational.

Replication Disadvantages   Although replication provides a number of advantages, it also creates significant problems. Recall the problems that data duplication caused in file processing systems: Data duplication uses additional storage; it can require additional personnel time to enter the data in multiple files; and there is the potential for data inconsistency—different copies of the same data item having different values. The use of additional data storage space is an inescapable consequence of data replication; however, distributed databases allowing data replication can, and must, avoid the latter two problems.

A user authorized to modify a unit of data should be able to initiate an update from any node. The value she or he enters for the data unit being updated must be automatically copied to all its storage locations. The system must be able to ensure that all copies have been updated and have the same value for the updated item before the update transaction is allowed to successfully terminate.

Guaranteeing data consistency with replicated data in a multiuser environment is a complex problem. Locks must be applied to *each* copy of the affected data. This locking is needed because two updates initiated at different nodes and processed over an overlapping time period could lead to inconsistent data. A substantial amount of communication among nodes is required in the locking and update processes. The node where the modification is initiated must request locks from each node containing a copy of the affected data, and the acquisition of a lock at each node must be confirmed by the initiating node before it requests the actual update of the data. Next, each node must notify the initiating node that it has completed its update. Finally, when confirmation of the update has been received from each node, the initiating node sends a message indicating that the transaction can be committed.

This set of communications clearly adds substantial complication and processing overhead to update transactions. Recovery from failures also becomes more complicated. If one of the nodes fails and the other nodes continue to process updates, how will the failing node be restored to a consistent state upon recovery? If communications failures isolate certain nodes of the system, can the remaining nodes continue to process updates without compromising the integrity and consistency of data? All these issues must be dealt with by DDBMS systems allowing data replication.

Because of all this complexity, it is generally impractical to consider using fully replicated storage for data elements that are updated on a frequent basis. However, as we noted earlier, data replication improves the efficiency of query operations by allowing them to be performed locally at any node. Thus, fully replicated storage can be quite effective for data that is queried frequently but rarely updated. For example, the names and addresses of customers are used on a frequent basis in a wide variety of query operations but are not frequently modified. Thus, replication of name and address data might improve the processing speed and efficiency of a DDBMS.

Horizontal Partitioning

Horizontal partitioning of a database table assigns different rows of the table to different nodes. For our CUSTOMER table, the logical way to assign rows would be to store the data for each customer at the site of that customer's Home Branch. An example of this type of partitioning is shown in Figure 12.4. We would expect the majority of transactions on each customer's data to be initiated at his or her home branch, and no remote communications would be required to support such transactions. Transactions not originating at the customer's home branch would be routed via the system's data directory to the correct node for processing.

Horizontal partitioning of data is most efficient when all of the data relating to a particular instance of an entity are normally accessed from a particular (home) node, but different occurrences of the entity class have different home nodes.

Springfield Database

Customer ID#	Customer Name	Customer Address	Phone Number	Home Branch	Mother's Maiden Name	Contact _Date	Credit _Rating	Credit _Eval._ Date
46732	Jones, J.	228 S. 1st	793-6812	Springfield	Bates	08/03/95	AA	06/01/92
50213	Norris, A.	140 E. Main	791-4371	Springfield	Jones	03/17/95	A	02/04/95
60613	Coles, D.	314 S. Elm	788-9208	Springfield	Downs	04/26/95	A	03/14/91

Ash Grove Database

Customer ID#	Customer Name	Customer Address	Phone Number	Home Branch	Mother's Maiden Name	Contact _Date	Credit _Rating	Credit _Eval._ Date
49316	Davis, W.	1313 W. Pine	821-6346	Ash Grove	Lewis	01/06/95	AAA	06/21/94
56071	West, J.	702 N. Ash	821-6119	Ash Grove	Aaron	07/19/95	AAA	07/19/95

Greenville Database

Customer ID#	Customer Name	Customer Address	Phone Number	Home Branch	Mother's Maiden Name	Contact _Date	Credit _Rating	Credit _Eval._ Date
53802	Boyd, B.	2602 N. 7th	603-1702	Greenville	Adams	06/11/95	AAA	09/04/95
59132	Evans, R.	2803 W. 3rd	601-3491	Greenville	Yates	05/02/95	AA	08/03/93

FIGURE 12.4
CUSTOMER Table
Distributed by
Horizontal
Fragmentation

Transactions for each customer will most often originate at the node of her or his Home Branch, but different customers have different home branches. Thus, horizontal partitioning is generally a good fit for this data. However, there are some limitations. All transactions originating at the Loan Office, plus any transactions originating at a bank branch other than the customer's home branch, would require communications across the nodes of the database. This would be true for queries as well as updates.

Vertical Partitioning

Vertical partitioning of a database table assigns different columns of the table to different nodes. For our CUSTOMER table, the Credit_Rating and Credit_Eval_Date columns contain attributes that are normally created and maintained at the bank's Compton Heights Loan Office. Thus, we might want to store those two attributes at the Compton Heights node of the database. All the other table attributes are used in processing normal banking transactions and would be stored at a different location—perhaps at the bank's main offices in Greenville. Figure 12.5 shows this type of partitioning. Customer ID# appears in both partitions because it is the primary key of the CUSTOMER table. The Customer ID# attribute is needed to uniquely identify occurrences in each partition of the table and would be needed to join the partitions to recreate the full CUSTOMER table.

Greenville Processing Center Database

Customer ID#	Customer Name	Customer Address	Phone Number	Home Branch	Mother's Maiden Name	Contact _Date
46732	Jones, J.	228 S. 1st	793-6812	Springfield	Bates	08/03/95
49316	Davis, W.	1313 W. Pine	821-6346	Ash Grove	Lewis	01/06/95
50213	Norris, A.	140 E. Main	791-4371	Springfield	Jones	03/17/95
53802	Boyd, B.	2602 N. 7th	603-1702	Greenville	Adams	06/11/95
56071	West, J.	702 N. Ash	821-6119	Ash Grove	Aaron	07/19/95
59132	Evans, R.	2803 W. 3rd	601-3491	Greenville	Yates	05/02/95
60613	Coles, D.	314 S. Elm	788-9208	Springfield	Downs	04/26/95

Compton Heights Loan Office Database

Customer ID#	Credit _Rating	Credit _Eval._ Date
46732	AA	06/01/92
49316	AAA	06/21/94
50213	A	02/04/95
53802	AAA	09/04/95
56071	AAA	07/19/95
59132	AA	08/03/93
60613	A	03/14/91

FIGURE 12.5
CUSTOMER Table Distributed by Vertical Fragmentation

Vertical partitioning can be effective when the processing of the table originating at some database nodes normally requires only a subset of the table's attributes. If processing at each of two or more nodes requires only a subset of the table's attributes, and if those subsets of attributes do not overlap, vertical partitioning of a table will be highly efficient. Here we are assuming that each node processes information about all the occurrences of an entity, but that each site deals with only selected characteristics of the entities—Compton Heights handles loan-related data across all customers while another node handles other forms of transactions. With vertical partitioning, remote database access can be avoided for all transactions requiring access only to those attributes of a table stored at the local node. However, any transaction (query or update) requiring access to attributes stored in a nonlocal partition will require remote database access.

One aspect of our CUSTOMER table fits vertical partitioning very well. The Compton Heights Loan Office does deal only in loan-related information, and it processes this information for all customers. However, there are some significant problems. Customer names and addresses are really needed by most transactions

Springfield Database

Customer ID#	Customer Name	Customer Address	Phone Number	Home Branch	Mother's Maiden Name	Contact _Date
46732	Jones, J.	228 S. 1st	793-6812	Springfield	Bates	08/03/95
50213	Norris, A.	140 E. Main	791-4371	Springfield	Jones	03/17/95
60613	Coles, D.	314 S. Elm	788-9208	Springfield	Downs	04/26/95

Ash Grove Database

Customer ID#	Customer Name	Customer Address	Phone Number	Home Branch	Mother's Maiden Name	Contact _Date
49316	Davis, W.	1313 W. Pine	821-6346	Ash Grove	Lewis	01/06/95
56071	West, J.	702 N. Ash	821-6119	Ash Grove	Aaron	07/19/95

Greenville Database

Customer ID#	Customer Name	Customer Address	Phone Number	Home Branch	Mother's Maiden Name	Contact _Date
53802	Boyd, B.	2602 N. 7th	603-1702	Greenville	Adams	06/11/95
59132	Evans, R.	2803 W. 3rd	601-3491	Greenville	Yates	05/02/95

Compton Heights Loan Office Database

Customer ID#	Customer Name	Customer Address	Phone Number	Home Branch	Credit _Rating	Credit _Eval._ Date
46732	Jones, J.	228 S. 1st	793-6812	Springfield	AA	06/01/92
49316	Davis, W.	1313 W. Pine	821-6346	Ash Grove	AAA	06/21/94
50213	Norris, A.	140 E. Main	791-4371	Springfield	A	02/04/95
53802	Boyd, B.	2602 N. 7th	603-1702	Greenville	AAA	09/04/95
56071	West, J.	702 N. Ash	821-6119	Ash Grove	AAA	07/19/95
59132	Evans, R.	2803 W. 3rd	601-3491	Greenville	AA	08/03/93
60613	Coles, D.	314 S. Elm	788-9208	Springfield	A	03/14/91

FIGURE 12.6

Distribution of the CUSTOMER Table Using a Combination of Replication and Fragmentation Methods

originating at either of the partition sites. Thus, if those attributes are stored exclusively at either site, most transactions originating at the other site will require remote database access. Because our Compton Heights node did not include these attributes, most of its transactions will have to access the partition at Greenville to get this information. A further problem is the fact that the partition located at Greenville does not fit the model for vertical partitioning. Transactions on different rows in this partition have very different access patterns. The pattern of access is actually a horizontal one in which most transactions for each customer originate at the home branch of that customer.

Combining Distribution Methods

What is really desirable in our CUSTOMER table example, and in most databases, is the use of combinations of these distribution methods. Figure 12.6 shows a distribution scheme for the CUSTOMER table that combines all the distribution methods. A vertical partition is applied to place loan-related data for all customers at the Compton Heights node. Horizontal partitioning divides the information relating to normal banking transactions among the nodes at the various bank branches, based on the customer's Home Branch. Finally, information for both loan processing and normal banking transactions is replicated. The name, address, and phone number of each customer is stored both at the Compton Heights node and at one of the branch nodes.

Thus far, our example has dealt with only a single table. The task of appropriately distributing data becomes still more complex when multiple tables, and the relationships among them, are considered. Suppose we add some additional tables to our bank example. The bank issues checking accounts to customers. Each customer may have one or more checking accounts and a CHECKING-ACCOUNT table is maintained. Numerous checks and deposits can be processed against each checking account, and a CHECKING-ACTIVITY table is used to store data about these transactions. Similarly, each customer can have one or more loans, and numerous payments may be made on a loan account. Tables named LOAN-ACCOUNT and LOAN-ACTIVITY are used to store this information, and all loan-related processing is handled by personnel at the Loan Office. Figure 12.7 shows how this database might look if a centralized DBMS were used.

How would this combination of tables be distributed for use in a distributed database system? Figure 12.8 illustrates a possible distribution. In this case, the distribution of the CUSTOMER table dictates the distribution of the other tables. The checking accounts belonging to customers whose Home Branch is Springfield will most frequently be accessed from the Springfield branch, as will the CHECKING-ACTIVITY records associated with those checking accounts. Thus, the Home Branch attribute of the CUSTOMER table establishes the criterion for the horizontal partitioning of the CUSTOMER, CHECKING-ACCOUNT, and CHECKING-ACTIVITY tables. On the other hand, all records of the LOAN-ACCOUNT and LOAN-ACTIVITY tables will be accessed primarily from the Compton Heights node. So the entire contents of these tables are placed at Compton Heights. The replication of some customer attributes is retained, but no additional replication is needed in this instance.

DATA DISTRIBUTION IN CURRENT CLIENT-SERVER RELATIONAL DBMSs

As we have seen, a true DDBMS should provide users with transparent access to the data of a distributed database system. However, the distributed database capabilities

FIGURE 12.7
The Apex Bank
Customer Database

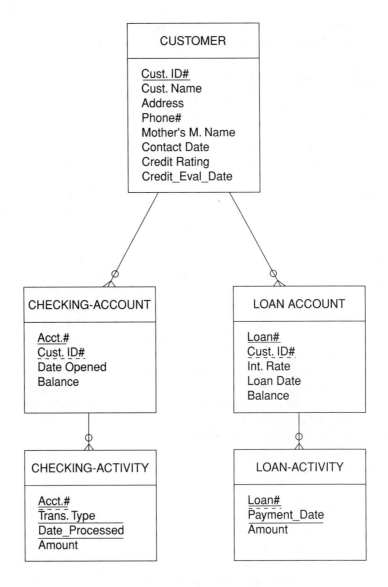

FIGURE 12.7
The Apex Bank
Customer Database

currently available in commercial DBMS products fall considerably short of this goal. Distributed versions of several of the major relational DBMSs are available that provide some DDBMS features. In addition, the standard versions of many client-server–oriented relational DBMSs provide some limited capabilities to support the distribution of data. In this section, we will discuss some features of Access and Oracle that support the use of distributed data. These features do not fully integrate the distributed data into a single database. Rather, they facilitate the sharing of data among separate databases at different locations. Essentially, this represents an extension of the client-server model to allow for multiple servers.

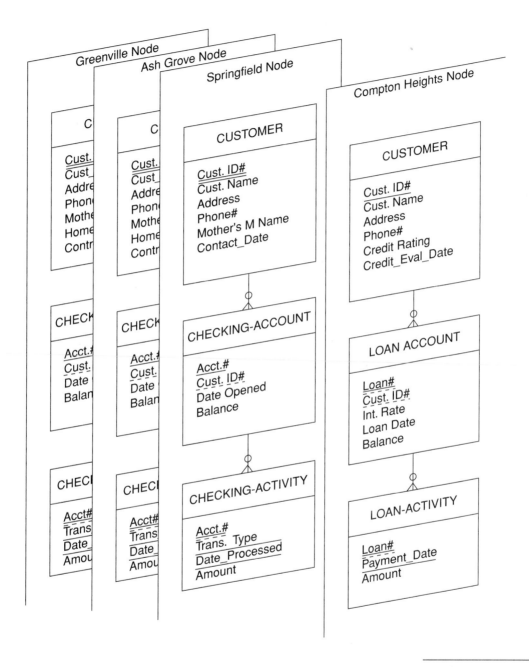

FIGURE 12.8
Distribution Pattern for the Apex Bank Customer Databases

DATABASES WITH ATTACHED OR LINKED TABLES

One database can provide access to data from another (external) database by linking to, or attaching to, that external database. Once this type of connection is established, tables from the external database can be accessed by users as if they were a part of the internal database.

Attached Tables under Access

Attached table
A table from a different (external) database that has been linked to the current database so that most database operations can be performed on it as if it were an internal table. Attached tables are a feature of Access.

The Access DBMS provides this type of connection by allowing the user to create attached tables. **Attached tables** are relational database tables from an external database that are to be used with, and treated as part of, your Access database. The data of these attached tables are still managed by the external database, but Access copies information about the structure of these tables into your Access database.

Figure 12.9 shows an example of the table list for an Access database with attached tables. This database might be maintained by a salesperson. The salesperson needs to be able to use information about her customers and their orders that is maintained in an organizational database. At the same time, she wants to maintain additional information about each call she makes on a customer. This information is needed only by our salesperson and does not need to be in the organizational database. To support her needs, our salesperson has created an Access database consisting of three attached tables (CUSTOMER, ORD, and ORDER-ITEM), from an external (organizational) database and one local CUSTOMER-CONTACT table, which she will maintain from within Access. The globe symbol next to the three external tables in Figure 12.9 indicates that they are attached tables. A set of table structure diagrams showing these tables and the logical relationships among them is presented in Figure 12.10.

Figure 12.11 shows the relationships among these tables that have been defined in Access. There are no cardinality indicators on the links between the tables because Access is not maintaining the referential integrity between the tables.

FIGURE 12.9
Attached Tables in an Access Database

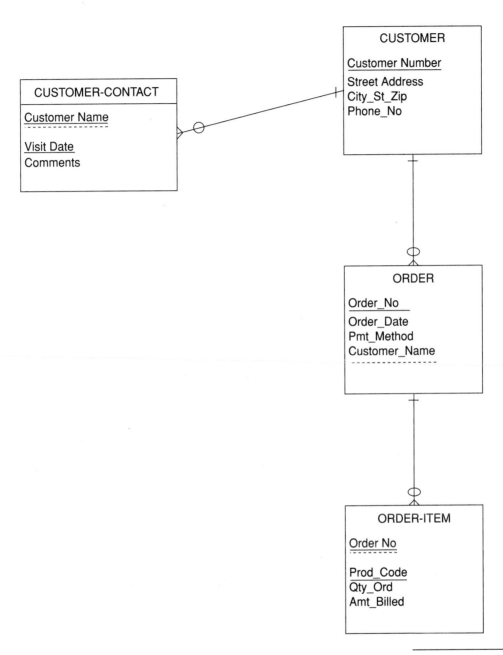

FIGURE 12.10

Table Structure Diagrams for the Salesperson Database Example

The external database we are attaching to could be another Access database or it could be an Oracle or a DB2 database or any other common relational DBMS. We can even use attached tables from more than one external database. An Open Database Connectivity (ODBC) linkage between the databases must be established in order to set up our table attachment. The ODBC linkage translates between the two

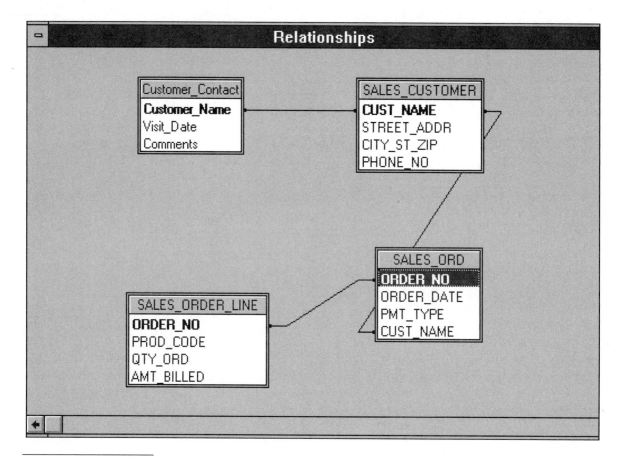

FIGURE 12.11
Relationships
Diagram in Access

DBMSs and ensures that the commands and data that are exchanged are put in a form that can be understood by the DBMS on the receiving side. Software to provide this service, called ODBC drivers, must be installed before attachments can be made.

Once an attachment has been established, the attached tables appear as tables in your Access database, and most operations that can be performed on your internal tables can also be performed on attached tables. Attached tables can be used in queries, reports, and forms. Can you insert, update, and delete records in attached tables from within Access? Yes, but only if you have been granted the rights to perform these operations within the DBMS of the external database. Recall that the data of attached tables are still stored in the external database and are managed by it. Whenever you open an Access database that contains attached tables, you are immediately required to log in to the external database, which must determine that you have rights to the attached tables before you are allowed to use them. In essence, the local Access database has become a client requesting services from a server that provides the data from the attached tables (see Figure 12.12). Applications, such as forms, reports, or queries, address their requests to the local Access database as if it contained all the required data.

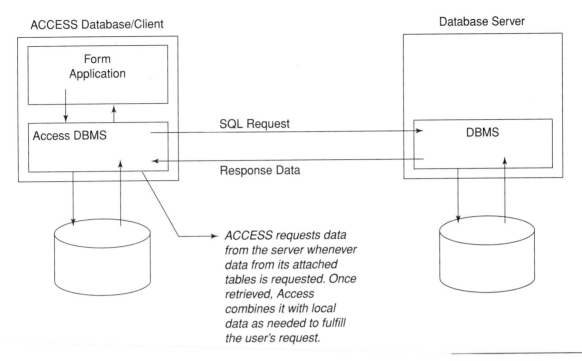

ACCESS Database/Client

Database Server

Form
Application

Access DBMS

SQL Request

Response Data

DBMS

*ACCESS requests data
from the server whenever
data from its attached
tables is requested. Once
retrieved, Access
combines it with local
data as needed to fulfill
the user's request.*

FIGURE 12.12
An Access Database
Using Attached Tables

Attached tables operate in a fashion similar to views. When a view or an attached table is created, what is saved is not a set of data, but a set of instructions that allow the current data for the view, or in this case the attached table, to be retrieved whenever a SQL statement using it is issued. If our salesperson issues a query in Access that requests retrieval of data from the CUSTOMER table, that query is translated into a SQL select statement which, through ODBC linkages, is sent to the external database. That database checks to ensure that the user is authorized to see the requested data. If the user is authorized, the data are returned to Access, which displays the data just as it would display the data of an internal table. A similar procedure would be followed for Insert, Update, and Delete operations.

There are some limitations on the operations that can be performed on attached tables. Suppose that a change to the structure of a table in the external database, such as the addition of a field or an index, is made. If the table that was modified was an attached table, the attachment must be *refreshed* within Access in order for these changes to be available to users of the Access database. Also, these changes to the structure of an attached table cannot be made from within Access even if the user has the appropriate rights. The attached tables are still managed by the external database and any changes to the structure of the tables must be made from within that database. Attached tables can be examined in *design view* within Access, but most of the design characteristics cannot be modified. Characteristics that affect only the way in which data are displayed in Access, but do not affect how the data are stored in the external database, can be modified as shown in Figure 12.13.

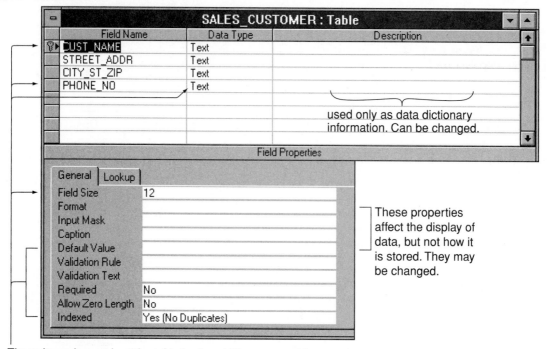

These items impact how the table is stored. They may not be changed for attached tables.

FIGURE 12.13
The Table Design Options for an Attached Access Table

There are limitations on the referential integrity services that can be provided within this type of database. The external database is responsible for enforcing referential integrity rules among the attached tables. It would, for instance, prevent our salesperson from inserting an order whose Customer Number does not exist in the CUSTOMER table. Access could provide similar referential integrity for relationships between its internal tables. But, can we provide referential integrity for a relationship between an attached table and an internal table? This type of referential integrity cannot be provided, because it would require a coordinated rule across two separate database management systems. In our example database, there is nothing to prevent our salesperson from creating a CUSTOMER-CONTACT record whose Customer Number does not exist in the attached CUSTOMER table even though such a record would be meaningless.

It should be noted that it is also possible to create an Access database that consists entirely of attached tables from another database. In fact, this approach is used when we simply want to run client applications using Access.

Creating Database Links in Oracle

In Oracle, a CREATE DATABASE LINK command can be used to link to data in an external database. This statement does not create a permanent linkage between the databases or copy in information about tables in the external database. Once a CRE-ATE DATABASE LINK statement is issued, the user is allowed to issue SQL commands on the external database, including commands that join related data from internal and external tables. The CREATE DATABASE LINK statement includes user, password, and network routing information required to link to the external database and establish the appropriate access rights. It also establishes a link name that is used as a qualifier whenever data from the external database are to be used.

The basic syntax of the CREATE DATABASE LINK statement is as follows:

```
CREATE DATABASE LINK db_link_name
CONNECT TO user IDENTIFIED BY password USING 'connect_string'
```

The statement establishes a name for the database link and gives user name, password, and the connect_string used by the network to identify the external location. Suppose we wish to establish a link named *custinfo* for a user named *salesp01* whose password is *id28439*. This link is to be to a database identified to the network as *'X:CORP-SALES'*. In this case the CREATE DATABASE LINK Statement would be:

```
CREATE DATABASE LINK custinfo
CONNECT TO salesp01 IDENTIFIED BY id28439 USING 'X:CORP-SALES'
```

Once this statement has been issued, the user salesp01 would be able to execute select, insert, update, and delete operations on tables in this external database if he or she has authorization based on the user rights granted to him or her in that database. (We are assuming use of Oracle with the distributed option. Without this option only select operations are allowed.) However, Oracle copies no information about the structure of tables in the external database into the internal database. The user must either know the names of the tables and attributes he or she will be using or must make inquiries on the external database to get this information. The linkage lasts only for the duration of a session and must be reestablished when a new session begins. As with our Access example, referential integrity cannot be maintained by the DBMS for relationships between internal and external tables. Also, the external database could be another Oracle database or it could be another relational DBMS subject to the availability of appropriate linking software.

To reference data from the external database, the user appends its table names with the @ character followed by the link name. We can use the salesperson database example of Figure 12.10 to illustrate this. Assume that the CUSTOMER-CONTACT table has been created in the database that is currently open and that the CUSTOMER, ORD, and ORDER-ITEM tables exist in the CORP-SALES database. We created a database link (named custinfo) to this database in the preceding CREATE DATABASE LINK statement. We could now use the following SELECT statement to retrieve a listing of related CUSTOMER and CUSTOMER-CONTACT information.

```
SELECT * FROM CUSTOMER@custinfo, CUSTOMER-CONTACT
```

If the user salesp01 has the authorization to perform updates on the CUSTOMER table, the following statement could be used to modify a customer's address:

```
UPDATE CUSTOMER@custinfo
    SET address = "318 New Street"
```

The same principle is followed for insert and delete statements. Operations on an external, linked database require that any table names from the external database are qualified by *@db_link_name*. Because of limitations in coordinating locking between the separate DBMSs involved, statements that require locking operations in both the internal and the external databases are prohibited.

The example we have been using is a hierarchical one. Data flowed from an organizational database on a server to an individual workstation, but the data stored in the internal tables of our Access or Oracle database were only used locally. However, there is no reason that data cannot flow in both directions. We could have two databases on separate servers, each linked to data stored in the other. Figure 12.14 illustrates this type of structure in which each node is both a server handling requests for the data it holds and a client requesting externally held data.

In addition to nodes that act as servers for a portion of the database, there may be nodes of the system that operate only as clients. In Figure 12.15, client nodes are attached to each of the nodes containing portions of the database. Whenever Client workstation C2 needs data, it sends a SQL request to its server at node A. After appropriate authorization checking, node A begins to retrieve the requested data. If any of the requested data is held by node B, node A sends a SQL request to node B. In responding to node C2's request, node A not only acts as a server, but also serves as an intermediary to secure resources from another site for the original client.

This type of attachment or linkage between databases is available in a variety of client-server–oriented relational DBMSs on the market today. In Figure 12.15, for example, server A could have been running an Oracle DBMS while server B was running DB2 or Sybase. The attached client nodes could have been using Access, Paradox, or Powerbuilder. A wide variety of relational DBMS products can

FIGURE 12.14
**Two Database Servers
Sharing Data**

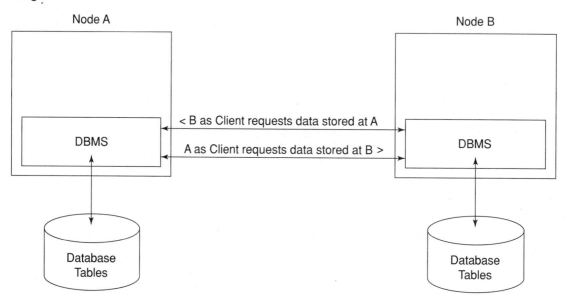

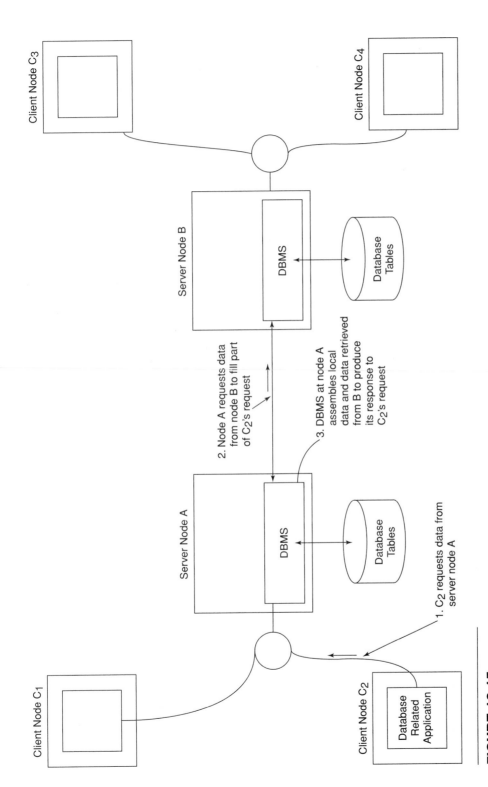

FIGURE 12.15
Servers Sharing Data
and Supporting Clients

be connected in this manner, although there can be some difficulties, such as poor translation of data types, when linking diverse products.

This linkage mechanism provides rather flexible access to distributed data without the expense and processing overhead that would be required by a DDBMS. However, it does require significant user knowledge of the structure of the system as well as the use of explicit commands issued by the data administrators, developers, and/or users to create and maintain the linkages. Also, this type of system creates a hole in the referential integrity structure provided by the DBMS.

SNAPSHOT TABLES

Snapshot table
A table consisting of data copied from another "master" table. The snapshot table is to be used only for data retrieval operations and is designed to be automatically refreshed (its data recopied from the master table) on a regular basis.

A **snapshot table** is created from data stored in one or more other tables and is designed to be automatically updated on a periodic basis. Typically, the snapshot table is created from a table in an external database. The snapshot table can only be read; no insertions into or modifications of the data in a snapshot table are allowed. Any additions, deletions, or changes to data must be made to the master table that is the source for the snapshot table. These changes will then be reflected in the snapshot table whenever it is updated.

The process of updating a snapshot table is called *refreshing* the snapshot. In some cases a snapshot can be refreshed by posting from a *snapshot log* where changes to the master table have been maintained. This process is similar to posting entries in a transactions log to recover a database that has failed, as was described in Chapter 12. When the master table is large and does not have frequent changes, updating from a snapshot log can save a substantial amount of processing.

A snapshot table is much like the idea of a replicated table in a DDBMS, except that the snapshot table is not continuously updated and, thus, will at times contain obsolete data. However, managing snapshot tables is much simpler and requires much less overhead than managing replicated data. A snapshot table is most effective for tables whose values are not frequently changed. For example, suppose that product information, including product pricing, for a department store chain is set by central headquarters and applies to all stores. Further assume that changes to the set of products available or the pricing of products are made only on a weekly basis and become effective at the beginning of the following week. In this situation, we could maintain a master PRODUCT table at the corporate headquarters and create a snapshot table from that master at each local department store. We would ensure that the snapshot tables were updated each weekend to reflect any changes made to the master PRODUCT table. In this case, the data in the local databases would be completely accurate and would allow all product pricing information to be retrieved locally. The basic syntax of Oracle's CREATE SNAPSHOT statement is as follows:

```
CREATE SNAPSHOT snapshot_table_name
    REFRESH START WITH date NEXT date
    AS subquery
```

The snapshot_table_name is the name we wish to assign to the snapshot table. The refresh clause indicates the times when refreshes will occur. START WITH specifies the date when the snapshot table will first be created. NEXT indicates when the snapshot will first be refreshed after its initial creation. The length of the interval between these two dates determines the interval between refreshes thereafter.

Assuming that a database link named *corp-prod* has been established to the database containing the master PRODUCT table, the following statement could be used to create a local snapshot table called LOC-PRODUCT. Because no START WITH date is given, the snapshot table will be created immediately. It will be refreshed automatically 7 days from now and will be refreshed every 7 days thereafter.

```
CREATE SNAPSHOT LOC-PRODUCT
     REFRESH NEXT sysdate + 7
     AS SELECT * FROM PRODUCT@corp-prod
```

   Where snapshot tables are used, we must be willing to accept some inaccuracy in the data that is being read. This inaccuracy can be reduced, but never eliminated, by updating snapshot tables more frequently.

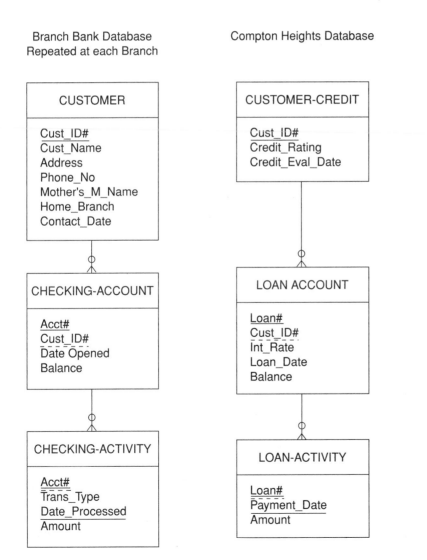

Branch Bank Database
Repeated at each Branch

Compton Heights Database

FIGURE 12.16
Table Structures for
Apex Bank Database

THE BANKING EXAMPLE REVISITED

At this point we have examined the mechanisms commonly available to support data distribution in current commercial DBMS products. To get a better view of the capabilities and limitations of these mechanisms, let's apply them to the Apex Bank example presented earlier in the chapter. Figure 12.8 presents the distribution scheme we will use and Figure 12.7 shows additional details of the crucial CUSTOMER table.

Recall that the CUSTOMER table is partially replicated. Each customer's ID#, Name, Address, Phone Number, and Home Branch are stored both at his or her home branch and at the Compton Heights Loan Office. We must decide which copy is to be the master. In this case, the principal users of the data are likely to be located at the customer's home branch. Thus, we will place the master copy of the data there and create snapshot copies at the Loan Office. Figure 12.16 on page 499 shows the data structure of the tables to be created at the Loan Office and the structure of the tables to be created at each bank branch. The structure of the tables is identical for all branches because each will store a parallel set of data for its home customers.

Note that the CUSTOMER-CREDIT table of the Compton Heights database contains only the Customer ID#, Credit-Rating, and Credit-Eval-Date for each customer. To provide the set of Customer information needed at Compton Heights, we will need to create snapshot tables to provide the other attributes needed and then join the snapshot table data with the appropriate data from the CUSTOMER-CREDIT table.

Figure 12.17 shows the set of statements required. The snapshot (replicated) data that is to be used actually comes from horizontal partitions of the CUSTOMER table at each of the three branch banks. Thus, three distinct snapshot tables must be created. The data in these snapshot tables is then combined using the UNION clause of the SELECT statement. The UNION clause links sets of data with a common column structure and produces one row for each row that appears in any of the tables that are being linked. Once the UNION operation has been performed, the resulting BASE-CUST view must be joined with the internally stored CUSTOMER-CREDIT table. The result is a view called LOAN-CUSTOMER, which contains the desired set of Customer information. This set of commands would be written by the data administration staff. However, users would be able to run queries using the LOAN-CUSTOMER view without being concerned with the steps used to generate it.

Some limitations should be noted. First, the customer data used at the Compton Heights office will not always be accurate. If a customer reports an address change at her or his home branch in the middle of the week, that change will only be reflected in the Compton Heights data at the beginning of the following week. Also, remember that the snapshot tables cannot be updated. If a customer wishes to report an address change to a loan officer at Compton Heights, the update would have to be made to the master table at the customer's home branch.

The structure of the tables stored at the branch bank offices is not affected by our distribution—for them it is simply a horizontal partitioning where each branch uses a parallel set of tables for its customers' data. However, processing of customer transactions will be affected by the distribution of data. The customer might be required to tell the cashier the name of her or his home branch. This information would then be used to retrieve that customer's data from the appropriate location. Alternatively, an application might be developed that would first search the appropriate tables in the local database. If the desired record is not found locally, the application would then search the parallel tables of the other branches. To support this type of processing, database links would be established from each branch to all other branches. It might be possible to create applications where the location of data is largely transparent to

FIGURE 12.17
Creating the
CUSTOMER-LOAN
View with Snapshot
Data

Create links to all external databases:

```
CREATE DATABASE LINK grnvle
    CONNECT TO loan-user IDENTIFIED BY ID2834 USING 'X:GRNVLE'
CREATE DATABASE LINK ashgrv
    CONNECT TO loan-user1 IDENTIFIED BY ID4837 USING 'X:ASHGRV'
CREATE DATABASE LINK spfld
    CONNECT TO loan-usera IDENTIFIED BY ID3704 USING 'X:SPFLD'
```

Create snapshot tables:

```
CREATE SNAPSHOT GRNVLE-CUST REFRESH NEXT sysdate + 7
    AS SELECT Cust_ID#, Cust_Name, Cust_Address, Phone_Number,
        Home_Branch from CUSTOMER@grnvle
CREATE SNAPSHOT ASHGRV-CUST REFRESH NEXT sysdate + 7
    AS SELECT Cust_ID#, Cust_Name, Cust_Address, Phone_Number,
        Home_Branch from CUSTOMER@ashgrv
CREATE SNAPSHOT SPFLD-CUST REFRESH NEXT sysdate + 7
    AS SELECT Cust_ID#, Cust_Name, Cust_Address, Phone_Number,
        Home_Branch from CUSTOMER@spfld
```

Create a view that is a union of the snapshot table:

```
CREATE VIEW BASE-CUST
    AS SELECT * FROM GRNVLE-CUST
        UNION SELECT * FROM ASHGRV-CUST
            UNION SELECT * FROM SPFLD-CUST
```

Join this view with the internal CUSTOMER-CREDIT table:

```
CREATE VIEW LOAN-CUSTOMER
    AS SELECT cc.Cust_ID#, Cust_Name, Cust_Address, Phone_Number,
        Home_Branch, Credit_Rating, Credit_Eval_Date
            FROM BASE-CUST bc, CUSTOMER-CREDIT cc
                WHERE bc.Cust_Id# = cc.Cust_ID#
```

the end-user. However, the applications developers would be required to explicitly reference the locations of the tables used by their applications.

It should be clear from this example that current data distribution techniques fall far short of the ideal of DDBMS structures. However, they can still be used to provide a rather significant range of access to distributed data.

DATA WAREHOUSING

Data warehouse databases are designed specifically to support the analysis needs of management. Normally, the data stored in a data warehouse database are organized differently than that of operational databases. The warehouse database is generally to be used for retrieval only. It is not updated by its users. The data stored in the warehouse are extracted from operational databases of the organization and/or obtained from external sources. The warehouse database is updated on a periodic basis by extracting updated data from their various sources.

Although data warehouses are normally separate databases, many of the capabilities of a data warehouse can be provided within existing operational databases. We will begin our discussion of key features of data warehouse systems by examining how views and snapshot tables within an existing operational database can be used to support the analysis needs of managers.

SUPPORTING THE DATA ANALYSIS NEEDS OF MANAGERS

Let's look at a simple example of the types of data required to support managers. Managers in the marketing department of an organization need to be able to examine sales trends in numerous categories of sales. Sales by product and/or product line, by the location of the customer, and by time period are just a few of the categories that a marketing department might want to use. This type of data would typically be recorded on a transaction-by-transaction basis in an operational sales database. An extremely simplified version of a set of transaction tables storing this data is shown in Figure 12.18. The table structure is similar to that of the Apex Products example used in earlier chapters. Customers place orders and each order may have multiple order-lines. Each of the order-lines pertains to one product.

Suppose a manager frequently needs to examine quarterly sales trends by product line for each state (based on the customer's address). Within the existing operational database, we could create a VIEW using SQL to produce this set of data using the following SQL CREATE VIEW statement:

```
CREATE VIEW SALES_SUM (State, Prod_Line, Month, Qty_Sold, Sales_Val)
  AS
SELECT State, Prod_Line, TRUNC(Order_Date, 'Q'), SUM(Qty_Ord),
  SUM(Amt_Billed)
FROM CUSTOMER C, ORD O, ORDER_LINE OL, PRODUCT P
  WHERE C.C_No = O.C_No
  AND O.Order_No = OL.Order_No
  AND OL.Prod_Code = P.Prod_Code
```

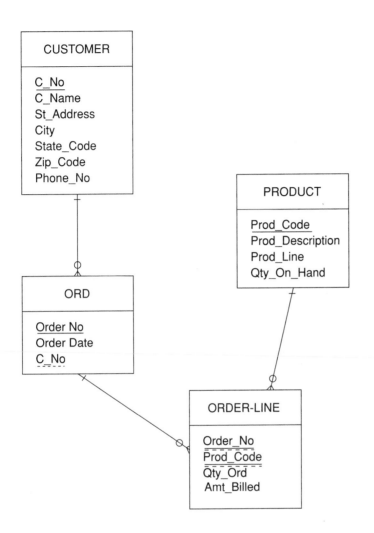

FIGURE 12.18
A Set of Sales-
Related Tables

```
AND Order_Date
   GROUP BY State, Prod_Line, TRUNC(Order_Date, 'Q')
```

The syntax used here should be familiar to you with the exception of the TRUNC function performed on the Order_Date. This TRUNC operation is the method Oracle SQL uses to truncate dates. Similar functions are available in most current relational DBMSs. The 'Q' parameter tells the function to truncate to the quarterly level. After truncation, all dates in the first quarter of 1998 would be recorded as January 1, 1998. The last condition in the WHERE clause excludes data from the current (presumably uncompleted) quarter from being included in the VIEW that is created. The GROUP BY clause contains the same truncation of dates to the quarterly level so that the data generated for the SALES_SUM view are aggregate values of units sold and dollar value of sales for each product line in each state for each quarter.

The Sales_Sum view would allow our marketing managers to retrieve the data they needed for analysis at any time. However, this approach might seriously degrade the performance of the database. Each time the Sales_Sum view is retrieved, a substantial volume of data across four tables of the database must be retrieved and processed to repopulate the view. Also, because it is a group view, it cannot be used to add or modify data.

Because the data described above will be used only for retrieval purposes and new observations are added only on a quarterly basis, this set of data could easily be provided in a snapshot table by executing the following **CREATE SNAPSHOT** statement:

```
CREATE SNAPSHOT SALES_SUM (State, Prod_Line, Month, Qty_Sold, Sales_Val)
   REFRESH START WITH '10-JAN-98' NEXT '10-APR-98'
     AS
   SELECT State, Prod_Line, TRUNC(Order_Date, 'Q'), SUM(Qty_Ord),
       SUM(Amt_Billed)
     FROM CUSTOMER C, ORD O, ORDER_LINE OL, PRODUCT P
       WHERE C.C_No = O.C_No
         AND O.Order_No = OL.Order_No
         AND OL.Prod_Code = P.Prod_Code
         AND Order_Date <TRUNC(SYSDATE,'Q')
           GROUP BY State, Prod_Line, TRUNC(Order_Date, 'Q')
```

The statement, as written, would create the snapshot table at midnight on the tenth day of January and would **REFRESH** the snapshot table at midnight on the tenth day of each quarter thereafter. This snapshot table would be generated only one time each quarter and could be scheduled to be produced at a time when use of the database is low, such as at midnight.

This snapshot table should meet the needs of our marketing manager just as well as the view we showed earlier. However, it substantially reduces the load on the operational tables of the database caused by this user. Now our manager can run queries and statistical analyses on the data of the snapshot table without interfering with ongoing transactions. In addition, the snapshot table is based on grouped data—there may be hundreds or even thousands of sales per quarter of a product line in a state. Thus, the number of records retrieved each time the snapshot table is accessed is substantially smaller than the number of records that would need to be retrieved to repopulate the view.

Our example was designed to produce a summary table to meet the needs of one manager. In practice, a number of managers will need to do analysis on summary information from the same sets of operational tables. There may be managers who need to examine trends in sales for individual products rather than product lines. Others may want to look at sales trends based on the telephone area code of the customer rather than the state of residence. In addition, some managers may want to use annual increments in their analysis while others may need time intervals as short as a month.

How can we produce a snapshot table to meet the needs of all these users? Essentially, we must consolidate the requirements of all the users and produce a snapshot table (or set of snapshot tables) that will support the needs of all. Figure 12.19 shows a **CREATE SNAPSHOT** statement that might be used, and presents a sample of the type of data that this table would contain. We have created a snapshot table at the greatest level of detail that managers might need to perform an analysis. One

Syntax:
```
CREATE SNAPSHOT SALES_SUMMARY
   REFRESH START WITH '05-NOV-97' NEXT '05-DEC-97'
     AS
   SELECT State, Substr(Phone_No,1,3) As Area_Code, Prod_Line, P.Prod_Code,
         TRUNC(Order_Date, 'MONTH') AS Sales_Month, SUM(Qty_Ord) AS Units_Sold,
              SUM(Amt_Billed) AS Sales_$
       FROM CUSTOMER C, ORD O, ORDER_LINE OL, PRODUCT P
     WHERE C.C_No = O.C_No
       AND O.Order_No = OL.Order_No
       AND OL.Prod_Code = P.Prod_Code
     GROUP BY State, Substr(Phone_No,1,3), Prod_Line, P.Prod_Code, TRUNC(Order_Date,
     'MONTH')
```

Sample of the Resulting Data

State	Area Code	Prod_Line	Prod_Code	Sales_Month	Units_Sold	Sales_$
AZ	520	PC	AR28	01-APR-97	5148	5142852.00
AZ	520	PC Component	KB12	01-FEB-97	2178	130571.10
AZ	520	PC Component	KB12	01-APR-97	396	23740.20
AZ	520	PC Component	MC22	01-FEB-97	12375	983812.50
AZ	520	PC Component	MO43	01-FEB-97	3465	380976.75
AZ	602	PC	AR28	01-APR-97	594	593406.00
AZ	602	PC	AR28	01-JUL-97	1485	1483515.00
AZ	602	PC	AR35	01-FEB-97	1188	1543212.00
AZ	602	PC Component	KB12	01-APR-97	594	35610.30
AZ	602	PC Component	MC22	01-APR-97	376	188892.00
AZ	602	PC Component	MC22	01-JUL-97	7425	590287.50
AZ	602	PC Component	MO43	01-FEB-97	1188	130620.60
AZ	602	PC Component	MO43	01-APR-97	594	65310.30
AZ	602	PC Component	MO43	01-JUL-97	1485	163275.75
CA	213	PC	AR28	01-APR-97	396	395604.00
CA	213	PC	AR28	01-JUL-97	1584	1582416.00
CA	213	PC	AR35	01-JUL-97	396	514404.00

FIGURE 12.19
A Snapshot Table Designed to Support a Group of Managers

Sample of the Resulting Data

State	Area Code	Prod_Line	Prod_Code	Sales_Month	Units_Sold	Sales_$
CA	213	PC Component	MC22	01-APR-97	1584	125928.00
CA	213	PC Component	MC22	01-JUL-97	1584	125928.00
CA	310	PC	AR28	01-APR-97	495	494505.00
CA	310	PC	AR28	01-JUL-97	396	395604.00
CA	310	PC	AR35	01-APR-97	792	1028808.00
CA	310	PC Component	MO43	01-APR-97	1188	130620.60

FIGURE 12.19 (Cont.)
A Snapshot Table Designed to Support a Group of Managers

row is produced for each distinct combination of State, Area_Code, Prod_Line, Prod_Code, and Sales_Month. Where full detail is not needed, the data in the SALES_SUMMARY snapshot table can be further aggregated as needed. In this example, our original marketing manager could use the following SQL query to retrieve quarterly sales data by State and Prod_Line:

```
SELECT State, Prod_Line, TRUNC(Sales_Month, 'Q') AS Sales_Qtr,
    SUM(Units_Sold) AS Tot_Units, SUM(Sales_$) AS Tot_Sales
      FROM SALES_SUMMARY
        GROUP BY State, Prod_Line, TRUNC(Sales_Month, 'Q')
```

If necessary, we could create views populated by the snapshot table to support frequently needed sets of data, such as the preceding query. As long as the level of detail is sufficiently fine and all the appropriate grouping categories are included, our snapshot table should support both repeated and ad hoc analysis needs of a variety of managers.

WAREHOUSE DATABASES

The preceding example clearly demonstrates that the data requirements to support managerial analysis are substantially different from the data requirements of operational databases. We saw that performance could be substantially enhanced by placing data to support management applications in tables separate from the operational tables of a database. Data warehousing databases carry this concept much farther. They store interrelated sets of tables designed to support management in a database that is completely separate from the operational databases of the organization. Data in the warehouse database are extracted (and summarized) from one or more operational databases. External data acquired from outside sources, such as government demographic and income estimates or industry sales estimates, may also be included in the warehouse database.

Warehouse databases tend to have a rather flat table structure. Because warehouse data are used only for retrieval, tables frequently are not fully normalized. For instance, the Prod_Line attribute in the snapshot table in Figure 12.19 could be derived from the Prod_Code attribute and thus would be placed in a separate table (the PROD-UCT table) in a fully normalized database. However, because this table is for retrieval only, the anomalies caused by unnormalized data are not a problem. If sales data will frequently be requested by product line categories, substantial processing time may be saved by avoiding the joining of multiple tables to satisfy this request.

At the same time, the table structure of warehouse databases tends to be broad—each child (many side) table has relationships to numerous parent tables. For instance, the SALES_TOTAL snapshot table presented in Figure 12.19 could have been linked to as many as five parent tables—one for each grouping category.

Warehouse databases also tend to be broader in scope than operational databases and they need to retain data over longer periods of time. In creating our snapshot table in the previous section, we considered only managers in the marketing department. However, sales data would also be of interest to many other groups within the organization. Sales trends affect and are affected by production and distribution processes in an organization. Managers across all these areas may need to analyze summary sales, production, and distribution data and evaluate interrelationships among them in order to effectively plan their operations.

Figure 12.20 provides a very simplified view of the type of table structures that might be found in a data warehouse database. We have extended our previous example by assuming that our company produces the products it sells and that it has a single production plant and a single warehouse. Thus, there will be one row in the Production-Summary table for each distinct combination of Product, Product-Line, and Month. The geographic groupings of state and area code do not apply here.

In addition, we are assuming that monthly estimates of Per Capita Income, Total Retail Sales, and Population for each area code within each state have been obtained from some external source. This demographic information has no product or product line groupings. Finally, some of our grouping categories may have characteristics of their own that sometimes need to be used in analysis, such as the geographic size of a state or region or the number of workdays in a particular month. Four of our original grouping categories have characteristics of this type and are included as tables in Figure 12.20.

In developing the examples presented here, we have overlooked a number of complicating factors. Snapshot tables from operational databases cannot be directly used in a data warehouse for a number of reasons. First, data in the data warehouse are maintained indefinitely, while data in operational databases are removed to archival storage rather quickly. Thus, data from operational databases can be used only to add new observations to the warehouse tables or to update recent observations. In addition, operational data will normally need to be "cleaned up" before it is stored in the warehouse. Order cancellations may need to be posted against orders to adjust sales figures. Adjustments to resolve conflicting regional boundaries, product line categories, and/or time period definitions may be needed. Extensive manipulation of the data extracted from operational databases is normally required before it is stored in a data warehouse database. A number of software products are available to support these cleaning and transformation operations or they may be performed by programs written by the organization's IS staff.

Because of the unique features of data warehouse systems, the processes required to develop them differ substantially from the standard database development

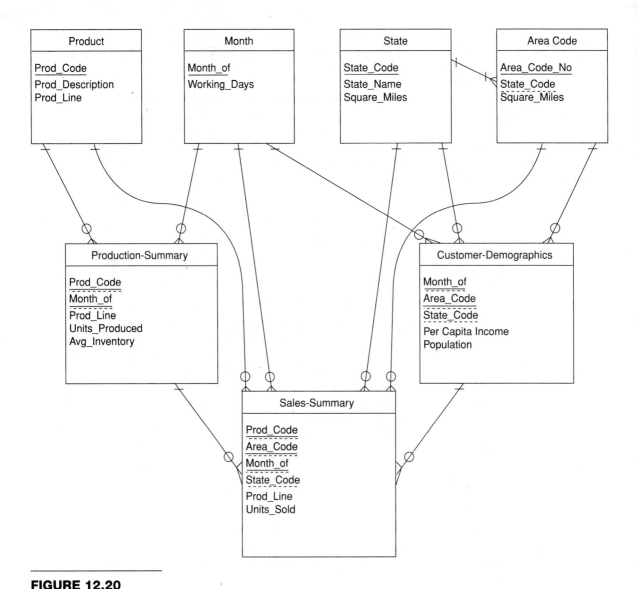

FIGURE 12.20
Table Structures for a
Data Warehouse
Database

processes described in this text. In addition, specialized DBMS packages designed specifically to support data warehouse operations may be required to obtain optimal performance. For a discussion of data warehouse development methods and data warehousing software and hardware requirements, see Gill and Rao (1996).

SUMMARY

Distributed database systems move a step beyond client-server systems by allowing the data of the system, as well as processing activities, to be distributed across multiple nodes of the system. Ideally, this distributed data should be managed by a single, integrated, distributed database management system (DDBMS). Commercially available DBMS products today fall far short of the ideal of the DDBMS, but do provide significant capabilities to access data distributed across separate DBMSs.

In DDBMSs, data may be distributed across the various nodes of the database in a variety of ways. Data may be fully replicated at all the nodes of the system. This maximizes the availability of data at each location. However, replication makes insert, update, and deletion operations substantially more complex. The alternative to replication of data is partitioning, which can be either horizontal or vertical. Horizontal partitioning assigns different rows of a table to different nodes. Vertical partitioning assigns different tables or different attributes of a table to different nodes.

In order for a DDBMS to serve users effectively, users must be able to treat the database exactly as if it were a centralized database. To achieve this, the database employs several types of transparency, enabling the user to go about his or her work without having any knowledge of or being affected by a number of factors: the *location* of data, how data have been *fragmented* across nodes, whether and how data are *replicated,* any *failures* that may have occurred in the system, and the activities of others who are *concurrently* using the database.

Capabilities for working with distributed data using current DBMSs come largely through the ability to link to external data using such statements as ATTACH TABLE (Access) or CREATE DATABASE LINK (Oracle) and through the ability to create *snapshot* tables. Attachment or linkage to an external database allows users to retrieve data from the external database when requested and link it to internal tables or perform most types of operations that the user is allowed to perform on those external tables. When this type of linkage is used, there is no way of enforcing referential integrity constraints on relationships between internal and external tables. In addition, statements that would require locking in both the internal and external databases are not allowed. Snapshot tables provide a copy of an external master table's data as of some point in time. The snapshot table is designed to be *refreshed* on a periodic basis. Its function is similar to a replicated table. However, we cannot be sure that the data in a snapshot table are completely accurate. Snapshot tables are designed to be used for retrieval (SELECT) only.

Data warehousing operations are designed to meet the data analysis requirements of managers. Managers require summary data that are related to key internal and external performance measures and that are organized to support retrieval based on a wide variety of categories. Snapshot tables within operational databases can be developed to support some of these needs. However, separate data warehouse databases may be required to fully support managerial information requirements. Warehouse databases store data (often in summary form) extracted from operational and/or external databases. The warehouse database is designed to support retrieval only and commonly has a flat, but broad, table structure.

REVIEW QUIZ

_____ Recovery from failures is achieved without users having to know how data are distributed.

_____ Each user feels that she or he is the only user of the system.

_____ A table copied from a master table, refreshed on a periodic basis, and used only for retrieval operations.

_____ In order to use a database, users do not need to know whether data elements have been copied at multiple locations.

_____ To use a database, users do not need to know whether different data elements are stored at different locations.

_____ A table from an external database that has been linked to the current database.

_____ Redundant copies of a data element are maintained at multiple nodes of a database.

_____ Data and applications in a database system can be distributed across multiple nodes, but the data are managed as an integrated whole.

_____ Different rows of a table are stored at different nodes.

_____ Users of a distributed database system do not need to be aware of the location of a particular data element.

_____ Data within or across tables of a database are divided between different locations for storage, but only one copy of each data element is maintained.

_____ Different columns of a table, or different tables within a database, are stored in different locations.

1. Distributed database management system
2. Replication
3. Partitioning
4. Horizontal partitioning
5. Vertical partitioning
6. Location transparency
7. Fragmentation transparency
8. Replication transparency
9. Failure transparency
10. Concurrency transparency

11. Attached table

12. Snapshot table

1. Discuss the dimensions of transparency as it pertains to distributed databases. Why does transparency become a more complex problem when data are distributed?

2. Describe and distinguish between replication and fragmentation.

3. Replication of data makes data retrieval simpler and quicker, but data insertion, modification, and deletion are more complex and time consuming. Why? What are the implications of this fact?

4. Distinguish between horizontal and vertical partitioning of data. Give an example of a situation where horizontal partitioning would be appropriate. Where vertical partitioning would be appropriate.

5. Assess the advantages and disadvantages of distributed database management systems. Where is this type of system most likely to be used?

6. Describe how attached tables are used in Access. What operations can be performed on attached tables? What operations are prohibited?

7. Describe the CREATE DATABASE LINK statement in Oracle. How do its capabilities compare to the attached tables used by Access?

8. Discuss the referential integrity hole that exists when attached or externally linked tables are used. How would you deal with the data integrity problems created by this hole?

9. Describe a snapshot table. How does it differ from a replica table? How does it differ from simply importing a table from another database?

10. What determines the frequency with which a snapshot table should be refreshed? What problems arise if it is refreshed too rarely? Too frequently?

11. How do the data requirements to support managers' analyses differ from the requirements of transaction processing?

12. What are the advantages of using a snapshot table, as compared to a view, to support managers' needs for summary data for analysis? Are there any disadvantages?

13. Why do data warehouse databases tend to have a "flat but broad" table structure?

14. How is the data of a data warehouse created and updated?

15. Investigate three operating databases at your school or at businesses in your area. Are any of them operating as distributed databases? Select one database and discuss the advantages and disadvantages of operating it as a distributed database system.

16. Suppose you are to be an analyst on a project involving development of a distributed database management system. What additional types of questions would you ask users in order to do an effective job of designing a distributed database system?

17. Suppose you are the database administrator at Air West Airlines. A proposal is made to develop the database system described in Chapter 5 as a distributed database system. Would you support or oppose this proposal? What arguments would you use to convince others to support your position?

18. Assuming that the Air West Airlines database were to be developed as a distributed database, which table or tables should be replicated? Why? Are there any tables that should be fragmented horizontally? Vertically? Explain and justify. Refer to Chapter 5 for information about the Air West Airlines database.

19. Assume that the set of airline reservation tables shown in Figure 6.3 have been created. You are now asked to create some linkages and snapshot tables to support distribution of this data. Assume all nodes are using an Oracle DBMS. The reservation tables are stored at Phoenix and you are working for a user group at San Francisco who want to get access to this data through their local DBMS. This group's user name and password for the Phoenix database are SFOUSERS and OLDENBAIT, respectively. The connect string to link to the Phoenix database is SUNCONN.

Write the statements required to make snapshot copies of the AIRPORT and FLIGHT tables that are to be updated at midnight next Sunday and at that same time every week thereafter. You are also to write the statements needed to establish links to the PASSENGER and TICKET tables.

20. Bipolar Products Co. has its headquarters in Dallas and has employees working for divisions based in Dallas, Phoenix, and St. Louis. Bipolar is developing a personnel database that is to be distributed across its three work sites. The accompanying sample listings show the data needed for this database. All processing of insurance claims and other information on the insurance report will be handled out of the headquarters in Dallas. On the other hand, employee wage and hour transactions will originate almost exclusively from the location where the employee works. There will actually be a separate Employee Wage Report for each work location for each pay period.

Each insurance plan is provided by only one provider. Each division of the company is assigned to only one location. There is a single assigned wage rate for each employee class. The wage rate for each employee class is assigned by headquarters and is changed only about once a year. Based on this information and assuming that this personnel database is to be implemented as a distributed database, indicate how the data shown in the following table should be distributed across the three locations.

Employee Insurance Report

Emp. ID#	Emp. Name	Hire Date	Insur. Plan#	Insurance Provider	Dep. ID#	Dep. Name	Dependent's Bir. Date
2674	J. Evans	07/02/85	03	Aetner	1784	D. Evans	02/18/81
					2846	R. Evans	05/03/88
3072	L. Ray	01/16/89	05	Cosmopolitan			
1028	W. Smith	02/28/83	03	Aetner	4072	L. Smith	11/03/88
3714	A. Adams	04/08/90	04	Cosmopolitan	3785	H. Adams	03/07/84
					3786	D. Adams	03/07/84
					3787	L. Adams	03/07/84

Employee Wage Report

Emp. ID#	Emp. Name	Assigned Division	Work Location	Period Ending	Hours Worked	Pay Class	Hourly Wage	Gross Pay
2674	J. Evans	PLM	St. Louis	11/26/97	72	V	$7.50	$540
3072	L. Ray	PLM	St. Louis	11/26/97	80	W	$7.00	$560
1028	W. Smith	HTD	St. Louis	11/26/97	80	V	$7.50	$600
3714	A. Adams	ALV	Dallas	11/26/97	40	W	$7.00	$280
4971	P. Powers	ALV	Dallas	11/26/97	80	X	$9.00	$720
6314	D. Davis	ALV	Dallas	11/26/97	80	V	$7.50	$600
1822	F. Funny	DPR	Phoenix	11/26/97	80	X	$9.00	$720
2674	J. Evans	PLM	St. Louis	12/10/97	80	V	$7.50	$600

21. Based on your answer to question 20, write the statements you would use to create needed database links, snapshot tables, and views users will need to support this database system. Assume that the system is to be implemented as three Oracle databases, one located at each work site.

OBJECT-ORIENTED DATABASE SYSTEMS

LEARNING OBJECTIVES

After completing this chapter you should be able to

- Describe the key features of the semantic data model (SDM) and assess how these features are supported by various DBMS products.

- Distinguish between aggregation and generalization relationships.

- Use the semantic object model to develop a conceptual model of a small database system.

- Describe the basic components of the object-oriented model including: objects, object classes, attributes, and methods.

- Describe how messages are used to access methods and data in encapsulated objects and write a simple example of this concept using pseudocode.

- Understand and give examples of inheritance, multi-inheritance, and polymorphism.

- Understand the difference between an object-oriented programming language (OOPL) and an object-oriented database management system (OODBMS).

- Describe and assess the availability of object-oriented features within commercial relational DBMS products.

In this chapter we examine the object-oriented data model. Three central features of the object-oriented data model distinguish it from other database models. First, the data representing a thing and methods to be applied to that data are stored together as an object. Methods describe the behavior of an object, the processes that can be performed on its data. Second, the data and methods of an object are *encapsulated*— they cannot be directly viewed by other objects or processes. Data are accessed and processes performed by sending messages to the methods of an object activating them to perform the needed work. Finally, object-oriented systems support inheritance. Lower level (child) objects inherit both the data and the methods of the higher level (parent) objects with which they are associated.

Full implementation of these object-oriented principles requires a rethinking of the database development process from the conceptual design stage through the choice of a DBMS for implementation. Object-oriented modeling uses data structures that are more complex than those commonly provided by the E-R model. Representations and structures that have evolved from the semantic data model, or SDM, are often used in the conceptual design process for object-oriented databases. An object-oriented database management system (OODBMS) is needed to implement a database that conforms fully to the object-oriented data model. However, object-oriented analysis and design methods can be, and often are, used with the relational data model to develop database systems incorporating many features of the object-oriented model.

In the sections that follow, we will give an overview of the object-oriented data model and OODBMSs. We will describe key elements of the SDM and see how it can be used in conceptual modeling of object-oriented databases. We will describe the semantic object model (SOM) and use it to graphically represent the object-oriented data model at the conceptual level. We will present a description of the basic components of the object-oriented model. Finally, we will discuss how these components are being implemented in OODBMS, and will examine how selected object-oriented concepts are being incorporated into relational DBMS products.

THE SEMANTIC DATA MODEL

The term **semantic data model (SDM),** refers to a whole family of related conceptual modeling methodologies that have grown out of the work of Hammer and McLoed (1981). The semantic data model uses object terminology. The "things" that are to be modeled are referred to as objects rather than entities. For now, we can think of the term *object* as corresponding to an entity occurrence in the E-R model. The term *object class* corresponds to an entity class, and attributes have essentially the same meaning they had in the E-R model. We will define these terms more formally in a later section of this chapter.

The SDM provides a *semantically complete* model of the structure of data by supporting a more complex set of data structures than that commonly provided by the E-R model. The SDM insists that two alternative types of relationships can exist between objects (entities) in a hierarchy—*generalization* and *aggregation.* These two

Semantic data model (SDM)
A type of conceptual data modeling methodology that emphasizes completeness in capturing complex logical relationships within the conceptual model.

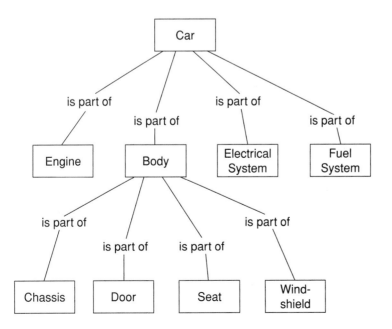

FIGURE 13.1
A Car Is an Aggregation of Components

alternative relationship types are fundamentally different and should have distinct representations. Current E-R modeling structures recognize the distinction between these two relationship types. However, this distinction was first drawn and is still a central feature of the SDM. The SDM also supports richer specifications of the nature of attributes. Any form of *domain restrictions* on attributes is allowed and *derived attributes* can be specified as a part of the data model. As we will see, many of these SDM data structures are well suited for implementation using an object-oriented approach but are difficult to implement in traditional (hierarchical, network, and relational) models.

THE AGGREGATION RELATIONSHIP TYPE

An aggregation object is related to its components by an *is-part-of* relationship. For example, as Figure 13.1 suggests, a Car might be thought of as an aggregation of Engine, Body, Electrical-System, and Fuel-System objects. Each of these subcomponents *is-part-of* a Car, and each might, in turn, be seen as an aggregation object. For example, a Body object is an aggregation of Chassis, Door, Seat, and Windshield objects, and so on. The relationship between an aggregation object and its subcomponents may be one to one or one to many. Each Car has only one engine. However, a car body might have two or more door or seat subcomponents.

Aggregation relationship
A relationship between a parent object and a set of child (subclass) objects in which each child object is a part or component of the parent object.

A hierarchy of **aggregation relationships** is shown in Figure 13.1. The aggregation object class Car contains not only its subcomponents, but also all subcomponents of those subcomponents. Thus, the Chassis, Door, Seat, and Windshield object classes are part of the Car object class because they are part of the Body object class, which is, in turn, part of the Car object class.

Aggregations are quite prevalent in our descriptions of everyday things. For instance, a customer's name and address are each potentially aggregation objects.

FIGURE 13.2
Name and Address as Aggregations

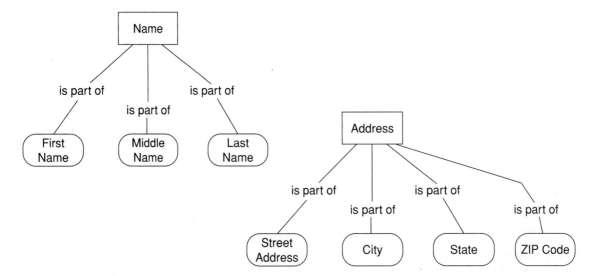

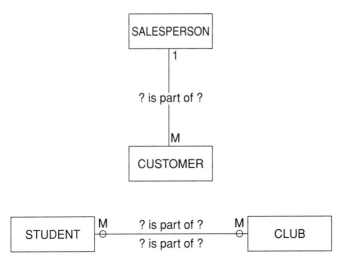

FIGURE 13.3
The Salesperson-
Customer Relationship

FIGURE 13.4
The Student-Club
Relationship

As Figure 13.2 indicates, a Name can be thought of as an aggregation of First Name, Middle Name (or initial), and Last Name.

Similarly, an Address is an aggregation of Street Address, City, State, and ZIP Code. These aggregations are not commonly represented by tables in Relational models because the components of these aggregations can be stored along with other attributes of a customer in a single customer table without violating normalization rules. However, these aggregations are meaningful metadata. When we ask what someone's address is, we are asking for exactly the aggregation of attributes shown in Figure 13.2.

Most one to many relationships between objects can be interpreted as aggregation relationships. Take, for instance, the relationship between salespersons and customers shown in Figure 13.3. We are assuming that each customer is assigned to one salesperson, but each salesperson may be responsible for more than one customer. Are the Customers assigned to a Salesperson "part of" that Salesperson? Physically, no! However, information about the customers assigned to a salesperson is a "part of" the set of information describing that salesperson.

Following the same line of reasoning, many to many relationships between objects can often be thought of as bidirectional aggregation relationships. For instance, the relationship between students and clubs in Figure 13.4 shows that a club can have many students as members and a student can belong to more than one club. From the student perspective, information about clubs to which the student belongs is "part of" the set of information describing the student. At the same time, from the club perspective, information about students who belong to a particular club is "part of" the set of information about the club.

This broad definition of aggregation is particularly useful in conceptual modeling. At the same time, it is useful to retain a special designation for those aggregation relationships in which the *is-part-of* relationship can be thought of in a physical sense. We will refer to these physical aggregation relationships as *class composition hierarchies.*

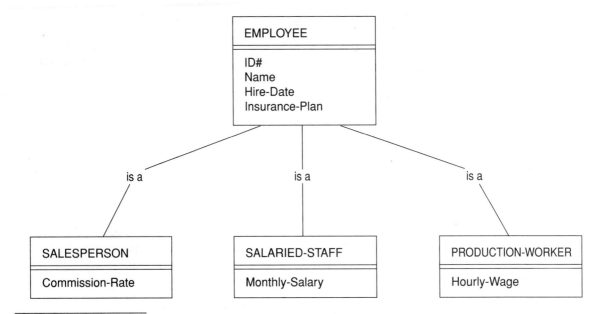

FIGURE 13.5
A Generalization
Relationship

**Generalization
relationship**
A relationship between a
parent object and a set of
child (subclass) objects in
which each child object
is a specialization or type
of the parent object.

THE GENERALIZATION RELATIONSHIP TYPE

The **generalization relationship** is actually a generalization-specialization relationship. Figure 13.5 illustrates this type of relationship. Suppose that a firm has three categories of employees: Salesperson, Salaried-Staff, and Production-Worker. Each type of worker can be thought of as a *specialization* of the object-type (entity class) Employee. At the same time, the Employee object-type can be thought of as a *generalization* of the Salesperson, Salaried-Staff, and Production-Worker object-types. This relationship is also described as an *is-a* relationship. Each Salesperson, Salaried-Staff, or Production-Worker *is-a*(n) Employee. This *is-a* notation was used in representing class-subclass relationships in the E-R model.

Characteristics (attributes) are defined for the objects at each level of the hierarchy. Attributes defined for objects higher in the hierarchy are *inherited* by all their specializations that appear below them in the hierarchy. As Figure 13.5 indicates, Employee ID#, Employee Name, Hire-Date, and Insurance-Plan attributes might be defined for the Employee object. These characteristics would be inherited by members of each of the specialized subcategories of the Employee object. Other attributes may be defined only for a specific specialization object. For example, a Commission-Rate attribute might be defined for Salespersons only.

The fundamental differences between aggregation and generalization should be clear. First, an instance of an aggregate object class contains instances of each of its related subclasses, whereas each instance of a generalization object normally contains only one of the related subclass specializations. An employee is a Salesperson *or* a Salaried-Staff member *or* a Production-Worker. However, a Car has an Engine *and* a Body *and* a Fuel System *and* an Electrical System. Second, generalization relationships logically have the property of inheritance, but aggregation relationships do not. The characteristics defined for the Employee object class logically apply to each of its specialization subclasses: Every Salesperson or Production-Worker has an ID#, a Name, a Hire-Date, and so forth. However, an engine does not have all the characteristics of the car of which it is a component.

ATTRIBUTE SPECIFICATIONS IN THE SDM

The SDM model also provides broad capabilities to describe attributes in a complete manner. In the original Hammer and McLoed specification, the SDM was presented in text rather than graphical form. Characteristics of attributes were described in narrative form. These descriptions could include any form of domain restriction. In addition to key restrictions—a primary key attribute must be unique—other, more complex forms of restrictions could be specified. For instance, in the Airline database, we might want to specify that the Meal attribute can only be assigned the values B, L, D, or S.

More complex types of restrictions could be conceived involving interactions between attributes perhaps belonging to different objects. A particular plane should be assigned to a flight only if that plane will be at the airport at least 30 minutes prior to the time the flight is scheduled to depart. Such a restriction is quite complex, and yet it is a legitimate expression of metadata.

The SDM also provides for the specification of derived attributes as a part of the structure of data. For example, seniority is often a meaningful attribute of an employee, but how is the level of seniority determined? It can be derived by subtracting the date an employee was hired from the current date. Under the SDM, seniority would be defined as a derived attribute and its method of derivation would be recorded as a part of the conceptual model.

IMPLEMENTING SDM STRUCTURES

Two important features of the object-oriented model give it strong capabilities to implement the SDM structures that we have been discussing. The object-oriented model supports inheritance, and it allows methods, as well as data, to be stored in objects. Other data models are much more limited in their ability to support these structures, although the capabilities of many relational DBMSs are being expanded to incorporate many key object-oriented capabilities.

Characteristics of an object should automatically be inherited by its subclasses. However, traditional data models do not support inheritance: Characteristics stored in an object can be accessed by one of its subclasses only by walking pointer chains (hierarchical and network models) or by joining tables (relational model). This limitation is eliminated under the object-oriented model, which supports automatic inheritance by a subclass of the characteristics defined for its superclass.

The importance of being able to store methods as a part of objects becomes apparent when one examines the SDM's treatment of attributes. Many types of domain restrictions on attributes have been difficult to implement using the traditional data models. The simple restriction that the Meal attribute of a flight can have only the values of B, L, D, or S is readily implemented in most current relational DBMSs through use of a CHECK statement.

A more complex restriction, such as that requiring a plane assigned to a specific flight to be chosen only from among those planes at the departure airport at the appropriate flight time, requires the execution of a fairly sophisticated module of code to test the condition. Under the object-oriented model, this restriction is simply stored as a method associated with the Flight-Schedule object. The TRIGGER statement, used in some relational DBMS products, is essentially a restricted type of method that allows this type of restriction to be imposed in the relational model. We will discuss the trigger statement later in this chapter.

Some forms of restrictions on the relationships between object classes are difficult or impossible to impose under traditional data models. For example, in Figure 13.5, Salesperson, Salaried-Staff, and Production-Worker are mandatory, but mutually exclusive, specializations of Employee. Each Employee must be a Salesperson, a Salaried-Staff member, or a Production-Worker, and no employee can belong to more than one of these subclasses. This restriction involves interactions among more than two tables (the EMPLOYEE table and each of its subclass tables) and cannot be enforced by most current relational DBMSs.

Many current DBMSs also prohibit the storage of derived attributes in the database. Take, for example, the Seniority characteristic of an employee described earlier. The value of seniority is determined by data manipulation—subtracting an employee's Hire-Date from the current date. Storing it as an attribute would create data redundancy and is inefficient because the seniority level changes continuously with the passage of time. This type of data can be included in a database only by causing its derivation formula to be executed in response to a query.

Fundamentally, these limitations of current models come from the sharp distinction they draw between data and processes. The database is to contain only the *permanent* data of the organization and not the *transitory* processes that manipulate the data. However, the domain restrictions and derived attribute specifications we have described earlier are inherent, permanent properties of the data. Ideally, these properties should be a part of our data model. By incorporating methods as well as data in its objects, an object-oriented database is easily able to build properties of this type into the data model.

THE SEMANTIC OBJECT MODEL

BASIC STRUCTURE

Semantic object model (SOM)
A conceptual modeling tool designed to provide diagrammatic representations of data in a form consistent with the SDM and the object oriented-model.

Hammer and McLoed's original formulation of the SDM presented all model components in textual form. A number of researchers have developed extensions of the original SDM that use graphical representations of the model components to improve understanding. **Semantic object modeling (SOM)** (Kroenke, 1995) is a graphical modeling methodology that uses object-oriented terminology and incorporates many features of the SDM. We will use the SOM to illustrate key SDM concepts graphically.

Semantic object modeling uses a rectangle to represent each object class. The name of the object is given above the rectangle representing its contents, and

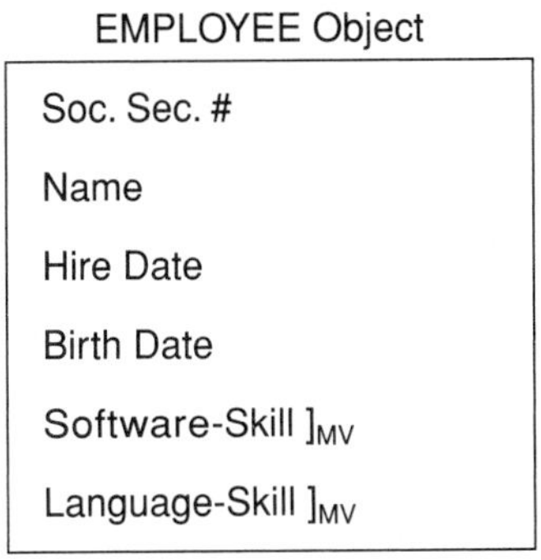

EMPLOYEE Object

```
Soc. Sec. #

Name

Hire Date

Birth Date

Software-Skill ]MV

Language-Skill ]MV
```

FIGURE 13.6
The Employee
Object Class

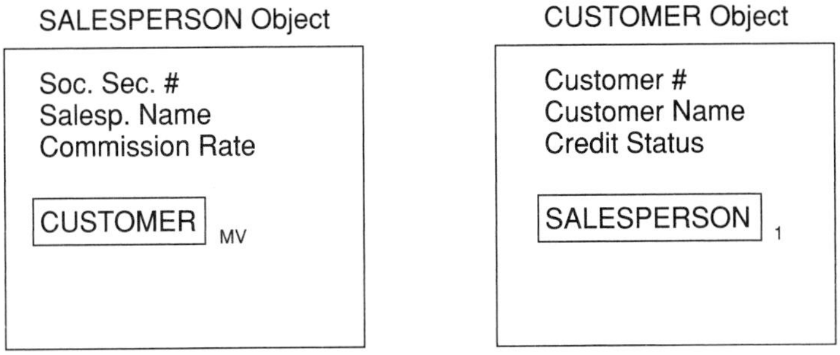

SALESPERSON Object

```
Soc. Sec. #
Salesp. Name
Commission Rate

CUSTOMER   MV
```

CUSTOMER Object

```
Customer #
Customer Name
Credit Status

SALESPERSON   1
```

FIGURE 13.7
Compound Objects

the attributes and *other objects* that make up the object are described within the rectangle.

Figure 13.6 shows a simple example of how an Employee object class might be represented. Attributes' names are listed in the rectangular box representing the Object.

The Software-Skill and Language-Skill attributes are of particular interest. An employee might have language skills in French, Spanish, and German or software skills in the use of both word processors and spreadsheets. Under semantic object modeling, the MV label is used to indicate that the attributes are multivalued and are treated as part of the base Employee object. Using Kroenke's terminology, an object with only single-valued attributes is a **simple object,** while one containing multivalued attributes is a **composite object.**

Simple object
An object containing only single-valued attributes.

Composite object
An object containing multivalued attributes.

COMPOUND OBJECTS

Aggregation relationships are represented through the use of compound objects. A **compound object** is one that includes another object. One object can be included as "a part of" another object by placing the included object's Name in a rectangular box inside the object being described (see Figure 13.7). Information about Customers assigned to a Salesperson is a part of the information describing that Salesperson, so the Customer object is included in the Salesperson object. The aggregate object includes its component subclass objects.

Compound object
An object type that includes or contains another object type, where an aggregation relationship exists between the two object types.

Note, however, that the Salesperson object is also included in the description of the Customer object class. From the Customer object's perspective, information about the Salesperson who serves a Customer is a part of the set of data describing that Customer. The broad definition of aggregation relationships is being used here. Thus, each of two related object classes can be thought of as containing the other.

The MV next to the Customer box in the Salesperson object representation indicates that this is a multivalued relationship. More than one Customer can be assigned to a Salesperson. The 1 next to the Salesperson box in the Customer object representation indicates the *minimum* cardinality of the relationship. Every Customer object must be associated with a Salesperson.

The compound object type can also be used to represent many to many relationships between objects, like the one between Student and Club. A Student can

FIGURE 13.8
The STUDENT and
CLUB Object Classes

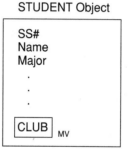

FIGURE 13.9
An Association Object

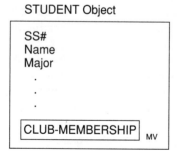

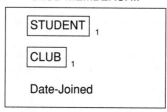

belong to many Clubs and each Club can have many Students as members. This is the bidirectional aggregation relationship that we described in an earlier section and presented in Figure 13.4. To represent this type of relationship in the SOM, each object is included in the other's object definition with an MV next to it, as shown in Figure 13.8.

ASSOCIATION OBJECTS

Of course, there may be attributes that are identified by the relationship between Student and Club. For example, we might want to record the date when a particular Student joined a particular Club. To store this data we would need to create a Student-Club object with Date-Joined as its attribute, as shown in Figure 13.9. This type of object is sometimes referred to as an **association object,** and it has the same role as the intersection entity described for E-R modeling.

Association object
An object type that represents an association between two other (parent) object types.

GENERALIZATION OBJECTS

Generalization relationships are also represented by placing the name of an object in the description of a related object. Figure 13.10 shows how the Employee generalization

FIGURE 13.10
A Generalization Object

EMPLOYEE Object

ID #

Name

Hire-Date

Insurance Plan

SALESPERSON

OR

SALARIED-STAFF

OR

PRODUCTION-WORKER ₁

SALESPERSON Object

Commission-Rate

EMPLOYEE ₁

SALARIED-STAFF Object

Monthly-Salary

EMPLOYEE ₁

PRODUCTION-WORKER Object

Hourly-Wage

EMPLOYEE ₁

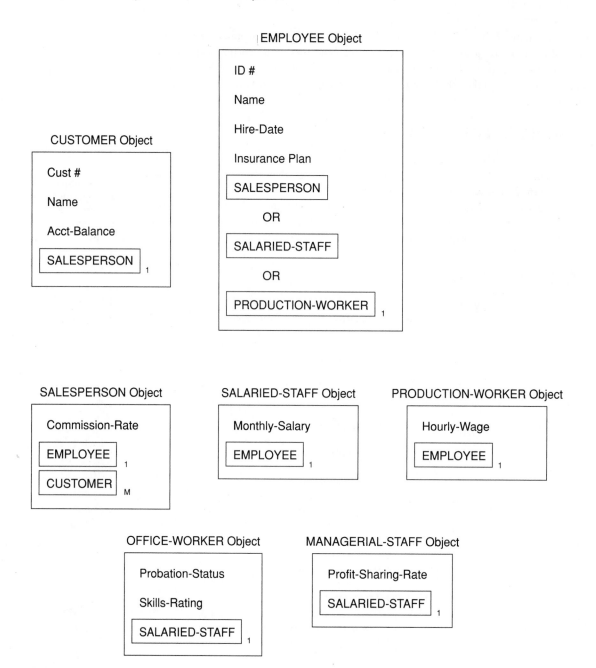

FIGURE 13.11
A Complex Object Structure

hierarchy, previously presented in Figure 13.5, would be represented using semantic object modeling. The word OR between the subclass names indicates that each member of the generalization class belongs to only one of its subclasses. An Employee can be a Salesperson *OR* a Salaried-Staff member *OR* a Production-Worker. The 1 after the last subclass indicates that the relationship is mandatory—every employee must be in one of these groups.

On the subclass side, each specialization object instance contains an instance of the related **generalization object** *and inherits characteristics from it.* The SALES-PERSON, SALARIED-STAFF, and PRODUCTION-WORKER class descriptions each inherit characteristics from the EMPLOYEE object class. Thus, Name and Hire-Date can be thought of as characteristics of SALESPERSON or of PRODUCTION-WORKER, and so on.

Generalization object
An object type that includes or contains related subclass object types, where a generalization relationship exists between the object type and the subclass object types.

COMPLEX OBJECT STRUCTURES

An object may have multiple types of relationships with other object classes. The OFFICE-WORKER and MANAGERIAL-STAFF object classes that have been added to Figure 13.10 to produce Figure 13.11 are specializations of the Salaried-Staff object class. Thus, the SALARIED-STAFF object class is both a specialization of EMPLOYEE and a generalization of the OFFICE-WORKER and MANAGERIAL-STAFF classes.

The CUSTOMER object class has also been added. Note the aggregation relationship between salespersons and customers, represented by making each a compound object containing the other.

METHODS IN THE SOM

Methods associated with an object are not normally included in its SOM representation. However, we can extend the SOM to include methods by adding a double line across the rectangle representing an object class and listing methods below that line. Figure 13.12 shows the EMPLOYEE object class representation with the Seniority method added. Recall that seniority is a derived characteristic of an employee. The Seniority method performs the computations necessary to derive the value of seniority for an employee.

A similar technique is commonly used to add methods to E-R diagrams. Figure 13.13 illustrates a form of E-R notation that has been expanded to include attribute names and methods names.

EMPLOYEE Object

Soc. Sec. #
Name
Hire Date
Birth Date
Software-Skill]$_{MV}$
Language-Skill]$_{MV}$
Methods: Seniority

FIGURE 13.12
The Employee Object Class with Methods Represented in the SOM

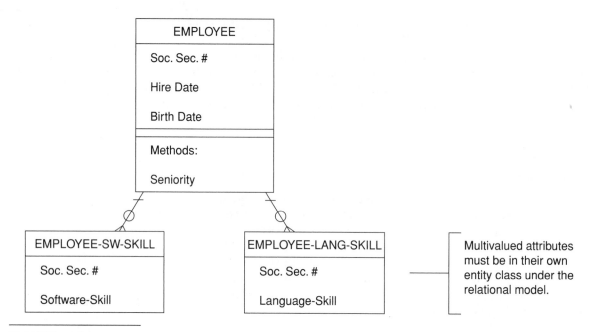

FIGURE 13.13
The Employee Entity
Type with Methods
Represented in the
E-R Model

THE SOM AS A CONCEPTUAL MODELING TOOL

Proponents of the semantic object model argue that it describes data in a way that is easier for users to understand than the relationship arrows provided by the E-R model. However, the semantic object model has not yet gained wide use among practitioners. Perhaps its most distinctive feature is the manner in which it depicts objects as containing each other. This provides a good method for visualizing the concept of inheritance and will be used for illustration purposes later in this chapter.

OBJECT-ORIENTED DATABASE MANAGEMENT SYSTEMS

Object-oriented database management systems (OODBMSs) have taken many of their key features from Object-Oriented Programming Languages (OOPLs). Although an object-oriented language called ALGOL had been in existence since 1960, object-oriented programming began to enter the mainstream of programming languages with the emergence of SmallTalk, which originated in 1977, and the subsequent development of object-oriented versions of the C language, Such as C++.

OOPLs provide database-like data structures. However, the object structures created by the programming languages do not provide for the persistent storage of data between executions of a program. Thus, the development of OODBMSs to provide for the persistent storage of objects (and more efficient handling of large volumes of data) can be seen as a natural extension of OOPL concepts. For a full discussion of object-oriented design principles, see Booch (1991).

In previous sections, we have used several terms associated with the object-oriented model without fully describing them. These terms will now be formally defined and discussed in greater detail as we begin to describe the key features of OOPLs and OODBMSs.

OBJECTS

The most fundamental building block of the object-oriented model is the object. An **object** is an abstract representation of the properties of a real-world thing. The properties of the object include both data attributes and behavior. As we will see, the behavior portion of an object is represented by methods that can be applied to and stored with the object's data.

Each object must have an Object ID (OID), which is assigned by the system and guaranteed to be unique. The OID is different from a primary key attribute assigned by users. The OID for an object can never be modified and, once assigned, is never reused even if the object associated with it is deleted. The OID performs functions somewhat similar to the pointers used in network and hierarchical databases. The OID is used to link related objects. However, the OID does not in any way reference a physical storage location. Thus, OIDs are unaffected by changes in physical storage structures. Primary key attributes may still be employed by users to help them identify objects. However, the primary keys are no longer used for navigation of relationships among objects.

Object
An abstract representation of the properties of a real-world thing that has a unique identity and can have embedded attributes and behavior.

OBJECT CLASSES

Objects that share a common structure are organized into **object classes.** As shown in Figure 13.14, Joe Barnes and Ann Evans are each represented by a unique object. The objects representing these individuals and all other individuals employed by XZY Company might constitute an Employee Object Class. A set of objects belong together in an object class if they have common properties. There should be a common set of attributes possessed by all the objects in the class and common methods that can be applied to all objects in the class. In our example, each Employee has a name, an assigned department, and a hire date.

Object class
A grouping of related object instances and their methods. Objects organized into an Object Class share common attributes and/or methods.

ATTRIBUTES

Attributes essentially have the same meaning under the object-oriented model that they had in the E-R model. Attributes of an object are simply characteristics that describe the object. However, as we will see, an attribute of an object can be the OID of another object.

METHODS

Object classes also contain methods. **Methods** are a unique feature of the object-oriented model that allow it to capture the behavior of objects. Figure 13.15 illustrates the relationship between methods and objects. Objects are accessed by sending messages to their methods. Any process or operation performed on an object or a class of objects must be performed by a method. A method is identified by a method name.

Method
A named set of instructions that is part of an object class and that can be used to perform operations on object instances or on the object class.

FIGURE 13.14
Objects with Common
Properties Form a
Class

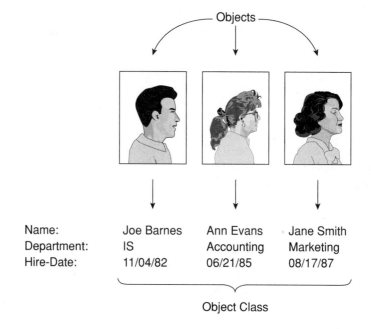

Name:	Joe Barnes	Ann Evans	Jane Smith
Department:	IS	Accounting	Marketing
Hire-Date:	11/04/82	06/21/85	08/17/87

Object Class

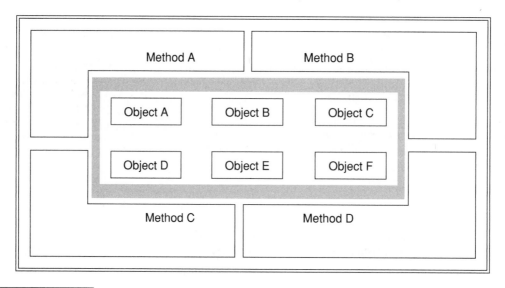

FIGURE 13.15
An Object Class
Contains Objects
and Methods

The body of a method is a set of computer instructions in some programming language. Methods are used to change the state of an object's attribute values, to print or display attribute values or information derived from them, and even to create object instances. Methods may operate on individual objects or may operate on an object class.

ENCAPSULATION

Encapsulation means that the methods and objects of an object class are hidden from view. Neither the contents of a method nor the data values assigned to an object may be directly viewed or modified by external entities. Only the names of methods and the names of attributes are public information. Messages sent to the object can request that a named method be performed on an object having a certain value for a named attribute. Methods are executed in a black box fashion. A method accesses data as needed and executes its instructions to produce a result. However, only the result is visible externally. Neither the contents of the method nor the object data values are visible externally.

An example of a method operating on individual objects in Figure 13.16 is Seniority. Seniority, the length of service with the company, can be determined by subtracting an employee's hire date from the current date. This method is associated with the Employee object class because it determines the length of service for any employee of the company.

Methods and objects are accessed by sending them messages. A message specifies the receiver object (or object class), the method, and one or more parameters, if needed. For example, suppose we want to find the Seniority level of Ann Evans. Figure 13.17 illustrates this using pseudocode to describe the message and method

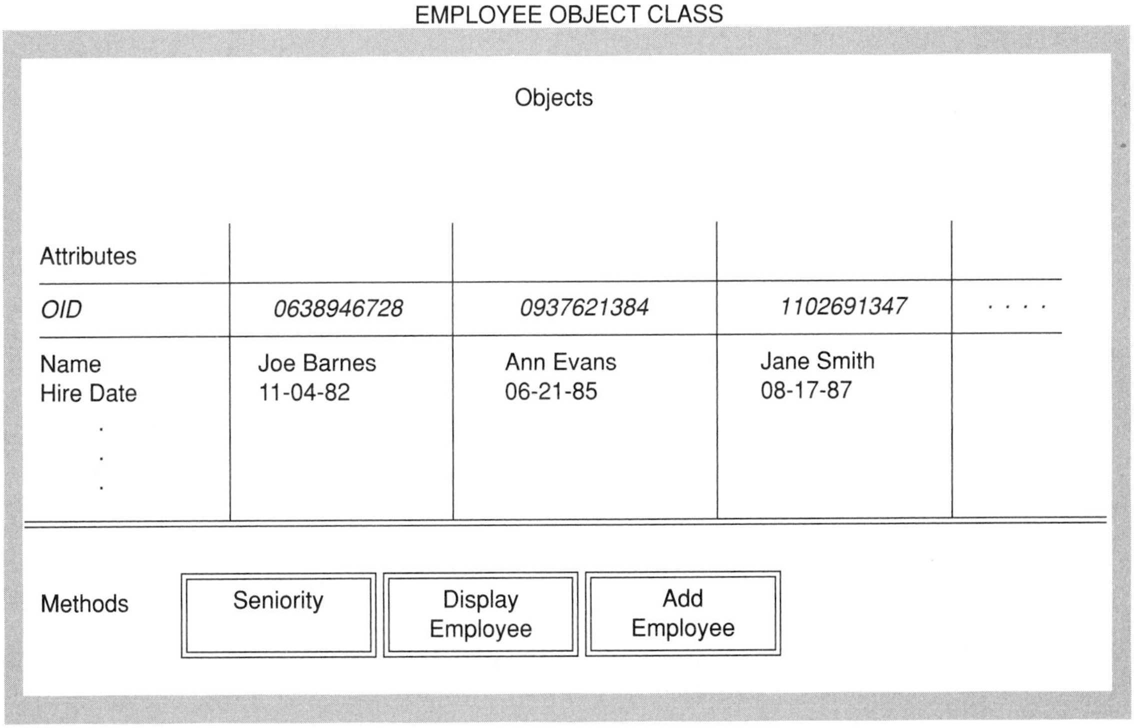

Encapsulation
The process of hiding the contents of objects and methods from view by entities external to the object class.

FIGURE 13.16
An Example of
an Object Class

EMPLOYEE OBJECT CLASS

Objects				
Attributes				
OID	*0638946728*	*0937621384*	*1102691347*	. . . .
Name Hire Date	Joe Barnes 11-04-82	Ann Evans 06-21-85	Jane Smith 08-17-87	

Methods	Seniority	Display Employee	Add Employee

Message: Perform the SENIORITY Method
　　　　　on the EMPLOYEE Object whose Name is "Ann Evans"
　　　　　Parameter -> System_Date

Method SENIORITY:　　　　　　　　　　　　　　　EMPLOYEE OBJECT INSTANCES

Accept Parameter Value into Current_Date

Seniority_Level = Current_Date - Hire_Date

Return Seniority_Level

Attributes		
OID	OI5267	OI1847
Name	Joe Barnes	Ann Evans
Hire Date	11-04-82	06-21-85

FIGURE 13.17
A Message Causes a
Method to Be
Executed

content. A message would be sent to the Employee object class requesting that the Seniority method be applied to the "Ann Evans" object. (Note that the message identifies the object by a key attribute. The OID is used only by the system.) In this case one data value external to the object class must be supplied to the method. The system date is sent to the method as a parameter value. This message causes the method Seniority to be performed on the "Ann Evans" object. Ann Evans's hire date is subtracted from the system date and the answer is returned by the method.

A method can call (send a message to) another method. For example, suppose we need to know the average seniority level of all employees. An AVE-SENIORITY method might be created to generate this result. AVE-SENIORITY would be a class method because its value is a characteristic of the EMPLOYEE object class as a whole. To determine the average seniority level across all employees, we must determine the seniority level for each EMPLOYEE object and then take an average across all objects in the class. Figure 13.18 shows a set of pseudocode for the AVE-SENIORITY method. The AVE-SENIORITY method takes advantage of the fact that we already have a SENIORITY method that returns the seniority level of an individual EMPLOYEE object. The AVE-SENIORITY method is designed to find the first object in the EMPLOYEE object class and then work through each object instance. The SENIORITY method is performed and the results are accumulated for each EMPLOYEE object. Once the last EMPLOYEE object has been processed, the Ave_Seniority is computed and returned as the result of the AVE-SENIORITY method.

In the preceding case, one method called another method defined on the same object class. However, a method can call another method defined on its own *or a different* object class, which could, in turn, call another method defined on its own or another object class, and so on.

One type of method that is of particular interest to us is a method used to create a new object (add a record). Such a method (let's call it CREATE-OBJECT) must address the object class and not a specific *existing* object instance. The CREATE-OBJECT method must cause a set of attribute values for the new object to be collected,

Message: Perform the AVE-SENIORITY Method
            on the EMPLOYEE Object Class
            Parameter -> System_Date

Method AVE_SENIORITY:
    Accept Parameter Value into Current_Date
    Total_Seniority = 0
    Employee_Count = 0
    Find first EMPLOYEE Object
    Current_Name = Name

While there are more EMPLOYEE Objects to process
        Send message: Perform SENIORITY Method
                on the EMPLOYEE whose Name is Current_Name
                Parameter -> Current_Date
      Accept Return into Seniority_Level
      Total_Seniority = Total_Seniority + Seniority_Level
      Employee_Count = Employee_Count + 1
      Find next EMPLOYEE object
Ave_Seniority = Total_Seniority / Employee Count
Return Ave_Seniority

Attributes				
OID	0638946728	0937621384	1102691347	· · ·
Name	Joe Barnes	Ann Evans	Jane Smith	
Hire Date	11-04-82	06-21-85	08-17-87	
·				
·				
·				

FIGURE 13.18
An Example of a
Class Method

it must associate a unique OID with the object, and it must cause the data for this object instance to be stored. The CREATE-OBJECT method is also responsible for enforcing any necessary domain restrictions on attributes. Restrictions involving retrieval and processing of data from other object classes can be enforced, because the CREATE-OBJECT method can use programming language processing instructions and is able to call methods defined on other objects.

OBJECTS AS ATTRIBUTES OF OTHER OBJECTS

Under the object-oriented model the values of attributes may contain a value expressed in the form of some base data type—an integer, a string, and so on. Alternatively, an attribute can be defined as an **abstract data type (ADT).** An ADT is a chunk of data whose structure is not known by the object in which it appears as an attribute. An ADT can contain a combination of attributes in various forms. Its structure is user defined and self-contained. This should sound very much like the

Abstract data type (ADT)
A chunk of data that appears as an attribute of an object, but whose structure is not known by the object in which it appears. An object can be included in another object by specifying the second object as an ADT in the first object.

definition of an object class. Essentially, that is what an ADT is. One object can be included in another object by specifying it as an ADT attribute of that object. What is stored in the ADT attribute is the OID of the object to be referenced. The OID is not treated as a value, but rather is used to link to the location of the referenced object. Once there, the structure and methods associated with the referenced object become available. This, in effect, allows one object to be included in another object.

MULTIMEDIA DATA

The ability of an object to contain another object gives the object-oriented model powerful capabilities to handle data in varied forms. For example, suppose we want to store a picture of each employee in our database. The data needed to produce a picture have a different structure than standard numeric and text data. A picture is stored

FIGURE 13.19
A Picture as
an Object

EMPLOYEE

Structure	Objects		
Identity (OID)	OI5267	OI1847	OI2837
Attributes			
Name	Joe Barnes	Ann Evans	Jane Smith
Hire-Date	11-04-82	06-21-85	08-17-87
Birth Date	07-18-59	09-03-63	01-22-61
E-Picture	OI89234	OI91673	OI88674
Methods	SENIORITY	AVE-SENIORITY	

EMPLOYEE-PICTURE

Structure	Objects		
Identity (OID)	OI89234	OI91673	OI88674
Picture (Stored as a BLOB)			
Methods	Display	Print	

as a huge chunk of data describing the picture dot-by-dot (pixel-by-pixel). This chunk of data must be processed by a set of instructions that understand its structure in order to display or print the picture appropriately. In the object-oriented model, the chunk of data describing the picture and the methods required to process that data would simply be stored as an object. This type of object is sometimes called a *binary large object* (BLOB). In the case of our employee example, we might create an EMPLOYEE-PICTURE object class to store this information (Figure 13.19). The picture of an employee would then be defined as an ADT attribute in the employee object class, making it possible to display or print the employee's picture.

This same mechanism can be used for other data media as well. For instance, digitized voice messages and instructions for processing them could be stored in an object. Thus, the object-oriented model provides a very powerful and flexible mechanism for storing and using multimedia databases.

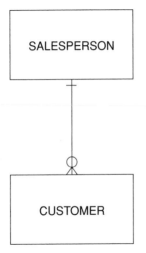

FIGURE 13.20
Entity-Relationship Model Representation of the Salesperson-Customer Relationship

Semantic Object Model Representation

SALESPERSON Object

CUSTOMER Object

CLASS COMPOSITION HIERARCHIES

The idea of making one object a part of another object through the ADT mechanism is also used to represent physical aggregation relationships (class composition hierarchies). Because the subclass objects in this type of aggregation hierarchy are physically part of the aggregation object, their OIDs are included as ADT attributes of the aggregation object. For example, an Engine, a Body, an Electrical System, and a Fuel System are all physical parts of a Car. Thus, when representing this type of relationship in the object-oriented model, each Car object would contain OIDs associated with its Engine, its Body, its Electrical System, and its Fuel System as ADT attributes.

Can this concept of containing one object in another be extended to other types of relationships? Let's examine the CUSTOMER object class and its relationship with the SALESPERSON object class. The SOM and E-R representations of the relationship are shown in Figure 13.20. CUSTOMER and SALESPERSON are compound objects. We are assuming that each customer is assigned to only one salesperson, but a salesperson can serve many customers.

Each SALESPERSON object is a parent object type that can have zero to many CUSTOMER objects as children. Because each CUSTOMER is related to only one

FIGURE 13.21
An Aggregate Relationship Between Object Classes

SALESPERSON

Structure	Objects	
Identity (OID)	OI2837	OI3462

Attributes
  Name
  Hire-Date
  Commission-Rate
  Customers (ADT)
	Lewis
	12/12/96
	.030
	OI16293, OI19011, ...
		Thomas
		10/05/97
		.025
		OI13745, OI18113, ...

CUSTOMER

Structure	Objects			
Identity (OID)	OI13745	OI16293	OI18113	OI19011

Attributes
  Customer-No
  Name
  Credit-Status
	272
	Smith, J.
	B
		714
		Evans, R.
		A
			381
			Norris, P.
			C
				407
				Allen, A.
				B

SALESPERSON, this relationship can be viewed as a hierarchy. SALESPERSON is at a higher level of the hierarchy, and Customers can be viewed as "parts of" the SALESPERSON object. To represent this, we simply add an ADT attribute to the SALESPERSON object, which might be called Customers. It contains a list of the OIDs of each CUSTOMER object associated with a particular SALESPERSON, as shown in Figure 13.21. This type of specification could be used if an attribute of an object is allowed to have a set of values.

When the standard class specification does not allow for multivalued attributes, a special type of object class called a *collection class* is commonly used to implement

FIGURE 13.22
Using a Collection
Object Class

SALESPERSON

Structure	Objects	
Identity (OID)	OI2837	OI3462
Attributes Name Hire-Date Commission-Rate Customers (ADT)	Lewis 12/12/96 .030 OI2814	Thomas 10/05/97 .025 OI2922

COLLECTION-OF-CUSTOMERS

Structure	Objects	
Identity (OID)	OI2814	OI2922
Attributes Set-of- Customers (ADT)	OI16293, OI19011, .	OI13745, OI18113, .

CUSTOMER

Structure	Objects			
Identity (OID)	OI13745	OI16293	OI18113	OI19011
Attributes Customer-No Name Credit-Status	272 Smith, J. B	714 Evans, R. A	381 Norris, P. C	407 Allen, A. B

one to many associations. A collection object class stores collections of OIDS. Each object instance contains the OIDs of all the objects on the many side of a relationship that are associated with a particular occurrence of the object class on the one side of the relationship (see Figure 13.22). The COLLECTION-OF-CUSTOMERS object class stores sets of OIDS of CUSTOMER objects, where each COLLECTION-OF-CUSTOMERS object occurrence contains the OIDs of all customers assigned to a particular salesperson. Each SALESPERSON object class contains the OID of the one COLLECTION-OF-CUSTOMERS associated with that customer.

It is tempting to use this same ADT mechanism to document the reverse association from customer to salesperson. Could we place in each CUSTOMER object the OID of his or her associated SALESPERSON object? This is the type of inclusive relationship that the SOM implies. However, at the implementation level, this cannot be allowed. Under such a system, when we retrieved a SALESPERSON object it would retrieve several CUSTOMER objects and they, in turn, would each retrieve the SALESPERSON object as parts of them, and so on. To avoid this sort of endless looping, the ADT mechanism is restricted to creating hierarchies of objects very similar in structure to those produced by the hierarchical data model. Join operations similar to the relational join are used when it is necessary to bring together data from multiple related hierarchies.

SUPERCLASSES, SUBCLASSES, AND INHERITANCE

FIGURE 13.23
Superclass
Identification in Objects

The superclass-subclass relationship is a central concept of the object-oriented model. When an object class is defined, in addition to identifying its attributes and methods,

EMPLOYEE

Structure	Objects		
Identity (OID)	OI5267	OI1847	OI2837
Super Class Universal	OI0242	OI0242	OI0242
Attributes Name Hire-Date Birth Date	Joe Barnes 11-04-82 07-18-59	Ann Evans 06-21-85 09-03-63	Jane Smith 08-17-87 01-22-61
Methods	SENIORITY	AVE-SENIORITY	

SALESPERSON

Structure	Objects	
Identity (OID)	OI2837	OI3462
Super Class EMPLOYEE	OI2837	OI1847
Attributes Commission-Rate	.030	.025

its **superclass** (or superclasses) is also identified. For our Employee hierarchy, the SALESPERSON object class would be defined as a subclass of the EMPLOYEE class. This is illustrated in Figure 13.23. The SALARIED-STAFF and PRODUCTION-WORKER object classes would also be defined as subclasses of EMPLOYEE, but are not presented in Figure 13.23. Each of these object classes can, in turn, have additional subclasses.

    Note that the EMPLOYEE class is identified as being a subclass of the UNIVERSAL class. Within the object-oriented model there is a universal class that forms the top of the class-subclass hierarchy and contains all other classes. The name of a class's superclass is specified as a part of the structure of the class when it is created. Each object instance created for that class must store the OID of the superclass object to which it belongs. The OID is used to traverse the database.

    We know that **subclasses** inherit data and methods from their superclasses. If a message sent to an object requests a method or data attribute that cannot be found in that object class, the superclass of that class is searched. Suppose, for example, a message is sent requesting that the Seniority method be performed on an identified SALESPERSON whose object OID is OI3462. Because the method Seniority cannot be found in the SALESPERSON object class, the Superclass OID would be used to link to the associated EMPLOYEE superclass object. In this case the Superclass OID of OI1847 links to the MPLOYEE object instance for Ann Evans. The Seniority method is found within the EMPLOYEE class, so it is executed and the answer is returned.

    The concept of **inheritance** also applies to multilevel hierarchies. Figure 13.24 shows semantic object modeling diagrams for a portion of our Employee object hierarchy. Suppose a message was sent to the MANAGERIAL-STAFF class requesting execution of the Seniority method on one of its objects. The Seniority method is not found in the MANAGERIAL-STAFF class. The shading of SALARIED-STAFF in the MANAGERIAL-STAFF description indicates that SALARIED-STAFF is a superclass of MANAGERIAL-STAFF. Thus, the SALARIED-STAFF class would next be searched. It does not contain the Seniority method either. However, it has a superclass—EMPLOYEE. The message is sent on to the EMPLOYEE class, which does have the Seniority method and can respond to the message. In general, messages sent to a class are forwarded to its superclass and on to superclasses of that superclass until a response to the message can be made or until the entire hierarchy has been searched.

Superclass
A class that has a parent relationship to another class (is directly above it in an aggregation or generalization hierarchy).

Subclass
A class that has a child relationship to another class (is directly below it in an aggregation or generalization hierarchy).

Inheritance
Refers to the concept that subclasses take on (*inherit*) the characteristics of their superclasses.

MULTIPLE INHERITANCE

In our example each subclass belongs to only one superclass. Conceptually, it is possible for a subclass to belong to, and inherit characteristics from, more than one superclass. Some object-oriented languages allow this and some do not. A system in which a subclass can be a member of more than one superclass is called a multiple-inheritance system. Multiple inheritance can add power and flexibility to the object-oriented model, but it also increases complexity. Suppose a subclass has two superclasses that each have an attribute called Name and a method called Seniority. Which characteristics should the subclass inherit? If multiple inheritance is allowed, a mechanism for resolving these conflicts must be provided. Methods for controlling multiple inheritance are beyond the scope of this text.

FIGURE 13.24
Inheritance in a
Multilevel Hiearchy

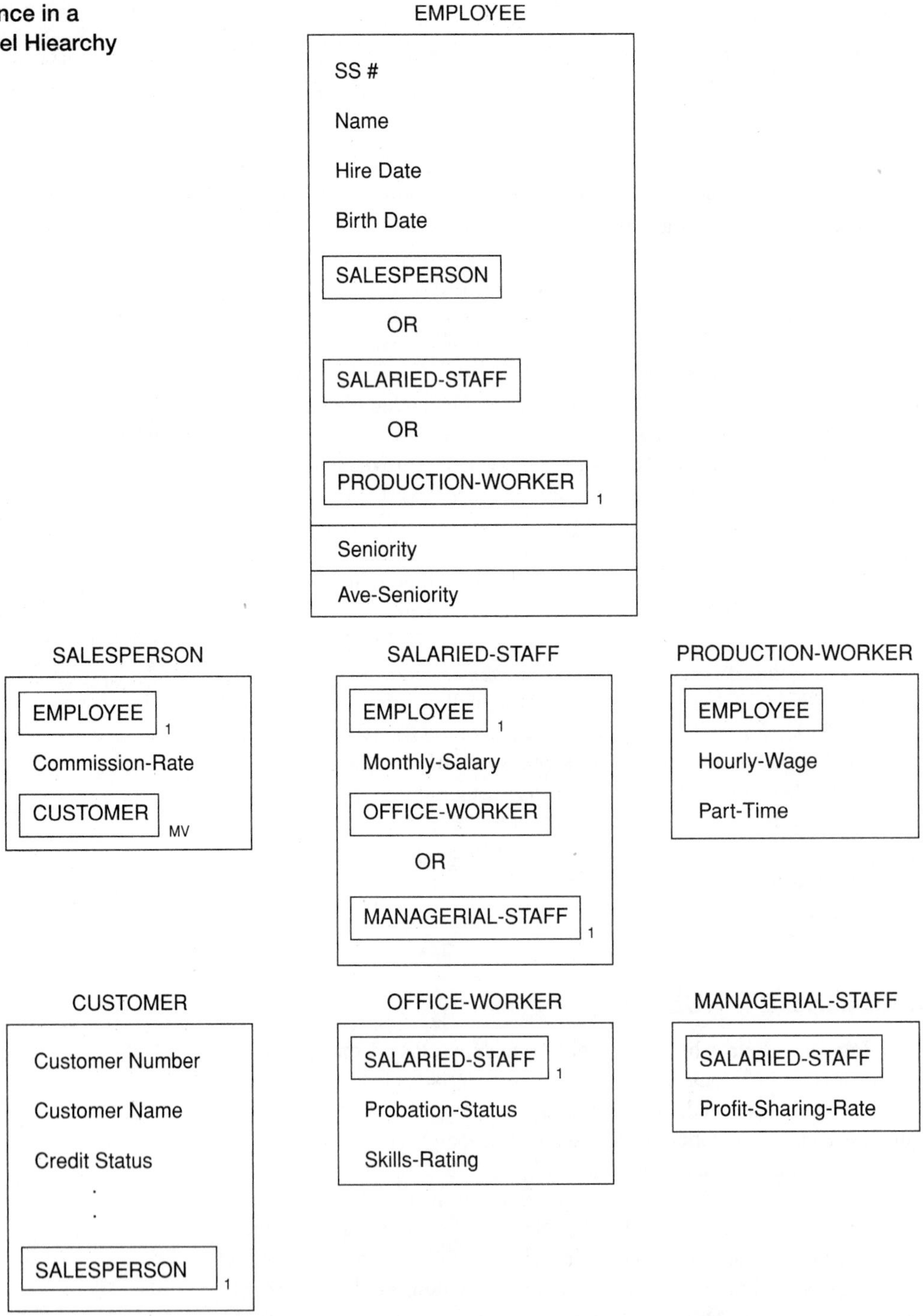

EMPLOYEE

SS #

Name

Hire Date

Birth Date

SALESPERSON

OR

SALARIED-STAFF

OR

PRODUCTION-WORKER 1

Seniority

Ave-Seniority

SALESPERSON

EMPLOYEE 1

Commission-Rate

CUSTOMER MV

SALARIED-STAFF

EMPLOYEE 1

Monthly-Salary

OFFICE-WORKER

OR

MANAGERIAL-STAFF 1

PRODUCTION-WORKER

EMPLOYEE

Hourly-Wage

Part-Time

CUSTOMER

Customer Number

Customer Name

Credit Status

.
.

SALESPERSON 1

OFFICE-WORKER

SALARIED-STAFF 1

Probation-Status

Skills-Rating

MANAGERIAL-STAFF

SALARIED-STAFF

Profit-Sharing-Rate

POLYMORPHISM

Polymorphism means that the same method may have different meanings to different object classes. Suppose our employee example were modified a bit so that some of the members of the OFFICE-WORKER class are part-time workers. This situation might be handled by adding a new attribute, Part-Time, to the OFFICE-WORKER class and giving it a value of Y for part-time workers. They will accumulate only a half year of seniority for each year they have been employed. Thus, for office workers, the method Seniority will need to consider whether an employee is full-time or part-time and adjust the seniority computation accordingly.

This situation could be handled by placing a revised version of the Seniority method in the OFFICE-WORKER class. Suppose a message requesting execution of the Seniority method is sent to the OFFICE-WORKER class. Because it has a method named Seniority, its version of the Seniority method will be executed. If the same message were sent to the SALESPERSON or MANAGERIAL-STAFF class, the original Seniority method stored in the EMPLOYEE object would be executed through the inheritance process.

Polymorphism
Condition in which the same method may have different meanings for different object classes. A method may be defined for some superclass, but redefined for certain subclasses that need to use a specialized version of the method.

OODBMS EXTENSIONS OF THE OBJECT-ORIENTED MODEL

Most of the features of the object-oriented model that have been discussed thus far can be found in OOPLs as well as in OODBMSs. As we noted earlier, OODBMSs must provide for persistent storage of objects. In OOPLs, objects do not persist between program executions. Objects are created and used by a single program, and normally serve a single user. OODBMSs are designed to provide for persistent objects. The OODBMS must support simultaneous access to the database by multiple users and must be able to serve users with differing needs and levels of expertise.

A number of features are required to achieve these goals. The OODBMS must provide access controls to ensure the privacy of sensitive data and methods. It also must provide locking procedures to ensure the integrity of data and methods while still maintaining adequate access to the database. Finally, the OODBMS should provide query access to the data stored in its objects. No standard exists for these OODBMS features. Different approaches have been used by different OODBMS developers. We will be describing the approach used in the ORION OODBMS (Kim, 1991).

ACCESS CONTROL

Access control measures for OODBMSs are similar to those used under other data models. Access privileges to various elements can be granted to or revoked from specified users. However, the object-oriented model has a more complex structure and this, in turn, adds complexity to access control measures. Access to read, write, or modify *methods* associated with an object must be controlled. The hierarchical structure of objects also adds complexity to the access control problem. Should a user who is granted access to a subclass automatically receive rights to access the characteristics of superclass objects which that subclass inherits, or should access to the superclass be handled separately? Should access to a superclass automatically imply access to its subclasses? Who should be authorized to create a new subclass? The access control procedures of the OODBMS must address these issues.

LOCKING

The hierarchical structure of objects also complicates locking procedures. When a lock is acquired on an object, all its subclasses in the object hierarchy may also need to be locked to prevent them from inheriting characteristics that are in the process of being changed. OODBMSs generally provide for implicit locking of the related objects in this situation. However, automatic extension of locks to all elements of a hierarchy of objects may limit the accessibility of the database. As with other data models, the timing of lock acquisitions and types of locks acquired may be adjusted to optimize performance. In any case, the need to provide implicit locking of related objects in a hierarchy adds additional complexity to this task.

VERSIONING

One response to the access problems associated with OODBMSs is to allow multiple versions of objects and object hierarchies to exist. A user may need to make an extensive set of interrelated changes to a number of related objects in an object hierarchy. For example, if an engineer is changing a design feature in a Computer Aided Design database, his or her change is likely to require changes to a number of objects representing interrelated components. Normally, the entire class hierarchy would need to be locked for the exclusive use of that engineer until the set of related changes was completed. Other users would be locked out of a whole set of objects for a prolonged period of time. What happens if there is a mistake in some aspect of the engineer's modifications that is not found until the transaction has been completed? What if it is necessary to scrap the set of modifications?

Versioning
Occurs if updates to a database do not cause the old version of the data to be destroyed, but rather cause both the new and old copies of the data to be stored as *versions.*

Versioning provides for the maintenance of different *versions* of the same object. Someone can make experimental changes to a set of objects and save them as new versions of the objects without destroying the previous versions. When one user is in the process of making changes to a versioned object, other users may still access that object, but will be told that their version of the object may not be current.

These advantages come at the expense of increased complexity. Versions of interrelated objects must be coordinated. In our design example, a user would want to access either the updated versions of all the objects that had been changed by the engineer, or the prior versions of all those objects. The use of alternative versions of the same object by different users can create what is, in effect, a data consistency problem unless there is strong coordination of the versions accessed by alternative users. Normally, one version of each versionable object will be designated as the default version. It will be supplied when a user requests the object without specifying which version she wishes to access.

QUERY LANGUAGE

Most OODBMSs provide query language capabilities. Queries in an OODBMS typically look very similar to SQL queries and, in fact, OODBMS developers are working toward SQL compatibility in their query languages. The chief difference from SQL queries is that joins are not necessary to retrieve data from related objects in a class hierarchy. Thus, we should be able to use the following sort of select statement:

```
SELECT Name, Hire-Date from SALESPERSON
WHERE Commission-Rate > .02
```

Although Name and Hire-Date are stored in the EMPLOYEE class, its characteristics are inherited by its SALESPERSON subclass and, thus, can be accessed without joining the two object classes. In general, we should be able to retrieve data from any set of objects that are interconnected in a hierarchical relationship without the use of the join operation. An explicit join would be required to retrieve data from multiple objects whose relationship is not hierarchical. For example, a join operation would be required to retrieve data from related occurrences of the STUDENT and CLUB objects, because their relationship is many to many and cannot be expressed as a hierarchy.

ADVANTAGES AND LIMITATIONS
OF THE OBJECT-ORIENTED MODEL

We have noted several advantages of the object-oriented model. It supports storage of multimedia data. It supports the inheritance characteristics by subclasses in a generalization hierarchy. Because objects contain methods, the object-oriented model allows full flexibility to define derived attributes and to establish complex domain restrictions on attributes. All these capabilities are either missing or very limited in other data models.

The chief limitation of the object-oriented model is its complexity. The need to specify methods and class hierarchy relationships increases the complexity of the database structure that must be defined. End-users may find it more difficult to comprehend and work with the OODBMS structure. The added complexity of the model is likely to slow system performance by increasing the overhead required to handle database management tasks, such as access and concurrency control.

COMMERCIAL USE OF THE OBJECT-ORIENTED MODEL

Thus far, OODBMSs have not received wide commercial use. The complexity of the object-oriented model, the lack of established standards for object-oriented databases, and the costs of conversion to a new form of DBMS are all factors limiting the commercial penetration of OODBMSs.

Traditional network, hierarchical, and especially relational database models have proven quite effective for modeling a wide variety of business applications. These applications are often transaction oriented and tend to require the handling of large volumes of data that were organized in relatively simple and stable structures. The object-oriented model is not a good fit for database applications of that type. Such databases have little need for the additional structures supported by the OODBMS, and the additional overhead incurred in maintaining the OODBMS structures is substantial.

The object-oriented model is a better fit for serving database applications that have not been effectively supported by traditional data models. Traditional data models have been less effective in supporting such design applications as Computer Aided Design (CAD), Computer Aided Manufacturing (CAM), and Computer Aided Software Engineering (CASE). The traditional models have also been less effective in supporting applications involving multimedia data, such as geographic information systems (GIS). Several expert systems software packages are now using object-based storage structures. Expert systems developers have found that traditional data models do a poor job of supporting the complex and evolving structures of data. The object-oriented data model appears to best fit applications characterized by relatively complex data structures that are evolving over time and that may involve multiple media.

OODBMS SOFTWARE PACKAGES

The use of object-oriented concepts in the data management arena remains in an evolutionary state. One set of developers has built OODBMSs by extending the data management facilities of object-oriented programming languages. At the same time, other developers have been extending the relational model to produce OODBMS, or OODBMS-like, data management capabilities.

There is very limited experience, as of this writing, with the commercial use of true OODBMSs. Examples of OODBMSs that are commercially available include GEMSTONE, VBASE, and ORION. GEMSTONE provides data management extensions to the SmallTalk object-oriented programming language. VBASE extends the C++ programming language to handle the data management requirements of an OODBMS. ORION is not formally based on any OOPL, but uses structures like those of OOPLs. Significant differences exist among these products with respect to such features as the type of inheritance supported, the degree of access control and concurrency management services provided, and query language capabilities provided. However, these and other OOPL-based OODBMSs are attempting to provide full support for the use of object-oriented principles in a database environment. A number of fully object-oriented DBMSs are now commercially available. However, these products, thus far, have seen very little use in business-oriented database systems.

Relational DBMS products that have been modified to accommodate object-oriented features are having a substantial impact on business-oriented database systems. These modifications vary from attempts to radically extend the relational model so that it fully supports object-oriented concepts, to much more limited extensions of the relational model that encompass one or two key object-oriented features.

Examples of relational DBMS products that have been extensively modified to incorporate object-oriented features include POSTGRES and STARBURST. Each of these systems uses system generated and managed identifiers (OIDs) as key fields to interconnect tables. Each system also provides for inheritance, encapsulation, and user-defined (abstract) data types. Methods are also supported. In POSTGRES, an attribute can be of the data type *procedure,* which is, in essence, a method.

Adoption of selected object-oriented features in common relational DBMSs represents the most important impact of the object-oriented model on current mainstream business database systems. Many popular relational DBMS packages now support the storage and retrieval of multimedia data in the form of binary large objects (BLOBs). In addition, many relational DBMSs use triggers that perform some of the functions of methods. Triggers are sequences of SQL statements that are "triggered" (moved to action) when a specified table is updated, created, or deleted. These sequences of statements are, in fact, procedures that can be used to enforce domain restrictions and related business rules. Triggers provide only a portion of the functionality of methods. Triggers cannot be called, they are applied only in response to predefined events, and they encompass only a portion of the types of processes that can be performed on a table of data. However, triggers do represent a promising mechanism for improving the ability of relational databases to incorporate and enforce business rules.

SUMMARY

The major concepts of object-oriented database systems have evolved from the semantic data model (SDM) at the conceptual modeling level and from object-oriented programming languages at the physical level.

Several key SDM concepts are crucial to the object-oriented data model. The relationships between objects can be divided into two basic types. *Generalization* relationships are ones in which each subclass member *is a* member of the generalization class. *Aggregation* relationships are ones in which each subclass is *part of* the aggregation class. The SDM also allows complete freedom to fully define the domains of attributes, including any form of domain restrictions, and it provides the ability to define attributes whose value will be computed. Object-oriented database management systems are designed to support all these features of the SDM.

The semantic object model (SOM) provides a graphical representation of the SDM that can be used in the conceptual design of object-oriented (and other) databases. The SOM represents each object class as a rectangular box that contains the attributes of the object and can contain other objects as well. One unique feature of the SOM is that related objects can be described as mutually including each other.

Object-oriented database management systems (OODBMSs) extend many of the structures used by object-oriented programming languages. Both data and methods to be applied to data are stored in objects. Objects are uniquely identified by a system-managed object identifier (OID). Objects are encapsulated so that data in an object may be accessed only by sending a message to one method in the object class. Subclasses can inherit the characteristics of their superclass, and this structure is used to represent generalization relationships. One class can contain another class as an abstract data type (ADT) attribute.

Object-oriented database systems are just beginning to be used commercially. A variety of methods are being used to build object-oriented capabilities into DBMSs. Some developers are building DBMSs using structures from object-oriented programming languages. Others are attempting to adapt relational DBMSs in ways that support many or all of the key elements of the object-oriented model.

It is too early to tell how extensively OODBMSs will be used commercially. However, we can say that the first uses are occurring in such areas as CAD/CAM, CASE tools, and GIS systems, which are characterized by the need to support complex data structures that evolve over time and involve multiple media.

REVIEW QUIZ

_____ *Part of* relationship.

_____ An object containing multivalued attributes.

_____ A representation of a real-world thing that can have embedded properties and behavior.

_____ *Is a* relationship.

_____ An object type that contains another object type in an aggregation relationship.

_____ An object type that contains another object type in a generalization relationship.

_____ A diagrammatic tool for object-oriented conceptual design.

_____ A chunk of data that is an attribute of an object, but whose structure is not known to the object.

_____ Changes to data in a database do not cause the old values to be removed from the database.

_____ An object containing only single-valued attributes.

_____ A class in a child relationship to another class.

_____ A named set of instructions that is part of an object class and operates on object instances in that class.

_____ Means that the contents of objects and methods are hidden from view by entities outside their object class.

_____ A class in a parent relationship to another class.

_____ The same method may have different meanings to different object classes.

_____ A grouping of related object instances.

_____ An object type used to represent a relationship between two other object types.

_____ A conceptual modeling methodology emphasizing semantic completeness in representing metadata.

_____ Subclasses take on the characteristics of their superclasses.

1. Semantic data model
2. Aggregation relationship
3. Generalization relationship
4. Semantic object model
5. Simple object
6. Composite object
7. Compound object
8. Association object
9. Generalization object
10. Object
11. Object class
12. Method
13. Encapsulation
14. Abstract data type
15. Superclass
16. Subclass
17. Inheritance
18. Polymorphism
19. Versioning

---

1. Describe and distinguish between aggregation and generalization relationships. Give examples of each type of relationship.
2. Describe and assess the treatment of domain specifications and derived attributes under the SDM. Describe the role of methods in implementing these features of the SDM.
3. Describe the basic features of the semantic object model. Use an example to illustrate how fundamental data elements and relationships are represented in this model.
4. Describe and distinguish between the simple, composite, compound, association, and generalization object types in the SOM.

REVIEW QUESTIONS AND EXERCISES

5. Compare and contrast the SOM with the E-R model. What do you see as advantages and limitations of each model?

6. Describe each of the following elements of the object-oriented model: objects, object classes, attributes, and methods. How do these elements correspond to elements in the relational model? In file-oriented processing?

7. Describe encapsulation and discuss how messages are used to access methods and data and to communicate between methods.

8. What is a class method? Give an example of a class method.

9. What is an abstract data type (ADT)? What capabilities does the ADT provide in the object-oriented model?

10. Describe how the object-oriented model uses ADTs to build class composition hierarchies.

11. What is a BLOB? What is the relationship between a BLOB and an ADT?

12. What is an object identifier (OID)? How are OIDs created and maintained? How does the concept of an OID relate to the concept of a primary key in the relational model?

13. Describe the concepts of superclass, subclass, and inheritance.

14. What does the term *multiple inheritance* mean?

15. Describe polymorphism. Give an example of how the concept of polymorphism can be used in designing methods to be applied to various object classes in a hierarchy.

16. What extensions to the object-oriented model used with object-oriented programming languages are needed to support object-oriented database management systems?

17. Describe versioning in OODBMSs. Why is this an important feature in OODBMSs?

18. How do OODBMS query languages differ from the standard query language of the relational model? When is a join required in performing a query on an OODBMS?

19. A public library keeps the following table of data about its patrons. Draw an appropriate diagram to represent the data in the semantic object model diagram. What type(s) of object(s) did you find (simple, composite, compound, etc.)?

Patron Name	Home Phone#	Library Card#	ID#	Due Date	ID#	Due Date	ID#	Due Date
			- - - - - - -	- Books	Checked Out	- - - - - - -	- - - - -	- -
J. Smith	3-7285	L19673	L282.9	9/23/98	HC12.1	9/23/98		
A. Ault	2-1793	L84361						
S. Davis	3-1983	L24639	LV302	9/25/98	QC17/5	9/28/98	BA81.3	10/01/98
R. Jones	2-1793	L41925	HA1.25	10/13/98				
R. Ault	2-1793	L82630	BC12.3	09/22/98				

20. A company keeps the following set of information about employees. Draw an appropriate SOM diagram to represent this data. What types of objects did you find (simple, composite, compound, etc.)?

ID #	Employee Name	Wage Class	Wage Rate	Department Name	Department Head	Birth Date
46823	Jan Jones	B	$8.50	Packing	L. Davis	08/06/57
37910	Al Evans	A	$7.25	Shipping	S. Smith	01/04/51
52907	Sam Smith	C	$9.75	Shipping	S. Smith	02/23/44
63015	Ann Adams	A	$7.25	Packing	L. Davis	09/27/59
29414	Tom Bates	B	$8.50	Sales	J. Kerns	11/03/66

21. Based on your SOM representation of the data in question 20, draw a set of diagrams (similar to Figure 13.21) showing the structure of the object classes you would use to implement this set of object classes. Use the sample data to illustrate your structure.

22. Suppose you are asked to write a method for the Employee object class which will derive the age of a selected employee. Write a set of pseudocode for this method. How would you cause your method to be executed?

23. A payroll clerk gives you the following information: "Data for hours worked are taken from daily time sheets and recorded in computerized form on a weekly basis. Wage rates are uniform for each employee class and are set by management. I produce this report each week":

XYZ COMPANY PAY REPORT
Week of: 9/21/98

Emp. #	Emp. Name	Hours Worked	Emp. Class	Wage Rate	Gross Pay
110	Jones	40	2	$6.00	$240.00
120	Smith	48	1	$5.00	$260.00
130	Alda	40	2	$6.00	$240.00
140	Bates	40	1	$5.00	$200.00
150	Adams	32	3	$7.00	$224.00

a. Create a set of objects to represent this data using the semantic object model.

b. Assume that a method is to be used to generate the value for Gross Pay. Write appropriate pseudocode for this method.

24. Through personal contact or by reading current information systems' periodicals, identify a real-life company that is using an object-oriented DBMS. Describe how it is being used and discuss the experiences (good and bad) that the company has had with the product.

THE HIERARCHICAL
MODEL—IMS

LEARNING OBJECTIVES

After completing this chapter you should be able to

- Design a data structure diagram that models a hierarchical data structure for some application.

- Convert a data structure diagram to an IMS database definition (schema).

- Set up a Program Communication Block for a COBOL program to communicate with an IMS database.

- Set up a Search Argument to retrieve data from an IMS database.

- Develop logic using either pseudocode or COBOL to store data in the database, update that data, delete data, and retrieve data using the various IMS data calls.

- Lay out the steps required to design and initialize a database using IMS.

- Lay out the steps required to code and test procedures using COBOL and IMS DML statements.

IMS (Information management system)
A hierarchical database system developed by IBM in the 1960s that continues to be used today in a large number of legacy systems.

The hierarchical database model has been implemented in a number of database software products over the years. These include IMAGE from Hewlett-Packard, TOTAL from Cincom, System 2000 from MRI Systems, and IMS from IBM. Hierarchical-based systems were implemented in more applications than any other database model during the 1970s and 1980s. IMS has been the most widely used hierarchical database due to the dominance of IBM mainframes. IBM continues to market and support IMS along with its relational database system, DB2.

A large customer base continues to use IMS for large transaction systems, including banks, insurance companies, credit card companies, and large production and manufacturing organizations. The use of **IMS (information management systems)** along with CICS enables customers with large transaction-based systems to continue to achieve performance that is difficult to match with some of the relational models.

The current version of IMS is called IMS/ESA (Extended System Architecture). IBM is also providing a Web interface to IMS that allows developers to bridge the gap between legacy database systems and the Web. For the latest information about IMS, go to IBM's IMS Web home page (Figure 14.1). If the URL in the figure has changed, go to www.ibm.com and follow the links to IMS.

IMS DATABASE SYSTEMS

ORIGINS OF IMS

The space projects of the early 1960s provided the need to maintain large assembly structures containing many parts and relationships. These are referred to as "Bills of

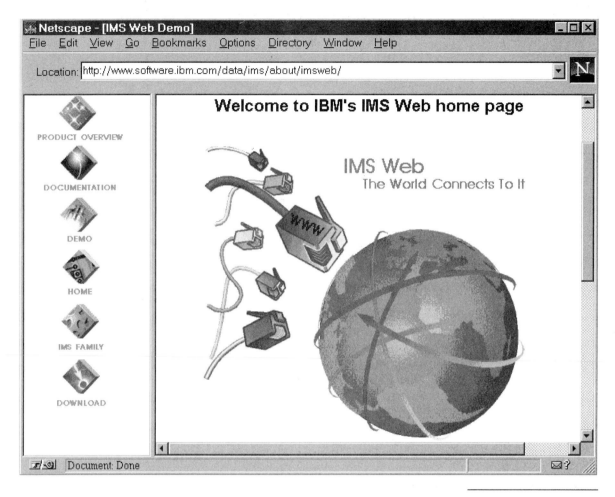

FIGURE 14.1
IBM's IMS Web
Home Page

Materials," or parts lists. A parts list has a hierarchical structure. A high-level assembly is made up of a number of lower level assemblies. Each lower level assembly is also made up of a number of lower level assemblies and piece parts. A piece part is an individual component, like a bolt or housing. The complexities of tracking large and complex components in the production of space equipment led to the development of software that would manage data with hierarchical attributes. The first project in the development of IMS was a joint project between IBM and North American Aviation.

HIERARCHICAL STRUCTURE

Hierarchical structure is the most common data structure for modeling applications. The real world is full of hierarchical relationships. A hierarchy is also referred to as an inverted tree structure. The base, or root, divides into one or more parts called branches. Each branch can also divide into multiple branches. This branching can continue to any level. The point at which the branch splits is called a *node* (see Figure 14.2).

FIGURE 14.2
Inverted Tree
Structure

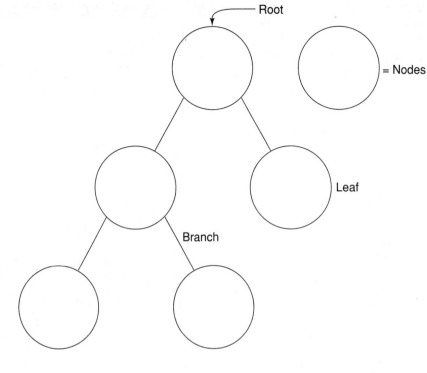

FIGURE 14.3
Air West
Hierarchical
Structure

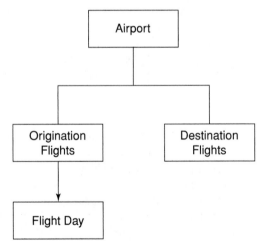

Child
A segment that is defined at
a subsidiary level to another
segment.

The key principle in a tree structure is that an upper level node can split into
any number of lower level nodes, but a lower level node can be connected to only one
upper level node. An upper level node can be called a *parent* and the lower level node
a **child.** Multiple occurrences of a child node from the same parent node are referred
to as *twins.* A node without children is referred to as a *leaf.* Each node in a tree structure is equivalent to a record type in database structures.

Figure 14.3 shows an example of a hierarchical structure in which the airport record type is the root. Airport is the parent of Origination Flights and Destination Flights. Origination Flights is also the parent of Flight Day. Figure 14.4 shows the same database as occurrences of the structure shown in Figure 14.3. Many flights leave Phoenix for Los Angeles and Minneapolis at different times of the day. Each flight operates on most days of the year, so there is one record in the database for each day a specific flight operates. Flights also arrive (destination Phoenix) from Los Angeles and Minneapolis at different times of the day.

DEFINING THE IMS DATABASE STRUCTURE

IMS refers to record types in a database as **segments.** Each segment is defined to IMS with a unique name. Segments normally have a unique key or sequence field. Segments with a key field are maintained by IMS in a sequence based on the values in the key field. Other fields in the segment can be defined as additional search fields.

The database structure for the Air West example used in this chapter is shown in Figure 14.5. This is a simple hierarchical portion of the Airline database. Examples

Segment
A record that is defined as part of the IMS database structure.

FIGURE 14.4
Air West
Occurrence
Diagram

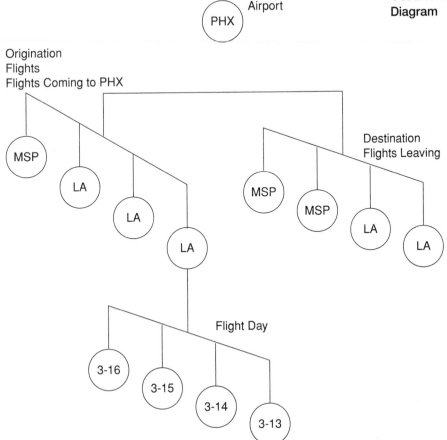

FIGURE 14.5
Air West IMS
Database

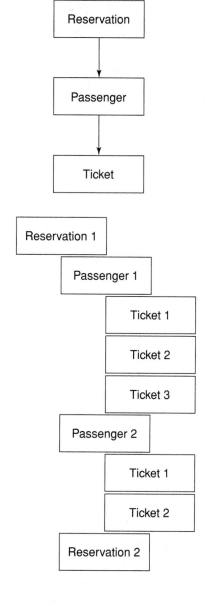

FIGURE 14.6
IMS Sequence of
Occurrence Records in
Database

of additional structures will be covered briefly in an advanced topics section later in the chapter. The Air West database has been implemented using the Micro Focus Workbench along with the IMS emulator that runs on the PC. The examples shown in the chapter have all been done on this platform (see the complete program at the Dryden Web site: **www.dryden.com/infosys/lorents**). The software is completely compatible with IMS on the mainframe.

The database consists of three segments: Reservation, Passenger, and Ticket. A reservation can be for one or more passengers, and a passenger can have multiple

```
DBD   NAME=AIRWEST,ACCESS=(HIDAM,VSAM)
DATASET DD1=AIRWEST,DEVICE=3380,SIZE=4096
SEGM NAME=RESERVAT,PARENT=0,BYTES=54,PTR=TB
    FIELD NAME=(SEQFIELD,SEQ,U),BYTES=6,START=1
SEGM  NAME=PASSENGR,PARENT=RESERVAT,BYTES=36,PTR=TB
    FIELD NAME=(SEQFIELD,SEQ,U),BYTES=6,START=7
SEGM  NAME=TICKET,PARENT=PASSENGR,BYTES=38,PTR=TB
DBDGEN
FINISH
END
```

FIGURE 14.7

Sample Database Description (DBD) for the Air West Database

tickets for a trip. An occurrence diagram of this structure is shown in Figure 14.6. IMS stores the data in the database in the logical or physical order of its hierarchical structure depending on the access method that is used. A passenger that is related to a reservation is stored right after the reservation record. Any ticket records for that passenger are stored immediately following the passenger record. Another reservation record is not stored until all data related to the first reservation have been stored.

Various access methods can be used with IMS. The most common is HIDAM, or Hierarchic Indexed Direct Access Method. This was used with the sample airline database. The **root** segments (reservation records) can be accessed directly using an index. The database can also be processed sequentially. Using HIDAM, the database consists of a segment area and an index area requiring multiple data sets. The segments are not necessarily maintained in physical order because the index maintains a logical ordering.

The first step in defining an IMS database is to set up a **database description (DBD).** An example of a DBD is shown in Figure 14.7. The first line (DBD) gives the database a name and describes the access method as HIDAM using a VSAM data set. The second line **(DATASET)** describes the physical data set by giving it a name, the device type, and the block size to use. The third line (SEGM) defines a segment by giving it a name, the parent name (zero = root segment), the length in bytes, and the pointer structure to use. A pointer designation of TB means that there are twin pointers forward and backward on each occurrence of a passenger record. The multiple occurrences of passenger records are called **twins.** The set of passenger records is also connected to the reservation record with a pointer to the first passenger and a pointer to the last passenger. This allows the passengers to be processed in either direction.

The fourth line is a field definition for the segment. Multiple field definitions can exist, but normally only those fields that are used as key fields and secondary indexes are defined. IMS does not care about the definition of other data in the segments. The field name used in the example is a generic name called SEQFIELD. The SEQ parameter specifies the index key that will be used to access the segments. The key starts in byte one and is six bytes long. The actual field in this location for reservation

Root
The parent segment of a tree structure.

Database description (DBD)
The description of the record structures in the database system; similar to the concept of a schema in CODASYL terminology.

Dataset
A physical file that can hold multiple logical files on IBM mainframes; similar to the concept of a directory in a DOS file system.

Twin
Multiple occurrences of the same segment type.

Logical child

A segment set up to carry a pointer that references another segment.

Program specification block (PSB)

A description of the record structures that can be accessed and the processing options that can be used on those records; similar to the concept of a subschema in CODASYL terminology.

Program communication block (PCB)

A description of the individual records and fields that can be accessed by a program. The PCBs make up the main content of a PSB.

SENsitive SEGment (SENSEG)

A parameter in a Program Specification Block that allows a developer to specify the fields a program can reference in a DML command.

SENsitive FieLD (SENFLD)

A parameter in a Program Specification Block that allows a developer to specify fields that are sensitive to DML statements in the host program.

is confirmation number. Each segment of the database is defined in the same manner. The last segment, TICKET, does not have a sequence field. This means that the only way to get to a ticket is to know the reservation confirmation number and the passenger itinerary number. The itinerary number starts in byte seven of Passenger and is six bytes long. The last lines in the DBD are control lines to the IMS compiler to set up the definitions for IMS. An application of any complexity will have multiple database files, requiring multiple DBDs. The segments in the multiple databases can be linked together through **logical child** indexes.

The DBD is similar to a database schema combined with its physical description. The next step is to define the logical schema, or program view. This is referred to as the **program specification block (PSB).** The PSB defines the segments that are going to be used in a particular program, which is similar to a subschema in CODASYL terminology. The PSB used for the Airline database is shown in Figure 14.8.

The PSB consists of one or more **program communication blocks (PCBs).** A PSB can consist of multiple PCBs that come from different database descriptions (DBDs). The PCB defines the name of the database and the processing options in a parameter referred to as PROCOPT. The processing options include G for GET, I for INSERT, R for replace, D for delete, and A for all options. The processing options can be specified for each segment, so you can allow read-only on some segments and updates on others. The term **SENsitive SEGment (SENSEG)** means that the application program is sensitive to that segment. *Sensitivity* means that the program is allowed to manipulate data on a segment with different levels of sensitivity, such as read, write, update, and delete. There is also a **SENsitive FieLD (SENFLD)** that allows the developer to specify sensitivity down to the field level. An example of the SENFLD statement is SENFLD NAME=PHONE,START=32. SENFLD names can be used only if they have been defined in the DBD.

Once the DBD and PCB have been set up as a source file in an editor, they can be compiled. The compile process sets up the database and formats it for processing. A utility is run to zero load the database before storing application data in it. Normally the initial load of data into the database is done with a utility. The data are presented to the database sorted into the same hierarchical sequence maintained by the database. The initial database loading can also be done by writing an application program to load the data.

APPLICATION PROGRAMMING USING IMS—MESSAGE PROCESSING

Data Language One (DL/1 or DL/I)

The data manipulation language for IMS.

The language used to communicate with IMS databases and message queues is called **Data Language One (DL/I).** The host language most commonly used is COBOL. The examples used in this chapter were done with Micro Focus Workbench COBOL and IMS using a PC. A complete example of the application program used to illustrate the various sections of this chapter is listed in the chapter appendix. The following describes how the program is set up to send and receive data between the application program and DL/I and the IMS messaging system. The data includes both database data and control data. Control data are used to tell IMS

```
PCB   TYPE=DB,NAME=AIRWEST,PROCOPT=A
SENSEG NAME=RESERVAT,PARENT=0
SENSEG NAME=PASSENGR,PARENT=RESERVAT
SENSEG NAME=TICKET, PARENT=PASSENGR
PSBGEN LANG=COBOL, PSBNAME=AIRWEST1
END
```

what to do, and to control the processing in the program based on IMS return (status) codes.

An execution environment for a typical **IMS Data Communications (IMS/DC)** system is made up of a number of components. The IMS/VS Control Region in an MVS environment normally includes a Communication Control Processor, Editing Modules such as Message File Services (MFS), a Queue Manager, Logging functions, the DL/I processor and the address spaces for the database definitions, and the database and terminal I/O buffers. Other regions of the MVS address space include the application programs that run in Message Processing Program (MPP) regions or in Batch Message Processing Program (BMP) regions.

BMP applications are normally batch-oriented and can be run during off hours. MPP applications are scheduled by IMS to respond to on-line terminals that are updating or requesting data on a real-time basis.

A message (transaction) from a terminal is received by the Communications Processor, edited by MFS, and queued by the Queue Manager. DL/I processes transactions (messages) that are in the queue and schedules MPP applications based on the transaction code (tran code) for each transaction. Scheduling an MPP means that the specific application needed for a transaction must be loaded into an available MVS region, if that application is not already loaded. The MPP processes the transaction by issuing database calls through the DL/I processor and by sending a message back to the Queue Manager through the DL/I processor. Message processing of transactions (input and output) that DL/I does with the Queue Manager is similar to some of the message processing that DL/I handles between the database and the application program. For a more detailed explanation of data communication and message processing, see Eckols ("IMS for the Cobol Programmer," Mike Murach & Associates, 1987).

HOST PROGRAM LINKAGES TO IMS

The COBOL program sets up a linkage section that is a shared communication area between DL/I and the application program, called the Program Communication Block (PCB) mask. It must be in the same format as Figure 14.9 and must contain the fields as shown. The PCB-MASK-1 in Figure 14.9 is used to pass parameter data between DL/I and the COBOL program. The database name, segment name, processing options, status code, and key value are all set in this area on each call to DL/I as it is executed.

Another shared area is the **input/output program communication block (IO-PCB),** which is used to support message processing in an IMS/DC environment and to

FIGURE 14.8
Sample Program Specification Block (PSB) for the Airline Database

IMS Data Communications (IMS/DC)
A separate component of IMS that supports the interface and message queues between an IMS database, a program, and terminals.

Input/output program communication block (IO-PCB)
A PCB used to define a logical terminal that is used as part of the IMS/DC (Data Communication) environment.

```
LINKAGE SECTION.
01 PCB-MASK-1.
      03 DBDNAME-1              PIC X(8).
      03 LEVEL-NUMBER-1         PIC X(2).
      03 STATUS-CODE-1          PIC X(2).
      03 PROC-OPTIONS-1         PIC X(4).
      03 JCB-ADDRESS-1          PIC X(4).
      03 SEGMENT-NAME-1         PIC X(8).
      03 KEY-LENGTH-1           PIC S9(5) COMP.
      03 NUMBER-SEGS-1          PIC S9(5) COMP.
      03 KEY-FEEDBACK.
         05 RES-KEY             PIC X(6).
         05 PASS-KEY            PIC X(6).


01 IO-PCB.
      03 FILLER PIC X(12).
      03 A   PIC S9(7).
      03 B   PIC S9(7).
      03 C   PIC S9(7).
```

FIGURE 14.9
COBOL Linkage
Section for IMS

schedule the application. The sample program in this chapter has been simplified by not using a terminal interface. It emulates typical transactions that would come from a terminal by reading them from a sequential file. The IO-PCB is still necessary in this example to emulate scheduling the application to get it started.

WORKING STORAGE AREAS USED IN IMS APPLICATIONS

The working storage section of a COBOL program is coded to accept the segments retrieved from an IMS database. Here the entire record is defined to COBOL. As stated before, IMS does not need to know the definition of the fields except for key fields and fields used in SENFLD statements. This is similar to coding COBOL records coming from any file in the file section. Normally the detail field breakdown is done in the working storage section.

Another area coded in the working storage section is the qualification formats for setting up key structures to find records in the database. These are called **segment search arguments (SSAs).** Examples of SSAs used in the Air West application are shown in Figure 14.10.

The first example is an unqualified SSA where we specify only the segment name. The next two examples are qualified SSAs where we also specify the key values of the records we want to locate. In these SSA formats we specify the key name that was defined in the DBD, the relational operator EQ meaning equal, the segment name, and the key value. The key value is moved to the SSA just before the call is

Segment search argument (SSA)
A set of parameters that are placed in a host program to allow DML commands such as GET UNIQUE to retrieve a specific record based on a key.

```
01  UNQUAL-SSA.
    03  SEG-NAME           PIC X(8).
    03  FILLER             PIC X   VALUE SPACE.


01  RESERVATION-SSA.
    03  FILLER             PIC X(8) VALUE'RESERVAT'.
    03  FILLER             PIC X   VALUE'('.
    03  FILLER             PIC X(8) VALUE'SEQFIELD'.
    03  FILLER             PIC XX  VALUE'EQ'.
    03  SSA-CONFIRM-NO     PIC X(6).
    03  FILLER             PIC X   VALUE')'.


01  PASSENGER-SSA.
    03  FILLER             PIC X(8) VALUE'RESERVAT'.
    03  FILLER             PIC X   VALUE'('.
    03  FILLER             PIC X(8) VALUE'SEQFIELD'.
    03  FILLER             PIC XX  VALUE'EQ'.
    03  SSA-CONFIRM-NO1    PIC X(6).
    03  FILLER             PIC X   VALUE')'.
    03  FILLER             PIC X(8) VALUE'PASSENGR'.
    03  FILLER             PIC X   VALUE'('.
    03  FILLER             PIC X(8) VALUE'SEQFIELD'.
    03  FILLER             PIC XX  VALUE'EQ'.
    03  SSA-ITINERY-NO     PIC X(6).
    03  FILLER             PIC X   VALUE')'.
```

FIGURE 14.10
Sample Segment
Search Arguments
(SSA)

issued to IMS (DL/I). In the case of a hierarchical retrieval, the key fields of the hierarchy (parent and child) must be set before issuing the call.

Another area defined in working storage are the codes for the different calls that can be made to IMS (DL/I). A sample of these definitions can be seen in Figure 14.11.

The commands are used as parameters in calls to IMS (DL/I). A more detailed explanation of these commands will follow in the command processing section.

APPLICATION PROGRAMMING
USING IMS/DML

Once the communication areas have been set up within a program, the programmer can focus on the processing calls to retrieve data from the database and to put data into the database. These database calls are part of the IMS DL/I language. More generically, in database terminology, they can be referred to as the **IMS data manipulation language (IMS/DML).** IMS and DL/I are used

Data manipulation language (IMS/DML)
Called DL/I, a data manipulation language used in a host language to store, retrieve, and maintain data.

```
01 IMS-FUNCTIONS.
      03 GU           PIC X(4)        VALUE'GU'.
      03 GN           PIC X(4)        VALUE'GN'.
      03 GNP          PIC X(4)        VALUE'GNP'.
      03 ISRT         PIC X(4)        VALUE'ISRT'.
      03 GHNP         PIC X(4)        VALUE'GHNP'.
      03 REPL         PIC X(4)        VALUE'REPL'.
      03 DLET         PIC X(4)        VALUE'DLET'.
      03 GHN          PIC X(4)        VALUE'GHN'.
      03 CHNG         PIC X(4)        VALUE'CHNG'.
      03 PURG         PIC X(4)        VALUE'PURG'.
      03 GHU          PIC X(4)        VALUE'GHU'.
```

FIGURE 14.11

An Example of
IMS Function Codes
Used in IMS

somewhat interchangeably in the following discussion even though DL/I is a component of IMS.

PROCESSING INITIALIZATION

The first entry in the procedure division must be a call to set up a linkage with the IMS system. The call is ENTRY 'DLITCBL' USING IO-PCB PCB-MASK-1. This command, which is a representation of the function DL/I to COBOL, sets up the linkage with IMS using the **IO-PCB** and the segment PCB. The exit is done with a GOB-ACK statement in COBOL instead of a STOP RUN because the application program is operating as a called application under the control of IMS. Therefore, you want to return control to IMS. Normally IMS is running in its own region and the user is communicating with IMS using IMS/DC (data communications).

IO-PCB (Input/Output Program Communication Block)
A PCB used to define a logical terminal that is used as part of the IMS/DC (data communication) environment.

DATABASE DML CALLS

The database processing calls in the procedure division are calls to insert, update, delete, and retrieve segments. Figure 14.12 provides a summary of these IMS processing calls.

The calls to IMS are part of the DL/I language, and are somewhat standard for COBOL, PL/1, and assembly language. The parameter list specifies the function, the PCB mask to use, the data area to receive or transfer data, and the SSA that contains the key or keys of the hierarchical structure of segments to retrieve, update, or delete. The example in Figure 14.13 shows a GET UNIQUE using a specific confirmation number to find the reservation record in the database.

The reservation segment search argument (SSA) is coded in the exact format shown. The first field names the segment to be retrieved, the second field specifies the key field to search on, and the third field is the value of the specific confirmation number to search for. The search argument, **'SEQFIELD=001005'** is placed in parenthesis. The call, COBOL to DL/I, is made with the parameters, function code, PCB, data area, and SSA in that order. The retrieval process works as follows:

SEQFIELD
A parameter used in a segment search argument that specifies a field as a sequence field.

```
GU = GET UNIQUE
     Used to get a specific segment using a qualified SSA with a key
     value.

GN = GET NEXT
     Used to get the next logical segment from the current position in
     the database. It can be any segment type.

GNP = GET NEXT WITHIN PARENT
      Used to get segments that are children within the same parent.

GHU = GET HOLD UNIQUE
      Used to retrieve segments that are going to be updated or
      deleted.

GHN = GET HOLD NEXT
      Same as GET NEXT with the GHU functions.

GHNP = GET HOLD NEXT PARENT
       Same as GET NEXT within parent with GHU functions.

ISRT = INSERT
       Used to insert new records.

REPL = REPLACE
       Used to modify existing records.

DLET = DELETE
       Used to delete existing records.
```

FIGURE 14.12
Summary of IMS (DL/I)
Processing Calls

1. Accept confirmation number from user.
2. Move confirmation number '001005' to the SSA.
3. Execute the call GU using the SSA.
4. Check the status code.

Each time a call is made to IMS, IMS returns a **status code** to the status code area of the program specification block (PSB) in the linkage section. A status code of blank means that the call executed successfully. Figure 14.14 lists some useful status codes.

Status code
The code used to check the result of a DL/I command that is returned from IMS.

LOADING AND INSERTING RECORDS

There are multiple ways to perform the various functions of IMS just like there are multiple ways to program any problem. The most efficient way to load an IMS

```
01 RESERVATION-SSA.
   03 FILLER                PIC X(8) VALUE'RESERVAT'.
   03 FILLER                PIC X    VALUE'('.
   03 FILLER                PIC X(8) VALUE'SEQFIELD'.
   03 FILLER                PIC XX   VALUE'EQ'.
   03 SSA-CONFIRM-NO        PIC X(6).
   03 FILLER                PIC X    VALUE')'.


   MOVE 520-CONFIRM-NO TO SSA-CONFIRM-NO.
   CALL 'CBLTDLI' USING GU
          PCB-MASK-1
          610-RESERVATION
          RESERVATION-SSA.
```

FIGURE 14.13
Example of Using
GET UNIQUE

database is to use a load utility and sort the records in the correct hierarchical sequence before executing the load utility. Another approach is to assume that the database is a new application, and the on-line COBOL program accepts data from screens. An application program is executed to add data to a database that has just been initialized (zero loaded). The Air West COBOL program used in this chapter illustrates this process. However, we are not using IMS/DC, the data communications package of IMS, or CICS, another IBM transaction processing system. Instead we are emulating the on-line transactions by using a file. The call format for most of the IMS calls is very similar. The call is to CBLTDLI, which means COBOL to DL/I, with the parameters being the function code, program control block mask, the data area, and the search arguments. The example in Figure 14.15 is an insert of the reservation record into the database. The reservation record is the root record, so it is the easiest to set up. The function code is ISRT for insert. All function codes are four characters or less and are normally set up in working storage. The segment search argument in this illustration is simple and is referred to as an unqualified SSA because it has no keys to search for. All the unqualified SSA requires is the segment name that was defined in the DBD. The status code in the PCB is checked to see if a duplicate is already in the database. A duplicate occurrence of a segment (Reservation with the same confirmation number) will not be added to the database if the DBD was defined with a unique designation on the sequence field (confirmation number).

Inserting children into the database can be done in the same way as the parent is inserted by using the unqualified SSA as long as they are inserted in sequence. If the transactions come in at different times (randomly) as they normally do in an on-line system, then the parent must be found before inserting the child. Finding the parent is done with the qualified SSA shown in Figure 14.13. The qualified SSA contains the segment name and the key value (confirmation number). The insert process

Function	Status Code	Meaning
GN, GHN	GE	Segment not found
GNP, GHNP	GE	No more segments under parent
GN (unqualified)	GA	Moved up in level
	GK	New segment type at same level
	GB	End of Database
ISRT (Load mode)	LB	Segment already exists
	LC	Key values out of sequence
	LD	No parent for segment being loaded
	LE	Segment types out of sequence
ISRT (Insert mode)	II	Segment already exists
	IX	Insert rule violation
DLET, REPL	DJ	No previous get hold call
	DA	Key field modified
	DX	Delete rule violation
	RX	Replace rule violation
	AJ	Qualified SAA was used with replace

FIGURE 14.14
List of Status Codes
Returned from IMS

requires two steps. First, the parent is located (Figure 14.16) with a GET UNIQUE (GU), and, if the parent is found, the child can be inserted (Figure 14.17).

The status code GE means that the segment was not located. The status code LB means that the segment is already in the database and it cannot be inserted again.

Positioning two levels into the hierarchy requires multiple SSAs. The example in Figure 14.18 shows a GET UNIQUE on a passenger that is stored within a reservation.

```
MOVE 'RESERVAT' TO SEG-NAME.
CALL 'CBLTDLI' USING ISRT
        PCB-MASK-1
        610-RESERVATION
        UNQUAL-SSA.
IF STATUS-CODE-1 = 'LB'
 DISPLAY ' ' 500-SCREEN-DATA
    '..RESERVATION ALREADY EXISTS'
```

FIGURE 14.15

Sample Code for
Inserting the
Reservation Record
into the Database

```
CALL 'CBLTDLI' USING GU
    PCB-MASK-1
    610-RESERVATION
    RESERVATION-SSA.
IF STATUS-CODE-1 = 'GE'
 DISPLAY ' ' 500-SCREEN-DATA
    '..NO RESERVATION FOR THIS PASSENGER'
```

FIGURE 14.16

Sample Code to Find a
Parent (Reservation)
before Inserting a
Child (Passenger)

The confirmation number key field is put into the reservation SSA and the itinerary number key field is put into the passenger SSA. The call is made using both segment search arguments (SSAs), which obtain the correct reservation/passenger combination. Segment inserts made at this point will store the segments under this specific passenger occurrence that is under a specific reservation occurrence in the database. This would be done if we wanted to insert ticket occurrences for this passenger.

RETRIEVING RECORDS

The primary way to obtain data from the database is to use the GET UNIQUE function. You already have a good understanding of how this function works from the earlier discussion on inserting data into the database. A GET UNIQUE not only positions within the database, but the data are also transferred from the database segment to the COBOL working storage area specified in the call. The 620-PASSENGER in the Air West program is an example of an area specified to receive the data.

Any segment that has been defined with a sequence field in the DBD can be obtained directly with the GET UNIQUE function. There are a number of other

```
MOVE 'PASSENGR' TO SEG-NAME.
CALL 'CBLTDLI' USING ISRT
          PCB-MASK-1
          620-PASSENGER
          UNQUAL-SSA.
IF STATUS-CODE-1 = 'LB'
   DISPLAY ' ' 500-SCREEN-DATA
          '..PASSENGER ALREADY EXISTS'
```

FIGURE 14.17
Sample Code to Insert
the Child (Passenger)

```
MOVE 550-ITIN-NO TO SSA-ITINERY-NO.
MOVE 550-CONFIRM-NO TO SSA-CONFIRM-NO.
CALL 'CBLTDLI' USING GU
          PCB-MASK-1
          620-PASSENGER
          RESERVATION-SSA
          PASSENGER-SSA.
```

FIGURE 14.18
Sample Code Using
Multiple SSAs

```
MOVE 'TICKET' TO SEG-NAME.
CALL 'CBLTDLI' USING GNP
          PCB-MASK-1
          650-TICKET
          UNQUAL-SSA.
```

FIGURE 14.19
Sample Code to Get
the Next Segment
within a Parent

GET functions. The GET NEXT WITHIN PARENT (GNP) retrieves sequential segments of the same level once a position has been established in the database. The call returns a status code of GE when there are no more segments (children) associated with this parent. The GET NEXT WITHIN PARENT in Figure 14.19 will get ticket segments until the next passenger or reservation segment is located. This would be true even if the ticket segment had lower level segments attached to it.

```
MOVE 520-PASS-NAME  TO 620-PASS-NAME.
CALL 'CBLTDLI' USING REPL
     PCB-MASK-1
     620-PASSENGER.
```

FIGURE 14.20
Sample Code to
Modify Data after
Using a Get Hold
Unique

FIGURE 14.21
Air West Database
with a Logical Child

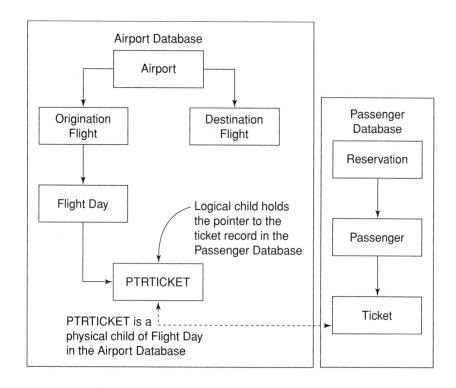

Processing records in the database sequentially is done by the GET NEXT (GN) command. Using an unqualified SSA with the segment name PASSENGER, we can process all the passenger records in the database in sequence by confirmation number. The records are in sequence by confirmation number because they are stored under the reservation segment, which is in sequence by confirmation number. Multiple passengers under the same reservation are in sequence by itinerary number. Processing GET NEXT without an SSA will retrieve any record in sequence starting at the last position in the database. You should be aware of some important status codes when using GET NEXT without an SSA. GA means the segment retrieved is a level above the last record retrieved. GK means that a different segment type was retrieved at the same level, and GB means you have come to the end of the database.

MODIFYING RECORDS

Modifying data in the database requires locating the record, changing the data, and rewriting it back to the database. Locating the record is done with a GET HOLD UNIQUE (GHU), which is the same as a GET UNIQUE (GU) except that *replace* and *delete* statements can be processed against the retrieved segment after it is located. The *replace* statement must be the next IMS call after the GET HOLD UNIQUE. The example in Figure 14.20 illustrates the replacement of a segment assuming the GHU has already been executed. In this example the passenger name is changed and rewritten to the database. Notice that it is not necessary to have an SSA to specify which segment to replace. The replacement is done on the segment that was just retrieved with a preceding GHU.

DELETING RECORDS

Deleting segments follows the same logic used for replacing segments. The segment is located with a GET HOLD UNIQUE (GHU), and the next call is a DELETE (DLET). The call is exactly the same, except for the function code, which is DLET. Other GET HOLD calls can also be used. The GHN is the same at the GET NEXT, and the GHNP is the same at the GET NEXT WITHIN PARENT. Depending on the delete or replace logic, these GET statements may be used instead of a GET UNIQUE to locate the records.

ADVANCED TOPICS IN IMS

The Air West example presented in this chapter used a simple hierarchical database structure. Most databases involve more entities and relationships. The airline example can be expanded to include airports, flights originating from those airports, and the execution of flights on specific days. These flights have a relationship to the tickets stored for each passenger. The entity relationship structure shown in Figure 14.21 is set up in IMS as two databases with separate DBD descriptions. A PSB is set up with two PCBs (program communication blocks). Two PCB masks are set up in the linkage section with the database entry call referencing both PCBs. Calls can be made to either database from the application program. A ticket that is accessed in one database can use the flight number and airport code on that ticket to access flight information in the other database.

LOGICAL STRUCTURES IN IMS

IMS supports various pointer systems to model logical database structures. The most common approach is to set up a segment that is referred to as a *logical child*.

The segment is normally defined in one database as a physical child of another segment. The contents of the segment hold a pointer to a parent in another database. It is a logical child of the parent in the other database.

Figure 14.21 shows an example of how this could be used to connect a ticket with flight information on a specific day. The DBD for the airport database would contain the segment PTRTICKET, listing its parents as both the FLTDAY in the airport database and TICKET in the passenger database. The DBD for the passenger database would have an LCHILD entry after the ticket segment that would name the segment PTRTICKET in the airport database. The pointer options defining the segment PTRTICKET would include LP, meaning that it can store a pointer to its logical parent. Pointer segments can be defined throughout multiple databases to set up relationships between them.

SUMMARY

IMS is one of the first major database systems to be used for large production database applications. It is still one of the major systems used because of the inability or lack of desire of organizations to convert legacy COBOL/IMS systems to a relational environment. IMS is built to process hierarchical (tree) type data structures. The main feature of hierarchical structures is that a child can have only one parent. IMS provides a way to connect to other parents through the use of pointer structures referred to as logical child and logical parent. A large percentage of applications that are built can be supported by tree structure data models.

IMS databases are defined by setting up database definitions called DBDs. The DBD contains information about each segment (record) in the database along with the definition of each field within each segment. The database is further defined to an application by using a PSB (program specification block). A program specification block consists of multiple program communication blocks (PCBs). A PCB defines the access ability of an application for each segment. Access ability is defined as insert, get, delete, and update. The PCB also defines the sensitive segments, meaning the segments that the application can access within the application.

Applications access the database through calls embedded in the host language, such as COBOL. Calls include such operations as GU (Get Unique), GN (Get Next), IN (Insert), and RE (Replace). The statements use search definitions set up in the working storage area of the program that are referred to as segment search arguments (SSAs). The SSAs are used to hold the keys related to the segments that are retrieved or sent to the database for processing. The program also defines the communication areas where the records will be stored or transferred to the database. The PCB (program communication block) areas are used by the IMS engine to communicate information on the status of calls back and forth between the engine and COBOL.

_____ The term given to the database definition.

_____ The term given to the program specification block.

_____ The term given to the specification within the PSB to specify a sensitive segment.

_____ The term given to the specification within the DBD to define a segment.

_____ The code used to communicate the results of a DML code.

_____ The name given to the segment that is at the top of the hierarchy.

_____ The name given to a segment that is owned by another segment.

_____ The name given to multiple occurrences of the same segment.

_____ The name given to a segment that is used to store a pointer that is a link to another segment.

_____ The DML code used to obtain a specific record using a key value.

_____ The DML code used to obtain child segments of the same parent.

_____ The DML code used to obtain a segment that is to be updated or deleted.

_____ The status code for a segment that is not found.

_____ The status code for a segment that is retrieved at a higher level than the previous segment.

_____ A communication area that is part of the COBOL linkage section.

_____ The transaction processing component of IMS.

_____ The processing option parameter.

_____ The library routine called in COBOL to process a COBOL to DL/I command.

_____ The parameter used in a DL/I call in COBOL to code the values for a search argument.

_____ The parameter used in a DL/I call in COBOL to pass the data for the I-O control block.

1. PSB
2. SSA
3. DBD
4. IMS
5. IO-PCB
6. IMS/DC
7. Status code
8. GU
9. GHU
10. GN
11. GA
12. GE
13. GK
14. CBLTDLI
15. Root
16. Child
17. Parent
18. Twin
19. Logical child
20. Segment
21. SENSEG
22. SEGM
23. PROCOPT
24. GNP

REVIEW QUESTIONS AND EXERCISES

1. Define and describe the following terms.
   a. SSA
   b. IMS
   c. DBD
   d. SENSEG
   e. SENFIELD
   f. Segment
   g. SEQFIELD
   h. Ptr=TB
   i. DBD gen
   j. HIDAM

k. Node

l. Tree

m. Parent

n. MPP

o. Root segment

p. PSB

q. PCB

r. PROCOPT (A, D, U)

s. DL/I

2. Set up a DBD for the following database.

- Automobile record (License No., Make, Year, Value)
- Owner record (Name, SSN, Phone)
- An owner can have many automobiles.

3. Set up an SSA for retrieving owners sequentially.

4. Set up an SSA for retrieving a specific owner on SSN.

5. Set up an SSA for retrieving automobiles for a specific owner.

6. Set up an SSA for retrieving a specific owner and automobile using License No.

7. Write the COBOL code to store an owner.

8. Write the COBOL code to store an automobile.

9. Write the COBOL code to delete an owner.

10. Write the COBOL code to modify the Phone for an owner.

11. Write the COBOL code to list all automobiles for an owner.

12. Write the COBOL code to list all owners with names > 'C'.

13. Write the COBOL code to list all automobiles with a year of 1990.

14. Describe how the COBOL program communicates with IMS.

15. Describe how children are related to their parents in IMS.

16. Set up a hierarchical database design for the Airline database using reservation, passenger, ticket, and flight. How would the tickets reference the flight segments?

17. Explain the following commands:

    a. GHU

    b. GNP

    c. GHNP

    d. REPL

    e. DLET

    f. ISRT

18. What logical operators can be used in the SSA?

19. Explain the following status codes:

   a. GE

   b. GA

   c. GK

   d. GB

20. Explain the following status codes:

   a. LB

   b. DJ

   c. LD

21. Where is the status code returned in the COBOL program? Give an example of a COBOL statement to check the status code.

22. Go to IBM's page on IMS (www.software.ibm.com/data/ims/) and write a report on the latest features of IMS and related IMS products.

THE NETWORK
DATA MODEL

15

LEARNING OBJECTIVES

After completing this chapter you should be able to

- Design a data structure diagram that models a network data structure for some application.
- Develop entity definitions for a network data structure that include location mode, data definitions, and key definitions.
- Develop set definitions for a network data structure that include set order, insertion mode, deletion mode, parentage, and pointer structure such as prior, next, and owner.
- Convert a data structure diagram to an IDMS schema.
- Set up an IDMS subschema for an application.
- Develop the device media control language DMCL file to set up the physical environment for the database.
- Develop logic using either pseudocode or COBOL to store data in the database, update that data, delete data, and retrieve data using IDMS commands.
- Lay out the steps required to design and initialize a database using IDMS.
- Lay out the steps required to code and test procedures using COBOL and IDMS DML statements.

Conference on Data Systems Languages (CODASYL)
An organization formed to develop COBOL standards; later formed a task group to work on database standards.

Database Task Group (DBTG)
The committee formed under the CODASYL umbrella to develop standards for a network architecture database system.

Data description language (DDL)
The language used to describe the data structure of the database, both in the schema definition and in the subschema definition.

Data manipulation language (DML)
The language used within the host language that is an interface between the database system and the host language to add, modify, and delete data and data relationships.

Device media control language (DMCL)
The language used to define the physical database structure, including files, journals and the mapping of the logical database descriptions to the physical files.

Charles Bachman
A database specialist with General Electric who was responsible for the early design of CODASYL-type databases within GE. The DSD is often called a *Bachman diagram.*

The network data model was developed in the 1960s through efforts by industry and by a **Conference on Data Systems Languages (CODASYL)** committee known as the **Database Task Group (DBTG)**. The main feature of the network data model is its ability to model a data structure in which there can be multiple parents for a child. In the hierarchical model, a child can have only one parent. The network model makes it very easy to model a many to many relationship that exists between two entities in many data models by supporting an intersection entity (child) that is related to both parents.

The DBTG consisted of representatives from IBM, Honeywell, Computer Sciences Corporation, General Electric, Bell Labs, the Navy, and other organizations. This group delivered the DBTG April 1971 Report that outlined the components of the network database system. Included were the **data description language (DDL)** for describing schemas (database descriptions); the DDL for describing subschemas (user views of the database); the **data manipulation language (DML)** used in a host language such as COBOL to store, maintain, and retrieve data; and the **device media control language (DMCL)** for describing the physical database. The 1971 report was updated in 1973, 1978, and 1981. The work of the CODASYL committee became the basis of the ANSI standard for network data models. General Electric contributed much of its early work in Integrated Data Store (IDS) and that of **Charles Bachman's** data structure diagramming methods (DSD) to this effort. Later, Honeywell bought General Electric and continued to market the product as IDS II. Other companies developed databases using the CODASYL model, including UNIVAC with its DMS 1100 and DMS 90 products, Digital Equipment Corporation with its DMS product, and the XEROX DBMS product. IBM had a heavy investment in IMS and did not choose to implement a network database product. John Cullinane, an IBM employee, left IBM to form **Cullinane** Corporation, which developed a product called **Integrated Data Management System (IDMS).** The product ran on IBM mainframes and was widely used. The company changed its name to **Cullinet** and was later sold to Computer Associates (CA). Computer Associates has continued to upgrade the product and has a significant customer base that continues to use IDMS. Release 14.0 was scheduled to appear in 1997.

MAPPING A LOGICAL SCHEMA INTO THE NETWORK MODEL

This chapter uses the Airline database and IDMS to illustrate the implementation of the network model. The **data structure diagram (DSD)** is used as the most common

Cullinane/Cullinet
The company that first developed IDMS and brought it to the market.

Integrated Data Management System (IDMS)
A database system developed by the Cullinane Corporation in the 1970s that supported the CODASYL network data model.

Data structure diagram (DSD)
A diagram similar to an E-R diagram that shows entity relationships, entity properties and set properties; often called a *Bachman diagram.*

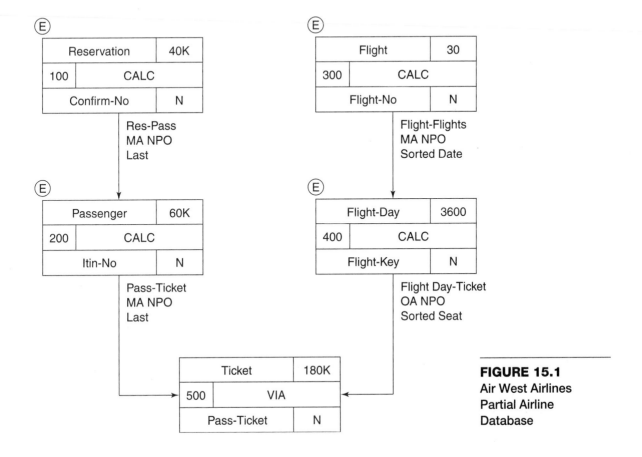

FIGURE 15.1
Air West Airlines
Partial Airline
Database

Schema
The overall description of the database logical structures that is defined by the DDL.

tool to model a network database. The DSD in Figure 15.1 diagrams a portion of the Airline database that has been implemented in IDMS for the illustrations in this chapter. The boxes and sets (relationship lines) in the DSD contain some additional information to make it easier for the database administrators and programmers to match the specific names and definitions used in the **schema** with those used in the programs.

RECORD TYPE DEFINITIONS

Record type
The logical definition and specifications of a record.

CALC, DIRECT, VIA
A DDL parameter that specifies the insertion mode of a record into the database. VIA means that a member record will be stored close to its owner. CALC means that the record will be stored based on a hashed key. DIRECT means that the record will be stored in a page where the direct key is known.

The first line in the box contains the name of the entity or record type and the approximate volume of occurrences of that record type in the database at any one time. The second line contains the record type number and the location mode of the record. **Record type** numbers are unique numbers assigned by the database administrator to each record type in the schema. Location modes can be either **CALC, DIRECT,** or **VIA.** CALC stores record occurrences in pages (storage blocks) based on a hashing algorithm using a primary key. DIRECT stores record occurrences based on a direct address of the storage block (page number and record or line number within the page). VIA stores record occurrences of a member record close (same page or adjacent page) to the occurrence of one of its owner records. The third line specifies the primary key to use for the CALC key when the record is CALC, or the set name of the owner/member relationship that specifies which owner to use when a record is VIA. The last box in line three specifies the handling of duplicate keys. N means that duplicates are not allowed. If the record is VIA location mode, the duplicates not allowed pertains to the sort key in sorted sets.

Set Type Definitions

Set type
The logical definition and specifications of a set.

Most of the set definitions are listed on the DSD next to the line defining the set relationship between the record types. These definitions are referred to as the **set type.** Each set type is given a name that normally reflects the names of the record types that participate in the set. Other characteristics of the set are specified, including set participation, set order, and types of pointers. These will be defined more specifically in the schema section.

COMPONENTS OF THE IDMS DATABASE MANAGEMENT SYSTEM (DBMS)

Setting up a network database using IDMS involves working with various processors included with the IDMS software. A diagram of these components is shown in Figure 15.2. The first stage requires the database administration group (DBA) to build a schema from the DSD in Figure 15.1, using the data description language (DDL). The schema is a complete definition of a database, including all record types, set types, and field definitions. The building of a schema results in a source program that is compiled by a schema processor that updates the IDMS data dictionary assigned to the project.

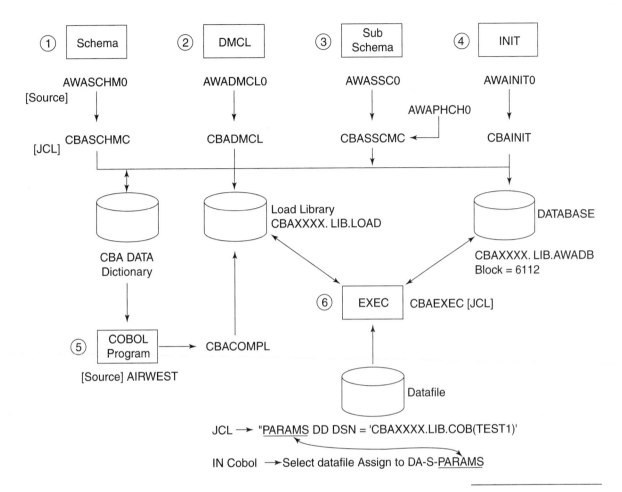

FIGURE 15.2
IDMS Process

The next stage is to define the physical file structures to be used for the database, backups, and journals. This is done with the device media control language (DMCL), which creates another source file. This source is compiled by a processor that references the definitions produced by the schema and creates a module that is stored in the load library.

The third stage is to create subschemas for each application that uses the database by writing copy statements. These commands copy the specific record type and set type definitions from the schema that are needed for a particular application, such as updating flight data. Subschemas are sometimes referred to as user views. The subschema source is compiled by another processor referencing the schema, with the resulting object module stored in the load library.

The fourth stage is to initialize the database and get it ready to accept data. This is a process that uses the results of the DMCL compilation to format and insert control bytes for each of the data blocks so that the database processor can read and write these blocks. There are a variety of DASD devices on different types of hardware.

The DMCL and the initialization process provide a means to define different physical structures to the same database processor or engine.

The database is now ready to accept data. Data can be loaded by using utilities or by using host language programs with an embedded data manipulation (DML) code. Normally the host language is COBOL. COBOL programs that have embedded DML are passed through a precompiler supplied with IDMS that converts the DML to library calls that can be handled by COBOL compilers. The compiled programs produce object programs that can be linked and set up as executable run modules in the load library (See the complete program and sample data at the Dryden Web site: **www.dryden.com/infosys/lorents**).

Other components of IDMS include management utilities that can be used to back up, restore, monitor, and control the database.

CREATING THE SCHEMA IN IDMS—THE DATA DESCRIPTION LANGUAGE (DDL)

A sample schema for the partial Airline database DSD (Figure 15.1) is shown in Figure 15.3. The schema is given a name—in this case, AWASCHM0 (Air West Airline Schema version 0). Schemas can be maintained by completely deleting the old one and adding a new one, or by modifying parts of the schema with the verb MODIFY. The schema sets up a logical file name for the database, which will be linked with the physical file through the link name called CBALINK when an application is run. The area concept is similar to a logical file concept. Databases can consist of multiple areas where some record types are in some areas and other record types are in other areas. The areas can be assigned to different physical files or data **sets.** This allows for parts of the database to be backed up and restored while other parts of the database are in production. In the Air West database one area has been defined to include 100 pages with the addresses from 801001 to 801100. The remainder of the schema defines records types and sets.

Record Type Definitions

Most of the record type definitions come directly from the DSD (Figure 15.1). These include the name, record ID, location mode, key, and duplicates designation. Each record type is also assigned to an area. The remainder of the record type definition includes the field definitions in COBOL format. Field names must also be in COBOL format. Because there are five record types in the DSD, there will be five record descriptions defined in the schema.

The content of the TICKET record type is quite different in the IDMS database structure compared to the relational structure. It has only one field, which is 'SEAT'. Because it is hooked to Flight-day and Passenger by pointers, and the additional data regarding a ticket is in the **owner** records, the additional data does not have to be repeated in the **member** records. There tends to be less data redundancy, but this is compensated for by the space carrying pointers. A pointer is a database key (DBKey) consisting of the page number (block number) and the line number (relative record number within the block) that references another record in the database. The Ticket carries pointer lists (NEXT, PRIOR, and OWNER pointers) for the Pass-Ticket set and the Flight-Day–Ticket set. The NEXT pointer is used to point to the next record

Set
The term used in a CODASYL database definition that refers to the relationship between two entities. A set is managed by a linked list of pointers.

Owner
The term used to refer to the entity that is the parent of a one to many relationship.

Member
The term used to refer to the entity that is a child in a one to many relationship.

```
SET OPTIONS FOR SESSION INPUT 1 THRU 72.
DELETE SCHEMA AWASCHM0.
ADD
     SCHEMA NAME IS AWASCHM0 VERSION IS 1
     SCHEMA DESCRIPTION IS 'AIR WEST'.
ADD
     FILE NAME IS AWADB            ASSIGN TO CBALINK
                                   DEVICE TYPE IS 3380.
ADD
     AREA NAME AWA-DB              RANGE IS 801001 THRU 801100
                                   WITHIN FILE AWADB
                                   FROM 1 THRU 100.
ADD
     RECORD NAME 100-RESERVATION
     RECORD ID 100
     LOCATION MODE CALC            USING 100-CONFIRM-NO
                                   DUPLICATES NOT ALLOWED

     WITHIN AREA AWA-DB.
       02 100-CONFIRM-NO           PIC 9(6).
       02 100-RES-DATE             PIC 9(6).
       02 100-RES-NAME             PIC X(20).
       02 100-RES-PHONE            PIC X(12).
       02 100-RES-FLIGHT-NO        PIC 9(4).
       02 100-RES-FLIGHT-DATE      PIC 9(6).
ADD
     RECORD NAME 200-PASSENGER
     RECORD ID 200
     LOCATION MODE CALC            USING 200-ITIN-NO
                                   DUPLICATES NOT ALLOWED

     WITHIN AREA AWA-DB.
       02 200-PASS-NAME            PIC X(20).
       02 200-ITIN-NO              PIC 9(6).
       02 200-PRICE                PIC 9(4)V9(2).
ADD
     RECORD NAME 300-FLIGHT
     RECORD ID 300
     LOCATION MODE CALC            USING 300-FLIGHT-NO
                                   DUPLICATES NOT ALLOWED

     WITHIN AREA AWA-DB.
       02 300-FLIGHT-NO            PIC 9(4).
       02 300-ORIG                 PIC X(3).
```

FIGURE 15.3
Air West Schema

```
           02 300-DEST                    PIC X(3).
           02 300-ORIG-TIME               PIC 9(4).
           02 300-DEST-TIME               PIC 9(4).
           02 300-MEAL                    PIC X.
           02 300-PRICE                   PIC 9(4)V9(2).

   ADD
       RECORD NAME                    400-FLIGHT-DAY
       RECORD ID                      400
       LOCATION MODE CALC             USING 400-FLIGHT-KEY
                                      DUPLICATES NOT ALLOWED

       WITHIN AREA AWA-DB.
          02 400-FLIGHT-KEY.
          04 400-FLIGHT-NO            PIC 9(4).
          04 400-FLIGHT-DATE          PIC 9(6).
          02 400-EQUIP-NO             PIC 9(3).
          02 400-PASS-CTR             PIC 9(3).
          02 400-DEPART-TIME          PIC 9(4).
          02 400-ARRIVE-TIME          PIC 9(4).
          02 400-FUEL-USED            PIC 9(6).
          02 400-STATUS-NOTE          PIC X(20).
   ADD
       RECORD NAME 500-TICKET
       RECORD ID 500
       LOCATION MODE VIA PASS-TICKET SET
       WITHIN AREA AWA-DB.
          02 500-SEAT                 PIC X(3).
   ADD
   SET NAME RES-PASS
   ORDER IS LAST
   MODE IS CHAIN LINKED PRIOR
   OWNER IS 100-RESERVATION
   MEMBER IS 200-PASSENGER
       LINKED TO OWNER
       MANDATORY AUTOMATIC.
   ADD
   SET NAME PASS-TICKET
   ORDER IS LAST
   MODE IS CHAIN LINKED PRIOR
   OWNER IS 200-PASSENGER
```

FIGURE 15.3 (Cont.)
Air West Schema

```
MEMBER IS 500-TICKET
    LINKED TO OWNER
    MANDATORY AUTOMATIC.
ADD
SET NAME FLIGHT-FLIGHTDAY
ORDER IS SORTED
MODE IS CHAIN LINKED PRIOR
OWNER IS 300-FLIGHT
MEMBER IS 400-FLIGHT-DAY
    LINKED TO OWNER
    MANDATORY AUTOMATIC
    ASCENDING KEY IS 400-FLIGHT-DATE
    DUPLICATES NOT.
ADD
SET NAME FLIGHTDAY-TICKET
ORDER IS SORTED
MODE IS CHAIN LINKED PRIOR
OWNER IS 400-FLIGHT-DAY

MEMBER IS 500-TICKET
    LINKED TO OWNER
    OPTIONAL AUTOMATIC
    ASCENDING KEY IS 500-SEAT
    DUPLICATES NOT.
VALIDATE.
```

FIGURE 15.3 (Cont.)
Air West Schema

in the list, the PRIOR pointer is used to point to the previous record in the list, and the OWNER pointer is used to point to the owner or parent record for that set occurrence.

Set Type Definitions

A set is added to the schema for each relationship between entities in the DSD. Most of the information for defining the set has been recorded on the DSD in Figure 15.1 next to the line defining each set relationship. The line in the set definition gives the set a name. The remaining lines describe the characteristics of the set. These include:

ORDER Order can be **last, first, next, prior, or sorted.** This tells IDMS where to put the record in the logical order in the set relationship. The physical placement of the record in the database is controlled by the location mode clause in the record description. There is only one location mode per record type because a record occurrence can exist only once in the database. However, the record can participate in many relationships, so the logical order must be specified for each relationship. The order tells IDMS how to maintain the pointers for the linked list that maintains each relationship. LAST means the record is always put at the end of the list. Consequently, it will be the last of a set of

Last, first, next, prior, or sorted
A set ordering system parameter that specifies the insertion sequence of a record into a logical set occurrence. FIRST means that the record will be at the beginning of the set (LIFO—Last In, First Out). LAST means that the new record will be at the end of the set (LILO—Last In, Last Out). NEXT and PRIOR mean that the record will be inserted just after or just before the record at which we are currently positioned.

records retrieved when sequentially walking the set. The first record stored in the list will be the first one retrieved (First In, First Out/FIFO). Order is FIRST is the opposite, meaning that the most recent record stored in the list is first in the list. This is equivalent to Last In, First Out (LIFO). Order is NEXT or PRIOR means that the record is stored in front of or behind the current record. This order requires the program to obtain the position of a record in the list before issuing the store command. Order is SORTED means the list is always in sequence by some key. When another record is added to the list, it is linked into the list by the value of its key relative to the other keys in the list. The sorted list can be ascending or descending. Duplicate keys can be allowed or not allowed.

MODE IS CHAIN LINKED PRIOR tells IDMS that the list is to be controlled by pointers, including a prior or backward pointer.

OWNER IS 100-RESERVATION specifies the name of the owner record type of the set.

MEMBER IS 200-PASSENGER specifies the name of the member record type of the set.

LINKED TO OWNER tells IDMS to set up owner pointers as a part of the pointer list. This means every member record carries the database key of the owner record. Owner pointers speed processing when there is a need to obtain repeated owner information requests. The requests can still be handled by IDMS without owner pointers, but IDMS can get to the owner only by following the list of members instead of going directly to the owner.

MANDATORY AUTOMATIC tells IDMS how to set up the membership retention options of the member records. There are four possible combinations made up from the choices of using MANDATORY or OPTIONAL and the choices of using **AUTOMATIC** or **MANUAL. MANDATORY/OPTIONAL** controls the fate of member records when owner records are deleted. An **ERASE ALL** MEMBERS will erase the specified record and all mandatory and optional members. An **ERASE SELECTIVE** MEMBERS will erase the specified record and all mandatory child records. Optional child records will be erased only if they do not participate as members in other sets. An **ERASE PERMANENT** MEMBERS will erase the specified record and all mandatory members. Optional members are disconnected. OPTIONAL also allows processing to disconnect a member from one owner and reconnect to another owner without deleting and restoring the record. AUTOMATIC means that IDMS will connect the member to the owner automatically based on the current position (last record occurrence either obtained or stored) of the owner record type. The processing program must find the correct owner before storing the member. AUTOMATIC requires the owners to be in the database before a member can be stored. MANUAL means that the program must use a CONNECT command to connect the member to the correct owner. If membership is OPTIONAL the connect can be done after the record has been stored. The use of OPTIONAL MANUAL allows for the storing of member records into sets where some of the members participate in the set and some of the members do not participate. It also allows members to be stored before the owners are stored.

VALIDATE tells the schema processor to compile the schema.

AUTOMATIC/MANUAL
A record insertion parameter that is used to control how a record is connected to a set occurrence when a record is added to the database.

MANDATORY/ OPTIONAL
A record retention parameter that is used to control how member records are retained when an owner record is removed from the database given different delete parameters.

ERASE ALL, PERMANENT, SELECTIVE
A DML Erase parameter that allows the database system to erase or not erase member records of erased owner records depending on the retention parameter.

DEVICE MEDIA CONTROL (DMCL)

Figure 15.4 shows an example of the source language for setting up the physical file definitions for the database system. This source has been written in the device media control language (DMCL). The language supports ADDS, DELETES, and MODIFIES of

FIGURE 15.4
DMCL Source for
Air West Airlines

```
        MODIFY
            DMCL NAME IS              AWADMCL0
                OF SCHEMA AWASCHM0 VERSION 1.
  *+    DATE.                      02/01/96.
  *+    INSTALLATION.              IDMS  CV/DC/UCF USER
  *+
  *+    ************************************************************
  *+    *********  AWA BUFFER
  *+    ************************************************************
        MODIFY
            BUFFER NAME IS AWA-BUFFER
                PAGE CONTAINS 6112 CHARACTERS
                BUFFER CONTAINS 3 PAGES.

  *+    ************************************************************
  *+    *********  AWA AREA
  *+    ************************************************************
        ADD
            AREA NAME IS AWA-DB
            OF  SCHEMA NAME   AWASCHM0 VERSION 1
            BUFFER NAME IS AWA-BUFFER

  *+    ************************************************************
  *+    *********  AWA JOURNAL
  *+    ************************************************************

        MODIFY
            DISK JOURNAL FILE NAME IS J1JRNL
            BLOCK CONTAINS 1508 CHARACTERS
            FILE CONTAINS 24000 BLOCKS
            ASSIGN TO J1JRNL
            DEVICE TYPE IS 3380.
        MODIFY
            DISK JOURNAL FILE NAME IS J2JRNL
            BLOCK CONTAINS 1508 CHARACTERS
            FILE CONTAINS 24000 BLOCKS
            ASSIGN TO J2JRNL
            DEVICE TYPE IS 3380.
```

```
MODIFY
    ARCHIVE JOURNAL FILE NAME IS SYSJRNL
    BLOCK CONTAINS 8000 CHARACTERS
    ASSIGN TO SYSJRNL
    DEVICE TYPE IS 3420.
GENERATE.
```

FIGURE 15.4 (Cont.)
MCL Source for
Air West Airlines

the various objects that are part of the device media control. These objects are maintained in the central dictionary. The DMCL for this database is given a name, which is associated with the schema that was developed in Figure 15.3. Buffer space is assigned based on the block size that was set up when the data set was allocated. The area name is defined for the DMCL based on the schema definitions and associated with the buffer space. The journal and archive file spaces are defined, named, and allocated to devices. Journals 1 and 2 are used for recording the transaction images and the database images before and after they are modified. The archive journal has been assigned to a tape device and is also used as part of the backup and recovery in the event of a database failure. The final statement is to generate the DMCL, which updates the central dictionary, compiles the source, and stores a load module in the load library for the database system to reference when using the defined database.

CREATING SUBSCHEMAS

Subschema
A portion of the overall database description (schema) that will be used by a particular application. An application that requires access to data from just two entities needs access only to the definitions for that part of the database.

The **subschema** is a subset of the schema that is generated for each application. It serves two primary purposes. It sets up only the resources necessary in the database to run that application, and access to the data is limited to what has been defined in the subschema. The subschema source for Air West is shown in Figure 15.5. It specifies the subschema name and the DMCL name and ADDS the area, records, and sets necessary for the application. The subschema copies all the objects in the schema so it is a full subset of the schema. This has been done to allow the program in this chapter to be used for examples of accessing all parts of the database. The subschema statements also put restrictions on record locks for retrieval and updates. In this case no locks have been allowed.

One other source file is required to do the subschema compilation. This source file contains the command information to tell the subschema compiler the load module name when it is stored in the load library. The source file used for Air West was named AWAPNCH and contained one statement as follows: PUNCH LOAD MODULE AWASSC0.

INITIALIZING THE DATABASE

The database can be initialized as soon as the schema and DMCL have been successfully compiled, and the data set allocated for the database file. The initialization

```
DELETE SUBSCHEMA NAME IS AWASSC0.
    ADD SUBSCHEMA NAME IS AWASSC0 OF SCHEMA NAME IS AWASCHM0
                            VERSION IS 1
        DMCL NAME IS AWADMCL0 OF SCHEMA NAME IS AWASCHM0
                            VERSION IS 1.
    ADD AREA AWA-DB
        PROTECTED RETRIEVAL IS NOT ALLOWED
        PROTECTED UPDATE IS NOT ALLOWED
        EXCLUSIVE RETRIEVAL IS NOT ALLOWED
        EXCLUSIVE UPDATE IS NOT ALLOWED.

    ADD RECORD 100-RESERVATION  KEEP NOT ALLOWED.
    ADD RECORD 200-PASSENGER    KEEP NOT ALLOWED.
    ADD RECORD 300-FLIGHT       KEEP NOT ALLOWED.
    ADD RECORD 400-FLIGHT-DAY   KEEP NOT ALLOWED.
    ADD RECORD 500-TICKET       KEEP NOT ALLOWED.

    ADD SET  RES-PASS           KEEP NOT ALLOWED.
    ADD SET  PASS-TICKET        KEEP NOT ALLOWED.
    ADD SET  FLIGHT-FLIGHTDAY   KEEP NOT ALLOWED.
    ADD SET  FLIGHTDAY-TICKET   KEEP NOT ALLOWED.
GENERATE.
```

FIGURE 15.5
Subschema
for Air West

process involves formatting the dataset blocks with control bytes based on the parameters in the DMCL. This is the only way the database processor can read and write the blocks in the database file. The initialization run requires a source file specifying the initialization process to follow and the DMCL to reference. The source file used for Air West was named AWAINIT and contained the statement PROCESS= TOTAL, DMCL=AWADMCL0.

APPLICATION PROGRAMMING USING IDMS

Most application programming in IDMS is done with the host language COBOL. Other processors that come with IDMS allow the user other alternatives for setting up applications. IDMS-DC is a communication interface that allows the user to use screens with COBOL. There are two application development systems, one for batch applications (ADSB) and one for on-line applications (ADSO). Other products include Online English, CULPRIT, Online QUERY, and INTERACT.

THE DATA MANIPULATION LANGUAGE (DML)

All the products rely on basic IDMS functions that are referred to as the data manipulation language (DML). These functions are shown in Figure 15.6. The BIND and

Function	Services Performed
BIND	Associates IDMS record types and control blocks with space in variable storage
READY	Prepares database areas for processing
FINISH	Releases database areas
IF	Tests whether a set is empty or whether a record occurrence is a member of a particular set
COMMIT	Effects a checkpoint for recovery procedures
ROLLBACK	Requests recovery of the database
KEEP	Locks a record occurrence against access or update by another run unit
FIND*	Locates a record occurrence in the database
GET*	Delivers a record occurrence to variable storage
ERASE	Deletes a record occurrence from the database
CONNECT	Links a record occurrence to a set
MODIFY	Rewrites a record occurrence in the database
DISCONNECT	Dissociates a record occurrence from a set
STORE	Adds a record occurrence to the database
ACCEPT	Returns database key pointers, run-time statistics, a bind address, or database procedure control information to variable storage
RETURN	Returns a database key and associated symbolic key to variable storage; used only with the Sequential Processing Facility

*FIND and GET can be combined into the dual-function OBTAIN, which both locates and delivers record occurrences.

FIGURE 15.6
IDMS Functions

COMMIT
A DML statement that makes all changes to a database permanent to that point in the processing stream.

ROLLBACK   A DML statement to roll back all changes made to a database to the last point of a commit statement within a processing stream of transactions.

STORE, MODIFY
DML commands to add and rewrite records in the database.

DISCONNECT, CONNECT
The DML commands to disconnect and connect records from a set occurrence.

READY functions are used in the initialization routines of an application to establish communication between the program, the IDMS engine, and the database itself. The READY is like an OPEN statement. FINISH is like a close statement and is used in the end routine. **COMMIT** and **ROLLBACK** are used to maintain the integrity of the database. A COMMIT sets a processing point for the ROLLBACK to go back to if a ROLLBACK is executed. In effect, it says that all processing is okay to this point. A ROLLBACK is executed by the program if a fatal error occurs in processing the database. This could happen for various reasons, including physical file problems, corruption of pointers, programming errors, and other inconsistencies in processing the database.

The commands that maintain the database include STORE, ERASE, MODIFY, DISCONNECT, and CONNECT. **STORE,** ERASE, and **MODIFY** are the same as add, delete, and change. **DISCONNECT** and **CONNECT** are used to move a record logically out of one set occurrence and into another set occurrence without deleting and adding the record. The record stays in the database, but the pointers are changed to connect it to a different owner. Another use of CONNECT is to connect a member to an owner in a manual set where some records of that record type participate in the set and some do not. A third use of CONNECT is to connect a member to an owner after the owner record shows up in the database. Sometimes member records are entered into the database before all the owner information is available.

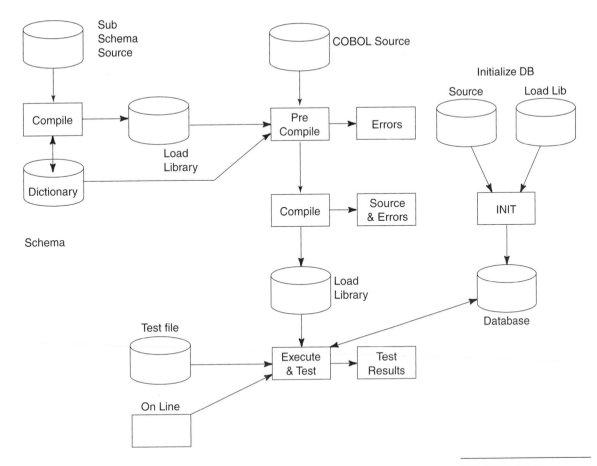

FIGURE 15.7
Steps in Developing a COBOL Program Using IDMS

FIND, OBTAIN
DML commands to position to and retrieve the data from specific records in the database.

Retrieval of records in the database is done with the **FIND,** GET, and **OBTAIN** commands. OBTAIN is a combination of the FIND and GET. Often in processing it is only necessary to position the processing on a record occurrence. The data does not have to be transferred to the program work area. This is accomplished with the FIND command. A GET will transfer the data to the program work area after the record is located with a FIND command. OBTAIN combines the two functions.

IF, KEEP, and ACCEPT are special functions. IF is used in an application program to determine if a set is empty or if a record occurrence is a member of a particular set. KEEP is used with an OBTAIN to prevent other run units (users) from accessing the record until the current run unit is finished with the record. This would be used in update routines. ACCEPT is used to save database keys, statistics, and bind addresses for use in the program for later processing or reporting.

The steps in developing a COBOL application are shown in Figure 15.7. The subschema compilation, the allocation of a data set (file) to the database, and the initialization of the database are normally done by the database group. The development of the application using COBOL goes through the normal systems development cycle of creating COBOL source from the systems specifications. Once the COBOL source has been developed, it goes through a precompiler to convert the DML statements to calls that the COBOL compiler can handle. If there are syntax errors at this point, such as incorrect schema names or incorrect use of the DML, the precompiler prints a list of the errors and stops the run. If there are no errors, the precompiler sends its output to the regular COBOL compiler. After a successful compilation, the program can be tested against the database. Programs can be written to load the database from flat files, or to load data on an interactive basis. The database could also be preloaded by using utilities supplied by the database vendor.

CONCEPTS OF CURRENCY

Currency
The current position of the last accessed record within a record type, within a set type, and for a run unit.

Database processing using IDMS is completely dependent on establishing current positions on records and sets called *currencies*. There are four currencies established when DML instructions such as FIND and OBTAIN are executed. They are Current of Run Unit, Current of Area, Current of Record, and Current of Set. At the time the database is opened, no currencies have been established. The execution of an OBTAIN or FIND for a flight record will set up the following currencies. The record obtained will be current of that record type, current of all sets it participates in, current of run unit, and current of area. If another record type such as Passenger is obtained, then Passenger becomes current of its record type, current of all sets it participates in, and current of area and run unit. Flight will still be current of its record type, and current of any sets that it participates in as long as the Passenger record does not participate in the same sets. Why is currency important? **Currency** establishes single positions within database record occurrences as reference points to process records associated with those records. Figure 15.8 shows a simple network structure for records A, B, and C. The C record occurrences must be linked to the proper A and B record occurrences. This is done by locating an A occurrence based on its key and locating a B occurrence based on its key before storing C in the database. When C is stored, it is linked to whatever A record is current of the A record type and linked to whatever B record is current of the B record type at the time it is stored.

Currency is also important when retrieving records. If a B record is obtained for a specific key and an OBTAIN FIRST is executed on the B–C set, a C record will be obtained that is related to that specific B record occurrence. If an OBTAIN

FIGURE 15.8
DML Parts of a
COBOL Program

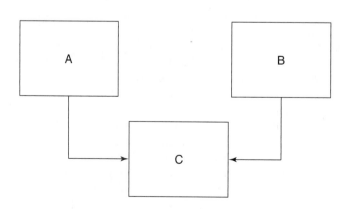

NEXT is executed on the same B–C set, then another C record is obtained that also relates to that same B record. If a new B record is obtained and the obtains on the B–C set are repeated, then C records will be obtained that relate to the new B record. Retrieving a C record that relates to a specific A and a specific B record when C does not have a CALC key illustrates an interesting phenomenon regarding currencies. Many students want to obtain the specific A and B records, establishing currency on the A and B record types, and then obtain a C record, thinking that the C record obtained will relate to the current of record type in both A and B. This does not work. The only way to do this is to obtain either the A or the B record and then obtain C records by processing the A–C or B–C related set. Let's look at an example. If we obtain an A record based on the key, then obtain a C record by doing an OBTAIN FIRST on the A–C set, we can obtain an owner record of the B–C set and find out if that B record satisfies the A and B combination for the C we are looking for. Obtaining the owner record does not alter the currency of the A–C set.

The COBOL program has some entries in each of the three major divisions. The IDMS-CONTROL section is added to the environment division after file-control along with the statements:

```
PROTOCOL. MODE IS BATCH DEBUG
  IDMS-RECORDS WITHIN WORKING-STORAGE SECTION.
```

The subschema to be used for the application is identified to the program under the SCHEMA SECTION, which is the first section in the Data Division. The entry DB AWASSC0 WITHIN AWASCHM0 informs the precompiler that the subschema records and sets in AWASSC0 of Schema AWASCHM0 are to be included in the working storage section of the program. These statements set up the communication mode between IDMS and the application program, and also tell the precompiler where to place the record and communications areas within the COBOL program. An example of the communication area for the Air West application is shown in Figure 15.9. It is referred to as the SUBSCHEMA-CTRL area and is used by the program and the IDMS database processor to pass information back and forth. The communication area consists of a number of fields that contain status information that is updated after each DML command, and a record area to store the data for each record defined in the schema that has been referenced in the subschema for this application. The record descriptions contain the field descriptions used in the schema. These field descriptions are used in the COBOL program to reference the data that is passed to and from the database. It is important for the programmer to have a copy of the schema when starting to program a new application in order to know the field names and the definitions that will be used in this area.

One status field referenced frequently in the COBOL program is the ERROR-STATUS field. IDMS returns a four-digit code after each DML statement is executed. A code of 0000 means that the DML command was successful. Any other code means that the command was not successful. The program must determine if the resulting condition is an error or a normal situation. Frequently the resulting condition is a record not found or an end of set condition. These conditions are not errors but information the program can use to take the proper course of action. The first two digits of the code refer to the type of command being executed. The second two

```
000098    01 600-ABORT-MESSAGE          PIC X(55).
000099
000100    01 SUBSCHEMA-CTRL.
000101        03  PROGRAM-NAME           PIC X(8) VALUE SPACES.
000102        03  ERROR-STATUS           PIC X(4) VALUE '1400'.
000103                           88  DB-STATUS-OK VALUE '0000'.
000104                           88  ANY-STATUS
000105                               VALUE '0000' thru '9999'.
000106                           88  ANY-ERROR-STATUS
000107                               VALUE '0001' THRU '9999'.
000108                           88  DB-END-OF-SET VALUE '0307'.
000109                           88  DB-REC-NOT-FOUND VALUE '0326'.
000110        03  DBKEY                  PIC S9(8)
000111                                   USAGE COMP
000112                                   SYNC.
000113        03  RECORD-NAME            PIC X(16) VALUE SPACES.

000114        03  RRECORD-NAME           REDEFINES RECORD-NAME.

000115            05   SSC-NOON          PIC X(8).
000116            05   SSC-DBN           PIC X(8).
000117        03  AREA-NAME              PIC X(16) VALUE SPACES.

000118        03  AREA-RNAME             REDEFINES AREA-NAME.

000119            05   SSC-DNO           PIC X(8).
000120            05   SSC-DNA           PIC X(8).
000121        03  ERROR-SET              PIC X(16) VALUE SPACES.

000122        03  ERROR-RECORD           PIC X(16) VALUE SPACES.

000123        03  ERROR-AREA             PIC X(16) VALUE SPACES.

000124        03  IDBMSCOM-AREA          PIC X(100) VALUE LOW-VALUE.

000125        03  IDBMSCOM               REDEFINES IDBMSCOM-AREA

000126                                   PIC X
000127                                   OCCURS 100.
```

FIGURE 15.9
IDMS Communi-
cation Area

```
000128          03  RIDBMSCOM               REDEFINES IDBMSCOM-AREA.

000129              05  DB-SUB-ADDR         PIC X(4).
000130              05  FILLER              PIC X(96).
000131          03  DIRECT-DBKEY            PIC S9(8)
000132
                                            USAGE COMP
000133                                      SYNC.
000134          03  DIRECT-DBK              REDEFINES DIRECT-DBKEY

000135                                      PIC S9(8)
000136                                      USAGE COMP
000137                                      SYNC.
000138          03  DATABASE-STATUS.
000139              05  DBSTATMENT-CODE PIC X(2).
000140              05  DBSTATUS-CODE       PIC X(5).
000141          03  FILLER                  PIC X.
000142          03  RECORD-OCCUR            PIC S9(8)
000143                                      USAGE COMP
000144                                      SYNC.
000145          03  DML-SEQUENCE            PIC S9(8)
000146                                      USAGE COMP
000147                                      SYNC.
000148      01  SUBSCHEMA-SSNAME    PIC X(8) VALUE  AWASSC0'.
000149      01  SUBSCHEMA-RECNAMES.
000150          03  SRI                     PIC X(16)
000151                                      VALUE 'SRI              '.
000152          03  SR500                   PIC X(16)
000153                                      VALUE '500-TICKET       '.
000154          03  SR400                   PIC X(16)
000155                                      VALUE '400-FLIGHT-DAY   '.
000156          03  SR300                   PIC X(16)
000157                                      VALUE '300-FLIGHT       '.
000158          03  SR200                   PIC X(16)
000159                                      VALUE '200-PASSENGER    '.
000160          03  SR100                   PIC X(16)
000161                                      VALUE '100-RESERVATION  '.
000162      01  SUBSCHEMA-SETNAMES.
000163          03  RES-PASS                PIC X(16)
```

FIGURE 15.9 (Cont.)
IDMS Communi-
cation Area

```
000164                                               VALUE 'RES-PASS              '.
000165        03  PASS-TICKET                         PIC X(16)
000166                                               VALUE 'PASS-TICKET           '.
000167        03  FLIGHT-FLIGHTDAY                    PIC X(16)
000168                                               VALUE 'FLIGHT-FLIGHTDAY '.
000169        03  FLIGHTDAY-TICKET                    PIC X(16)
000170                                               VALUE 'FLIGHTDAY-TICKET '.
000171        03  CALC                               PIC X(16)
000172                                               VALUE 'CALC                  '.
000173   01  SUBSCHEMA-AREANAMES
000174        03  AWA-DB                             PIC X(16)
000175                                               VALUE 'AWA-DB                '.
000176   01  500-TICKET.
000177        02  500-SEAT                           PIC X(3).
000178        02  FILLER                             PIC X(5).
000179   01  400-FLIGHT-DAY.
000180        02  400-FLIGHT-KEY.
000181            04  400-FLIGHT-NO                  PIC 9(4).
000182            04  400-FLIGHT-DATE                PIC 9(6).
000183        02  400-EQUIP-NO                       PIC 9(3).
000184        02  400-PASS-CTR                       PIC 9(3).
000185        02  400-DEPART-TIME                    PIC 9(4).
000186        02  400-ARRIVE-TIME                    PIC 9(4).
000187        02  400-FUEL-USED                      PIC 9(6).
000188        02  400-STATUS-NOTE                    PIC X(20).
000189        02  FILLER                             PIC X(6).
000190   01  300-FLIGHT.
000191        02  300-FLIGHT-NO                      PIC 9(4).
000192        02  300-ORIG                           PIC X(3).
000193        02  300-DEST                           PIC X(3).
000194        02  300-ORIG-TIME                      PIC 9(4).
000195        02  300-DEST-TIME                      PIC 9(4).
000196        02  300-MEAL                           PIC X.
000197        02  300-PRICE                          PIC 9(4)V9(2).
000198        02  FILLER                             PIC X(7).
000199   01  200-PASSENGER.
000200        02  200-PASS-NAME                      PIC X(20).
000201        02  200-ITIN-NO                        PIC 9(6).
000202        02  200-PRICE                          PIC 9(4)V9(2)
```

FIGURE 15.9 (Cont.)
IDMS Communi-
cation Area

```
000203     01   100-RESERVATION.
000204          02   100-CONFIRM-NO              PIC 9(6).
000205          02   100-RES-DATE               PIC 9(6).
000206          02   100-RES-NAME               PIC X(20).
000207          02   100-RES-PHONE              PIC X(12).
000208          02   100-RES-FLIGHT-NO          PIC 9(4).
000209          02   100-RES-FLIGHT-DATE        PIC 9(6).
000210          02   FILLER                     PIC X(2).
```

FIGURE 15.9 (Cont.)
IDMS Communi-
cation Area

digits refer to the type of error or condition. You will note that IDMS sets up some common 88 levels for some conditions, such as DB-STATUS-OK, ANY-ERROR-STATUS, DB-END-OF-SET, and DB-REC-NOT-FOUND. The major code 03 is for a FIND, GET, or OBTAIN, and the minor code 07 is for end of set. The minor code 26 is for record not found.

GENERAL PROCEDURE ROUTINES

The typical database processes include storing (loading or adding) new records to the database, modifying existing records, erasing existing records, and retrieving data in the form of queries or reports.

STORING a Parent Record with No Parents

The process logic to store a record differs depending on the location of the record in the data structure. The process to store a parent record that has no parents is very easy. The process involves setting up the key, determining if the record already exists, and storing the record. The pseudocode for this procedure is:

```
Move record key from screen buffer to record
Find record in database
IF record found
   Set Screen message to "Duplicate Record"
ELSE
   Move remaining screen data to record
   Store record
   Set Screen message to "Record Stored"
END-IF
```

The COBOL routine that illustrates this logic is 01-A100-STORE-RESERVA-TION along with the STORE statement in 99-U110-STORE-RESERVATION (Figure 15.10). Note that the store statement is a very simple command: STORE 100-RESERVATION. The database system does the CALC routine on the key, determines the block number, and stores the record in that block.

The second statement in the DML store routine is to check the error-status code by executing IDMS-STATUS. This routine checks the status code to see if it is other

```
01-A100-STORE-RESERVATION.
     MOVE '01-A100-STORE-RESERVATION' TO 600-ABORT-MESSAGE.
     DISPLAY '***  THIS MODULE STORES RESERVATION ***'.
     MOVE 510-CONFIRM-NO TO 100-CONFIRM-NO.
     PERFORM 99-U100-OBTAIN-RESERVATION.
     IF  DB-REC-NOT-FOUND
          MOVE 510-RES-DATE          TO 100-RES-DATE
          MOVE 510-RES-NAME          TO 100-RES-NAME
          MOVE 510-RES-PHONE         TO 100-RES-PHONE
          MOVE 510-RES-FLIGHT-NO     TO 100-RES-FLIGHT-NO
          MOVE 510-RES-FLIGHT-DATE   TO 100-RES-FLIGHT-DATE
          PERFORM 99-U110-STORE-RESERVATION
          DISPLAY ' ' 500-SCREEN-DATA '..RESERVATION STORED'
     ELSE
          DISPLAY ' ' 500-SCREEN-DATA
                              '..RESERVATION ALREADY EXISTS'.
99-U110-STORE-RESERVATION.
     STORE 100-RESERVATION.
     PERFORM IDMS-STATUS.
```

FIGURE 15.10
COBOL Code to
Store a Parent with
No Parents

Record occurrence
The actual insertion of a
specific record into a
database.

Set occurrence
The actual occurrence of a
set in the database that
takes place when an owner
record of the set is inserted
into the database.

than zero. If it is not zero, the status routine prints out various messages that show the status of what happened, rolls back the database to the last commit, and shuts down the run.

Storing a record of any type creates a **record occurrence** of that record type. Storing a parent record (owner) in the database initiates a **set occurrence** of any set type where this record participates as owner. The set occurrence is established even though there are no child records (members).

STORING a Child Record with One Parent

Storing a child record has the same logic as storing a parent except the parent record of the child must be located first. This process is necessary so IDMS can connect the child to the proper parent occurrence in the database. If the store was executed without finding the parent, the child would be connected to the last parent that was current of the parent record type. The pseudocode to store a child is:

```
Move record key of parent from screen buffer to record
Find parent
IF parent not found
   Display "No parent message"
ELSE
   Move record key of child from screen buffer to record
   Find child record in database
   IF child record not found
      Move remaining screen data to record
```

```
        Store record
    ELSE
        Set Screen message to "Duplicate Record"
    END-IF
END-IF
```

An example of the code for this procedure is shown in the 02-A100-STORE-PAS-SENGER routine. The DML store command is STORE 200-PASSENGER.

```
02-A100-STORE-PASSENGER.
   MOVE '02-A100-STORE-PASSENGER' TO 600-ABORT-MESSAGE.
   DISPLAY '*** THIS MODULE STORES PASSENGER ***'.
   MOVE 520-CONFIRM-NO TO 100-CONFIRM-NO.
   PERFORM 99-U100-OBTAIN-RESERVATION.
   IF DB-REC-NOT-FOUND
      DISPLAY ' ' 500-SCREEN-DATA
         'NO RESERVATION FOR THIS CONFIRMATION NO'
   ELSE
      PERFORM 02-B100-STORE-PASSENGER.
```

The schema structure is referenced by IDMS, so IDMS knows to connect the child (PASSENGER) to the parent (RESERVATION) using prior, next, and owner pointers defined by the set description.

STORING a Child with Multiple Parents

The logic to store a child with multiple parents follows the same logic as storing a child with one parent. The process of locating each parent is repeated until all parents are located. IDMS will automatically link the child into each set occurrence for each parent based on the set definitions in the schema assuming mandatory automatic as the insertion definition.

```
05-A100-STORE-TICKET.
   MOVE '05-A100-STORE-TICKET' TO 600-ABORT-MESSAGE.
   DISPLAY '*** THIS MODULE STORES TICKET***'.
   MOVE 550-ITIN-NO TO 200-ITIN-NO.
   PERFORM 99-U200-OBTAIN-PASSENGER.
   IF DB-REC-NOT-FOUND
      DISPLAY ' ' 500-SCREEN-DATA
         '..NO PASSENGER FOR THIS TICKET'
   ELSE
      PERFORM 05-B100-STORE-TICKET.

05-B100-STORE-TICKET.
   MOVE '05-B100-STORE-TICKET' TO 600-ABORT-MESSAGE.
   MOVE 550-FLIGHT-DAY-KEY TO 400-FLIGHT-KEY.
   PERFORM 99-U400-OBT-FLIGHT-DAY.
   IF DB-REC-NOT-FOUND
      DISPLAY ' ' 500-SCREEN-DATA
         '..NO FLIGHT DAY FOR THIS TICKET'
```

```
      ELSE
        PERFORM 05-C100-STORE-TICKET.
    05-C100-STORE-TICKET.
      MOVE '05-C100-STORE-TICKET' TO 600-ABORT-MESSAGE.
      PERFORM 99-U500-OBTAIN-TICKET.
      IF DB-REC-NOT-FOUND
      MOVE 550-SEAT TO 500-SEAT
      PERFORM 99-U510-STORE-TICKET
        DISPLAY ' ' 500-SCREEN-DATA '..TICKET STORED'
      ELSE
        DISPLAY ' ' 500-SCREEN-DATA
          '..SEAT ALREADY TAKEN                   '.
```

Module 5 in the sample program shows an example of storing a child with two parents. The parents are Passenger and Flight-Day. The first routine in the module (05-A100-STORE-TICKET) finds and sets currency on the Passenger record; the second routine (05-B100-STORE-TICKET) finds and sets currency on the Flight-Day record. The last routine (05-C100-STORE-TICKET) is the standard routine to store a record. Because currency for both parents was previously established, the pointer chains will be linked automatically for both sets.

Retrieving Existing Records in the Database

Procedures to find records in the database for modifying, erasing, and retrieving all use the same retrieval logic. Finding a record depends on how it is stored. If the record is a CALC record, it can be retrieved directly using the key. If the record is a VIA record, it must be retrieved through one of its owners or parents. This is done by obtaining the parent and then processing child records connected to that parent via the set. This is referred to as *walking the set*. It is basic sequential processing logic. The first record of the set is obtained, and then a processing routine is performed until end of set or the record is found. This processing routine does what it needs to do to identify and process the record. If the record is not found, the routine obtains the next record in the set. The following pseudocode illustrates the logic to process all child records (B) for a specific parent record (A).

```
Process-A
  Move the Key for the desired A record to the database record (A)
  Obtain the Parent (A)
  IF found
    Obtain first child (B) of parent-child set (A-B)
    DO UNTIL End-of-Set
      Process child data
      Obtain next child (B) in parent-child set (A-B)
    END-DO
  ELSE
    Message "Parent not found"
  END-IF
```

```
IDENTIFICATION DIVISION.

PROGRAM-ID. program-name [VERSION version-no]

ENVIRONMENT DIVISION.

IDMS-CONTROL SECTION.


PROTOCOL  MODE IS  ┌ BATCH ──────┐
                   │ mode-name   │ [DEBUG]
                   └─────────────┘

                 ┌ MANUAL
IDMS-RECORDS ────┤ WITHIN WORKING-STORAGE SECTION [LEVELS INCREMENTED BY level-count]
                 └ WITHIN LINKAGE SECTION [LEVELS INCREMENTED BY level-count]


DATA DIVISION.
SCHEMA SECTION.
DB subschema-name WITHIN schema-name [VERSION version-no].


PROCEDURE DIVISION.
COPY IDMS SUBSCHEMA-BINDS .
COPY IDMS module-name [VERSION version-no].
```

Control Statements

```
BIND RUN-UNIT [FOR subschema-name] [TO subschema-ctrl-identifier]


BIND  ┌ record-name [TO identifier]            ┐
      └ identifier WITH record-name-identifier ┘


BIND PROCEDURE FOR proc-name-identifier TO proc-comm-area


READY [area-name]  ┌ USAGE-MODE IS ┌ PROTECTED ┐ ┌ RETRIEVAL ┐ ┐
                   │               └ EXCLUSIVE  ┘ └ UPDATE    ┘ │
                   └                                            ┘


FINISH
IF set-name IS [NOT] EMPTY imperative-statement
IF [NOT] set-name MEMBER imperative-statement
COMMIT
ROLLBACK

                                 ┌ record-name        ┐
KEEP [EXCLUSIVE] CURRENT         │ WITHIN set-name    │
                                 └ WITHIN area-name   ┘
```

FIGURE 15.11
COBOL DML Syntax

Retrieval Logic for Multi-Hierarchical Levels   If the hierarchical structure drops to another level (grandchildren), the same logic is used at the next level. Notice that the outer loop logic (processing B records) is repeated again for the inner loop logic (processing D records).

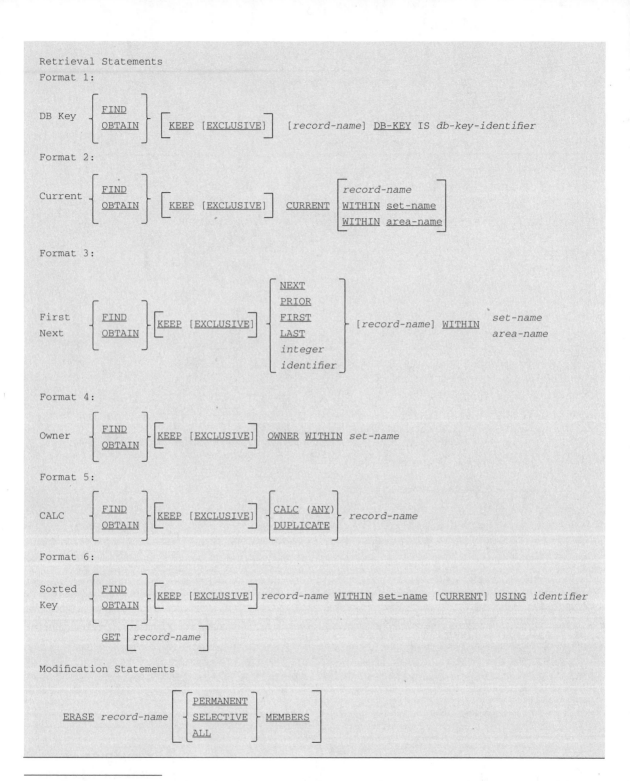

FIGURE 15.11 (Cont.)
COBOL DML Syntax

```
      CONNECT record-name TO set-name

      MODIFY record-name

      DISCONNECT record-name FROM set-name

      STORE record-name


Save Statements

                                    ┌─                    ─┐
                                    │ record-name          │
      ACCEPT db-key-identifier FROM │ set-name   CURRENCY  │
                                    │ area-name            │
                                    └─                    ─┘

                                                 ┌─      ─┐
                                                 │ NEXT   │
      ACCEPT db-key-identifer FROM set-name     ─┤ PRIOR  ├─ CURRENCY
                                                 │ OWNER  │
                                                 └─      ─┘

      ACCEPT identifier FROM IDMS-STATISTICS

      ACCEPT identifier FROM record-name BIND

      ACCEPT proc-comm-area FROM proc-name-identifier PROCEDURE
```

For more information, refer to CA-IDMS DML Reference-COBOL Computer Associates.

FIGURE 15.11 (Cont.)
COBOL DML Syntax

```
Process-A
  Move the Key for the desired A record to the database record (A)
  Obtain the Parent (A)
  IF found
    Obtain first child (B) of parent-child set (A-B)
    DO UNTIL End-of-Set
      Obtain first child (D) of parent-child set (B-D)
      Do until End-of-Set
        Process D data
        Obtain next child (D) in parent-child set (B-D)
      END-DO
      Obtain next child (B) in parent-child set (A-B)
    END-DO
  ELSE
    Message "Parent not found"
  END-IF
```

Frequently the process of identifying the desired child record requires obtaining the owner on another set. This is done with the obtain owner (format 4) in Figure 15.11. When the correct owner of the other parent-child set is found, then the correct child record has been isolated. See the pseudocode example that follows.

Pseudocode to Retrieve a Specific Child Record with Multiple Parents

```
Process-A
  Move the Key for the desired A record to the database record (A)
  Obtain the Parent (A)
  IF found
    Obtain first child (B) of parent-child set (A-B)
    Do Until End-of-Set
      Obtain Owner (C) of parent-child set (C-B)
      If C Key or data = desired C data
        Process existing A, B, C data
      Else
        Obtain next child (B) in parent-child set (A-B)
      End-if
    End-Do
    If End-of-Set
      Message "No B found matching desired C data"
    End-if
  ELSE
    Message "Parent (A) not found"
  END-IF
```

Child records defined as VIA using a sorted set on a key field can be obtained directly by using the sort key on that set, after currency (position) has been established on the parent. This is done by using format 6 of the OBTAIN commands defined in the DML commands in Figure 15.11. The following is an example of using this format of the OBTAIN, where the TICKETS are sorted on seat within the FLIGHTDAY-TICKET set.

```
OBTAIN 500-TICKET WITHIN FLIGHTDAY-TICKET USING 500-SEAT.
```

Modifying Records

Modifying a record requires finding the desired record, altering the data in the database record area in working storage, and rewriting the record. The record is rewritten with the MODIFY command. A sample routine to modify passenger data is shown in module six of the sample program. The routine is modifying all data from the screen section that is not blank. This routine finds the Passenger record directly, because the Passenger record has a CALC key on itinerary number.

Sample Code to Modify a Record

```
06-A100-MODIFY-PASSENGER.
    MOVE '06-A100-MODIFY-PASSENGER' TO 600-ABORT-MESSAGE.
    DISPLAY '*** THIS MODULE MODIFIES PASSENGER DATA ***'.
    MOVE 520-ITIN-NO TO 200-ITIN-NO.
    PERFORM 99-U200-OBTAIN-PASSENGER.
    IF DB-REC-NOT-FOUND
        DISPLAY ' ' 500-SCREEN-DATA
            '..NO PASSENGER FOR THIS ITINERARY NO'
    ELSE
        PERFORM 06-B100-MODIFY-PASSENGER
        DISPLAY ' ' 500-SCREEN-DATA
                '..PASSENGER DATA MODIFIED'.
06-B100-MODIFY-PASSENGER.
    MOVE '06-B100-MODIFY-PASSENGER' TO 600-ABORT-MESSAGE.
    IF 520-PASS-NAME NOT = SPACE
        MOVE 520-PASS-NAME TO 200-PASS-NAME.
    IF 520-PRICE NOT = SPACE
        MOVE 520-PRICE TO 200-PRICE.
    PERFORM 99-U230-MODIFY-PASSENGER.
99-U230-MODIFY-PASSENGER.
    MODIFY 200-PASSENGER.
    PERFORM IDMS-STATUS.
```

Erasing Records

Erasing a record is the same process as modifying a record. The record is located and then erased. Module seven in the sample program shows an example of deleting a record. The Flight record is a CALC record on Flight Number so it can be retrieved directly. The erase command in 99-U320-ERASE-FLIGHT is an ERASE 300-FLIGHT SELECTIVE MEMBERS, which means the Flight records and the related Flight-Day child records will be deleted. The Ticket records will not be deleted because they are children of the Passenger record.

Sample Code to Delete a Record

```
07-A100-ERASE-FLIGHT.
   MOVE '07-A100-ERASE-FLIGHT ' TO 600-ABORT-MESSAGE.
   DISPLAY '*** THIS MODULE ERASES FLIGHT DATA ***'.
   MOVE 530-FLIGHT-NO TO 300-FLIGHT-NO.
   PERFORM 99-U300-OBTAIN-FLIGHT.
   IF DB-REC-NOT-FOUND
      DISPLAY ' ' 500-SCREEN-DATA
                   '..NO FLIGHT FOR THIS FLIGHT NO'
   ELSE
      PERFORM 99-U320-ERASE-FLIGHT
      DISPLAY ' ' 500-SCREEN-DATA
                   '..FLIGHT AND RELATED FLIGHT DAYS ERASED'.
99-U320-ERASE-FLIGHT.
   ERASE 300-FLIGHT SELECTIVE MEMBERS.
                   PERFORM IDMS-STATUS.
```

An ERASE 300-FLIGHT ALL MEMBERS would also erase the Ticket records. An ERASE 300-FLIGHT PERMANENT MEMBERS would erase the Flight records but not the Flight-Day records because Flight-Day records are defined as optional.

Retrieving Data for Queries and Reports

Retrieving data for reports and queries is a process of starting somewhere in the database and processing down the structure while processing owner data at each level in the structure. This is a combination of the hierarchical processing of multiple levels with the obtain owner logic built in at each level. Module eight in the Air West sample program shows an example of this logic. This module sets up a query of all itinerary data for a particular reservation. The reservation is located directly by confirmation number, and then each passenger that is linked to this reservation is obtained in sequence. The processing for each passenger obtains each ticket in sequence, and for each ticket obtains owner information on flight-day and then obtains owner information on flight.

Once both owners are obtained, all the data necessary to report the itinerary schedule for the specific flight represented by that ticket can be reported back to the screen. This process is repeated for each ticket until the end of set on the tickets, and then the entire ticket process is repeated again for each passenger until end of set on passengers. Retrieval generally means coming into the database on a CALC key as the entry point. Processing down the structure is done by obtaining first record and then obtaining next record on a set until the set is completely processed. Processing up the structure is done by obtaining owner on other sets. If more levels up the structure are necessary, then you obtain owner again on the set above the current owner you just obtained.

Sample Code to Retrieve Multiple Levels with Owners on Other Sets

```
08-A100-RETRIEVE-RES-DATA.
   MOVE '08-A100-RETRIEVE-RES-DATA ' TO 600-ABORT-MESSAGE.
   DISPLAY '*** THIS MODULE RETRIEVES RESERVATION DATA ***'.
   MOVE 510-CONFIRM-NO TO 100-CONFIRM-NO.
   PERFORM 99-U100-OBTAIN-RESERVATION.
   IF DB-REC-NOT-FOUND
     DISPLAY ' ' 500-SCREEN-DATA
                 '..NO RESERVATION FOR THIS CONFIRMATION'
   ELSE
     DISPLAY ' RESERVATION FOR ' 100-RES-NAME
     PERFORM 08-B100-RETRIEVE-PASSENGER.
     DISPLAY ' ' 500-SCREEN-DATA
                 '..END OF DATA FOR THIS RESERVATION          '.
08-B100-RETRIEVE-PASSENGER.
   MOVE '08-B100-RETRIEVE-PASSENGER' TO 600-ABORT-MESSAGE.
   PERFORM 99-U250-OBT-FIRST-PASSENGER.
   IF DB-END-OF-SET
                 DISPLAY ' NO PASSENGER DATA UNDER THIS RESERVATION'
   ELSE
     PERFORM 08-C100-TICKET-PROCESSING UNTIL DB-END-OF-SET.
08-C100-TICKET-PROCESSING.
   MOVE '08-C100-TICKET-PROCESSING' TO 600-ABORT-MESSAGE.
   DISPLAY ' PASSENGER ' 200-PASS-NAME
   PERFORM 99-U560-OBT-FIRST-PASS-TICKET.
   IF DB-END-OF-SET
                 DISPLAY ' NO TICKETS FOR THIS PASSENGER'
   ELSE
     PERFORM 08-D100-PROCESS-TICKETS UNTIL DB-END-OF-SET.
   PERFORM 99-U250-OBT-NEXT-PASSENGER.
08-D100-PROCESS-TICKETS.
   MOVE '08-D100-PROCESS-TICKETS' TO 600-ABORT-MESSAGE.
   PERFORM 99-U570-OBT-FLIGHT-DAY-OWNER.
   PERFORM 99-U470-OBT-FLIGHT-OWNER.
   DISPLAY '    ' 300-ORIG ' ' 300-ORIG-TIME ' '
                  300-DEST ' ' 300-DEST-TIME ' '
                  300-MEAL ' ' 300-PRICE ' '
                  400-FLIGHT-NO ' ' 400-FLIGHT-DATE ' '
                  500-SEAT.
   PERFORM 99-U560-OBT-NEXT-PASS-TICKET.
99-U250-OBT-FIRST-PASSENGER.
   OBTAIN FIRST 200-PASSENGER WITHIN RES-PASS.
   IF NOT DB-END-OF-SET
     PERFORM IDMS-STATUS.
```

```
99-U250-OBT-NEXT-PASSENGER.
    OBTAIN NEXT 200-PASSENGER WITHIN RES-PASS.
    IF NOT DB-END-OF-SET
      PERFORM IDMS-STATUS.
99-U560-OBT-FIRST-PASS-TICKET.
    OBTAIN FIRST 500-TICKET WITHIN PASS-TICKET.
    IF NOT DB-END-OF-SET
      PERFORM IDMS-STATUS.
99-U560-OBT-NEXT-PASS-TICKET.
    OBTAIN NEXT 500-TICKET WITHIN PASS-TICKET.
    IF NOT DB-END-OF-SET
      PERFORM IDMS-STATUS.
99-U470-OBT-FLIGHT-OWNER.
    OBTAIN OWNER WITHIN FLIGHT-FLIGHTDAY.
    PERFORM IDMS-STATUS.
99-U570-OBT-FLIGHT-DAY-OWNER.
    OBTAIN OWNER WITHIN FLIGHTDAY-TICKET.
```

Connecting and Disconnecting Records

IDMS controls data structures by linking records together in sets. All the child records for a parent or owner are linked together with pointers. There are times when it is nice to be able to have control over this linking so that it is not automatic. One example of this relates to storing a child in the database before all parent occurrences exist. The child can be linked to the parents after the parent is entered into the database.

Another example is that not all occurrences of child records have to participate in all set occurrences. If the set definition is constructed as manual, the program can determine when to link a child record to a parent in that particular set occurrence. This can be done by connecting the child record to the parent record after the child record has been stored. Another example is being able to change the record from one set occurrence to another set occurrence within the same set definition. This is done by disconnecting the record from one set occurrence and connecting the record to another set occurrence. Module nine in the sample program illustrates an example of the processing required to do this.

The first step is to find the record that needs to be changed. In this example we are changing the ticket from one flight to another flight. Instead of leaving at 9:00, the passenger wants to leave on the 11:00 flight. The change is accomplished by finding the ticket for the passenger that is related to the 9:00 flight. When the ticket is found, it is disconnected from the its current Flight-Day record occurrence or Flight Day–Ticket set occurrence.

The next step is to find (establish currency on) the new Flight-Day occurrence and connect the ticket to its related Flight-Day–Ticket set occurrence. Note that the parent of the set does not have to be present in order to disconnect. However, the parent must be current of its record type in order to execute a connect so IDMS knows which parent occurrence to connect the record to.

HELPFUL HINTS IN TESTING

Once the program has been compiled successfully, testing can be done. The sample program is not set up with any screen front end such as **CICS, ISPF,** or **IDMS/DC.** The program emulates getting data from a screen by reading data records from a file. Each record on the input file is like a transaction that came from a screen that had been completed by a user. Each screen can execute any one of nine routines in the program. Each routine is related to a specific transaction type.

Normally the first phase of testing is to store the various record types in the database. The next phase is to test modifications to records, erasing records, and the disconnect and connect of records. The last phase is to test the retrieval of data for query and report purposes. The testing can be done in phases or a complete test suite can be executed as one run that includes storing data, modifying the database, and retrieving data. If a test run fails, the output report will display various status lines that show the status of the program and IDMS. An example of this report is shown in Figure 15.12. The figure shows the routine name, the DML command number, the error status code, and the error record and error set name. The error status codes are shown in Figure 15.13.

It is important to be aware that when the database is aborted, very often a code is set within the database locking it so you can not access it again. You can unlock it with proper utilities, or you can reinitialize the database and reload the data up to the point where you want to start testing again. Initializing the database during testing can be convenient for starting tests over again from common starting points, because of the modification to the database that is done by the testing.

Customer Information Control System (CICS)
An on-line screen interface system from IBM that manages communication between COBOL and a 3270 terminal.

Interactive System Productivity Facility (ISPF)
A programmer interface that is used by application developers on IBM MVS systems to manage data sets, build files, edit files, build JCL, compile programs, and test applications.

Integrated Data Management System/Data Communications (IDMS/DC)
The IDMS data communications interface used to build and manage 3270 terminal user interfaces with host programs like COBOL.

```
***  THIS MODULE RETRIEIVES RESERVATION DATA ***
ABORTED IN PARAGRAPH    08-A100-RETRIEVE-RES-DATA
PROGRAM NAME ------ AIRWEST
ERROR STATUS ------ 0306
ERROR RECORD ------
ERROR SET --------- FLIGHTDAY-TICKET
ERROR AREA -------- AWA-DB
LAST GOOD RECORD -- 100-RESERVATION
LAST GOOD AREA ---- AWA-DB
DML SEQUENCE--------0000000043
```

FIGURE 15.12
Sample Messages from Program Abort

Major DB Status Codes

Code	Database Function
00	Any DML statement
01	FINISH
02	ERASE
03	FIND/OBTAIN
05	GET
06	KEEP
07	CONNECT
08	MODIFY
09	READY
11	DISCONNECT
12	STORE
14	BIND
15	ACCEPT
16	IF
17	RETURN
18	COMMIT
19	ROLLBACK
20	LRF requests

Minor DB Status Codes

Code	Database Function Status
00	Combined with a major code of 00, this code indicates successful completion of the DML operation. Combined with a non-zero major code, this code indicates that the DML operation was not completed successfully due to central version causes, such as time-outs and program checks.
01	An area has not been readied. When this code is combined with a major code of 16, an IF operation has resulted in a valid false condition.
02	Either the db-key used with a FIND/OBTAIN DB-KEY statement or the direct db-key suggested for a STORE is not within the page range for the specified record name.
04	The occurrence count of a variably occurring element has been specified as either less than zero or greater than the maximum number of occurrences defined in the control element.
05	The specified DML function would have violated a duplicates-not-allowed option for a CALC, sorted, or index set.
06	No currency has been established for the named record, set, or area.

FIGURE 15.13
Error Status Codes
Run-Time Error-
Status Codes

Code	Database Function Status
07	The end of a set, area, or index has been reached or the set is empty.
08	The specified record, set, procedure, or LR verb is not in the subschema or the specified record is not a member of the set.
09	The area has been readied with an incorrect usage mode.
10	An existing access restriction or subschema usage prohibits execution of the specified DML function. For LRF users, the subschema in use allows access to database records only. Combined with a major code of 00, this code means the program has attempted to access a database record, but the subschema in use allows access to logical records only.
11	The record cannot be stored in the specified area due to insufficient space.
12	There is no db-key for the record to be stored. This is a system internal error and should be reported.
13	A current record of run unit either has not been established or has been nullified by a previous ERASE statement.
14	The CONNECT statement cannot be executed because the requested record has been defined as a mandatory automatic member of the set.
15	The DISCONNECT statement cannot be executed because the requested record has been defined as a mandatory member of the set.
16	The record cannot be connected to a set of which it is already a member.
18	The record has not been bound.
20	The current record is not the same type as the specified record name.
21	Not all areas being used have been readied in the correct usage mode.
22	The record name specified is not currently a member of the set name specified.
23	The area name specified is either not in the subschema or not an extent area; or the record name specified has not been defined within the area name specified.
25	No currency has been established for the named set.
26	No duplicates exist for the named record or the record occurrences cannot be found.
28	The run unit has attempted to ready an area that has been readied previously.
29	The run unit has attempted to place a lock on a record that is locked already by another run unit. A deadlock results. Unless the run unit issued either a FIND/OBTAIN KEEP EXCLUSIVE or a KEEP EXCLUSIVE, the run unit is aborted.
30	An attempt has been made to erase the owner record of a nonempty set.
31	The retrieval statement format conflicts with the record's location mode.
32	An attempt to retrieve a CALC/DUPLICATE record was unsuccessful; the value of the CALC field in variable storage is not equal to the value of the CALC control element in the current record of run unit.

FIGURE 15.13 (Cont.)
Error Status Codes
Run-Time Error-
Status Codes

Code	Database Function Status
33	At least one set in which the record participates has not been included in the subschema.
40	The WHERE clause in an OBTAIN NEXT logical-record request is inconsistent with a previous OBTAIN FIRST or OBTAIN NEXT command for the same record. Previously specified criteria, such as reference to a key field, have been changed. A path status of LR-ERROR is returned to the LRC block.
41	The subschema contains no path that matches the WHERE clause in a logical-record request. A path status of LR-ERROR is returned to the LRC block.
42	An ON clause included in the path by the DBA specified return of the LR-ERROR path status to the LRC block; an error has occurred while processing the LRF request.
43	A program check has been recognized during evaluation of a WHERE clause; the program check indicates that either a WHERE clause has specified comparison of a packed decimal field to an unpacked non-numeric data field, or data in variable storage or a database record does not conform to its description. A path status of LR-ERROR is returned to the LRC block unless the DBA has included an ON clause to override this action in the path.
44	The WHERE clause in a logical-record request does not supply a key element (sort key, CALC key, or db-key) expected by the path. A path status of LR-ERROR is returned to the LRC block.
45	During evaluation of a WHERE clause, a program check has been recognized because a subscript value is neither greater than 0 nor less than its maximum allowed value plus 1. A path status of LR-ERROR is returned to the LRC block unless the DBA has included an ON clause to override this action in the path.
46	A program check has revealed an arithmetic exception (for example: overflow, underflow, significance, divide) during evaluation of a WHERE clause. A path status of LR-ERROR is returned to the LRC block unless the DBA has included an ON clause to override this action in the path.
53	The subschema definition of an indexed set does not match the indexed set's physical structure in the database.
54	Either the prefix length of an SR51 record is less than zero or the data length is less than or equal to zero.
55	An invalid length has been defined for a variable-length record.
56	An insufficient amount of memory to accommodate the CA-IDMS/DBcompression/decompression routines is available.
60	A record occurrence type is inconsistent with the set named in the ERROR-SET field in the IDMS communications block. This code usually indicates a broken chain.
61	No record can be found for an internal db-key. This code usually indicates a broken chain.
62	A system-generated db-key points to a record occurrence, but no record with that db-key can be found. This code usually indicates a broken chain.
63	The DBMS cannot interpret the DML function to be performed. When combined with a major code of 00, this code means invalid function parameters have been passed on the call to the DBMS. For LRF users, a WHERE clause includes a keyword that is longer than the 32 characters allowed.
64	The record cannot be found; the CALC control element has not been defined properly in the subschema.

FIGURE 15.13 (Cont.)
Error Status Codes
Run-Time Error-
Status Codes

Code	Database Function Status
65	The database page read was not the page requested.
66	The area specified is not available in the requested usage mode.
67	The subschema invoked does not match the subschema object tables.
68	The CICS interface was not started.
69	A BIND RUN-UNIT may not have been issued; the CV may be inactive or not accepting new run units; or the connection with the CV may have been broken due to time out or other factors. When combined with a major code of 00, this code means the program has been disconnected from the DBMS.
70	The database will not ready properly; a JCL error is the probable cause.
71	The page range or page group for the area being readied or the page requested cannot be found in the DMCL.
72	There is insufficient memory to dynamically load a subschema or database procedure.
73	A central version run unit will exceed the MAXERUS value specified at system generation.
74	The dynamic load of a module has failed. If operating under the central version, a subschema or database procedure module either was not found in the data dictionary or the load (core image) library or, if loaded, will exceed the number of subschema and database procedures provided for at system generation.
75	A read error has occurred.
76	A write error has occurred.
77	The run unit has not been bound or has been bound twice. When combined with a major code of 00, this code means either the program is no longer signed on to the subschema or the variable subschema tables have been overwritten.
78	An area wait deadlock has occurred.
79	The run unit has requested more db-key locks than are available to the system.
80	The target node is either not active or has been disabled.
81	The converted subschema requires specified database name to be in the DBNAME table.
82	The subschema must be named in the DBNAME table.
83	An error has occurred in accessing native VSAM data sets.
91	The subschema requires a DBNAME to do the bind run unit.

FIGURE 15.13 (Cont.)
Error Status Codes
Run-Time Error-
Status Codes

SUMMARY

This chapter has presented an example of implementing a network type database. The example was done using IDMS and COBOL on a mainframe. IDMS is still heavily used in industry because it was adopted by a number of large companies for their primary database system before relational database systems were available. Like IMS, IDMS is embedded with COBOL in many large legacy systems with tremendous investments, and it is difficult to change these systems without additional large investments.

Code	Database Function Status
92	No subschema areas map to DMCL.
93	A subschema area symbolic was not found in DMCL.
94	The specified dbname is neither a dbname defined in the DBNAME table, nor a SEGMENT defined in the DMCL.
95	The specified subschema failed DBTABLE mapping using the specified dbname.

Release 12.0, July 1992

This quick reference applies to Release 12.0 of CA-IDMS/DB and CA-IDMS/DC and accompanies the following manuals: *CA-IDMS Navigational DML Programming, CA-IDMS DML Reference—COBOL, CA-IDMS DML Reference—Assembler, and CA-IDMS DML Reference—PL/I.*

CA-IDMS, CA-IDMS/DC, CA-IDMS/DB and CA-IDMS/UCF are registered trademarks of Computer Associates International, Inc.

All product names referenced herein are trademarks of their respective companies.

FIGURE 15.13 (Cont.)
Error Status Codes
Run-Time Error-
Status Codes

IDMS has four major components used to build database systems. The components are schema, subschema, DMCL, and DML. Other components exist as tools to help manage and initialize loads of the database. The schema is the overall description of the database. It defines the entity (record) names, field names, types, and sizes, the relationships between records, the location of records in the database, and the definition of the various sets that link the records. The subschema is used to set up various definitions of the database that are subsets of the schema definition. Subschemas are used to provide security to the database by allowing only certain views to an application. If a specific application is only updating certain records in the database, the subschema provides a view that includes only those records. The DMCL is used to describe the physical requirements of the database to the IDMS system. This includes information about the physical size of the blocks, the number of blocks to use, the mapping of entities to different areas, and the use of journals to maintain database security and tracking. The DML (data manipulation language) is the language embedded into the host language COBOL to provide the communication between the COBOL program and IDMS. It includes commands like OBTAIN, MODIFY, ERASE, STORE, CONNECT and DISCONNECT. The DML is also used to set up the open and close of the database and the communication areas within working storage.

The process of setting up a database in IDMS starts with the E-R (entity relationship) diagram. Normally this diagram is expanded to include many of the definitions that are a part of the IDMS schema definitions. This diagram is referred to as a Data Structure Diagram or DSD, or a Bachman diagram. The diagram is used as a map to build the schema. The schema is compiled, which updates all the definitions in an IDMS dictionary. The next step is to build the DMCL and compile it. The result of the DMCL compilation is stored in the load library. Any number of subsets (subschemas) can now be defined and compiled. The results of these compiles are also stored in a load library. The last step in preparing the database to accept data is to initialize it. This is a process of formatting it much like formatting a disk so that it is set up with the blocks and addresses that IDMS can read. The database is now ready to accept data. Data can be loaded into the database using a utility, or through a COBOL program that has been written especially to load data. The regular production on-line computer programs can also be used to start loading the database; however, in most cases an application already has large amounts of data associated with it that must be preloaded.

The last step in the process is to build the application programs. References to the subschema and the schema are contained in the schema section of the COBOL program. This reference provides the COBOL precompiler with all the information necessary to set up the communication area in the COBOL program with all the record definitions and control area necessary for this application. The procedure division contains DML commands that execute various database routines to store, delete, update, and retrieve data using the IDMS database. These calls are converted to calls the COBOL compiler can understand by the IDMS COBOL precompiler. Once the COBOL program is written and successfully compiled, the object program is linked to the various libraries and stored in the load library. The last step is to execute the COBOL program with data that comes either from a file or from on-line screens. Screen-driven COBOL programs on a mainframe require screen processors such as IDMS/DC, IMS/DC, or CICS with calls embedded into the COBOL program. These processors along with COBOL are beyond the scope of this book and were not covered.

REVIEW QUIZ

_____ The language used to set up and define a schema.

_____ The language used to set up and define the physical file system and journals for the database system.

_____ The language used in a host language to make database calls to the database.

_____ The committee responsible for developing the CODASYL database standard.

_____ Name used for a parent record of a set.

_____ Name used for a child record of a set.

_____ The term used to refer to a specific entity stored in the database.

_____ The term used to refer to the definition of an entity within a database.

_____ The term used to refer to a specific set that has been initiated in the database.

_____ The term used to refer to the definition of a set.

_____ Use of Last or Next in a set definition.

_____ Use of Optional or Mandatory in a set definition.

_____ Use of Manual or Automatic in a set definition.

_____ The DML command to add a record to the database.

_____ The DML command to delete a record from the database.

_____ The DML command to add a record to a set occurrence.

_____ The DML command to remove a record from a set occurrence.

_____ The DML command to delete an owner record and all its members.

_____ The DML command to delete an owner record and all members that do not participate in other sets.

_____ The DML command to cause all changes to a database to become permanent even in the event of a Rollback.

_____ The DML command to remove all changes to the database up to the last commit point.

_____ The record position within a set that is the last record accessed in that set occurrence.

_____ The specific record occurrence of specific type that was last accessed.

_____ The insertion mode for a specific record type.

_____ The DML command to get the first record in a set occurrence.

_____ The DML command to get the owner record in a set occurrence.

_____ The code used to check the status of a DML command.

_____ The main difference between a network database and a hierarchical database.

_____ The process of sequentially processing records within a set occurrence.

_____ The founder of IDMS.

_____ The developer of a CODASYL database called IDS at General Electric.

_____ Page number and line number where a record is stored.

1. IDMS
2. CODASYL
3. DBTG
4. DDL
5. DMCL
6. DML
7. IDS
8. DSD
9. Set type
10. Set occurrence
11. Record type
12. Schema
13. Subschema
14. Record occurrence
15. Area
16. Database key
17. Page number
18. Line number
19. Cullinane
20. Charles Bachman
21. Owner
22. Member
23. Walking a set
24. A child can have more than one parent
25. Obtain first
26. Obtain next
27. Obtain owner
28. AUTOMATIC or MANUAL
29. Current of set
30. Current of record type
31. ERASE ALL
32. ERASE SELECTIVE

33. ERASE PERMANENT

34. ROLLBACK

35. COMMIT

36. CONNECT

37. DISCONNECT

38. Record occurrence

39. Insertion mode

40. Deletion mode

41. Sort order

42. STORE

43. Error status

REVIEW QUESTIONS AND EXERCISES

1. Describe the history of the development of network type databases.

2. Explain the functionality of each of the following commands.

   a. BIND

   b. READY

   c. FINISH

   d. COMMIT

   e. ROLLBACK

   f. FIND

   g. GET

   h. ERASE

   i. MODIFY

   j. CONNECT

   k. DISCONNECT

   l. STORE

   m. OBTAIN

   n. ACCEPT

   o. IF

   p. KEEP

3. Set up a DSD for the following car rental database:

   ■ Automobile record (License No., Make, Year, Value)

   ■ Customer record (Name, SSN, Phone)

   ■ Rental Record (Date, Pickup date, Return date, Total Charges)

   ■ A customer can rent many automobiles and an automobile can be rented by many customers.

4. Set up a schema for the car rental DSD.

5. Write the COBOL code to store a customer.

6. Write the COBOL code to store an automobile.

7. Write the COBOL code to delete a customer.

8. Write the COBOL code to modify the Phone for a customer.

9. Write the COBOL code to list all automobiles ever rented for a customer.

10. Write the COBOL code to list all customers with names >C.

11. Write the COBOL code to list all automobiles with a year of 1996.

12. Describe how the COBOL program communicates with IDMS.

13. Describe how children are related to their parents in IDMS.

14. Modify the network database design for the Airline database to add an entity that maintains seat address, location, and type, where address is 16A; location is window, aisle, or middle; and type is first class, exit row, bulk head, and so on. Set up another entity to maintain the assignment of these seats to tickets in the Airline database as seat assignments are made to passengers. Set up a schema for this portion of the Airline database.

15. Where is the status code returned in the COBOL program? Give an example of a COBOL statement to check the status code. List the most common status codes that are used in a COBOL program.

16. Explain how currency is used when storing child (member) records.

17. Explain how currency is used when retrieving owner records from different set occurrences.

18. Explain how currency is used when walking one set occurrence using FIND NEXT and retrieving owner data in another set occurrence that a record participates in.

19. Explain the use of currency for erase and modify.

20. Explain the use of ERASE ALL, ERASE PERMANENT, and ERASE SELECTIVE.

21. Explain the use of currency when doing a disconnect and a connect of the same record to a different parent (owner).

22. Set up an example of a network-type database where there are multiple sets between two entity types similar to the AIRPORT/FLIGHT structure. Other possibilities include bill of materials, debit and credits of accounts, and genealogy structures. Draw a DSD and show some sample occurrences using longhand diagrams.

23. Explain the different location modes CALC, DIRECT, and VIA.

24. Explain the different orders PRIOR, NEXT, FIRST, LAST, SORTED.

25. Explain the different insertion modes (manual, automatic).

26. Explain the different deletion modes (mandatory, optional).

27. Explain the difference between location mode and order.

28. How would you design the Airline database to retrieve airports in sequence by airport name from the database on a regular basis?

APPENDIX A:
INTRODUCTION TO XDB,
ORACLE, AND ACCESS

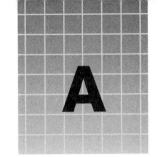

CHAPTER OUTLINE

XDB can be installed either on a local system on a server. The engine can be started under Windows by starting the XDB DDE server icon. A new database can be set up by executing a create location SQL command such as: CREATE LOCATION AIRLINE IN C:\DB\XDBAIR. This sets up the database location within the XDB system tables. The SQL commands are executed in the interactive SQL utility (Figure A.1). The commands can be built, edited, saved, and run from the various menus on this window. The figure shows the SQL to build the reservation table within the airline location. The airline location is selected by using Profile and the Browse menu under profile to change the location.

Once the table is created, you can go to the dictionary and select tables, select a table and select DESCRIBE, and you can view a description of the table (Figure A.2).

The window in Figure A.3 shows the use of the SQL utility window to insert data into the reservation table.

Figure A.4 shows the window after executing the SQL command: SELECT * FROM RESERVATION;. This window can also be used to insert, delete, and modify data in the table.

XDB/DB2 FUNCTIONS

XDB/DB2 have a number of functions that are in addition to the aggregate functions covered earlier in Chapter 6. These functions can be used in the SELECT in the same way. A definition of these functions follow:

XSTDDEV (x):	Standard deviation of x.
XVAR (x):	Variance of x.

FIGURE A.1

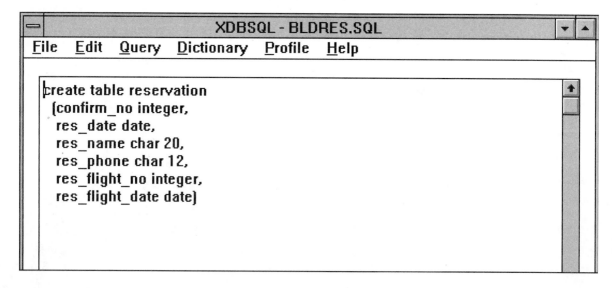

```
XDBSQL - BLDRES.SQL
File   Edit   Query   Dictionary   Profile   Help

create table reservation
 (confirm_no integer,
  res_date date,
  res_name char 20,
  res_phone char 12,
  res_flight_no integer,
  res_flight_date date)
```

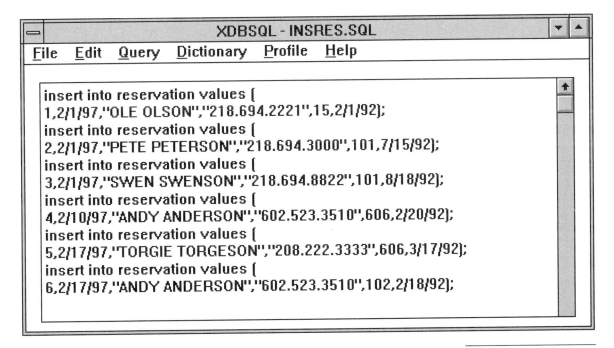

FIGURE A.2

FIGURE A.3

```
┌─────────────────────────────────────────────────────────────────────┐
│ ▭                        QUERY RESULTS                               ▯│
├─────────────────────────────────────────────────────────────────────┤
│ File    Record    Help                                                │
├─────────────────────────────────────────────────────────────────────┤
│                                                                       │
│  ☒ Automatic Record Update                                            │
│  Record 1                                                             │
│                                                                       │
│  ┌────────────┬────────────┬───────────────────────┬──────────┬─┐   │
│  │ confirm_no │  res_date  │      res_name         │   res_p  │▲│   │
│  ├────────────┼────────────┼───────────────────────┼──────────┤ │   │
│  │ 1          │ 02/01/1997 │ ┃LE OLSON             │ 218.69   │ │   │
│  │ 2          │ 02/01/1997 │ PETE PETERSON         │ 218.69   │ │   │
│  │ 3          │ 02/01/1997 │ SWEN SWENSON          │ 218.69   │ │   │
│  │ 4          │ 02/10/1997 │ ANDY ANDERSON         │ 602.52   │ │   │
│  │ 5          │ 02/17/1997 │ TORGIE TORGESON       │ 208.22   │ │   │
│  │ 6          │ 02/17/1997 │ ANDY ANDERSON         │ 602.52   │ │   │
│  │            │            │                       │          │ │   │
│  │            │            │                       │          │ │   │
│  │            │            │                       │          │ │   │
│  │            │            │                       │          │▼│   │
│  └────────────┴────────────┴───────────────────────┴──────────┴─┘   │
│  ◄ ▭                                                          ▭ ►    │
│                                                                       │
│  Field type is CHARACTER.                                             │
└─────────────────────────────────────────────────────────────────────┘
```

FIGURE A.4

AGE(date1,date 2):	Number of years between date 2 and date1.
AGE(date1):	Number of years between today and date1.
DATE(expres):	Converts expres to date format where expres = mm/dd/yyyy or expres = positive number where 1 = 1–1–0001.DAY(date-expr):Extracts day of the month (1–31) from date expression (date or timestamp).
DAYS(date-expr):	Calculates number of days from 1–1–0001 to the date in the date expression.
HOUR(time-expr):	Extracts hour (1–24) from time expression.
MICROSECOND(time-expr):	Extracts microsecond (0–99999) from time expression.

MINUTE(time-expr):	Extracts minute (0–59) from time expression.
MONTH(date-expr):	Extracts month (1–12) from date.
SECOND(time-expr):	Extracts second (0–59) from time expression.
TIME(expres):	Converts expres into time format where expres = hh:mm:AM or PM or expres = hh:mm:ss in 2400 time format or express is a timestamp.
TIMESTAMP(expres1[,exprs2]):	Generates a timestamp where expres1 can be the string yyyymmddhhmmss, or expres1 is the date string and expres2 is the time string.
YEAR(date-expr):	Extracts the year from date.
XDATE(m,d,y):	Generates a date from the integers m, d and y. m could be the month from some other date such as month(birthdate).
DECIMAL(x[,p [,s]]):	Converts x to decimal with precision (1-15) and scale (0-p).
FLOAT(x):	Converts x to floating point.
INTEGER(x):	Converts x to integer.
CHAR(x):	Converts date, time or timestamp into a string.
DIGITS(x):	Converts a numeric x to string.
HEX(x):	Converts x to Hexadecimal string.
LENGTH(x):	Finds the length of x.
SUBSTR(x,m [,n]):	Extracts n characters from x starting at m.
XCONCAT(expres1,expres2):	Concatenates two strings. This can also be done with the ‖. Select fname ‖ lname is the same as Select xconcat(fname,lname).
XLEFT(x,n):	Extracts the left n characters from x.
XLOWER(x):	Converts x to lowercase.
XRIGHT(x,n):	Extracts the last n characters from x.
XTRIM(x):	Trims off trailing spaces from x.
XUPPER(x):	Converts x to upper case.

INTRODUCTION TO ORACLE

If you are using Oracle, the Oracle software is normally running on a mainframe or a server somewhere within the university environment. Personal Oracle is also available on PC workstations. Access to Oracle's SQL interface is done through Oracle's product called SQL Plus, which runs under windows on a client workstation. The first window that comes up under SQL Plus for Windows is a log-on window that

```
┌──────────────────────────────────────────────────────────────────┐
│ ─                    Oracle SQL*Plus              [icons]    ▼ ▲   │
├──────────────────────────────────────────────────────────────────┤
│ File   Edit   Search   Options   Help                              │
│ ORACLE7 Server Release 7.0.16.4.2 - Production                  ↑  │
│ With the procedural and distributed options                       │
│ PL/SQL Release 2.0.18.1.0 - Production                             │
│                                                                    │
│ SQL>                                                               │
│   1  select * from flight                                          │
│   2* where orig = 'PHX' and dest = 'LAX'                           │
│ SQL>                                                               │
│   1  select * from flight                                          │
│   2* where orig = 'PHX' and dest = 'LAX'                           │
│                                                                    │
│ FLIGHT_NO ORI DES ORIG_TIME DEST_TIME M     PRICE                  │
│ --------- --- --- --------- --------- - ---------                  │
│        15 PHX LAX 01-NOV-94 01-NOV-94 B        49                  │
│        17 PHX LAX 01-NOV-94 01-NOV-94 B        79                  │
│        31 PHX LAX 01-NOV-94 01-NOV-94 S        49                  │
│        33 PHX LAX 01-NOV-94 01-NOV-94 S        49                  │
│        35 PHX LAX 01-NOV-94 01-NOV-94 S        49                  │
│        40 PHX LAX 01-NOV-94 01-NOV-94 N        49                  │
│                                                                    │
│ 6 rows selected.                                                   │
│                                                                    │
│ SQL>                                                            ↓  │
│ ←                                                               →  │
└──────────────────────────────────────────────────────────────────┘
```

FIGURE A.5

allows you to put in the log-on ID and password to your database and the location of that database. To log onto the sample database from ORACLE, you would enter SCOTT for the log-on, TIGER for the password, and X:orasrv (installation dependent) for the remote location of the server database. Once connected, you can build and execute SQL statements from a window (see window example in Figure A.5) that has the SQL prompt. Figure A.5 shows a command that was loaded from a file (File Open on the menu bar), and run (File Run on the menu bar).

Commands are built in a buffer. The following commands allow you to edit and manipulate the lines in that buffer.

Append ...add text to the end of the current line

Change /old/new/ ...change old to new in the current line

Change /old ...delete old from the line

Clear Buffer ....delete all lines in the buffer

Del ....delete the current line

Input ....add 1 or more lines

List ...list all lines in the buffer

List n ....list line n

List * ...list the current line

List m n ...list the range of lines m through n

A sample of the SQL buffer appears as follows:

```
SQL> SELECT *
2 FROM TICKET
3 WHERE flight_no = 101
4
```

There are 3 lines in this buffer. When you press return on line four without entering anything, you return to the SQL prompt. The buffer edit commands can be run from the SQL prompt to modify the buffer and list what is in the buffer. The following commands can also be used at the SQL prompt to execute and save the query.

Run ....runs the query

Save file_name ....saves the query as a file on your disk

Get file_name ....retrieves a file into the buffer that was previously saved

Start file_name .... retrieves and runs a file

SQL Plus adds the .SQL extension to all files it saves and automatically looks for that extension on the GET command.

It is much easier to use the windows Notepad editor to modify and save SQL commands. The editor can be invoked by using the Edit and Invoke Editor from the menu bar. This puts you directly into the notepad editor. You can make your modifications in notepad, save the file, switch to the SQL Plus window, select File Open from the menu bar, and then run the command by selecting File Run from the menu bar.

ORACLE FUNCTIONS

DATE FUNCTIONS

ORACLE carries both the date and time in a DATE variable type. Stored are the century, year, month, day, hour, minute, and second. The default date format is entered in ORACLE with the NLS_DATE_FORMAT, which is a string like MM-DD-YY. ORACLE supports the entire range of date and time specifications.

Example (TO_DATE ('30-OCT-96 20:32:23' 'DD-MON-YY HH24:MI:SS') will convert this date so it can be stored or used in ORACLE date functions. Some of the other formats that can be used are:

YYYY	1996
MM	10
MONTH	OCTOBER
DAY	WEDNESDAY
DY	WED

D	(1-7) where day 1 is set by an NLS_TERRITORY parameter
J	Julian day, number of days since 1-1- 4712 B.C.
AM	
PM	
HH or HH12	

TO_CHAR converts date format to character format
Example TO_CHAR(res_date, 'month dd yyyy')

1. ADD_MONTHS(d,n) d= date, n= number of months

   Example: SELECT TO_CHAR (ADD_MONTHS(res_date,2), 'DD-MON-YYYY')

   FROM ticket WHERE res_name ='OLE OLSON'

   If the value of res_date is 2–1–1996, the date returned will be 4–1–1996.

2. LAST_DAY(d) d=date

   Example: SELECT SYSDATE, LAST_DAY(SYSDATE),

   LAST_DAY(SYSDATE) - SYSDATE

   Results will be today's date, last date of the month, and the number of days left.

3. MONTHS BETWEEN(d1,d2) d1 = first date, d2 = second date

4. NEW_TIME(d,z1,z2) d=date, z1 = time zone of date, z2=new time zone date and time

AST, ADT:	Atlantic Standard or Atlantic Daylight
BST, BDT:	Bering
CST, CDT:	Central
EST, EDT:	Eastern
GMT:	Greenwich
HST, HDT:	Alaska–Hawaii
MST, MDT:	Mountain
NST:	Newfoundland
PST, PDT:	Pacific
YST, YDT:	Yukon

5. NEXT_DAY(d, char) d= date, char = date of week like WEDNESDAY

   This will return the date of the next Wednesday after the date.

SOME ORACLE CHARACTER FUNCTIONS

1. CHR(n) Returns the character assigned to the value of n in the character set.
2. CONCAT(char1, char1) Concatenates into char1, char1 + char2. Same as char1 || char2.
3. INITCAP(char) Returns all words in char with the first letter in uppercase.
4. LOWER(char) Returns all words in lowercase.
5. LTRIM(char,[,set]) Trims all leading 'set' characters. If set is + all leading + would be eliminated, default set is blank.
6. RTRIM same as LTRIM except that is does trailing characters.
7. SOUNDEX(char)   returns equal sounding names. Example where SOUNDEX(res_name) = SOUNDEX(jonson).
8. SUBSTR(char,m [,n]) Returns the first m characters of char beginning at n. Default for n is 1.
9. UPPER(char) changes all characters to uppercase.
10. ASCII(char) returns the decimal value representing the ASCII value of the first character in char.

OTHER ORACLE FUNCTIONS

POWER (m,n) same as m^n or m**n

SQRT(n)

AVG

COUNT

MIN

MAX

STDDEV

SUM

VARIANCE

INTRODUCTION TO USING ACCESS

Access can be used with most of the SQL presented in Chapter 6. Access has a very up-to-date GUI front end and will become one of the more popular micro database systems in database courses. Using Access with the course should be supplemented with a quick reference on Access or with books that are available in the lab. The student can also use the cue cards within Access to help in getting started on the system. The windows in Access have the look and feel of other Microsoft office products, which also helps students who have used these products before. Figure A.6 shows an example of opening a database (the airline database that is used through-

FIGURE A.6

out the text) in Access. The figure shows various tables that are a part of this database. You can access SQL by clicking on the Query icon.

Clicking on the Query icon brings up a window that allows you to use queries that have been defined, or you can define a new query using the NEW button (Figure A.7).

The query design window allows you to work in either QBE or SQL. As you build the QBE definition by selecting columns and attributes of those columns, the SQL is built in the SQL window, and you can switch to that window with the SQL button. Figure A.8 shows the query in design mode using the design button (first icon on the icon bar).

The next example (Figure A.9) shows the query in SQL by using the SQL button. If you build the query in this window, the design window is built automatically by Access. Or if you build the query in QBE mode, the SQL is built automatically by Access. This is a great learning tool for students starting to learn SQL.

Run the query by clicking the datasheet view button or the run button (!). Figure A.10 shows an example of running this query or SQL statement.

You can use the file menu to save the query results or print the query results. In the definition window, the same features are available: save the query definition or

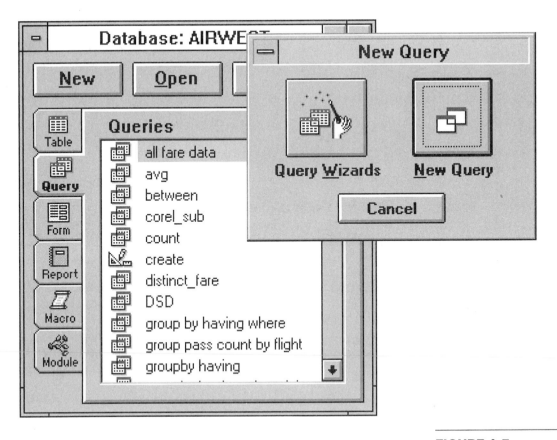

FIGURE A.7

print the query definition. You can also bring the outputs into a WORD document by printing to a file or by doing print screens to the clipboard and pasting them into the WORD document.

ACCESS FUNCTIONS

Access has many different functions to use with SQL statements. The functions can be looked up in Access help under the following categories. Go to Help, Search, Function Categories to look at how to use any specific function.

Arrays	Inspection of Variables
Control of Program Flow	Math
Conversion	Object Linking and Embedding (OLE)
Date/Time	Object Manipulation

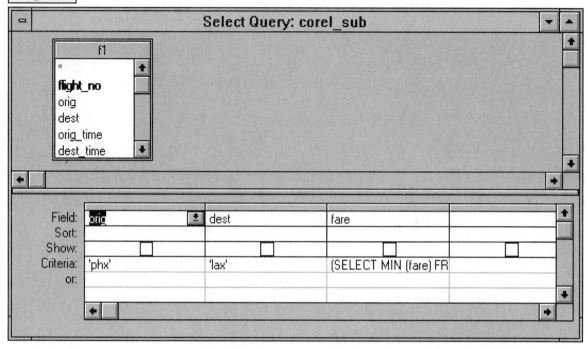

FIGURE A.8

```
Select Query: corel_sub

SELECT *
FROM flight AS f1
WHERE orig = 'phx'
      AND   dest = 'lax'
      AND   fare =
          (SELECT MIN (fare) FROM flight f2
               WHERE f1.orig = f2.orig
               AND   f1.dest = f2.dest);
```

FIGURE A.9

Datasheet View

flight_no	orig	dest	orig_time	dest_time	meal
15	PHX	LAX	7:00	8:20	B
31	PHX	LAX	17:55	19:10	S
33	PHX	LAX	18:55	19:15	S
35	PHX	LAX	20:20	21:40	S
40	PHX	LAX	22:25	23:42	
0					

Select Query: corel_sub

Record: 1 of 5

FIGURE A.10

Domain	Operators
Dynamic Data Exchange (DDE)	Procedures
Error Handling	SQL
File Input/Output (I/O)	Strings
Financial	Variables and Constants

Date Functions

DateAdd(interval, number, date)
DateDiff(interval, date1, date2[, firstweekday][, firstweek])

Time period:	interval
Year:	yyyy
Quarter:	q
Month:	m
Day of year:	y
Day:	d
Weekday:	w
Week:	ww
Hour:	h
Minute:	n
Second:	s

String Functions

Ltrim, Rtrim, Trim:	Removes left spaces, right spaces and space on both the left and right.
Mid, Right, Left:	Returns a middle, right, or left substring.
Len:	Obtains the length of a string.

Data Conversion and Special Purpose

IsNull	
IsDate	
IsNumeric	
ANSI value to string	Chr
String to ANSI value	Asc
Number to string	Format, Str
String to number	Val
One numeric data type to another	CCur, CDbl, CInt, CLng, CSng, CStr, CVar, CVDate
Decimal number to other radix string	Hex, Oct
Date to serial number	DateSerial, DateValue
Serial number to date	Day, Month, Weekday, Year
Time to serial number	TimeSerial, TimeValue
Serial number to time	Hour, Minute, Now, Second

GLOSSARY

Abstract data type (ADT) - A chunk of data that appears as an attribute of an object, but whose structure is not known by the object in which it appears. An object can be included in another object by specifying the second object as an ADT in the first object.

Access - A relational database system supplied by Microsoft that runs primarily on local workstations. The database can be on a server and shared within a workgroup environment.

Access granularity - Refers to the degree of control over access to a database. Its dimensions are the size of the unit of data accessed and the scope of actions allowed on the data.

Aggregation relationship - A relationship between a parent object and a set of child, or sub-class, objects, in which each child object is a part of or component of the parent object.

Anomaly - A condition that may prevent the storage or retention of relevant data or may create the potential for inconsistent data. Anomalies may arise in the process of creating, modifying, or deleting a table.

ANSI - American National Standards Institute - An organization of the U.S. government that defines standards used in all professions.

Association object - An object type represents an association between two other (parent) object types.

Associations - An association can exist from one set of objects to another. A one-to-one association from set A to set B exists if only one item in B may be associated with a given item in A.

Attached table - A table from a different (external) database which has been linked to the current database so that most database operations can be performed on it as if it were an internal table. Attached tables are a feature of Access.

Attribute - A column or field in a table; a characteristic or property of an Entity.

AUTOMATIC, MANUAL - A record insertion parameter that controls how a record is connected to a set occurrence when a record is added to the database.

B+ tree index structure - An index structure which has all of the properties of the B-Tree structure and which additionally has pointers in its sequence set which support sequential processing without reference to higher levels of the index.

B- tree index structure - An index structure which has an algorithm that incrementally adjusts the index structure to maintain balanced depth of index ranges as data are added to or deleted from the database.

Bachman - A database specialist with GE who was responsible for the early design of CODASYL type databases within GE. The DSD diagram is often called a Bachman diagram.

Boyce-Codd Normal form (BCNF) - A table is in Boyce-Codd Normal form if it is in third normal form and it contains no nonkey determinants.

Business process reengineering - A methodology or approach to data planning and IS development that requires the reorganization and streamlining of business processes as a part of the implementation of the information system.

CASE - Computer Aided Software Engineering - A tool that defines systems using an information engineering methodology in which business rules and data are defined and stored in a repository, and the COBOL or C code is generated from the definition.

Check box - A control on a window that allows the user to select from one or more selections in a group where the selections are not mutually exclusive. More than one selection can be selected at any one time. The control supports a Yes/No response.

Checkpoint - A point of time when there are no transactions on a database that are in process. Checkpoints are used to limit the processing required for recovery from database failures.

Child - A segment that is defined at a subsidiary level to another segment.

CICS - Customer Information Control System - An online screen interface system from IBM that manages communication between COBOL and a 3270 terminal.

Client/Server Database System - A database system featuring cooperative processing. A single server processor performs all database management, storage, and retrieval functions, but applications using database data are executed on one or more client processors.

CODASYL - Conference on Data System Languages - An organization that was formed to develop COBOL standards and later formed a task group to work on database standards.

Cold-site - A site which contains a duplicate copy of all of the hardware and software required to operate a database system and is designed to be quickly brought on-line should a disaster damage or destroy an organization's data center.

Command button - A control on a window that allows the user to control the sequence of operations in an application by responding to major processing selections such as Cancel, Add, Delete, Modify, OK, Yes, No.

COMMIT - A DML statement that makes all changes to a database permanent to that point in the processing stream. Once COMMITted, a transaction's effects cannot be rolled back.

Composer by IEF - A CASE tool marketed by Texas Instruments.

Composite object - An object containing multivalued attributes.

Compound object - An object type that includes or contains another object type, where an aggregation relationship exists between the two object types.

Computer assisted software engineering (CASE) tools - Software products designed to support one or more phases of the planning and/or development of information systems.

Concatenated key - A primary key consisting of two or more attributes which together uniquely identify an occurrence of an entity.

Conceptual data model - A model that provides representations of the structure of a database in a form that is independent of the physical structures required for implementation.

Concurrency transparency - Occurs when the distributed database appears to each user as if he/she is the only user of the system.

Concurrent access - Occurs if multiple users access a database over the same time period. Under concurrent access, control measures must be taken to assure that this multiple access does not compromise the integrity of the database.

Control break properties - The attributes that describe the fields that control the grouping of data into various control groups that include separate header, detail, and footer sections within the report.

Correlated subquery - A subquery that refers to the same table used in the main query.

Crystal reports - A report generator software package that runs under Windows-based operating systems that can be used to generate reports using SQL through ODBC connections to database systems such as Oracle and Sybase.

Cullinane/Cullinet - The company that first developed and brought IDMS to the market.

Currency - The current position of the last accessed record within a record type, within a set type, and for a run unit.

Cursor - A pointer system used to process SQL statements that result in a multiple row response from the SQL engine. The SQL statement is defined as a Cursor early in the host program, and then it is executed with OPEN, FETCH, and CLOSE statements.

Cylinder - A set of parallel tracks across all surfaces of a disk pack that can be accessed when the read/write arm is in a stationary position.

Data administration - An information systems function with responsibility for data planning and for the administrative and technical management of an organization's databases.

Data definition language - The set of statements used by a DBMS to define the structure of a database.

Data dictionary - Information describing the structure of a set of data which can be readily retrieved by users. A data dictionary is a common feature of DBMS software.

Data planning - A process used to identify information needed to support strategic plans of the organization. Data planning identifies basic entities that need to be represented in databases and helps to define their scope.

Data redundancy - Occurs when more than one copy of the same item of data is stored and maintained by an organization. Data redundancy can lead to data inconsistency, where different copies show different values for the same item of data.

Data steward - An end user of a database system who has the responsibility and authority to control the granting of access rights to some portion of a database.

Data transfer time - The time required to physically transfer a set of data from secondary to primary storage once the read/write head has been positioned over the beginning point of the requested data.

Data type - A data property that defines an attribute as text, numeric, date, currency, or some other variation of text and numeric.

Data warehouse - A database system designed to support the query and reporting needs of management. A data warehouse typically contains summary data extracted from one or more operational databases that have been organized to facilitate managerial analysis.

Database - An integrated, self-describing collection of data about related sets of things and the relationships that interconnect them.

Database administration - An information systems function with responsibility for the technical management of an organization's databases.

Database development - The analysis, design, and implementation of a database system.

Database management system - The set of software used to develop, implement, manage, and maintain the data stored in a database.

Database space - A physical space on a disk (file) for storing database tables and indexes.

Database system - A database system includes the data stored in the database, the DBMS used to develop it, and the applications developed to create and maintain the data of the database.

Database tuning - The adjustment of physical storage structures of a database to improve its operational efficiency.

Dataset - A physical file that can hold multiple logical files on IBM mainframes. Similar to the concept of a directory in a DOS file system.

DB2 - A relational database system that runs under most IBM platforms, including the PC (OS/2), the AS400, and the larger mainframes (MVS). It also runs on UNIX platforms from both IBM and other vendors.

DBD - Data Base Description - The description of the record structures in the database system. Similar to the concept of a schema in CODASYL terminology.

DBTG - Database Task Group - The committee formed under the CODASYL umbrella to develop standards for a network architecture database system.

DCLGEN processor - A processor used by IBM and XDB to convert relational table definitions to COBOL data definitions for the COBOL program.

DDL - Data Description Language - The language used to describe the data structure of the database both in the schema definition and the subschema definition. Also referred to as a Bachman diagram.

Deadlock - A deadlock occurs for a set of transactions if each of the transactions has each requested access to data that has been locked by another transaction in the set. None of the transactions can complete and release its locks.

Denormalization - The intentional maintenance of a database table (or tables) in less than fully normalized form. The purpose of denormalization is to enhance performance. Denormalization of tables creates the potential for anomalies that must be prevented.

Derived attribute - An attribute whose value can always be determined by performing some calculation on values of other attributes in the database. Derived attributes are not normally stored in a database.

Direct access storage device (DASD) - A storage device that allows data to be accessed in approximately the same amount of time no matter where it is stored on the medium and regardless of its logical ordering in a data structure. Magnetic disk is the most common device.

DISCONNECT, CONNECT - The DML commands to disconnect and connect a record from a set occurrence.

Distributed database - A database configuration in which data are distributed across multiple computers but managed as a single database.

Distributed database management system (DDBMS) - A database management system which supports the distribution of data across multiple nodes while managing the database as an integrated whole. A DDBMS should allow users to access data throughout the system.

Distributed database system - A database system in which database management storage and retrieval functions are distributed across multiple nodes (processors), but the database is managed as a unified whole.

DL/1 or DL/I - data language one - The data manipulation language for IMS.

DMCL - Device Media Control Language - The language used to define the physical database structure including files, journals and the mapping of the logical database descriptions to the physical files.

DML - Data Manipulation Language - The language used within the host language that is an interface between the database system and the host language to add, modify, and delete data and data relationships.

Domain- The domain of an attribute is the set of all values that can validly be assigned to that attribute.

Domain/key normal form (DKNF) - A table is in domain/key normal form if every logical restriction on the value of attributes in the relation is a result of the definition of keys and domains. A table that is in domain/key normal form cannot contain anomalies.

Drop down menu - A menu on a window that drops down from a main menu when the main menu is accessed.

DSD - Data Structure Diagram - A diagram that is similar to an E-R diagram that shows entity relationships, entity properties, and set properties.

Dynamic SQL - SQL statements that are partially built before the precompile process and then modified while the program is executing using input from the user. An example might be to modify the conditions of the WHERE clause in the SQL statement.

Encapsulation - Encapsulation of objects and methods means that their contents are hidden from view by entities external to the object class.

Entity-Relationship Model - The entity-relationship model is a popular conceptual data model which is designed to provide a description of a database in visual form.

Entity - A person, place, thing, or event of importance to the organization. Anything that can be a noun can be an entity.

Entity class - The set of all occurrences of a given type of entity.

Entity occurrence - One individual instance of a type of entity; the set of data describing an instance of an entity.

Equi join - Same as inner join.

ERASE ALL, PERMANENT, SELECTIVE - A DML Erase parameter that allows the database system to erase or not erase member records of erased owner records depending on the retention parameter.

Exclusive lock - An exclusive lock completely prohibits other transactions from accessing the locked data.

External model - The model of a database from the perspective of an individual user or group of users, a user view.

Failure transparency - Means that recovery from failures in a distributed system should not require users to have knowledge of how the data are distributed.

Fault tolerant system - A system which contains redundant copies of crucial system elements and is designed to continue operating at or near normal capacity when certain common types of failures occur.

Field properties - The attributes such as type, size, label, format that describe the various characteristics of a field.

FIND, OBTAIN - DML commands to position and to retrieve the data from specific records in the database.

First normal form (1NF) - A table is in first normal form if it contains no repeating groups of attributes.

Fixed relationship - A fixed relationship exists if, once an occurrence in an entity class is associated with a given occurrence of a related entity, it must remain associated with that specific occurrence.

Footers - An area at the end of a section of a report to display labels and data that pertain to that section.

Foreign key - An attribute in one table that is or refers to the primary key of another table. It is a way of linking one table to another.

Fourth normal form (4NF) - A table is in fourth normal form if it is in third normal form and it contains no multivalued dependencies.

Fragmentation transparency - Means that a user can retrieve data that are stored in fragments on multiple nodes without being aware that it is fragmented.

Functional determination - X functionally determines Y if there is only one possible value for Y associated with each values of X.

Generalization object - An object type that includes or contains related sub-class object types, where a generalization relationships exists between the object type and the sub-class object types.

Generalization relationship - A relationship between a parent object and a set of child, or subclass, objects, such that, each sub-class object is a specialization, a type of, the parent object.

Group box - A box with a label that is also referred to as an option group; a visual way of grouping controls on a window to logically put controls that are related to each other together as a group.

GUI - Graphical User Interface - A windowing system with various window controls such as buttons, check boxes, menus bars, and list boxes.

Hashing - Hashing is an access method which determines the storage location of a record based upon a mathematical algorithm performed on some key attribute of that record. Hashing supports direct access, but not sequential access.

Headers - An area at the beginning of a section of a report to display heading lines and data that pertain to that section of the report.

Heading lines - Lines that are displayed on top of each type of section in a report or form that describe the remaining content of that section.

Hierarchical data model - A database model which uses pointer based data retrieval and support only hierarchical data structures.

Horizontal partitioning - In horizontal partitioning, different rows of a table are stored at different nodes, but all columns for a given row of the table are stored at the same node.

Host language - Language used to write the main server procedures that hosts the embedded SQL accessing the database systems.

Host language interface - A software component of the DBMS which allows commands to manipulate a database to be combined with standard programming language commands to create applications.

Host variable - A variable in a host language program that has be defined to the precompiler so that is can be referenced in SQL statements as well as referenced by statements in the host language.

Hot-site - An alternate data center site which is operated to continuously maintain a redundant copy of a database to protect against damage or destruction of the organization's main data center.

HTML - Hyper Text Mark Up Language - Used to build window displays that can be used by browsers such as Netscape.

Hyper-diagrams - Sets of interconnected diagrams produced by a CASE or I-CASE tool. Hyper-diagrams allow a virtually unlimited number of objects to be interconnected, thus, supporting the complex interrelationships among design components.

IDMS - Integrated Data Management System - A database system developed by the Cullinane Corporation in the 1970s that supported the CODASYL network data model.

IDMS/DC - The IDMS data communications interface used to build and manage 3270 terminal user interfaces with host programs like COBOL.

IMS - Information Management System - A hierarchical database system developed by IBM in the 1960s that continues to be used in a large number of legacy systems today.

IMS/DML - The data manipulation language called DL/I used in a host language to store, retrieve and maintain data.

IMS/DC - IMS Data Communications - The IMS/DC is a separate component of IMS that supports the interface and message queues between an IMS database, a program, and terminals.

Index - An ordered list of items coupled with an indication of where those items can be found; a data structure that allows a table to be retrieved in sorted order based upon some column or set of columns.

Information engineering (IE) - An information systems development methodology whose phases are: planning, analysis, design, and implementation. The IE methodology calls for computer generation of applications based on conceptual level specifications.

Information resource management - Information resource management is a concept that views information as a resource that can be used to strategic advantage. To achieve this, the information resource must be effectively planned and must be readily accessible.

Information systems architecture - An overall plan for the structure of information systems in an organization described in terms of data, process and network elements.

Inheritance - Refers to the concept that subclasses take-on (inherit) the characteristics of their superclasses.

Inner join - A join that includes the matching rows of all tables within the join operation. All attributes of the result table derive their values from their respective tables.

Integrated CASE (I-CASE) products - Products that provide an integrated set of tools supporting all stages of the planning and development of information systems from data and IS planning through automated generation of programs to implement applications.

Internal model - The model that describes how data are physically stored in a database system.

Internet - Same as the World Wide Web.

Intersection entity - An intersection entity resolves a many to many relationship between two other entities. It appears on the many side of a one to many relationship with each of them.

Intra-table relationship - A relationship between occurrences of the same entity class.

Intranet - Use of WWW technology, Java applets, and a browser like Netscape to develop internal networks to work with organizational databases. Similar to client-server using Web technology.

IO-PCB (Input/output program communication block) - A PCB that is used to define a logical terminal that is used as part of the IMS/DC (Data Communications) environment.

ISAM (Indexed sequential access method) file structure - A file structure that supports both random and sequential access by physically storing data in sequential order, but providing an index structure to allow random access.

Isolation level - The degree of protection that each user of a database has from the effects of other user's transactions. A high isolation level protects data integrity very well, but may cause substantial deadlock problems.

ISPF (Interactive system productivity facility)+A153 - A programmer interface that is used by application developers on IBM MVS systems to manage datasets, build files, edit files, build JCL, compile programs, and test applications.

Java - A language useful in building applications on servers and client stations to process data coming from the WWW or internal databases using web technology.

Join - A relational operation that combines attributes from two or more tables to create another table or table result.

Label - A control on a window that displays the titles and text to identify other objects on the window.

Last, next, prior, first - A set ordering system parameter that specifies the insertion sequence of a record into a logical set occurrence.

Left join - A special form of the outer join used on two tables where the non-matches from the first table (left table) are included in the result table.

Legacy system - A system that uses older technology that is no longer used in systems currently under development.

Linked list - A data structure in which each record in the linked set contains a pointer to the next record in the set. Thus the set of related records can be retrieved using data stored with each record, without reference to a separate index.

List box - A control on a window that allows a user to view, select, and deselect various rows of data within a separate window or box.

Location transparency - Means that a user can process data in a distributed system without knowing where it is located.

Logical child - A segment that is set up to carry a pointer that references another segment.

Look-ahead log - A look-ahead log is a transactions log which is always updated before the results of a transaction are actually recorded in the database.

Mandatory relationship - A relationship is mandatory if every occurrence in one entity class must be associated with at least one occurrence in the related class.

Mandatory, optional - A record retention parameter that is used to control how member records are retained when an owner record is removed from the database given different delete parameters.

Member - The entity that is a child in a one-to-many relationship.

Menu bar - A window control that allows the user to control the sequence of processing events by selecting options from a bar normally located at the top of the window.

Metadata - Information describing the nature and structure of an organization's data; data about data.

Method - A method is a named set of instructions that is part of an object class and can be used to perform operations on object instances or the object class.

Multivalued dependency - A dependency where an attribute has an independent relationship with two or more other attributes.

Network Data Model - A database model that uses pointer-based data retrieval and supports network data structures.

Normalization - A process of evaluating table structures and reorganizing them as necessary to produce a set of stable, well-structured relations.

NT (New technology) - A PC-based windows operating system from Microsoft that is a multi-tasking operating system that supports various network architectures.

Null - A nonvalue. The attribute has never been given a value. It is not the same as a zero or a blank. Database systems implement this by giving the attribute a special value that denotes it as a null to all other operations of that database system.

Null character - A special character representation in the database that represents a null value to all operations in that database system.

Object-oriented data model - A database model based upon objects which combine methods (processes) to be applied to data with the data itself, and which includes the concept that objects can inherit the properties of other (higher level objects).

Object - An object is an abstract representation of the properties of a real world thing which has a unique identity and can have embedded attributes and behavior.

Object class - An object class is a grouping of related object instances and their methods. Objects organized into an Object Class share common attributes and/or methods.

ODBC (Open database connectivity) - Software that standardizes the interface to a database system that allows various application systems to access any database system. An ODBC interface allows Access to obtain data from Oracle.

OLE - Object linking and embedding - A protocol that allows the linking or embedding of objects such as pictures, sounds, and graphs into other objects such as forms and reports.

Option button - A control on a window that allows the user to select from a group of options that are mutually exclusive. Only one option can be selected within that group at any one time. Also called a radio button. Example - Sex: Male, Female.

Optional relationship - A relationship is optional if it is not required that every occurrence of one entity be associated with an occurrence of the related entity.

Oracle - A relational database system that runs on various platforms and is very popular in mid-range client/server environments. Oracle supports a number of development tools such as Forms, Reports, Browsers, and CASE tools.

Outer join - A join that includes the non-matching rows of the various tables included in the join. The attributes from the non-matching tables are set to null in the result table.

Owner - The term used to refer to the entity that is the parent of a one to many relationship.

PAD logic - Process Action Diagram - An area in IEF where program logic and database actions are defined and stored in the IEF repository.

Partial dependency - A dependency where the value of a nonkey attribute can be uniquely identified (functionally determined) using only part of a concatenated primary key.

Partitioning - A data distribution schema that splits tables, or rows or columns within tables, into pieces that are stored at different nodes of a distributed database system.

PCB - Program communication block - Each PCB is a description of the individual records and fields that can be accessed by a program. The PCBs make up the main content of a PSB.

Pointer - A data element in a record which specifies the address of a related record.

Polymorphism - Means that the same method may have different meanings for different object classes. A method may be defined for some super-class, but redefined for certain subclasses which need to use a specialized version of the method.

Powerbuilder - A software system from Powersoft that is used to build applications with GUI and procedural code using SQL to database systems such as Oracle and Sybase.

Precompiler - A processor used by developers to precompile the SQL code within a COBOL program before sending the source code to the COBOL compiler. Some COBOL compilers (Micro Focus) allow the user to specify the precompilation dialect.

Predicate - A predicate is a search condition in a query such as logical operator, range test, null test, and pattern match using LIKE.

Primary key - An attribute (or combination of attributes) that uniquely identifies an occurrence of an entity; a unique identifier of a row in a table.

Projection - A result table that consists of some subset of attributes from another table or tables.

Properties - An attribute of another object such as a field, form, query, or report that describes a specific characteristic of that object such as color, font size, and position.

Prototyping development cycle - An information systems development methodology where systems are developed through rapid, iterative processes of gathering requirements, designing, and implementing a prototype for user feedback.

PSB - Program specification block - A description of the record structures that can be accessed and the processing options that can be used on those records. Similar to the concept of a subschema in CODASYL terminology.

QBE (Query by example) - A graphical software tool used by many products to assist end users in building queries. The tool specifies the data to be included, any calculations, any summarization, and the order of the query result.

Query language - A user-friendly language designed to support retrieval of selected data from a database.

Radio button - See option button.

Random access - When random access methods are used, all data items can be retrieved in approximately the same amount of time regardless of their position on the storage medium and regardless of any logical sequencing of records which might exist.

Read/write head - A read/write head is a device that can read or write magnetic spots on a disk surface. Multiple read/write heads are often attached to a common arm that can adjust their position over the disk surface.

Record occurrence - The actual insertion of a specific record into a database.

Record type - The logical definition and specifications of a record.

Referential integrity - Referential integrity is maintained by a DBMS if all logical relationships that exist between tables are implemented when data are added to tables and these relationships are accurately maintained when data are modified or deleted.

Relation - A two-dimensional array that has a single-valued entry in each cell, has no duplicate rows, and has columns whose meaning is identical across all rows; a table.

Relational algebra - The operations on tables using relational operators such as union, difference, intersection, product, projection, selection, and join.

Relational calculus - A nonprocedural language based on predicate calculus that is complex to understand and not used much in most commercial implementations of relational databases.

Relational data model - A database model that uses the repetition of key identifying data to link related data and features a query language widely accessible to end users.

Relationship - A relationship between any two entities is defined by the pair of associations that exist between them. The types of relationships that can exist are one-to-one, one-to-many, and many-to-many.

Replication - Replication is storage of multiple copies of the same data items in different nodes of a distributed database. A data element is said to be fully replicated if a copy of it is kept at every node of a distributed database system.

Replication transparency - Means that a user can retrieve, insert, modify, or delete data that are replicated across multiple nodes of the network without knowing that the data are replicated.

Report layout - The process of designing the report format into various heading, detail, and footing sections.

Result table - A table that is the result of a query. The result table is a temporary table that exists only during the time the query is in use.

Right join - A special form of the outer join used on two tables where the non matches from the second table (right table) are included in the result table.

Rollback - A DML statement to roll back all changes made to a database to the last point of a commit statement within a processing stream of transactions.

Rollback - The rollback of a database transaction means that all portions of the transaction that have been completed are undone. The database is restored to the state it would have been in had the transaction never occurred.

Root - The parent segment of a tree structure.

Rotational delay - The average wait time for the beginning of a set of data to be retrieved to rotate under the read/write head once it is in position.

Schema - The overall description of the database logical structures that is defined by the DDL.

Second normal form (2NF) - A table is in second normal form if it is in first normal form and it has no partial dependencies.

Seek time - The average time required for the read/write arm to be moved into position for the reading of a randomly selected record.

Segment - A record that is defined as part of the IMS database structure.

Selection - A result table that consists of some subset of rows from another table.

Self-join - A join of a table with another table where the other table is the same table.

Semantic data model (SDM) - A type of conceptual data modeling methodology. The SDM emphasizes completeness in capturing complex logical relationships within the conceptual model.

Semantic object model (SOM) - The semantic object model is a conceptual modeling tool designed to provide diagrammatic representations of data in a form consistent with the SDM and the object oriented model.

SENFLD - Sensitive field - A parameter in a Program Specification Block that allows a developer to specify fields that are sensitive to DML statements in the host program.

SENSEG - Sensitive segment - A parameter in a Program Specification Block that allows a developer to specify the fields a program can reference in a DML command.

SEQFIELD - A parameter used in a Segment Search Argument that specifies a field as a sequence field.

Sequential access - When sequential access methods are used, data must be retrieved in sequential order based upon some characteristic of the data.

Set - The term used in a CODASYL database definition that refers to the relationship between two entities. A set is managed by a linked list of pointers.

Set occurrence - The actual occurrence of a set in the database that takes place when an owner record of the set is inserted into the database.

Set type - The logical definition and specifications of a set.

Shared lock - A shared lock on a unit of data allows other transactions to read the locked data, but does not allow another transaction to modify the locked unit of data.

Simple object - An object containing only single valued attributes.

Snapshot table - A table consisting of data copied from another master table. The snapshot table is to be used only for data retrieval operations and it is designed to be automatically refreshed (its data recopied from the master table) on a regular basis.

SPUFI (SQL processor using file input) - A processor used by IBM to allow developers to test SQL against the database system before embedding the SQL in the COBOL program.

SQL (Structured query language) - A language that is used in relational databases to build and query tables.

SSA - Segment Search Argument - A set of parameters that are set up in a host program to allow DML command such as GET UNIQUE to retrieve a specific record based on a key.

Static SQL - SQL statements that are defined at compile time and do not change after the precompile process.

Status code - The code used to check the result of a DL/I command that is returned from IMS,

STORE, MODIFY - DML commands to add and rewrite records in the database.

Subclass - A class that has a child relationship to another class (is directly below it in an aggregation or generalization hierarchy) is said to be a subclass of that related class.

Subject area database - A database containing data that is needed to support a set of related processes within an organization. The set of data within a subject area database should be highly interrelated but as independent as possible of data in other subject area databases.

Subschema - A subset of a database that represents those components needed by a particular user or set of users. Users are able to access only the portion of a database that is included in their subschema.

Superclass - A class that has a parent relationship to another class (is directly above it in an aggregation or generalization hierarchy) is said to be a superclass of that related class.

SYBASE - A relational database system that runs on various platforms that is used in mid-range client-server environments.

Sybase - A relational database system that is supplied by Sybase that runs on IBM mainframes, UNIX platforms, and various PC based servers.

Systems development life cycle (SDLC) - A methodology for the development of information systems that divides the process into the five stages of: investigation, analysis, design, implementation, and maintenance.

Systems repository - A collection containing all forms of information required to develop information system including: planning information, business rules, and data and processing requirements.

Text box - A control on a window that is a field that accepts data from the user or displays data from other sources such as databases, files, or calculations done by a procedure.

Third normal form (3NF) - A table is in third normal form if it is in second normal form and it has no transitive dependencies.

Three schema architecture - An architecture for databases developed by ANSI/SPARC that identifies three levels of models: external models, the conceptual model, and the internal model.

Track - A track is a concentric circle on the surface of a disk platter. A read-write head will pass over the set of data for a track if the read-write head remains stationary while a disk makes one complete revolution.

Transaction - In the context of database processing, a transaction is an interrelated set of actions affecting a database.

Transactions log - Records the effect of each transaction on a database. This log normally records a before image and an after image of each unit of data that is changed by a transaction.

Transitive dependency - A dependency where the value of one nonkey attribute is functionally determined by another nonkey attribute.

Transparency - Refers to the ability of a user of a database system to process data in that system as if it were stored, managed, and maintained on the user's own computer.

Tuple - Relational terminology for a row in a table.

Twin - Multiple occurrences of the same segment type.

Two phase locking - A locking protocol which requires that all locks needed for a transaction be acquired before any of its locks are relinquished. This locking protocol is designed to ensure that actions taken by a transaction are based on current data.

Unique index - An index which requires the values of the indexed column to be unique. Rows with duplicate values for the index column will not be allowed if a unique index has been defined.

Unnormalized table - An unnormalized table is a table that does not meet the definition of a relation. A table containing rows with multiple values for an attribute or containing duplicate rows is an unnormalized table.

Versioning - Versioning occurs if updates to a database do not cause the old version of the data to be destroyed, but rather cause both the new and old copies of the data to be stored as versions.

Vertical partitioning - In vertical partitioning, different columns of a table or different tables in the database are stored at different nodes.

VIA, CALC, DIRECT - A DDL parameter that specifies the insertion mode of a record into the database.

View - A subset of data from one or more tables of a

database. Most commands that can be performed on
tables can be performed on views; however, a view does
not store data.

Visual basic - A software system from Microsoft that can
be used to build GUI applications using procedural code
that runs on the client.

VSAM (Virtual sequential access method) File Structure
- Supports both random and sequential access by storing
data within sequence sets that can be processed sequentially; provides an index structure to allow random
access.

WWW - World Wide Web also referred to as the Internet-
Network of Web servers around the world that can be
accessed by workstations using a Web Browser like
Netscape.

XDB - A relational database system that is used in conduc-
tion with other development tools on PC platforms to
develop, maintain and test applications that run in a
DB2 environment on mainframes. XDB is a DB2 lookalike that runs under Windows.

REFERENCES

WWW Sites

See www.dryden.com/database/morgan_lorents for the latest Web site references.

SQL Standards Home Page - http://www.jcc.com/sql_stnd.html
American National Standards Institute - http://www.ansi.org/
Oracle Magazine - http://www.oramag.com/
Oracle - http://www.oracle.com
IBM IMS - http://www.software.ibm.com/data/ims/

IBM
DB2 Database Server - http://www.software.ibm.com/is/sw-servers/database/
Data Management - http://www.software.ibm.com/data/
DB2 SQL Reference -
   http://www.software.ibm.com/data/db2/support/sqls00aa/
DB2 Application Programming -
   http://www.software.hosting.ibm.com/data/db2/support/sqla00aa

AIS Data Modeling Bibliography - http://www.aisintl.com/case/biblio.html
Database Systems Laboratory University of Massachusetts -
   http://www-ccs.cs.umass.edu/db.html

XDB - http://www.xdb.com
White Papers on Client Server Computing -
   http://www.xdb.com/wpapers/css_wpaper.htm

Sybase - http://cobweb.sybase.com
SQL Anywhere Summary - http://www.sybase.com/products/system11/anywp.html

Embedded SQL - www.uu.se/IT/MIMER/SQLProgrammers/Contents.html

Manuals

IBM Database 2

SQL Reference	SC26-4380-1
SQL Users Guide	SC26-4376-0
Application Programming and SQL Guide	SC26-4377-1
Messages and Codes	SC26-4379-01

Oracle

Programmer's Guide to the Oracle Precompiler	A21022-2
Pro*Cobol Supplement to the Precompiler Guide	A21027-2
Oracle 7 Server Messages and Codes Manual	3605-70-1292

XDB

XDB SQL Reference	Micro Focus Manual 3.00.01
XDB Utilities for Windowed Environments	Micro Focus Manual 3.00.01
XDB Error Messages	Micro Focus Manual 3.00.01

Standards

American National Standards Institute
1430 Broadway
New York, NY 10018
Phone (sales): 212-642-4900

Designation: ANSI X3.135-1992
Title: Information Systems-Database Language-SQL (includes ANSI X3.168-1989)

Designation: ANSI/ISO/IEC 9075-1992
Title: Information Technology-Database Languages-SQL Technical Corrigendum 1

Books

Stephen Cannan and Gerard Otten. *SQL—The Standard Handbook* (Berkshire, England: McGraw-Hill Book Company, 1992).

Joe Celko. *Joe Celko's SQl for Smarties* (San Mateo, CA: Morgan Kaufmann Publishers, Inc., 1995), 467 pages. (ISBN: 1-55860-323-9)

E.F. Codd. *The Relational Model for Database Management* (Reading, MA: Addison-Wesley, 1990), 538 pages. (ISBN: 0-201-14192-2)

C.J. Date. *An Introduction to Database Systems* (Reading, MA: Addison-Wesley, 1995),839 pages. (ISBN: 0-201-54329-X)

C.J. Date with Hugh Darwen. *A Guide to the SQL Standard, 3rd Edition* (Reading, MA: Addison-Wesley, 1993).

Steve Eckols. "IMS for the Cobol Programmer," Part 1: Data Base Processing with IMS/VS and DL/I and Part 2: Data Communications and Message Format Service (Mike Murach & Associates, 1987).

James R. Groff and Paul N. Weinberg. *Using SQL* (Berkeley, CA: Osborne McGraw-Hill, 1990).

H. Gill and P. Rao. *The Official Guide to Data Warehousing* (Indianapolis: Que Corporation, 1996), 382 pages.

Martin Gruber. *Technical Editor: Joe Celko, SQL Instant Reference* (Alameda, CA: SYBEX Inc., 1993).

W. Kim. *Introduction to Object-Oriented Databases* (Cambridge, MA: The MIT Press, 1991).

George Koch. *ORACLE 7—The Complete Reference* (Berkeley, CA: Osborne McGraw-Hill, 1994), 1,028 pages.

J. Martin. *Information Engineering: A Trilogy* (Englewood Cliffs, NJ: Prentice-Hall, 1990).

D. McGoveran and C.J. Date. *A Guide to SYBASE and SQL Server* (Reading, MA: Addison-Wesley, 1993), 548 pages.

Jim Melton and Alan R. Simon. *Understanding the New SQL: A Complete Guide* (San Mateo, CA: Morgan-Kaufmann Publishers, 1992).

F. Taylor. "Why Distribute," in *Distributed Databases* (Northwood, England: Online Publications, 1981), pages 3–22.

Composer Development Methods Series (Plano, TX: Texas Instruments, 1995).

Journals

D. Burleson. "Legacy Bumps Slow Trip to Relational." *Software,* March 1995, pages 1589–92.

P. Chen. "The Entity-Relationship Model—Toward a Unified View of Data." *ACM Transactions on Database Systems,* Vol. I, March 1976, pages 9–36.

E.F. Codd. "Recent Investigations into Relational Data Base Systems." IFIP Conference, Stockholm, Sweden, 1974.

R. Christoff. "Deals with the Devil." *Journal of Information Systems Management,* Vol. 7, Fall 1990, pages 61–4.

R. Fagin. "A Normal Form for Database that is based on Domains and Keys." *ACM Transactions on Database Systems,* Vol. 6 September 1981, pages 387–415.

C.C. Fleming and B. Von Halle. "An Overview of Logical Data Modeling." *Data Resources Management,* Vol. 1, Winter 1990, pages 5–15.

M. Frank. "Object-Relational Hybrids." *Database Management Systems,* Vol. 8, July 1995, pages 46–47+.

D. Friend. "Client/Server Vs. Cooperative Processing." *Information Systems Management,* Vol. 11, Summer 1994, pages 7–14.

T. Guimares. "Information Resource Management: Improving the Focus." *Information Resource Management Journal,* Vol. 1, Fall 1988, pages 10–21.

T. Holt. "Common Sense Normalization." *Mid Range Computing,* Vol. 13, September 1995, pages 71–5.

M. Hammer and D. McLeod. "Database Description with SDM: A Semantic Data Model." *ACM Transactions on Database Systems,* Vol. 6, September 1981, pages 351–386.

T.J. Teory, D. Yang, and J.P. Fry. "A Logical Design Methodology Using the Extended Entity-Relationship Model." *ACM Computing Surveys,* June 1986, pages 197–222.

I. Traiger, J. Gray, C. Galtieri, and B. Lindsay. "Transactions and Consistency in Distributed Database Systems." *ACM Transactions on Database Systems,* Vol. 7, September 1982, pages 323–342.

J.A. Zachman. "A Framework for Information Systems Architechture." *IBM Systems Journal,* Vol. 26, March 1987, pages 276–92.

INDEX